PROFESSIONAL
SQL SERVER® 2012 INTERNALS AND TROUBLESHOOTING

INTRODUCTION xxix

▶ **PART I**   **INTERNALS**

CHAPTER 1   SQL Server Architecture 3
CHAPTER 2   Demystifying Hardware 29
CHAPTER 3   Understanding Memory 53
CHAPTER 4   Storage Systems 77
CHAPTER 5   Query Processing and Execution 111
CHAPTER 6   Locking and Concurrency 149
CHAPTER 7   Latches and Spinlocks 181
CHAPTER 8   Knowing Tempdb 211

▶ **PART II**   **TROUBLESHOOTING TOOLS AND LESSONS FROM THE FIELD**

CHAPTER 9   Troubleshooting Methodology and Practices 241
CHAPTER 10   Viewing Server Performance with PerfMon and the PAL Tool 259
CHAPTER 11   Consolidating Data Capture with SQLdiag 295
CHAPTER 12   Bringing It All Together with SQL Nexus 325
CHAPTER 13   Diagnosing SQL Server 2012 Using Extended Events 349
CHAPTER 14   Enhancing Your Troubleshooting Toolset with PowerShell 379
CHAPTER 15   Delivering a SQL Server Health Check 405
CHAPTER 16   Delivering Manageability and Performance 445
CHAPTER 17   Running SQL Server in a Virtual Environment 469

INDEX 509

PROFESSIONAL

SQL Server® 2012
Internals and Troubleshooting

Christian Bolton
Justin Langford
Glenn Berry
Gavin Payne
Amit Banerjee
Rob Farley

WILEY

John Wiley & Sons, Inc.

Professional SQL Server® 2012 Internals and Troubleshooting

Published by
John Wiley & Sons, Inc.
10475 Crosspoint Boulevard
Indianapolis, IN 46256
www.wiley.com

Copyright © 2013 by John Wiley & Sons, Inc., Indianapolis, Indiana

Published simultaneously in Canada

ISBN: 978-1-118-17765-5
ISBN: 978-1-118-22730-5 (ebk)
ISBN: 978-1-118-24027-4 (ebk)
ISBN: 978-1-118-26490-4 (ebk)

Manufactured in the United States of America

10 9 8 7 6 5 4 3 2 1

For general information on our other products and services please contact our Customer Care Department within the United States at (877) 762-2974, outside the United States at (317) 572-3993 or fax (317) 572-4002.

Wiley publishes in a variety of print and electronic formats and by print-on-demand. Some material included with standard print versions of this book may not be included in e-books or in print-on-demand. If this book refers to media such as a CD or DVD that is not included in the version you purchased, you may download this material at http://booksupport.wiley.com. For more information about Wiley products, visit www.wiley.com.

Library of Congress Control Number: 2012946050

ABOUT THE AUTHORS

 CHRISTIAN BOLTON is the technical director for Coeo Ltd., a leading provider of SQL Server managed support and consulting in the U.K. and Europe. Christian is a Microsoft Certified Architect, Microsoft Certified Master, and MVP for SQL Server, and an experienced technical author. He is particularly interested in SQL Server infrastructure, scalability, and high availability, and is a highly rated speaker at technical conferences worldwide. Christian was the lead author and technical editor for this entire project.

 JUSTIN LANGFORD leads the Managed Support team for Coeo Ltd., delivering 24-7 remote DBA services for mission-critical SQL Server platforms. Before joining Coeo, Justin worked for Microsoft on the Premier Field Engineering team, delivering support consulting to some of Microsoft's largest finance and government customers in Europe. Justin co-authored Wrox's *Professional SQL Server 2005 Performance Tuning* and *Professional SQL Server 2008 Internals and Troubleshooting*. Justin is a SQL Server MVP and lives in London with his wife, Claire. When he's not working, he enjoys sailing and has a keen interest in classic British sports cars.

 GLENN BERRY is a principal consultant with SQLskills. He has worked as a SQL Server professional for many years in a variety of roles, most recently as database architect for Avalara in Parker, CO. Glenn has been a SQL Server MVP since 2007, and has many Microsoft certifications, including MCITP, MCDBA, MCSE, MCSD, MCAD, and MCTS. His expertise includes DMVs, high availability, hardware selection and configuration, and performance tuning. Glenn is heavily involved in the SQL Server community, and is a frequent speaker at user groups, SQLSaturdays, and the PASS Community Summit. He is the author of the book *SQL Server Hardware*, and he contributed chapters for *SQL Server MVP Deep Dives* and *SQL Server MVP Deep Dives, Volume 2*. He is also an adjunct faculty member at University College–University of Denver, where he completed the Master Teacher Program and has been teaching since 2000. Glenn's blog is at http://sqlserverperformance.wordpress.com/ and he can be reached by e-mail at glenn@SQLskills.com and on Twitter at @GlennAlanBerry.

 GAVIN PAYNE is a senior consultant for Coeo Ltd., and a Microsoft Certified Master for SQL Server. His focus as a technical architect and database consultant is on the scoping, designing, and implementation of SQL Server database platforms, as well as the optimization and improvement of existing environments. He also organizes regional SQL Server community events, and presents at European events such as SQLBits and SQLSaturdays. Prior to working for Coeo, Gavin was a solution architect for managed services providers, for whom he acted as a technical authority during the pre- and post-sale phases of outsourcing relationships. Originally from the historic Cotswolds region, Gavin now lives in the South of England, and outside of work his interests include reading about post-war politics and the history of electronic intelligence gathering, and travel. He can be contacted at gavin@coeo.com.

 AMIT BANERJEE currently works as a Senior Premier Field Engineer at Microsoft, specializing in proactive and advisory consulting assistance for SQL Server environments. In the past, he was part of the SQL Server Escalation Services team at Microsoft, which involved troubleshooting and fixing complex issues related to SQL Server in a wide range of environments. He has worked on SQL Server environments for leading corporations in various business domains, helping them to identify and rectify SQL Server-related issues for mission- and business-critical applications. Apart from his daily work, he also contributes to the SQL Nexus, SQL Server Backup Simulator, and SQLDiag/PSSDiag Configuration Manager tools.

 ROB FARLEY runs LobsterPot Solutions, a Gold Partner SQL Server and Business Intelligence consultancy in Adelaide, Australia. He presents regularly at PASS chapters and conferences such as TechEd Australia, SQL PASS, and SQLBits (UK), and heads up the Adelaide SQL Server User Group. He has been a SQL Server MVP since 2006, and is a Microsoft Certified Trainer, helping to create several of the MCP exams. He is also a director of the PASS organization. You can find his blog at http://sqlblog .com/blogs/rob_farley. Despite being busy with all these things, Rob is dedicated to his wife, his three children, his church, and the Arsenal Football Club.

ABOUT THE CONTRIBUTORS

MICHAEL ANDERSON is a senior systems engineer with Microsoft IT, based in Redmond, WA. He has worked for more than 15 years as a storage architect and database systems designer, optimizing Microsoft SQL Server systems starting with version 6.5. His industry experience includes more than a decade working in the Microsoft Information Technology and Online Services divisions. He was an early member of the Bing advertising engine, Microsoft adCenter, helping to shepherd the service from inception to the second-largest advertising engine on the Internet. He has experience designing SQL Server data warehouse and business intelligence systems. Michael now specializes in designing Microsoft IT's Hyper-V private cloud systems. He is an author and contributor to several Microsoft and EMC white papers and maintains his SQL I/O performance blog at `http://sqlvelocity.typepad.com`.

JAMES BOOTHER is a senior consultant for Coeo Ltd., a Microsoft Gold Partner. James started his career as a database developer and has more than a decade of broad IT experience working within Development and IT departments, performing development activities that include database administration, system administration, and departmental management. In his current role he architects, implements, and troubleshoots mission-critical SQL Server environments. He's a passionate .NET, PowerShell and SQL developer, and regularly presents on these subjects. He lives just north of London with his wife and three children. Outside of work, James enjoys motor sport and can often be found watching Formula 1 both on TV and trackside. James can be contacted at `james@coeo.com`.

STEVEN WORT has been working with SQL Server since 1993, starting with version 4.2 running on OS2. He has over 30 years of experience developing applications in the IT industry, working in a wide range of industries. Steven joined Microsoft in 2000 as an escalation engineer on the Systems Integration Engineering (SIE) team, where he co-authored multiple workshops on debugging Windows and .NET. In 2004 he moved to the SQL Server team to work on scalability for SQL Server 2005. After a short spell in the Windows group spent working on scaling large database systems, he is now back on the SQL Server team working on building a range of SQL Server-based appliances. Steven has co-authored several books on SQL Server administration, troubleshooting, and performance tuning.

ABOUT THE TECHNICAL EDITORS

ROBERT L. DAVIS is a senior product consultant and chief SQL Server evangelist for Idera Software, where he works closely with their development teams to help build better SQL Server tools. Previously, he was the program manager for the SQL Server Certified Master Program in Microsoft Learning. He was also a senior production DBA at Microsoft, with more than 12 years of experience with SQL Server. He is one of the authors of *Pro SQL Server 2008 Mirroring*, a writer for *SQL Server Magazine*, a Microsoft Certified Master of SQL Server 2008, as well as a speaker and trainer.

RICHARD DOUGLAS, MCITP, MCTS, MCP, is a systems consultant for Quest software, where he specializes in SQL Server, providing solutions and system health checks to organizations across the Europe, Middle East, and Africa region. Richard has recently assumed the position of editor-in-chief of the community site www.SQLServerPedia.com, which provides articles on SQL Server and a blog syndication service. He also regularly presents webinars to both U.S. and EMEA audiences. A keen member of the SQL Server community, he founded and runs a PASS-affiliated chapter in the U.K., and is on the organizing committee for a national event called SQLRelay.

LAERTE JUNIOR is a skilled principal database architect, developer, and administrator, specializing in SQL Server and PowerShell programming, with over eight years of hands-on experience. He holds a degree in computer science, has been awarded a number of certifications, and is an expert in SQL Server 2000, SQL Server 2005, and SQL Server 2008 technologies. An active member of the SQL Server and PowerShell community through his technology blog and Simple-Talk articles, he also organizes, and is a speaker at, Microsoft community events, attracting hundreds of attendees.

JONATHAN KEHAYIAS is a principal consultant and trainer for SQLskills. He is also a SQL Server MVP and one of the few Microsoft Certified Masters of SQL Server 2008 outside of Microsoft. He frequently blogs about SQL Server; presents sessions at PASS Summit, SQLBits, SQL Connections, and local SQL Saturday events; and has remained a main contributor of answers to questions on the MSDN SQL Server Database Engine forum since 2007. Jonathan is a performance-tuning expert for both SQL Server and hardware, and has architected complex systems as a developer, business analyst, and DBA. He also has extensive development (T-SQL, C#, and ASP.NET), hardware, and virtualization design expertise, Windows expertise, Active Directory experience, and IIS administration experience. Jonathan can be found online as @SQLPoolBoy on Twitter, or through his blog, http://sqlskills.com/blogs/jonathan.

THOMAS KEJSER holds a masters degree in computer science from DAIMI in Denmark and has industry experience across a diverse range of sectors, including telcos, software vendors, health care, manufacturing, retailers, and investment banks. His most recent achievements include building multi-terabyte-size data warehouses, setting up OLTP systems for extreme scale, and tuning world record data movement speed. When he is not coaching developers and DBAs, he publishes white papers for Microsoft and posts his musings on `http://blog.kejser.org`. Thomas lives in London and spends his spare time discussing philosophy with friends over a good glass of whiskey.

JAMES ROWLAND-JONES is a SQL Server consultant and Microsoft MVP for The Big Bang Data Company. His focus and passion is to architect and deliver highly scalable database systems that are creative, simple, and elegant in their design. He has worked for some of the world's largest institutions and been responsible for project delivery across EMEA. James has worked on both OLTP and BI and data warehouse engagements. Recently he has been spending a lot of time working on SQL Server reference architectures and appliances, notably Fast Track and PDW. James is a keen advocate for the SQL Server community, both internationally and in the U.K. He is a member of the SQLBits Organising Committee and is currently serving on the PASS board of directors. You can find him on twitter at `@jrowlandjones`, or feel free to e-mail him at `JRJ@BigBangData.co.uk`.

MIKE WALSH is a SQL Server consultant and MVP with his own consulting service, Straight Path IT Solutions, and a partner at Linchpin People, a SQL Server consultancy focused on service. He has been working with SQL Server since version 6.5 as a DBA, developer, and performance expert throughout his career. Most recently he has been helping numerous companies set up DBA best practices, get the most out of their SQL Server infrastructure, and design highly available and scalable systems. He provides mentoring and custom training for his clients and their DBA teams. Mike remains active in the SQL Server community as a speaker, blogger, user group leader, PASS volunteer, and local event organizer. He can be found on twitter at `@mike_walsh`, on his blog at `www.straightpathsql.com`, or through e-mail at `mike@straightpathsql.com`.

CREDITS

ACKNOWLEDGMENTS

WE ALL HAVE SQL SERVER books that are considered a must have; the ones that every serious SQL Server Professional displays proudly on their bookshelf but hardly ever reads. I don't like the thought of the books that I've helped to create being nothing more than bookshelf trophies, so the best feedback I ever had about the SQL Server 2008 version of this book was seeing a dog-eared, well-worn copy of it bristling with color-coded bookmarks while on a customer site. That unintentional feedback from a complete stranger meant a lot to me and helped enormously to keep spirits high during the development of this book, so I'd like to thank that anonymous IT Professional and everyone else that took the time to give us feedback — this book would not have been written without you.

I owe an enormous debt of gratitude to all the authors and contributors that allowed themselves to be drawn in to this project, particularly Justin Langford and Steven Wort as they knew full well what was in store — and signed-up anyway. The previous authoring team left big shoes to fill so I had to pull out all the stops to make this book a success. I never would have imagined being able to bring together a team like this, you only have to look at everyone's bio to see what I mean. They're all great guys and I'm proud to have my name associated with them.

Behind every great writing team, there's a great a team of technical editors and I've been very lucky to get some of the best people in the industry to critique our work during this project. I'm very grateful to those silent heroes for helping to make our work stand up to scrutiny.

Finally, I would like to thank my wife Gemma and my children Ava and Leighton for putting up with me and my fifth "last ever" authoring project in a row. I won't be so naïve as to say "never again," but I promise I'll take a long break this time.

— CHRISTIAN BOLTON

IN THE LAST 12 MONTHS I have learned the value of collaboration, especially while writing chapters, as I wouldn't normally do this kind of thing. First, I must thank Christian, as both my manager and the book's lead author, for giving me the opportunity to write two chapters — chapters that offered me the chance to write in my own style and from my own perspective. Second, I must thank my two technical editors: Jonathan Kehayias and Robert Davis. Jonathan's knowledge of virtualization gave my first chapter the quality benchmark it needed, while his community contributions about Extended Events provided invaluable research for the other chapter, which was accurately rounded out with the help of Robert's input. Finally, thank you to Neil and Chris.

— GAVIN PAYNE

I WANT TO ACKNOWLEDGE my wife and children — they are the reason behind almost everything I do. Also, when Christian asked me to be involved, I had no idea I would later become sick for a few months, so I greatly appreciate the support that I got from him, the team at Wiley, and James Roland-Jones (whose work on the first version of this book formed a strong foundation). The work on latches from Microsoft's SQLCAT team was very helpful, especially that of Thomas Kejser, who also reviewed that chapter for me. These are all terrific people who should be congratulated.

— ROB FARLEY

CONTENTS

INTRODUCTION   *xxix*

PART I: INTERNALS

CHAPTER 1: SQL SERVER ARCHITECTURE   3

Introduction   3
Database Transactions   4
  ACID Properties   4
  SQL Server Transactions   5
The Life Cycle of a Query   5
  The Relational and Storage Engines   6
  The Buffer Pool   6
  A Basic SELECT Query   7
  A Simple Update Query   15
  Recovery   18
SQL Server's Execution Model and the SQLOS   22
  Execution Model   22
  The SQLOS   25
Summary   26

CHAPTER 2: DEMYSTIFYING HARDWARE   29

The Importance of Hardware   29
How Workload Affects Hardware
  and Storage Considerations   30
  Workload Types   30
  Server Model Selection   32
  Server Model Evolution   33
Processor Vendor Selection   35
  Intel Processors   35
  AMD Processors and Numbering   43
Choosing and Configuring Hardware for Redundancy   46
Hardware Comparison Tools   48
  TPC-E Benchmark   48
  Geekbench Benchmark   50
Summary   51

CHAPTER 3: UNDERSTANDING MEMORY — 53

Introduction — 53
Physical and Virtual Memory — 54
Physical Memory — 54
Maximum Supported Physical Memory — 55
Virtual Memory — 56
NUMA — 59
SQL Server Memory — 63
Memory Nodes — 64
Clerks, Caches, and the Buffer Pool — 64
Optimizing SQL Server Memory Configuration — 70
Min and Max Server Memory — 70
Lock Pages in Memory — 72
Optimize for Ad-Hoc Workloads — 74
Summary — 76

CHAPTER 4: STORAGE SYSTEMS — 77

Introduction — 77
SQL Server I/O — 78
Storage Technology — 78
SQL Server and the Windows I/O Subsystem — 82
Choosing the Right Storage Networks — 84
Shared Storage Arrays — 86
Capacity Optimization — 86
Storage Tiering — 88
Data Replication — 89
Remote Data Replication — 92
Windows Failover Clustering — 93
SQL Server AlwaysOn Availability Groups — 94
Risk Mitigation Planning — 94
Measuring Performance — 95
Storage Performance Counters — 96
Disk Drive Performance — 97
Sequential Disk Access — 100
Server Queues — 101
File Layout — 101
Partition Alignment — 103
NTFS Allocation Unit Size — 104
Flash Storage — 104
Storage Performance Testing — 106
Summary — 110

CHAPTER 5: QUERY PROCESSING AND EXECUTION — 111

Introduction — 111
Query Processing — 112
  Parsing — 112
  Algebrizing — 112
Query Optimization — 113
  Parallel Plans — 114
  Algebrizer Trees — 115
  sql_handle or plan_handle — 115
  Understanding Statistics — 116
  Plan Caching and Recompilation — 117
  Influencing Optimization — 123
Query Plans — 129
  Query Plan Operators — 132
  Reading Query Plans — 135
Executing Your Queries — 140
  SQLOS — 140
Summary — 147

CHAPTER 6: LOCKING AND CONCURRENCY — 149

Overview — 149
Transactions — 150
  A Is for Atomic — 150
  C Is for Consistent — 151
  I Is for Isolated — 151
  D Is for Durable — 151
Database Transactions — 151
  Atomicity — 151
  Consistency — 152
  Isolation — 152
  Durability — 152
The Dangers of Concurrency — 153
  Lost Updates — 153
  Dirty Reads — 155
  Non-Repeatable Reads — 156
  Phantom Reads — 158
  Double Reads — 161
  Halloween Effect — 162
Locks — 163
  Monitoring Locks — 163
  Lock Resources — 165

Lock Modes 167
Compatibility Matrix 173
Lock Escalation **174**
Deadlocks **175**
Isolation Levels **175**
Serializable 176
Repeatable Read 177
Read Committed 177
Read Uncommitted/NOLOCK 178
Snapshot 178
Read Committed Snapshot 178
Summary **179**

CHAPTER 7: LATCHES AND SPINLOCKS **181**

Overview **181**
Symptoms **182**
Recognizing Symptoms 182
Measuring Latch Contention 183
Measuring Spinlock Contention 184
Contention Indicators 185
Susceptible Systems **185**
Understanding Latches and Spinlocks **186**
Definitions 186
Latching Example 187
Latch Types **194**
Latch Modes **194**
NL 195
KP 195
SH 195
UP 195
EX 195
DT 195
Latch Compatibility 196
Grant Order 196
Latch Waits 197
SuperLatches/Sublatches **198**
Monitoring Latches and Spinlocks **199**
DMVs 199
Performance Monitor 201
Extended Events 202
Latch Contention Examples **203**

Inserts When the Clustered Index Key Is an Identity Field 203
Queuing 205
UP Latches in tempdb 208
Spinlock Contention in Name Resolution 209
Summary **209**

CHAPTER 8: KNOWING TEMPDB **211**

Introduction **211**
Overview and Usage **212**
User Temporary Objects 213
Internal Temporary Objects 217
The Version Store 217
Troubleshooting Common Issues **220**
Latch Contention 220
Monitoring Tempdb I/O Performance 229
Troubleshooting Space Issues 231
Configuration Best Practices **232**
Tempdb File Placement 232
Tempdb Initial Sizing and Autogrowth 234
Configuring Multiple Tempdb Data Files 237
Summary **237**

PART II: TROUBLESHOOTING TOOLS AND LESSONS FROM THE FIELD

CHAPTER 9: TROUBLESHOOTING METHODOLOGY AND PRACTICES **241**

Introduction **241**
Approaching Problems **242**
Ten Steps to Successful Troubleshooting 242
Behavior and Attitude 244
Success Criteria 245
Working with Stakeholders 245
Service-Level Agreements 246
Engaging External Help 247
Defining the Problem **248**
Guidelines for Identifying the Problem 248
Isolating the Problem 249
Performance Bottlenecks 250
Data Collection **252**
Focused Data Collection 253
Understanding Data Gathering 253

Tools and Utilities   254

Data Analysis   **255**

Validating and Implementing Resolution   **256**

Validating Changes   256

Testing Changes in Isolation   256

Implementing Resolution   257

Summary   **257**

CHAPTER 10: VIEWING SERVER PERFORMANCE WITH PERFMON AND THE PAL TOOL   **259**

Introduction   **259**

Performance Monitor Overview   **260**

Reliability and Performance Monitor   260

New PerfMon Counters for SQL Server 2012   263

Getting Started with PerfMon   268

Getting More from Performance Monitor   **278**

Bottlenecks and SQL Server   278

Prescriptive Guidance   279

Wait Stats Analysis   284

Getting a Performance Baseline   285

Performance Analysis of Logs   **285**

Getting Started with PAL   285

Other PerfMon Log Analysis Tools   **289**

Using SQL Server to Analyze PerfMon Logs   289

Combining PerfMon Logs and SQL Profiler Traces   289

Using Relog   290

Using LogMan   291

Using LogParser   293

Summary   **293**

CHAPTER 11: CONSOLIDATING DATA CAPTURE WITH SQLDIAG   **295**

The Data Collection Dilemma   **295**

An Approach to Data Collection   **296**

Getting Friendly with SQLdiag   **297**

Using SQLdiag in Snapshot Mode   298

Using SQLdiag as a Command-line Application   299

Using SQLdiag as a Service   303

Using SQLdiag Configuration Manager   **305**

Configuring SQLdiag Data Collection Using Diag Manager   307

Adding Trace Filters to a SQLdiag Configuration   310

Employing Best Practices   **318**

Gearing Up for Long-Term Data Collection 319
Filtering Out the Noise 320
Alert-Driven Data Collection with SQLdiag 322
Summary 323

CHAPTER 12: BRINGING IT ALL TOGETHER WITH SQL NEXUS 325

Introducing SQL Nexus 325
Getting Familiar with SQL Nexus 326
Prerequisites 326
Loading Data into a Nexus Database 328
Analyzing the Aggregated Data 331
Customizing SQL Nexus 340
Using ReadTrace.exe 341
Building Custom Reports for SQL Nexus 342
Running SQL Nexus Using the Command Prompt 342
Creating Your Own Tables in the SQL Nexus Database 342
Writing Your Own Queries 344
The OSTRESS Executable 344
Resolving Common Issues 346
Issue #1 346
Issue #2 346
Issue #3 346
Issue #4 347
Summary 348

CHAPTER 13: DIAGNOSING SQL SERVER 2012 USING EXTENDED EVENTS 349

Introduction to Extended Events 349
Getting Familiar with Extended Events 350
Why You Should Be Using Extended Events 351
SQL Server Roadmap 351
Graphical Tools 351
Low Impact 351
When You Might Use Extended Events 352
What Are Extended Events? 352
Where the Name Extended Events Comes From 353
Extended Events Terminology 354
Creating Extended Events Sessions in SQL Server 2012 363
Introduction to the New Session Form 363
Monitoring Server Logins 366
Monitoring for Page Splits with Extended Events 367

Counting the Number of Locks Acquired per Object   369
Creating Sessions Using T-SQL   370
Viewing Data Captured by Extended Events   **371**
Viewing Event File Data   371
Summary   **376**

**CHAPTER 14: ENHANCING YOUR TROUBLESHOOTING
TOOLSET WITH POWERSHELL**   **379**

Introducing PowerShell   **379**
Getting Started with PowerShell   **380**
The PowerShell Environment   381
The Basics — Cmdlets, Variables, Advanced Functions,
and Modules   383
Working Remotely   390
What's New in SQL Server 2012   391
Using PowerShell to Investigate Server Issues   **393**
Interrogating Disk Space Utilization   393
Interrogating Current Server Activity   394
Interrogating for Warnings and Errors   396
Interrogating Server Performance   396
Proactively Tuning SQL Server Performance with PowerShell **397**
Index Maintenance   397
Managing Disk Space Utilization of Backups   398
Extracting DDL Using SMO   398
Scheduling Script Execution   403
Summary   **404**

CHAPTER 15: DELIVERING A SQL SERVER HEALTH CHECK   **405**

The Importance of a SQL Server Health Check   **405**
Running DMV and DMF Queries   **406**
SQL Server Builds   **408**
Database-Level Queries   **426**
Summary   **442**

CHAPTER 16: DELIVERING MANAGEABILITY AND PERFORMANCE   **445**

Improve Efficiency with SQL Server Manageability Features **445**
Manageability Enhancements in SQL Server 2012   **446**
Policy-Based Management   **447**
Overview   447
Other Microsoft Tools for Managing SQL Server   **460**

System Center Advisor   461
System Center Operations Manager   464
Summary   **466**

CHAPTER 17: RUNNING SQL SERVER IN A VIRTUAL ENVIRONMENT   469

The Shift to Server Virtualization   **469**
An Overview of Virtualization   **470**
History of Virtualization   471
The Breadth of Virtualization   472
Platform Virtualization   472
Cloud Computing   473
Why Virtualize a Server?   **473**
Business Benefits   474
Technical Benefits   474
Encapsulation   475
SQL Server 2012 and Virtualization   476
Limitations of Virtualization   477
Common Virtualization Products   **477**
VMware   477
Microsoft Hyper-V   478
Xen   479
Hardware Support for Virtualization   479
Virtualization Concepts   **480**
Host Server   480
Hypervisor   480
Virtual Server (or Guest Server or Virtual Machine)   482
Extended Features of Virtualization   **483**
Snapshotting   483
High-Availability Features   483
Online Migration   484
Highly Available Virtual Servers   486
Host and Guest Clustering   487
Deploying SQL Server with Virtualization's High-Availability Features   487
Managing Contention   **488**
Good Contention   488
Bad Contention   488
Demand-Based Memory Allocation   489
Weighting   490
Identifying Candidates for Virtualization   **491**
Guiding Principles   491
Server Workload   491

Gathering Sizing Data | 492
Sizing Tools | 493
Non-Performance Related Requirements | 493
Architecting Successful Virtual Database Servers | **494**
Architecting Virtual Database Servers vs. Physical Database Servers | 494
Virtual Database Server Design | 495
Monitoring Virtualized Database Servers | **502**
Information and Misinformation from Performance Monitor | 503
Summary | **507**

INDEX | *509*

INTRODUCTION

IF YOU'RE TROUBLESHOOTING an apparent "SQL Server" issue, you need to be able to troubleshoot the underlying operating system and storage as well as SQL Server. The aim of this book is to bring together and simplify the architectural details of these components before introducing you to the tools and techniques that very successful SQL Server Professionals use every day to get great results.

A fair amount of Windows and hardware internals' information is available already, but very little of it condenses and filters the right material to be easily consumed by SQL Server professionals. The available material is either too light or too in-depth — with nothing to help bridge the gap.

Combining this need with the need for practical internals' information on SQL Server and comprehensive introductions to troubleshooting tools available from the SQL Server Community and that come with SQL Server itself, three goals were established for this book:

➤ To provide in-depth architectural information on SQL Server (and the environment on which it depends) that is easy to consume

➤ To present a practical introduction to free and included SQL Server troubleshooting tools

➤ To deliver against both of these goals using real-world examples and anecdotes to help SQL Server professionals efficiently and accurately determine the root cause of issues on systems running SQL Server

WHO THIS BOOK IS FOR

This book is intended for readers who regard themselves as, or who aspire to be, SQL Server professionals in predominantly relational environments. What we mean by SQL Server professionals are those who consider SQL Server to be one of their core product skills and who continually strive to increase their knowledge of the product and how to use it.

Because it is not a beginner's book, we assume that readers know the basics about installing, configuring, and using SQL Server, and are aware of some of the challenges presented by troubleshooting SQL Server problems using only the native tools provided. However, for readers who are not entirely confident about some of the topics presented, every effort has been made to present enough foundational information to get started.

The book is presented in two parts. The first part covers internals, which provides an in-depth grounding in core concepts and therefore the knowledge necessary to understand the output and positioning of the tools covered in the second part of the book. Readers who are confident with the subject matter presented in Part I will find that they can start reading from Part II, dipping back into Part I as required to clarify any understanding.

WHAT THIS BOOK COVERS

Before launching into a description of the book's structure and the contents of each chapter, the following sections describe the key drivers and assumptions that originally dictated which topics the book needed to cover.

Understanding Internals

You don't really need to understand a lot about how SQL Server works to be successful in many SQL Server–based job roles. You can find numerous well-established, prescriptive guidelines and a very active and helpful community. Eventually, however, you will reach a point when that's just not enough (usually when something serious has gone wrong).

During an unexpected service outage, for example, you need to make quick decisions in order to balance the demands of restoring the service as quickly as possible while gathering enough data to help you diagnose the issue so you can prevent it from happening again. In that situation you cannot depend on external help or goodwill; it won't arrive fast enough to help you. Understanding SQL Server internals enables you to make quick and effective decisions for resolving problems independently.

Several years ago, a Microsoft customer encountered corruption in a large business-critical database running on SQL Server. The business decided to take the database offline until it was fixed because it held financial trade data, and mistakes would have been disastrous.

They ran DBCC CHECKDB, which can be used in SQL Server to help detect and resolve corruption, but killed it after eight hours in favor of a database restore. The backup was corrupt, however, so they had no option but to run CHECKDB again, which fixed the problem after another 12 hours. This time-consuming disaster ultimately forced the company to pay a large fine for failing to provide a service to the financial markets.

The simple lessons to learn from this example are to test your backups and to know how long CHECKDB takes to run (and to understand that it takes longer when corruption is detected, as it takes another pass with deeper checks). These are best practices that can be followed with little understanding of actual internals.

The main reason for including this example, however, is the information that resulted from the postmortem. The original error message that detected the problem contained details about a corrupt page. Armed with a data page number, the troubleshooting team could have used DBCC PAGE to look at the header and determine to which database object it belonged. In this case it belonged to a nonclustered index that could have been rebuilt without having to take the entire database down to run CHECKDB or restore the entire database. This is why it's useful to know the "internals"; so you can work things out for yourself and take the best course of action.

This book covers internals' information for Windows and SQL Server that will help you understand the environment in which your application(s) work; configure your server to optimize for different requirements; and avoid making blind decisions in the heat of the moment because you don't know why you're seeing a particular behavior.

Troubleshooting Tools and Lessons from the Field

The second part of this book deals with a range of free troubleshooting tools that you can use together to form a structured, effective troubleshooting strategy. Because the tools can seem overly complicated and difficult to learn to the uninitiated, these chapters form a comprehensive and practical guide that can make your life much easier — both on a daily basis and when faced with a serious problem.

This part of the book also gives you the advantage of looking at topics that are based on real-world experiences, offering concrete examples rather than boilerplate "how it works" advice — this approach received a lot of positive feedback for the previous version of this book, covering SQL Server 2008, so we have retained and expanded on that idea.

HOW THIS BOOK IS STRUCTURED

The first part of the book starts with a high-level overview of SQL Server's architecture, leading into chapters on the core resources that are important to SQL Server, including hardware, memory, and storage. After these chapters you'll find material that is critical to understand for effective troubleshooting: query processing and execution, locking and concurrency, latches and spinlocks, and Tempdb.

Part II begins with both a human-oriented and process-driven look at how to approach troubleshooting. Then it jumps into the tools and technologies that work well independently but are brought together into one easy solution for analysis with SQL Nexus.

The next chapters get you started with Extended Events and the new user interface introduced with SQL Server 2012, easing you gently into using PowerShell for troubleshooting, building your own health checks with dynamic management views (DMVs), and meeting the challenges of managing large SQL Server estates.

Finally, you will learn about what server virtualization means for SQL Server and how to identify good candidates to move into a virtual environment.

The following overview of each chapter puts them into context within the book so you can decide where to start reading.

Chapter 1: SQL Server Architecture

This chapter takes you lightly through the life cycle of a query, with enough depth to help you understand fundamental concepts and architectures without getting lost in the complexities of individual components (some of which are looked at closely in later chapters). This chapter will appeal to readers at all levels of skill, whether you're a developer, a DBA, or a seasoned SQL Server veteran.

Chapter 2: Demystifying Hardware

Having modern, appropriately sized and selected hardware and storage is the absolute foundation of good database server performance and scalability. Unfortunately, many database professionals struggle to keep up with the latest developments in server hardware and I/O subsystems, often relying on someone else (who may not be familiar with SQL Server) to select their hardware and I/O subsystems. This can result in inappropriately sized and matched hardware that does not perform well for different types of SQL Server workloads. This chapter describes the tools and techniques you need to make intelligent decisions regarding database server hardware and sizing.

Chapter 3: Understanding Memory

Memory is an important aspect of troubleshooting SQL Server because problems here can cause problems everywhere else. An understanding of memory is one of the first areas you should master if you want to differentiate yourself as a SQL Server professional.

This chapter looks at fundamental memory concepts common to any application running on Windows, how SQL Server interacts with memory through Windows, and how SQL Server manages memory internally.

Chapter 4: Storage Systems

Understanding I/O has always been a key part of a DBA's role. However, separation of duties is now very common in many environments and the responsibility for delivering both I/O performance and high availability has become the domain of the SAN administrator. Over time this has led to a frustrating disconnect between these two groups, with each using a separate language to describe its respective requirements and solutions.

However, there is also a "battle royale" currently in play in the storage world. Direct-attached storage (DAS) is regaining popularity — primarily through the advent of solid-state devices (SSDs). SSDs have breathed fresh life into the storage market, delivering exponential performance improvements while significantly reducing device count, energy costs, and data center floor space.

DAS solutions are interesting because they also return the power (and responsibility) back to the owner of the server — and for database platforms that means the DBA. SQL Server 2012 offers some very compelling application-centric availability options that will again give users the opportunity to evaluate DAS as their platform of choice.

This chapter helps readers understand the needs of both the SAN administrator and the DBA. It explores the design options facing a SAN administrator and some of the trade-offs required when provisioning storage in the enterprise. You will see the benefits that a SAN can provide and the functionality and features that are typically available, enabling you to bridge the terminology gap between these two parties. The chapter concludes with a review of the information a SAN administrator requires from a DBA in order to make the right decisions when provisioning storage.

Chapter 5: Query Processing and Execution

Query processing within SQL Server involves many components, and in this chapter you'll learn about the query optimization framework and how statistics and costing are used to find a good way to execute your code. In this chapter you'll also discover how to read execution plans, as well as explore code optimization techniques that give SQL Server a better chance of creating a good plan.

Chapter 6: Locking and Concurrency

Transactions are the life source of an RDBMS. A database that cannot handle thousands of transactions per second is quickly derided by the community. However, good throughput is worthless without the assurance of data integrity. High-end database platforms such as SQL Server have very sophisticated mechanisms for not only delivering great throughput but also managing integrity of the data, thereby delivering predictable results.

This chapter demonstrates that a database system is only as good as its transactions. Because a poorly designed or heavy transaction can seriously affect the performance of your SQL Server, this chapter provides a thorough grounding in SQL Server's mechanisms for managing data integrity through the use of transactions, locking architecture, and enhanced performance by leveraging optimistic concurrency models.

Chapter 7: Latches and Spinlocks

As data volumes continue to rise, DBAs are faced with larger and more demanding systems. Today's workloads can place tremendous strain on the internals of SQL Server — especially in its default configuration. One of these internal areas that can feel this strain is latches. In a perfect world, a DBA would never need to worry about latches. They exist only to ensure the integrity of the data in memory. However, all too often database resources are left waiting for a latch resource, thereby slowing the whole system down.

This chapter guides you through the fundamentals of latch architecture, explains how to troubleshoot a latch contention issue, and finishes with best practice guidance to minimize and mitigate any risk going forward.

Chapter 8: Knowing Tempdb

Tempdb is used by applications to store temporary objects and by SQL Server to store temporary result sets used internally to process queries. There is only one tempdb for an instance of SQL Server, and its importance has grown significantly since SQL Server 2005 introduced new features such as online indexing and snapshot isolation levels that use tempdb heavily.

In this chapter you'll find out which features use tempdb and what the performance implications can be for enabling them, as well as how to monitor and tune the database for best performance and availability.

Chapter 9: Troubleshooting Methodology and Practices

This chapter provides a framework for effectively troubleshooting complex problems. It includes content describing how to identify SQL Server problems, when to use the tools discussed in this book, and diagnosis for complex issues. This chapter outlines an approach to tackling SQL Server problems using real-world examples and offering guidance that will enable you to promptly focus on the root cause of a problem.

Chapter 10: Viewing Server Performance with PerfMon and the PAL Tool

Performance Monitor has a been a staple data gathering and reporting tool since Windows NT4, but it has continued to increase in terms of size and scope since those early days.

In this chapter you will learn how to optimize your data collection using Performance Monitor to reduce the impact on the monitored system, and how to load the data straight into SQL Server to run your own T-SQL queries against the results. It also introduces you to the Performance Analysis of Logs tool (PAL), which greatly simplifies the analysis of large data captures.

Chapter 11: Consolidating Data Capture with SQLdiag

SQLdiag, first introduced in SQL Server 2005, is a great tool that helps to coordinate the collection of Performance Monitor logs and SQL traces, as well as gather other system data.

In this chapter you'll learn how to configure, customize, and run SQLdiag, as well as be introduced to the Performance Statistics script from Microsoft, which adds locking, blocking, and wait stats to the list of collectors that SQLdiag coordinates. This tool is an important secret of the trade for efficient data collection, and this chapter is a must read for anyone not using it extensively already.

Chapter 12: Bringing It All Together with SQL Nexus

SQL Nexus is a freeware tool written by SQL Server escalation engineers at Microsoft, and it is the crown jewel of the troubleshooting tools because it consolidates the analysis and reporting capabilities of all the other tools mentioned previous to this chapter.

Using the consolidated data collection from the Performance Statistics script, SQL Nexus will load into a database and analyze Performance Monitor log data; SQL trace files using ReadTrace, which is embedded into the tool; locking and blocking information, including blocking chains with the actual statements and execution plan details; as well SQL Server waits data, which is also aggregated.

In this chapter you'll read about how to configure, run, and draw conclusions from the reports created by this tool, which is by far the most useful piece of software in the troubleshooting kit bag of users who have taken the time to learn it.

Chapter 13: Diagnosing SQL Server 2012 Using Extended Events

This chapter describes the Extended Event architecture and how you can use it to take your troubleshooting capabilities to a higher level. Extended Events provides a low-impact, very flexible, and powerful method for capturing troubleshooting information — one that enables you to gain insight into difficult and intermittent problems that were impossibly hard to diagnose using traditional methods.

Chapter 14: Enhancing Your Troubleshooting Toolset with PowerShell

Administrative activities on the Windows platform have traditionally been carried out within GUI applications, such as SQL Server Management Studio. PowerShell has changed the administrative landscape, especially for activities such as troubleshooting and performance tuning.

This chapter demonstrates how PowerShell integrates with Windows, WMI, the Registry, and the file system, and in particular its deep integration with SQL Server. You will then explore how SQL Server troubleshooting can be performed with PowerShell, focusing on identifying which key resources are being used where, and how PowerShell can help address the issues discovered.

The chapter concludes with some proactive performance tuning scripts that you can use to monitor and tune your SQL Server environment.

Chapter 15: Delivering a SQL Server Health Check

Dynamic management views (DMVs) were first added to SQL Server 2005, and they have been enhanced in every version of SQL Server since then. They provide a wealth of extremely valuable information about the configuration, health, and performance of your SQL Server instance, along with useful metrics about individual user databases.

This chapter covers an extensive set of DMV queries that you can use as a diagnostic tool to assess the health and performance of your SQL Server instances and databases. It also provides valuable background information and specific tips you can use to properly interpret the results of each query.

Chapter 16: Delivering Manageability and Performance

This chapter covers the challenges of managing a SQL Server estate. It considers all aspects of manageability, such as configuration management, performance, capacity planning, and automation. Also covered are features within SQL Server such as Policy-Based Management and multi-server management. The chapter provides real-world advice on the benefits and limitations of the out-of-the-box tools, community solutions such as the Enterprise Policy Management Framework, and monitoring tools such as System Center Operations Manager.

Chapter 17: Running SQL Server in a Virtual Environment

This chapter begins by looking at virtualization concepts and the difference between good and bad contention. It then describes how to identify good candidates for virtualization before architecting successful virtualized database platforms, focusing on memory, storage, CPU, and high availability. The chapter concludes by discussing how to monitor the performance of virtualized systems post-implementation.

WHAT YOU NEED TO USE THIS BOOK

The samples in this book were written and tested on SQL Server 2012 Standard, Enterprise, and Developer Editions. Both the Developer Edition and the Evaluation Edition of SQL Server 2012 are very easy to obtain, and they perform identically to the Enterprise Edition.

The source code for the samples is available for download from the Wrox website at:

```
www.wrox.com/remtitle.cgi?isbn=1118177657
```

CONVENTIONS

To help you get the most from the text and keep track of what's happening, we've used a number of conventions throughout the book.

> **WARNING** *Warnings hold important, not-to-be-forgotten information that is directly relevant to the surrounding text.*

> **NOTE** *Notes indicate tips, hints, tricks, or asides to the current discussion.*

As for styles in the text:

➤ We *highlight* new terms and important words when we introduce them.

➤ We show keyboard strokes like this: Ctrl+A.

➤ We show filenames, URLs, and code within the text like so: `persistence.properties`.

➤ We present code in two different ways:

```
We use a monofont type with no highlighting for most code examples.
```

```
We use bold to emphasize code that is particularly important in the present context
or to show changes from a previous code snippet.
```

SOURCE CODE

As you work through the examples in this book, you may choose either to type in all the code manually, or to use the source code files that accompany the book. All the source code used in this book is available for download at www.wrox.com. Specifically for this book, the code download is on the Download Code tab at:

        www.wrox.com/remtitle.cgi?isbn=1118177657

You can also search for the book at www.wrox.com by ISBN (the ISBN for this book is 978-1-118-17765-5) to find the code. A complete list of code downloads for all current Wrox books is available at www.wrox.com/dynamic/books/download.aspx.

At the beginning of each chapter, we've provided information on where to download the major code files for the chapter. Throughout each chapter, you'll also find references to the names of code files as needed in listing titles and text.

Most of the code on www.wrox.com is compressed in a .ZIP, .RAR archive, or similar archive format appropriate to the platform.

Once you download the code, just decompress it with your favorite compression tool. Alternately, you can go to the main Wrox code download page at www.wrox.com/dynamic/books/download.aspx to see the code available for this book and all other Wrox books.

ERRATA

We make every effort to ensure that there are no errors in the text or the code. However, no one is perfect, and mistakes do occur. If you find an error in one of our books, such as a spelling mistake or a faulty piece of code, we would be very grateful for your feedback. By sending in errata, you may save another reader hours of frustration, and at the same time, you will be helping us provide even higher quality information.

To find the errata page for this book, go to www.wrox.com/remtitle.cgi?isbn=1118177657 and click the Errata link. On this page you can view all errata submitted for this book and posted by Wrox editors.

If you don't spot "your" error on the Book Errata page, go to www.wrox.com/contact/techsupport.shtml and complete the form there to send us the error you have found. We'll check the information and, if appropriate, post a message to the book's errata page and fix the problem in subsequent editions of the book.

P2P.WROX.COM

For author and peer discussion, join the P2P forums at http://p2p.wrox.com. The forums are a web-based system for you to post messages relating to Wrox books and related technologies and interact with other readers and technology users. The forums offer a subscription feature to e-mail you topics of interest of your choosing when new posts are made. Wrox authors, editors, other industry experts, and your fellow readers are present on these forums.

At http://p2p.wrox.com, you will find a number of different forums that will help you, not only as you read this book, but also as you develop your own applications. To join the forums, just follow these steps:

1. Go to http://p2p.wrox.com and click the Register link.

2. Read the terms of use and click Agree.

3. Complete the required information to join, as well as any optional information you wish to provide, and click Submit.

4. You will receive an e-mail with information describing how to verify your account and complete the joining process.

> **NOTE** *You can read messages in the forums without joining P2P, but in order to post your own messages, you must join.*

Once you join, you can post new messages and respond to messages other users post. You can read messages at any time on the web. If you would like to have new messages from a particular forum e-mailed to you, click the Subscribe to this Forum icon by the forum name in the forum listing.

For more information about how to use the Wrox P2P, be sure to read the P2P FAQs for answers to questions about how the forum software works, as well as many common questions specific to P2P and Wrox books. To read the FAQs, click the FAQ link on any P2P page.

PART I
Internals

▶ **CHAPTER 1:** SQL Server Architecture

▶ **CHAPTER 2:** Demystifying Hardware

▶ **CHAPTER 3:** Understanding Memory

▶ **CHAPTER 4:** Storage Systems

▶ **CHAPTER 5:** Query Processing and Execution

▶ **CHAPTER 6:** Locking and Concurrency

▶ **CHAPTER 7:** Latches and Spinlocks

▶ **CHAPTER 8:** Knowing Tempdb

SQL Server Architecture

WHAT'S IN THIS CHAPTER?

➤ Understanding database transactions and the ACID properties

➤ Architectural components used to fulfill a read request

➤ Architectural components used to fulfill an update request

➤ Database recovery and the transaction log

➤ Dirty pages, checkpoints, and the lazy writer

➤ Where the SQLOS fits in and why it's needed

WROX.COM CODE DOWNLOADS FOR THIS CHAPTER

The wrox.com code downloads for this chapter are found at www.wrox.com/remtitle .cgi?isbn=1118177657 on the Download Code tab. The code is in the Chapter 1 download and individually named according to the names throughout the chapter.

INTRODUCTION

A basic grasp of SQL Server's database engine architecture is fundamental to intelligently approach troubleshooting a problem, but selecting the important bits to learn about can be challenging, as SQL Server is such a complex piece of software. This chapter distills the core architecture of SQL Server, putting the most important components into the context of executing a simple query to help you understand the fundamentals of the core engine.

You will learn how SQL Server deals with your network connection, unravels what you're asking it to do, decides how it will execute your request, and finally how data is retrieved and modified on your behalf.

You will also discover when the transaction log is used and how it's affected by the configured recovery model; what happens when a checkpoint occurs and how you can influence the frequency; and what the lazy writer does.

The chapter starts by defining a "transaction" and outlining the database system's requirements to reliably process them. You'll then look at the life cycle of a simple query that reads data, looking at the components employed to return a result set, before examining how the process differs when data needs to be modified.

Finally, you'll learn about the components and terminology that support the recovery process in SQL Server, and the SQLOS "framework" that consolidates a lot of the low-level functions required by many SQL Server components.

> **NOTE** *Coverage of some areas of the life cycle described in this chapter is intentionally shallow in order to keep the flow manageable; where that's the case, you are directed to the chapter or chapters that cover the topic in more depth.*

DATABASE TRANSACTIONS

A *transaction* is a unit of work in a database that typically contains several commands that read from and write to the database. The most well-known feature of a transaction is that it must complete all the commands in their entirety or none of them. This feature, called *atomicity*, is just one of four properties defined in the early days of database theory as requirements for a database transaction, collectively known as ACID properties.

ACID Properties

The four required properties of a database transaction are atomicity, consistency, isolation, and durability.

Atomicity

Atomicity means that *all* the effects of the transaction must complete successfully or the changes are rolled back. A classic example of an atomic transaction is a withdrawal from an ATM machine; the machine must both dispense the cash *and* debit your bank account. Either of those actions completing independently would cause a problem for either you or the bank.

Consistency

The consistency requirement ensures that the transaction cannot break the integrity rules of the database; it must leave the database in a consistent state. For example, your system might require that stock levels cannot be a negative value, a spare part cannot exist without a parent object, or the data in a sex field must be male or female. In order to be consistent, a transaction must not break any of the constraints or rules defined for the data.

Isolation

Isolation refers to keeping the changes of incomplete transactions running at the same time separate from one another. Each transaction must be entirely self-contained, and changes it makes must not be readable by any other transaction, although SQL Server does allow you to control the degree of isolation in order to find a balance between business and performance requirements.

Durability

Once a transaction is committed, it must persist even if there is a system failure — that is, it must be durable. In SQL Server, the information needed to replay changes made in a transaction is written to the transaction log before the transaction is considered to be committed.

SQL Server Transactions

There are two types of transactions in SQL Server, *implicit* and *explicit,* and they are differentiated only by the way they are created.

Implicit transactions are used automatically by SQL Server to guarantee the ACID properties of single commands. For example, if you wrote an update statement that modified 10 rows, SQL Server would run it as an implicit transaction so that the ACID properties would apply, and all 10 rows would be updated or none of them would.

Explicit transactions are started by using the BEGIN TRANSACTION T-SQL command and are stopped by using the COMMIT TRANSACTION or ROLLBACK TRANSACTION commands.

Committing a transaction effectively means making the changes within the transaction permanent, whereas rolling back a transaction means undoing all the changes that were made within the transaction. Explicit transactions are used to group together changes to which you want to apply the ACID properties as a whole, which also enables you to roll back the changes at any point if your business logic determines that you should cancel the change.

THE LIFE CYCLE OF A QUERY

To introduce the high-level components of SQL Server's architecture, this section uses the example of a query's life cycle to put each component into context to foster your understanding and create a foundation for the rest of the book.

It looks at a basic SELECT query first in order to reduce the scope to that of a READ operation, and then introduces the additional processes involved for a query that performs an UPDATE operation. Finally, you'll read about the terminology and processes that SQL Server uses to implement recovery while optimizing performance.

Figure 1-1 shows the high-level components that are used within the chapter to illustrate the life cycle of a query.

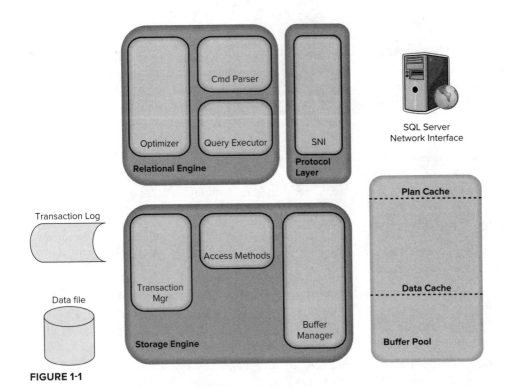

FIGURE 1-1

The Relational and Storage Engines

As shown in Figure 1–1, SQL Server is divided into two main engines: the Relational Engine and the Storage Engine. The Relational Engine is also sometimes called the query processor because its primary function is query optimization and execution. It contains a Command Parser to check query syntax and prepare query trees; a Query Optimizer that is arguably the crown jewel of any database system; and a Query Executor responsible for execution.

The Storage Engine is responsible for managing all I/O to the data, and it contains the Access Methods code, which handles I/O requests for rows, indexes, pages, allocations and row versions; and a Buffer Manager, which deals with SQL Server's main memory consumer, the buffer pool. It also contains a Transaction Manager, which handles the locking of data to maintain isolation (ACID properties) and manages the transaction log.

The Buffer Pool

The other major component you need to know about before getting into the query life cycle is the buffer pool, which is the largest consumer of memory in SQL Server. The buffer pool contains all the different caches in SQL Server, including the plan cache and the data cache, which is covered as the sections follow the query through its life cycle.

> **NOTE** *The buffer pool is covered in detail in Chapter 3.*

A Basic SELECT Query

The details of the query used in this example aren't important — it's a simple SELECT statement with no joins, so you're just issuing a basic read request. It begins at the client, where the first component you touch is the SQL Server Network Interface (SNI).

SQL Server Network Interface

The SQL Server Network Interface (SNI) is a protocol layer that establishes the network connection between the client and the server. It consists of a set of APIs that are used by both the database engine and the SQL Server Native Client (SNAC). SNI replaces the net-libraries found in SQL Server 2000 and the Microsoft Data Access Components (MDAC), which are included with Windows.

SNI isn't configurable directly; you just need to configure a network protocol on the client and the server. SQL Server has support for the following protocols:

➤ **Shared memory** — Simple and fast, shared memory is the default protocol used to connect from a client running on the same computer as SQL Server. It can only be used locally, has no configurable properties, and is always tried first when connecting from the local machine.

➤ **TCP/IP** — This is the most commonly used access protocol for SQL Server. It enables you to connect to SQL Server by specifying an IP address and a port number. Typically, this happens automatically when you specify an instance to connect to. Your internal name resolution system resolves the hostname part of the instance name to an IP address, and either you connect to the default TCP port number 1433 for default instances or the SQL Browser service will find the right port for a named instance using UDP port 1434.

➤ **Named Pipes** — TCP/IP and Named Pipes are comparable protocols in the architectures in which they can be used. Named Pipes was developed for local area networks (LANs) but it can be inefficient across slower networks such as wide area networks (WANs).

To use Named Pipes you first need to enable it in SQL Server Configuration Manager (if you'll be connecting remotely) and then create a SQL Server alias, which connects to the server using Named Pipes as the protocol.

Named Pipes uses TCP port 445, so ensure that the port is open on any firewalls between the two computers, including the Windows Firewall.

➤ **VIA** — Virtual Interface Adapter is a protocol that enables high-performance communications between two systems. It requires specialized hardware at both ends and a dedicated connection.

Like Named Pipes, to use the VIA protocol you first need to enable it in SQL Server Configuration Manager and then create a SQL Server alias that connects to the server using VIA as the protocol. While SQL Server 2012 still supports the VIA protocol, it will be removed from a future version so new installations using this protocol should be avoided.

Regardless of the network protocol used, once the connection is established, SNI creates a secure connection to a TDS endpoint (described next) on the server, which is then used to send requests and receive data. For the purpose here of following a query through its life cycle, you're sending the SELECT statement and waiting to receive the result set.

Tabular Data Stream (TDS) Endpoints

TDS is a Microsoft-proprietary protocol originally designed by Sybase that is used to interact with a database server. Once a connection has been made using a network protocol such as TCP/IP, a link is established to the relevant TDS endpoint that then acts as the communication point between the client and the server.

There is one TDS endpoint for each network protocol and an additional one reserved for use by the dedicated administrator connection (DAC). Once connectivity is established, TDS messages are used to communicate between the client and the server.

The SELECT statement is sent to the SQL Server as a TDS message across a TCP/IP connection (TCP/IP is the default protocol).

Protocol Layer

When the protocol layer in SQL Server receives your TDS packet, it has to reverse the work of the SNI at the client and unwrap the packet to find out what request it contains. The protocol layer is also responsible for packaging results and status messages to send back to the client as TDS messages.

Our SELECT statement is marked in the TDS packet as a message of type "SQL Command," so it's passed on to the next component, the Query Parser, to begin the path toward execution.

Figure 1-2 shows where our query has gone so far. At the client, the statement was wrapped in a TDS packet by the SQL Server Network Interface and sent to the protocol layer on the SQL Server where it was unwrapped, identified as a SQL Command, and the code sent to the Command Parser by the SNI.

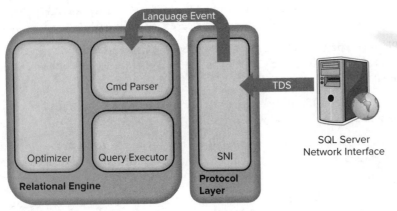

FIGURE 1-2

Command Parser

The Command Parser's role is to handle T-SQL language events. It first checks the syntax and returns any errors back to the protocol layer to send to the client. If the syntax is valid, then the next step is to generate a query plan or find an existing plan. A query plan contains the details about how SQL Server is going to execute a piece of code. It is commonly referred to as an *execution plan*.

To check for a query plan, the Command Parser generates a hash of the T-SQL and checks it against the plan cache to determine whether a suitable plan already exists. The plan cache is an area in the buffer pool used to cache query plans. If it finds a match, then the plan is read from cache and passed on to the Query Executor for execution. (The following section explains what happens if it doesn't find a match.)

Plan Cache

Creating execution plans can be time consuming and resource intensive, so it makes sense that if SQL Server has already found a good way to execute a piece of code that it should try to reuse it for subsequent requests.

The plan cache, part of SQL Server's buffer pool, is used to store execution plans in case they are needed later. You can read more about execution plans and plan cache in Chapters 3 and 5.

If no cached plan is found, then the Command Parser generates a query tree based on the T-SQL. A query tree is an internal structure whereby each node in the tree represents an operation in the query that needs to be performed. This tree is then passed to the Query Optimizer to process. Our basic query didn't have an existing plan so a query tree was created and passed to the Query Optimizer.

Figure 1-3 shows the plan cache added to the diagram, which is checked by the Command Parser for an existing query plan. Also added is the query tree output from the Command Parser being passed to the optimizer because nothing was found in cache for our query.

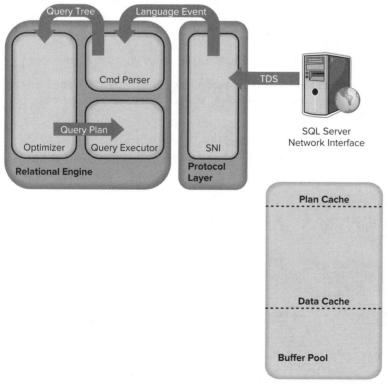

FIGURE 1-3

Query Optimizer

The Query Optimizer is the most prized possession of the SQL Server team and one of the most complex and secretive parts of the product. Fortunately, it's only the low-level algorithms and source code that are so well protected (even within Microsoft), and research and observation can reveal how the Optimizer works.

It is what's known as a "cost-based" optimizer, which means that it evaluates multiple ways to execute a query and then picks the method that it deems will have the lowest cost to execute. This "method" of executing is implemented as a query plan and is the output from the Query Optimizer.

Based on that description, you would be forgiven for thinking that the Optimizer's job is to find the *best* query plan because that would seem like an obvious assumption. Its actual job, however, is to find a *good* plan in a reasonable amount of time, rather than the *best* plan. The optimizer's goal is most commonly described as finding the most *efficient* plan.

If the Optimizer tried to find the "best" plan every time, it might take longer to find the plan than it would to just execute a slower plan (some built-in heuristics actually ensure that it never takes longer to find a good plan than it does to just find a plan and execute it).

As well as being cost based, the Optimizer also performs multi-stage optimization, increasing the number of decisions available to find a good plan at each stage. When a good plan is found, optimization stops at that stage.

The first stage is known as *pre-optimization*, and queries drop out of the process at this stage when the statement is simple enough that there can only be one optimal plan, removing the need for additional costing. Basic queries with no joins are regarded as "simple," and plans produced as such have zero cost (because they haven't been costed) and are referred to as *trivial plans*.

The next stage is where optimization actually begins, and it consists of three search phases:

➤ **Phase 0** — During this phase the optimizer looks at nested loop joins and won't consider parallel operators (parallel means executing across multiple processors and is covered in Chapter 5).

   The optimizer will stop here if the cost of the plan it has found is < 0.2. A plan generated at this phase is known as a *transaction processing*, or *TP*, plan.

➤ **Phase 1** — Phase 1 uses a subset of the possible optimization rules and looks for common patterns for which it already has a plan.

   The optimizer will stop here if the cost of the plan it has found is < 1.0. Plans generated in this phase are called *quick plans*.

➤ **Phase 2** — This final phase is where the optimizer pulls out all the stops and is able to use all of its optimization rules. It also looks at parallelism and indexed views (if you're running Enterprise Edition).

   Completion of Phase 2 is a balance between the cost of the plan found versus the time spent optimizing. Plans created in this phase have an optimization level of "Full."

HOW MUCH DOES IT COST?

The term *cost* doesn't translate into seconds or anything meaningful; it is just an arbitrary number used to assign a value representing the resource cost for a plan. However, its origin was a benchmark on a desktop computer at Microsoft early in SQL Server's life.

In a plan, each operator has a baseline cost, which is then multiplied by the size of the row and the estimated number of rows to get the cost of that operator — and the cost of the plan is the total cost of all the operators.

Because cost is created from a baseline value and isn't related to the speed of your hardware, any plan created will have the same cost on every SQL Server installation (like-for-like version).

The statistics that the optimizer uses to estimate the number of rows aren't covered here because they aren't relevant to the concepts illustrated in this chapter, but you can read about them in Chapter 5.

Because our SELECT query is very simple, it drops out of the process in the pre-optimization phase because the plan is obvious to the optimizer (a *trivial plan*). Now that there is a query plan, it's on to the Query Executor for execution.

Query Executor

The Query Executor's job is self-explanatory; it executes the query. To be more specific, it executes the query plan by working through each step it contains and interacting with the Storage Engine to retrieve or modify data.

> **NOTE** *The interface to the Storage Engine is actually OLE DB, which is a legacy from a design decision made in SQL Server's history. The development team's original idea was to interface through OLE DB to allow different Storage Engines to be plugged in. However, the strategy changed soon after that.*
>
> *The idea of a pluggable Storage Engine was dropped and the developers started writing extensions to OLE DB to improve performance. These customizations are now core to the product; and while there's now no reason to have OLE DB, the existing investment and performance precludes any justification to change it.*

The SELECT query needs to retrieve data, so the request is passed to the Storage Engine through an OLE DB interface to the Access Methods.

Figure 1-4 shows the addition of the query plan as the output from the Optimizer being passed to the Query Executor. Also introduced is the Storage Engine, which is interfaced by the Query Executor via OLE DB to the Access Methods (coming up next).

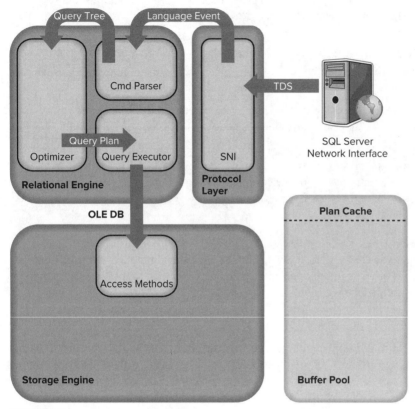

FIGURE 1-4

Access Methods

Access Methods is a collection of code that provides the storage structures for your data and indexes, as well as the interface through which data is retrieved and modified. It contains all the code to retrieve data but it doesn't actually perform the operation itself; it passes the request to the Buffer Manager.

Suppose our SELECT statement needs to read just a few rows that are all on a single page. The Access Methods code will ask the Buffer Manager to retrieve the page so that it can prepare an OLE DB rowset to pass back to the Relational Engine.

Buffer Manager

The Buffer Manager, as its name suggests, manages the buffer pool, which represents the majority of SQL Server's memory usage. If you need to read some rows from a page (you'll look at writes when we look at an UPDATE query), the Buffer Manager checks the data cache in the buffer pool to see if it already has the page cached in memory. If the page is already cached, then the results are passed back to the Access Methods.

If the page isn't already in cache, then the Buffer Manager gets the page from the database on disk, puts it in the data cache, and passes the results to the Access Methods.

> **NOTE** *The* PAGEIOLATCH *wait type represents the time it takes to read a data page from disk into memory. Wait types are covered later in this chapter.*

The key point to take away from this is that you only ever work with data in memory. Every new data read that you request is first read from disk and then written to memory (the data cache) before being returned as a result set.

This is why SQL Server needs to maintain a minimum level of free pages in memory; you wouldn't be able to read any new data if there were no space in cache to put it first.

The Access Methods code determined that the SELECT query needed a single page, so it asked the Buffer Manager to get it. The Buffer Manager checked whether it already had it in the data cache, and then loaded it from disk into the cache when it couldn't find it.

Data Cache

The data cache is usually the largest part of the buffer pool; therefore, it's the largest memory consumer within SQL Server. It is here that every data page that is read from disk is written to before being used.

The sys.dm_os_buffer_descriptors DMV contains one row for every data page currently held in cache. You can use this script to see how much space each database is using in the data cache:

```
SELECT count(*)*8/1024 AS 'Cached Size (MB)'
    ,CASE database_id
        WHEN 32767 THEN 'ResourceDb'
        ELSE db_name(database_id)
        END AS 'Database'
FROM sys.dm_os_buffer_descriptors
GROUP BY db_name(database_id),database_id
ORDER BY 'Cached Size (MB)' DESC
```

The output will look something like this (with your own databases, obviously):

```
Cached Size (MB)   Database
3287               People
34                 tempdb
12                 ResourceDb
4                  msdb
```

In this example, the People database has 3,287MB of data pages in the data cache.

The amount of time that pages stay in cache is determined by a *least recently used (LRU) policy*.

The header of each page in cache stores details about the last two times it was accessed, and a periodic scan through the cache examines these values. A counter is maintained that is decremented if the page hasn't been accessed for a while; and when SQL Server needs to free up some cache, the pages with the lowest counter are flushed first.

The process of "aging out" pages from cache and maintaining an available amount of free cache pages for subsequent use can be done by any worker thread after scheduling its own I/O or by the lazy writer process, covered later in the section "Lazy Writer."

You can view how long SQL Server expects to be able to keep a page in cache by looking at the MSSQL$instance:Buffer Manager\Page Life Expectancy counter in Performance Monitor. Page life expectancy (PLE) is the amount of time, in seconds, that SQL Server expects to be able to keep a page in cache.

Under memory pressure, data pages are flushed from cache far more frequently. Microsoft has a long standing recommendation for a minimum of 300 seconds for PLE but a good value is generally considered to be 1000s of seconds these days. Exactly what your acceptable threshold should be is variable depending on your data usage, but more often than not, you'll find servers with either 1000s of seconds PLE or a lot less than 300, so it's usually easy to spot a problem.

The database page read to serve the result set for our SELECT query is now in the data cache in the buffer pool and will have an entry in the sys.dm_os_buffer_descriptors DMV. Now that the Buffer Manager has the result set, it's passed back to the Access Methods to make its way to the client.

A Basic SELECT Statement Life Cycle Summary

Figure 1-5 shows the whole life cycle of a SELECT query, described here:

1. The SQL Server Network Interface (SNI) on the client established a connection to the SNI on the SQL Server using a network protocol such as TCP/IP. It then created a connection to a TDS endpoint over the TCP/IP connection and sent the SELECT statement to SQL Server as a TDS message.

2. The SNI on the SQL Server unpacked the TDS message, read the SELECT statement, and passed a "SQL Command" to the Command Parser.

3. The Command Parser checked the plan cache in the buffer pool for an existing, usable query plan that matched the statement received. When it didn't find one, it created a query tree based on the SELECT statement and passed it to the Optimizer to generate a query plan.

4. The Optimizer generated a "zero cost" or "trivial" plan in the pre-optimization phase because the statement was so simple. The query plan created was then passed to the Query Executor for execution.

5. At execution time, the Query Executor determined that data needed to be read to complete the query plan so it passed the request to the Access Methods in the Storage Engine via an OLE DB interface.

6. The Access Methods needed to read a page from the database to complete the request from the Query Executor and asked the Buffer Manager to provision the data page.

7. The Buffer Manager checked the data cache to see if it already had the page in cache. It wasn't in cache so it pulled the page from disk, put it in cache, and passed it back to the Access Methods.

8. Finally, the Access Methods passed the result set back to the Relational Engine to send to the client.

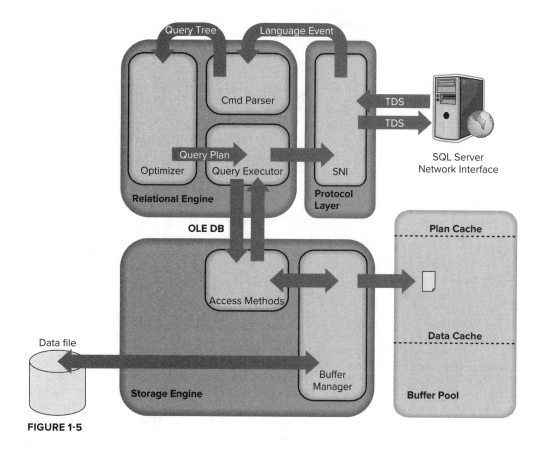

FIGURE 1-5

A Simple Update Query

Now that you understand the life cycle for a query that just reads some data, the next step is to determine what happens when you need to write data. To answer that, this section takes a look at a simple UPDATE query that modifies the data that was read in the previous example.

The good news is that the process is exactly the same as the process for the SELECT statement you just looked at until you get to the Access Methods.

The Access Methods need to make a data modification this time, so before the I/O request is passed on, the details of the change need to be persisted to disk. That is the job of the Transaction Manager.

Transaction Manager

The Transaction Manager has two components that are of interest here: a Lock Manager and a Log Manager. The Lock Manager is responsible for providing concurrency to the data, and it delivers the configured level of *isolation* (as defined in the ACID properties at the beginning of the chapter) by using locks.

> **NOTE** *The Lock Manager is also employed during the* SELECT *query life cycle covered earlier, but it would have been a distraction; it is mentioned here because it's part of the Transaction Manager, but locking is covered in depth in Chapter 6.*

The real item of interest here is actually the Log Manager. The Access Methods code requests that the changes it wants to make are logged, and the Log Manager writes the changes to the transaction log. This is called *write-ahead logging (WAL)*.

Writing to the transaction log is the only part of a data modification transaction that always needs a physical write to disk because SQL Server depends on being able to reread that change in the event of system failure (you'll learn more about this in the "Recovery" section coming up).

What's actually stored in the transaction log isn't a list of modification statements but only details of the page changes that occurred as the result of a modification statement. This is all that SQL Server needs in order to undo any change, and why it's so difficult to read the contents of a transaction log in any meaningful way, although you can buy a third-party tool to help.

Getting back to the UPDATE query life cycle, the update operation has now been logged. The actual data modification can only be performed when confirmation is received that the operation has been physically written to the transaction log. This is why transaction log performance is so crucial.

Once confirmation is received by the Access Methods, it passes the modification request on to the Buffer Manager to complete.

Figure 1-6 shows the Transaction Manager, which is called by the Access Methods and the transaction log, which is the destination for logging our update. The Buffer Manager is also in play now because the modification request is ready to be completed.

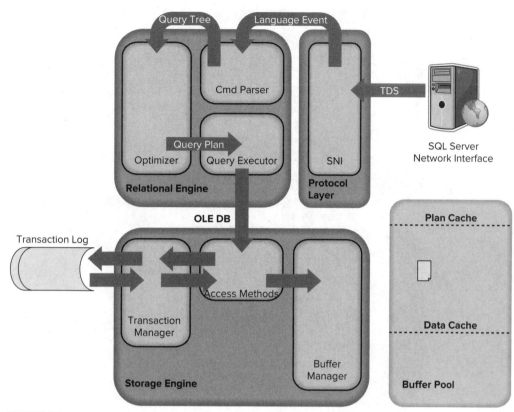

FIGURE 1-6

Buffer Manager

The page that needs to be modified is already in cache, so all the Buffer Manager needs to do is modify the page required by the update as requested by the Access Methods. The page is modified in the cache, and confirmation is sent back to Access Methods and ultimately to the client.

The key point here (and it's a big one) is that the UPDATE statement has changed the data in the data cache, *not* in the actual database file on disk. This is done for performance reasons, and the page is now what's called a *dirty page* because it's different in memory from what's on disk.

It doesn't compromise the *durability* of the modification as defined in the ACID properties because you can re-create the change using the transaction log if, for example, you suddenly lost power to the server, and therefore anything in physical RAM (i.e., the data cache). How and when the dirty page makes its way into the database file is covered in the next section.

Figure 1-7 shows the completed life cycle for the update. The Buffer Manager has made the modification to the page in cache and has passed confirmation back up the chain. The database data file was not accessed during the operation, as you can see in the diagram.

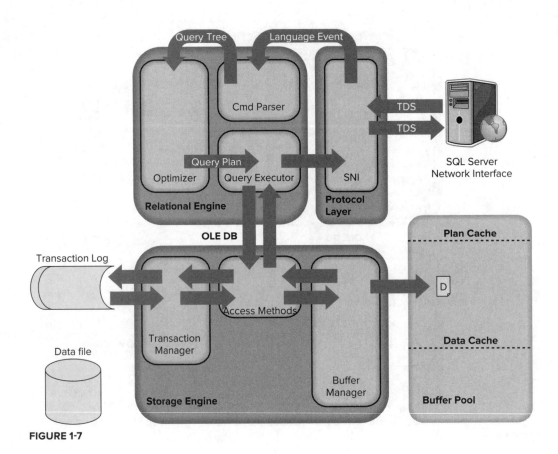

FIGURE 1-7

Recovery

In the previous section you read about the life cycle of an UPDATE query, which introduced write-ahead logging as the method by which SQL Server maintains the *durability* of any changes.

Modifications are written to the transaction log first and are then actioned in memory only. This is done for performance reasons and enables you to recover the changes from the transaction log if necessary. This process introduces some new concepts and terminology that are explored further in this section on "recovery."

Dirty Pages

When a page is read from disk into memory it is regarded as a *clean page* because it's exactly the same as its counterpart on the disk. However, once the page has been modified in memory it is marked as a *dirty page*.

Clean pages can be flushed from cache using dbcc dropcleanbuffers, which can be handy when you're troubleshooting development and test environments because it forces subsequent reads to be fulfilled from disk, rather than cache, but doesn't touch any dirty pages.

A dirty page is simply a page that has changed in memory since it was loaded from disk and is now different from the on-disk page. You can use the following query, which is based on the sys.dm_os_buffer_descriptors DMV, to see how many dirty pages exist in each database:

```
SELECT db_name(database_id) AS 'Database',count(page_id) AS 'Dirty Pages'
FROM sys.dm_os_buffer_descriptors
WHERE is_modified =1
GROUP BY db_name(database_id)
ORDER BY count(page_id) DESC
```

Running this on my test server produced the following results showing that at the time the query was run, there were just under 20MB (2,524*8\1,024) of dirty pages in the People database:

```
Database Dirty Pages
People   2524
Tempdb   61
Master   1
```

These dirty pages will be written back to the database file periodically whenever the *free buffer list* is low or a *checkpoint* occurs. SQL Server always tries to maintain a number of free pages in cache in order to allocate pages quickly, and these free pages are tracked in the free buffer list.

Whenever a worker thread issues a read request, it gets a list of 64 pages in cache and checks whether the free buffer list is below a certain threshold. If it is, it will try to age-out some pages in its list, which causes any dirty pages to be written to disk. Another thread called the *lazy writer* also works based on a low free buffer list.

Lazy Writer

The *lazy writer* is a thread that periodically checks the size of the free buffer list. When it's low, it scans the whole data cache to age-out any pages that haven't been used for a while. If it finds any dirty pages that haven't been used for a while, they are flushed to disk before being marked as free in memory.

The lazy writer also monitors the free physical memory on the server and will release memory from the free buffer list back to Windows in very low memory conditions. When SQL Server is busy, it will also grow the size of the free buffer list to meet demand (and therefore the buffer pool) when there is free physical memory and the configured Max Server Memory threshold hasn't been reached. For more on Max Server Memory, see Chapter 3.

Checkpoint Process

A checkpoint is a point in time created by the checkpoint process at which SQL Server can be sure that any *committed* transactions have had all their changes written to disk. This checkpoint then becomes the marker from which database recovery can start.

The checkpoint process ensures that any dirty pages associated with a committed transaction will be flushed to disk. It can also flush uncommitted dirty pages to disk to make efficient use of writes but unlike the lazy writer, a checkpoint does not remove the page from cache; it ensures the dirty page is written to disk and then marks the cached paged as clean in the page header.

By default, on a busy server, SQL Server will issue a checkpoint roughly every minute, which is marked in the transaction log. If the SQL Server instance or the database is restarted, then the recovery process reading the log knows that it doesn't need to do anything with log records prior to the checkpoint.

LOG SEQUENCE NUMBER (LSN)

LSNs are used to identify records in the transaction log and are ordered so SQL Server knows the sequence in which events occurred.

A *minimum LSN* is computed before recovery does any work like roll forward or roll back. This takes into account not only the checkpoint LSN but other criteria as well. This means recovery might still need to worry about pages before a checkpoint if all dirty pages haven't made it to disk. This can happen on large systems with large numbers of dirty pages.

The time between checkpoints, therefore, represents the amount of work that needs to be done to *roll forward* any committed transactions that occurred after the last checkpoint, and to *roll back* any transactions that were not committed. By checkpointing every minute, SQL Server is trying to keep the recovery time when starting a database to less than one minute, but it won't automatically checkpoint unless at least 10MB has been written to the log within the period.

Checkpoints can also be manually called by using the CHECKPOINT T-SQL command, and can occur because of other events happening in SQL Server. For example, when you issue a backup command, a checkpoint will run first.

Trace flag 3502 records in the error log when a checkpoint starts and stops. For example, after adding it as a startup trace flag and running a workload with numerous writes, my error log contained the entries shown in Figure 1-8, which indicates checkpoints running between 30 and 40 seconds apart.

2009-04-26 22:31:33.070	spid10s	About to log Checkpoint begin.
2009-04-26 22:31:33.070	spid10s	About to log Checkpoint end.
2009-04-26 22:32:05.910	spid10s	About to log Checkpoint begin.
2009-04-26 22:32:05.910	spid10s	About to log Checkpoint end.
2009-04-26 23:33:29.280	spid10s	About to log Checkpoint begin.
2009-04-26 23:33:29.370	spid10s	About to log Checkpoint end.
2009-04-26 23:34:12.000	spid10s	About to log Checkpoint begin.
2009-04-26 23:34:12.090	spid10s	About to log Checkpoint end.

FIGURE 1-8

ALL ABOUT TRACE FLAGS

Trace flags provide a way to change the behavior of SQL Server temporarily and are generally used to help with troubleshooting or for enabling and disabling certain features for testing. Hundreds of trace flags exist but very few are officially documented; for a list of those that are and more information on using trace flags, see http://msdn.microsoft.com/en-us/library/ms188396.aspx.

Recovery Interval

Recovery Interval is a server configuration option that can be used to influence the time between checkpoints, and therefore the time it takes to recover a database on startup — hence, "recovery interval."

By default, the recovery interval is set to 0; this enables SQL Server to choose an appropriate interval, which usually equates to roughly one minute between automatic checkpoints.

Changing this value to greater than 0 represents the number of minutes you want to allow between checkpoints. Under most circumstances you won't need to change this value, but if you were more concerned about the overhead of the checkpoint process than the recovery time, you have the option.

The recovery interval is usually set only in test and lab environments, where it's set ridiculously high in order to effectively stop automatic checkpointing for the purpose of monitoring something or to gain a performance advantage. Unless you're chasing world speed records for SQL Server, you shouldn't need to change it in a real-world production environment.

SQL Server evens throttles checkpoint I/O to stop it from affecting the disk subsystem too much, so it's quite good at self-governing. If you ever see the SLEEP_BPOOL_FLUSH wait type on your server, that means checkpoint I/O was throttled to maintain overall system performance. You can read all about waits and wait types in the section "SQL Server's Execution Model and the SQLOS."

Recovery Models

SQL Server has three database recovery models: full, bulk-logged, and simple. Which model you choose affects the way the transaction log is used and how big it grows, your backup strategy, and your restore options.

Full

Databases using the full recovery model have all their operations fully logged in the transaction log and must have a backup strategy that includes full backups *and* transaction log backups.

Starting with SQL Server 2005, full backups don't truncate the transaction log. This is done so that the sequence of transaction log backups isn't broken and it gives you an extra recovery option if your full backup is damaged.

SQL Server databases that require the highest level of recoverability should use the full recovery model.

Bulk-Logged

This is a special recovery model because it is intended to be used only temporarily to improve the performance of certain bulk operations by *minimally logging* them; all other operations are fully logged just like the full recovery model. This can improve performance because only the information required to roll back the transaction is logged. Redo information is not logged, which means you also lose point-in-time-recovery.

These bulk operations include the following:

➤ BULK INSERT

➤ Using the bcp executable

➤ SELECT INTO

➤ CREATE INDEX

➤ ALTER INDEX REBUILD

➤ DROP INDEX

BULK-LOGGED AND TRANSACTION LOG BACKUPS

Using bulk-logged mode is intended to make your bulk-logged operation complete faster. It does not reduce the disk space requirement for your transaction log backups.

Simple

When the simple recovery model is set on a database, all committed transactions are truncated from the transaction log every time a checkpoint occurs. This ensures that the size of the log is kept to a minimum and that transaction log backups are not necessary (or even possible). Whether or not that is a good or a bad thing depends on what level of recovery you require for the database.

If the potential to lose all changes since the last full or differential backup still meets your business requirements, then simple recovery might be the way to go.

SQL SERVER'S EXECUTION MODEL AND THE SQLOS

So far, this chapter has abstracted the concept of the SQLOS to make the flow of components through the architecture easier to understand without going off on too many tangents. However, the SQLOS is core to SQL Server's architecture so you need to understand why it exists and what it does to complete your view of how SQL Server works.

In short, the SQLOS is a thin user-mode layer that sits between SQL Server and Windows. It is used for low-level operations such as scheduling, I/O completion, memory management, and resource management. To explore exactly what this means and why it's needed, you first need to understand SQL Server's execution model.

Execution Model

When an application authenticates to SQL Server it establishes a connection in the context of a *session*, which is identified by a *session_id* (in older versions of SQL Server this was called a SPID). You can view a list of all authenticated sessions by querying the sys.dm_exec_sessions DMV.

When an execution request is made within a session, SQL Server divides the work into one or more *tasks* and then associates a *worker thread* to each task for its duration. Each thread can be in one of three states (that you need to care about):

➤ **Running** — A processor can only execute one thing at a time and the thread currently executing on a processor will have a state of *running*.

➤ **Suspended** — SQL Server has a co-operative scheduler (see below) so running threads will yield the processor and become *suspended* while they wait for a resource. This is what we call a *wait* in SQL Server.

➤ **Runnable** — When a thread has finished waiting, it becomes *runnable* which means that it's ready to execute again. This is known as a *signal wait*.

If no worker threads are available and *max worker threads* has not been reached, then SQL Server will allocate a new worker thread. If the max worker threads count *has* been reached, then the task will *wait* with a wait type of THREADPOOL until a thread becomes available. Waits and wait types are covered later in this section.

The default max workers count is based on the CPU architecture and the number of logical processors. The formulas for this are as follows:

For a 32-bit operating system:

➤ Total available logical CPUs <= 4

  ➤ Max Worker Threads = 256

➤ Total available logical CPUs > 4

  ➤ Max Worker Threads = 256 + ((logical CPUs − 4)*8)

For a 64-bit operating system:

➤ Total available logical CPUs <= 4

  ➤ Max Worker Threads = 512

➤ Total available logical CPUs > 4

  ➤ Max Worker Threads = 512 + ((logical CPUs − 4)*16)

As an example, a 64-bit SQL Server with 16 processors would have a Max Worker Threads setting of 512 + ((16−4)*16) = 704.

You can also see the max workers count on a running system by executing the following:

```
SELECT max_workers_count
FROM sys.dm_os_sys_info
```

> ### INCREASING THE MAX WORKER THREADS SETTING
>
> Running out of worker threads (THREADPOOL wait type) is often a symptom of large numbers of concurrent parallel execution plans (since one thread is used per processor), or it can even indicate that you've reached the performance capacity of the server and need to buy one with more processors. Either way, you're usually better off trying to solve the underlying problem rather than overriding the default Max Worker Threads setting.

Each worker thread requires 2MB of RAM on a 64-bit server and 0.5MB on a 32-bit server, so SQL Server creates threads only as it needs them, rather than all at once.

The sys.dm_os_workers DMV contains one row for every worker thread, so you can see how many threads SQL Server currently has by executing the following:

```
SELECT count(*) FROM sys.dm_os_workers
```

Schedulers

Each thread has an associated *scheduler,* which has the function of scheduling time for each of its threads on a processor. The number of schedulers available to SQL Server equals the number of logical processors that SQL Server can use plus an extra one for the dedicated administrator connection (DAC).

You can view information about SQL Server's schedulers by querying the sys.dm_os_schedulers DMV.

Figure 1-9 illustrates the relationship between sessions, tasks, threads, and schedulers.

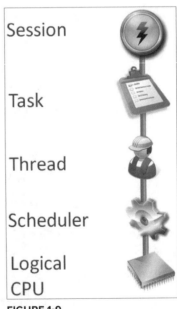

FIGURE 1-9

Windows is a general-purpose OS and is not optimized for server-based applications, SQL Server in particular. Instead, the goal of the Windows development team is to ensure that all applications, written by a wide variety of developers inside and outside Microsoft, will work correctly and have good performance. Because Windows needs to work well in a broad range of scenarios, the development team is not going to do anything special that would only be used in less than 1% of applications.

For example, the scheduling in Windows is very basic to ensure that it's suitable for a common cause. Optimizing the way that threads are chosen for execution is always going to be limited because of this broad performance goal; but if an application does its own scheduling then there is more intelligence about what to choose next, such as assigning some threads a higher priority or deciding that choosing one thread for execution will avoid other threads being blocked later.

The basic scheduler in Windows is known as a *pre-emptive scheduler* and it assigns slices of time known as *quantums* to each task to be executed. The advantage of this is that application developers don't have to worry about scheduling when creating applications; the downside is that execution can be interrupted at any point as Windows balances execution requests from multiple processes.

All versions of SQL Server up to and including version 6.5 used the Windows scheduler to take advantage of the work that the Windows team had done through a long history of optimizing processor usage. There came a point, however, when SQL Server 6.5 could not scale any further and it was limited by the general-purpose optimizations of the pre-emptive scheduler in Windows.

For SQL Server 7.0, Microsoft decided that SQL Server should handle its own scheduling, and created the User Mode Scheduler (UMS) to do just that. The UMS was designed as a *co-operative* scheduling model whereby threads aren't forcibly interrupted during execution but instead voluntarily yield the processor when they need to wait for another resource. When a thread yields the processor, a *wait type* is assigned to the task to help describe the wait and aid you in troubleshooting performance issues.

The SQLOS

Prior to SQLOS (which was first implemented in SQL Server 2005), low-level operations such as scheduling, I/O completion, memory management, and resource management were all handled by different teams, which resulted in a lot of duplication of effort as the product evolved.

The idea for SQLOS was to consolidate all these efforts of the different internal SQL Server development teams to provide performance improvements on Windows, putting them in a single place with a single team that can continue to optimize these low-level functions. This enables the other teams to concentrate on challenges more specific to their own domain within SQL Server.

Another benefit to having everything in one place is that you now get better visibility of what's happening at that level than was possible prior to SQLOS. You can access all this information through dynamic management views (DMVs). Any DMV that starts with `sys.dm_os_` provides an insight into the workings of SQLOS, such as the following:

➤ **sys.dm_os_schedulers** — Returns one row per scheduler (remember, there is one user scheduler per logical processor) and displays information about scheduler load and health. See Chapter 5 for more information.

➤ **sys.dm_os_waiting_tasks** — Returns one row for every executing task that is currently waiting for a resource, as well as the wait type

➤ **sys.dm_os_memory_clerks** — Memory clerks are used by SQL Server to allocate memory. Significant components within SQL Server have their own memory clerk. This DMV shows all the memory clerks and how much memory each one is using. See Chapter 3 for more information.

Relating SQLOS back to the architecture diagrams shown earlier, many of the components make calls to the SQLOS in order to fulfill low-level functions required to support their roles.

Just to be clear, the SQLOS doesn't replace Windows. Ultimately, everything ends up using the documented Windows system services; SQL Server just uses them in a way optimized for its own specific scenarios.

> **NOTE** *SQLOS is not a way to port the SQL Server architecture to other platforms like Linux or Mac OS, so it's not an OS abstraction layer. It doesn't wrap all the OS APIs like other frameworks such as .NET, which is why it's referred to as a "thin" user-mode layer. Only the things that SQL Server really needs have been put into SQLOS.*

DEFINING DMVS

Dynamic management views (DMVs) enable much greater visibility into the workings of SQL Server than any version prior to SQL Server 2005. They are basically just views on top of the system tables or in-memory system counters, but the concept enables Microsoft to provide a massive amount of useful information through them.

The standard syntax starts with `sys.dm_`, which indicates that it's a DMV (there are also dynamic management functions, but DMV is still the collective term in popular use), followed by the area about which the DMV provides information — for example, `sys.dm_os_` for SQLOS, `sys.dm_db_` for database, and `sys.dm_exec_` for query execution.

The last part of the name describes the actual content accessible within the view; `sys.dm_db_index_usage_stats` and `sys.dm_os_waiting_tasks` are a couple of examples, and you'll come across many more throughout the book.

SUMMARY

In this chapter you learned about SQL Server's architecture by following the flow of components used when you issue a read request and an update request. You also learned some key terminology and processes used for the recovery of SQL Server databases and where the SQLOS fits into the architecture.

Following are the key points from this chapter:

➤ The Query Optimizer's job is to find a good plan in a reasonable amount of time; not the *best* plan.

➤ Anything you want to read or update needs to be read into memory first.

➤ Any updates to data are written to the transaction log on disk before being updated in memory, so transaction log performance is critical; the update isn't written directly to the data file.

➤ A database page that is changed in memory but not on disk is known as a dirty page.

➤ Dirty pages are flushed to disk by the checkpoint process and the lazy writer.

➤ Checkpoints occur automatically, roughly every minute, and provide the starting point for recovery.

➤ The lazy writer maintains space available in cache by flushing dirty pages to disk and keeping only recently used pages in cache.

➤ When a database is using the full recovery model, full backups will not truncate the transaction log. You must configure transaction log backups.

➤ Tasks are generated to provide the context for a unit of work executed in a session. Worker threads handle the execution of work within a task, and a scheduler is the mechanism by which threads are given time on a processor to execute.

➤ The SQLOS is a framework used by components in SQL Server for scheduling, I/O, and memory management.

2

Demystifying Hardware

WHAT'S IN THIS CHAPTER?

➤ Understanding SQL Server workload types

➤ Server model selection and evolution

➤ Processor selection and SQL Server 2012 licensing considerations

➤ Understanding processor model numbering

➤ Choosing hardware to increase redundancy

➤ Using hardware comparison tools

WROX.COM CODE DOWNLOADS FOR THIS CHAPTER

There are no code downloads for this chapter.

THE IMPORTANCE OF HARDWARE

The underlying foundation of SQL Server 2012 performance and scalability is the actual hardware and storage subsystem on which your instance of SQL Server 2012 is running. This is true whether you are running in a virtualized environment or in a bare metal configuration. Regardless of what type of database workload you may have to deal with, and irrespective of how well designed and optimized your databases are, the characteristics and performance of your database hardware and storage subsystem are extremely important. Even the most well-designed and carefully tuned database application can be crippled by poorly chosen or inadequate hardware. This is not to say that hardware can solve all performance or scalability problems. A frequently executed, expensive query on an extremely large dataset can quickly overwhelm even the best hardware and storage subsystem. Despite this, having modern, properly sized hardware and a good storage subsystem gives you a much better chance of being able to handle any type of workload that you may see on SQL Server 2012, and makes your life as a DBA much easier!

Unfortunately, far too many database administrators (DBAs) are blissfully ignorant about the important details regarding their database hardware infrastructure. Given the pace of recent and ongoing advances in new processors and chipsets, along with changes in both magnetic and flash storage, trying to stay current with hardware technology can be daunting. Many DBAs simply give up, and let someone else make all the hardware and storage decisions. No matter who makes these decisions, however, the DBA is usually blamed for any performance or scalability issues that show up later. Even if you don't get to make the final decisions regarding hardware selection, being knowledgeable and informed about server hardware puts you in a much stronger position during the decision-making process. Being educated about database hardware also helps you understand whether your existing hardware and storage subsystem is woefully underpowered by today's standards, which is extremely valuable information for a DBA. This chapter is designed to give you the foundational concepts and knowledge that you need to make informed decisions about your database hardware and storage systems.

HOW WORKLOAD AFFECTS HARDWARE AND STORAGE CONSIDERATIONS

If you are ready to accept the challenge of learning some of the mysteries of database server hardware and storage, where should you begin? The first step is to have a good understanding of your current or planned workload. You need to know whether your database server will be running only the actual SQL Server Database Engine, or also other SQL Server components such as SQL Server Analysis Services (SSAS), SQL Server Integration Services (SSIS), or SQL Server Reporting Services (SSRS). Ideally, you would want these other SQL Server components running on separate dedicated servers, but you might not have that luxury because of the extra hardware and licensing costs. Even if you are only going to be running the Database Engine on your database server, you need to understand what kind of workload you will be handling.

Workload Types

Several different types of workload are common with SQL Server, or any other relational database management server (RDBMS), including online transaction processing (OLTP), data warehousing (DW), relational reporting, and online analytical processing (OLAP). Depending on your applications and what SQL Server components are running on your database server, you might have a relatively pure version of one of these workload types or a mixture of several.

Other variables include the number of user databases running on your database instance, and the volume and intensity of your workload — that is, how many batch requests per second, how many new rows are inserted or updated per second, and so on. All these different variables affect your hardware selection decisions, and how you decide to configure your hardware and storage subsystem to get the best performance possible for that type of workload.

OLTP Workloads

One extreme is a pure OLTP workload, which is typically characterized by numerous short-duration queries and transactions with a relatively high percentage of write activity. Processors with higher base clock speeds and higher turbo speeds (within the same processor family) tend to perform better on most OLTP queries. A pure OLTP workload usually has a high degree of data volatility, especially in some of the database's key tables. Having a pure OLTP workload will influence your hardware options and how you configure your hardware and storage subsystem. These workloads generate more input/output (I/O) operations per second (IOPS) than an equivalent data warehouse (DW) system.

With a single OLTP database, you will see mostly sequential write activity to your transaction log file, and more random write activity to your data file(s). If you have more than one OLTP database on your instance of SQL Server, and the transaction log files for these databases are located on the same drive array, you will see more random write activity because the drive array is forced to service all the transaction log files for multiple OLTP databases. If you are using technologies such as SQL Server transactional replication, database mirroring, or AlwaysOn availability groups, you will also see sequential read activity against your transaction log file(s).

Data Warehousing Workloads

Another completely different type of workload is a pure DW workload, which has long-running, complex queries that are often parallelized by the Query Optimizer; this places a premium on having processors with higher physical core counts and better memory controllers in order to execute these types of queries as quickly as possible. Also very important for DW workloads is having a large amount of memory to ensure you have adequate room for the buffer pool.

A DW workload has more sequential reads from your data files and very little write activity to your data files and log file during normal operations. During data loads, you will see predominantly sequential write activity to your transaction log file and a combination of sequential and random write activity to your data files. You want to consider sequential read and write performance as you select and configure your I/O subsystem for a DW workload.

Relational Reporting Workloads

Many organizations maintain a second copy of an OLTP database for reporting usage. This is ideally located on a dedicated server that is separate from the primary OLTP database server. This "reporting" database will have many additional nonclustered indexes added to the existing OLTP tables and it may also have additional reporting tables containing calculated summary data for reporting purposes.

In some cases, this reporting database is restored from a backup of the production OLTP database, perhaps once a day. After the restore is finished, all the additional nonclustered indexes are created and the reporting tables are loaded and indexed. In terms of sequential read and write performance, this type of pattern places a lot of stress on the I/O subsystem. Restoring a database from a backup and creating many new indexes is a sequential operation, so having a lot of sequential I/O performance is very important. After the reporting database is ready for use, the overall workload becomes very similar to a DW workload. If you have this type of pattern, you should consider using the new *columnstore index* feature in SQL Server 2012.

Another scenario for a relational reporting database is to use transactional replication between the production OLTP database, which acts as a publisher, to the "reporting" database, which acts as a subscriber. Usually, many additional nonclustered indexes are added to the subscriber to improve query performance for reporting queries. Maintaining acceptable INSERT, UPDATE, and DELETE performance in this database is more difficult because of these additional indexes. This places more stress on your I/O subsystem, so you will see sequential writes to the log file and random writes to the data files. The reporting queries cause sequential reads from the data files. Overall, this is a relatively challenging mixed workload type.

OLAP Workloads

OLAP workloads have several different components, including reading data from the source(s) to initially build or update the cube, processing the cube when changes are made, and then actually running various types of OLAP queries to retrieve the data for users. Having processors with higher physical core counts, with better memory controllers in order to execute these types of queries as quickly as possible, is very valuable. Also very important for OLAP workloads is having a large amount of memory so that you can process large cubes quickly. OLAP workloads tend to have a lot of random I/O, so flash-based storage (see Chapter 4) for the cube files can be very beneficial. Flash-based storage includes solid-state drives (SSDs) and other devices such as Fusion-io cards that use solid-state flash memory for permanent storage. These types of devices offer extremely high random I/O performance, which is very useful for OLAP workloads.

Server Model Selection

In order to choose an appropriate server model for your database server, you must first decide whether you want to use an Intel processor or an AMD processor, as this absolutely dictates which server models you can consider from your system vendor. Next, you need to decide whether you will be using a one-socket, two-socket, or four-socket database server, or something even larger, as that constrains your available processor options. You also have to decide what vertical form factor you want for the server — that is, whether it will be a 1U, 2U, 4U, or even larger server. These designations, (1U, 2U, etc.) refer to how tall the server is in rack units, with a rack unit being roughly 1.75 inches tall. This affects how many servers will fit in a rack, and how many internal drive bays will fit inside a rack-mounted server.

These choices also affect the maximum amount of physical memory (RAM) that you can have, the number of Peripheral Component Interconnect Express (PCIe) expansion slots that are available, and the number of internal drive bays that are available in the server.

Here are some things to consider as you decide whether to purchase a two-socket database server or a four-socket database server. Traditionally, it was very common to use a four-socket machine for most database server scenarios, while two-socket servers were most often used for web servers or application servers. However, given recent advances in processors, improvements in memory density, and the increase in the number and bandwidth of PCIe expansion slots over the past several years, you might want to seriously reconsider that conventional wisdom.

Historically, two-socket database servers did not have enough processor capacity, memory capacity, or I/O capacity to handle most intense database workloads. Processors have become far more powerful in the last few years, and memory density has increased dramatically. It is also possible to achieve much more I/O capacity connected to a two-socket server than it was a few years ago, especially with the latest processors and chipsets that have PCIe 3.0 support.

Another reason to carefully consider this issue is the cost of SQL Server 2012 Enterprise Edition processor core licenses. If you can run your workload on a two-socket server instead of a four-socket server, you could save up to 50% on your SQL Server processor core license costs, which can be a very substantial savings! With SQL Server 2012 Enterprise Edition, the cost of a few processor core licenses would pay for a very capable two-socket database server (exclusive of the I/O subsystem).

Server Model Evolution

To provide some history and context, this section describes how the capabilities and performance of commodity two- and four-socket servers have changed over the past seven years. In 2005, you could buy a two-socket Dell PowerEdge 1850 with two hyperthreaded Intel Xeon "Irwindale" 3.2GHz processors and 12GB of RAM (with a total of four logical cores). This was fine for an application or web server, but it really didn't have the CPU horsepower (the Geekbench score was about 2200) or memory capacity for a heavy-duty database workload (more details about Geekbench appear later in the chapter). This model server had relatively few expansion slots, with either two PCI-X or two PCIe 1.0 slots being available.

By early 2006, you could buy a four-socket Dell PowerEdge 6850 with four dual-core, Intel Xeon 7040 "Paxville" 3.0GHz processors and up to 64GB of RAM (with a total of 16 logical cores with hyperthreading enabled). This was a much better choice for a database server at the time because of the additional processor, memory, and I/O capacity compared to a PowerEdge 1850. Even so, its Geekbench score was only about 4400, which is pretty pathetic by today's standards, even compared to a new Core i3–2350M entry-level laptop. In 2005 and 2006, it still made sense to buy a four-socket database server for most database server workloads because two socket servers simply were not powerful enough in terms of CPU, memory, or I/O.

By late 2007, you could buy a two-socket Dell PowerEdge 1950 with two, quad-core Intel Xeon E5450 processors and 32GB of RAM (with a total of eight logical cores), which provided a relatively powerful platform for a small database server. The Intel Xeon 5400 series did not have hyperthreading. A system like this would have a Geekbench score of about 8000. With only two PCIe 1.0 × 8 slots it had limited external I/O capability, but the gap compared to four socket servers was beginning to narrow.

In late 2008, you could get a four-socket Dell PowerEdge R900 with four, six-core Intel Xeon X7460 processors and 256GB of RAM (with a total of 24 logical cores). This system had seven PCIe 1.0 expansion slots, divided into four × 8 and three × 4 slots. (The × 4 and × 8 refer to the number of lanes. The more lanes, the higher the maximum bandwidth.) This was a very power-ful but costly platform for a database server, with a Geekbench score of around 16,500. This was the last generation of Intel Xeon processors to use a symmetrical multiprocessing (SMP) architecture, rather than a non-uniform memory access (NUMA) architecture, so it did not scale very well when additional processor sockets were added to servers. The Intel Xeon 7400 series did not have hyperthreading. Many four-socket servers of this vintage are still in use today, even though their performance and scalability has long been eclipsed by modern two-socket servers.

By early 2009, you could get a two-socket Dell PowerEdge R710 with two, quad-core Intel Xeon X5570 processors, and 144GB of RAM (with a total of 16 logical cores with hyperthreading enabled). This system had four PCIe 2.0 expansion slots, divided into two × 8 and two × 4 slots. This provided a very powerful database server platform in a very compact package. Such a system would have a Geekbench score of around 15,000. It used the 45nm Nehalem-EP family processor, which had NUMA support. This was when the tide began to turn in favor of two-socket servers instead of four-socket servers, as this system had enough CPU, memory, and I/O capacity to compare favorably with existing four-socket servers. If you were concerned about 144GB of RAM not being enough memory in the R710, you could buy two R710s, nearly doubling the CPU capacity and the I/O capacity of a single R900. This assumes that you could split your database workload between two database servers, by moving databases or doing something such as vertical or horizontal partitioning of an existing large database.

By early 2011, you could buy that same Dell PowerEdge R710 with more powerful six-core 32nm Intel Xeon X5690 processors and up to 288GB of RAM (with a total of 24 logical cores with hyperthreading enabled), and push the Geekbench score to about 24,000. This gives you quite a bit more CPU capacity and memory than the PowerEdge R900 that you could buy in late 2008. An R710 with those processors would give you the absolute best single-threaded OLTP performance available until March 2012, when the Dell R720 with the 32nm Xeon E5–2690 became available.

In March of 2012, you could purchase a two-socket Dell PowerEdge R720 with two, eight-core 32nm Intel Xeon E5–2690 processors and up to 768GB of RAM (with 32GB DIMMs) and seven PCIe 3.0 expansion slots, split between six × 8 and one × 16 slots. This provides a total of 32 logical cores (with hyperthreading enabled) visible to Windows, and this system has a Geekbench score of about 41,000, a significant improvement over the previous generation R710 server. It also has more memory capacity, better memory bandwidth, and much more I/O capacity due to the higher number of improved PCIe 3.0 expansion slots. This two-socket system has a Geekbench score that is roughly comparable to a 2011 vintage four-socket Dell PowerEdge R910 server that is using the 32nm Xeon E7–4870 processor. We now have a two-socket server that compares extremely well with the latest model four-socket servers in nearly every respect.

This overall trend has been continuing over the past several years, with Intel introducing new processors in the two-socket space about 12–18 months ahead of introducing a roughly equivalent new processor in the four-socket space. This means that you will get much better single-threaded OLTP performance from a two-socket system than from a four-socket system of the same age (as long as your I/O subsystem is up to par). The latest model two-socket servers with the Sandy Bridge-EP Intel Xeon E5–2690 processor compare very favorably to four-socket servers with the Sandy Bridge-EP Intel Xeon E5–4650, and even more favorably to four-socket servers with the older Westmere-EX Intel Xeon E7–4870 for all but the largest workloads.

Given the choice, two, two-socket machines instead of one, four-socket machine would be preferable in almost all cases. The only major exception would be a case in which you absolutely needed far more memory in a single server than you can get in a two-socket machine (a Dell PowerEdge R720 can now handle up to 768GB if you are willing to pay for 32GB DIMMs) and you are unable to do any reengineering to split up your workload.

From a SQL Server 2012 licensing perspective, a fully loaded Dell R720 is much more affordable than a fully loaded Dell R910, as we are talking about 16 physical cores for the R720 vs. 40 physical cores for the R910. At the time of writing, the full retail cost of 16 processor core licenses for SQL Server 2012 Enterprise Edition would be $109,984, whereas the retail cost for 40 processor core licenses would be $274,960. This means that you could buy two very well equipped R720 servers and their required SQL Server licenses for significantly less money than the cost of a single well-equipped R910 and its required SQL Server licenses. If you can split your workload between two servers, you would get *much* better performance and scalability from two R720 servers compared to a single R910 server.

PROCESSOR VENDOR SELECTION

The critical first question is whether you want an Intel processor or an AMD processor for your database server. Unfortunately, it is very hard to make a viable case for choosing an AMD processor-based server for SQL Server 2012, for two main reasons. The first reason is performance. The cold, hard fact is that AMD has simply been unable to compete with Intel from a single-threaded performance perspective since the introduction of the Intel Nehalem microarchitecture in 2008. This gap has only increased over the past several years with the introduction of the Westmere, Sandy Bridge, and Ivy Bridge processors. The second reason is the licensing cost for SQL Server 2012 Enterprise Edition. AMD processors have higher physical core counts in their processors compared to Intel, and they provide lower performance per physical core. This forces you to pay for more SQL Server 2012 core licenses but get lower single-threaded performance, which is not a very good combination.

Because SQL Server 2012 Enterprise Edition is licensed by physical core, this makes it much more expensive to use a relatively poorly performing AMD processor for SQL Server 2012. One argument in favor of AMD is that their high-end processors are significantly less expensive than the high-end Intel models. If your primary consideration is getting the absolute lowest hardware cost, regardless of the effect on performance or scalability, then you should be considering a low core count, AMD processor-based system. In fairness to AMD, many typical SQL Server workloads would run perfectly fine on a modern AMD system; therefore, if low hardware cost is your first priority, you can buy an AMD server with a low core count processor to save some money.

Intel Processors

Until the introduction of the Intel Xeon E7 processor family in 2011 and the Intel Xeon E5 processor family in 2012, Intel had different processor families for different socket count servers. For example, the Intel Xeon 3xxx family was for single-socket servers, the Intel Xeon 5xxx family was for two-socket servers, and the Intel Xeon 7xxx family was for four-socket (or more) servers. Now you can get an Intel Xeon E5 family processor for a one-, two-, or four-socket server. You can choose a Xeon E5–2400 series processor for a one- or two-socket server, a Xeon E5–2600 series processor for a two-socket server, or a Xeon E5–4600 series processor for a four-socket server. You can also get an Intel Xeon E7 family processor for a two-, four-, or eight-socket server. You can choose a Xeon E7–2800 series processor for a two-socket server, a Xeon E7–4800 series processor for a four-socket server, or a Xeon E7–8800 series processor for an eight-socket (or more) server. These new options from Intel can be quite confusing to sort out unless you pay attention to the details.

Prior to the release of SQL Server 2012, paying the price premium for the absolute best processor available for each socket in your database server was an effective strategy for database server processor selection. The SQL Server processor license cost was pretty high (even for Standard Edition), so you wanted to get as much performance and scalability capacity as possible for each expensive processor socket license that you purchased.

This is still a valid strategy for SQL Server 2008 R2 and earlier, but the licensing changes in SQL Server 2012 Enterprise Edition dictate a few modifications to this line of thinking. In early November 2011, Microsoft announced some rather fundamental changes regarding how SQL Server 2012 will be licensed compared to previous versions. SQL Server 2012 has three main editions: Enterprise Edition, Business Intelligence Edition, and Standard Edition. The old Data Center Edition and Workgroup Edition have been eliminated, which is probably no big loss. The existing Developer and Express Editions are still available, along with Web Edition for hosting providers.

Rather than the old, familiar socket-based licensing used in SQL Server 2008 R2 and earlier, SQL Server 2012 uses a combination of core-based and Server + Client Access License (CAL) licensing, depending on which edition you buy, and which choice you make for Standard Edition. With Standard Edition, you can choose core-based licensing or Server + CAL-based licensing. With Business Intelligence Edition, you have to use Server + CAL-based licensing, while Enterprise Edition requires the use of core-based licensing. Standard Edition is the base edition, with a limit of 16 physical processor cores. Microsoft decided to maintain the 64GB RAM limit for SQL Server 2012 Standard Edition (just like the 64GB RAM limit in SQL Server 2008 R2 Standard Edition). Business Intelligence Edition includes all the functionality of Standard Edition, plus extra BI features and functionality. Enterprise Edition includes everything in BI Edition, plus all the extra Enterprise Edition features and functionality. Enterprise Edition is the top-of-the-line edition of SQL Server 2012, now including all the features that were available in SQL Server 2008 R2 Data Center Edition. As a DBA, you really want to use Enterprise Edition if you have any choice in the matter, as it offers so many useful features, such as online index operations, data compression, and AlwaysOn availability groups, to name a few.

If you are using core-based licensing (as you must for SQL Server 2012 Enterprise Edition), each physical socket in your server must use a minimum of four core licenses. That means if you have old hardware that uses dual-core processors, you still have to buy four core licenses for each socket. That is yet another reason to not use ancient hardware for SQL Server 2012. Any Intel Xeon or AMD Opteron processor that has only two physical cores was at least four to five years old by the time SQL Server 2012 was released, so it really should be retired. Keep in mind that only physical cores count for licensing purposes (on non-virtualized servers), so Intel hyperthreading is free from a licensing perspective.

Core licenses are now sold in two-core packs, again with a minimum of four cores per physical socket. The full retail license cost per physical core is $6,874 for SQL Server 2012 Enterprise Edition. This is pretty grim news for AMD, with their higher physical core counts and lower per-socket performance compared to Intel. This situation was so obvious that Microsoft released a SQL Server 2012 Core Factor Table on April 1, 2012, that reduces the per-core license cost by 25% for a number of modern AMD processors that have six or more cores. Even with this change, the latest AMD processors are not a very cost-effective choice for SQL Server 2012. The numbers in Table 2-1 show the cost differential in pretty graphic detail, even with the .75 AMD Core Factor (see the "AMD Processors and Numbering" section later) applied to the license costs for the AMD processors.

TABLE 2-1: SQL Server 2012 License Cost Comparison

PROCESSOR	CORES	PER SOCKET COST	TOTAL SOCKETS	TOTAL LICENSE COST PER SERVER
Intel Xeon X5690	6	$41,244	2	$82,488
AMD Opteron 6282SE	16	$82,488	2	$164,976
Intel Xeon E5–2690	8	$54,992	2	$109,984
Intel Xeon E5–4650	8	$54,992	4	$219,968
Intel Xeon X7560	8	$54,992	4	$219,968
Intel Xeon E7–4870	10	$68,740	4	$274,960
AMD Opteron 6180SE	12	$61,866	4	$247,464
AMD Opteron 6282SE	16	$82,488	4	$329,952

For an OLTP workload on a two-socket server, an Intel Xeon E5–2690 processor would be preferable to an Intel Xeon E7–2870 processor because of its better single-threaded performance, a result of being a newer-generation model (Sandy Bridge-EP vs. Westmere-EX), higher clock speed, better memory bandwidth, and PCIe 3.0 support. For a DSS/DW workload, the E5–2690 would be preferable for the same reasons, even though it has a lower core count and a smaller L3 cache size.

For most OLTP workloads, you would also be far better off, from a performance perspective, with an older two-socket Intel Xeon X5690 server or a two-socket Intel Xeon E5–2690 server than you would be with a four-socket AMD Opteron 6282SE server. The extremely large difference in license cost between those two options makes Intel an even more compelling choice. As shown in Table 2-2, one way to partially confirm this assessment is to look at TPC-E scores for different systems and divide them by the total physical core count for the system (not by the thread count).

TABLE 2-2: TPC-E Scores by Total Physical Cores

SYSTEM	PROCESSOR	TPC-E	SOCKETS	TOTAL CORES	SCORE PER CORE
HP Proliant DL380 G7	Intel Xeon X5690	1284.14	2	12	107.01
IBM System × 360 M4	Intel Xeon E5–2690	1863.23	2	16	116.45
HP Proliant DL385 G7	AMD Opteron 6282SE	1232.84	2	32	38.53
HP Proliant DL585 G7	AMD Opteron 6176SE	1400.14	4	48	29.17
IBM System × 3850 × 5	Intel Xeon E7–4870	2862.61	4	40	71.57
NEC Express 5800/A1080a	Intel Xeon E7–8870	4614.22	8	80	57.68

It is very unlikely that you would ever upgrade to a better processor in an existing database server, so you will be stuck with your processor choice for the life of the server. If you have "excess" processor capacity, consider using it to trade CPU utilization for I/O utilization by using backup compression and data compression (if you have the Enterprise Edition of SQL Server 2008 or newer). Unlike a laptop or web server, it is a mistake to buy a processor that is a couple of steps down from the top-of-the-line model for database server usage. Trading some extra CPU utilization for less I/O utilization is usually a net win, especially if you have a modern, multi-core processor that can readily handle the extra work.

Of course, a new two-socket server will have a lower total RAM limit than a new four-socket server. For example, a two-socket Xeon X5690 would be limited to 288GB of RAM, which is probably enough for most workloads. A two-socket server will also have less total I/O capacity than a new four-socket server because it has fewer PCIe expansion slots. Still, you can easily get 5–6GB/sec of sequential throughput out of a modern two-socket server, which should be plenty for most workloads. After the Intel 32nm Sandy Bridge-EP Xeon E5–2600 series was released in early 2012, the wisdom of choosing a two-socket Intel-based server was even clearer, as it has higher memory density, more I/O bandwidth, and even better per-core performance than the Xeon 5600 series did.

If you are looking at the lower end of the cost and workload spectrum, you have several options. The one-socket 22nm Intel Xeon E3–1290 v2 processors (which are basically the same as the desktop Ivy Bridge Core i7 processor) are limited to 32GB of RAM, which somewhat limits their utility for larger database usage. If 32GB of RAM is not enough for your workload, a single-socket Dell R320 server with one Intel Xeon E5–2400 series processor and up to 96GB of RAM is available. Keep in mind that the memory limit for SQL Server 2012 Standard Edition is still 64GB, which is too low considering the memory density of modern hardware. One possible way around it with good hardware (with more than 128GB of RAM) is to install more than one instance of SQL Server 2012 Standard Edition on the same physical server.

Classic Intel Processor Numbering

In order to understand older Intel processor numbers, you need to know how to decode "classic" Intel processor numbers. By classic we mean Intel Xeon processors produced from about 2006 until April 2011 (when Intel introduced a new processor numbering system for new and upcoming processors).

Knowing how to decode the processor model number is a very handy skill to have when you want to understand the capabilities, relative age, and relative performance of a particular processor. An example of an Intel processor number is shown in Figure 2-1.

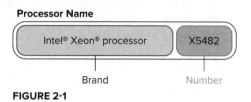

FIGURE 2-1

Intel Xeon processor numbers are categorized in four-digit numerical sequences, plus an alpha prefix that indicates whether it is optimized for electrical power usage or performance. The alpha prefixes are as follows:

- ➤ X, meaning performance
- ➤ E, meaning mainstream
- ➤ L, meaning power optimized

The model number starts with 3, 5, or 7, depending on the server form factor for which the processor is designed. If the processor number starts with a 3, it is designed for a single-socket server; if it starts with a 5, it is designed for a two-socket server; and if it starts with a 7, it is designed for a four-socket or more server. The second digit of the model number designates the generation, or relative age, of a processor. For example, the Xeon 5100 series was launched in Q2 2006, while the Xeon 5300 series was launched in Q4 2006, and the Xeon 5400 series was launched in Q4 2007.

For a more complete example, a Xeon X7560 is a high-end performance processor for multi-processor systems, an Intel Xeon E5540 is a mainstream processor for dual-processor systems, while an Intel Xeon L5530 is a power-optimized processor for dual-processor systems. The final three digits denote the generation and performance of the processor; for example, a Xeon X7560 processor would be newer and probably more capable than a Xeon X7460 processor. Higher numbers for the last three digits of the model number mean a newer generation in the family — for example, 560 is a newer generation than 460.

You should *always* choose the performance models, with the X model prefix, for SQL Server usage. The additional cost of an X series Xeon processor, compared to an E series, is minimal compared to the overall hardware and SQL Server license cost of a database server system. You should also avoid the power-optimized L series, as these can reduce processor performance by 20% to 30% while only saving 20 to 30 watts of power per processor, which is pretty insignificant compared to the overall electrical power usage of a typical database server (with its cooling fans, internal drives, power supplies, etc.). Of course, it would be a different story if you needed dozens or hundreds of web servers instead of a small number of mission-critical database servers, as the overall power savings would be pretty significant in that case.

Current Intel Processor Numbering

This section explains the current processor numbering system for Xeon processors that Intel introduced on April 5, 2011. This new system, shown in Figure 2-2, is used for the new processor families that Intel released on that date (the E3 series and the E7 series) and the E5 series that was released in March of 2012. The model numbers for the older existing Xeon processors remain unchanged in this system.

The first two digits in the processor number represent the Product Line designation, which will be E3, E5, or E7, depending on their place in the overall product lineup. After the Product Line designation is a four-digit number that provides more details about the particular processor. The first digit is the "wayness," which is the number of physical CPUs that are allowed in a node (which is a physical server). This

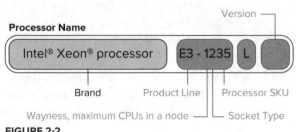

FIGURE 2-2

first digit can be 1, 2, 4, or 8. The second digit is the socket type, in terms of its physical and electrical characteristics. The last two digits are the processor SKU, with higher numbers generally indicating higher performance. Finally, an L at the end indicates energy-efficient, low electrical power processors. For SQL Server database server usage, you should avoid these power-optimized processors, as the performance impact of the reduced power usage is pretty dramatic.

The E3 Product family is for single-processor servers or workstations. The first generation of this family (E3–1200 series) is essentially the same as the desktop 32nm Sandy Bridge processors that were released in January 2011. The second generation of this family is the E3–1200 v2 series, which is basically the same as the desktop 22nm Ivy Bridge processors that were released in May 2012. They are both limited to 32GB of RAM.

The E5 Product family (the 32nm Sandy Bridge-EP) includes the E5–2600 series that was released in March 2012, and the E5–2400 series (32nm Sandy Bridge-EN) and E5–4600 series that were released in May 2012. You should probably avoid the entry-level Sandy Bridge-EN series, which has less memory bandwidth and lower clock speeds compared to the Sandy Bridge-EP series.

The E7 Product family (the 32nm Westmere-EX) has different models that are meant for two-socket servers, four-socket servers, and eight-socket and above servers. The E7–2800 series is for two-socket servers, the E7–4800 series is for four-socket servers, while the E7–8800 series is for eight-socket and above servers. Just in case you are wondering, the "EP" designation at the end of the family code word (such as Westmere-EP) stands for "efficient performance," while the "EX" designation stands for "expandable."

Intel's Tick-Tock Release Strategy

Since 2006, Intel has adopted and implemented a Tick-Tock strategy for developing and releasing new processor models. Every two years, they introduce a new processor family, incorporating a new microarchitecture; this is the tock release. One year after the tock release, they introduce a new processor family that uses the same microarchitecture as the previous year's tock release, but using a smaller manufacturing process technology and usually incorporating other small improvements, such as larger cache sizes or improved memory controllers. This is the tick release. This Tick-Tock release strategy benefits the DBA in a number of ways. It offers better predictability regarding when major (tock) and minor (tick) releases will be available. This helps you plan hardware upgrades to possibly coincide with your operating system and SQL Server version upgrades.

Tick releases are usually socket-compatible with the previous year's tock release, which makes it easier for the system manufacturer to make the latest tick release processor available in existing server models quickly, without completely redesigning the system. In most cases, only a BIOS update is required to enable an existing model system to use a newer tick release processor. This makes it easier for the DBA to maintain servers that are using the same model number (such as a Dell PowerEdge R710 server), as the server model will have a longer manufacturing life span. For example, the Dell PowerEdge R710 was able to use the original 45nm Nehalem-EP Xeon 5500 series processors and the newer 32nm Westmere-EP Xeon 5600 series processors, so that model server was available for purchase for over three years.

As a DBA, you need to know where a particular processor falls in Intel's processor family tree in order to meaningfully compare the relative performance of two different processors. Historically, processor performance has nearly doubled with each new tock release, while performance usually increases by around 20–25% with a tick release. Some of the recent and upcoming Intel Tick-Tock releases are shown in Figure 2-3.

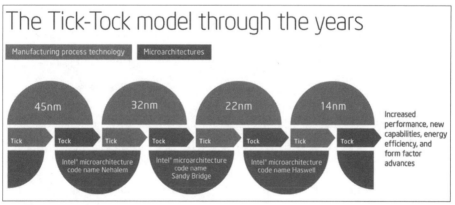

FIGURE 2-3

The manufacturing process technology refers to the size of the individual circuits and transistors on the chip. The Intel 4004 (released in 1971) series used a 10-micron process; the smallest feature on the processor was 10 millionths of a meter across. By contrast, the Intel Xeon "Ivy Bridge" E3–1200 v2 series (released in May 2012) uses a 22nm process. For comparison, a nanometer is one billionth of a meter, so 10 microns would be 10,000 nanometers. This ever-shrinking manufacturing process is important for two main reasons:

➤ **Increased performance and lower power usage** — Even at the speed of light, distance matters, so having smaller components that are closer together on a processor means better performance and lower power usage.

➤ **Lower manufacturing costs** — This is possible because more processors can be produced from a standard silicon wafer. This helps to create more powerful and more power-efficient processors available at a lower cost, which is beneficial to everyone but especially the database administrator.

The first tock release was the Intel Core microarchitecture, which was introduced as the dual-core "Woodcrest" (Xeon 5100 series) in 2006, with a 65nm process technology. This was followed up by a shrinkage to 45nm process technology in the dual-core "Wolfdale" (Xeon 5200 series) and quad-core "Harpertown" processors (Xeon 5400 series) in late 2007, both of which were Tick releases. The next tock release was the Intel "Nehalem" microarchitecture (Xeon 5500 series), which used a 45nm process technology, introduced in late 2008. In 2010, Intel released a Tick release, code-named "Westmere" (Xeon 5600 series) that shrank to a 32nm process technology in the server space. In 2011, the 32nm "Sandy Bridge" tock release debuted with the E3–1200 series for single-socket servers and workstations. This was followed up by the "Ivy Bridge" tick release of the E3–1200 v2 series for single-socket servers and workstations that had a process shrink to 22nm. Table 2-3 shows the recent and upcoming Tick-Tock releases in the two-socket server space.

TABLE 2-3: Intel Tick-Tock Release History for Two Socket Servers

TYPE	YEAR	PROCESS	SERIES	CODE NAME
Tock	2006	65nm	5100, 5300	Woodcrest, Clovertown
Tick	2007	45nm	5200, 5400	Wolfdale, Harpertown
Tock	2008	45nm	5500	Nehalem-EP
Tick	2010	32nm	5600	Westmere-EP
Tock	2012	32nm	E5–2400, E5–2600	Sandy Bridge-EP
Tick	2013	22nm	TBA (E5–2600 v2?)	Ivy Bridge-EP
Tock	2014	22nm	TBA	Haswell
Tick	2015	14nm	TBA	Rockwell
Tock	2016	14nm	TBA	Skylake

Intel Hyperthreading

Intel originally implemented a feature called hyperthreading back in 2002, as part of the NetBurst architecture in the Northwood-based Pentium 4 processors and the equivalent Xeon family. Hyperthreading was created to address the frequently wasted processor cycles that resulted when the central processor in a system waited on data from main memory. Instead of wasting processor cycles during this wait time, the idea was to have two logical processors inside a single physical core that could each work on something different when the other logical processor was stalled waiting on data from main memory.

Hyperthreading is Intel's marketing term for its simultaneous multi-threading architecture whereby each physical processor core is split into two logical cores. The "simultaneous" term is a little misleading, as you cannot actually have two threads running simultaneously on the two logical cores in a single physical core of the same physical processor. What actually happens is that the threads run alternately, with one working while the other one is idle.

Hyperthreading works quite well for desktop applications. The classic example is running a complete anti-virus scan while the user is still able to work interactively with another application in the foreground. Unfortunately, the initial implementation of hyperthreading on the Pentium 4 NetBurst architecture did not work very well on many server workloads such as SQL Server. This was because the L2 data cache for each physical core was shared between the two logical cores, which caused performance issues because the L2 cache had to be constantly refreshed as the application context switched between the two logical processors. This behavior was known as *cache thrashing*, and it often led to a decrease in overall performance for SQL Server workloads. Another factor that made this situation even worse was the very deep processor pipeline that was used in the Pentium 4 architecture, which made it even more costly when the data needed by the logical processor was not found in the L2 cache.

Because of these factors, it became very common for database administrators to disable hyperthreading for *all* SQL Server workloads, which is really a mistake. Different types of SQL Server workloads react differently to having hyperthreading enabled, with OLTP workloads generally performing better with hyperthreading enabled, and data warehouse workloads sometimes performing worse with hyperthreading enabled. Before you decide whether to enable or disable hyperthreading, test it both ways with your actual workload.

Modern Intel processors (Nehalem, Westmere, Sandy Bridge, and Ivy Bridge) seem to work much better with hyperthreading because of larger L2 and L3 cache sizes, newer processor architectures, and faster access to main memory. Because of this, we advise you to enable hyperthreading for SQL Server, especially for OLTP workloads, unless you have done testing that actually shows a performance decrease with your workload. It is significant that every single TPC-E OLTP benchmark submission for these modern Intel processors has been done with hyperthreading enabled on the database server, which is certainly intentional.

AMD Processors and Numbering

This section discusses AMD Opteron processor numbering. Advanced Micro Devices (AMD) has various versions of the Opteron family that are meant for server use. When assessing AMD processors, it is very helpful to understand what the model numbers actually mean. Recent AMD Opteron processors are identified by a four-character model number in the format ZYXX, where the Z character indicates the product series:

➤ 1000 Series = 1-socket servers

➤ 2000 Series = Up to 2-socket servers and workstations

➤ 4000 Series = Up to 2-socket servers

➤ 6000 Series = High performance 2- and 4-socket servers

➤ 8000 Series = Up to 8-socket servers and workstations

The Y character differentiates products within a series:

➤ Z2XX = Dual-Core.

➤ Z3XX = Quad-Core.

➤ Z4XX = Six-Core.

➤ First-generation AMD Opteron 6000 series processors are denoted by 61XX.

➤ Second-generation AMD Opteron 6000 series processors are denoted by 62XX.

The XX digits indicate a change in product features within the series (for example, in the 8200 series of dual-core processors, you can find models 8214, 8216, 8218, and so on), and are not a measure of performance. It is also possible to have a two-character product suffix after the XX model number, as follows:

➤ No suffix — Indicates a standard power AMD Opteron processor

➤ SE — Performance optimized, high-powered

➤ HE — Low-powered

➤ EE — Lowest power AMD Opteron processor

For example, an Opteron 6282 SE would be a 6000 series, 16-core, performance-optimized processor; an Opteron 8439 SE would be an 8000 series, six-core, performance-optimized processor; while an Opteron 2419 EE would be a 2000 series, six-core, energy-efficient processor. For mission-critical database servers, we recommend selecting an SE suffix processor, if it is available for your server model. The reason why it isn't available in every server model is due to its higher electrical power requirements.

It should also be noted that AMD has broken their own processor numbering rules with the most recent versions of the Opteron (including the 4100, 4200, 6100, and 6200 series), as they do not follow the standard numbering scheme just described.

Recent Opteron AMD releases, plus planned releases, are summarized in Table 2–4. Since 2011, the 16-core Interlagos processor has been AMD's best-performing model, even though it did not live up to expectations for that release.

TABLE 2-4: Recent AMD Processor Releases

YEAR	PROCESS	SERIES	CODE NAME
2006	90nm	1200, 2200, 8200	Santa Ana, Santa Rosa
2007–8	65nm	1300, 2300, 8300	Budapest, Barcelona
2009	45nm	2400, 8400	Shanghai, Istanbul
2010	45nm	4100, 6100	Lisbon, Magny-Cours

2011	32nm	4200, 6200	Valencia, Interlagos
2013	32nm	4300, 6300	Seoul, Abu Dhabi
2014	28nm	TBA	TBA

SQL Server 2012 Core Factor Table

Looking at recent TPC-E benchmark submissions for both AMD and Intel processors, it is pretty difficult to avoid noticing how poorly the few tested AMD systems have done compared to the latest Intel systems. For example, in January 2012, a new Hewlett-Packard TPC-E benchmark submission showed a 1232.84 TpsE score for a two-socket AMD system with 32 physical cores, compared to a 1284.14 TpsE score for a two-socket Intel system with 12 physical cores. Both of these TPC-E benchmark submissions were on SQL Server 2008 R2. With these results, you would be paying 2.66 times as much for SQL Server 2012 Enterprise Edition core licenses for the AMD system compared to the Intel system (32 physical cores vs. 12 physical cores). This is rather dire news for AMD, with their higher physical core counts and lower per physical core OLTP performance compared to Intel.

Likely in response to this situation, on April 1, 2012, Microsoft released a new SQL Server 2012 Core Factor Table for AMD processors, which is shown in Table 2–5. Note that not all processors are included in the table.

TABLE 2-5: SQL Server 2012 Core Factor Table for AMD Processors

PROCESSOR TYPE	CORE FACTOR
All other AMD Processors	1
AMD 31XX, 32XX, 41XX, 42XX, 61XX, 62XX Series Processors with 6 or more cores	0.75
Single-Core Processors	4
Dual-Core Processors	2

The most relevant part of this table regards the newer AMD 31XX, 32XX, 41XX, 42XX, 61XX, and 62XX series of processors with six or more cores that have a core factor of 0.75. Having a core factor of 0.75 means that you multiply the actual number of physical cores times the core factor to arrive at the number of cores for SQL Server licensing purposes; for example, if you had a four-socket server, where each socket was populated with an AMD Opteron 6284 SE processor. That particular processor has 16 physical cores, so 4 times 16 would give you a result of 64 SQL Server 2012 core licenses that would be required for that server (before the Core Factor table was introduced). Using the new licensing rules from the Core Factor table, you would be able to multiply 64 times 0.75 to get a new result of 48 SQL Server 2012 core licenses that would be required for that server (after the Core Factor table was introduced). This means that AMD cores for some processors are somewhat more affordable now for SQL Server 2012 than they would be without the core factor calculation.

Based on the SQL Server 2012 Core Factor Table, you would only be paying *twice as much* for SQL Server 2012 Enterprise Edition licenses for the 32-core AMD system compared to the 12-core Intel system (32 AMD physical cores times 0.75 vs. 12 Intel physical cores). That is a slightly better story for AMD, but it is still a pretty hard sell.

Based on the TPC-E benchmark results, both the older Intel Xeon X5600 Westmere-EP series and the new Intel Xeon E5–2600 Sandy Bridge-EP series perform much better per physical core on OLTP workloads than the latest AMD Opteron 6200 series processors. These Intel processors simply have significantly better single-threaded performance, which is very important for OLTP workloads.

As a result of this new Core Factor Table, SQL Server 2012 processor licenses will be a little less expensive than they were previously for those AMD processor families that have more than six cores, but they will still be much more expensive in total than a better-performing Intel solution. The somewhat lower hardware cost for the AMD processor compared to the hardware cost of the Intel processor is rather trivial compared to the difference in the licensing cost. Hopefully AMD can do better with the upcoming Piledriver core-based Opteron series expected in 2013.

CHOOSING AND CONFIGURING HARDWARE FOR REDUNDANCY

This section describes the most important items that you should consider from a hardware perspective when you are trying to increase the basic resiliency and availability of an individual database server. These are some of the first steps you would take as part of designing a high-availability solution for your data tier. The basic goal here is to eliminate as many single points of failure as possible at the hardware and configuration level. Therefore, when choosing components for a database server and including them as part of the server configuration (as opposed to a web server, for example), you should consider these aspects regardless of any other high-availability techniques you decide to use.

You should always get two internal drives in a RAID 1 (mirrored) configuration for the operating system and the SQL Server binaries. These drives should be using the integrated hardware RAID controller that is available on most new rack-mounted servers. Using an integrated hardware RAID controller (which usually has a 256MB–512MB cache) provides better performance than using software RAID through Windows. Having two drives in RAID 1 offers a basic level of redundancy for the operating system and the SQL Server binaries, so the server will not stop functioning if one of the drives fails.

Try to get at least 146GB, 15K 2.5″ drives for this purpose. Using 15K drives helps Windows Server boot a little faster, and it will help SQL Server load a bit faster when the service first starts up. Using 146GB (or larger) drives provides more room to accommodate things like the Windows page file, SQL Server Error Log files, dump files, and so on, without being worried about drive space. As SSD prices continue to fall, you might want to consider using two SSDs for your mirrored boot drive. Reducing your boot time and reducing the time it takes for SQL Server to start up using SSDs could help you meet your recovery time objective (RTO) goals.

Ensure that you have dual power supplies for the database server, each plugged into separate circuits in your server room or data center. You should also be plugged into an uninterruptable power supply (UPS) on each circuit, and ideally have a backup power source, such as a diesel generator for your data center. The idea here is to protect against an internal power supply failure, a cord being kicked out of an electrical socket, a circuit breaker tripping, or loss of electrical power from the utility grid. Adding a second power supply is relatively inexpensive insurance, typically less than $300. Despite this, we have seen many battles with economizing bosses about this item over the years. Power supplies do fail, cords are accidentally unplugged, and circuit breakers do get tripped. Therefore, stick to your guns about dual power supplies for a database server. You should have multiple network ports in the server, with Ethernet connections into at least two different network switches. These network switches (which should also have dual power supplies) should be plugged into different electrical circuits in your data center. Most new rack-mounted servers have at least four gigabit Ethernet ports embedded on the motherboard. All of this is designed to prevent an outage caused by the loss of a single network port or a single network switch.

You should have multiple RAID controller cards (if you are using direct-attached or internal storage); multiple host bus adapters (HBAs) (if you are using a Fibre Channel SAN); or multiple PCIe Gigabit, or better Ethernet cards with an iSCSI SAN. This will give you better redundancy and better throughput, depending on your configuration. Again, the idea here is to try to avoid an outage caused by the loss of a single component.

Wherever your SQL Server data files, log files, tempdb files, and SQL Server backup files are located, they should be protected by an appropriate RAID level, depending on your budget and performance needs. You want to prevent your databases from going down due to the loss of a single drive. Keep in mind that RAID is not a substitute for an appropriate SQL Server backup and restore strategy! *Never* let anyone, whether it is a SAN vendor, a server administrator from your operations team, or your boss, talk you into not doing SQL Server backups as appropriate for your recovery point objective (RPO) and recovery time objective (RTO) requirements. This cannot be emphasized enough! There is absolutely no substitute for having SQL Server backup files, although you will undoubtedly be pressured throughout your career, by different people, into not running SQL Server database backups. Stand your ground. The old saying is true: "If you don't have backups, you don't have a database."

To reduce the boot and SQL Server startup time on your database servers, note the following BIOS configuration setting. For a standalone database server, reducing your total reboot time has a direct effect on your high-availability numbers. Therefore, go into the BIOS setup for the server and disable the memory testing that normally occurs during the POST sequence, which shaves a significant amount of time off of it (often many minutes, depending on how much RAM is installed), so the server will boot faster. This carries little risk, as this testing only occurs during the POST sequence; it has nothing to do with detecting a memory problem while the server is running later, which is the job of your hardware or system-monitoring software.

While you are in the BIOS setup, also access the Power Management section and either disable the power management settings or set them to OS control. By default, Windows Server 2008 and Windows Server 2008 R2 use the Windows Balanced Power Plan. This saves electrical power usage by reducing the multiplier setting for the processors, which reduces their clock speed when the system is not under a heavy load. This sounds like a good idea, but it can actually have a very significant negative effect on performance, as some processors do not react quickly enough to an increase in workload. This is particularly important if you have an Intel Nehalem or Westmere family processor. The latest Intel Sandy Bridge and Ivy Bridge family processors react to power state changes much more quickly than Nehalem or Westmere did, which makes them much less sensitive to those changes from a performance perspective.

Regardless of what processor you have, power management can have other negative effects on your database server. One example is when you are using Fusion-io cards in your server. Some forms of hardware management can affect the PCIe slots in the server, so Fusion-io specifically recommends that you disable power management settings in your main BIOS setup and in Windows. The easy solution to all of this is to ensure that you are using the High Performance Windows Power Plan, and that you disable the power management settings in your BIOS.

Finally, after ensuring that you have followed all the guidelines described thus far, you still are not done. Depending on your RPO and RTO requirements, you should be planning and hopefully implementing some sort of overall high-availability and disaster-recovery (HA/DR) strategy to provide you with an even more robust system that will be able to handle as many different types of issues and "disasters" as possible. This strategy could include technologies such as Windows failover clustering, database mirroring, log shipping, transactional replication, and SQL Server 2012 AlwaysOn Availability Groups, along with an actual plan that outlines the policies and procedures needed to successfully handle a disaster.

HARDWARE COMPARISON TOOLS

We are firm proponents of using readily available benchmark tools and some common sense and analysis as a means of comparing different hardware types and configurations. Rather than simply guess about the relative and absolute performance of different systems, you can use the results of standardized database benchmarks and specific component benchmarks to more accurately evaluate and compare different systems and components. This section discusses two such benchmarking tools: the TPC-E OLTP benchmark and the Geekbench processor and memory performance benchmark.

TPC-E Benchmark

The TPC Benchmark E (TPC-E) is an OLTP performance benchmark that was introduced in early 2007. TPC-E is a not a replacement for the old TPC-C benchmark, but rather a completely new OLTP benchmark. Even though this newer benchmark has been available for over five years, there are still no posted results for any RDBMS other than SQL Server. Fortunately, many results are posted for SQL Server, which makes it a very useful benchmark when assessing SQL Server hardware. At the time of writing, there are 54 published TPC-E results, using SQL Server 2005, 2008, 2008 R2, and SQL Server 2012. This gives you many different systems and configurations from which to choose as you look for a system resembling one that you want to evaluate.

The TPC-E benchmark is an OLTP, database-centric workload that is meant to reduce the cost and complexity of running the benchmark compared to the older TPC-C benchmark. Unlike TPC-C, the storage media for TPC-E must be fault tolerant (which means no RAID 0 arrays). Overall, the TPC-E benchmark is designed to have reduced I/O requirements compared to the old

TPC-C benchmark, which makes it both less expensive and more realistic because the sponsoring hardware vendors will not feel as much pressure to equip their test systems with disproportionately large, expensive disk subsystems in order to get the best test results. The TPC-E benchmark is also more CPU intensive than the old TPC-C benchmark, which means that the results tend to correlate fairly well to CPU performance, as long as the I/O subsystem can drive the workload effectively.

It simulates the OLTP workload of a brokerage firm that interacts with customers using synchronous transactions and with a financial market using asynchronous transactions. The TPC-E database is populated with pseudo-real data, including customer names from the year 2000 U.S. Census, and company listings from the NYSE and NASDAQ. Having realistic data introduces data skew, and makes the data compressible. The business model of the brokerage firm is organized by customers, accounts, and securities. The data model for TPC-E is significantly more complex, and more realistic, than TPC-C, with 33 tables and many different data types. The data model for the TPC-E database also enforces referential integrity, unlike the older TPC-C data model.

The TPC-E implementation is broken down into a Driver and a System Under Test (SUT), separated by a network. The Driver represents the various client devices that would use an N-tier client-server system, abstracted into a load generation system. The SUT has multiple application servers (Tier A) that communicate with the database server and its associated storage subsystem (Tier B). The TPC provides a transaction harness component that runs in Tier A, while the test sponsor provides the other components in the SUT. The performance metric for TPC-E is transactions per second, tpsE. The actual tpsE score represents the average number of Trade Result transactions executed within one second. To be fully compliant with the TPC-E standard, all references to tpsE results must include the tpsE rate, the associated price per tpsE, and the availability date of the priced configuration. The current range of published TPC-E scores ranges from a low of 144.88 tpsE to a high of 4614.22. There are scores for two-socket, four-socket, eight-socket and 16-socket systems, using several different processor families from Intel and AMD. Reflecting the performance deficit of recent AMD processors, only four AMD results have been published out of the 54 total submissions.

When assessing the OLTP performance of different server platforms using different processor families and models, you want to look for a TPC-E result that uses the same type and number of processors as the system you are considering. If you cannot find an exact match, look for the closest equivalent system as a starting point, and then adjust the results upward or downward using component benchmark results and common sense.

For example, let's say that you are considering the potential performance of a new two-socket, 2.6GHz Intel Xeon E5–2670 system. After looking at the published TPC-E results, the nearest match that you can find is a two-socket, 2.9GHz Intel Xeon E5–2690 system that has a tpsE score of 1863.23. After looking at other component-level benchmarks for CPU and memory performance, you might feel relatively safe reducing that score by about 10% to account for the clock speed difference on the same generation and family processor(with the same number of cores, cache sizes, and memory bandwidth), coming up with an adjusted score of about 1676 tpsE.

You want to compare the potential performance of this system to an older four-socket system that uses the 2.66GHz Intel Xeon X7460 processor, and you find a TPC-E benchmark for a similar system that has a score of 671.35 tpsE. Just looking at these raw scores, you could be relatively confident that you could replace the old four-socket system with that new two-socket system and see better performance with more scalability headroom. You should also drill into the actual TPC-E submissions to better understand the details of each system that was tested. For each tested system, you want to know things such as operating system version, SQL Server version, the amount of RAM in the database server, the initial database size, the type of storage, and the number of spindles. All of this gives you a better idea of the validity of the comparison between the two systems.

When assessing the relative OLTP performance of different processors, take the raw TPC-E tpsE score for a system using the processor and divide it by the number of physical cores in the system to get an idea of the relative "per physical core performance." Using the preceding example, the proposed new two-socket Xeon E5-2670 system would have 16 physical cores. Taking your adjusted score of 1676 and dividing by 16 would give you a figure of 104.75. The old four-socket Xeon X7460 system has 24 physical cores, so taking the actual raw score of 671.35 and dividing it by 24 gives you a figure of 27.97, which is a pretty dramatic difference between the two processors for single-threaded OLTP performance.

Geekbench Benchmark

Geekbench is a cross-platform, synthetic benchmark tool from a company called Primate Labs. It offers a rather comprehensive set of benchmarks designed to measure the processor and memory performance of a system, whether it is a laptop or a multi-processor database server. There is no measurement of I/O performance in this benchmark. One convenient feature of Geekbench is that there are no configuration options to worry about. You simply install it and run it, and within about three minutes you will see the scores for the system you have tested. These are broken down into an overall Geekbench score and a number of scores for processor and memory performance. This is very useful for comparing the relative processor and memory performance of different processors and different model servers that may be configured in a variety of ways.

This test can be a very reliable and useful gauge of processor and memory performance. Thousands of Geekbench score reports have been submitted to the online Geekbench database, which is available at http://browser.primatelabs.com. It is highly likely that you can find a score in their database for nearly any processor or model server that you want to compare. This is very handy, especially if you don't have a large dedicated testing lab with a lot of different model servers and processors.

For example, suppose you have an older Dell PowerEdge 2950 server with two Intel Xeon E5440 processors and 32GB of RAM. It turns out that a system like this has a Geekbench score of around 7950. You are trying to justify the purchase of a new Dell PowerEdge R720 server with two Intel Xeon E5-2690 processors and 128GB of RAM, and you discover a result in the online database that shows a Geekbench score of about 41,000. That's a rather dramatic increase compared to a score of 7950. Using Geekbench scores in conjunction with TPC-E scores is a fairly reliable way to compare relative processor and memory performance, especially for OLTP workloads. Using these two benchmarks together is a very useful technique that will likely serve you well.

SUMMARY

As you go through the process of evaluating, selecting, sizing, and configuring your database hardware and storage subsystem, it is extremely important that you are familiar with the characteristics of the type(s) of workload that your system will be handling. Different types of workloads and mixed workloads place varying demands on your server hardware and storage subsystem. You need to take this into account early in the process, as it influences many of your decisions.

After considering your workload, you need to decide whether you want an Intel or an AMD-based database server, as that dictates which model servers from your selected system vendor are eligible for consideration. Unfortunately, given the relatively poor single-threaded performance and high physical core counts of the last two generations of AMD Opteron processors, it is very hard to justify their use with SQL Server 2012 Enterprise Edition, even after considering the SQL Server 2012 Core Factor Table license discounts. If AMD continues to be unable to compete in the high end of the market, it will reduce the incentives for Intel to maintain their aggressive product release cycle, and slow the pace of innovation. This will be bad for the IT industry in the long run.

After selecting your processor vendor, you need to decide whether your workload and volume requirements dictate the use of a one-, two-, four-, or eight-socket database server. With the latest generation of processors and improved memory and storage densities, many smaller SQL Server workloads may be able to run quite well on a single-socket database server.

Because processors have become much more powerful, and memory and storage density have improved over the past several years, it has become increasingly feasible to use two-socket servers for database usage. Intel continues to release newer-generation processors more quickly in the two-socket space, and the equivalent generation Intel two-socket processors have better single-threaded performance than their Intel four-socket counterparts. This means that you may be able to run a much higher percentage of SQL Server workloads on a two-socket server, rather than a four-socket server, and save a great deal of money in SQL Server license costs. Despite these improvements in the two-socket space, some workloads still require more resources than you can obtain from a two-socket server. If you need even more RAM, PCIe expansion slots, or total processor cores than you can get in a two-socket server, you have to make the jump to a four-socket or larger server.

With the new core-based licensing in SQL Server 2012 Enterprise Edition, you need to pay much closer attention to your physical core counts and the relative performance and scalability you get for each physical core. You are likely to be stuck with the processor(s) you choose for the lifetime of the server, which is probably several years, so choose wisely. Choosing wisely means getting the most performance and scalability with the lowest total physical core count in the server. Choosing poorly means getting less performance and scalability but paying the same or a higher total cost for your SQL Server licenses. Put some serious thought into your processor decision, using benchmark results to help justify it.

Because server RAM is relatively inexpensive, with costs continuing to decline, it makes sense to get a large amount of RAM, subject to any SQL Server license limits. Both SQL Server 2008 R2 Standard Edition and SQL Server 2012 Standard Edition have a license limit of 64GB. Physical RAM is an inexpensive, partial substitute for I/O capacity. If you have enough physical RAM that your entire database fits into memory, that's an ideal situation. In many cases you may not have that luxury, but you should still try to get as much RAM as you can afford or as much as will fit in your server.

Finally, take advantage of the readily available component and application-level benchmarks to compare and evaluate different systems and components, rather than just guess. This approach will give you much more accurate estimates about different systems; and no matter what else you do, make an effort to learn more about hardware and stay current with new developments over time. This knowledge is critical to your career as a database professional.

3

Understanding Memory

WHAT'S IN THIS CHAPTER?

➤ Understanding physical memory and how to use virtual memory addressing

➤ NUMA architecture and how SQL Server uses it

➤ SQL Server's memory clerks, caches, and pools

➤ Looking at SQL Server's plan cache

➤ An in-depth look at Query/Workspace memory

➤ Memory configuration options including Max Server Memory, Lock Pages in Memory, and Optimize for Ad-hoc Workloads

WROX.COM CODE DOWNLOADS FOR THIS CHAPTER

The wrox.com code downloads for this chapter are found at www.wrox.com/remtitle .cgi?isbn=1118177657 on the Download Code tab. The code is in the Chapter 3 download and individually named according to the names throughout the chapter.

INTRODUCTION

Memory, disk, and CPU are the holy trinity of resources in a computer system, and memory is first because it's the area you're most likely to have an issue with. Memory issues can cause both disk and CPU saturation, so when troubleshooting a server issue (or at least a performance issue), you need to start by looking at the memory profile of the system.

Understanding how Windows and SQL Server interact with and manage memory is crucial for gaining an understanding of the actual memory usage of a server you're troubleshooting.

The first part of this chapter explains the fundamentals of how Windows manages memory and explains the difference and relationship between physical and virtual memory. The second part focuses on SQL Server's internal memory structures, how they are managed, and how you can break down their usage for effective troubleshooting. The chapter concludes with a look at different memory configuration options for SQL Server, helping you to understand what they do and how to decide on an appropriate configuration.

THE 32-BIT AND 64-BIT ARCHITECTURES

Support for 32-bit architectures (or more specifically x86) continues with SQL Server 2012, although there is one major change: removal of the Address Windowing Extensions (AWE) feature, which allows 32-bit processes to access more than 4GB of RAM.

The removal of AWE from SQL Server 2012 is really the final nail in the coffin for 32-bit SQL Server, so we anticipate that nearly all installations will be 64-bit. Additionally, Windows Server 2012 is 64-bit only. For this reason, the rest of the chapter focuses on and refers to only 64-bit SQL Server unless explicitly stated.

If you still have a requirement for 32-bit, the /3GB tuning parameter is still supported in SQL Server 2012 and is covered in detail in the "Tuning 32-Bit Systems" section in Chapter 2 of the previous edition of this book, *Professional SQL Server 2008 Internals and Troubleshooting* (Bolton et al., Wrox, 2010).

PHYSICAL AND VIRTUAL MEMORY

This section covers topics — often considered to be outside the scope of a database professional — that are fundamental to the way that Windows manages memory and the applications running on it, including SQL Server. Understanding this information is a great differentiator among database professionals and it will give you the right foundation of knowledge to understand how all applications work with Windows.

Physical Memory

When the term *physical memory* is used, it's usually in relation to RAM (random access memory), but it actually also includes the system page file (explained later in the chapter). RAM is also referred to as primary storage, main memory, or system memory because it's directly addressable by the CPU. It is regarded as the fastest type of storage you can use, but it's volatile, meaning you lose what was stored when you reboot the computer. It's also expensive and limited in capacity compared to nonvolatile storage such as a hard disk.

For example, Windows Server 2012 supports up to 4TB of RAM, but buying a server with that much memory will cost you millions of U.S. dollars, whereas it's possible to buy a single 4TB hard disk for a few hundred dollars. Combine a few of those and you can have tens of TBs of very cost-effective storage space. Consequently, servers use a combination of hard disks to store data, which is then loaded into RAM where it can be worked with much faster.

By way of comparison, throughput for RAM modules is measured in gigabytes per second (GB/s) with nanosecond (ns) response times, whereas hard disk throughput is measured in megabytes per second (MB/s) with millisecond (ms) response times. Even solid-state storage technology, which is much faster than traditional disk, is typically still measured in MB/s throughput and with microsecond (μs) latency. You can read more about storage in Chapter 4.

> **NOTE** *Just to be clear on the relationship between the time units mentioned here, a millisecond is a thousandth of a second (0.001 seconds), a microsecond is a thousandth of a millisecond (0.000001 seconds), and a nanosecond is a thousandth of a microsecond (0.000000001 seconds).*

Maximum Supported Physical Memory

For ease of reference, Table 3-1 shows the maximum usable RAM for SQL Server 2012 by feature and edition.

TABLE 3-1: SQL Server 2012 Usable Memory by Edition and Feature

FEATURE	ENTERPRISE	BUSINESS INTELLIGENCE	STANDARD	WEB	EXPRESS W/ADVANCED SERVICES	EXPRESS
Database Engine	Windows Maximum	64GB	64GB	64GB	1GB	1GB
Analysis Services	Windows Maximum	Windows Maximum	64GB	N/A	N/A	N/A
Reporting Services	Windows Maximum	Windows Maximum	64GB	64GB	4GB	N/A

```
http://msdn.microsoft.com
```

SQL Server 2012 Enterprise Edition and SQL Server 2012 Business Edition support the maximum RAM of the underlying operating system, the most popular of which at the time of writing are Windows Server 2008 R2 Standard Edition, which supports 32GB, and Windows Server 2008 R2 Enterprise Edition, which supports 2TB.

Windows Server 2012, due for release at the end of 2012, supports a maximum of 4TB of RAM.

Virtual Memory

If all the processes running on a computer could only use addresses in physical RAM, the system would very quickly experience a bottleneck. All the processes would have to share the same range of addresses, which are limited by the amount of RAM installed in the computer. Because physical RAM is very fast to access and cannot be increased indefinitely (as just discussed in the previous section), it's a resource that needs to be used efficiently.

Windows (and many other mainstream, modern operating systems) assigns a virtual address space (VAS) to each process. This provides a layer of abstraction between an application and physical memory so that the operating system can choose the most efficient way to use physical memory across all the processes. For example, two different processes can both use the memory address 0xFFF because it's a virtual address and each process has its own VAS with the same address range.

Whether that address maps to physical memory or not is determined by the operating system or, more specifically (for Windows at least), the Virtual Memory Manager, which is covered in the next section.

The size of the virtual address space is determined largely by the CPU architecture. A 64-bit CPU running 64-bit software (also known as the *x64 platform*) is so named because it is based on an architecture that can manipulate values that are up to 64 bits in length. This means that a 64-bit memory pointer could potentially store a value between 0 and 18,446,744,073,709,551,616 to reference a memory address.

This number is so large that in memory/storage terminology it equates to 16 *exabytes* (EBs). You don't come across that term very often, so to grasp the scale, here is what 16 exabytes equals when converted to more commonly used measurements:

➤ 16,384 petabytes (PB)

➤ 16,777,216 terabytes (TB)

➤ 17,179,869,184 gigabytes (GB)

17 billion GB of RAM, anyone?

As you can see, the *theoretical* memory limits of a 64-bit architecture go way beyond anything that could be used today or even in the near future, so processor manufacturers implemented a *44-bit* address bus instead. This provides a virtual address space on 64-bit systems of 16TB.

This was regarded as being more than enough address space for the foreseeable future and logically it is split into two ranges of 8TB: one for the process and one reserved for system use. These two ranges are commonly referred to as *user mode* and *kernel mode* address space and are illustrated in Figure 3-1. Each application process (i.e., SQL Server) can access up to 8TB of VAS, and therefore up to 8TB of RAM (depending on operating system support — remember Windows Server 2012 supports 4TB of RAM, so we're halfway there).

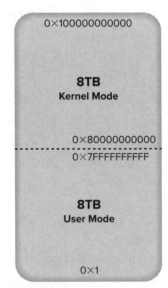

FIGURE 3-1

> **NOTE** *x64 is the predominant 64-bit architecture in use today, but Intel developed an alternative architecture known as IA-64 that is implemented in its Itanium processors. It was designed as a high-end alternative to mainframes, but the platform didn't have very many production implementations of SQL Server and has subsequently been dropped from SQL Server 2012. Windows has also dropped support for IA-64 with the release of Windows Server 2012, which runs only on x64.*

> **NOTE** *The virtual address space for a 32-bit system is only 4GB, which when broken down into 2GB for kernel mode and 2GB for user mode, doesn't provide much space at all. It is this memory addressing limitation that is the key driver for the adoption of 64-bit.*
>
> *Chapter 2 of the previous edition of this book,* Professional SQL Server 2008 Internals and Troubleshooting, *provides extensive coverage of 32-bit Windows and SQL Server environments, including all of the tuning options.*

Virtual Memory Manager

The *Virtual Memory Manager (VMM)* is the part of Windows that links together physical memory and virtual address space. When a process needs to read from or write something into memory, it references an address in its VAS; and the VMM will map it to an address in RAM. It isn't guaranteed, however, to still be mapped to an address in RAM the next time you access it because the VMM may determine that it needs to move your data to the page file temporarily to allow another process to use the physical memory address. As part of this process, the VMM updates the VAS address and makes it invalid (it doesn't point to an address in RAM anymore). The next time you access this address, it has to be loaded from the page file on disk, so the request is slower — this is known as a *page fault* and it happens automatically without you knowing.

The portion of a process's VAS that currently maps to physical RAM is known as the *working set*. If a process requests data that isn't currently in the working set, then it needs to be reloaded back into memory before use. This is called a *hard page fault* (a *soft page fault* is when the page is still on the standby list in physical memory); and to fix it, the VMM retrieves the data from the page file, finds a free page of memory, either from its list of free pages or from another process, writes the data from the page file into memory, and then maps the new page back into the process's virtual address space.

> **NOTE** *The* Memory: Page Faults/sec *counter in Performance Monitor includes both hard and soft page faults; therefore, if you want to monitor just the performance that is sapping hard page faults, you need to look at* Memory: Page Reads/sec *to get the number of times the disk was accessed to resolve hard page faults, and then compare it to* Memory: Pages Input/sec *to calculate the average number of pages being read in each disk access.*

On a system with enough RAM to give every process all the memory it needs, the VMM doesn't have to do much other than hand out memory and clean up after a process is done with it. On a system without enough RAM to go around, the job is a little more involved. The VMM has to do some work to provide each process with the memory it needs when it needs it. It does this by using the page file to temporarily store data that a process hasn't accessed for a while. This process is called *paging*, and the data is often described as having been paged out to disk.

The Virtual Memory Manager keeps track of each mapping for VAS addresses using page tables, and the mapping information itself is stored in a page table entry (PTE). This is illustrated in Figure 3-2 using two SQL Server instances as an example. Note that the dashed arrow indicates an invalid reference that will generate a hard page fault when accessed, causing the page to be loaded from the page file.

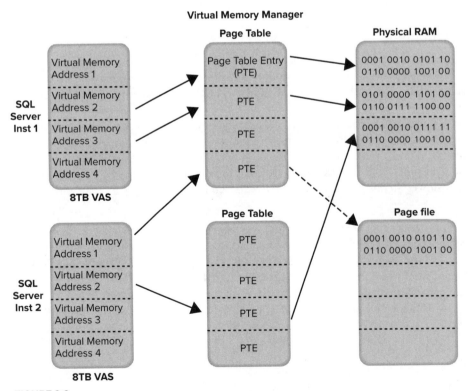

FIGURE 3-2

Sizing the Page File

Determining the optimal size of a page file has been a long-running debate for years. By default, Windows will manage the size of your page file *recommending* a page file size of 1.5 times the size of RAM.

It won't hurt performance to leave the default in place but the debates start to ensue when there are large amounts of RAM in a server and not enough disk space on the system drive for a full-size page file.

The primary purpose of a page file is to allow Windows to temporarily move data from RAM to disk to help it manage resources effectively. When a page file is heavily used, it indicates memory pressure; and the solution is to optimize your memory resources or buy more RAM, rather than to optimize your page file.

If you have disk space concerns on your page file drive, then setting the page file to 50% of total available RAM would be a safe bet.

At one client, where I was delivering a SQL Server Health Check, one of their servers had 96GB of RAM and a 96GB page file. Page file usage was minimal during the day, but every night a SQL Server Analysis Services cube was being rebuilt, which required so much memory that 20GB of the page file was being used during the build. This amount of page file usage is extreme but even a page file sized at 50% would have been more than enough. They upgraded the RAM to 128GB the next week.

Another argument for full-size page files is that they are required to take full memory dumps. While that is correct, it is extremely unlikely that Microsoft support will ever investigate a full memory dump because of the sheer size of it, and certainly never on the first occurrence of an issue. This then gives you time to increase the size of your page file temporarily at Microsoft's request to gather a full dump should the need ever actually arise.

NUMA

Non-Uniform Memory Architecture (NUMA) is a hardware design that improves server scalability by removing motherboard bottlenecks. In a traditional architecture, every processor has access to every memory bank across a shared system bus to a central memory controller on the motherboard. This is called *symmetric multiprocessing (SMP)* and it has limited scalability because the shared system bus quickly becomes a bottleneck when you start to increase the number of processors.

In a NUMA system, each processor has its own memory controller and a direct connection to a dedicated bank of RAM, which is referred to as *local* memory, and together they're represented as a NUMA *node*.

> **NOTE** *To ensure the consistency of data held in the small amount of cache memory present on each CPU, all mainstream implementations use cache-coherent NUMA (ccNUMA), which ensures that when data held in one CPU's cache is modified, any other copies of that data cached on other CPUs are also updated.*

A NUMA node can access memory belonging to another NUMA node but this incurs additional overhead and therefore latency — this is known as *remote memory*.

Coreinfo, a free tool from Sysinternals that can be found on the TechNet website, displays a lot of interesting information about your processor topology, including a mapping of the access cost for remote memory, by processor. Figure 3-3 shows a screenshot from a NUMA system with two nodes, indicating the approximate cost of accessing remote memory as 1.3 times that of local — although latency in the tests can produce outlying results as you can see in the figure. 00 to 00 is actually local and should report a cost of 1.0.

FIGURE 3-3

> **NOTE** *NUMA nodes are fundamental to SQL Server's architecture, so you'll be using them even if you don't have NUMA-capable hardware. On your laptop, for example, SQL Server treats everything as being in NUMA node 0.*

SQL Server's Use of NUMA

SQL Server creates its own internal nodes on startup that map directly on to NUMA nodes, so you can query SQL Server directly and get a representation of the physical design of your motherboard in terms of the number processors, NUMA nodes, and memory distribution.

For example, Figure 3-4 shows a representation of a server with two processors, each with four cores and a bank of local memory that makes up a NUMA node. When SQL Server starts, the SQLOS identifies the number of logical processors and creates a scheduler for each one in an internal node (SQLOS and Schedulers are covered in Chapter 1 and Chapter 5).

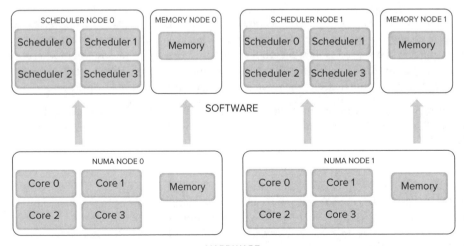

FIGURE 3-4

The memory node is separate from the scheduler node, not grouped together as it is at the hardware level. This provides a greater degree of flexibility and independence; it was a design decision to overcome memory management limitations in earlier versions of Windows.

> **NOTE** *Intel's* Hyper-Threading (HT) *technology duplicates the state of each CPU core and presents two logical processors to Windows per core. SQL Server sees whatever Windows presents, so if the processors in Figure 3-4 subsequently had HT enabled, you would see eight schedulers being created per node. You can read more about HT in Chapter 2.*

SQL Server NUMA CPU Configuration

You can view information about the NUMA configuration in SQL Server using several DMVs. Figure 3-5 shows results from sys.dm_os_schedulers on a server with 24 logical processors and two NUMA nodes. The parent_node_id column shows the distribution of schedulers and CPU references across the two NUMA nodes. You can also see a separate scheduler for the dedicated administrator connection (DAC), which isn't NUMA aware.

The sys.dm_os_nodes DMV also returns information about CPU distribution, containing a node_id column and a cpu_affinity_mask column, which when converted from decimal to binary provides a visual representation of CPU distribution across nodes. A system with 24 logical processors and two NUMA nodes would look like the following:

	scheduler_id	cpu_id	parent_node_id	status
1	0	0	0	VISIBLE ONLINE
2	1	1	0	VISIBLE ONLINE
3	2	2	0	VISIBLE ONLINE
4	3	3	0	VISIBLE ONLINE
5	4	4	0	VISIBLE ONLINE
6	5	5	0	VISIBLE ONLINE
7	6	6	0	VISIBLE ONLINE
8	7	7	0	VISIBLE ONLINE
9	8	8	0	VISIBLE ONLINE
10	9	9	0	VISIBLE ONLINE
11	10	10	0	VISIBLE ONLINE
12	11	11	0	VISIBLE ONLINE
13	12	12	1	VISIBLE ONLINE
14	13	13	1	VISIBLE ONLINE
15	14	14	1	VISIBLE ONLINE
16	15	15	1	VISIBLE ONLINE
17	16	16	1	VISIBLE ONLINE
18	17	17	1	VISIBLE ONLINE
19	18	18	1	VISIBLE ONLINE
20	19	19	1	VISIBLE ONLINE
21	20	20	1	VISIBLE ONLINE
22	21	21	1	VISIBLE ONLINE
23	22	22	1	VISIBLE ONLINE
24	23	23	1	VISIBLE ONLINE
25	1048576	0	64	VISIBLE ONLINE (DAC)

FIGURE 3-5

```
node_id       dec-to-bin CPU mask
0             000000000000111111111111
1             111111111111000000000000
```

When SQL Server starts, it also writes this information to the Error Log, which you can see for the same server in Figure 3-6.

Node configuration: node 0: CPU mask: 0x0000000000000fff:0 Active CPU mask: 0x0000000000000fff:0. This message provides a description of the NUMA configuration for this computer.
Node configuration: node 1: CPU mask: 0x0000000000fff000:0 Active CPU mask: 0x0000000000fff000:0. This message provides a description of the NUMA configuration for this computer.

FIGURE 3-6

SQL Server NUMA Memory Configuration

As you learned earlier in the chapter, SQL Server memory nodes map directly onto NUMA nodes at the hardware level, so you can't do anything to change the distribution of memory across nodes.

SQL Server is aware of the NUMA configuration of the server on which it's running, and its objective is to reduce the need for remote memory access. As a result, the memory objects created when a task is running are created within the same NUMA node as the task whenever it's efficient to do so. For example, if you execute a simple query and it's assigned a thread on scheduler 0 in node 0, then SQL Server will try to use the memory in node 0 for all new memory requirements to keep it local.

How much memory SQL Server tries to use in each hardware NUMA node is determined by the target server's memory, which is affected by the max server memory option (see the section "Min and Max Server Memory" later in the chapter).

Whether you configure Max Server Memory or not, SQL Server will set a target server memory, which represents the target for SQL Server memory usage. This target is then divided by the number of NUMA nodes detected to set a target for each node.

If your server doesn't have an even distribution of RAM across the hardware NUMA nodes on your motherboard, you could find yourself in a situation in which you need to use remote memory just to meet SQL Server's target memory. Figure 3-7 illustrates this; the target server memory of node 3 cannot be fulfilled with local memory because the RAM has not been evenly distributed across NUMA nodes on the motherboard.

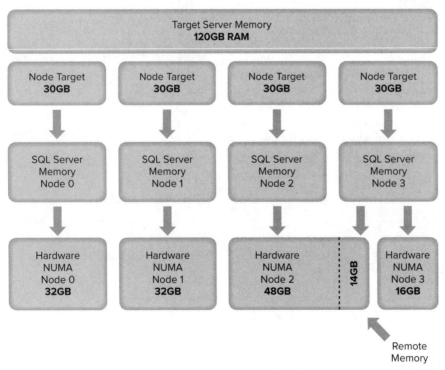

FIGURE 3-7

SQL SERVER MEMORY

The first part of this chapter dealt mainly with the memory environment external to SQL Server — that is, understanding and configuring memory before SQL Server starts. This second part looks at how SQL Server manages memory.

DROPPING WINDOWS SERVER 2003 SUPPORT

SQL Server 2012 doesn't support Window Server 2003, which was a huge relief for the SQL Server development team, as it enabled them to drop all the code required to deal with legacy memory models used prior to Windows Server 2008.

The effect of this is lower development costs for Microsoft (and therefore quicker product releases) and an increase in the efficiency with which SQL Server can be supported.

Memory management in SQL Server has a three-level structure. At the bottom are memory nodes, which are the lowest-level allocators for SQL Server memory. The second level consists of memory clerks, which are used to access the memory nodes, and cache stores, which are used for caching. The top level contains memory objects, which provide a smaller degree of granularity than the memory clerks allow directly.

Only clerks can access memory nodes to allocate memory, so every component that needs to allocate substantial amounts of memory needs to create its own memory clerk when the SQL Server service starts.

NEW MEMORY MANAGER FOR SQL SERVER 2012

Previous versions of SQL Server required VAS space outside of SQL Server's memory allocation for Multi-Page Allocations (MPA) and CLR memory requirements.

The MPA was used whenever a component required a single allocation greater than 8KB and a single page allocator dealt with anything less than or equal to 8KB. In SQL Server 2012, there is only one page allocator for all requests and they all come directly from SQL Server's memory allocation.

CLR allocations also come directly from SQL Server's memory allocation in SQL Server 2012, which makes it much easier to size SQL Server's memory requirements (See Min and Max Server Memory later in the chapter).

Memory Nodes

Memory nodes map directly onto NUMA nodes as described earlier in the chapter, and you can view details about these nodes on your server using the sys.dm_os_memory_nodes DMV. You will always have at least one memory node, which has a memory_node_id of 0, and you may have several if your CPU architecture supports NUMA.

Each memory node has its own memory clerks and caches, which are distributed evenly across all the nodes (although some objects will only be found in node 0). SQL Server's total usage is calculated using the sum of all the nodes.

Clerks, Caches, and the Buffer Pool

Memory clerks are the mechanism by which memory caches are used, and the buffer pool is by far the largest consumer of memory in SQL Server. All three are discussed in this section.

Memory Clerks

Whenever a memory consumer within SQL Server wants to allocate memory, it needs to go through a memory clerk, rather than going straight to a memory node. There are generic memory clerks like MEMORYCLERK_SQLGENERAL, but any component that needs to allocate significant amounts will have been written to create and use its own memory clerk.

The buffer pool for instance has its own memory clerk (MEMORYCLERK_SQLBUFFERPOOL), as do query plans (MEMORYCLERK_SQLQUERYPLAN), which makes troubleshooting much easier because you can view the memory allocations made by each clerk and see who has what.

You can view details about all the memory clerks using the sys.dm_os_memory_clerks DMV. For example, running the following query against a SQL Server 2012 Enterprise Edition instance running a production workload produced the results shown in Figure 3-8:

```
SELECT     [type],
           memory_node_id,
           pages_kb,
           virtual_memory_reserved_kb,
           virtual_memory_committed_kb,
           awe_allocated_kb
FROM       sys.dm_os_memory_clerks
ORDER BY virtual_memory_reserved_kb DESC;
```

The query orders the results by virtual_memory_reserved_kb, so what you see in the figure are the top eight memory clerks ordered by the amount of VAS that they have reserved.

	type	memory_node_id	pages_kb	virtual_memory_reserved_kb	virtual_memory_committed_kb	awe_allocated_kb
1	MEMORYCLERK_SQLBUFFERPOOL	0	12398056	51989208	1017280	0
2	MEMORYCLERK_SQLCLR	0	62424	9481344	579968	0
3	MEMORYCLERK_SOSMEMMANAGER	0	0	412712	412088	0
4	OBJECTSTORE_LOCK_MANAGER	0	1002264	131076	131076	0
5	MEMORYCLERK_SQLSTORENG	0	4944	11520	11520	0
6	MEMORYCLERK_SQLCLRASSEMBLY	0	0	4856	4856	0
7	MEMORYCLERK_XE_BUFFER	0	0	3072	3072	0
8	MEMORYCLERK_XE_BUFFER	1	0	1536	1536	0

FIGURE 3-8

Caches

SQL Server uses three types of caching mechanism: object store, cache store, and user store.

Object stores are used to cache homogeneous types of stateless data, but it's the cache and user stores that you'll come across most often. They are very similar in that they're both caches — the main difference between them is that user stores must be created with their own storage semantics using the development framework, whereas a cache store implements support for the memory objects mentioned previously to provide a smaller granularity of memory allocation.

Essentially, the user stores are mainly used by different development teams within Microsoft to implement their own specific caches for SQL Server features, so you can treat cache stores and user stores the same way.

To view the different caches implemented on your SQL Server, use the sys.dm_os_memory_cache_counters DMV. For example, running the following query will show you all the caches available, ordered by the total amount of space they consume:

```
SELECT    [name],
          [type],
          pages_kb,
          entries_count
FROM      sys.dm_os_memory_cache_counters
ORDER BY pages_kb DESC;
```

Sample output showing the top three caches by size is shown in Figure 3-9.

	name	type	pages_kb	entries_count
1	SQL Plans	CACHESTORE_SQLCP	344664	1300
2	Object Plans	CACHESTORE_OBJCP	64696	190
3	Bound Trees	CACHESTORE_PHDR	30008	284

FIGURE 3-9

Here, the caches you see are all related to query processing (discussed further in Chapter 5). These specific caches are used for the following:

➤ CACHESTORE_OBJCP — Compiled plans for objects such as stored procedures, functions, and triggers

➤ CACHESTORE_SQLCP — Cached plans for SQL statements or batches that aren't in stored procedures. If your application doesn't use stored procedures, then the plans are cached here. However, they are much less likely to be reused than stored procedure plans, which can lead to a bloated cache taking a lot of memory (see the "Optimize for Ad-Hoc Workloads" section later in the chapter).

➤ CACHESTORE_PHDR — Algebrizer trees for views, constraints, and defaults. An algebrizer tree is the parsed SQL text that resolves table and column names.

Buffer Pool

The buffer pool contains and manages SQL Server's data cache. Information on its contents can be found in the `sys.dm_os_buffer_descriptors` DMV. For example, the following query returns the amount of data cache usage per database, in MB:

```
SELECT    count(*)*8/1024 AS 'Cached Size (MB)'
          ,CASE database_id
          WHEN 32767 THEN 'ResourceDb'
          ELSE db_name(database_id)
          END AS 'Database'
FROM      sys.dm_os_buffer_descriptors
GROUP BY db_name(database_id),database_id
ORDER BY 'Cached Size (MB)' DESC
```

Monitoring SQL Server's buffer pool is a great way to look out for memory pressure, and Performance Monitor provides numerous counters to help you do this for quick insight, including the following:

➤ `MSSQL$<instance >:Memory Manager\Total Server Memory (KB)` — Indicates the current size of the buffer pool

➤ `MSSQL$<instance >:Memory Manager\Target Server Memory (KB)` — Indicates the ideal size for the buffer pool. Total and Target should be almost the same on a server with no memory pressure that has been running for a while. If Total is significantly less than Target, then either the workload hasn't been sufficient for SQL Server to grow any further or SQL Server cannot grow the buffer pool due to memory pressure, in which case you can investigate further.

➤ `MSSQL$<instance >:Buffer Manager\Page Life Expectancy` — Indicates the amount of time, in seconds, that SQL Server expects a page that has been loaded into the buffer pool to remain in cache. Under memory pressure, data pages are flushed from cache far more frequently. Microsoft recommends a minimum of 300 seconds for a good PLE; this threshold continues to be debated within the SQL Server community, but one thing everyone agrees on is that less than 300 seconds is bad. In systems with plenty of physical memory, this will easily reach thousands of seconds.

Plan Cache

Execution plans can be time consuming and resource intensive to create; therefore, it makes sense that if SQL Server has already found a good way to execute a piece of code, it should try to reuse it for subsequent requests. The *plan cache* (also referred to as the procedure cache) is used to cache all the execution plans in case they can be reused.

You can view the contents of the plan cache and determine its current size by using the `sys.dm_exec_cached_plans` DMV or by running DBCC MEMORYSTATUS and looking for the "Procedure Cache" section, where you'll find the number of plans in cache and the cache size, in 8KB pages.

> **NOTE** DBCC MEMORYSTATUS *provides a lot of useful information about SQL Server's memory state but you'll find that DMVs provide far more flexibility with the output, so try to get used to finding the same information from DMVs whenever possible. The following DMVs are a good place to start:*
>
> ➤ sys.dm_os_memory_nodes
>
> ➤ sys.dm_os_memory_clerks
>
> ➤ sys.dm_os_memory_objects
>
> ➤ sys.dm_os_memory_cache_counters
>
> ➤ sys.dm_os_memory_pools

The following example script uses sys.dm_exec_cached_plans to show the number of cached plans and the total size in MB:

```
SELECT count(*) AS 'Number of Plans',
sum(cast(size_in_bytes AS BIGINT))/1024/1024 AS 'Plan Cache Size (MB)'
FROM sys.dm_exec_cached_plans
```

Running this on a production SQL Server 2012 instance with Max Server Memory set to 32GB produced the following results:

```
Number of Plans    Plan Cache Size (MB)
14402              2859
```

> **NOTE** *This server-level option can help to reduce* plan cache bloat *by not caching single-use ad-hoc plans. You can read about it in the section "Optimizing SQL Server Memory Configuration" later in the chapter.*

The *maximum* size for the plan cache is calculated by SQL Server as follows:

➤ 75% of server memory from 0–4GB +

➤ 10% of server memory from 4GB–64GB +

➤ 5% of server memory > 64GB

Therefore, a system with 32GB of RAM would have a maximum plan cache of 3GB + 2.8GB = 5.8GB.

Query/Workspace Memory

In SQL Server, query memory (also known as workspace memory) is used to temporarily store results during hash and sort operations when executing a query. It's not very widely known or documented, but if you look at an execution plan (also known as an query plan) for a query and you see hash and/or sort operators, that query needs to use query memory to complete execution.

Query memory is allocated out of the buffer pool, so it's definitely something to be aware of when you're building a picture of the memory usage on a server.

You can find out how much query memory an individual query uses by looking at the properties of an actual execution plan in Management Studio, as opposed to an estimated execution plan. The estimated plan contains information about how SQL Server will run the query, and it shows any hash or sort operators; but the actual plan reflects what SQL Server used to execute the query, and it contains additional runtime data, including how much query memory was used.

You can view the details of any queries that already have an allocation of query memory (memory grant) and those that are waiting for a memory grant using the sys.dm_exec_query_memory_ grants DMV.

Query memory also has its own memory clerk, which means you can view the sizing information for outstanding memory grants by querying the sys.dm_exec_query_memory_grants DMV where type = 'MEMORYCLERK_SQLQERESERVATIONS'.

The memory requirements for all hash and sort operators in a plan are added together to get the total query memory requirement.

The amount of space available as query memory is dynamically managed between 25% and 75% of the buffer pool but it can grow larger than that if the buffer pool is not under pressure.

Five percent of query memory is reserved for small queries that require less than 5MB of memory and have a "cost" of less than 3. SQL Server assigns a cost to queries based on how many resources will be needed to run the query. You can read more about how SQL Server assigns and uses "cost" in Chapter 5.

No individual query will get a grant for more than 20% of the total query memory, to ensure that other queries can still be executed. In addition to this safeguard, SQL Server also implements a query memory grant queue. Every query that contains a hash or sort operation has to pass through the global query memory grant queue before executing, which is organized as five queues organized by query cost query cost.

Each query is put into the appropriate queue based on cost, and each queue implements a first-come first-served policy. This method enables smaller queries with lower memory requirements to be processed even if larger queries are waiting for enough free memory.

Figure 3-10 shows a representation of the five queues based on query cost that make up the global memory grant queue on a server with 1GB of query memory. The box at the bottom of the picture contains eight existing memory grants totaling 920MB, leaving 104MB free. The first request to arrive was for 120MB and went into Q3. This request can't be allocated immediately because only 104MB are free. The next request is only for 20MB and goes into Q2. This request can be fulfilled immediately because having multiple queues means that it isn't stuck behind the first request that is still waiting.

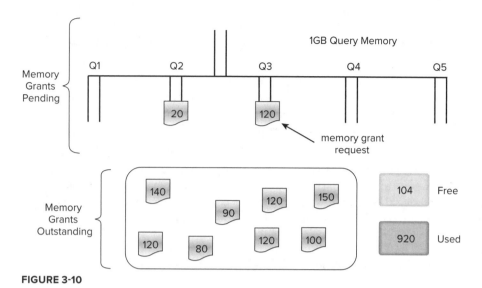

FIGURE 3-10

The Query Wait Option

Queries can time out if they spend too much time waiting for a memory grant. The time-out duration is controlled by the Query Wait option, which can be modified either using sp_configure or on the Advanced page of Server Properties in Management Studio. The default value is -1, which equates to 25 times the cost of the query, in seconds. Any positive value for Query Wait will be used as the time-out value in seconds.

It is possible for a transaction that contains a query waiting for a memory grant to hold locks open and cause a blocking problem before it times out. In this situation, a lower Query Wait value would reduce the impact on other tasks by causing the query to time out sooner.

However, first try to reduce the memory requirement for the query or increase the available memory to avoid the timeout before changing a global option like Query Wait because doing so affects all queries running on the server. The default setting allows for a dynamic time-out value that varies according to the query cost, so it's generally the best option.

Query Memory Diagnostics

There are a number of different ways to get information on query memory usage on your SQL Server in addition to the DMVs already discussed at the beginning of the section. Performance Monitor provides the following counters, all of which are found within the instance's Memory Manager:

➤ **Granted Workspace Memory (KB)** — Total amount of query memory currently in use

➤ **Maximum Workspace Memory (KB)** — Total amount of memory that SQL Server has marked for query memory

➤ **Memory Grants Pending** — Number of memory grants waiting in the queue

➤ **Memory Grants Outstanding** — Number of memory grants currently in use

The RESOURCE_SEMAPHORE wait type is a wait on a memory grant, so if you see this near the top in your results from the sys.dm_os_wait_stats DMV, then your system is struggling to provide memory grants fast enough.

You can also encounter performance issues other than just a query timing out while it waits for a memory grant. Within an execution plan or when analyzing a SQL trace, you may notice *hash warning* or *sort warning* messages if you have selected the relevant events. These occur when the memory grant was insufficient for a query's requirements.

A hash warning occurs when the hash build doesn't fit in memory and must be spilled to disk (its actually written to tempdb). A sort warning occurs when a multi-pass sort is required because the granted memory was insufficient. Both warnings generally occur because the SQL Server Query Optimizer made the wrong choice, usually because of inaccurate statistics or a lack of useful statistics. For more details about this, see Chapter 5.

OPTIMIZING SQL SERVER MEMORY CONFIGURATION

This section discusses some of the most common memory configuration options for SQL Server.

Min and Max Server Memory

Min Server Memory (MB) and Max Server Memory (MB) control the allowable size of *all* SQL Server's memory usage. With the introduction of a new Memory Manager described earlier in the chapter, this is a change for SQL Server 2012. This makes sizing SQL Server's memory requirements much easier than with previous versions.

As its name suggests, Min Server Memory controls the minimum amount of physical memory that SQL Server will try to keep committed. We say "try" because it can fall under that value if Windows is desperate enough, but to all intents and purposes it sets a floor for SQL Server's memory usage.

When the SQL Server service starts, it does not acquire all the memory configured in Min Server Memory but instead starts with only the minimum required, growing as necessary. Once memory usage has increased beyond the Min Server Memory setting, SQL Server won't release any memory below that amount.

Not surprisingly, Max Server Memory is the opposite of Min Server Memory, setting a ceiling for memory usage. Both values can be set using sp_configure or through Management Studio on the Memory page of the SQL Server Properties window.

Configuring a maximum value for the buffer pool is the more important of the two settings and will prevent SQL Server from taking too much memory. This is particularly significant on 64-bit systems, where a lack of free physical memory can cause Windows to trim SQL Server's working set. See the section "Lock Pages in Memory" for a full description of this issue.

There are several different ways to calculate an appropriate value for configuring Max Server Memory, but two of the most straightforward are as follows:

➤   Look at SQL Server's maximum usage.

➤   Determine the maximum potential for memory requirements outside SQL Server.

Each of these options is covered in the following sections.

Looking at the SQL Server's Maximum Usage

With this method, you set SQL Server to dynamically manage memory and then monitor the `MSSQL$<instance>:Memory Manager\Total Server Memory (KB)` counter using Performance Monitor. This counter measures SQL Server's total buffer pool usage.

The Total Server Memory value will decrease if other requirements outside SQL Server need more physical memory than is currently free, and then increase again to use any free memory. If you monitor this counter for a period of time that is representative for your business (i.e., it includes busy and slack periods), you can then set Max Server Memory to the lowest value that was observed for Total Server Memory (KB), and you won't have to worry about SQL Server having to shrink its usage during normal operations.

Determining the Maximum Potential for Requirements Outside SQL Server

This option is the most popular, as the aim is to calculate the worst-case scenario for memory requirements other than SQL Server's. You should allow for the following:

➤ 2GB for Windows

➤ xGB for SQL Server worker threads. You can find your max workers count by querying `sys.dm_os_sys_info`. Each thread will use 0.5MB on x86, and 2MB on x64.

➤ 512MB, if you use linked servers, extended stored procedure dlls, or objects created using Automation procedures (sp_OA calls)

➤ 1–3GB, for other applications that might be running on the system, such as backup programs or anti-virus software

For example, on a server with eight CPU cores and 64GB of RAM running SQL Server 2012, a third-party backup utility, and virus checker, you would allow for the following:

➤ 2GB for Windows

➤ 1GB for worker threads (576 × 2MB rounded down)

➤ 512MB for linked servers, etc.

➤ 1GB for the backup program and virus checker

For a total of 4.5GB, you would configure Max Server Memory to 59.5GB.

Both of these options can be valid in different circumstances. On a single SQL Server from which you need to squeeze every drop of performance, you might use option 1 and monitor Total Server Memory to see how often SQL Server has to give memory back to Windows. However, if you had dozens of SQL Servers to manage or a mission-critical server, you might go with option 2, as it would be easier to calculate across multiple servers and is less likely to cause a failure under exceptional circumstances.

Checking That Your Max Server Memory Is Effective

How you decide to configure Max Server Memory when you build a server (there are many opinions on the matter) isn't as important as measuring its effectiveness and adjusting it when the server has run its expected workload. An easy way to do this is using performance monitor counters, specifically, `MSSQL$<instance>:Buffer Manager\Page Life Expectancy` (PLE) (also see the section "Clerks, Caches, and the Buffer Pool") and `Memory\Available MBytes`. The balance between these two counters shows you how effective your Max Server Memory setting is.

➤ **PLE:** Shows you how many seconds SQL Server expects to keep a page in the data cache and is a good measure of memory pressure on SQL Server

➤ **Available MBytes:** Shows how much physical RAM Windows has that isn't doing anything

If your PLE is low (<300 is definitely low but you might choose a higher threshold), then check your Available MBytes to see how much unused RAM is available. Windows starts to aggressively trim (see next section) all application working sets when it has less than 5MB available, so anything close to this on a production server should be considered an urgent problem.

The minimum Available MBytes you should have is 100MB but even this is cutting it too close because any application that is run on your SQL Server can easily use that up. Instead, try aiming for 500 or 600MB as a minimum or even 1GB to be sure. That way, if you need to run any support tools on the server, there will be plenty of RAM for them.

So, if your PLE is low and you have plenty of Available MBytes because you were conservative with your Max Server Memory setting, then you have scope to increase your Max Server Memory, thereby increasing your PLE. Conversely, if your Available MBytes is low because you were aggressive with your Max Server Memory setting and your PLE is very high, then you can reduce your Max Server Memory to give some RAM back to Windows.

Here are some example scenarios to illustrate this point:

➤ Max Server Memory is 30GB on a server with 32GB RAM. PLE averages 10,000 and Available MBytes is 90MB. **Solution:** Lower Max Server Memory by at least 500MB.

➤ Max Server Memory is 46GB on a server with 50GB RAM. PLE averages 10 and Available MBytes is 1500MB. **Solution:** Increase Max Server Memory by 500MB to 1000MB.

➤ Max Server Memory is 60GB on a server with 64GB RAM. PLE averages 50 and Available MBytes is 20MB. **Solution:** Lower Max Server Memory by 100MB and buy more RAM (quickly).

Lock Pages in Memory

Lock Pages in Memory (LPIM) is used as a work-around for a problem than can occur between Windows and SQL Server, and it was especially bad on older versions of SQL Server, which could run on Windows Server 2003 and earlier.

If there isn't enough free physical memory in Windows to service a request for resources from a driver or another application, Windows will trim the working set (which refers to the physical memory usage of a process) of all applications running on the server. This is normal behavior and shouldn't have much noticeable impact.

Windows Server 2003 didn't cope very well with badly written drivers and could actually force all applications to empty their working sets. This is known as *aggressive working set trimming* and had a devastating effect on SQL Server's memory allocation — and therefore performance. So that you could see when this happened, Microsoft added a message to the SQL Server Error Log. Here is an example:

```
A significant part of sql server process memory has been paged out.
This may result in a performance degradation. Duration: 0 seconds.
Working set (KB): 1086400, committed (KB): 2160928, memory
utilization: 50%.
```

This behavior significantly changed in Windows Server 2008 and later thus preventing the biggest problem — badly written drivers causing application working sets to be emptied. This won't affect SQL Server 2012 because it only runs on Windows Server 2008+.

In SQL Server 2012, you will still get messages logged when Windows performs working set trimming. Several messages can indicate a gradual decline of SQL Server's working set (which is still a problem).

Resolving this issue (or avoiding it all together) can be approached in two ways:

➤ Set Max Server Memory appropriately to ensure that Windows and other processes running on the server have enough physical memory to perform their work without asking SQL Server to trim. See the previous section on Min and Max Server Memory for more details.

➤ If you're still seeing the issue (or if its effects are so severe you don't want to risk seeing it again), you can configure your SQL Server to use Locked Pages in Memory (LPIM).

When LPIM is enabled, SQL Server's buffer pool pages are "locked" and non-pageable so Windows can't take them when trimming.

Once the pages are locked, they're not considered part of available memory for working set trimming. However, only SQL Server buffer pool allocations can be locked — Windows can still trim the working sets of other processes, affecting resources on which SQL Server depends.

LPIM should be used if you continue to get working set trimming after setting a suitable max server memory *or* the cost of SQL Server's working set being trimmed again is too risky.

Whether or not it should be used as a default best practice on all your SQL Servers is a common debate. One perspective is that it's a work-around and not intended to replace the default behavior on every SQL Server implementation. Administrators who believe this don't set it unless they know it's going to fix a problem. Another perspective is that setting it by default on every implementation is a good preventative measure, which avoids working set trimming ever happening.

Ultimately, it's down to personal choice; and whether or not you choose to enable it by default is less important than understanding what it does and making an educated decision rather than blindly enabling the feature because someone advised it.

> **NOTE** *Having read what LPIM was introduced to fix, it's also worth noting that a side-effect of using locked pages is that they require slightly less overhead to manage (because they can't be moved). This can translate into a real performance benefit on large scale, high-throughput SQL Servers. So it's definitely worth testing on your most performance sensitive servers to see if it helps.*

If LPIM is working, you'll see the following message in the SQL Server Error Log:

```
Using Locked Pages in the Memory Manager.
```

You can read about Microsoft support for this feature and how to enable it at http://support.microsoft.com/kb/2659143.

Optimize for Ad-Hoc Workloads

Every time an execution plan (see Chapter 5) is generated, it is stored in the plan cache in the hope that it can be reused — this is one of the efficient ways that SQL Server manages its workload.

If an execution plan is never reused, then it's just taking up resources unnecessarily; and the use of unparameterized ad-hoc T-SQL is the most likely cause.

When you execute code in SQL Server, it generates a hash value of your code and uses that to determine plan reuse. If you execute a stored procedure, a hash value is generated from the stored procedure name, and the plan will be reused on each subsequent procedure call regardless of the parameter values used.

If you run the same code outside of a stored procedure (*ad-hoc T-SQL*), the hash is taken on the whole statement, including any literal values. When you then change the literal values for another execution, the hash is different, so SQL Server doesn't find a match and generates a new execution plan instead of reusing the previous one.

This situation can lead to a scenario called *plan cache bloat*, whereby potentially thousands of ad-hoc plans are generated and cached with a *usecount* of 1 even though the code is fundamentally the same.

The ideal solution is to use stored procedures or functions, or to parameterize all your ad-hoc T-SQL; but this can be very challenging, and often unachievable due to complexity and company politics, so Microsoft introduced the *Optimize for Ad-hoc Workloads* server-level option in SQL Server 2008 to help.

When this option is enabled, SQL Server will cache only a *plan stub* the first time a piece of ad-hoc T-SQL is executed, rather than the full plan. If SQL Server subsequently tries to reuse that plan, it will be generated again but this time cached in full. This avoids the scenario of thousands of single-use plans taking up valuable space in cache.

For example, recall this script used earlier in the chapter:

```
SELECT count(*) AS 'Number of Plans',
sum(cast(size_in_bytes AS BIGINT))/1024/1024 AS 'Plan Cache Size (MB)'
FROM sys.dm_exec_cached_plans
```

The preceding code produced the following results on a SQL Server 2012 instance with Max Server Memory set to 32GB:

Number of Plans	Plan Cache Size (MB)
14402	2859

Almost 3GB of memory is being used to cache plans, so it's significant enough to investigate the usage details. The following script breaks down the plan cache size by cached object type:

```
SELECT objtype AS 'Cached Object Type',
count(*) AS 'Number of Plans',
sum(cast(size_in_bytes AS BIGINT))/1024/1024 AS 'Plan Cache Size (MB)',
avg(usecounts) AS 'Avg Use Count'
FROM sys.dm_exec_cached_plans
GROUP BY objtype
```

The results are as follows:

Cached Object Type	Number of Plans	Plan Cache Size (MB)	Avg Use Count
UsrTab	10	0	222
Prepared	286	72	4814
View	216	20	62
Adhoc	13206	**2223**	39
Check	30	0	7
Trigger	22	5	1953
Proc	738	554	289025

As you can see, most of the plan cache is taken up with ad-hoc plans, with an average use of 39, which is quite low; therefore, you now want to determine how many of those are single-use plans by modifying the earlier cache sizing script:

```
SELECT count(*) AS 'Number of Plans',
sum(cast(size_in_bytes AS BIGINT))/1024/1024 AS 'Plan Cache Size (MB)'
FROM sys.dm_exec_cached_plans
WHERE usecounts = 1
AND objtype = 'adhoc'
```

Here are the results:

Number of Plans	Plan Cache Size (MB)
12117	332

This indicates that 332MB of cache is being used for plans that aren't being reused, which isn't a huge amount on this server, but it's completely wasted, so there's no reason not to get rid of these plans.

The Optimize for Adhoc Workloads option ensures that this scenario will never occur — and because it only affects ad-hoc plans, we recommend switching it on by default in all installations of SQL Server.

SUMMARY

In this chapter, you've learned the difference between physical and virtual memory and the limited support SQL Server 2012 has for 32-bit environments.

You've also read about NUMA architectures and how SQL Server's memory model structures itself around NUMA. And you've seen the Clerks and Caches that SQL Server uses, including the buffer pool and the plan cache.

You've also learned about Workspace Memory, which supports hashing and sort operations; how to determine an effective Max Server Memory setting; and that all of SQL Server's memory requests are now governed by this setting.

Other configuration settings you read about were Optimize for AdHoc Workloads, which prevents cache bloat from single-use ad-hoc plans; and Lock Pages in Memory, which prevents Windows trimming SQL Server's working set.

Storage Systems

WHAT'S IN THIS CHAPTER?

➤ Storage and RAID technology

➤ Choosing the right storage network

➤ The SQL I/O system

➤ Windows I/O system

➤ Configuration best practices

➤ Storage performance

➤ Storage validation and testing

WROX.COM CODE DOWNLOADS FOR THIS CHAPTER

There are no code downloads for this chapter.

INTRODUCTION

Storage systems have been confounding database administrators and designers since Microsoft first released SQL Server. Today DBAs are not only required to design and maintain SQL Server, but are also often pressed into service as storage administrators. For DBAs working in the enterprise, communication with the server, networking, and especially storage teams are always a challenge.

This chapter will equip you, the humble database professional, with the knowledge needed to define proper storage performance. More important, you will gain insight and a common language that enables you to communicate with storage networking teams. We will follow SQL server reads and writes as they traverse the Windows and storage stacks.

By examining various storage hardware components, you will learn how best to protect your data with RAID technology. You will also see how storage area networks assist in data protection. Finally, you will learn how to validate your functional configuration and performance.

SQL SERVER I/O

Let's begin by investigating how SQL Server generates I/O. We are concerned with reading existing data and writing new data. At its most basic SQL Server is made up of a few files that reside within the server file system. As a rule, different computer system components perform at different rates. It is always faster to process items in the CPU than it is to serve requests from processor cache. As detailed in the hardware chapter, L2 and L3 CPU cache is faster than computer memory. Server memory is faster than any I/O component.

SQL attempts to mitigate the relatively slow I/O system by caching whatever it can in system memory. Newly received data is first written to the SQL transaction log by SQL Server write-ahead logging (WAL) as you saw in Chapter 1. The data is then written to buffer pages hosted in server memory. This process ensures that the database can be recovered in the event of failure.

Storing the buffer pages in memory ensures that future reads are returned to the requestor promptly. Unfortunately, server memory is not infinite. At some point SQL server will need to write data. In Chapter 1 you learned about how SQL Server writes data to disk using the Lazy Writer and Checkpoint processes. This chapter will cover the mechanics of how the operating system and storage subsystems actually get this data onto disk storage.

Contrast these write operations with read requests that are generated by SQL Server worker threads. The workers initiate I/O read operations using the SQL Server asynchronous I/O engine. By utilizing an asynchronous operation worker threads can perform other tasks while the read request is completed. The asynchronous I/O engine depends on Windows and the underlying storage systems to successfully read and write data to permanent storage.

SQL Server takes advantage of the WriteFileGather and ReadFileScatter Win32 APIs. WriteFileGather collects data from discontinuous buffers and writes this data to disk. ReadFileScatter reads data from a file and disperses data into multiple discontinuous buffers. These scatter/gather APIs allow the bundling of potential I/O operations thus reducing the actual number of physical read and write operation.

Understanding Windows storage is the key to tuning SQL Server I/O performance and guaranteeing data integrity. This chapter aims to arm database administrators and designers with the appropriate nomenclature to enable communication with other information technology disciplines. Open, reliable communication is the ultimate key to successful relational data management.

STORAGE TECHNOLOGY

The Host Bus Adapter (HBA) handles connections from the server to storage devices and can also perform several other roles. While a basic HBA provides connectivity to storage, more advanced HBAs have embedded Array controllers. When the storage is located within or attached to the server, it is called Direct Attached Storage (DAS). A storage device managed by a dedicated external array controller is called Storage Area Network (SAN) attached storage. Figure 4-1 shows the basic building blocks of a storage subsystem.

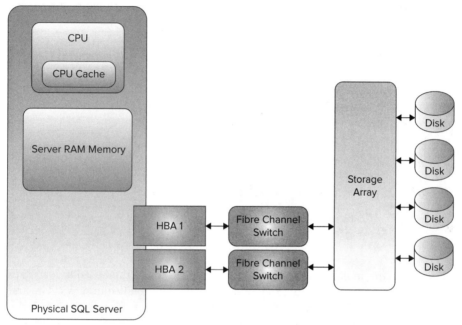

FIGURE 4-1

Storage devices connected to a storage network that are not logically grouped are called, rather inelegantly, a JBOD, for "just a bunch of disks (or drives)." Figure 4-2 shows an example of a JBOD. JBODs can be accessed directly by SQL Server as individual physical disk drives. Just remember that JBODs do not offer any protection against failure.

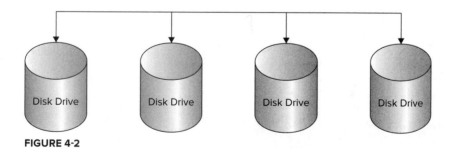

FIGURE 4-2

Storage array controllers group disks into volumes called a redundant array of inexpensive disks (RAID). RAID-constructed volumes offer capacity without failure protection. The simplest type of unprotected RAID set is often called *disk striping*, or RAID 0.

To understand a RAID 0 set, imagine a series of four disk drives lined up in a row. Data written to a stripe set will fill the first drive with a small amount of data. Each subsequent drive will then be filled with the same amount of data, at which point the process is repeated starting with the first disk drive. Figure 4-3 shows how data looks after it has been written to a RAID 0 disk subsystem. Each data stripe is made up of some uniform data size. Most RAID systems allow the user to modify the size of the data stripe.

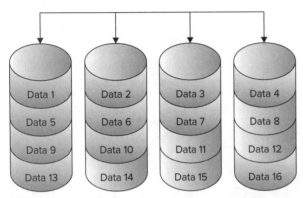

FIGURE 4-3

Concatenated disk arrays are similar to stripe datasets, differing in the method used to load data. You can think of concatenated datasets as a group of disk drives that are filled in series. The first group is filled, then the second group, and so on. We will investigate the performance implications of different RAID configurations later in the Disk Drive Performance section of this chapter.

Figure 4-4 shows the contrast between striped RAID, which is serpentine in its layout, and the waterfall pattern of a concatenated disk array. Concatenated systems don't necessarily lack data protection. Many storage arrays layer different types of RAID. One example is a system that combines mirrored physical disks into a concatenated RAID set. This combined system offers the benefits of protected data and the ease of adding more capacity on demand since each new concatenated mirror will be appended to the end of the overall RAID set.

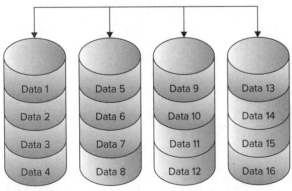

FIGURE 4-4

RAID defines two ways to provide failure protection: disk mirroring and parity generation. RAID 1, often called *disk mirroring*, places data in equal parts on separate physical disks. If one disk fails, the array controller will mirror data from the remaining good disk onto a new replacement disk. Figure 4-5 details the frequent combination of mirroring and striping. This system is often called RAID 1 + 0 or simply RAID 10.

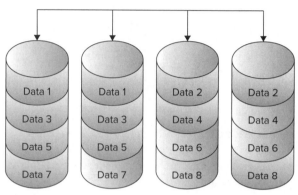

FIGURE 4-5

The storage array uses an *exclusive or (XOR)* mathematical calculation to generate parity data. Parity enables the array to recreate missing data by combining parity information with the data that is distributed across the remaining disks. This parity data enables you to make efficient use of your capacity but at the cost of performance, as the XOR calculation needed to generate the parity data is resource intensive. More details about the performance implications of data protection can be found in the Disk Drive Performance section of this chapter.

Many different parity RAID configurations have been defined. The two most common types are disk striping with parity (RAID 5) and disk striping with double parity (RAID 6). Examples of both are shown in Figure 4-6 and Figure 4-7. RAID 5 protects a system against a single disk drive failure. RAID 6 protects against a double disk failure. RAID 5 and 6 offer disk failure protection while minimizing the amount of capacity dedicated to protection. Contrast this with RAID 1, which consumes half of the available storage in order to protect the data set.

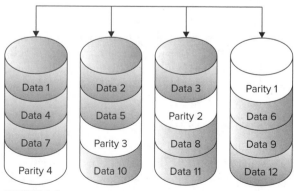

FIGURE 4-6

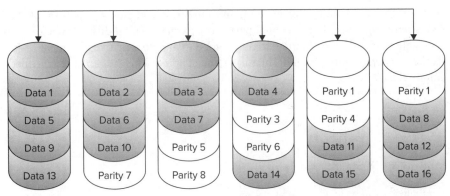

FIGURE 4-7

To create the parity information the RAID engine reads data from the data disks. This data is computed into parity by the XOR calculation. The parity information is written to the next data drive. The parity information is shifted to a different drive with each subsequent stripe calculation thus ensuring no single drive failure causes catastrophic data loss.

RAID 6 generates two parity chunks and diversifies each across a different physical disk. This double parity system protects against a double disk drive fault. As disk drives become larger and larger, there is a significant chance that before the failed data can be repaired a second failure will occur.

RAID 5 and RAID 6 become more space efficient on larger sets of disk drives. A RAID 5 disk set using seven data drives and one parity drive will consume less relative space than a disk set using three data drives and one parity drive.

Each of these RAID sets represents a failure domain. That is to say, failures within the domain affect the entire dataset hosted by a given failure domain. Large failure domains can also incur a performance penalty when calculating the parity bits. In a four-disk RAID 5 set, only three data drives are accessed for parity calculation. Given an eight-disk RAID set, seven drives are accessed.

You can combine RAID types into the same volume. Striping or concatenating several RAID 5 disk sets enables the use of smaller failure domains while increasing the potential size of a given volume. A striped, mirrored volume is called RAID 1+0 (or simply RAID 10). This RAID construct can perform extremely well at the cost of available capacity.

Many storage controllers monitor how RAID sets are accessed. Using a RAID 10 dataset as an example, several read requests sent to a given mirrored drive pair will be serviced by the drive with the least pending work. This work-based access enables RAID sets to perform reads more rapidly than writes. We will cover much more about the effects of RAID on I/O performance in the Disk Drive Performance section of this chapter.

SQL Server and the Windows I/O Subsystem

Microsoft SQL Server is an application that utilizes the Windows I/O subsystem. Rather than covering the minutia of how SQL Server reads and writes from the NTFS file system, we are going to explore the specific Windows I/O systems that will report errors to the Windows event logs. This should aid you in troubleshooting many storage errors.

The storage system components, shown in Figure 4-8, report errors to the Windows system Event Log. SQL Server reports errors to the Windows application log. You can either directly check the Event Logs or use System Center to scrape the Event Logs for actionable errors.

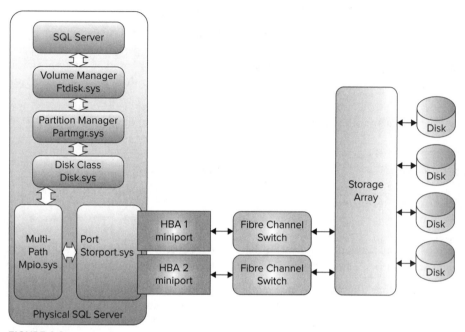

FIGURE 4-8

The Volume Manager driver (ftdisk.sys) creates a new I/O request packet that is passed to the Partition Manager driver (partmgr.sys). Once the request packet is created, the Volume Manager passes this packet to the Disk Class driver (disk.sys). Ftdisk.sys continues to monitor for successful delivery of the request packet. If problems are detected, then ftdisk.sys reports the errors to the system Event Log. These ftdisk errors usually represent very serious storage system issues.

At this point the Disk Class driver passes the storage request to either the Multipath System driver (mpio.sys) or the Port driver (storport.sys). Multipath I/O is a Microsoft technology that is utilized in storage area networks (SANs). Vendors can create an MPIO device-specific module (DSM) driver that details how the Multipath driver should load balance I/O across different storage pathways. Microsoft offers a generic DSM that provides limited failover capabilities. Non-SAN technologies do not use MPIO.

The HBA is the physical piece of hardware that interfaces with disk drives and other storage devices. HBA manufacturers create a miniport driver that interfaces with storport.sys. Most HBA drivers will independently report communication errors to the application Event Log.

Ideally, this entire chain of events takes no longer than 20 milliseconds. Performance is governed by a myriad of factors, the most important of which is latency. Both ftdisk.sys and SQL Server time each I/O. If the round-trip duration exceeds 15 seconds (for SQL Server or 1 minute for ftdisk.sys), then errors are reported to the SQL logs and the Windows application Event Log. As you hopefully noticed, a normal operation is measured in milliseconds, so one second is an eternity.

Choosing the Right Storage Networks

This chapter opened with an example of a SQL Server using a single disk drive. More complex storage networks link multiple hosts, or initiators, to many storage devices, or targets. These advanced storage area networks facilitate low-latency, high-throughput communication.

The storage network can facilitate the sharing of storage resources. Direct attached storage offers good performance for a relatively low cost, but DAS storage can orphan performance and capacity. Imagine several applications that grow in capacity at different rates or are used at different times. Consolidated storage that is attached to a SAN network enables users to share both storage capacity and available performance.

Complex storage networks are often built using Fibre Channel (FC) technology.

> **NOTE** *The spelling of "Fibre" is no accident. The creators of FC wanted to differentiate the technology from fiber optic technologies that did not support copper cabling at the time.*

FC differs from most server network protocols in that it is not routed. Routing enables the creation of large and resilient networks, but routed networks require a lot of overhead to operate.

If you are familiar with Fibre Channel you may already be aware of routing solutions for it. Several products exist to fulfill this role; their use is extremely complex and beyond the scope of this chapter.

Because it is not routed, FC defines a standard for both direct and switched storage network connections. Modern FC networks utilize high-speed network switches to communicate.

Storage networks are not limited to Fibre Channel. Several protocols define methods for sending storage data over existing server IP networks. Fibre Channel Internet Protocol (FCIP) allows Fibre Channel data frames to be encapsulated within an IP packet. Internet Small Computer Systems Interface (iSCSI) allows the transmission of SCSI data over IP networks.

FCIP and iSCSI transport different layers of the storage network. Fibre Channel frames are analogous to Ethernet data frames. SCSI is a storage control system comparable to Internet Protocol. Transmission Control Protocol is an Internetworking protocol and therefore has no analogue in storage networking. Emerging technologies such as Fibre Channel Over Ethernet (FCOE) combine the attributes of existing Fibre Channel networks with Ethernet routed networks.

Regardless of the specific network technology that is used to transport storage traffic, keep in mind that bandwidth is not infinite. Excessive storage traffic not only negatively impacts the performance of a single system, it can hamper all connected components. Many applications must meet minimum performance requirements spelled out in *service-level agreements (SLAs)*. Storage network performance is critical to overall application performance.

Block-Based Storage vs. File-Based Storage

The operating system, in this case Windows, uses NTFS to create a structure that enables it to use one or more blocks to store files. When a server accesses a physical disk directly, it is called block-based access. When data is accessed over a server network, such as TCP/IP, it is called file data. Devices that provide file access are called network-attached storage (NAS).

Disk drives store data in blocks. Each block contains 512 bytes of data (some storage arrays use 520-byte blocks — the extra 8 bits define a checksum used to guarantee data integrity).

> **NOTE** *Disk technology changes over time. In order to facilitate larger disk drive sizes, disk manufacturers are now implementing a larger 4KB data block. SQL Server is designed to utilize this new block size. See this Microsoft customer support blog for more information:* http://blogs.msdn.com/b/psssql/archive/2011/01/13/sql-server-new-drives-use-4k-sector-size.aspx

Disk drive data blocks are individually numbered by the disk firmware in a scheme using what are called *logical block numbers (LBNs)*.

> **NOTE** *SQL Server best practices recommend that NTFS partitions used for data and log files be formatted using 64K allocation clusters. This setting maximizes efficiency by minimizing wasted space. NTFS reserves space for the MFT$ based on the partition's size. Each file needs a 1KB allocation record in the MFT$. Because only a few data and log files are stored on a partition, and 64KB clusters align with 64KB data extents used by SQL Server, it makes perfect sense to minimize the size of an MFT$. If the partition is used for storing many smaller files then it should be formatted using the standard 4KB cluster size. Running out of allocation units will result in a fragmented MFT$, thus significantly harming file access performance on that partition.*

Starting with SQL Server 2008 R2, storage administrators have the option of using Server Message Block (SMB) networks to access data files. Technet offers a detailed overview of the advantages of SMB here: http://technet.microsoft.com/en-us/library/ff625695(WS.10).aspx.

SQL Server 2012 supports SMB version 3.0 which offers improved performance over earlier versions. For more information on configuring SQL Server 2012 with SMB 3.0 visit: http://msdn.microsoft.com/en-us/library/hh759341.aspx.

Setting up an SMB network enables you to connect to your file over a UNC path (*server_name*\ *share*). This access can greatly simplify the setup of network-based storage, although you should use caution and specifically check to ensure that your particular system is supported, as NAS devices often are not supported for use in this configuration.

Contrast SMB with the use of an iSCSI network. iSCSI is a protocol used for accessing block data over a server network. It requires the use of initiator software on the host server and a compatible iSCSI storage target.

Both SMB and iSCSI utilize a server network to communicate. You must ensure that the server network is low latency and has the bandwidth available to handle the demands that will be placed on it by either technology. Most Fibre Channel networks are dedicated to handling only storage traffic.

If you utilize a server network to transport block or file SQL Server traffic, it may need to be dedicated to transferring only the storage traffic. In lieu of dedicated networks, consider implementing Quality of Service (QoS) that puts a higher priority on storage traffic over normal network packets.

Keep in mind that no technology provides a magic bullet. Even robust networks can be filled with traffic. Storage transfers are extremely sensitive to delay.

Shared Storage Arrays

Shared array controllers are primarily responsible for logically grouping disk drives. Sharing the storage controller enables the creation of extremely large volumes that are protected against failure. In addition to the normal features of direct attached storage controllers, a shared array controller provides both storage performance and capacity.

Shared array controllers, often called SAN controllers, offer more advanced features than direct attached systems. The feature sets are divided into three categories:

➤ Efficient capacity utilization

➤ Storage tiering

➤ Data replication

Before diving into the features of SAN arrays, however, it would be helpful to look at some of the language that storage administrators use to describe their systems.

Capacity Optimization

It has been our experience that most information technology professionals are not very good at predicting the future. When asked how much performance and space they anticipate needing over the next three to five years, administrators do their best to come up with an accurate answer, but unfortunately real life often belies this estimate.

Meet Bob. Bob forecasted that his new OLTP application would start at 10GB and grow at 10GB per year over the next five years. Just to be on the safe side, Bob asked for 100GB in direct-attached storage. Bob's new widget sells like hotcakes and his database grows at 10GB per month. Seven months in, Bob realizes that he is in trouble. He asks his storage administrators for another 500GB in space to cover the next five years of growth.

Unfortunately, the storage and server administrators inform Bob that other users have consumed all the space in his data center co-location. The information technology group is working diligently to expand the space, but it will be six months before they can clear enough space to accommodate his storage. Bob notes that never again will he come up short on storage and go through the pain of expanding his system.

Moving forward Bob always asks for 10 times his original estimate. In his next venture Bob finds that his database will also grow at 10GB per year over 5 years but this time Bob, having "learned his lesson" asks for 10GB a month. Unfortunately Bob's actual storage requirement was closer to 5GB per year.

Bob has unwittingly become his own worst enemy. When Bob needs storage for his second application there isn't any storage available because Bob is simultaneously holding on to unused storage for his first application. He has underprovisioned his storage requirements for his second application while massively overprovisioning his first.

Bob's example is not unique. IT shops the world over consistently overprovision storage. Imagine the implications; over the life of the storage and server, companies purchase a significant amount of excess storage that requires powering and servicing. To combat this wasteful use of space, several storage array manufacturers now sell a technology called *thin provisioning*.

Thin provisioning uses the concept of just-in-time storage allocation within storage pools, whereby many physical disk drives are amalgamated into one large pool. Appropriate RAID protection is applied to the disk drives within the pool. Many volumes can be created from each pool. Synthetic or virtual volumes are presented to the host servers.

When a volume is created as a thin device it allocates only a minimum amount of storage. From the perspective of the operating system, the volume is a certain set size, but the actual data usage within the thin pool closely matches the size of written data. As new data is written to the volume, the storage array allocates more physical storage to the device. This enables the storage administrator to directly regulate the amount of storage that is used within the storage environment.

Because over-forecasting is no longer under-utilizing space, the database administrator can focus on easing operational complexity, versus trying to optimally forecast storage. Creating a single data file within a file group and later adding files while maintaining performance is an extremely painful operation. If a database is built without planning for growth and instead is concatenated over time by adding files, then data access is not uniform.

One possible growth-planning solution is to create several data files on the same volume. If that volume becomes full, the original data files can be moved. This data file movement will require downtime, but it is preferable to reloading the entire dataset. When utilizing storage pools it is possible to create large thin volumes that may never be fully utilized. This is possible because the storage systems are provisioning storage only as it is needed. Many SAN array controllers also facilitate online volume growth.

Unfortunately, many DBAs subvert the concept of thin provisioning by fully allocating their database at creation time. Most database administrators realize that growing a data file can be a painful operation, so they often allocate all the space they will ever need when the database is created. Unfortunately, for our thin pool, SQL Server allocates data and log files by writing zeros to the entire data file.

If the Windows Server is set to use instant file initialization, the file will be created in a thin-pool-friendly way. New storage will be allocated in the pool only as the data actually increases (http://msdn.microsoft.com/en-us/library/ms175935(v=SQL.105).aspx). The DBA can also ensure that the file is thin-pool-friendly by creating data and log files that are only as large or slightly larger than the data the file will contain.

> **NOTE** *Database files are created using zeroes for security purposes. Physically writing zeroes to new space helps to ensure that previous data is not accidently exposed to the new host. Check your security requirements prior to enabling instant file initialization.*

If the data file has already been created as a large file filled with zeros, then a feature called Zero Page Reclaim can be used on the array to reclaim the unused space. Running Zero Page Reclaim allows the array to return the zero space to the available storage pool so it can be allocated to other applications.

Deleting data from within a database or even deleting files from a volume will not return free space to the thin storage pool. In the case of reclaiming deleted file space, most storage vendors offer a host-side tool that checks the NTFS Master File Table and reallocates space from deleted space. If you decided to delete space from within a SQL Server data or log file you need to run the DBCC SHRINKFILE command to first make the file smaller, and then run the host-side storage reclamation tool to return space to a given thin pool.

Unfortunately, thin storage pools have a dirty little secret. In order to optimize storage use in a world where storage forecasting is an inexact science, it is necessary to overprovision the thin pools. This means that storage teams must closely monitor the growth rate at which new storage is being used.

> **WARNING** *If Microsoft Windows makes a write request against a thin volume that no longer has free space, it will blue screen the server. To prevent this, storage administrators have a few options: Run a storage array tool like Zero Page Reclaim to gather unused space, add more physical storage to the thin pool, or migrate the volume to a different array with more space. It is critical to catch growth issues before they become a serious problem.*

Storage Tiering

Non-volatile storage is generally manufactured to offer either high performance or high capacity. High-performance disk and flash drives are much more costly than high-density storage. In an effort to make the most efficient use of both capacity and performance, SAN arrays allow several types of storage to be mixed within a given array.

Our database administrator, Bob, is now stinging after submitting his budget to his manager, Stan. Bob needs to come up with a plan for reducing his storage requests for the next fiscal year. He bumps into Eddy, who works for Widget Company's storage department, at the water cooler.

Eddy has heard of Bob's plight and suggests that Bob place his backup files on less costly high-capacity SATA drives. This will reduce Bob's budget request and make Stan happy. Bob will keep his log and tempdb files on higher-performance SAS RAID 10 volumes and shift his data files onto less expensive RAID 5 SAS drives.

Because the server is tied to a storage network, the different tiers of disks don't even need to exist within the same array. Bob could place his data, log, and tempdb files on one array and move his backup data to a completely different storage system. This approach offers the added benefit of shrinking the possible failure domain. If the primary array suffers a catastrophic failure, the backup data still exists on a separate array.

This mixing and matching of storage within a SAN array is called storage tiering. Some storage arrays provide automated *storage tiering*, monitoring volumes or pieces of volumes for high performance. When predetermined performance characteristics are detected, the array will migrate data onto a higher tier of storage. Using this model, Bob only needs to put all his data on a storage volume; the array determines where to place the data and when to move it.

Different storage vendors have implemented storage tiering in unique ways. One of the most unique features is the granularity of data that is migrated. Some arrays use a transfer size of a few kilobytes. Other arrays migrate gigabytes of data. Each system offers different performance. Be sure to evaluate any potential system to ensure it meets your needs.

> **WARNING** *Storage tiering has the effect of changing performance over time. Many financial systems always require consistent performance. If your specific system requires repeatable performance then storage tiering should not be used.*

Data Replication

SAN arrays offer both internal and external storage data replication. Internal replication consists of data snapshots and clones. Some storage arrays offer inner array data migration features. Both a snapshot (also called a snap) and a clone offer a point-in-time data copy. This data copy can be used for backup or reporting.

> **NOTE** *For more information on increasing the performance of reporting systems please visit:* http://sqlvelocity.typepad.com/blog/2010/09/ scalable-shared-data-base-part-1.html.

Both snapshots and clones need to be created in sync with the database log and data files. In order to maintain SQL data integrity, both the log file and data files need to be copied at exactly the same time. If the log and data files are not in sync, the database can be rendered unrecoverable.

Prior to creating the point-in-time data copy, you need to decide on the type of SQL Server recovery that is needed. You can create application-consistent copies using the SQL Server Virtual Backup Device Interface (VDI). VDI is an application programming interface specification that coordinates the freezing of new write operations, the flushing of dirty memory buffer pages to disk (thus ensuring that the log and data base files are consistent), and the fracturing of the clone or snap volume. Fracturing is the process of stopping the cloning operation and making the snapshot or clone volume ready for use. Once the fracture is complete, the database resumes normal write operations. Reads are not affected.

> **WARNING** *VDI imposes a ten-second timer for the completion of the freeze and fracture operation. When implementing VDI on busy SQL Servers, especially those with large memory, it may be necessary to stop running SQL Server jobs prior to executing the freeze and fracture operation. If the SQL Server can't write all the dirty data pages to disk in ten seconds, the operation will fail.*

Crash-consistent data copies depend on the fact that SQL Server uses a write-ahead logging model, as described earlier. New data is first written to the disk or storage volume. As soon as the write operation is complete, it is acknowledged. Only after the data has been successfully written and acknowledged will SQL Server write data to its buffer pool.

> **WARNING** *SQL server offers features to improve data loading. These features change how data is written and can affect SQL Server replication. Microsoft offers detailed information on data loading with Trace Flag 610:* `http://msdn` `.microsoft.com/en-us/library/dd425070(v=SQL.100).aspx.`

If the database is shut down before it has a chance to flush dirty buffer-page data to disk, the write-ahead logging feature enables SQL Server to recover data that was written to the log but not to the database files. This recovery model enables the use of advanced replication technologies.

Clone data volumes create an exact replica of the source volume as of the point in time when the clone was created (Figure 4-9). Because the clone is an exact copy it enables the isolation of I/O performance. The source volume can continue to operate normally while the clone can be mounted to a different host. This enables a workload to be distributed among many machines without affecting the source volume. Such a scenario is extremely useful to enable high-performance reporting systems. Keep in mind that the clone volume requires the same amount of space within the storage array as the original volume requires.

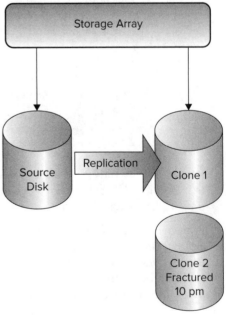

FIGURE 4-9

A hardware storage snapshot, shown in Figure 4-10, is a point-in-time data copy. The snapshot differs from a clone data copy in that it keeps only the original copy of changed data.

> **NOTE** *A hardware snapshot differs from a SQL Server database snapshot. The SQL Server snapshot provides a read only static view of the database based on a point in time. For more information on SQL Server database snapshots visit:* `http://msdn.microsoft.com/en-us/library/ms175158.aspx.`

When a change is written to the storage volume, the array stores the original data and then writes the new data to disk. All the changes are tracked until the user requests a point-in-time data copy. The array correlates all the changed data blocks that now represent the state of the volume at that moment in time.

The user can continue to create as many snap volumes as the array supports. Snapshots utilize capacity based on the rate of data change. It is possible to churn so much data that the snapshots consume more data than the actual data volume. Expiring snap volumes can reduce the amount of space consumed.

Snapshots do not isolate performance. Any I/O executed against the snap volume is accessing both the source volume and any saved changes. If the primary database server is so busy that you have decided to utilize a second server that performs reporting functions, a clone volume may be a better choice than a snapshot.

For business continuance and disaster recovery (BCDR) you could also consider a layered approach. The clone volume will provide a unique data copy. Keep in mind that the clone is a mirror of the original data and will consume the same capacity as the original volume. Keeping several clone copies can be cost prohibitive.

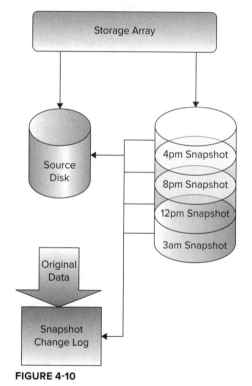

FIGURE 4-10

Snapshots can offer many inexpensive point-in-time copies, but they won't work if the primary data volume is compromised. You can enable a data clone to protect against a catastrophic data failure. The snapshots can be taken much more frequently and enable the DBA to roll back to a specific point in time (which is extremely useful in case of user error or computer virus).

> **WARNING** *A successful recovery requires all user database log and data files to be recoverable to the exact point in time.*

Remote Data Replication

Both SAN and NAS array controllers offer external data replication. This feature enables two or more array controllers to synchronize data. Vendors provide either a real-time or a point-in-time data migration framework.

Real-time frameworks replicate changes as they are written to the array. This replication is performed synchronously or asynchronously. Synchronous data replication is extremely sensitive to latency and is therefore not used over great distances.

Synchronous Replication

When SQL Server writes changes to either the data or the log, remember that both the user database and the log files must be replicated; a synchronous replication system writes the I/O to its battery-backed data cache. The array then sends the I/O to its replication partner. The partner writes the I/O to its own cache and then sends a successful acknowledgment to the source array.

At this point, based on proprietary caching algorithms, the storage arrays write the data from their cache to disk, and a success acknowledgment is sent to the SQL Server. As you can see, this process adds latency to the entire write process. Distance directly translates to latency. If the systems are asked to handle too much replicated data, or are placed too far apart, the database will slow considerably.

Asynchronous Replication

Rather than wait for a single change to be committed to both arrays, asynchronous replication sends a stream of changes between the arrays. As I/O is successfully written to cache, the source array returns a success acknowledgment to SQL Server. This way, changes are written without slowing the SQL Server processes.

The primary array sends changes to the remote array in a group. The remote array receives the group of changes, acknowledges the successful receipt, and then writes the changes to physical media. Each vendor offering asynchronous remote replication has a property method for ensuring successful delivery and recovering from communication issues between the arrays.

From a BCDR prospective, the drawback to implementing asynchronous replication is the potential for some data loss. Because the write I/O is instantly acknowledged on the source array, some amount of data is always in transit between the arrays. Most unplanned failover events will result in transit data being lost. Due to the design of SQL server lost data does not mean that the remote database is corrupt.

> **NOTE** *All of these replication technologies must provide the capability to keep I/O exchanges intact. If only part of a write is delivered and written to a log file or data page, it is considered* torn. *A torn I/O is not recoverable by SQL Server DBCC. For this reason, SQL Server requires storage arrays to maintain atomic I/O. The SQL Server team offers a compliance program called SQL Server I/O Reliability. This program requires storage vendors to guarantee that they are fully compliant with all SQL Server data integrity standards.*

Several storage vendors combine point-in-time technology with remote replication. These features enable the administrator to take a clone or snapshot of the user databases (using VDI to create an application-consistent data copy if desired) and send the data to a remote array.

As with asynchronous replication, point-in-time remote replication offers the advantage of low server impact. Remotely sending a snapshot enables you to specifically control the potential for data loss. If you set the snap interval for five minutes, you can be reasonably certain that in the event of unplanned failure you will lose no more than five minutes of changes. Identifying an exact amount of expected data loss can offer huge advantages when negotiating the parameters of BCDR with the business.

Windows Failover Clustering

Many SQL Server installations utilize Windows Failover Clustering to form high-availability SQL Server clusters. These systems create a virtual SQL Server that is hosted by an active server and at least one passive server. SQL Server 2008 and 2008 R2 failover clusters supported only shared storage failover clustering. The SAN storage array allows all SQL Server clusters to access the same physical storage and move that storage between nodes.

SQL Server failover clusters are based on the concept of "shared nothing"; the SQL Server instance (or instances) can live on only one active server. SQL Server places an active lock on log and data files, preventing other servers or programs from accessing the files. This is incorporated to prevent data changes that SQL Server would have no way to detect. In addition to file locks, the failover cluster also actively prevents other systems from using the storage volumes by using SCSI reservation commands.

Failover clustering can be set to automatically fail the instance over to a standby server when a failure occurs. SQL Server failover clusters also support the use of *geo-clustering*. A geo-cluster uses storage replication to ensure that remote data is in-sync with the source data. Storage vendors provide a proprietary cluster resource dynamic link library (DLL) that facilitates cluster-to-storage-array communication.

The use of a resource DLL enables a rapid failover between sites with little or no administrator involvement. Traditional failover systems require the interaction of many teams. Returning to our example, assume that Widget Company has just implemented a local SQL Server with a remote failover system.

The system in use by Widget uses traditional storage replication. When the Widget DBAs try to execute a failover they first need to contact the storage administrators so they can run failover scripts on the storage arrays. Once the storage is failed to the remote site, the DBAs can bring the database online. Because the server name is different, the DBAs need to reconfigure the database to do that. Now the application owners need to point all the middle-tier systems to the new server.

Even when the failover is planned it is extremely resource intensive to implement. The use of a geo-cluster greatly simplifies the failover process. The failover is implemented automatically whenever the SQL Server geo-cluster is failed over to a remote node. Unfortunately, SQL Server 2008 and 2008R2 only supported geo-clustering when both servers shared the same IP subnet.

This networking technology is called a *stretch virtual local area network*, or *stretch VLAN*. The stretch VLAN often requires that network engineers implement complex networking technologies. SQL Server 2012 solves this through AlwaysOn Failover Cluster Instances. This new feature enables each SQL Server to utilize an IP address that is not tied to the same IP subnet as the other hosts.

> **NOTE** *Multi-subnet SQL Server failover cluster network names enable the* `RegisterAllProvidersIP` *property. This provides all the IP addresses that SQL Server is configured to use. It is important that newer SQL Server client drivers (such as the SQL Server Native Client) be utilized, as they support this configuration. The use of older SQL Server client drivers requires advanced configuration.*

SQL Server AlwaysOn Availability Groups

The configuration and setup of AlwaysOn Availability Groups is beyond the scope of this chapter. From a storage perspective, Availability Groups offer a new, server-based method for replicating data that is application centric rather than platform centric. As discussed earlier, storage systems can use point-in-time data copies to facilitate data backup and performance isolation. Deciding between application based failover and hardware based failover is an architecture choice.

Earlier versions of SQL Server utilized log shipping, and later SQL Server mirroring, to keep standby SQL Servers updated with information. In the case of both log shipping and storage replication, the remote database must be taken offline prior to data synchronization. Availability Groups enable the use of near-real-time readable secondary database servers.

The read-only data copy can facilitate reporting offload or even backup. In addition, Availability Groups support synchronous or asynchronous data replication and also multiple secondary servers. You can configure one secondary as a reporting system that is hosted locally, and a second server can be hosted remotely, thus providing remote BCDR.

From a storage perspective, note the following caveats: Each remote secondary server needs as much storage capacity (and usually performance) as the primary database. In addition, it is critical that your network infrastructure is designed to handle the increased network traffic that can be generated by replicating data locally and remotely. Finally, all your servers must have enough performance available to handle the replication. If your server is already processor, storage, or memory bound, you are going to make these conditions worse. In these cases it is often advantageous to enable storage-based replication. Think of AlwaysOn Availability Groups as a powerful new tool that now enhances your SQL Server toolkit.

Risk Mitigation Planning

All of the replication and backup technologies described here are designed to mitigate risk. To properly define the specific procedures and technologies that will be used in your BCDR strategy, you need to decide how soon you need the system online and how much data your business is willing to lose in the process.

The projected time that it will take to bring a failed system online is called the *recovery time objective (RTO)*. The estimated amount of original data that may be lost while the failover is being executed is called the *recovery point objective (RPO)*. When designing a recovery plan it is important to communicate clear RTO and RPO objectives.

Ensure that the recovery objectives will meet business requirements. Be aware that systems that provide a rapid failover time with little or no data loss are often extremely expensive. A good rule of thumb is that the shorter the downtime and the lower the expected data loss, the more the system will cost.

Let's look at an example failover system that has an RTO of 1 hour and an RPO of 10 minutes. This imaginary system is going to cost $10,000 and will require DBAs to bring up the remote system within one hour. If we enhance this example system to automatic failover it will reduce our RTO to 10 minutes, and we should not lose any data with an RPO of 0. Unfortunately, this system will cost us half a million dollars.

MEASURING PERFORMANCE

The single most important performance metric is latency. Latency is a measure of system health and the availability of system resources. Latency is governed by queuing theory, a mathematical study of lines, or queues. An important contribution to queuing theory, now known as Little's Law, was introduced in a proof submitted by John D. C. Little (http://or.journal.informs.org/content/9/3/383) in 1961.

Put simply, Little's Law states that given a steady-state system, as capacity reaches maximum performance, response time approaches infinity. To understand the power of Little's Law, consider the typical grocery store. If the store only opens one cash register and ten people are waiting in line, then you are going to wait longer to pay than if the store opened five or ten cashiers.

Storage systems are directly analogous to a grocery store checkout line. Each component has a certain performance maximum. Driving the system toward maximum performance will increase latency. We have found that most users and application owners directly correlate latency with failure. For example, it won't matter that a payroll system is online if it can't process transactions fast enough to get everyone's paycheck out on time.

You test I/O performance using several tools that are described later. You test storage using a logarithmic scale, starting with one I/O, moving to two, then four, then eight, and finally peaking at 256 I/Os that are all sent to storage in parallel (see Figure 4-1). As it turns out, this test perfectly demonstrates Little's Law by defining how storage operates.

As you can see in Figure 4-11 the storage response time remains less than our goal of 10 milliseconds through eight outstanding I/Os. As we increase the workload to 16 outstanding I/Os, the latency increases to 20 milliseconds. We can determine from this test that our configuration is optimal when we issue between 8 and 16 I/Os. This is called the *knee of the curve*. The system is capable of a lot more work, but the latency is higher than our tolerance.

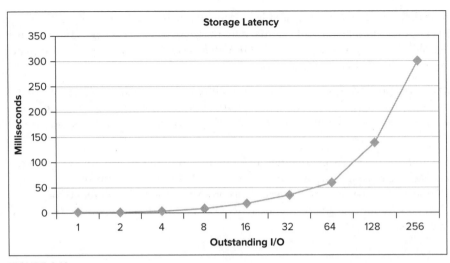

FIGURE 4-11

> **NOTE** *The goal of less than 10 milliseconds of latency is no accident. SQL Server best practices call for no more than 20 milliseconds of delay. If you implement synchronous data replication with AlwaysOn Availability Groups, you can't tolerate more than 10 milliseconds of delay; and many applications are even more sensitive!*

The remainder of this chapter explores how to accurately measure performance and latency. Techniques for establishing performance baselines are demonstrated, and then you will examine how the application of advanced storage pooling technology is changing how database systems are designed.

Storage Performance Counters

Windows Performance Monitor (perfmon) allows Windows Server users to capture storage performance metrics. For the purposes of storage monitoring, you utilize the LogicalDisk performance monitor object. Both logical and physical disk counters deliver storage performance metrics. The logical disk counters show the performance of a specific partition, while the physical disk counters cover the entire LUN (a Logical Unit Number is a term that describes a storage volume that is hosted by a storage controller). Table 4-1 shows a list of the available Windows storage performance counters.

The Average Disk Sec/Read and Write counters measure the time it takes for an input output (I/O) operation to be sent from the server to the storage system and back. This latency measure is the single biggest indicator of I/O system health. Reads and writes are treated separately because most storage systems perform one operation faster than the other. If you are using a storage array with a battery-backed cache, it will often write in just a few milliseconds, whereas a random read will take longer.

TABLE 4-1: Windows Storage Performance Counters

LOGICALDISK PERFMON OBJECT
Average Disk sec/Read
Average Disk sec/Write
Disk Reads/sec
Disk Writes/sec
Disk Read Bytes/sec
Disk Write Bytes/sec

The latency counters are measured in milliseconds. A reading of 0.001 is one millisecond, 0.010 is 10 milliseconds, and .100 is 100 milliseconds. SQL Server best practices call for latency that is under 20 milliseconds. This is not a hard-and-fast rule, however, as many applications will not tolerate latency that exceeds several milliseconds.

It is important to understand the underlying hardware configuration, application, and workload. In some cases, such as a SQL Server standard backup, large I/O sizes will drastically increase latency. If you change the backup I/O size to 8MB, the latency will increase, but you can still achieve a lot of work.

If you are implementing a specialized system, such as a SQL Server Fast Track Data Warehouse, you will actively configure the data files so they issue sequential I/O. Be sure to test your specific configuration so you can properly interpret the results.

The Disk Reads and Writes per second counters list how many I/Os are generated each second (Storage administrators often refer to this as IOPS). Disk Read and Write Bytes per second demonstrate the throughput of your storage system. To calculate average I/O sizes, simply divide bytes per second by the number of operations per second.

Knowing the size of the I/O can reflect application behavior. When performing highly random I/O access, SQL Server will write 8K data pages and read 64KB data extents from the data files. Performing sequential operations, such as a table scan, will generate I/O that is dynamically sized from 8K to 512KB. Dynamic I/O sizing, also known as Read-Ahead, is one of the hidden gems of SQL Server. Increasing I/O size decreases the number of I/Os and increases efficiency.

Disk Drive Performance

A disk drive (see Figure 4-12) is made up of an external logic board and an internal hard drive assembly. The logic board provides connectivity between the disk and the host. Each drive interface supports one of many available communications protocols. Modern interfaces use a high-speed serial connection. The interfaces that are most commonly used for database applications are SATA (Serial Advanced Technology Attachment), FC (Fibre Channel), and SAS (Serial Attached SCSI).

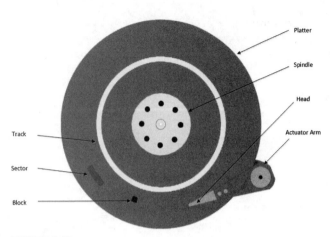

FIGURE 4-12

The hard drive assembly is serviceable only inside a high-technology clean room. Opening the cover on a hard disk drive will void the warranty. The drive platter rotates around a spindle and is powered by a spindle motor. A drive is made up of several platters that are stacked. Each platter is double-sided and coated with a magnetic oxide.

Data is physically read and written by a hard drive head. Each drive platter has a dedicated drive head. An actuator arm houses all the drive heads, and a magnetic actuator moves the arm. You can think of a hard drive as a record player. The platter spins and the head reads and writes data. Unlike a record player, however, the disk drive head can move back and forth. The head actually rides just above the disk surface on a cushion of high-pressure air that is created when the platter spins at high speed.

SATA disk drives provide commodity storage. They offer much larger capacity than FC or SAS drives. At the time of this writing, SATA drives are available with a capacity of three terabytes (3TB). SATA drives spin at lower speeds — 5,400 to 7,200 RPM. They are sold for both the consumer and the enterprise markets. Enterprise drives are designed for more continuous use and higher reliability.

Both FC and SAS drives are considered enterprise-class disk drives. They are available in 7,200, 10,000, and 15,000 RPM models. With the exception of Nearline SAS (NL-SAS) drives, these disk drives are generally lower in capacity than SATA disk drives. SAS 6GB/s drives are displacing Fibre Channel 4GB/s drives in the marketplace.

Modern SAS drives are manufactured in a 2.5^2 form factor, unlike the traditional 3.5^2 form factor of Fibre Channel and SATA drives. This smaller drive enables more disk drives to be housed in a given space. NL-SAS drives offer a high-reliability enterprise SATA drive with a SAS interface.

The logic board governs how the disk operates. Each disk contains buffers, and some disk drives contain cache. For the proper operation of SQL Server write-ahead logging, volatile cache must be bypassed for write operations. Most array vendors will guarantee cached data with battery backing. When using disks directly in a JBOD, it is important to ensure that they meet SQL Server reliability requirements.

A disk drive is made of both electronic and mechanical components. When data is read sequentially, the drive can read it as fast as the drive spins. When the data needs to be accessed out of order, the head needs to move to the appropriate track. Head movement, or seeking, is not instantaneous.

A sequential read consists of a head movement followed by the sequential reading or writing of data. When data is not sequentially located, the disk drive executes a series of random operations. Random access patterns are much slower because the head needs to physically move between tracks.

Drive manufacturers provide a measurement called *maximum seek time* that reflects how long it will take for the drive head to move from the innermost tracks to the outermost tracks. The manufacturer also provides what is known as *average seek time*, the average time it will take to move the drive head to any location on the disk.

Disk Drive Latency

You can calculate the time it takes to move the head to a location on the disk mathematically. The number of times a disk can rotate in a millisecond limits the amount of data the drive can generate, a limitation called *rotational latency*. To calculate how many random I/Os a hard disk can perform, the following equation is used:

$$IOPS = 1,000 \div (Seek\ Time + ((60,000 \div RPM) \div 2)$$

This equation works by normalizing all calculations to milliseconds. To find IOPS, you start by dividing 60,000 (because there are 60,000 milliseconds in a minute) by the hard disk rotations per minute. Dividing the revolutions per millisecond by 2 accounts for the fact that the head needs to exit the first track and enter the second track at specific points, requiring about two rotations. You add the revolutions result to the seek time and convert the result back to seconds by dividing 1,000 by this sum.

For example, consider a 10,000-RPM disk. This drive will rotate about 6 times per second. You account for the fact that it will take your drive two rotations to move between tracks and then add the seek time. This drive has a read seek time of 4 milliseconds. Dividing 1,000 by 7 results in 143 I/Os per second:

$$143 = 1000 \div (4 + ((60,000 \div 10,000) \div 2))$$

We have tested many drives over the years and this formula has proven reliable. Remember that each individual model of disk drive varies. Having said that, you can calculate IOPS for the most frequently used disk drives:

$$7,500\ RPM\ SATA: 80 = 1,000 \div (8.5 + ((60,000 \div 7,500) \div 2))$$

$$15,000\ RPM\ SAS: 185 = 1,000 \div (3.4 + ((60,000 \div 15,000) \div 2))$$

If you need more IOPS, then simply add more disks. If one disk will perform 150 IOPS, then two will perform 300. When you need 10,000 IOPS, you only need 54 physical disks. If you actually want to keep the data when one of the drives fails, then you need 108 disks. Those 108 disks will provide 10,000 IOPS when the database needs to read, but only 5,000 IOPS for writes. RAID causes overhead for both space and performance. RAID 1+0 is fairly easy to calculate. You will receive N number of reads and N divided by 2 writes. RAID 5 is much trickier to calculate.

> **NOTE** *For more information on how SQL Server actions translate into IOPS please visit* http://Sqlvelocity.typepad.com.

To generate the parity information, a RAID controller reads relevant data and performs an XOR calculation. Let's take a small RAID set of four disks as an example. One write operation will generate two writes and two reads. We are assuming that there are two existing data chunks and we are writing the third. We need to write the resultant parity and the new data block.

RAID controllers vary greatly in design, but generally speaking, they utilize their internal cache to assist in the generation of parity information. Typically, Raid 5 enables N number of reads and N divided by 4 writes.

RAID 6 protects against double disk failure and therefore generates double the parity. An 8-disk RAID set consists of two parity chunks and six data chunks. You need to write the new data chunk and two parity chunks, so you know that you have three writes. You need to read the other five data chunks, so you are looking at eight operations to complete the RAID 6 write. Luckily, most RAID controllers can optimize this process into three reads and three writes.

Table 4-2 provides a guide to calculating common RAID overhead. Please remember that each system is different and your mileage may vary.

TABLE 4-2: RAID Overhead

RAID TYPE	READ	WRITE
0	N	N
1+0	N	N ÷ 2
5	N	N ÷ 4
6	N	N ÷ 6

Sequential Disk Access

Microsoft SQL Server and various hardware manufacturers partner to provide guidance for data warehouse systems. This program is called SQL Server Fast Track Data Warehouse. A data warehouse system is designed to hold a massive amount of data. The Fast Track program takes great care to design storage hardware that is perfectly sized for a specific server platform.

The data warehouse is architected such that data is sequentially loaded and sequentially accessed. Typically, data is first loaded in a staging database. Then it is bulk loaded and ordered so that queries generate a sequential table access pattern. This is important because sequential disk access is far more efficient than random disk access. Our 15,000-RPM disk drive will perform 180 random operations or 1,400 sequential reads. Sequential operations are so much more efficient than random access that SQL Server is specifically designed to optimize sequential disk access.

In a worst-case scenario, SQL Server will read 64KB data extents and write 8K data pages. When SQL Server detects sequential access it dynamically increases the request size to a maximum size of 512KB. This has the effect of making the storage more efficient.

Designing an application to generate sequential disk access is a powerful cost-saving tool. Blending sequential operations with larger I/O is even more powerful. If our 15,000-RPM disk performs

64KB random reads, it will generate about 12MBs per second. This same drive will perform 88MBs per second of sequential 64KB reads. Changing the I/O size to 512KB will quickly cause the disk drive to hit its maximum transfer rate of 600MBs per second.

Increasing the I/O size has its limitations. Most hardware RAID controllers are designed to optimally handle 128KB I/Os. Generating I/Os that are too big will stress the system resources and increase latency.

One example is a SQL Server backup job. Out-of-the-box, SQL Server backup will generate 1,000KB I/Os. Producing I/Os this large will cause a lot of stress and high latency for most storage arrays. Changing the backup to use 512KB I/Os will usually reduce the latency and often reduce the time required to complete the backup. Each storage array is different, so be sure to try different I/O sizes to ensure that backups run optimally.

Henk Van Der Valk has written several articles that highlight backup optimization:

    http://henkvandervalk.com/how-to-increase-sql-database-full-backup-speed-using-
    compression-and-solid-state-disks

    http://henkvandervalk.com/how-to-increase-the-sql-database-restore-speed-using-db-
    compression-and-solid-state-disks

This Backup statement will set the maximum transfer size to 512KB.

```
BACKUP DATABASE [DBName] TO  DISK = N'E:\dump\BackupFile.bak'
WITH MAXTRANSFERSIZE=524288,  NAME = BackupName
GO
```

Server Queues

Each physical disk drive can perform one operation and can queue one operation. Aggregating disks into a RAID set increases the pool of possible I/O. Because each physical disk can perform two operations, a viable queue setting is determined by multiplying the number of disks in a RAID set by two. A RAID set containing 10 disk drives, for example, will work optimally with a queue of 20 outstanding I/Os.

Streaming I/O requires a queue of I/Os to continue operating at a high rate. Check the HBA settings in your server to ensure they are maximized for the type of I/O your application is generating. Most HBAs are set by the manufacturer to a queue of 32 outstanding I/Os. Higher performance can often be achieved by raising this value to its available maximum. The SQL Server FAST Track program recommends that queue depth be set at 64.

Keep in mind that in a shared storage SAN environment, the performance gains of one application are often achieved at the cost of overall performance. As a SQL Server administrator, be sure to advise your storage administrators of any changes you are making.

File Layout

This section divides the discussion about how to configure storage into traditional disk storage and array-based storage pools. Traditional storage systems offer predictable performance. You expect Online Transaction Processing (OLTP) systems to generate random workload. If you know how many transactions you need to handle, you can predict how many underlying disks will be needed in your storage array.

For example, assume that you will handle 10,000 transactions, and your storage is made up of 10K SAS drives that are directly attached to your server. Based on the math described earlier, you know that a 10K SAS drive will perform about 140 IOPS; therefore, you need 142 of them. Seventy-one disks would be enough to absorb 10K reads, but you are going to configure a RAID 1+0 set, so you need double the number of disks.

If you need to handle a lot of tempdb operations, then you need to appropriately size the tempdb drive. In this case, you are going to design tempdb to be about 20 percent of the expected I/O for the main data files, so you expect 2,000 IOPS. This will require that 28 disks in a RAID 1+0 configuration back the tempdb database.

You expect that a backup load will be entirely sequential in nature. Remember that SATA drives perform sequential operations extremely well, so they are a great candidate for dump drives. These drives are usually less expensive and offer greater capacity than SAS or Fibre Channel disks.

Large SATA disks store data in an extremely dense format, which puts them at greater risk for a failure and at the same time increases the chance that a second failure will occur before the RAID system can regenerate data from the first failure. For this reason, RAID 6 is an ideal candidate to protect the data drives. RAID 6 has the greatest performance overhead, so it is important to adjust the backup I/O appropriately. In most cases backup I/O should not exceed a 512KB transfer size.

Finally, you need to plan for your log drives. Logs are extremely latency sensitive. Therefore, you should completely isolate the log onto its own set of RAID 1+0 SAS disk drives. You expect sequential I/O, so the number of disks is governed by capacity rather than random performance I/O.

Why wouldn't you mix the log drive with the backup drive? Sequential disk access assumes that the drive head enters a track and reads sequential blocks. If you host applications that sequentially access a set of disk drives, you will cause the disk drive head to seek excessively.

This excessive head seeking is called *large block random access*. Excessive seeking can literally drop the potential IOPS by half:

$$15K \text{ SAS Max Seek: } 90 = 1{,}000 \div (9 + ((60{,}000 \div 15{,}000) \div 2))$$

Isolating sequential performance not only applies to log files. Within a database you can often identify specific data tables that are sequentially accessed. Separating this sequential access can greatly reduce the performance demand on a primary storage volume.

In large databases with extremely heavy write workloads, the checkpoint process can often overwhelm a storage array. SQL Server checkpoints attempt to guarantee that a database can recover from an unplanned outage within the default setting of one minute. This can produce an enormous spike of data in an extremely short time.

We have seen the checkpoint process send 30,000 write IOPS in one second. The other 59 seconds are completely idle. Because the storage array will likely be overwhelmed with this workload, SQL Server is designed to dial back the I/O while trying to maintain the one-minute recovery goal. This slows down the write process and increases latency.

In SQL Server 2008 and 2008 R2, you can start SQL Server with the –k command-line option (–k followed by a decimal representing the maximum MB per second the checkpoint is allowed to flush). This option can smooth the impact of a checkpoint at the potential risk of a long recovery and changed writing behavior. SQL Server 2012 includes a new feature called Indirect Checkpoint. The following Alter Database statement will enable Indirect Checkpoint:

```
ALTER DATABASE <Database_Name>
SET TARGET_RECOVERY_TIME = 60 SECONDS
```

Indirect Checkpoint has a smoothing effect on the checkpoint process. If the system would normally flush 30K IOPS in one second, it will now write 500 IOPS over the one-minute recovery interval. This feature can provide a huge savings, as it would take 428 10K disks configured in a RAID 1+0 stripe to absorb the 30,000 I/O burst. With Indirect Checkpoint you can use only eight disks. As with any new database feature, ensure that you fully test this configuration prior to turning it loose in a production environment.

Many organizations use shared storage arrays and thin storage pools to increase storage utilization. Keep in mind that storage pools amalgamate not only capacity, but also performance. We have previously recommended that data, log, backup, and temporary database files be isolated onto their own physical storage. When the storage is shared in a storage pool, however, this isolation no longer makes sense.

The current reason for separation is to protect the data, diversifying it across failure domains. In other words, don't keep all your eggs in one basket. It is advisable to ensure that database backups and physical data reside on different storage groups, or even different storage arrays.

Many IT groups maintain separate database, server, networking, and storage departments. It is important that you communicate the expected database performance requirements to the storage team so they can ensure that the shared storage arrays are designed to handle the load.

Once your application is running on a shared thin storage pool, performance monitoring is critical. Each of the applications is intertwined. Unfortunately, many systems are active at the exact same time — for example, end of month reporting. If your application negatively impacts other applications, it is often more beneficial and cost effective to move it out of the shared storage environment and onto a separate system.

Partition Alignment

Windows versions prior to Windows Server 2008 did not properly align Windows Server partitions to the underlying storage geometry. Specifically, the Windows hidden sector is 63KB in size. NTFS allocation units default to 4K and are always divisible by 2. Because the hidden sector is an odd size, all of the NTFS allocation units are offset. This results in the possibility of generating twice the number of NTFS requests.

Any partition created using the Windows 2008 or newer operating systems will automatically create sector alignment. If a volume is created using Windows 2003 or older operating systems, it has the possibility of being sector unaligned. Unfortunately, a misaligned partition must be recreated to align it properly.

For more information on sector alignment, please see this blog post: http://sqlvelocity.typepad
.com/blog/2011/02/windows-disk-alignment.html.

NTFS Allocation Unit Size

When formatting a partition you are given the option to choose the allocation unit size, which
defaults to 4KB. Allocation units determine both the smallest size the file will take on disk and
the size of the Master File Table ($MFT). If a file is 7KB in size, it will occupy two 4KB allocation
clusters.

SQL Server files are usually large. Microsoft recommends the use of a 64KB allocation unit size for
data, logs, and tempdb. Please note that if you use allocation units greater than 4KB, Windows will
disable NTFS data compression (this does not affect SQL Server compression).

It is more efficient to create fewer larger clusters for large SQL Server files than it would be to create
more small-size clusters. While large clusters are efficient for a few small files, the opposite is true
for hosting a lot of small files. It is possible to run out of clusters and waste storage capacity.

There are exceptions to these cluster size best practices. When using SQL Server FILESTREAM
to store unstructured data, ensure that the partition used to host FILESTREAM data is formatted
with an appropriate sector size, usually 4K. SQL Server Analysis Services (SSAS) will read and write
cube data to small XML files and should therefore also utilize a 4K-sector size.

Flash Storage

So far, you have seen that hard disk drives are mechanical devices that provide varying performance
depending on how the disk is accessed. NAND (Not AND memory which is a type of electronic
based logic gate)-based flash storage is an alternative technology to hard disks. Flash has no moving
parts and therefore offers consistent read performance that is not affected by random I/O.

Flash drives are significantly more expensive than traditional hard disks, but this cost is offset by
their I/O performance. A single 15K disk drive will only perform about 180 IOPS, whereas a single
flash drive can perform 20,000 or more. Because you often need to trade capacity for performance,
the flash drives offer a potentially huge cost savings. You can conceivably replace 220 15K disk
drives configured in a RAID 1+0 set with two flash drives!

The ideal scenario for flash disks is when you have an application that has a relatively small dataset
and an extremely high performance requirement. A high-transaction OLTP database or SQL Server
Analysis Services data cube are excellent examples of applications that can take advantage of the
increased random flash performance.

NAND flash drives are most efficient when responding to read requests. Writing to a flash disk is
a more complex operation that takes longer than a read operation. Erasing a NAND data block is
an even more resource-intensive operation. Blending reads and writes will reduce the potential performance of the flash drive. If a disk is capable of 20,000 or 30,000 reads, it may only be able to
sustain 5,000 writes.

Not all flash is created equally. Flash memory is created in both single (SLC) and multi-layer (MLC)
technology. SLC memory is more expensive to manufacture but offers higher performance. MLC

is manufactured using multiple stacked cells that share a single transistor. This enables MLC to be manufactured more economically, but it has the drawback of lowering performance and increasing the potential failure rate.

Enterprise MLC (eMLC) is a newer generation of flash technology that increases the reliability and performance of multi-level flash. Before choosing a type of flash, it is important to understand the number of reads and writes that your flash will be subjected to. The acts of writing and erasing from flash cells degrade the cells over time. Flash devices are built with robust error correcting and checking, but they will fail due to heavy write cycles. Ensure that the flash technology you implement will survive your application performance requirements. Unfortunately, flash devices are not a one-size-fits-all solution. If your application generates an extremely high number of random I/O requests, flash will probably perform well. Conversely, if your application creates a few large requests, such as a data warehouse application, then you won't necessarily see a great benefit.

Several manufacturers sell a flash-based PCI express NAND flash device. These cards offer extremely low latency at high I/O rates. A single card will respond in tens of microseconds and generate hundreds of thousands of IOPS. Contrast this with a shared array that responds in hundreds of micro-seconds, or even milliseconds. If your application can generate this type of I/O load, these cards can greatly increase your potential performance. Not only can the card sustain hundreds of thousands of I/Os, each is returned much faster. This can relieve many SQL blocking issues.

We stress that your application must be able to generate appropriate I/O because we have seen many instances in which customers have installed flash as a panacea only to be disappointed with low performance increases. If a given application is hampered by poor design, throwing money at it in the form of advanced technology will not always fix the problem!

There are now hybrid PCI express–based solutions that combine server software, the PCI express flash card, and shared storage arrays. These systems monitor I/O access patterns. If a given workload is deemed appropriate, data will be stored and accessed on the PCI express flash card. To maintain data integrity, the data is also stored on the shared storage array. This hybrid approach is useful for extremely large datasets that simply won't fit on a series of server flash cards. In addition, SAN features such as replication can be blended with new technology.

Many shared storage arrays offer flash solutions that increase array cache. These systems work just like the PCI express hybrid solution, except the flash is stored inside the shared storage array. Appropriate data is migrated to the flash storage, thereby increasing its performance. As stated before, if the access pattern is deemed not appropriate by the array, data will not be moved. Heavy write bursts are one example. A massive checkpoint that attempts to write 30,000 IOPS will probably never be promoted to flash because the accessed data changes every minute!

Shared storage arrays blend tiering and automated tiering with flash drives. When you consider most databases, only a subset of the data is in use at any given time. In an OLTP system, you care about the data that is newly written and the data you need to access over a short window of time to derive metrics. Once a sales quarter or year has passed, this data is basically an archive.

Some DBAs migrate this archive data. Automated tiering offers a low-overhead system that actively monitors data use. Active data is promoted to a flash storage tier; moderately accessed data is migrated to a FC or SAS tier; and archival data is automatically stored on high-capacity SATA.

Storage Performance Testing

You have likely noticed how we have stressed that each workload is different. No single storage system will solve every technical or business problem. Any system must be validated prior to its production deployment.

You should draw a distinction between validation and testing. If you are able to re-create your production system with an exact replica and run exactly the same workload, your results should mirror production. Unfortunately most administrators are not fortunate enough to field duplicate test and production systems. Validation allows these administrators to collect useful data and later apply the data to real problems.

It is important to understand how your system will perform given specific parameters. If you are able to predict and verify the maximum number of IOPS a given system will tolerate, you can then apply this knowledge to troubleshooting performance issues. If latency performance counters are high, and you notice that a 20-drive RAID 1+0 volume is trying to absorb 5,000 IOPS, it should be clear that you have exceeded the system I/O capacity.

> **WARNING** *Prior to beginning any storage testing it is important to alert relevant system owners. Running a peak load test on a shared storage system will impact all the storage-connected systems. If the testing is executed against an array with automatic storage tiering, it can cause the system to migrate test data into higher storage tiers and depreciate important production data. It is critical to understand the effects of testing, so be sure to exercise care!*

Microsoft has created two tools that are useful for performance testing: SQLIOSim for system validation, and SQLIO for performance measurement.

SQLIOSim is designed to simulate SQL Server I/O, and you can think of it as a functional test tool. It will stress SQL Server, the Windows Server, and storage, but it won't push them to maximum performance. SQLIOSim can be downloaded at `http://support.microsoft.com/kb/231619`.

Before getting started, note that SQLIOSim will report an error if latency exceeds 15 seconds. It is perfectly normal for storage I/O to show occasional high latency. We recommend using the GUI to run functional system testing (Figure 4-13), although the tool can be also be executed from a command prompt.

> **WARNING** *Many advanced storage arrays offer automated tiering and de-duplicating features. Synthetic test tools like SQLIO and SQLIOSim generate test files by writing repeating data, usually zeros. Advanced storage arrays will de-duplicate or return data with artificial velocity. It is especially important to use a test tool that creates data on top of an NTFS data partition. If the storage array answers a read request from data pages that have not been written, it will return zero data directly from the storage processor. Any of these conditions will produce performance data that is not representative of actual production performance. Be sure you understand the capabilities of the storage platform you are testing. If you receive test performance data that seems too good to be true, it probably is.*

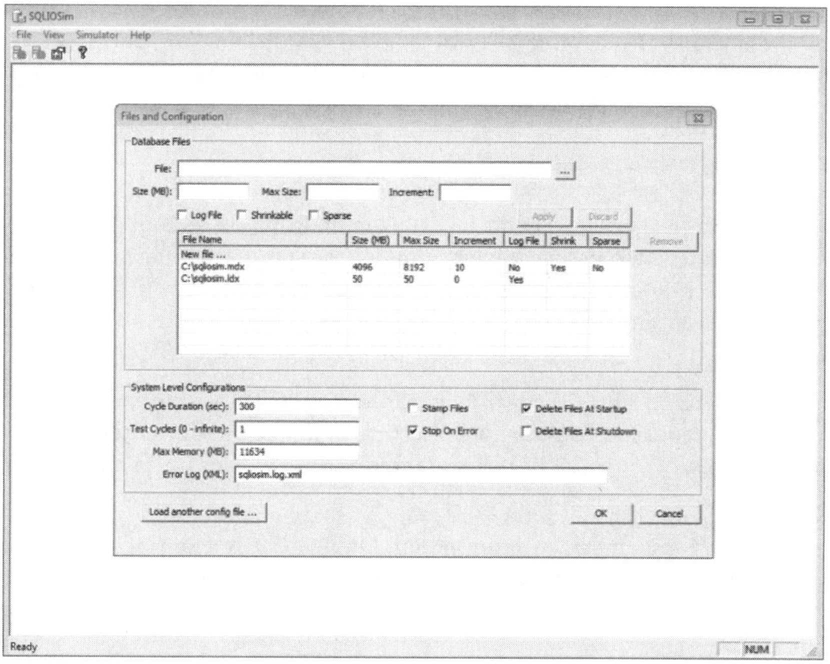

FIGURE 4-13

SQLIO is a tool that simply generates I/O. This application is executed from the command line and does not need SQL Server to run. Download SQLIO from `http://www.microsoft.com/download/en/details.aspx?displaylang=en&id=20163`.

We recommend testing the storage system to performance maximums and setting up a test that mimics your best guess at a production workload. SQLIO is executed from the Windows command line. After installing SQLIO, open the `param.txt` file located in the installation directory. The default path is C:\Program Files (x86)\SQLIO. The `param.txt` file contains the following code:

```
c:\testfile.dat 2 0x0 100
#d:\testfile.dat 2 0x0 100
```

The first line in the param file defines where the test file is located. Use the pound sign (#) to comment out a line in the `param.txt` file. The first number following the test file defines the number of threads per test file. Microsoft recommends setting this to the number of CPU cores running on the host machine. Leave the mask set at 0x0. Finally, the size of the test file in MB is defined.

Ensure that the test file is large enough to exceed the amount of cache dedicated to your storage volumes. If the host file is too small it will eventually be stored within the array cache.

SQLIO is designed to run a specific workload per instance. Each time you execute `SQLIO.exe` with parameters, it will define a specific type of I/O. It is entirely permissible to run many instances of SQLIO in parallel against the same test file.

Be sure to coordinate testing with your storage administrator before you start these tests, as they are designed to heavily stress your I/O system. It is best to begin by confirming any calculated assumptions. If you have 100 10K SAS disks configured in a RAID 1+0 set, you can assume random I/O will perform 14,000 reads. To test these assumptions run a single SQLIO.exe instance:

```
sqlio -kR -s300 -frandom -o1 -b8 -LS -Fparam.txt
```

The -k option sets either R (read) or W (write). Set the test run length using the –s function. We recommend testing for at least a few minutes (this example uses 5 minutes). Running a test for too short a time may not accurately demonstrate how a large RAID controller cache will behave. It is also important to pause in between similar tests. Otherwise, the array cache will reuse existing data, possibly skewing your results.

The -f option sets the type of I/O to run, either random or sequential. The -o parameter defines the number of outstanding I/O requests. You use the -b setting to define the size of the I/O request, in KB. This example tests very small I/O. SQL Server normally reads at least a full 64KB extent.

You use the -LS setting to collect system latency information. On a 64-bit system you can add the -64 option to enable full use of the 64-bit memory system. Finally, you define the location for the param.txt file using the -F option. Following is the test output:

```
sqlio v1.5.SG
using system counter for latency timings, 14318180 counts per second
parameter file used: param.txt
        file c:\testfile.dat with 2 threads (0-1) using mask 0x0 (0)
2 threads reading for 300 secs from file c:\testfile.dat
        using 8KB random IOs
        enabling multiple I/Os per thread with 8 outstanding
size of file c:\testfile.dat needs to be: 104857600 bytes
current file size:      0 bytes
need to expand by:      104857600 bytes
expanding c:\testfile.dat ... done.
using specified size: 100 MB for file: c:\testfile.dat
initialization done
CUMULATIVE DATA:
throughput metrics:
IOs/sec: 13080.21
MBs/sec:    102.18
latency metrics:
Min_Latency(ms): 0
Avg_Latency(ms): 0
Max_Latency(ms): 114
histogram:
ms: 0 1  2 3 4 5  6  7  8  9 10 11 12 13 14 15 16 17 18 19 20 21 22 23 24+
%: 37 59 3 0 0 0  0  0  0  0  0  0  0  0  0  0  0  0  0  0  0  0  0  0  0
```

This single 8K random test started by creating the 100MB test file. In this case, the test was generated on a VM guest using a flash drive, so the results are not representative of what you might see in a real-world test. The test ran for five minutes with one outstanding I/O, and generated 13,080 IOPS and 102 MB/sec. It peaked at 114 milliseconds of latency but averaged under a millisecond for access.

This test is a perfect demonstration of how a system can fail to utilize its maximum potential performance. Only eight outstanding I/Os completed, which failed to push the I/O subsystem. To properly test a given system, it is a good idea to scale the workload dynamically to determine how it will perform under increasing loads. To accomplish this you can script SQLIO:

```
sqlio -kR -s300 -frandom -o1 -b8 -LS -Fparam.txt
sqlio -kR -s300 -frandom -o2 -b8 -LS -Fparam.txt
sqlio -kR -s300 -frandom -o4 -b8 -LS -Fparam.txt
sqlio -kR -s300 -frandom -o8 -b8 -LS -Fparam.txt
sqlio -kR -s300 -frandom -o1 -b16 -LS -Fparam.txt
sqlio -kR -s300 -frandom -o1 -b32 -LS -Fparam.txt
sqlio -kR -s300 -frandom -o1 -b64 -LS -Fparam.txt
sqlio -kR -s300 -frandom -o1 -b128 -LS -Fparam.txt
sqlio -kR -s300 -frandom -o1 -b256 -LS -Fparam.txt
```

Run this batch file from the command line and capture the results to an output file:

```
RunSQLIO.bat > Result.txt
```

Ideally, you will test several different scenarios. Create a batch file with each scenario that scales from 1 to 256 outstanding I/Os, such as the following:

➤ Small-block random read performance:

```
sqlio -kR -s300 -frandom -o1 -b8 -LS -Fparam.txt
```

➤ Small-block random write performance:

```
sqlio -kW -s300 -frandom -o1 -b8 -LS -Fparam.txt
```

➤ Large-block sequential read performance:

```
sqlio -kR -s300 - fsequential -o1 -b8 -LS -Fparam.txt
```

➤ Large-block sequential write performance:

```
sqlio -kR -s300 -fsequential -o1 -b8 -LS -Fparam.txt
```

Running these scenarios as a single batch file will automate the I/O system testing process. The most important data points are the latency and performance measurements. When the tests exceed your maximum latency tolerance, usually not more than 20 milliseconds, you have exceeded the capabilities of your I/O subsystem. If the system does not meet your overall performance requirements with adequate response times, then you need to investigate the system for errors or configuration issues. Ultimately, you may need to optimize the storage system's performance to ensure that previously specified requirements are met.

SUMMARY

Database professionals can avoid I/O problems by designing, testing, and monitoring storage systems. You don't need to be a dedicated storage professional to ensure reliable system performance; just follow these simple guidelines:

➤ Include I/O systems when designing and planning database systems.

➤ Always test the storage systems for functionality and performance.

➤ Continuously monitor storage performance. Establish lines of communication with storage administrators to ensure that the storage systems meet your requirements.

➤ Plan for recovery and/or disaster. Document your plan and test it to ensure that it can be executed.

5

Query Processing and Execution

WHAT'S IN THIS CHAPTER?

➤ How SQL Server processes queries

➤ Understanding query optimization

➤ Reading query plans

➤ Using options to affect query plans

➤ Using plan hints to affect query plans

WROX.COM CODE DOWNLOADS FOR THIS CHAPTER

The wrox.com code downloads for this chapter are found at www.wrox.com/remtitle .cgi?isbn=1118177657 on the Download Code tab. The code is in the Chapter 5 download and individually named according to the names throughout the chapter.

This section uses the AdventureWorks 2012 database, so now is a good time to download it from the SQL Server section on CodePlex if you haven't already. The AdventureWorks 2012 samples can be found at http://www.codeplex.com/SqlServerSamples.

INTRODUCTION

Query processing is one of the most critical activities that SQL Server performs in order to return data from your T-SQL queries. Understanding how SQL Server processes queries, including how they are optimized and executed, is essential to understanding what SQL Server is doing and why it chooses a particular way to do it.

In this chapter you will learn how SQL Server query processing works, including the details of query optimization and the various options that you can use to influence the optimization process; and how SQL Server schedules activities and executes them.

QUERY PROCESSING

Query processing is performed by the Relational Engine in SQL Server. It is the process of taking the T-SQL statements you write and converting them into something that can make requests to the Storage Engine and retrieve the results needed.

SQL Server takes four steps to process a query: parsing, algebrizing, optimizing, and execution. They are shown in Figure 5-1.

The first three steps are all performed by the Relational Engine. The output of the third step is the optimized plan that is scheduled, and during which calls are made to the Storage Engine to retrieve the data that becomes the results of the query you are executing.

Query optimization and execution are covered later in this chapter. The following sections briefly discuss parsing and algebrizing.

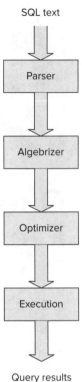

FIGURE 5-1

Parsing

During the parsing stage SQL Server performs basic checks on the source code (your T-SQL batch). This parsing looks for invalid SQL syntax, such as incorrect use of reserved words, column and table names, and so on.

If parsing completes without errors, it generates a parse tree, which is passed onto the next stage of query processing, binding. The parse tree is an internal representation of the query. If parsing detects any errors, the process stops and the errors are returned.

Algebrizing

The algebrization stage is also referred to as the binding stage. In early versions of SQL Server this stage was referred to as *normalization*. During algebrizing, SQL Server performs several operations on the parse tree and then generates a query tree that is passed on to the Query Optimizer.

The steps performed during algebrizing follow this model:

➤ **Step 1: Name resolution** — Confirms that all objects exist and are visible in the security context of the user. This is where the table and column names are checked to ensure that they exist and that the user has access to them.

➤ **Step 2: Type derivation** — Determines the final type for each node in the parse tree

➤ **Step 3: Aggregate binding** — Determines where to do any aggregations

➤ **Step 4: Group binding** — Binds any aggregations to the appropriate select list

Syntax errors are detected during this stage. If a syntax error is encountered, the optimization process halts and the error is returned to the user.

QUERY OPTIMIZATION

The job of the Query Optimizer is to take the query tree that was output from the algebrizer and find a "good" way to retrieve the data (results) needed. Note the use of "good" here, rather than "best," as for any nontrivial query, there may be hundreds, or even thousands, of different ways to achieve the same results, so finding the absolutely best one can be an extremely time-consuming process. Therefore, in order to provide results in a timely manner, the Query Optimizer looks for a "good enough" plan, and uses that. This approach means that you may very well be able to do better when you manually inspect the query plan; and in the section "Influencing Optimization" you will look at different ways you can affect the decisions that SQL Server makes during optimization.

The query optimization process is based on a principle of *cost*, which is an abstract measure of work that is used to evaluate different query plan options. The exact nature of these costs is a closely guarded secret, with some people suggesting that they are a reflection of the time, in seconds, that the query is expected to take. They also take into account I/O and CPU resources. However, users should consider cost to be a dimensionless value that doesn't have any units — its value is derived from comparisons to the cost of other plans in order to find the cheapest one. Therefore, there are no true units for cost values.

Although the exact details of what SQL Server does within the optimization phase are secret, it's possible to get a glimpse at some of what goes on. For the purposes of this book, you don't need to know every small detail, and in fact such a deep understanding isn't useful anyway. For one thing, there is nothing you can do to alter this process; moreover, with each new service pack or hotfix, the SQL Server team tunes the internal algorithms, thereby changing the exact behavior. If you were to know too much about what was occurring, you could build in dependencies that would break with every new version of SQL Server.

Rather than know all the details, you need only understand the bigger picture. Even this bigger picture is often too much information, as it doesn't offer any real visibility into what the Query Optimizer is doing. All you can see of this secretive process is what is exposed in the Dynamic Management View (DMV) `sys.dm_exec_query_optimizer_info`. This can be interesting, but it's not a great deal of help in understanding why a given T-SQL statement is assigned a particular plan, or how you can "fix" what you think may be a non-optimal plan.

The current model provided by the SQL Server team works something like this:

➤ Is a valid plan cached? If yes, then use the cached plan. If no plan exists, then continue.

➤ Is this a trivial plan? If yes, then use the trivial plan. If no, then continue.

➤ Apply simplification. Simplification is a process of normalizing the query tree and applying some basic transformations to additionally "simplify" the tree.

➤ Is the plan cheap enough? If yes, then use this. If no, then start optimization.

➤ Start cost-based optimization.

➤ **Phase 0** — Explore basic rules, and hash and nested join options.

➤ Does the plan have a cost of less than 0.2? If yes, then use this. If no, then continue.

➤ **Phase 1** — Explore more rules, and alternate join ordering. If the best (cheapest) plan costs less than 1.0, then use this plan. If not, then if MAXDOP > 0 and this is an SMP system, and the min cost > cost threshold for parallelism, then use a parallel plan. Compare the cost of the parallel plan with the best serial plan, and pass the cheaper of the two to phase 2.

➤ **Phase 2** — Explore all options, and opt for the cheapest plan after a limited number of explorations.

The output of the preceding steps is an executable plan that can be placed in the cache. This plan is then scheduled for execution, which is explored later in this chapter.

You can view the inner workings of the optimization process via the DMV sys.dm_exec_query_optimizer_info. This DMV contains a set of optimization attributes, each with an occurrence and a value. Refer to SQL Books Online (BOL) for full details. Here are a few that relate to some of the steps just described:

```
select *
from sys.dm_exec_query_optimizer_info
where counter in (
'optimizations'
, 'trivial plan'
, 'search 0'
, 'search 1'
, 'search 2'
)
order by [counter]
```

The preceding will return the same number of rows as follows, but the counters and values will be different. Note that the value for optimizations matches the sum of the trivial plan, search 0, search 1, and search 2 counters (2328 + 8559 + 3 + 17484 = 28374):

```
Counter              occurrencevalue
Optimizations 28374       1
search 0       2328       1
search 1       8559       1
search 2       3          1
trivial plan   17484      1
```

Parallel Plans

A parallel plan is any plan for which the Optimizer has chosen to split an applicable operator into multiple threads that are run in parallel.

Not all operators are suitable to be used in a parallel plan. The Optimizer will only choose a parallel plan if:

➤ the server has multiple processors,

➤ the maximum degree of parallelism setting allows parallel plans, and

➤ the `cost threshold for parallelism` sql server configuration option is set to a value lower than the lowest cost estimate for the current plan. Note that the value set here is the time in seconds estimated to run the serial plan on a specific hardware configuration chosen by the Query Optimizer team.

➤ The cost of the parallel plan is cheaper than the serial plan.

If all these criteria are met, then the Optimizer will choose to parallelize the operation.

An example that illustrates how this works is trying to count all the values in a table that match particular search criteria. If the set of rows in the table is large enough, the cost of the query is high enough, and the other criteria are met, then the Optimizer might parallelize the operation by dividing the total set of rows in the table into equal chunks, one for each processor core. The operation is then executed in parallel, with each processor core executing one thread, and dealing with one/number of cores of the total set of rows. This enables the operation to complete in a lot less time than using a single thread to scan the whole table. One thing to be aware of when dealing with parallel plans is that SQL Server doesn't always do a great job of distributing the data between threads, and so your parallel plan may well end up with one or two of the parallel threads taking considerably longer to complete.

Algebrizer Trees

As mentioned earlier, the output of the parser is a parse tree. This isn't stored anywhere permanently, so you can't see what this looks like. The output from the algebrizer is an algebrizer tree, which isn't stored for any T-SQL queries either, but some algebrizer output *is* stored — namely, views, defaults, and constraints. This is stored because these objects are frequently reused in other queries, so caching this information can be a big performance optimization. The algebrizer trees for these objects are stored in the cache store, where `type = CACHESTORE_PHDR`:

```
select *
from sys.dm_os_memory_cache_entries
where type = 'CACHESTORE_PHDR'
```

It's only at the next stage (i.e., when you have the output from optimization) that things start to get really interesting, and here you can see quite a bit of information. This very useful data provides details about each optimized plan.

sql_handle or plan_handle

In the various execution-related DMVs, some contain a `sql_handle`, while others contain the `plan_handle`. Both are hashed values: `sql_handle` is the hash of the original T-SQL source, whereas `plan_handle` is the hash of the cached plan. Because the SQL queries are auto-parameterized, the relationship between these means that many `sql_handles` can map to a single `plan_handle`.

You can see the original T-SQL for either using the dynamic management function (DMF) `sys.dm_exec_sql_text` (`sql_handle` | `Plan_handle`).

To see the XML showplan for the plan, use the DMF `sys.dm_exec_query_plan` (`plan_handle`).

Understanding Statistics

Statistics provide critical information needed by SQL Server when performing query optimization. SQL Server statistics contain details about the data, and what the data looks like in each table within the database.

The query optimization process uses statistics to determine how many rows a query might need to access for a given query plan. It uses this information to develop its cost estimate for each step in the plan. If statistics are missing or invalid, the Query Optimizer can arrive at an incorrect cost for a step, and thus choose what ends up being a bad plan.

You can examine the statistics for any table in the database by using SQL Server Management Studio, expanding the Object Explorer to show the table you are interested in. For example, Figure 5-2 shows the person.Address table in the AdventureWorks2012 database. Expand the table node, under which you will see a Statistics node. Expand this, and you will see a statistic listed for each index that has been created, and in many cases you will see additional statistics listed, often with cryptic names starting with _WA. These are statistics that SQL Server has created automatically for you, based upon queries that have been run against the database. SQL Server creates these statistics when the AUTO_CREATE_STATISTICS option is set to ON.

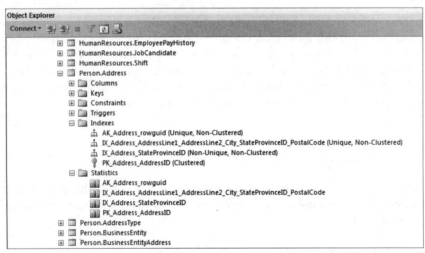

FIGURE 5-2

To see the actual statistic values, you can select an individual statistic, right-click it, and select the Properties option from the menu options. This will show you the Properties dialog for the statistic you selected. The first page, General, displays the columns in the statistic and when it was last updated. The Details page contains the real guts of the statistic, and shows the data distribution. For the PK_Address-AddressID statistic on the person.Address table in AdventureWorks2012, you should see something similar to Figure 5-3.

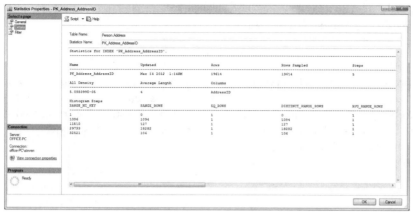

FIGURE 5-3

This figure shows just part of the multi-column output, which is the same output that you get when running the following DBCC command:

```
DBCC SHOW_STATISTICS ("Person.Address", PK_Address_AddressID);
```

The following SQL Server configuration options control how statistics are created.

Auto_create_statistics

When this is on (default), SQL Server automatically creates statistics when it thinks they would result in a better plan. That usually means when it is optimizing a query that references a column without statistics.

Auto_update_statistics

When this is on (default), SQL Server automatically updates statistics when a sufficient amount of the data in the relevant columns has changed. By default, this is done synchronously, which means that a query has to wait for the statistics to be updated before the optimization process can be completed.

Auto_update_statistics_asynchronously

When this option is on, SQL Server updates statistics asynchronously. This means that when it's trying to optimize a query and the statistics are outdated, it will continue optimizing the current query using the old stats, and queue the stats to be updated asynchronously. As a result, the current query doesn't benefit from the new stats, but it does not have to wait while stats are being updated before getting a plan and running. Any future queries can then benefit from the new stats.

Plan Caching and Recompilation

Once the Query Optimizer has come up with a plan, which may have taken a considerable amount of work, SQL Server does its best to ensure that you can leverage all that costly work again. It does this by caching the plan it just created, and taking steps to ensure that the plan is reused as widely as possible. It does this by using parameterization options.

Parameterization

Parameterization is a process whereby SQL Server takes the T-SQL you entered and looks for ways to replace values that may be variables with a token, so that if a similar query is processed, SQL Server can identify it as being the same underlying query, apart from some string, or integer values, and make use of the already cached plan. For example, the following is a basic T-SQL query to return data from the AdventureWorks2012 database:

```
select *
from person.person
where lastname = 'duffy'
```

Parameterization of this query would result in the string `'duffy'` being replaced with a parameter such that if another user executes the following query, the same plan would be used, saving on compilation time:

```
select *
from person.person
where lastname = 'miller'
```

Note that this is just an example, and this particular query gets a trivial plan, so it isn't a candidate for parameterization.

The SQL Server Books Online topic on "Forced Parameterization" contains very specific details about what can and cannot be converted to a parameter.

To determine whether a query has been parameterized, you can search for it in the DMV `sys.dm_exec_cached_plans` (after first executing the query to ensure it is cached). If the SQL column of this DMV shows that the query has been parameterized, any literals from the query are replaced by variables, and those variables are declared at the beginning of the batch.

Parameterization is controlled by one of two SQL Server configuration options — simple or forced:

➤ **Simple parameterization** — The default operation of SQL Server is to use *simple parameterization* on all queries that are suitable candidates. Books Online provides numerous details about which queries are selected and how SQL Server performs parameterization. Using simple parameterization, SQL Server is able to parameterize only a relatively small set of the queries it receives.

➤ **Forced parameterization** — For more control over database performance, you can specify that SQL Server use *forced parameterization*. This option forces SQL Server to parameterize all literal values in any select, insert, update, or delete statement queries. There are some exceptions to this, which are well documented in SQL Server Books Online. Forced parameterization is not appropriate in all environments and scenarios. It is recommended that you use it only for a very high volume of concurrent queries, and when you are seeing high CPU from a lot of compilation/recompilation. If you are not experiencing a lot of compilation/recompilation, then forced parameterization is probably not appropriate. Using forced in the absence of these symptoms may result in degraded performance and/or throughput because SQL Server takes more time to parameterize a lot of queries that are not later reused. It can also lead to parameter sniffing, causing inappropriate plan use.

Forced parameterization can also be more finely controlled through the use of plan guides. You will learn about plan guides in more detail later in this chapter.

Looking into the Plan Cache

The plan cache is built on top of the caching infrastructure provided by the SQL OS. This provides objects called *cache stores*, which can be used to cache all kinds of objects. The plan cache contains several different cache stores used for different types of objects.

To see the contents of a few of the cache stores most relevant to this conversation, run the following T-SQL:

```
select name, entries_count, pages_kb
from sys.dm_os_memory_cache_counters
where [name] in (
'object plans'
, 'sql plans'
, 'extended stored procedures'
)
```

Example output when I ran the preceding on my laptop is as follows:

```
name                        entries_count pages_kbObject Plans
54              12312SQL Plans                  48          2904Extended
Stored Procedures 4         48
```

Each cache store contains a hash table that is used to provide efficient storage for the many plans that may reside in the plan cache at any time. The hash used is based on the plan handle. The hash provides buckets to store plans, and many plans can reside in any one bucket. SQL Server limits both the number of plans in any bucket and the total number of hash buckets. This is done to avoid issues with long lookup times when the cache has to store a large number of plans, which can easily happen on a busy server handling many different queries.

To find performance issues caused by long lookup times, you can look into the contents of the DMV sys.dm_os_memory_cache_hash_tables, as shown in the following example. It is recommended that no bucket should contain more than 20 objects; and buckets exceeding 100 objects should be addressed.

```
select *
from sys.dm_os_memory_cache_hash_tables
where type in (
'cachestore_objcp'
, 'cachestore_sqlcp'
, 'cacchestore_phdr'
, 'cachestore_xproc'
)
```

Use the following DMV to look for heavily used buckets:

```
select bucketid, count(*) as entries_in_bucket
from sys.dm_exec_cached_plans
group by bucketid
order by 2 desc
```

You can look up the specific plans in that bucket using this query:

```
select *
from sys.dm_exec_cached_plans
where bucketid = 236
```

If the plans you find within the same bucket are all variations on the same query, then try to get better plan reuse through parameterization. If the queries are already quite different, and there is no commonality that would allow parameterization, then the solution is to rewrite the queries to be dramatically different, enabling them to be stored in emptier buckets.

Another approach is to query sys.dm_exec_query_stats, grouping on query_plan_hash to find queries with the same query plan hash using the T-SQL listed here:

```
select query_plan_hash,count(*) as occurrences
from sys.dm_exec_query_stats
group by query_plan_hash
having count(*) > 1
```

Four different kinds of objects are stored in the plan cache. Although not all of them are of equal interest, each is briefly described here:

➤ **Algebrizer trees** are the output of the algebrizer, although only the algebrizer trees for views, defaults, and constraints are cached.

➤ **Compiled plans** are the objects you will be most interested in. This is where the query plan is cached.

➤ **Cursor execution contexts** are used to track the execution state when a cursor is executing, and are similar to the next item.

➤ **Execution contexts** track the context of an individual compiled plan.

The first DMV to look at in the procedure cache is sys.dm_exec_cached_plans. The following query gathers some statistics on the type of objects exposed through this DMV (note that this doesn't include execution contexts, which are covered next):

```
select cacheobjtype, objtype, COUNT (*)
from sys.dm_exec_cached_plans
group by cacheobjtype, objtype
order by cacheobjtype, objtype
```

Running the preceding on my laptop resulted in the following output; your results will vary according to what was loaded into your procedure cache:

```
CACHEOBJTYPE    OBJTYPE    (NO COLUMN NAME)
Compiled Plan   Adhoc      43
```

```
Compiled Plan   Prepared  20
Compiled Plan   Proc      54
Extended Proc   Proc      4
Parse Tree      Check     2
Parse Tree      UsrTab    1
Parse Tree      View      64
```

To see the execution contexts, you must pass a specific plan handle to sys.dm_exec_cached_plans_ dependent_objects. However, before doing that, you need to find a plan_handle to pass to this dynamic management function (DMF). To do that, run the following T-SQL:

```
-- Run this to empty the cache
-- WARNING !!! DO NOT TRY THIS ON A PRODUCTION SYSTEM !!!
dbcc freeproccache
```

Now see how many objects there are in the cache. There will always be a bunch of stuff here from the background activities that SQL is always running.

```
select cacheobjtype, objtype, COUNT (*)
from sys.dm_exec_cached_plans
group by cacheobjtype, objtype
order by cacheobjtype, objtype
```

The output of the query will look similar to this:

```
CACHEOBJTYPE    OBJTYPE     (NO COLUMN NAME)
Compiled Plan   Adhoc       5
Compiled Plan   Prepared    1
Compiled Plan   Proc        11
Extended Proc   Proc        1
Parse Tree      View        10
```

Run the following code in the AdventureWorks2012 database, from another connection:

```
select lastname, COUNT (*)
from Person.Person_test
group by lastname
order by 2 desc
```

The output of the prior query is not of interest, so it's not shown here. The following query goes back and reexamines the cache:

```
-- Check that we got additional objects into the cache
select cacheobjtype, objtype, COUNT (*)
from sys.dm_exec_cached_plans
group by cacheobjtype, objtype
order by cacheobjtype, objtype
```

The output of the query will look similar to this:

```
CACHEOBJTYPE    OBJTYPE     (NO COLUMN NAME)
Compiled Plan   Adhoc       9
```

```
Compiled Plan    Prepared    2
Compiled Plan    Proc       14
Extended Proc    Proc        2
Parse Tree       View       13
```

At this point you can see that there are four more ad hoc compiled plans, and a number of other new cached objects. The objects you are interested in here are the ad hoc plans.

Run the following T-SQL to get the SQL text and the plan handle for the T-SQL query you ran against the AdventureWorks2012 database:

```
select p.refcounts, p.usecounts, p.plan_handle, s.text
from sys.dm_exec_cached_plans as p
    cross apply sys.dm_exec_sql_text (p.plan_handle) as s
where p.cacheobjtype = 'compiled plan'
and p.objtype = 'adhoc'
order by p.usecounts desc
```

This should provide something similar to the results shown in Figure 5-4.

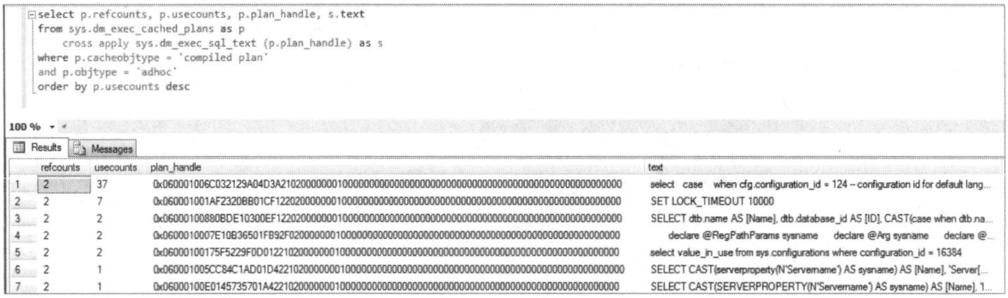

FIGURE 5-4

To see the execution context, take the `plan_handle` that you got from the preceding results and plug it into the DMF `sys.dm_exec_cached_plan_dependent_objects`, as shown in the following example:

```
select *
from sys.dm_exec_cached_plan_dependent_objects
(0x06000F005163130CB880EE0D0000000000000000000000000)
```

The preceding code returned the following results:

```
USECOUNTS  MEMORY_OBJECT_ADDRESS  CACHEOBJTYPE
1          0x0DF8A038             Executable Plan
```

Another interesting thing you can examine are the attributes of the plan. These are found in the DMF `sys.dm_exec_plan_attributes (plan_handle)` Note that you need to pass the DMF a plan handle, and then you will get the attributes for that plan:

```
select *
from sys.dm_exec_plan_attributes
(0x06000F00C080471DB8E06914000000000000000000000000)
```

The preceding query outputs a list of 28 attributes, a select few of which are shown here:

```
ATTRIBUTE        VALUE                                               IS_CACHE_KEY
set_options      135419                                              1
objectid         491225280                                           1
dbid             15                                                  1
language_id      0                                                   1
date_format      1                                                   1
date_first       7                                                   1
compat_level     100                                                 1
sql_handle       0x02000000C080471DB475BDA81DA97B1C6F2EEA51417711E8  0
```

The `sql_handle` in these results can then be used in a call to the DMF `sys.dm_exec_sql_`
`text (sql_handle)` to see the SQL that was being run.

Compilation/Recompilation

Compilation and recompilation are pretty much the same thing, just triggered at slightly different times. When SQL Server decides that an existing plan is no longer valid, which is usually due to a schema change, statistics changes, or some other event, it will re-compile the plan. This happens only when someone tries to run the query. If they try to run the query when no one else is using the plan, it is a compile event. If this happens when someone else is using a copy of the plan, it is a recompile event.

You can monitor the amount of compilation/recompilation that's occurring by observing the PerfMon Object SQL Server: SQL Statistics and then looking at the following two counters: SQL compilations/sec and SQL recompilations/sec.

Influencing Optimization

There are two main ways you can influence the Query Optimizer — by using *query hints* or *plan guides*.

Query Hints

Query hints are an easy way to influence the actions of query optimization. However, you need to very carefully consider their use, as in most cases SQL Server is already choosing the right plan. As a general rule, you should avoid using query hints, as they provide many opportunities to cause more issues than the one you are attempting to solve. In some cases, however, such as with complex queries or when dealing with complex datasets that defeat SQL Server's cardinality estimates on specific queries, using query hints may be necessary.

Before using any query hints, run a web search for the latest information on issues with query hints. Try searching on the keywords "SQL Server Query Hints" and look specifically for anything by Craig Freedman, who has written several great blog entries on some of the issues you can encounter when using query hints.

Problems with using hints can happen at any time — from when you start using the hint, which can cause unexpected side effects that cause the query to fail to compile, to more complex and difficult to find performance issues that occur later.

As data in the relevant tables changes, without query hints the Query Optimizer automatically updates statistics and adjusts query plans as needed; but if you have locked the Query Optimizer into a specific set of optimizations using query hints, then the plan cannot be changed, and you may end up with a considerably worse plan, requiring further action (from you) to identify and resolve the root cause of the new performance issue.

One final word of caution about using query hints: Unlike *locking hints* (also referred to in BOL as *table hints*), which SQL Server attempts to satisfy, query hints are stronger, so if SQL Server is unable to satisfy a query hint it will raise error 8622 and not create any plan.

Query hints are specified using the OPTION clause, which is always added at the end of the T-SQL statement — unlike locking or join hints, which are added within the T-SQL statement after the tables they are to affect.

> **NOTE** *Refer to the* Transact SQL Reference, Data Manipulation Language, Hints(Transact-SQL) *section, or search for* query hints *in SQL Server 2012* Books Online *for a complete list of query hints.*

The following sections describe a few of the more interesting query hints.

FAST number_rows

Use this query hint when you want to retrieve only the first *n* rows out of a relatively large result set. A typical example of this is a website that uses paging to display large sets of rows, whereby the first page shows only the first web page worth of rows, and a page might contain only 20, 30, or maybe 40 rows. If the query returns thousands of rows, then SQL Server would possibly optimize this query using hash joins. Hash joins work well with large datasets but have a higher setup time than perhaps a nested loop join. Nested loop joins have a very low setup cost and can return the first set of rows more quickly but takes considerably longer to return all the rows. Using the FAST <number_rows> query hint causes the Query Optimizer to use nested loop joins and other techniques, rather than hashed joins, to get the first *n* rows faster.

Typically, once the first *n* rows are returned, if the remaining rows are retrieved, the query performs slower than if this hint were not used.

{Loop | Merge | Hash } JOIN

The JOIN query hint applies to all joins within the query. While this is similar to the join hint that can be specified for an individual join between a pair of tables within a large more complex query, the query hint applies to *all* joins within the query, whereas the join hint applies only to the pair of tables in the join with which it is associated.

To see how this works, here is an example query using the AdventureWorks2012 database that joins three tables. The first example shows the basic query with no join hints.

NOTE *These examples include plan details that are discussed in more detail later in this chapter.*

```
use AdventureWorks2012
go

set statistics profile on
go

select p.title, p.firstname, p.middlename, p.lastname
, a.addressline1, a.addressline2, a.city, a.postalcode
from person.person as p inner join person.businessentityaddress as b
on p.businessentityid = b.businessentityid
inner join person.address as a on b.addressid = a.addressid
go

set statistics profile off
go
```

This returns two result sets. The first is the output from the query, and returns 18,798 rows; the second result set is the additional output after enabling the `set statistics profile` option. One interesting piece of information in the statistics profile output is the `totalsubtreecost` column. To see the cost for the entire query, look at the top row. On my test machine, this query is costed at 4.649578. The following shows just the `PhysicalOp` column from the statistics profile output, which displays the operator used for each step of the plan:

```
PHYSICALOP
NULL
Merge Join
Clustered Index Scan
Sort
Merge Join
Clustered Index Scan
Index Scan
```

The next example shows the same query but illustrates the use of a table hint. In this example the join hint applies only to the join between `person.person` and `person.businessentity`:

```
use AdventureWorks2012
go

set statistics profile on
```

```
go

select p.title, p.firstname, p.middlename, p.lastname
, a.addressline1, a.addressline2, a.city, a.postalcode
from person.person as p inner loop join person.businessentityaddress as b
on p.businessentityid = b.businessentityid
inner join person.address as a on b.addressid = a.addressid
go

set statistics profile off
go
```

The totalsubtree cost for this option is 8.155532, which is quite a bit higher than the plan that SQL chose, and indicates that our meddling with the optimization process has had a negative impact on performance.

The `PhysicalOp` column of the statistics profile output is shown next. This indicates that the entire order of the query has been dramatically changed; the merge joins have been replaced with a loop join as requested, but this forced the Query Optimizer to use a `hash match` join for the other join. You can also see that the Optimizer chose to use a parallel plan, and even this has not reduced the cost:

```
PhysicalOp
NULL
Parallelism
Hash Match
Parallelism
Nested Loops
Clustered Index Scan
Clustered Index Seek
Parallelism
Index Scan
```

The final example shows the use of a JOIN query hint. Using this forces both joins within the query to use the join type specified:

```
use AdventureWorks2012
go

set statistics profile on
go

select p.title, p.firstname, p.middlename, p.lastname
, a.addressline1, a.addressline2, a.city, a.postalcode
from person.person as p inner join person.businessentityaddress as b
on p.businessentityid = b.businessentityid
inner join person.address as a on b.addressid = a.addressid
option (hash join )
go

set statistics profile off
go
```

The total subtreecost for this plan is 5.097726. This is better than the previous option but still worse than the plan chosen by SQL Server.

The `PhysicalOp` column of the following statistics profile output indicates that both joins are now hash joins:

```
PhysicalOp
NULL
Parallelism
Hash Match
Parallelism
Hash Match
Parallelism
Index Scan
Parallelism
Clustered Index Scan
Parallelism
Index Scan
```

Using a query hint can cause both compile-time and runtime issues. The compile-time issues are likely to happen when SQL Server is unable to create a plan due to the query hint. Runtime issues are likely to occur when the data has changed enough that the Query Optimizer needs to create a new plan using a different join strategy but it is locked into using the joins defined in the query hint.

MAXDOP *n*

The MAXDOP query hint is only applicable on systems and SQL Server editions for which parallel plans are possible. On single-core systems, multiprocessor systems where CPU affinity has been set to a single processor core, or systems that don't support parallel plans (i.e. if you are running the express edition of SQL Server which can only utilize a single processor core), this query hint has no effect.

On systems where parallel plans are possible, and in the case of a query where a parallel plan is being generated, using MAXDOP (*n*) allows the Query Optimizer to use only *n* workers.

On very large SMPs or NUMA systems, where the SQL Server configuration setting for Max Degree of Parallelism is set to a number less than the total available CPUs, this option can be useful if you want to override the systemwide Max Degree of Parallelism setting for a specific query.

A good example of this might be a 16 core SMP server with an application database that needs to service a large number of concurrent users, all running potentially parallel plans. To minimize the impact of any one query, the SQL Server configuration setting Max Degree of Parallelism is set to 4, but some activities have a higher "priority" and you want to allow them to use all CPUs. An example of this might be an operational activity such as an index rebuild, when you don't want to use an online operation and you want the index to be created as quickly as possible. In this case, the specific queries for index creation/rebuilding can use the MAXDOP 16 query hint, which allows SQL Server to create a plan that uses all 16 cores.

OPTIMIZE FOR

Because of the extensive use of plan parameterization, and the way that the Query Optimizer sniffs for parameters on each execution of a parameterized plan, SQL Server doesn't always do the best job of choosing the right plan for a specific set of parameters.

The OPTIMIZE FOR hint enables you to tell the Query Optimizer what values you expect to see most commonly at runtime. Provided that the values you specify are the most common case, this can result in better performance for the majority of the queries, or at least those that match the case for which you optimized.

RECOMPILE

The RECOMPILE query hint is a more granular way to force recompilation in a stored procedure to be at the statement level rather than using the WITH RECOMPILE option, which forces the whole stored procedure to be recompiled.

When the Query Optimizer sees the RECOMPILE query hint, it forces a new query plan to be created regardless of what plans may already be cached. The new plan is created with the parameters within the current execution context.

This is a very useful option if you know that a particular part of a stored procedure has very different input parameters that can affect the resulting query plan dramatically. Using this option may incur a small cost for the compilation needed on every execution, but if that's a small percentage of the resulting query's execution time, it's a worthwhile cost to pay to ensure that every execution of the query gets the most optimal plan.

For cases in which the additional compilation cost is high relative to the cost of the worst execution, using this query hint would be detrimental to performance.

USE PLAN N 'xml plan'

The USE PLAN query hint tells the Query Optimizer that you want a new plan, and that the new plan should match the shape of the plan in the supplied XML plan.

This is very similar to the use of plan guides (covered in the next section), but whereas plan guides don't require a change to the query, the USE PLAN query hint does require a change to the T-SQL being submitted to the server.

Sometimes this query hint is used to solve deadlock issues or other data-related problems. However, in nearly all cases the correct course of action is to address the underlying issue, but that often involves architectural changes, or code changes that require extensive development and test work to get into production. In these cases the USE PLAN query hint can provide a quick workaround for the DBA to keep the system running while the root cause of a problem is found and fixed.

Note that the preceding course of action assumes you have a "good" XML plan from the problem query that doesn't show the problem behavior. If you just happened to capture a bunch of XML plans from all the queries running on your system when it was working well, then you are good to go, but that's not typically something that anyone ever does, as you usually leave systems alone when they are working OK; and capturing XML plans for every query running today just in case you may want to use the USE PLAN query hint at some point in the future is not a very useful practice.

What you may be able to do, however, is configure a test system with data such that the plan your target query generates is of the desired shape, capture the XML for the plan, and use that XML plan to "fix" the plan's shape on your production server.

Plan Guides

Plan guides, which were added in SQL Server 2005, enable the DBA to affect the optimization of a query without altering the query itself. Typically, plan guides are used by DBAs seeking to tune query execution on third-party application databases, where the T-SQL code being executed is proprietary and cannot be changed. Typical examples of applications for which plan guides are most likely to be needed would be large ERP applications such as SAP, PeopleSoft, and so on.

Although plan guides were first added in SQL Server 2005, significant enhancements, primarily regarding ease of use, were made to them in SQL Server 2008.

There are three different types of plan guide:

➤ **Object plan guide** — Can be applied to a stored procedure, trigger, or user-defined function

➤ **SQL plan guide** — Applied to a specific SQL statement

➤ **Template plan guide** — Provides a way to override database settings for parameterization of specific SQL queries

To make use of plan guides, the first step is to create or capture a "good" plan; the second step is to apply that plan to the object or T-SQL statement for which you want to change the Query Optimizer's behavior.

QUERY PLANS

Now that you have seen how your T-SQL is optimized, the next step is to look at the query plan that the Query Optimizer generated for it. There are several ways to view query plans, but perhaps the easiest is to view the graphical plan using SQL Server Management Studio (SSMS). SSMS makes this extra easy by providing a context-sensitive menu option that enables you to highlight any piece of T-SQL in a query window and display the estimated execution plan, as shown in Figure 5-5.

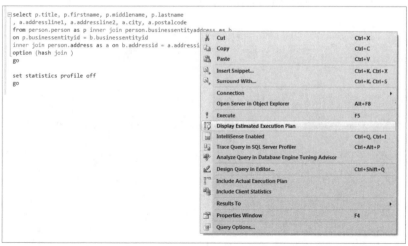

FIGURE 5-5

This provided the output shown in Figure 5-6.

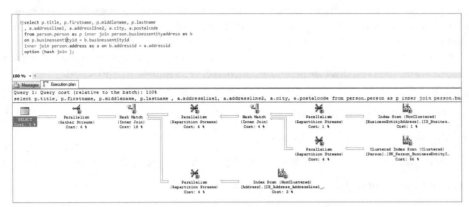

FIGURE 5-6

You can also include SET statements with your query to enable several options that provide additional output displaying the query plan for you. These options are SHOWPLAN_TEXT and SHOWPLAN_ALL. The following code example demonstrates how to use these options:

```
Use AdventureWorks2012
go
set showplan_text on
go
select * from person.person
go
set showplan_text off
go
```

Following are the two result sets returned by this query. Note that this is the output after setting the query result options to *results to text*, rather than *results to grid*:

```
StmtText

select * from person.person

(1 row(s) affected)

StmtText
   |--Clustered Index Scan(OBJECT:([AdventureWorks2012].[Person].[Person]
.[PK_Person_BusinessEntityID]))

(1 row(s) affected)
Use AdventureWorks2012
go
set showplan_all on
go
select * from person.person
go
```

```
set showplan_all off
go
```

Some of the output columns from this query are shown in Figure 5-7.

FIGURE 5-7

You can also use SHOWPLAN_XML to get the plan in an XML format:

```
Use AdventureWorks2012
go
set showplan_xml on
go
select * from person.person
go
set showplan_xml off
go
```

The results from the preceding query are shown in Figure 5-8.

Clicking on the XML will display the graphical execution plan shown in Figure 5-9.

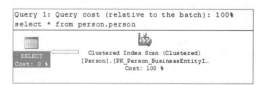

FIGURE 5-8

Another option is STATISTICS PROFILE. This is the first option to be discussed that executes the query, and returns a real plan. The previous options don't execute the query, they just return an estimated plan. Enabling this option adds statistical information to the showplan. This consists of the actual row count and the number of times each operator was run when the query was executed:

```
Query 1: Query cost (relative to the batch): 100%
select * from person.person
```

SELECT
Cost: 0 %

Clustered Index Scan (Clustered)
[Person].[PK_Person_BusinessEntityI...
Cost: 100 %

FIGURE 5-9

```
Use AdventureWorks2012
go
set statistics profile on
go
select * from person.person
go
set statistics profile off
go
```

Some of the columns' output from this query is shown in Figure 5-10.

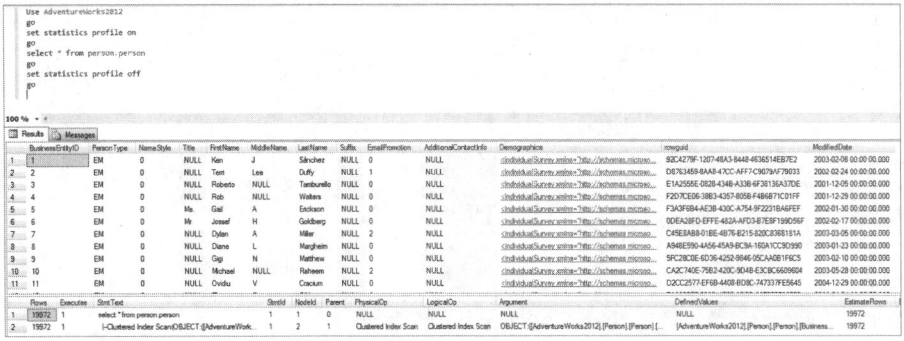

FIGURE 5-10

Another place to look for query plans is in the plan cache itself. When dealing with a lot of queries on a busy production system, it's often necessary to find the query plan for a particular query that's currently being used. To do this, use the following T-SQL to return either the XML for the plan or the text of the plan:

```
Select *
From sys.dm_exec_query_plan(plan_handle)

Select *
From sys.dm_exec_text_query_plan(plan_handle)
```

Note that you can use two DMFs here: One refers to returning the XML plan; whereas the name of the other implies it will return the text of the plan, suggesting it would be similar to the showplan_text output; but, in fact, both return the XML format of the plan. The difference is that the data type of the query_plan column in one is XML, whereas the data type in the other result set is text.

Query Plan Operators

The Query Optimizer can use many different operators to create your plan. Covering them all is beyond the scope of this book, so this section instead focuses on some examples demonstrating the most common operators you will come across. For a full list of operators, refer to SQL Server Books Online (SQL BOL). Search for the topic "Showplan Logical and Physical Operators Reference."

Join Operators

Join operators enable SQL Server to find matching rows between two tables. Prior to SQL Server 2005, there was only a single join type, the *nested loop join*, but since then additional join types have been added, and SQL Server now provides the three join types described in Table 5-1. These join types handle rows from two tables; for a self-join, the inputs may be different sets of rows from the same table.

TABLE 5-1: SQL Server Join Types

JOIN TYPE	BENEFIT
Nested loop	Good for small tables where there is an index on the inner table on the join key
Merge join	Good for medium-size tables where there are ordered indexes, or where the output needs to be ordered
Hash join	Good for medium to large tables. Works well with parallel plans, and scales well.

Nested Loop

The nested loop join is the original SQL Server join type. The behavior of a nested loop is to scan all the rows in one table (the outer table) and for each row in that table, it then scans every row in the other table (the inner table). If the rows in the outer and inner tables match, then the row is included in the results.

The performance of this join is directly proportional to the number of rows in each table. It performs well when there are relatively few rows in one of the tables, which would be chosen as the inner table, and more rows in the other table, which would be used as the outer table. If both tables have a relatively large number of rows, then this join starts to take a very long time.

Merge

The merge join needs its inputs to be sorted, so ideally the tables should be indexed on the join column. Then the operator iterates through rows from both tables at the same time, working down the rows, looking for matches. Because the inputs are ordered, this enables the join to proceed quickly, and to end as soon as any range is satisfied.

Hash

The hash join operates in two phases. During the first phase, known as the *build phase*, the smaller of the two tables is scanned and the rows are placed into a hash table that is ideally stored in memory; but for very large tables, it can be written to disk. When every row in the build input table is hashed, the second phase starts. During the second phase, known as the *probe phase*, rows from the larger of the two tables are compared to the contents of the hash table, using the same hashing algorithm that was used to create the build table hash. Any matching rows are passed to the output.

The hash join has variations on this processing that can deal with very large tables, so the hash join is the join of choice for very large input tables, especially when running on multiprocessor systems where parallel plans are allowed.

HASH WARNINGS

Hash warnings are SQL Profiler events that are generated when hash recursion, or hash bailout, occurs. Hash recursion happens when the output from the `hash` operation doesn't fit entirely in memory. Hash bailout occurs when hash recursion reaches its maximum level of recursion, and a new plan has to be chosen.

continues

continued

Anytime you see hash warnings, it is a potential indicator of performance problems and should be investigated.

Possible solutions to hash warnings include the following:

➤ Increase memory on the server.

➤ Make sure statistics exist on the join columns.

➤ Make sure statistics are current.

➤ Force a different type of join.

Spool Operators

The various spool operators are used to create a temporary copy of rows from the input stream and deliver them to the output stream. Spools typically sit between two other operators: The one on the right is the child, and provides the input stream. The operator on the left is the parent, and consumes the output stream.

The following list provides a brief description of each of the physical spool operators. These are the operators that actually execute. You may also see references to *logical operators*, which represent an earlier stage in the optimization process; these are subsequently converted to physical operators before executing the plan. The logical spool operators are Eager Spool, and Lazy Spool.

➤ **Index spool** — This operator reads rows from the child table, places them in tempdb, and creates a nonclustered index on them before continuing. This enables the parent to take advantage of seeking against the nonclustered index on the data in tempdb when the underlying table has no applicable indexes.

➤ **Row count spool** — This operator reads rows from the child table and counts the rows. The rows are also returned to the parent, but without any data. This enables the parent to determine whether rows exist in order to satisfy an EXISTS or NOT EXISTS requirement.

➤ **Table spool** — This operator reads the rows from the child table and writes them into tempdb. All rows from the child are read and placed in tempdb before the parent can start processing rows.

➤ **Window spool** — This operator expands each row into the set of rows that represent the window associated with it. It's both a physical and logical operator.

Scan and Seek Operators

These operators enable SQL Server to retrieve rows from tables and indexes when a larger number of rows is required. This behavior contrasts with the individual row access operators *key lookup* and *RID lookup*, which are discussed in the next section.

➤ **Scan operator** — The scan operator scans all the rows in the table looking for matching rows. When the number of matching rows is >20 percent of the table, scan can start to outperform seek due to the additional cost of traversing the index to reach each row for the seek.

There are scan operator variants for a clustered index scan, a nonclustered index scan, and a table scan.

➤ **Seek operator** — The seek operator uses the index to find matching rows; this can be either a single value, a small set of values, or a range of values. When the query needs only a relatively small set of rows, seek is significantly faster than scan to find matching rows. However, when the number of rows returned exceeds 20 percent of the table, the cost of seek will approach that of scan; and when nearly the whole table is required, scan will perform better than seek.

There are seek operator variants for a clustered index seek and a nonclustered index seek.

Lookup Operators

Lookup operators perform the task of finding a single row of data. The following is a list of common operators:

➤ **Bookmark lookup** — Bookmark lookup is seen only in SQL Server 2000 and earlier. It's the way that SQL Server looks up a row using a clustered index. In SQL Server 2012 this is done using either Clustered Index Seek, RID lookup, or Key Lookup.

➤ **Key lookup** — Key lookup is how a single row is returned when the table has a clustered index. In contrast with dealing with a heap, the lookup is done using the clustering key. The key lookup operator was added in SQL Server 2005 SP2. Prior to this, and currently when viewing the plan in text or XML format, the operator is shown as a clustered index seek with the keyword lookup.

➤ **RID lookup** — RID lookup is how a single row is looked up in a heap. RID refers to the internal unique *row id*entifier (hence RID), which is used to look up the row.

Reading Query Plans

Unlike reading a typical book such as this one, whereby reading is done from top left to bottom right (unless you're reading a translation for which the language is read in reverse), query plans in all forms are read bottom right to top left.

Once you have downloaded and installed the sample database, to make the examples more interesting you need to remove some of the indexes that the authors of AdventureWorks added for you. To do this, you can use either your favorite T-SQL scripting tool or the SSMS scripting features, or run the `AW2012_person_drop_indexes.sql` sample script (available on the book's website in the Chapter 5 Samples folder, which also contains a script to recreate the indexes if you want to return the AdventureWorks2012 database to its original structure). This script drops all the indexes on the `person.person` table except for the primary key constraint.

After you have done this, you can follow along with the examples, and you should see the same results.

> **NOTE** *Because you are looking at the inner workings of the Query Optimizer, and because this is a feature of SQL Server that is constantly evolving, installing any service pack or patch can alter the behavior of the Query Optimizer, and therefore display different results.*

You will begin by looking at some trivial query plans, starting with a view of the graphical plans but quickly switching to using the text plan features, as these are easier to compare against one another, especially when you start looking at larger plans from more complex queries.

Here is the first trivial query to examine:

```
select firstname, COUNT (*)
from Person.Person
group by firstname
order by COUNT (*) desc
```

After running this in SSMS after enabling the Include Actual Execution Plan option, which is shown in Figure 5-11, three tabs are displayed. The first is Results, but the one you are interested in now is the third tab, which shows the graphical execution plan for this query.

You should see something like the image shown in Figure 5-12.

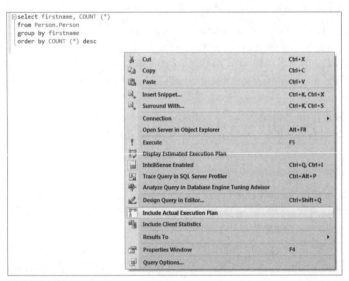

FIGURE 5-11

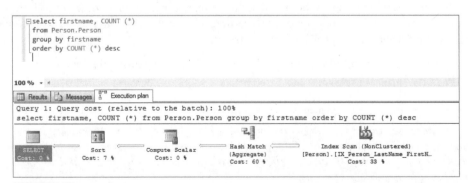

FIGURE 5-12

Starting at the bottom right, you can see that the first operator is the clustered index scan operator. While the query doesn't need, or get any benefit from, a clustered index, because the table has a clustered index and is not a heap, this is the option that SQL Server chooses to read through all the rows in the table. If you had removed the clustered index, so that this table was a heap, then this operator would be replaced by a table scan operator. The action performed by both operators in this case is identical, which is to read every row from the table and deliver them to the next operator.

The next operator is the hash match. In this case, SQL Server is using this to sort the rows into buckets by first name. After the hash match is the compute scalar, whereby SQL Server counts the number of rows in each hash bucket, which gives you the count (*) value in the results. This is followed by the sort operator, which is there to provide the ordered output needed from the T-SQL.

You can find additional information on each operation by hovering over the operator. Figure 5-13 shows the additional information available on the non-clustered index scan operator.

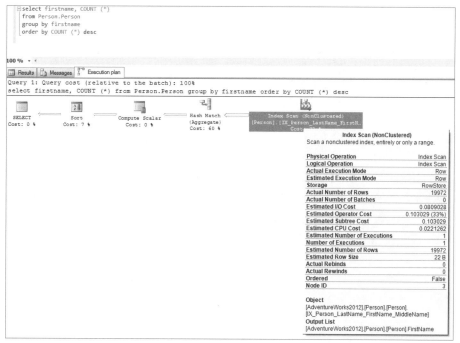

FIGURE 5-13

While this query seems pretty trivial, and you may have assumed it would generate a trivial plan because of the grouping and ordering, this is not a trivial plan. You can tell this by monitoring the results of the following query before and after running it:

```
select *
from sys.dm_exec_query_optimizer_info
where counter in (
'optimizations'
```

```
,  'trivial plan'
,  'search 0'
,  'search 1'
,  'search 2'
)
order by [counter]
```

Once the query has been optimized and cached, subsequent runs will not generate any updates to the Query Optimizer stats unless you flush the procedure cache using `dbcc freeproccache`.

On the machine I am using, the following results were returned from this query against the Query Optimizer information before I ran the sample query:

COUNTER	OCCURRENCE	VALUE
optimizations	10059	1
search 0	1017	1
search 1	3385	1
search 2	1	1
trivial plan	5656	1

Here are the results after I ran the sample query:

COUNTER	OCCURRENCE	VALUE
optimizations	10061	1
search 0	1017	1
search 1	3387	1
search 2	1	1
trivial plan	5656	1

From this you can see that the trivial plan count didn't increment, but the search 1 count did increment, indicating that this query needed to move onto phase 1 of the optimization process before an acceptable plan was found.

If you want to play around with this query to see what a truly trivial plan would be, try running the following:

```
select lastname
from person.person
```

The following T-SQL demonstrates what the same plan looks like in text mode:

```
set statistics profile on
go

select firstname, COUNT (*)
from Person.Person
group by firstname
order by 2 desc
go

set statistics profile off
go
```

When you run this batch, rather than see a third tab displayed in SSMS, you will see that there are now two result sets in the query's Results tab. The first is the output from running the query, and the second is the text output for this plan, which looks something like what is shown in Figure 5-14.

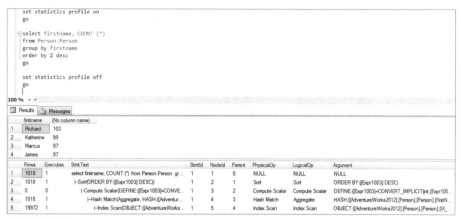

FIGURE 5-14

The following example shows some of the content of the StmtText column, which illustrates what the query plan looks like, just as in the graphical plan but this time in a textual format:

```
|--Sort(ORDER BY:([Expr1003] DESC))
     |--Compute Scalar(DEFINE:([Expr1003 ...
          |--Hash Match(Aggregate, ...
               |--Index Scan(OBJECT:( ...
```

As mentioned before, this is read from the bottom up. You can see that the first operator is the clustered index scan, which is the same operator shown in Figure 5-6. From there (working up), the next operator is the hash match, followed by the compute scalar operator, and then the sort operator.

While the query you examined may seem pretty simple, you have noticed that even for this query, the Query Optimizer has quite a bit of work to do. As a follow-up exercise, try adding one index at a time back into the `Person` table, and examine the plan you get each time a new index is added. One hint as to what you will see is to add the index `IX_Person_Lastname_firstname_middlename` first.

From there you can start to explore with simple table joins, and look into when SQL Server chooses each of the three join operators it offers: nested loop, merge, and hash joins.

EXECUTING YOUR QUERIES

So far in this chapter, you have learned how SQL Server parses, algebrizes, and optimizes the T-SQL you want to run. This section describes how SQL Server executes the query plan. First, however, it is useful to step back a little and look at the larger picture — namely, how the SQL Server architecture changed with SQL Server 2005 and the introduction of SQLOS.

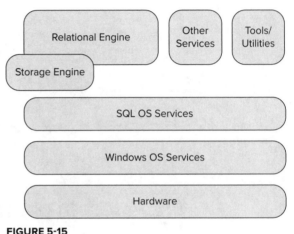

SQLOS

SQL Server 2005 underwent a major change in the underlying architecture with the introduction of SQLOS. This component provides basic services to the other SQL Server components, such as the Relational

FIGURE 5-15

Engine and the Storage Engine. This architecture is illustrated in the diagram shown in Figure 5-15.

The main services provided by SQLOS are scheduling, which is where our main interest lies; and memory management, which we also have an interest in because the memory management services are where the procedure cache lives, and that's where your query plans live. SQLOS also provides many more services that are not relevant to the current discussion. For more details on the other services provided by SQLOS, refer to Chapter 1 or SQL Server Books Online.

SQLOS implements a hierarchy of system objects that provide the framework for scheduling. Figure 5-16 shows the basic hierarchy of these objects — from the parent node, SQLOS, down to the workers, tasks, and OS threads where the work is actually performed.

The starting point for scheduling and memory allocation is the memory node.

Memory Nodes

The SQLOS memory node is a logical container for memory associated with a node, which is a collection of CPUs with shared memory. This can be either a "real" memory node, if the server has a NUMA architecture, or an artificial

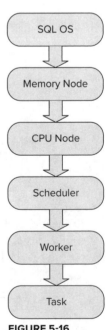

FIGURE 5-16

grouping that you created as a "soft" NUMA configuration. You'll find more details on NUMA in Chapter 3.

Along with the memory nodes created to model the physical hardware of the server, there is always one additional memory node used by the dedicated administrator connection (DAC). This ensures that some resources are always available to service the DAC, even when all other system resources are being used.

On an eight-processor SMP system without soft NUMA, there is one memory node for general server use, and one for the DAC. This is illustrated in Figure 5-17.

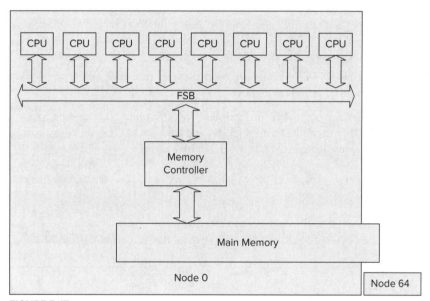

FIGURE 5-17

On an eight-processor NUMA system with two nodes of four cores, there would be two memory nodes for general use, and a third for the DAC. This is illustrated in Figure 5-18.

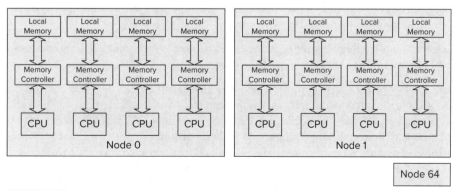

FIGURE 5-18

By querying the DMV sys.dm_os_memory_nodes, you can view the layout of memory nodes on your server. However, it makes more sense to include the node_state_desc column from sys.dm_os_nodes using this query. Note the join between node_id in sys.dm_os_nodes and memory_node_id in sys.dm_os_memory_nodes:

```
select c.node_id, c.memory_node_id, m.memory_node_id, c.node_state_desc
, c.cpu_affinity_mask, m.virtual_address_space_reserved_kb
from sys.dm_os_nodes as c inner join sys.dm_os_memory_nodes as m
on c.node_id = m.memory_node_id
```

Here is the output from the preceding query when run on a 16-way SMP server:

NODE_ID	MEMORY_NODE_ID	MEMORY_NODE_ID	NODE_STATE_DESC	CPU_AFFINITY_MASK	VIRTUAL_ADDRESS_SPACE_RESERVED_KB
0	0	0	ONLINE	65535	67544440
64	0	64	ONLINE DAC	0	2560

In this case, Node 0 has nearly all the 64GB of memory on this server reserved, and Node 64 is reserved for the DAC, which has just 2.5MB of memory reserved.

Following is the output from this query on a 192-processor NUMA system. The server is structured as eight NUMA nodes. Each NUMA node has four sockets, and each socket has six cores (using Intel Xeon hexa-core processors), resulting in 24 cores per NUMA node:

NODE_ID	MEMORY_NODE_ID	MEMORY_NODE_ID	NODE_STATE_DESC	CPU_AFFINITY_MASK	VIRTUAL_ADDRESS_SPACE_RESERVED_KB
0	0	0	ONLINE	16777215	268416
1	1	1	ONLINE	16777215	248827056
2	2	2	ONLINE	16777215	22464
3	3	3	ONLINE	16777215	8256
4	4	4	ONLINE	281474959933440	11136
5	5	5	ONLINE	281474959933440	4672
6	6	6	ONLINE	281474959933440	4672
7	7	7	ONLINE	281474959933440	5120
64	0	64	ONLINE DAC	0	2864

Soft NUMA

In some scenarios, you may be able to work with an SMP server and still get the benefit of having a NUMA-type structure with SQL Server. You can achieve this by using *soft NUMA*. This enables you to use Registry settings to tell SQL Server that it should configure itself as a NUMA system, using the CPU-to-memory-node mapping that you specify.

As with anything that requires Registry changes, you need to take exceptional care, and be sure you have backup and rollback options at every step of the process.

One common use for soft NUMA is when a SQL Server is hosting an application that has several different groups of users with very different query requirements. After configuring your theoretical 16-processor server for soft NUMA, assigning 2 NUMA nodes with 4 CPUs , and one 8-CPU node to a third NUMA node, you would next configure connection affinity for the three nodes to different ports, and then change the connection settings for each class of workload, so that workload A is "affinitized" to port x, which connects to the first NUMA node; workload B is affinitized to port y, which connects to the second NUMA node; and all other workloads are affinitized to port z, which is set to connect to the third NUMA node.

CPU Nodes

A CPU node is a logical collection of CPUs that share some common resource, such as a cache or memory. CPU nodes live below memory nodes in the SQLOS object hierarchy.

Whereas a memory node may have one or more CPU nodes associated with it, a CPU node can be associated with only a single memory node. However, in practice, nearly all configurations have a 1:1 relationship between memory nodes and CPU nodes.

CPU nodes can be seen in the DMV `sys.dm_os_nodes`. Use the following query to return select columns from this DMV:

```
select node_id, node_state_desc, memory_node_id, cpu_affinity_mask
from sys.dm_os_nodes
```

The results from this query, when run on a single-CPU system are as follows:

NODE_ID	NODE_STATE_DESC	MEMORY_NODE_ID	CPU_AFFINITY_MASK
0	ONLINE	0	1
32	ONLINE DAC	0	0

The results from the previous query, when run on a 96-processor NUMA system, comprising four nodes of four sockets, each socket with six cores, totaling 24 cores per NUMA node, and 96 cores across the whole server, are as follows:

NODE_ID	NODE_STATE_DESC	MEMORY_NODE_ID	CPU_AFFINITY_MASK
0	ONLINE	1	16777215
1	ONLINE	0	281474959933440
2	ONLINE	2	16777215
3	ONLINE	3	281474959933440
64	ONLINE DAC	0	16777215

> **NOTE** *The hex values for the* `cpu_affinity_mask` *values in this table are as follows:*
>
> ```
> 16777215 = 0x00FFFFFF
> 281474959933440 = 0x0F000001000000FFFFFF0000
> ```
>
> This indicates which processor cores each CPU node can use.

Processor Affinity

CPU affinity is a way to force a workload to use specific CPUs. It's another way that you can affect scheduling and SQL Server SQLOS configuration.

CPU affinity can be managed at several levels. Outside SQL Server, you can use the operating system's CPU affinity settings to restrict the CPUs that SQL Server as a process can use. Within SQL

Server's configuration settings, you can specify that SQL Server should use only certain CPUs. This is done using the *affinity mask* and *affinity64 mask* configuration options. Changes to these two options are applied dynamically, which means that schedulers on CPUs that are either enabled or disabled while SQL is running will be affected immediately. Schedulers associated with CPUs that are disabled will be drained and set to offline. Schedulers associated with CPUs that are enabled will be set to online, and will be available for scheduling workers and executing new tasks.

You can also set SQL Server I/O affinity using the affinity I/O mask option. This option enables you to force any I/O-related activities to run only on a specified set of CPUs. Using connection affinity as described earlier in the section "Soft NUMA," you can affinitize network connections to a specific memory node.

Schedulers

The scheduler node is where the work of scheduling activity occurs. Scheduling occurs against *tasks*, which are the requests to do some work handled by the scheduler. One task may be the optimized query plan that represents the T-SQL you want to execute; or, in the case of a batch with multiple T-SQL statements, the task would represent a single optimized query from within the larger batch.

When SQL Server starts up, it creates one scheduler for each CPU that it finds on the server, and some additional schedulers to run other system tasks. If processor affinity is set such that some CPUs are not enabled for this instance, then the schedulers associated with those CPUs will be set to a disabled state. This enables SQL Server to support dynamic affinity settings.

While there is one scheduler per CPU, schedulers are not bound to a specific CPU, except in the case where CPU affinity has been set.

Each scheduler is identified by its own unique scheduler_id. Values from 0–254 are reserved for schedulers running user requests. Scheduler_id 255 is reserved for the scheduler for the dedicated administrator connection (DAC). Schedulers with a scheduler_id > 255 are reserved for system use and are typically assigned the same task.

The following code sample shows select columns from the DMV sys.dm_os_schedulers:

```
select parent_node_id, scheduler_id, cpu_id, status, scheduler_address
from sys.dm_os_schedulers
order by scheduler_id
```

The following results from the preceding query indicate that scheduler_id 0 is the only scheduler with an id < 255, which implies that these results came from a single-core machine. You can also see a scheduler with an ID of 255, which has a status of VISIBLE ONLINE (DAC), indicating that this is the scheduler for the DAC. Also shown are three additional schedulers with IDs > 255. These are the schedulers reserved for system use.

```
PARENT_NODE_ID SCHEDULER_ID CPU_ID STATUS              SCHEDULER_ADDRESS
0              0            0      VISIBLE ONLINE       0x00480040
32             255          0      VISIBLE ONLINE (DAC) 0x03792040
0              257          0      HIDDEN ONLINE        0x006A4040
0              258          0      HIDDEN ONLINE        0x64260040
0              259          0      HIDDEN ONLINE        0x642F0040
```

Tasks

A task is a request to do some unit of work. The task itself doesn't do anything, as it's just a container for the unit of work to be done. To actually do something, the task has to be scheduled by one of the schedulers, and associated with a particular worker. It's the worker that actually does something, and you will learn about workers in the next section.

Tasks can be seen using the DMV sys.dm_os_tasks. The following example shows a query of this DMV:

```
Select *
from sys.dm_os_tasks
```

The task is the container for the work that's being done, but if you look into sys.dm_os_tasks, there is no indication of exactly what work that is. Figuring out what each task is doing takes a little more digging. First, dig out the request_id. This is the key into the DMV sys.dm_exec_requests. Within sys.dm_exec_requests you will find some familiar fields — namely, sql_handle, along with statement_start_offset, statement_end_offset, and plan_handle. You can take either sql_handle or plan_handle and feed them into sys.dm_exec_sql_text (plan_handle | sql_handle) and get back the original T-SQL that is being executed:

```
Select t.task_address, s.text
From sys.dm_os_tasks as t inner join sys.dm_exec_requests as r
on t.task_address = r.task_address
Cross apply sys.dm_exec_sql_text (r.plan_handle) as s
where r.plan_handle is not null
```

Workers

A worker is where the work is actually done, and the work it does is contained within the task. Workers can be seen using the DMV sys.dm_os_workers:

```
Select *
From sys.dm_os_workers
```

Some of the more interesting columns in this DMV are as follows:

➤ **Task_address** — Enables you to join back to the task, and from there back to the actual request, and get the text that is being executed

➤ **State** — Shows the current state of the worker

➤ **Last_wait_type** — Shows the last wait type that this worker was waiting on

➤ **Scheduler_address** — Joins back to sys.dm_os_schedulers

Threads

To complete the picture, SQLOS also contains objects for the operating system threads it is using. OS threads can be seen in the DMV sys.dm_os_threads:

```
Select *
From sys.dm_os_threads
```

Interesting columns in this DMV include the following:

➤ **Scheduler_address** — Address of the scheduler with which the thread is associated

➤ **Worker_address** — Address of the worker currently associated with the thread

➤ **Kernel_time** — Amount of kernel time that the thread has used since it was started

➤ **Usermode_time** — Amount of user time that the thread has used since it was started

Scheduling

Now that you have seen all the objects that SQLOS uses to manage scheduling, and understand how to examine what's going on within these structures, it's time to look at how SQL OS actually schedules work.

One of the main things to understand about scheduling within SQL Server is that it uses a non-preemptive scheduling model, unless the task being run is not SQL Server code. In that case, SQL Server marks the task to indicate that it needs to be scheduled preemptively. An example of code that might be marked to be scheduled preemptively would be any code that wasn't written by SQL Server that is run inside the SQL Server process, so this would apply to any CLR code.

> ### PREEMPTIVE VS. NONPREEMPTIVE SCHEDULING
>
> With preemptive scheduling, the scheduling code manages how long the code can run before interrupting it, giving some other task a chance to run.
>
> The advantage of preemptive scheduling is that the developer doesn't need to think about yielding; the scheduler takes care of it. The disadvantage is that the code can be interrupted and prevented from running at any arbitrary point, which may result in the task running more slowly than possible. In addition, providing an environment that offers preemptive scheduling features requires a lot of work.
>
> With nonpreemptive scheduling, the code that's being run is written to yield control at key points. At these yield points, the scheduler can determine whether a different task should be run.
>
> The advantage of nonpreemptive scheduling is that the code running can best determine when it should be interrupted. The disadvantage is that if the developer doesn't yield at the appropriate points, then the task may run for an excessive amount of time, retaining control of a CPU when it's waiting. In this case, the task blocks other tasks from running, wasting CPU resources.

SQL Server begins to schedule a task when a new request is received, after the Query Optimizer has completed its work to find the best plan. A task object is created for this user request, and the scheduling starts from there.

The newly created task object has to be associated with a free worker in order to actually do anything. When the worker is associated with the new task, the worker's status is set to *init*. When the initial setup has been done, the status changes to *runnable*. At this point, the worker is ready to go but there is no free scheduler to allow this worker to run. The worker state remains as runnable until a scheduler is available. When the scheduler is available, the worker is associated with that scheduler, and the status changes to *running*. It remains running until either it is done or it releases control while it waits for something to be done. When it releases control of the scheduler, its state moves to *suspended* (the reason it released control is logged as a wait_type. When the item it was waiting on is available again, the status of the worker is changed to runnable. Now it's back to waiting for a free scheduler again, and the cycle repeats until the task is complete.

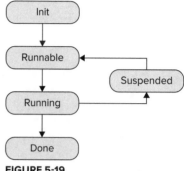

FIGURE 5-19

At that point, the task is released, the worker is released, and the scheduler is available to be associated with the next worker that needs to run. The state diagram for scheduling workers is shown in Figure 5-19.

SUMMARY

This chapter introduced you to the process of query execution, including the optimization process and some of the operators used by the Query Optimizer. Then you took a look at query plans, including the different ways that you can examine them, and how to read them. Finally, you learned about the objects that SQLOS uses to manage scheduling, and how scheduling works.

Some key points you should take away from this chapter include the following:

➤ SQL Server uses cost-based optimization to find what it thinks is a good enough plan. This won't always be the best plan.

➤ Statistics are a vital part of the optimization process.

➤ Many factors influence how SQL Server chooses a query plan.

➤ You can alter the plan chosen using a variety of plan hints and other configuration settings.

Locking and Concurrency

WHAT'S IN THIS CHAPTER?

➤ ACID: the properties of transactions worth protecting

➤ Avoiding concurrency dangers with locks

➤ Lock resources and modes

➤ A look at how lock escalation works

➤ A brief description of deadlocks

➤ Understanding how isolation levels affect locking behavior

WROX.COM CODE DOWNLOADS FOR THIS CHAPTER

The wrox.com code downloads for this chapter are found at www.wrox.com/remtitle .cgi?isbn=1118177657 on the Download Code tab. The code is in the Chapter 6 download and individually named according to the names within the chapter.

OVERVIEW

Tommy Cooper, the late great comic magician, did a trick in which he put two handkerchiefs, one white and one blue, into a bag. He said a magic word, pulled them out again, and then stated that the white one had turned blue, and the blue one had turned white. It's an excellent trick, though perhaps misunderstood, because the audience gets the impression that no change has occurred at all, and that he is simply pretending that the colors have swapped.

All joking aside, when you put something into a database, you have a certain level of expectation. You want to be assured that any data that has been entered can be retrieved in the same state, notwithstanding another process coming along and explicitly changing or deleting it.

You don't want any magic to wreak havoc while you're looking the other way. In short, you want your transaction to be protected.

This is a challenge that transactional database vendors have, which is investigated both in this chapter and in Chapter 7. It's something that database users (and by "users" I include database administrators, database developers, database architects and designers — anyone who uses a database in any way) take for granted. Having become so accustomed to the way that a database works, various things are now simply expected, just as you expect a letter to appear when you press a key on your computer keyboard, oblivious to the complex programming by software developers that makes it possible. When writing programs using very low-level languages, developers still need to consider those types of things, but for all the other developers, there is a lot that can be taken for granted.

Nonetheless, the concepts used to protect your data should be understood. After all, you need to allow many processes to access your databases at once, and therefore need to appreciate the difference between having some "magic" occur that has unexpected results, and controlling the behavior that occurs when multiple processes want to act on the same pieces of data. Nothing should give a database user the impression of magic, and the power of concurrency — coordinating multiple processes — should be appreciated and leveraged.

Protecting data from unexpected results is achieved through a system of locks and latches. Latches, which protect memory, are explained further in Chapter 7. This chapter is dedicated to locks, and how you can use them to provide a level of protection to the transactions in your system. You will look at what they are designed to preserve, how they do it, and the various options available for consideration. You will also look at the plusses and minuses of locking, and see how locks can be leveraged for your benefit. The point of this scrutiny is to enable as many processes as possible accessing the data.

Scalability continues to drive computing technology; and as your systems demand increasingly heavy workloads, locks become increasingly important also.

TRANSACTIONS

Just to ensure that we're all on the same page, let's quickly review what we're talking about when we discuss transactions. The most common analogy used to understand database transactions is the bank transaction. Beginning with the deposit, suppose you take $50 to the counter, resulting in a credit transaction in that amount to your account. When you look at your account statement when it arrives, you expect the transaction record to reflect that you deposited $50, not $48 or $52, depending on any fees or charges that might apply. This expectation actually stems from four aspects of transactions that have been identified by experts and that should be protected: atomicity, consistency, isolation, and durability, which form the neat acronym ACID. The following sections first examine these in the context of the bank transaction, and then you will revisit them in the context of your database.

A Is for Atomic

Atomic means indivisible — in this case, a collection of events being treated as a single unit. When you take your money to the bank and deposit it, you expect the transaction to be completed successfully. That is, you don't expect the teller to accept your money and then go to lunch, forgetting to credit your account. That kind of behavior would obviously ruin a bank; and when we revisit atomicity in the context of the database, you'll see that it would also ruin a database.

C Is for Consistent

Consistent means that everything is in agreement — in this case, the amount deposited is the amount credited. If you access a list of your recent transactions, the $50 that you deposited on Monday must be recorded as $50 on Monday, not $48 on Monday, not $52 on Tuesday, or any other combination of incorrect data. In other words, it is imperative that your records match the bank's records. Although you may feel personally slighted or ignored at the bank, or the teller may not remember you between visits, you need to feel confident that the bank can successfully process your transactions such that they are completed in a consistent manner.

I Is for Isolated

Banks understand discretion. If you are going through your dealings with a teller, you don't expect someone to be listening to the conversation and potentially making decisions based on what's going on. Isolation is the protection provided around the visibility of what's going on during each stage of the transaction, and extends out to whether your transaction can be affected by anything else that might be going on at the same time. Importantly, there are different levels of isolation that can be chosen.

For example, if your spouse is in another branch making a separate transaction, you might be okay with that branch seeing some information about your transaction part way through it, but you almost certainly wouldn't want to see a bank statement issued that only gave half the story.

D Is for Durable

Durability reflects the fact that your bank transaction cannot be accidentally deleted or otherwise compromised. After you deposit your money and receive a receipt, you are assured that your money is safe and available to you. Even in the event of system failure, the record of the fact that you deposited money should persist, no matter what happens next.

DATABASE TRANSACTIONS

Having looked at the ACID principles in the context of a bank transaction in the preceding section, this section examines how these four principles relate to your database environment, which you need to protect with just as much care as the bank affords to your monetary transactions.

Atomicity

When you make a change in the database that involves multiple operations, such as modifying two separate tables, if you have identified these operations as a single transaction, then you expect an all-or-nothing result — that is, the change is completely atomic. Recall from the bank analogy that depositing $50 must result in an additional $50 in your account. If the bank's server freezes or the teller's terminal stops working, then you expect your personal data to remain unchanged. In a database, locks help to achieve this, by ensuring that a transaction has exclusive access to anything that is being changed, so that it is either committed or rolled back completely. Anything short of that would break this very basic property of transactions.

Consistency

Databases enforce logic in many different ways. When a change is attempted, it can't be allowed to occur until the system is satisfied that no rules are going to be broken. For example, suppose you remove a value from a table but there are foreign keys referring to that column. The system must verify that these kinds of associations are handled before it can agree to that change; but in order to perform those checks and potentially roll them back if something has gone wrong, locks are needed. For another example, it should be impossible to delete a row while something else is being inserted in another table that relies on it.

Isolation

When the database engine inserts values into a table, nothing else should be able to change those values at the same time. Similarly, if the database engine needs to roll back to a previous state, nothing else should have affected that state or left it indeterminate. In other words, each action must happen in isolation from all others.

In terms of what other users see when they look at a transaction, or the data that is being considered, that's the domain of the isolation level, which is examined in much more detail later in this chapter. This concept of isolation is very important to understand, as you can exercise a lot of control over the environment.

Durability

Even if a failure occurs a split-second after your transaction has taken place, you need to be sure that the transaction has been persisted in the database. This is achieved through one of the most significant aspects of SQL Server — the behavior of the transaction log.

Most experienced database administrators have had to salvage MDF files, where the databases' data is stored, from a failed server, only to find that the MDF files alone do not provide enough information to recover the databases completely. Ideally, this situation prompts the DBA to learn why, after which they understand that MDF files without the accompanying LDF files (the transaction log) do not reflect the whole story.

That's because the transaction log is not like many of the other logs on a Windows server, such as the Windows Event Log. Those logs record information about what's going on, but only in order to provide a report of what has happened — typically for troubleshooting purposes. The SQL Server transaction log is much more than this.

When a transaction takes place, it is recorded in the transaction log. Everything that the transaction is doing is recorded there, while the changes to the actual data are occurring in memory. Once the transaction is complete and a commit command is sent, the changes are hardened, which is done in the transaction log. Locks are released at this point (as shown later in this chapter), but the record of the transaction appears in the transaction log files, rather than the data files. The data files are updated later. For the time being, the change exists in memory (where processes can access the updated data) and in the transaction log. Changes to the data files happen shortly afterward, when a separate CHECKPOINT operation takes place. Until then, the MDF files do not contain the current version of the database — for that, the MDF and LDF files are both needed.

Therefore, the durability of a transaction is provided by the existence and preservation of the database's transaction log. Database administrators protect their transaction logs above anything else; because in the event of a failure, the transaction log is the only record of the latest database changes.

For a minimally logged operation, the behavior is slightly different, and the transaction log contains only sufficient information to be able to commit or rollback the transaction fully; but the transaction log still performs a vital role in ensuring that transactions are durable.

THE DANGERS OF CONCURRENCY

Before tackling the subject of locks, it is important to understand concurrency. Database concurrency ensures that when multiple operations are occurring at once, the final result is still in agreement — that they concur. This agreement typically depends on a set of rules and constraints that coordinate the behaviors of transactions, making sure that different operations will play nicely together.

Having considered the attributes of your transactions that you need to protect, the following sections consider the types of things that can happen if you let transactions have a free-for-all environment — one where all the different transactions don't regard each other's boundaries, where isolation is completely ignored. Later, you'll look at the various isolation levels in more detail, but in this section if you look closely you'll often see the isolation level is set in the scripts.

The problems described next only occur when multiple sessions are occurring at once in your database. This is typical behavior, I'm sure, but it's worth noting that in a single-session environment, these problems won't happen.

Lost Updates

A lost update occurs when two processes read the same data and then try to update the data with a different value. Consider a scenario in which you and your partner have the romantic notion of a joint bank account. On pay day, your respective employers both deposit your salaries into the joint account. To perform the update, each process reads the data. At the time of the payments, all is well in the world and you have an outstanding balance of $10,000. Each process therefore reads $10,000 as its starting point. Your employer attempts to update the $10,000 figure with your monthly salary of $2,000, but at the same time your partner's employer updates the sum with his or her salary of $4,000. Your partner's salary is added just before yours, updating the $10,000 balance to $14,000. Your payment then runs and updates the $10,000 balance to $12,000. A look at the ATM shows $12,000. The first update has been lost, and even worse, it represented the bigger update!

This situation is one that the SQL Server platform handles automatically, regardless of the isolation level. However, database developers can introduce this behavior themselves by performing an update in two steps, rather than one. Consider this example (code file Ch6LostUpdates.sql):

```
/* SESSION 1*/
USE AdventureWorks2012;

DECLARE @SafetyStockLevel    int = 0
        ,@Uplift             int = 5;

BEGIN TRAN;
SELECT   @SafetyStockLevel = SafetyStockLevel
FROM     Production.Product
WHERE    ProductID = 1;

SET      @SafetyStockLevel = @SafetyStockLevel + @Uplift;

WAITFOR DELAY '00:00:05.000';

UPDATE   Production.Product
SET      SafetyStockLevel = @SafetyStockLevel
WHERE    ProductID = 1;

SELECT   SafetyStockLevel
FROM     Production.Product
WHERE    ProductID = 1;

COMMIT TRAN;
```

Does it look OK? The developer has wrapped the read and the write in an explicit transaction, but all this scenario needs is for some concurrent activity and a lost update will occur. The WAITFOR is only present to make it easier to detonate the code. In a separate session, have the following code ready:

```
/* SESSION 2*/
USE AdventureWorks2012;

DECLARE @SafetyStockLevel    int = 0
        ,@Uplift             int = 100;

BEGIN TRAN;
SELECT   @SafetyStockLevel = SafetyStockLevel
FROM     Production.Product
WHERE    ProductID = 1;

SET      @SafetyStockLevel = @SafetyStockLevel + @Uplift;

UPDATE   Production.Product
SET      SafetyStockLevel = @SafetyStockLevel
WHERE    ProductID = 1;

SELECT   SafetyStockLevel
FROM     Production.Product
WHERE    ProductID = 1;

COMMIT TRAN;
```

Now run Session 1; and then as soon as you have executed it, click over to Session 2 and execute that code. Session 2 should come back almost immediately showing that the transaction has raised the safety stock level from 1,000 to 1,100 (see Figure 6-1). If you return to Session 1, you should now be able to see that this transaction has also completed, except that the Safety Stock Level has gone from 1,000 to 1,005 (see Figure 6-2). The design of the transaction is flawed, causing an update to be lost.

FIGURE 6-1

FIGURE 6-2

What caused this loss? The developer wrote the transaction in such a way that both sessions are able to read the data and store the stock level in a variable. Consequently, when the update is made, both transactions start with the same value. This is a situation that should be avoided through more careful coding. Even raising the isolation level does not resolve this particular problem, which should be addressed by performing the addition as part of the update operation, as shown here:

```
UPDATE  Production.Product
SET     SafetyStockLevel += @Uplift
WHERE   ProductID = 1;
```

We know you are all too smart to code your transactions in a way that could allow lost updates, but it does show what can happen when insufficient consideration is given to the transaction design. Interestingly, SQL Server enables the syntax to support this behavior using the NOLOCK hint, although it is largely ignored.

Dirty Reads

A dirty read takes no notice of any lock taken by another process. The read is officially "dirty" when it reads data that is uncommitted. This can become problematic if the uncommitted transaction fails or for some other reason is rolled back.

Imagine a scenario in which you are shopping on a website and place an item into your basket and proceed to payment. The site's checkout process decrements the stock by one and starts to charge your card all in the one transaction. At that time, a second unrelated process starts. The website's back office stock interface runs and makes a dirty read of all the product inventory levels, reading the reduced value. Unfortunately, there is a problem with your transaction (insufficient funds), and your purchase transaction is rolled back. The website stock level has now reverted to the original level, but the stock interface has just reported a different value.

You can run the following example against the AdventureWorks2012 database. Session 1 starts an explicit transaction to update all persons with a last name of "Jones" to have the same first name of "James." This transaction will be rolled back after five seconds, and a SELECT is run to show the original values (code file Ch6DirtyReads.sql):

```
/* SESSION 1 */
USE AdventureWorks2012;

BEGIN TRANSACTION;

UPDATE  Person.Person
```

```
SET     FirstName = 'James'
WHERE   LastName = 'Jones';

WAITFOR DELAY '00:00:05.000';

ROLLBACK TRANSACTION;

SELECT  FirstName
       ,LastName
FROM    Person.Person
WHERE   LastName = 'Jones';
```

Once Session 1 is running, quickly switch over to a second session and execute the following SQL statement. The SQL in this second session will perform a dirty read. If you time it right and execute this query while the transaction in Session 1 is open (it has not yet been rolled back), then your output will match Figure 6-3 and every person with a surname of "Jones" now has a first name of "James":

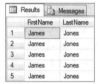

FIGURE 6-3

```
/* SESSION 2 */
USE AdventureWorks2012;

SET TRANSACTION ISOLATION LEVEL READ UNCOMMITTED;

SELECT  FirstName
       ,LastName
FROM    Person.Person
WHERE   LastName = 'Jones';
```

Non-Repeatable Reads

A non-repeatable read is one in which data read twice inside the same transaction cannot be guaranteed to contain the same value. This very behavior was discussed when looking at transactions earlier in the chapter. Depending on the isolation level, another transaction could have nipped in and updated the value between the two reads.

Non-repeatable reads occur because at lower isolation levels reading data only locks the data for the duration of the read, rather than for the duration of the transaction. Sometimes this behavior might be completely desirable. Some applications may want to know the absolute, real-time value, even mid transaction, whereas other types of transactions might need to read the same value multiple times.

Consider the following example. In Session 1 the transaction reads the data for the top five people from `Person.Person` and then waits for five seconds before repeating the step. Execute the code in Session 1 before flipping to a second session and executing the code in Session 2 (code file `Ch6NonRepeatableReads.sql`):

```
/*SESSION 1*/
USE AdventureWorks2012;

SET TRANSACTION ISOLATION LEVEL
```

```
READ COMMITTED;
--REPEATABLE READ;

BEGIN TRANSACTION;

SELECT TOP    5
              FirstName
              ,MiddleName
              ,LastName
              ,Suffix
FROM          Person.Person
ORDER BY      LastName;

WAITFOR DELAY '00:00:05.000';

SELECT TOP    5
              FirstName
              ,MiddleName
              ,LastName
              ,Suffix
FROM          Person.Person
ORDER BY      LastName;

COMMIT TRANSACTION;

/*SESSION 2*/
USE AdventureWorks2012;

BEGIN TRANSACTION;

UPDATE   Person.Person
SET      Suffix       = 'Junior'
WHERE    LastName     = 'Abbas'
AND      FirstName    = 'Syed';

COMMIT TRANSACTION;

/*
UPDATE   Person.Person
SET      Suffix       = NULL
WHERE    LastName     = 'Abbas'
AND      FirstName    = 'Syed';
*/
```

	First Name	Middle Name	Last Name	Suffix
1	Syed	E	Abbas	NULL
2	Catherine	R.	Abel	NULL
3	Kim	NULL	Abercrombie	NULL
4	Kim	NULL	Abercrombie	NULL
5	Kim	B	Abercrombie	NULL

	First Name	Middle Name	Last Name	Suffix
1	Syed	E	Abbas	Junior
2	Catherine	R.	Abel	NULL
3	Kim	NULL	Abercrombie	NULL
4	Kim	NULL	Abercrombie	NULL
5	Kim	B	Abercrombie	NULL

FIGURE 6-4

Providing you execute the update in Session 2 in time, your results will match Figure 6-4. The first read from Session 1, Syed Abbas, had no suffix; but in the second read he's now Syed Abbas Junior. The first read, therefore, hasn't been repeatable.

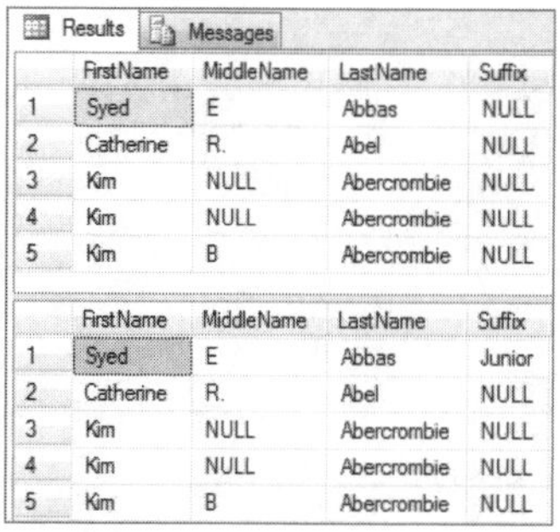

You can use the commented-out code in Session 2 to reset the data. Execute this code now. To get a repeatable read, change the transaction isolation level in Session 1 as indicated here:

```
SET TRANSACTION ISOLATION LEVEL
--READ COMMITTED;
REPEATABLE READ;
```

Now rerun Session 1 and Session 2 as before. You should notice that Session 2 has been blocked from performing its update until after the transaction has been completed. The first read in Session 1 is now repeatable. Your results from Session 1 should now match those in Figure 6-5.

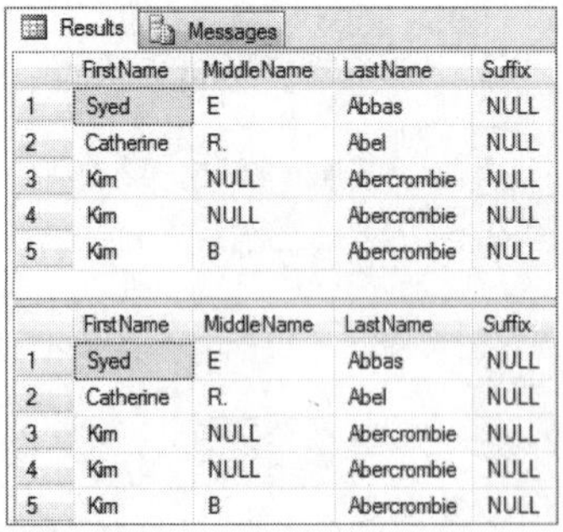

FIGURE 6-5

Phantom Reads

Phantom reads occur when a row is inserted into or deleted from a range of data by one transaction that is being read by another set of data. Recall the earlier work queue scenario. Suppose a user reads the work queue searching for new work items and gets back 10 records. Another user inserts a new work order. Shortly afterward, the first user refreshes the list of new work orders. There are now 11. This additional row is a phantom row.

Often this outcome is desirable. In cases when you need to be able to rely on the range of data previously read, however, it is not. The following example uses the `Person.Person` table to demonstrate a phantom (code file `Ch6PhantomReads.sql`):

```
/*SESSION 1*/
USE AdventureWorks2012;

SET TRANSACTION ISOLATION LEVEL
READ COMMITTED;
--SERIALIZABLE;

BEGIN TRANSACTION;

SELECT TOP    5
              FirstName
              ,MiddleName
              ,LastName
              ,Suffix
FROM          Person.Person
ORDER BY      LastName;

WAITFOR DELAY '00:00:05.000';

SELECT TOP    5
              FirstName
              ,MiddleName
              ,LastName
              ,Suffix
```

```
FROM        Person.Person
ORDER BY    LastName;

COMMIT TRANSACTION;
```

In Session 1 the transaction is again going to read the top five people from the `Person.Person` table twice in relatively quick succession. Session 2, however, inserts a new person who meets the criteria in the results of the query.

```
/*SESSION 2*/
USE AdventureWorks2012;

BEGIN TRANSACTION;

INSERT INTO [Person].[BusinessEntity]
            ([rowguid]
            ,[ModifiedDate])
     VALUES
            (NEWID()
            ,CURRENT_TIMESTAMP);

DECLARE @Scope_Identity int;

SELECT @Scope_Identity = SCOPE_IDENTITY();

INSERT INTO [Person].[Person]
            ([BusinessEntityID]
            ,[PersonType]
            ,[NameStyle]
            ,[Title]
            ,[FirstName]
            ,[MiddleName]
            ,[LastName]
            ,[Suffix]
            ,[EmailPromotion]
            ,[AdditionalContactInfo]
            ,[Demographics]
            ,[rowguid]
            ,[ModifiedDate])
     VALUES
            (@Scope_Identity
            ,'EM'
            ,'0'
            ,'Mr.'
            ,'James'
            ,'Anthony'
            ,'A'
            ,Null
            ,0
            ,Null
            ,Null
            ,NEWID()
```

```
                ,CURRENT_TIMESTAMP
                );

EXEC SP_EXECUTESQL
N'PRINT ''DELETE FROM Person.Person WHERE BusinessEntityID = '' +CAST(@Scope_
Identity as varchar(8));
  PRINT ''DELETE FROM Person.BusinessEntity WHERE BusinessEntityID = ''
+CAST(@Scope_Identity as varchar(8));'
  ,N'@Scope_Identity int',@Scope_Identity = @Scope_Identity

SELECT @Scope_Identity as BusinessEntityID

COMMIT TRANSACTION;
```

Run Session 1 now before switching over and executing Session 2. You should see in the results of the first query from Session 1 (see Figure 6-6) that Syed Abbas is the first person of five returned.

	First Name	Middle Name	Last Name	Suffix
1	Syed	E	Abbas	NULL
2	Catherine	R.	Abel	NULL
3	Kim	NULL	Abercrombie	NULL
4	Kim	NULL	Abercrombie	NULL
5	Kim	B	Abercrombie	NULL

FIGURE 6-6

However, in the result of the second query from Session 1 (see Figure 6-7) James Anthony A is now first. James Anthony A is a phantom.

	First Name	Middle Name	Last Name	Suffix
1	James	Anthony	A	NULL
2	Syed	E	Abbas	NULL
3	Catherine	R.	Abel	NULL
4	Kim	NULL	Abercrombie	NULL
5	Kim	NULL	Abercrombie	NULL

FIGURE 6-7

To demonstrate how phantoms can be prevented, first remove James Anthony A from the table. If you revert to Session 2 and look in your message tab, you should see two delete statements (see Figure 6-8 for details).

```
Results    Messages

(1 row(s) affected)

(1 row(s) affected)
DELETE FROM Person.Person WHERE BusinessEntityID = 20792
DELETE FROM Person.BusinessEntity WHERE BusinessEntityID = 20792

(1 row(s) affected)
```

FIGURE 6-8

Copy those two rows into a new window and execute them.

In Session 1, change the transaction isolation level from read committed to serializable, and repeat the example by running the code in Session 1 first, followed by that in Session 2:

```
SET TRANSACTION ISOLATION LEVEL
--READ COMMITTED;
SERIALIZABLE;
```

	Results		Messages	
	First Name	Middle Name	Last Name	Suffix
1	Syed	E	Abbas	NULL
2	Catherine	R.	Abel	NULL
3	Kim	NULL	Abercrombie	NULL
4	Kim	NULL	Abercrombie	NULL
5	Kim	B	Abercrombie	NULL

	First Name	Middle Name	Last Name	Suffix
1	Syed	E	Abbas	NULL
2	Catherine	R.	Abel	NULL
3	Kim	NULL	Abercrombie	NULL
4	Kim	NULL	Abercrombie	NULL
5	Kim	B	Abercrombie	NULL

FIGURE 6-9

This time the results for selects one and two from Session 1 are the same, as shown in Figure 6-9. Note that the insert from Session 2 still happened, but only after the transaction in Session 1 had been committed.

Don't forget to remove James Anthony A from your AdventureWorks2012 database before continuing by repeating the steps just outlined.

Double Reads

Double reads can occur when scanning data while using the default read committed isolation level, covered later in this chapter. During a period of concurrent activity, it is possible for one query to perform a range scan on a table and, as it is scanning, a second transaction can come in and move a row, thus causing it to be read twice. This can happen when the initial read during the range scan is not repeatable. The locks taken when reading data are by default released as soon as the data has been successfully read. Specific action is required to prevent this; you must increase the isolation level.

For example, the following code moves Bethany Raheem and so reads her record twice. There are only five Raheems in the AdventureWorks2012 database. However, in this example you will see six.

First, Session 1 creates a blocking update midway through the range scan of the Raheem data on a row that is further through the index than Bethany's row (code file Ch6DoubleReads.sql):

```
/* SESSION 1 PART 1 */
Use AdventureWorks2012;

BEGIN TRAN
UPDATE  Person.Person
SET     LastName    = 'Raheem_DOUBLE_READ_BLOCK'
WHERE   LastName    = 'Raheem'
AND     FirstName   = 'Kurt';
```

Now Session 2 starts a scan to return all persons whose surname begins with Raheem. This query will scan the index and be blocked by the uncommitted update in Session 1:

```
/* SESSION 2 */
USE     AdventureWorks2012;

SELECT  FirstName
        ,LastName
FROM    Person.Person
WHERE   LastName Like 'Raheem%';
```

Return to Session 1 and move Bethany Raheem, who has already been read, to a position in the index after the row being updated in Session 1:

```
/* SESSION 1 PART 2 */
UPDATE  Person.Person
SET     LastName    = 'Raheem_DOUBLE_READ_REAL'
WHERE   LastName    = 'Raheem'
AND     FirstName   = 'Bethany';

COMMIT TRAN;
```

The range scan query in Session 2 can now complete, and the results look like those in Figure 6-10.

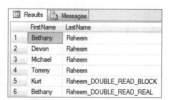

FIGURE 6-10

> **NOTE** *For more details on the double read, please see the blog post from Craig Freedman at* `http://blogs.msdn.com/craigfr/archive/2007/04/25/` `read-committed-isolation-level.aspx.`

Halloween Effect

The *Halloween effect* refers to a scenario in which data moves position within the result set and consequently could be changed multiple times. This effect is different from the double read because it is driven by data modification, rather than read queries.

In order to perform an update, the data must be read first. This is performed using two cursors: one for the read and the other for the write. If the data is updated by the write cursor before all the data was read in, then it is possible that a row will move position (courtesy of the update), potentially be read a second time, and consequently be updated again. In theory, this could go on forever. Reading the data using an index whose key is going to be updated by the query is an example of the Halloween effect.

This scenario is obviously highly undesirable, and thankfully the Storage Engine in SQL Server protects against it. As mentioned, SQL Server uses two cursors during an update: one to perform the read and another to perform the write. To ensure that the data available to the write has been read fully, SQL Server needs to inject a blocking operator such as a spool into the plan. It doesn't have to be the spool, but this operator is commonly selected because it invariably has the lowest cost attached to it. That said, it still isn't very efficient, as it means all the data has to be inserted into tempdb before it can be used by the write cursor. It does ensure that all the data is read before any modifications take place.

To achieve a greater level of efficiency, SQL Server actually looks out for the Halloween effect problem when creating the plan. It introduces the blocking operator only when there is a chance of the Halloween effect occurring. Even then it adds an extra one only if no blocking operator is already present in the plan performing this function.

In most update scenarios the index is used to locate data, and other non-key columns are updated in the table. You wouldn't normally expect the key to be frequently updated as well, so being able to remove the blocking operator is an important optimization.

It is worth remembering the performance penalty of the Halloween effect when deciding on your indexing strategy. Perhaps that index you were thinking of adding isn't such a great idea after all. When index or performance tuning, it is always worthwhile to keep an eye on the impact that your changes have on tempdb.

> **NOTE** *To learn more details about how SQL Server protects you from the Halloween effect, please see another excellent blog post from Craig Freedman at* `http://blogs.msdn.com/craigfr/archive/2008/02/27/` `halloween-protection.aspx.`

LOCKS

You've just read about blocking other users from seeing what's going on, or jumping in with other changes that stop a transaction from being able to behave in proper isolation. The mechanism in SQL Server that is used for this is a lock. By locking a piece of data, SQL Server prevents access to it. As you might expect, there are a variety of lock types (known as lock modes), and a variety of types of access they are designed to prevent. A lock is needed for almost every kind of data access, even reads, which means that locks actually do their blocking against other lock types. We don't say that an exclusive lock blocks reads; we say that an exclusive lock is incompatible with a shared lock — but the effect is the same. To picture the kind of blocking that will occur, imagine the kind of access that needs to take out the incompatible locks.

There are also many different types of things that can be locked. These are known as lock resources. By identifying what is locked, what caused it to be locked, and the type of lock that is taken out, you have the full set of information about the lock.

Monitoring Locks

Two main dynamic management views (DMVs) are used to monitor locks: sys.dm_tran_locks and sys.dm_os_wait_stats. The former lists all the locks that have currently been taken, and includes information identifying the lock resource and more, while the latter lists information about how often processes have had to wait when acquiring the various lock types.

The DMV sys.dm_tran_locks returns a lot of useful information about the locks currently held in the SQL Server instance. It shows not only the lock resource (as per the list of lock resources described next) and lock mode (also discussed later), but also the ID of the database in which the lock is located, plenty of information to identify the resource that has been locked, whether the lock was actually granted (it could be being converted, or it could be waiting), how many locks of that type are on the resource, the sessionid, and more.

There are a lot of columns, as described in Table 6-1.

TABLE 6-1: Currently Active Lock Resource Information Returned by sys.dm_tran_locks

COLUMN NAME	DESCRIPTION
resource_type	The type of lock resource that a transaction is trying to take a lock on, such as OBJECT, PAGE, KEY, etc.
Resource_subtype	Provides a subclassification of the resource requested. Not mandatory, but good for qualifying the resource; for example, if you create a table in a transaction you will get a subtype of DDL on the DATABASE resource_type lock.
Resource_database_id	The database in which the resource was requested

continues

TABLE 6-1 *(continued)*

COLUMN NAME	DESCRIPTION
Resource_description	Contains information describing the resource that isn't available in any other column
Resource_associated_entity_id	Describes the entity upon which the lock is being requested. It can be one of three things depending on the resource type: Object ID, HoBT ID, or Allocation Unit ID.
Resource_lock_partition	Normally 0. Lock partitioning must be available to you in order to see anything in this column, and only available on machines with 16 cores presented. It applies only to object locks, and even then only to those without a resource_subtype.
Request_mode	The mode in which the lock is requested. If the lock has a status of granted, then this is the lock mode under which the resource is currently operating — for example, IX (Intent Exclusive), X (Exclusive), etc.
Request_type	This value is always LOCK because this view only supports locks.
Request_status	This is one of three values: GRANT: The requested lock is in effect. WAIT: The lock is prevented from being acquired (blocked) because the resource is already locked with an incompatible locking mode. For instance one connection has a Grant X (Exclusive) lock on the object, and you are trying to also acquire an exclusive lock on the same object. CONVERT: The lock was previously granted with another status and is trying to upgrade to a more restrictive mode but is currently being blocked from doing so.
Request_reference_count	An approximate count of the number of times that a requestor has requested a lock on the given resource
Request_session_id	In most cases this is the session that requested the resource. Two special values: -2: A distributed transaction with no enlisted sessions -3: A deferred recovery transaction
Request_exec_context_id	Execution context of the process that owns the request
Request_request_id	Batch ID of the request that owns the resource
Request_owner_type	The entity type of the owner of the request. Possible types are as follows:

COLUMN NAME	DESCRIPTION
	TRANSACTION
	CURSOR
	SESSION
	SHARED_TRANSACTION_WORKSPACE
	EXCLUSIVE_TRANSACTION_WORKSPACE
Request_owner_id	Used when the owner type is TRANSACTION and represents the transaction ID
Request_owner_guid	Used when the owner type is TRANSACTION and the request has been made by a distributed transaction. In that circumstance, the value equates to the MSDTC GUID for that transaction.
Lock_owner_address	Represents the in-memory address of the request. Use this column to join to the resource_address column in sys.dm_os_waiting_tasks to see blocking lock information.

The DMV sys.dm_os_wait_stats shows the wait stats for the locks by their mode (the list of lock modes is shown later in this chapter), and you can see these in the wait_type column, with values such as LCK_M_IX for IX-locks, and LCK_M_S for S-locks. For each wait_type, the number of times waits have been required is shown, along with the total and maximum wait times and the total signal wait time. Using this DMV can highlight when the Database Engine must wait to acquire the various locks.

Lock Resources

Table 6-2 describes the many different types of things that can be locked, known as lock resources. It also gives an example of what each type of resource might look like.

TABLE 6-2: List of Lock Resources and Examples

RESOURCE TYPE	EXAMPLE OF RESOURCE	DESCRIPTION
RID	1:8185:4	A row identifier used to lock a single row when the table in question is a heap The RID format can be understood as: `<File : Page : Slot ID>`
		The lock resource RID can be retrieved with the undocumented %%lockres%% function.

continues

TABLE 6-2 *(continued)*

RESOURCE TYPE	EXAMPLE OF RESOURCE	DESCRIPTION
KEY	(3a01180ac47a)	A lock on a single row on an index. This includes row locks taken on tables that have a clustered index on them. The resource is a hash value that can be retrieved against your table with `%%lockres%%`.
PAGE	1:19216	A lock on an index or data page. Breaks down as `<FILE ID>:<PAGE NUMBER>`. These map to the `file_id` and `page_id` fields in the `sys.dm_os_buffer_descriptors` DMV.
EXTENT	1:19216	A contiguous set of eight pages. Pages are allocated to tables in extents. Breaks down as `<FILE ID> : <FIRST PAGE NO>`
HoBT	72057594058637312	HoBT is a Heap or Balanced Tree (BTree). When a table is a heap (no clustered index), it protects the heap. Otherwise, it protects the BTree of the index.
OBJECT	2105058535	Normally a table lock but it could be anything with an `OBJECT_ID`. If it's a table lock, then it covers both data pages and all indexes on the table.
APPLICATION	0:[MyAppLock]: (6731eaf3)	An application lock. Set by `sp_getapplock`.
METADATA	xml_collection_id = 65536	Used to lock SQL Server system metadata — e.g., when taking a schema stability lock on metadata of an XML column when querying a row.
ALLOCATION_UNIT	72057594039828480	Allocation Unit ID seen during deferred drop operations, such as on a large table. Also visible during minimally logged operations such as `SELECT INTO`.
FILE	0	Seen when adding or removing files from a database. No resource description information is published.
DATABASE	7	A lock against the entire database. This can be a shared transaction workspace lock to identify a connection in the DB or a transaction lock when altering the database. Changing from `read_write` to `read_only` requires an exclusive transaction against the database.

You may look at this table with a degree of hope that your locks never end up too far down the list. It's quite understandable and reasonable to expect that your normal querying behavior should be able to get away with just locking rows, pages, and occasionally a whole HoBT; but remember that a single object's locks can cover many HoBT locks, which in turn, might cover thousands or millions of pages, and who knows how many rows. A trade-off must be made between having a smaller number of locks with more data locked than strictly necessary and having less data locked with a larger number of locks.

Lock escalation occurs when a number of locks are converted into a smaller number of locks at levels further down that list (typically to the object level) — that is, making the trade-off to reduce the number of locks through coarser granularity. This can be beneficial in that it reduces the amount of overhead to manage the locks; but of course with more data locked, there is a higher likelihood of processes being blocked by encountering locked data. Details about how this escalation occurs are covered later in the chapter, after the lock modes and compatibility between the lock modes have been considered. For now, be aware of the kinds of things that can be locked.

Lock Modes

Data in a database is not like a book, which can only be in the possession of one person at a time. If you are reading a book, the book is in your hands and other people can't read it. Data is more like a notice on a board. You and other people can read it at the same time. However, if you want to change it, then you need to take the notice down off the board, and no one else can change it at the same time. Whether or not they can read it while it is being changed is a separate matter (the isolation level), but this scenario is related to the concept of *lock modes*, and the compatibility matrix between them, as described in the following sections.

Shared Lock Mode (S)

When a read request for a row of data is made by a task, by default, SQL Server will request a lock in shared mode. Shared mode is compatible with most other locks, as it is only permitted to read the row on the data page.

Update Lock Mode (U)

Update mode is a special kind of lock. It is used when searching data during a data modification request. The process is straightforward: SQL Server uses the update lock by locating the data and then preventing others from updating it. It prevents other requests from modifying the data by virtue of the update lock's compatibility with other locks. Any other requests wishing to lock the resource with an update or exclusive lock are forced to wait. However, in order to effect the data modification, the update lock must be converted to an exclusive lock. As the update lock has blocked all other data modification locks, all it needs to do is wait until it can get an exclusive lock when the last, if any, shared locks have been released. This allows for greater concurrency in the system as opposed to all writers just taking exclusive locks. If the latter were the case, then blocking would be a much greater problem. Concurrent queries would be blocked for the entire duration of the update (the read part and the write) as opposed to just the write.

Exclusive Lock Mode (X)

Exclusive locks are used for data modification via INSERT, UPDATE, and DELETE statements. In terms of compatibility, exclusive locks are not compatible with any other kind of lock, including other exclusive locks. All locks must wait for the exclusive lock to be released before they can proceed; provided your solution isn't using dirty reads and therefore bypassing the lock entirely. As mentioned earlier, exclusive locks are held until the end of the transaction, whether that is by commit or rollback.

Schema Lock Modes (Sch-S), (Sch-M)

There are actually two types of schema lock mode: *schema modification (Sch-M)* and *schema stability (Sch-S)*. These locks are taken by different processes but basically boil down to the same thing. A query takes a schema-modification lock when it wants to change the schema in some way. Schema stability is designed to block schema modification if needed. For example, when a stored procedure is compiled, a schema-stability lock is taken to ensure that no one changes the table during the compilation process. Alternatively, a schema-modification lock is taken when altering a table, as you have seen, but also when performing partition switching. In this case, a Sch-M is taken on both the source and the target.

Intent Lock Modes (IS), (IU), (IX)

As shown previously in the discussion of lock granularity, SQL Server can grant locks at various levels or degrees of granularity. These levels are used to form a hierarchy within SQL Server. A row is at the bottom of this hierarchy and belongs to a page; the page itself belongs to a table, and so on. The lock hierarchy is covered in detail in the next section, but the purpose of the intent lock is to indicate at the higher levels of the lock hierarchy that a part of the resource has a lock held against it. This allows checks to be performed at the level at which a lock is requested, which is a great performance optimization.

If an exclusive row lock is acquired on a table, the page and the table will have intent exclusive locks held against them. Consequently, if another process wants to take out a table lock, it can check at the table level, see that there is an intent exclusive lock present, and know it is blocked without having to scan the entire table looking for conflicting locks.

Intent locks shouldn't be considered as locks in the same vein as a shared, update, or exclusive lock. They act as indicators to SQL Server, pointing out that an actual lock has been acquired at a lower level in that hierarchy for that resource.

Consider an ALTER TABLE statement, which needs to be executed when no other users are trying to run queries against the table. If the table changed during the query, this would be very bad news indeed. However, it would also be a massive pain to check the locks for every row of the table to determine whether any are being read or modified. Instead, a table-level check takes place, which indicates immediately in a single request whether any other activity is occurring in the table.

Try this for yourself. In Session 1, run the following code (code file Ch6IntentLockModes.sql):

```
USE AdventureWorks2012;
/* SESSION 1 */

BEGIN TRANSACTION;
UPDATE       Production.Product
SET    SafetyStockLevel = SafetyStockLevel
```

```
WHERE    ProductID =1;
--ROLLBACK TRAN;

SELECT    resource_type
         ,resource_subtype
         ,resource_description
         ,resource_associated_entity_id
         ,request_mode
         ,request_status
FROM      sys.dm_tran_locks
WHERE     request_session_id = @@spid;
```

Note the intent locks (`request_mode` is `IX`) on page and object in Figure 6-11. Now try to run this `ALTER TABLE` statement in another query window:

	resource_type	resource_subtype	resource_description	resource_associated_entity_id	request_mode	request_status
1	DATABASE			0	S	GRANT
2	PAGE		1:709	72057594045595648	IX	GRANT
3	OBJECT			1717581157	IX	GRANT
4	KEY		(010086470766)	72057594045595648	X	GRANT

FIGURE 6-11

```
USE AdventureWorks2012;
/* SESSION 2 */

BEGIN TRANSACTION;
ALTER TABLE Production.Product
ADD TESTCOLUMN INT NULL;
--ROLLBACK TRANSACTION;
```

The `ALTER TABLE` statement should be blocked. How do you know this? First, it will take forever to make that change, as the explicit transaction in Session 1 hasn't been closed. However, more important, look at row 5 in the output shown in Figure 6-12 (the query for `sys.dm_tran_locks` has been rerun in the Session 1 window but also includes the SPID used for Session 2). Note that the `request_mode` contains a *schema modify lock*, and that the `request_status` is set to `WAIT`. This means it is on the wait list, which ties back to the fact that it is blocked. Finally, look at the `resource_type`. It's an object resource request. The database engine checks for the existence of an object `resource_type` for the same `resource_associated_entity_id` as the one requested. Because one exists, the `ALTER TABLE` cannot proceed.

	resource_type	resource_subtype	resource_description	resource_associated_entity_id	request_mode	request_status
1	DATABASE			0	S	GRANT
2	DATABASE			0	S	GRANT
3	PAGE		1:709	72057594045595648	IX	GRANT
4	OBJECT			1717581157	IX	GRANT
5	OBJECT			1717581157	Sch-M	WAIT
6	KEY		(010086470766)	72057594045595648	X	GRANT

FIGURE 6-12

You might want to roll back those transactions now to release the locks.

Conversion Lock Modes (SIX), (SIU), (UIX)

SQL Server also provides the facility to convert shared, update, or exclusive locks to shared with intent exclusive (SIX), shared with intent update (SIU), or update with intent exclusive (UIX). This happens when a statement inside a transaction already holds a lock at a coarse granularity (a table) but now needs to modify a component of the resource held at a much finer granularity (a row). The lock held against the coarse granularity needs to reflect this.

Consider the following example of a SIX lock (code file Ch6ConversionLockModes.sql):

```
USE AdventureWorks2012;

SET TRANSACTION ISOLATION LEVEL SERIALIZABLE;

BEGIN TRANSACTION;

SELECT  BusinessEntityID
        ,FirstName
        ,MiddleName
        ,LastName
        ,Suffix
FROM    Person.Person;

SELECT   resource_type
        ,resource_subtype
        ,resource_description
        ,resource_associated_entity_id
        ,request_mode
        ,request_status
FROM    sys.dm_tran_locks
WHERE   request_session_id = @@SPID;

UPDATE  Person.Person
SET     Suffix      = 'Junior'
WHERE   FirstName   = 'Syed'
AND     LastName    = 'Abbas';

SELECT   resource_type
        ,resource_subtype
        ,resource_description
        ,resource_associated_entity_id
        ,request_mode
        ,request_status
FROM    sys.dm_tran_locks
WHERE   request_session_id = @@SPID;

ROLLBACK TRANSACTION;
```

A transaction has selected all rows from the Person.Person table. This generates a table-level shared lock, as shown in Figure 6-13.

	resource_type	resource_subtype	resource_description	resource_associated_entity_id	request_mode	request_status
1	DATABASE			0	S	GRANT
2	OBJECT			1509580416	S	GRANT

FIGURE 6-13

The transaction continues through to update a single row. This triggers the need to convert the table-level shared lock to a SIX lock as the row must be exclusively locked. Figure 6-14 clearly shows that the row is locked with an exclusive KEY lock, but also that the table/object has converted its lock from shared (S) to shared with intent exclusive (SIX).

	resource_type	resource_subtype	resource_description	resource_associated_entity_id	request_mode	request_status
1	DATABASE			0	S	GRANT
2	KEY		(1d0096c50a7d)	72057594057981952	X	GRANT
3	METADATA	XML_COLLECTION	xml_collection_id = 65536	0	Sch-S	GRANT
4	METADATA	XML_COLLECTION	xml_collection_id = 65537	0	Sch-S	GRANT
5	KEY		(07038ce92446)	72057594058047488	RangeS-U	GRANT
6	PAGE		1:9992	72057594058047488	IU	GRANT
7	OBJECT			1509580416	SIX	GRANT
8	KEY		(3002fe6779f1)	72057594058047488	RangeS-U	GRANT
9	PAGE		1:36140	72057594057981952	IX	GRANT
10	OBJECT			1902629821	Sch-S	GRANT
11	OBJECT			1918629878	Sch-S	GRANT

FIGURE 6-14

Bulk Update Lock Mode (BU)

Bulk Update first appeared in SQL Server 2005. It is designed to allow multiple table-level locks on a single heap while using the Bulk API. This is important for parallel loading in data warehousing. However, in order to see it, you need to be loading into a heap and you must have specified a Tablock on the target table. The Tablock is a hint to say you'll take a table lock, but SQL Server sees that the Bulk API is making the assertion. So a BU lock is issued instead. Because multiple BU locks are permitted on the same table, you are therefore empowered to perform parallel loading into the heap, as each loader will take its own compatible BU lock. Note that dirty reads are also permitted against the target table.

> **NOTE** If you do not specify a Tablock hint when bulk loading data into a heap, then you will see exclusive page locks instead. If the target table has a clustered index, then use trace flag 610 and you will also see page locks on the bulk insert. See the Data Loading Performance Guide (http://msdn.microsoft.com/en-us/library/dd425070.aspx) from the SQLCAT team for further details.

The following SQL code example is using the BULK INSERT statement to load into a replica heap of the dbo.factinternetsales table. Notice that a Tablock hint has also been used. You can see the BU lock that is issued as a result in Figure 6-15 by querying sys.dm_tran_locks in a separate session as before. You'll have to be quick though! The sample data files contain only 60,398 rows (code file Ch6BulkUpdateLockMode.sql).

```
USE AdventureWorksDW2012;

CREATE TABLE [dbo].[TestFactInternetSales](
        [ProductKey] [int] NOT NULL,
        [OrderDateKey] [int] NOT NULL,
        [DueDateKey] [int] NOT NULL,
        [ShipDateKey] [int] NOT NULL,
        [CustomerKey] [int] NOT NULL,
        [PromotionKey] [int] NOT NULL,
        [CurrencyKey] [int] NOT NULL,
        [SalesTerritoryKey] [int] NOT NULL,
        [SalesOrderNumber] [nvarchar](20) NOT NULL,
        [SalesOrderLineNumber] [tinyint] NOT NULL,
        [RevisionNumber] [tinyint] NOT NULL,
        [OrderQuantity] [smallint] NOT NULL,
        [UnitPrice] [money] NOT NULL,
        [ExtendedAmount] [money] NOT NULL,
        [UnitPriceDiscountPct] [float] NOT NULL,
        [DiscountAmount] [float] NOT NULL,
        [ProductStandardCost] [money] NOT NULL,
        [TotalProductCost] [money] NOT NULL,
        [SalesAmount] [money] NOT NULL,
        [TaxAmt] [money] NOT NULL,
        [Freight] [money] NOT NULL,
        [CarrierTrackingNumber] [nvarchar](25) NULL,
        [CustomerPONumber] [nvarchar](25) NULL) ON [PRIMARY];

BULK INSERT dbo.TestFactInternetSales
FROM    'C:\factinternetsales.txt'
WITH    (TABLOCK
        ,FORMATFILE = 'C:\formatFIS.txt'
        );

/* SESSION 2 */
SELECT   resource_type
        ,resource_subtype
        ,resource_description
        ,resource_associated_entity_id
        ,request_mode
        ,request_status
FROM sys.dm_tran_locks
where request_session_id = <insert your session spid here,int, 0>
```

	resource_type	resource_subtype	resource_description	resource_associated_entity_id	request_mode	request_status
1	DATABASE	BULKOP_BACKUP_LOG		0	NULL	GRANT
2	DATABASE	BULKOP_BACKUP_DB		0	NULL	GRANT
3	DATABASE			0	S	GRANT
4	DATABASE	ENCRYPTION_SCAN		0	S	GRANT
5	OBJECT			142623551	BU	GRANT
6	HOBT	BULK_OPERATION		72057594193969152	IX	GRANT
7	ALLOCATION_UNIT	BULK_OPERATION_PAGE		72057594202357760	S	GRANT

FIGURE 6-15

Compatibility Matrix

Having looked at the list of lock modes that SQL Server uses, this section considers which of these are compatible with each other — that is, which locks prevent other locks from being taken out, and which ones are allowed. Two matrices of compatibility are shown — the first is explained, and the second one you can use for reference. Table 6-3 illustrates the first matrix.

TABLE 6-3: Sample Matrix of Compatibility

		EXISTING LOCK MODE					
		IS	S	U	IX	SIX	X
Requested Lock Mode	IS	Y	Y	Y	Y	Y	N
	S	Y	Y	Y	N	N	N
	U	Y	Y	N	N	N	N
	IX	Y	N	N	Y	N	N
	SIX	Y	N	N	N	N	N
	X	N	N	N	N	N	N

First, note the symmetry of this matrix. The labels "Existing Lock Mode" and "Requested Lock Mode" could be swapped without any of the Ys or Ns changing. The fact that a shared lock is incompatible with an intent exclusive lock is true whichever one is taken out first.

Next, look at the compatibility of the exclusive lock mode, the row and column marked with an X. Remember that this is the lock mode used when data is actually being modified. It's not compatible with any other lock modes. Therefore, if data is being modified, no other process can do anything with that data. It can't read it, and it definitely can't change it.

At the other end of the matrix, you can see that the intent shared lock mode is compatible with everything except the exclusive lock. This is the lock that is used on index pages and index objects, where a shared lock has been taken out at a more granular level. There is no problem taking out a lock of this type unless the resource itself is being changed. An intent exclusive lock is fine though — so if a single page of a table is locked with an exclusive lock, causing an object intent exclusive lock on the table/index itself, then a different part of the table can still be read. An intent shared lock can be taken out on the object despite the existence of the intent exclusive lock.

An intent exclusive doesn't prevent another intent exclusive lock from being taken out — two parts of a table can be changed at the same time without getting in each other's way. However, if part of a table is being changed, a shared lock cannot be taken out (remember, we're not talking about an intent shared lock).

The complete compatibility matrix found in SQL Server Books Online is shown in Figure 6-16. Although it seems dauntingly complex, if you take the time to study it you'll glean quite a bit of useful information.

	NL	SCH-S	SCH-M	S	U	X	IS	IU	IX	SIU	SIX	UIX	BU	RS-S	RS-U	RI-N	RI-S	RI-U	RI-X	RX-S	RX-U	RX-X
NL	N	N	N	N	N	N	N	N	N	N	N	N	N	N	N	N	N	N	N	N	N	N
SCH-S	N	N	C	N	N	N	N	N	N	N	N	N	N	I	I	I	I	I	I	I	I	I
SCH-M	N	C	C	C	C	C	C	C	C	C	C	C	C	I	I	I	I	I	I	I	I	I
S	N	N	C	N	N	C	N	N	C	N	C	C	C	N	N	N	N	N	C	N	N	C
U	N	N	C	N	N	C	N	C	C	C	C	C	C	N	C	N	N	C	C	C	C	C
X	N	N	C	C	C	C	C	C	C	C	C	C	C	C	C	N	C	C	C	C	C	C
IS	N	N	C	N	N	C	N	N	N	N	N	C	C	I	I	I	I	I	I	I	I	I
IU	N	N	C	N	C	C	N	N	N	N	N	C	C	I	I	I	I	I	I	I	I	I
IX	N	N	C	N	C	C	N	N	N	N	C	C	C	I	I	I	I	I	I	I	I	I
SIU	N	N	C	N	C	C	N	N	C	N	C	C	C	I	I	I	I	I	I	I	I	I
SIX	N	N	C	C	C	C	N	N	C	C	C	C	C	I	I	I	I	I	I	I	I	I
UIX	N	N	C	C	C	C	N	C	C	C	C	C	C	I	I	I	I	I	I	I	I	I
BU	N	N	C	C	C	C	C	C	C	C	C	C	N	I	I	I	I	I	I	I	I	I
RS-S	N	I	I	N	N	C	I	I	I	I	I	I	I	N	N	C	C	C	C	C	C	C
RS-U	N	I	I	N	N	C	I	I	I	I	I	I	I	N	C	C	C	C	C	C	C	C
RI-N	N	I	I	N	N	N	I	I	I	I	I	I	I	C	C	N	N	N	N	C	C	C
RI-S	N	I	I	N	N	C	I	I	I	I	I	I	I	C	C	N	N	C	C	C	C	C
RI-U	N	I	I	N	C	C	I	I	I	I	I	I	I	C	C	N	N	C	C	C	C	C
RI-X	N	I	I	C	C	C	I	I	I	I	I	I	I	C	C	N	C	C	C	C	C	C
RX-S	N	I	I	N	N	C	I	I	I	I	I	I	I	C	C	C	C	C	C	C	C	C
RX-U	N	I	I	N	N	C	I	I	I	I	I	I	I	C	C	C	C	C	C	C	C	C
RX-X	N	I	I	C	C	C	I	I	I	I	I	I	I	C	C	C	C	C	C	C	C	C

Key

N	No Conflict	SIU	Share with Intent Update
I	Illegal	SIX	Shared with Intent Exclusive
C	Conflict	UIX	Update with Intent Exclusive
		BU	Bulk Update
NL	No Lock	RS-S	Shared Range-Shared
SCH-S	Schema Stability Locks	RS-U	Shared Range-Update
SCH-M	Schema Modification Locks	RI-N	Insert Range-Null
S	Shared	RI-S	Insert Range-Shared
U	Update	RI-U	Insert Range-Update
X	Exclusive	RI-X	Insert Range-Exclusive
IS	Intent Shared	RX-S	Exclusive Range-Shared
IU	Intent Update	RX-U	Exclusive Range-Update
IX	Intent Exclusive	RX-X	Exclusive Range-Exclusive

FIGURE 6-16

LOCK ESCALATION

When more than 5,000 locks are taken out on the rows or pages of a particular table within a single T-SQL statement, lock escalation is triggered. During this process, the intent lock at the higher level is converted to a full lock — assuming this is possible and not prevented by other locks that may be already acquired — and then the locks at the more granular levels can be released, freeing up the resources needed to manage them.

As explained earlier, when a lock is taken out on a row or page, intent locks are taken out on the items higher up in the lock hierarchy — in particular, on the HoBTs and tables related to the locked row/page. In addition to providing a shortcut to determining whether something might be locking part of the table, these intent locks provide escalation points if the overhead of maintaining the locks becomes too high.

Escalation is to either the HoBT (for partitioned tables) or to the table itself (which is more typical). A page lock is not considered an escalation point — probably because by the time 5,000 locks are taken out, quite a large number of pages are locked, and a full table lock is a sensible solution to be able to reduce the number of locks.

If escalation can't occur, the more granular locks can't be released, and everything continues as before, with locks being taken out at the more granular points. This is typically because of other activity occurring in the affected table. Escalation will be attempted each time another 1,250 locks are acquired.

Lock escalation can be prevented by setting a table option to disallow it, or by forcing queries to take out table locks to start with. Ideally, you should let the system escalate locks as required, and only consider this kind of action when the number of escalations (monitored through `Lock:Escalation` events) becomes significantly higher than expected (compared to a benchmark of your system in a healthy state). You can also use trace flags (1211 and 1224) to disable lock escalation.

DEADLOCKS

Ideally, despite locks, your database system will allow a lot of users at once, and each transaction will get in, make the single change needed, and get out again; but locks inevitably mean blocking, and when transactions need to do multiple operations, this locking can even lead to deadlocks.

Although your application users will report that the application has deadlocked, this kind of behavior does not actually mean a deadlock has occurred. When a deadlock has been detected, the Database Engine terminates one of the threads, resolving the deadlock. The terminated thread gets a 1205 error, which conveniently suggests how to resolve it:

```
Error 1205 : Transaction (Process ID) was deadlocked on resources with another
process and has been chosen as the deadlock victim. Rerun the transaction.
```

Indeed, rerunning the transaction is often the best course of action here, and hopefully your application or even your stored procedure will have caught the error, recognized that it is a 1205, and tried the transaction again. Let's consider how a deadlock occurs, though.

It's quite straightforward really — one transaction locks a resource and then tries to acquire a lock on another resource but is blocked by another transaction. It won't be able to finish its transaction until such time as this second transaction completes and therefore releases its locks. However, if the second transaction does something that needs to wait for the first transaction, they'll end up waiting forever. Luckily this is detected by the Database Engine, and one of the processes is terminated.

When diagnosing these kinds of problems, it's worth considering that there are useful trace events such as `Lock:Deadlock` and Deadlock graph events. This enables you to see which combination of resources was being requested, and hopefully track down the cause. In most cases, the best option is to help the system get the quickest access to the resources that need updating. The quicker a transaction can release its resources, the less likely it is to cause a deadlock. However, another option is to lock up additional resources so that no two transactions are likely to overlap. Depending on the situation, a hint to lock an entire table can sometimes help by not letting another transaction acquire locks on parts of the table, although this can also cause blocking that results in transactions overlapping, so your mileage may vary.

ISOLATION LEVELS

Isolation levels determine how much transactions can see into other transactions, and can range from not-at-all to plenty. Understanding what the isolation levels do so that you can see how they prevent the concurrency side-effects described earlier can help you find an appropriate compromise between locking down too much and providing the necessary protection for your environment.

Many people misunderstand isolation levels. You may have seen large amounts of database code out there that use the NOLOCK hint, for example. To help combat this, you could find ways to educate people about isolation levels. Kendra Little has drawn a poster about them, shown in Figure 6-17. (You can find all her posters at www.littlekendra.com/sqlserverposters.) It could hang on a wall and serve as a conversation piece — people will ask you about it, providing an opportunity to talk to them about isolation levels.

Kendra's poster highlights the pessimism/optimism balance between the various isolation levels. There are four pessimistic isolation levels, and two optimistic ones. The optimistic levels involve the creation of snapshot data to allow additional concurrency, rather than the pessimistic behavior of blocking.

The following sections first describe the pessimistic isolation levels, followed by the optimistic ones.

FIGURE 6-17

Serializable

The serializable isolation level is the most pessimistic isolation level in SQL Server. It exhibits none of the concurrency problems that were shown earlier in the chapter. It simply locks everything up to ensure that no side-effects can take place. It does this by taking out range locks, which appear in the larger of the two lock compatibility matrices. These locks ensure that the whole range of any data that has been queried during the transaction is preserved, including avoiding insertions, to avoid the problem of phantom reads. These range locks typically conflict with each other, much more so than intent locks, thereby keeping the isolation as its utmost level.

Range locks can be seen in the following code (code file Ch6IsolationLevels.sql) and in Figure 6-18:

```
USE AdventureWorks2012;
GO

SET TRANSACTION ISOLATION LEVEL SERIALIZABLE;

BEGIN TRANSACTION;

SELECT  BusinessEntityID
FROM    Person.Person
where BusinessEntityID < 10;

SELECT    resource_type
        ,resource_subtype
        ,resource_description
        ,resource_associated_entity_id
        ,request_mode
        ,request_status
FROM    sys.dm_tran_locks
WHERE   request_session_id = @@SPID;

ROLLBACK TRAN;
```

	resource_type	resource_subtype	resource_description	resource_associated_entity_id	request_mode	request_status
1	DATABASE			0	S	GRANT
2	OBJECT			1765581328	IS	GRANT
3	KEY		(98ec012aa510)	72057594045595648	RangeS-S	GRANT
4	KEY		(a0c936a3c965)	72057594045595648	RangeS-S	GRANT
5	PAGE		1:1472	72057594045595648	IS	GRANT
6	KEY		(d08358b1108f)	72057594045595648	RangeS-S	GRANT
7	KEY		(40fd182c0dd9)	72057594045595648	RangeS-S	GRANT
8	KEY		(30b7763ed433)	72057594045595648	RangeS-S	GRANT
9	KEY		(8194443284a0)	72057594045595648	RangeS-S	GRANT
10	KEY		(b9b173bbe8d5)	72057594045595648	RangeS-S	GRANT
11	KEY		(c9fb1da9313f)	72057594045595648	RangeS-S	GRANT
12	KEY		(59855d342c69)	72057594045595648	RangeS-S	GRANT
13	KEY		(61a06abd401c)	72057594045595648	RangeS-S	GRANT

FIGURE 6-18

Repeatable Read

This level is not as strict as serializable, and it does not take out range locks. However, this means that data can be inserted into a set in such a way that the phantom reads scenario can occur.

Shared (S) locks are taken out and not released until the end of the transaction, including intent shared locks going up the lock hierarchy. These can be easily demonstrated by running the same block of code shown for the serializable example, but using SET TRANSACTION ISOLATION LEVEL REPEATABLE READ; instead of the first line. The results do not show range locks, but standard full locks instead (see Figure 6-19).

	resource_type	resource_subtype	resource_description	resource_associated_entity_id	request_mode	request_status
1	DATABASE			0	S	GRANT
2	OBJECT			1765581328	IS	GRANT
3	KEY		(98ec012aa510)	72057594045595648	S	GRANT
4	KEY		(a0c936a3c965)	72057594045595648	S	GRANT
5	PAGE		1:1472	72057594045595648	IS	GRANT
6	KEY		(40fd182c0dd9)	72057594045595648	S	GRANT
7	KEY		(30b7763ed433)	72057594045595648	S	GRANT
8	KEY		(8194443284a0)	72057594045595648	S	GRANT
9	KEY		(b9b173bbe8d5)	72057594045595648	S	GRANT
10	KEY		(c9fb1da9313f)	72057594045595648	S	GRANT
11	KEY		(59855d342c69)	72057594045595648	S	GRANT
12	KEY		(61a06abd401c)	72057594045595648	S	GRANT

FIGURE 6-19

Read Committed

Read committed is the default locking behavior of SQL Server 2012. In this environment, shared locks are released after the particular read operation, but, as in the more pessimistic isolation levels, they are still blocked by exclusive locks. This isolation level can exhibit some of the concurrency issues that were described earlier; but with fewer locks being taken out, the behavior is often considered good enough for many environments. It is entirely possible to read a piece of data in the transaction and then read it again later in the transaction, only to find that another transaction has snuck in and removed or changed that data — a non-repeatable read, which as implied, is not possible in the repeatable read isolation level.

If `SET TRANSACTION ISOLATION LEVEL READ COMMITTED;` is substituted in the preceding example, then both the shared locks from the repeatable read isolation level and the range locks of the serializable level will be eliminated, leaving only the shared lock on the whole database. See Figure 6-20.

	resource_type	resource_subtype	resource_description	resource_associated_entity_id	request_mode	request_status
1	DATABASE			0	S	GRANT

FIGURE 6-20

Read Uncommitted/NOLOCK

We mention the `NOLOCK` hint here because that is how many developers force the read uncommitted isolation level on their system. It is the least pessimistic isolation level, but it still is not classed as optimistic.

In the read uncommitted isolation level, shared (S) locks are not taken out at all. This also applies if the transaction is using a different isolation level but the `NOLOCK` hint is used. The upshot of this is the problem of dirty reads described earlier. Read transactions are not blocked by data with exclusive locks, but the data they read is of a potentially dubious value. Performance is increased, as without shared locks being acquired, there is no lock compatibility to be checked.

Note that some locks can still block reads in this isolation level — locks that stop anything getting near data, such as schema modification locks. The behavior of this isolation level has already been demonstrated as part of the dirty reads problem, so that code is not repeated here.

Snapshot

The optimistic snapshot isolation level is turned on using the command `SET TRANSACTION ISOLATION LEVEL SNAPSHOT;`. Before this can be done, however, the database must be configured to allow it, as shown here:

```
ALTER DATABASE AdventureWorks
SET ALLOW_SNAPSHOT_ISOLATION ON;
```

After the snapshot isolation level is set, the database can perform the extra work required when a transaction starts, ensuring that for the length of that transaction, the entire database appears as it did at the start of it. This has an interesting effect on the locking required for reads — no locks are required.

This may sound useful, but every time data is changed, the previous copy of the data must be stored until every transaction that was active when the change was made has been completed (except its own transaction, which naturally sees the newer copy of the data). The data to support this behavior is kept in the tempdb database.

Read Committed Snapshot

This isolation level is similar to the snapshot isolation level, but it only provides statement-level read consistency. Therefore, the behavior feels more like the read committed isolation level, with the same drawbacks of read committed regarding non-repeatable reads and the like, but it doesn't have the same blocking problems as read committed. When another transaction requests locked data using this isolation level, row versioning can provide a copy of it. However, the older versions of these rows are released when the transaction is over, thereby allowing more side-effects than are possible in the snapshot isolation level.

This last isolation level cannot be set using the SET TRANSACTION ISOLATION LEVEL command; it can only be set using the following:

```
ALTER DATABASE AdventureWorks
SET READ_COMMITTED_SNAPSHOT ON;
```

SUMMARY

In this chapter you looked at how locking protects your transactions and why it is important. You have seen what can happen if concurrency is ignored completely, and the various ways that these negative consequences can be prevented. You've also seen how you can determine what is going on with the locks in your system, and you should now understand the types of things that can cause the various types of locks to be acquired.

With a good understanding of locks, a database administrator should be able to find strategies for minimizing their impact. As you use the information in this chapter to investigate the locking patterns in your database, you should be able to get a good picture of the locking that is happening within your system, and then devise strategies using isolation levels and even perhaps hints (which have been deliberately avoided in this chapter, as they should only be a last resort) to control what's going on.

Finally, to return to the anecdote from the beginning of the chapter, Tommy Cooper's magic should be celebrated and enjoyed. It shouldn't cause you nightmares as you think of the problems you have with your database environment. Your "handkerchiefs" should only change color if you are expecting them to do that.

7

Latches and Spinlocks

WHAT'S IN THIS CHAPTER?

➤ Recognizing the symptoms of latch and spinlock contention

➤ Describing the types of systems which are susceptible to latch and spinlock contention

➤ Descriptions of latch types and modes

➤ Common contention-prone scenarios and how to resolve them

WROX.COM CODE DOWNLOADS FOR THIS CHAPTER

The wrox.com code downloads for this chapter are found at www.wrox.com/remtitle .cgi?isbn=1118177657 on the Download Code tab. The code is in the Chapter 7 download and individually named according to the names throughout the chapter.

OVERVIEW

When I speak to database consultants, many of them are familiar with SQL Server's locking behavior, and can even describe many of the principles covered in Chapter 6. They're far less confident about latches, however. Similarly, comparatively few can talk at any length about spinlocks, which are a very related topic. In light of this, I consider this chapter to be an important inclusion in this book.

The idea of this chapter is to offer practical advice to users trying to resolve issues identified to be related to both latch and spinlock behavior. We begin by describing some of the scenarios you might find yourself in, and the kind of symptoms you might see that betray a latch or spinlock problem. Even if they all seem alien (you might have never yet experienced latch contention) it would be useful to have a passing familiarity with these symptoms so that you can recognize various problems when you see them. By looking at the kinds of environments that lend themselves to latch and spinlock contention, you can assess your own situation and weigh the importance of this knowledge in your own skill set.

After introducing the symptoms, the chapter takes a detailed look at latches — what they are, how they work, and how to track them down using DMVs and extended events. The chapter also contains some real-world examples of latch contention, explaining how to resolve them

SYMPTOMS

In an ideal system, the number of transactions per second increases as traffic increases, and adding extra processor threads can help to resolve this. Having more processor threads should result in better performance, but it could lead to latch and spinlock contention instead. Over recent years, processors have not increased significantly, but the number of processors per server, cores per processor, and threads per core through hyperthreading have all been increasing, resulting in systems that are often scaled up by adding processor threads.

So it's important to recognize the signs of latch and spinlock contention.

Recognizing Symptoms

If your transactions per second figure is dropping as you enable extra processor threads, and your average latch waits are increasing at a rate greater than the throughput, then you quite possibly have a problem with latch contention. Consider the following two images. One represents how you want your system to behave, and the other, the effect of latch contention.

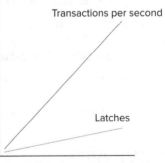

FIGURE 7-1

Both images show the number of transactions per second and average latch time (how to get this information will be shown soon).

Figure 7-1 represents the behavior that you should see when adding threads.

However, your chart may look more like the one shown in Figure 7-2. Notice the number of transactions per second starting to decrease after a point, and the number of latches increasing significantly.

In Figure 7-1, the ideal behavior shows the average latch time increasing a little as the number of processors increases, but not significantly. The number of transactions per second is happily increasing, suggesting that the processors are not conflicting with each other too much; and the more processors there are, the more can be done.

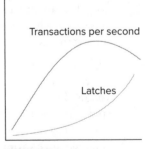

FIGURE 7-2

But in Figure 7-2, adding processors was proving useful but only up to a point. The effect of latch waits started to kick in, preventing the benefit of extra processors from being realized. It even got to the unhappy point of reducing the amount of work that could actually be done. This caused problems, rather than solving them. With the system spending so long waiting, the impact on real work becomes negative.

In order for spinlock contention to be a concern, behavior as described by the chart shown in Figure 7-3 would be exhibited, with the CPU rising exponentially as the load increases, with transactions dropping as with the latches. Keep in mind that you should also eliminate other factors that may be responsible for the increased CPU load.

Sometimes the obvious needs to be stated — you need a benchmark to tell you what "good performance" looks like, to weigh against what you're seeing when troubleshooting. When you examine a system without any historical background, you can sometimes recognize undesirable behavior, but a particular system could easily exhibit symptoms that are typical for it. Doctors use benchmarks when testing their patients — some of whom exhibit levels that are not typical across a broad population but are fine for them.

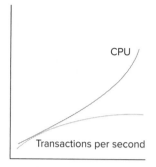

FIGURE 7-3

When you, in your role as database surgeon, open Performance Monitor, or PerfMon, and start looking at the various levels, it helps to know what those levels were before the problems started.

Measuring Latch Contention

A latch is like a lock on a piece of memory. As more threads get involved, they will start to compete to access the same pieces of memory, causing blocking. Blocking due to latch contention is exhibited in waits; but unlike a lock, a latch can be released as soon as the physical operation is completed.

The main sources of data about latches are two DMVs called sys.dm_os_wait_stats and sys.dm_os_latch_stats. The details of the values stored in these DMVs will be examined later in an explanation of latch modes and latch types, but for the purposes of recognizing the symptoms, a brief explanation will suffice. The DMVs are restarted when the service restarts, or when the DBCC SQLPERF command is called to clear them, as in the following code (code file Ch7Symptoms.sql):

```
DBCC SQLPERF('sys.dm_os_wait_stats', CLEAR);
DBCC SQLPERF('sys.dm_os_latch_stats', CLEAR);
```

Among the columns of the DMV sys.dm_os_wait_stats are ones called wait_type, wait_time_ms and waiting_tasks_count. These three columns represent the wait type, the total number of milliseconds that have been spent waiting on this wait type, and the number of times this type of wait has occurred, respectively. Wait types that associate with latches start with LATCH_, PAGELATCH_, or PAGEIOLATCH_.

Dividing the total wait time by the number of waits will give an average wait time (I'd recommend wrapping the waiting_tasks_count column in the NULLIF function to avoid a division by zero error). By querying this DMV repeatedly over time (as in the following example, code file Ch7Symptoms.sql, further illustrated in Figure 7-4), a picture can be built up of the frequency of latch waits, along with the amount of time the system must wait for these latches. This picture allows a database administrator to understand what kind of behavior is being exhibited — whether it matches Figure 7-1 or Figure 7-2.

```
SELECT
        wait_type,
        wait_time_ms,
        waiting_tasks_count,
        wait_time_ms / NULLIF(waiting_tasks_count,0) AS avg_wait_time
FROM    sys.dm_os_wait_stats
WHERE   wait_type LIKE 'LATCH_%'
OR      wait_type LIKE 'PAGELATCH_%'
OR      wait_type LIKE 'PAGEIOLATCH_%';
```

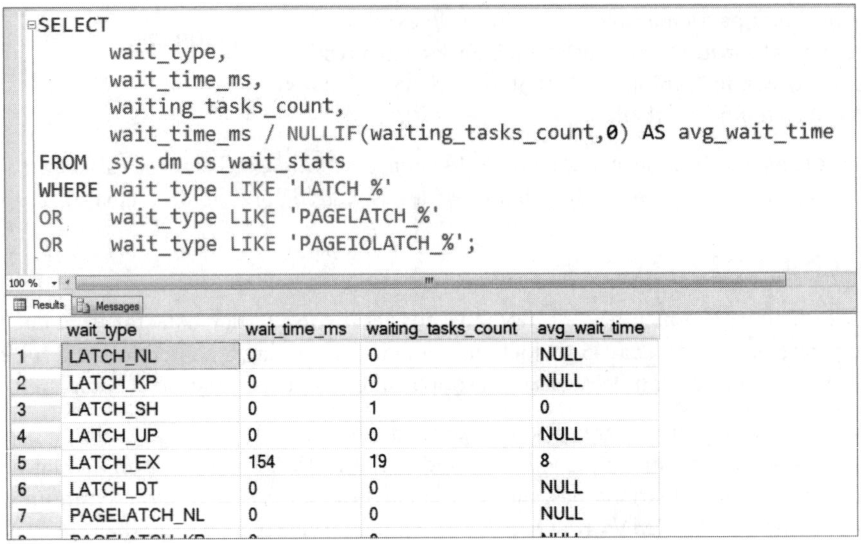

FIGURE 7-4

The DMV called `sys.dm_os_latch_stats` lists similar statistics for latch classes. This will be described further later in the chapter.

Measuring Spinlock Contention

For the time being, you can think of a spinlock as a latch, except that if the memory needing access is not available, the spinlock will keep checking it (known as spinning) for a while. There is slightly more to it, but that will be kept for later in the chapter.

The main DMV for spinlocks is `sys.dm_os_spinlock_stats`. The metrics of concern for spinlocks are around `collisions` and `spins_per_collision`, which are both columns in this DMV, along with the `name` column for the type of spinlock. Collisions and spins will be described later in the chapter. Here is an example of using `sys.dm_os_spinlock_stats` (code file `Ch7Symptoms.sql`), further illustrated in Figure 7-5:

```
SELECT name, collisions, spins_per_collision
FROM sys.dm_os_spinlock_stats
ORDER BY spins_per_collision DESC;
```

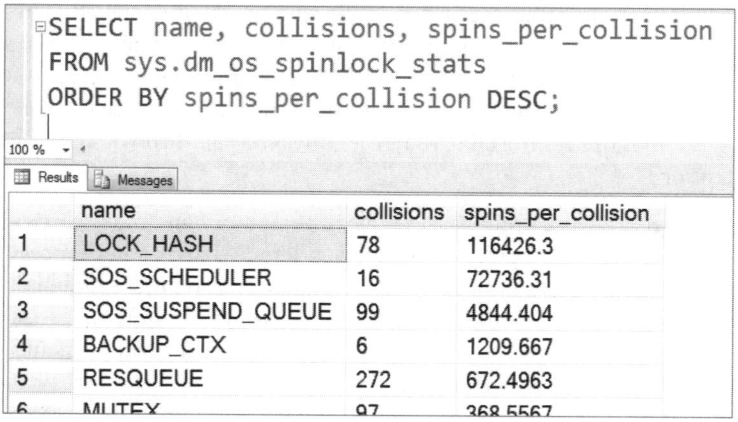

```
SELECT name, collisions, spins_per_collision
FROM sys.dm_os_spinlock_stats
ORDER BY spins_per_collision DESC;
```

	name	collisions	spins_per_collision
1	LOCK_HASH	78	116426.3
2	SOS_SCHEDULER	16	72736.31
3	SOS_SUSPEND_QUEUE	99	4844.404
4	BACKUP_CTX	6	1209.667
5	RESQUEUE	272	672.4963
6	MUTEX	97	368.5567

FIGURE 7-5

The sys.dm_os_spinlock_stats DMV can also be cleared using DBCC SQLPERF.

Contention Indicators

Locks are used to maintain the ACID properties of a transaction, but latches are used to provide consistency over a memory operation. A spinlock should be considered as similar, in that a resource is needed for a particular operation, but is not available.

Therefore, when you see higher than normal wait stats associated with latches and spinlocks, you may need to investigate further.

However, only seeing higher than normal wait stats does not in and of itself indicate a contention problem. It is perfectly reasonable to expect that if your system is busier now than when you took your benchmark, your wait stats would be higher. You should look for the proportion of wait stats compared to others, and compare this to the throughput being achieved. You might also want to consider how many transactions per second you're managing to achieve as you increase the load, and the effect of extra processors.

One strong indicator of latch contention can be seen when the proportion of latch-related wait stats increases unreasonably as your throughput increases, as shown in Figure 7-2.

For spinlock contention, a strong indicator is the number of spins per collision increasing, typically combined with increased CPU. Spinning is an activity that requires CPU effort, so if spinning increases disproportionally, CPU is likely to do the same. CPU may go up simply because of a busier system, but if the transactions per second counters are leveling off while CPU is increasing, then this would suggest the CPU is being used for something else — such as spinning. This is the behavior shown by the graph in Figure 7-3.

SUSCEPTIBLE SYSTEMS

In SQL Server, you lock something to use it. A latch is similarly applied to a piece of memory when it is used. In the physical world, suppose you want to sit in a chair. If it isn't occupied, then you have no problem. At home, even if you live with family, the chances of finding the chair unoccupied are relatively good. If you have people over, however, the chance of finding the chair occupied increases quickly. If there's a party going on, the chair might be occupied quite a lot. Even if people tend to sit down for just a few moments and then get up again, with enough people interested in sitting down now and then, the chance of the chair being occupied increases; and if that chair happens to be particularly popular (maybe it's a lot more comfortable than the other chairs), then you might have a great deal of chair-use contention.

In terms of latches and spinlocks, recall that a process uses a piece of memory and then releases it. Contention occurs when a process tries to use a piece of memory and finds that another process has already acquired a latch on it. If SQL Server were using only one processor core, there shouldn't be a problem (you can sit where you like if you're the only person at home); but that's yesterday's server, not today's. Increasingly, we're seeing systems with a number of cores that seem ridiculous; and much like we used to talk about memory in megabytes rather than gigabytes, the numbers available now will seem tiny in the future. It is already common to see six- or eight-core processors. Even my laptop, a few years old, is a quad-core machine, raised to eight through hyperthreading.

Furthermore, there are systems that encourage the use of a particular piece of memory. For example, when a lot of processes are trying to push data into a table, and that table always inserts data into the same page, latch contention could result. Database administrators don't always know exactly what the applications that use their databases are trying to do, but they often have a good idea of which tables meet these conditions, and therefore whether they might be candidates for latch contention.

I imagine by now you're convinced that latch contention is a very real possibility for your systems, and that if you're not suffering from it yet, it's only a matter of time. I think it's a good time to introduce what latches and spinlocks are, and take a deeper look at them.

UNDERSTANDING LATCHES AND SPINLOCKS

To understand latches and spinlocks, you will need to consider their actual definitions, and consider why they are required in SQL Server.

Definitions

You might recall from the discussion about locks that they are vital to the protection of data. In fact, it was suggested that without locks, there is no guarantee of data integrity, and all would be chaos. Latches perform the same function, but at another level. While locks protect our data from a logical perspective, ensuring that no one accesses the same table (or whatever) during someone else's transaction, latches do this for memory.

Books Online describes latches as "lightweight synchronization primitives that are used by the SQL Server engine to guarantee consistency of in-memory structures." In other words, despite the fact that you might think of your data as living in tables and indexes, these tables and indexes must be implemented in memory in order to enable the database engine to work its magic. To be used at all, data needs to be loaded off disk into RAM, making it available when needed. Latches protect this process of loading the data, and protect the data that has been already loaded. Similar to locks, latches are acquired when required, and have modes with various levels of compatibility. You'll learn more about these modes in a minute, and about some of the techniques that the SQL Server engine uses to efficiently manage latches.

You may already be thinking that because you can, to a certain extent, avoid locking trouble by simply setting the appropriate isolation level in your application, you ought to be able to do the same with latches. You can't.

A latch is an internal object, used by the SQL Server engine. It is not something that you, the database developer, can directly influence. If you need to get data from a particular page, the SQL Server engine needs to acquire a latch. You have no choice over this. Nor can you tell it what kind of latch to acquire — that's determined by the SQL Server engine. The difference is that this is not just about the protection of data, it's about the protection of server memory. Although you might be willing to tolerate dirty reads, and choose your locking strategy accordingly, you don't have that luxury with latches.

Spinlocks are a similar concept to latches, in that they are also lightweight synchronization primitives, but they act slightly differently. A lot of the effects can seem similar, and the kinds of systems that can exhibit spinlock contention are similar to those that can exhibit latch contention.

The main difference between a spinlock and a latch is this: If a thread fails to acquire a latch immediately, it yields, enabling the CPU to be used for other things. If a thread fails to acquire a spinlock, the thread starts looping (spinning), checking the resource repeatedly, with the expectation that it will become available soon. It won't spin forever, though. After a bit of time, it will back off, at which point it yields to other processes on the CPU.

Because we have no control over latching behavior or spinlocks, it isn't possible to demonstrate the impact of various latch scenarios using a real system, as shown for locks in Chapter 6. Instead, the following section presents a simulated example that uses real concepts.

Latching Example

All of the code in this section uses the Ch7Understanding.sql code file.

To begin, suppose you have a table that contains a single row of data. The following code will set up such an environment.

```
CREATE DATABASE LatchInAction;
GO
USE LatchInAction;

CREATE TABLE dbo.LatchTable
(        COL1 INT
        ,COL2 INT
);

INSERT INTO dbo.LatchTable ( COL1, COL2 )
VALUES (1,100);
```

Running DBCC IND will provide information about the pages that are used in the table. You will use the PagePID value of the row which has a PageType value of 1. The PageType column is the tenth column returned, so you may need to scroll. In my system, the value I'm looking for is 73, as seen in Figure 7-6.

```
DBCC IND(LatchInAction,'dbo.LatchTable',-1);
```

```
DBCC IND(LatchInAction,'dbo.LatchTable',-1)
```

100 %

Results | Messages

	PageFID	Page...	IAMFID	IAMPID	ObjectID	IndexID	Partition...	PartitionID	iam_chain_type	PageType
1	1	77	NULL	NULL	245575...	0	1	720575940...	In-row data	10
2	1	73	1	77	245575...	0	1	720575940...	In-row data	1

FIGURE 7-6

Now run DBCC PAGE to get the output of the table. Before doing that, though, you need to use DBCC TRACEON(3604) to output the results to the screen.

```
DBCC TRACEON(3604);
DBCC PAGE('LatchInAction',1,73,1);
```

The output is shown in Figure 7-7.

```
PAGE: (1:73)


BUFFER:


BUF @0x000000030057D5C0

bpage = 0x00000002F4E98000          bhash = 0x0000000000000000          bpageno = (1:73)
bdbid = 11                          breferences = 1                     bcputicks = 0
bsampleCount = 0                    bUse1 = 25104                       bstat = 0x9
blog = 0x15ab215a                   bnext = 0x0000000000000000

PAGE HEADER:


Page @0x00000002F4E98000

m_pageId = (1:73)                   m_headerVersion = 1                 m_type = 1
m_typeFlagBits = 0x0                m_level = 0                         m_flagBits = 0x8200
m_objId (AllocUnitId.idObj) = 84    m_indexId (AllocUnitId.idInd) = 256
Metadata: AllocUnitId = 72057594043432960
Metadata: PartitionId = 72057594039042048                                Metadata: IndexId = 0
Metadata: ObjectId = 245575913      m_prevPage = (0:0)                  m_nextPage = (0:0)
pminlen = 12                        m_slotCnt = 1                       m_freeCnt = 8079
m_freeData = 111                    m_reservedCnt = 0                   m_lsn = (32:72:24)
m_xactReserved = 0                  m_xdesId = (0:0)                    m_ghostRecCnt = 0
m_tornBits = 1864040631             DB Frag ID = 1

Allocation Status

GAM (1:2) = ALLOCATED               SGAM (1:3) = ALLOCATED
PFS (1:1) = 0x61 MIXED_EXT ALLOCATED  50_PCT_FULL                        DIFF (1:6) = CHANGED
ML (1:7) = NOT MIN_LOGGED

DATA:


Slot 0, Offset 0x60, Length 15, DumpStyle BYTE

Record Type = PRIMARY_RECORD        Record Attributes =  NULL_BITMAP    Record Size = 15

Memory Dump @0x000000001537A060

0000000000000000:   10000c00 01000000 64000000 020000            ........d......

OFFSET TABLE:

Row - Offset
0 (0x0) - 96 (0x60)
```

FIGURE 7-7

The noteworthy elements for this example are:

➤ In the PAGE HEADER section, the values m_slotCnt = 1 and m_freeData = 111

➤ In the DATA section, in Slot 0, the value Length 15

➤ In the OFFSET TABLE section, the Offset 96

This tells us that there is a single row (slot) in the page. This is Slot 0, which is 15 bytes long. This row starts at position 96 in the page. From position 111 on is empty (freedata). Not coincidentally, 111 = 96 + 15.

You can picture the page as in Figure 7-8.

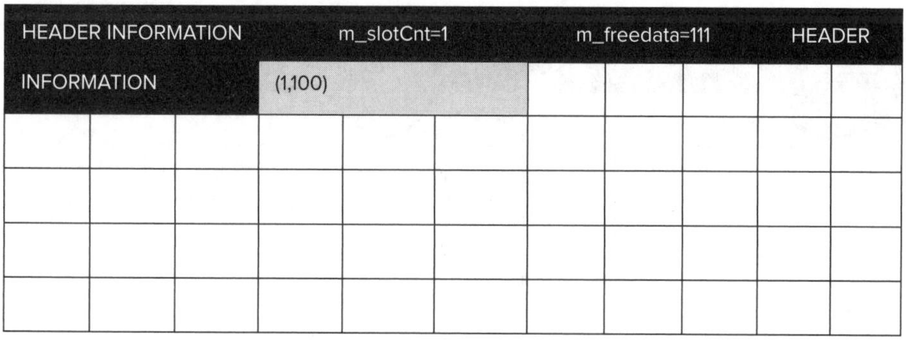

FIGURE 7-8

Consider that the white text on black background indicates the page header information, including the offset table. The grey background is the row containing (1,100), at position 96. The white background blocks are freedata, waiting to be allocated to further slots.

Now you can try doing some inserts, from two different sessions:

```
/*TRANSACTION 1 SESSION 1*/
    INSERT INTO LatchTable
    VALUES (2,200);

/*TRANSACTION 2 SESSION 2*/
    INSERT INTO LatchTable
    VALUES (3,300);
```

These inserts are concurrent and are received by the Lock Manager at the same time. Neither row exists, so there is no Exclusive (X) lock available on the row just yet. Both sessions receive an Intent Exclusive (IX) lock on the page, which are compatible with one another.

The transactions now proceed to the Buffer Manager to write their respective rows. The page is in memory, and both start to read it. The following two sections describe what can happen next. In the first fictitious scenario, latches do not exist. Then, once you have seen the problem that causes, the second section demonstrates how latches prevent it.

Without Latching

This part of the example represents a world without latches. Assume that the row containing the values (2,200) in Transaction 1 arrived at the page a fraction of a second before Transaction 2, when the values (3,300) are written. Transaction 1 writes to Slot 1, as seen in Figure 7-9 and Figure 7-10.

```
Slot 1, Offset 0x6f, Length 15, DumpStyle BYTE

Record Type = PRIMARY_RECORD          Record Attributes = NULL_BITMAP      Record Size = 15

Memory Dump @0x000000001580A06F

0000000000000000:    10000c00 02000000 c8000000 020000          ........È......
```

FIGURE 7-9

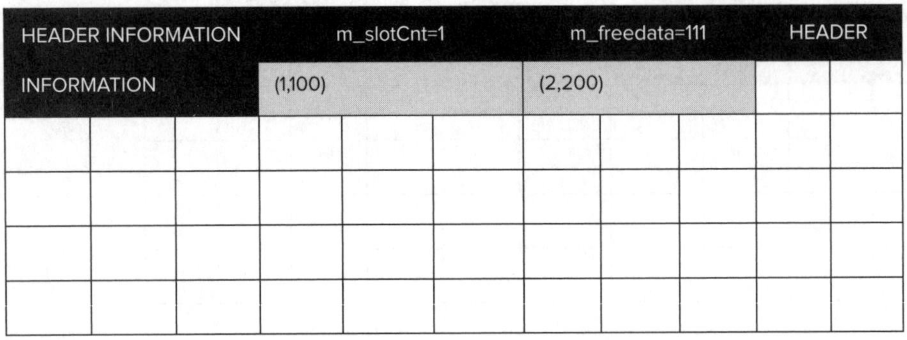

FIGURE 7-10

The update has gone through, as you have a second row in the page in slot 1 with the hex values 02 and c8 (which are the values 2 and 200, respectively). However, the page header is not yet updated. They still appear as in Figure 7-7. m_freedata is still 111, and the m_slotcnt value is still 1.

Before the header information is written, Transaction 2 arrives and wants to write a row with its values (3,300). Without a mechanism to stop it, Transaction 2 queries the m_freedata and m_slotcnt values, and writes its data into Slot 1, as seen in Figure 7-11 and Figure 7-12.

```
Slot 1, Offset 0x6f, Length 15, DumpStyle BYTE

Record Type = PRIMARY_RECORD          Record Attributes = NULL_BITMAP      Record Size = 15

Memory Dump @0x0000000011FEA06F

0000000000000000:    10000c00 03000000 2c010000 020000          .............,......
```

FIGURE 7-11

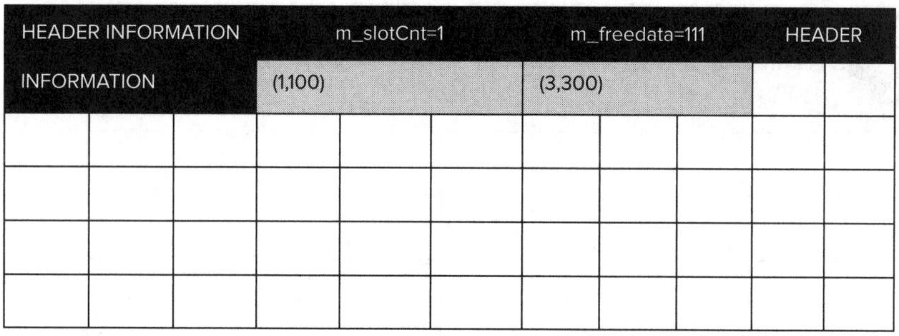

HEADER INFORMATION		m_slotCnt=1		m_freedata=111		HEADER	
INFORMATION		(1,100)		(3,300)			

FIGURE 7-12

Before the "2,200" transaction could update the metadata, the "3,300" transaction had arrived. This second transaction checked the m_freedata field, found the location to write the row, and made the change. By now Transaction 1 has updated the header information, but this is also overwritten by Transaction 2. The change made by Transaction 1 is gone, and we have a lost update, as seen in Figure 7-13 and Figure 7-14.

```
PAGE HEADER:


Page @0x00000002F9FA2000

m_pageId = (1:73)              m_headerVersion = 1           m_type = 1
m_typeFlagBits = 0x0           m_level = 0                   m_flagBits = 0x8200
m_objId (AllocUnitId.idobj) = 84   m_indexId (AllocUnitId.idInd) = 256
Metadata: AllocUnitId = 72057594043432960
Metadata: PartitionId = 72057594039042048
Metadata: ObjectId = 245575913     m_prevPage = (0:0)         Metadata: IndexId = 0
pminlen = 12                   m_slotCnt = 2                 m_nextPage = (0:0)
m_freeData = 126               m_reservedCnt = 2             m_freeCnt = 8062
m_xactReserved = 0             m_xdesId = (0:0)              m_lsn = (32:77:2)
m_tornBits = 1769750384        DB Frag ID = 1                m_ghostRecCnt = 0


Allocation Status

GAM (1:2) = ALLOCATED              SGAM (1:3) = ALLOCATED
PFS (1:1) = 0X61 MIXED_EXT ALLOCATED   50_PCT_FULL           DIFF (1:6) = CHANGED
ML (1:7) = NOT MIN_LOGGED

DATA:


Slot 0, Offset 0x60, Length 15, DumpStyle BYTE

Record Type = PRIMARY_RECORD        Record Attributes = NULL_BITMAP     Record Size = 15

Memory Dump @0x0000000011FEA060

0000000000000000:   10000c00 01000000 64000000 020000            ........d......

Slot 1, Offset 0x6f, Length 15, DumpStyle BYTE

Record Type = PRIMARY_RECORD        Record Attributes = NULL_BITMAP     Record Size = 15

Memory Dump @0x0000000011FEA06F

0000000000000000:   10000c00 03000000 2c010000 020000            ............,......

OFFSET TABLE:

Row - Offset
1 (0x1) - 111 (0x6f)
0 (0x0) - 96 (0x60)
```

FIGURE 7-13

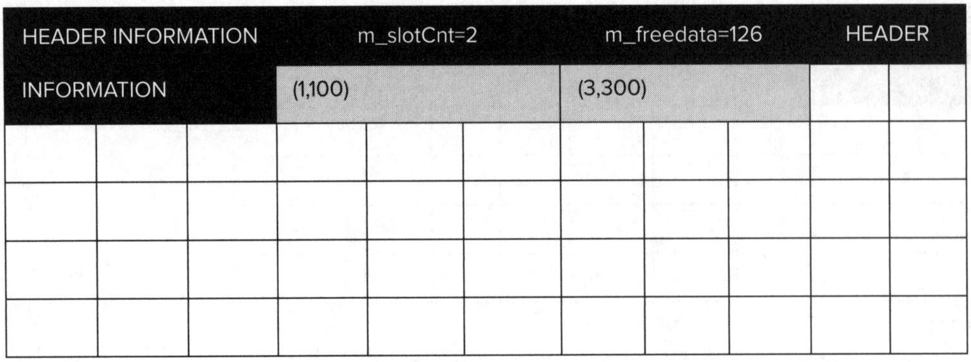

HEADER INFORMATION		m_slotCnt=2		m_freedata=126		HEADER	
INFORMATION		(1,100)		(3,300)			

FIGURE 7-14

This scenario reflects one of the prime uses for latches — serializing writes to prevent lost updates.

As mentioned before, you won't be able to repeat this demonstration. SQL Server wouldn't let you. In order to present it here, the output had to be massaged. Now take a look at what actually happens in a normal, i.e., latched, scenario. This you will be able to repeat.

With Latching

When these same steps are performed on a real SQL Server database, the behavior is affected by latches.

When Transaction 1 (2,200) gets to the page of memory, it acquires a latch. This is an EX latch, which you'll learn more about soon. A moment later, however, Transaction 2 (3,300) will also want an EX latch, which it won't be able to get. It has to wait for Transaction 1 to finish its business with that page (though not the whole transaction), and you will begin to see waits in sys.dm_os_wait_stats showing this.

With latches, Transaction 1 holds the EX latch for as long as it is needed to both write the row and update the page header and offset. Only then does it release the latch and allow another transaction in. Because of this, the page is never seen in the state shown in Figure 7-10 earlier.

Note that the 2,200 transaction does not wait for the completion of its transaction before releasing the latch. The latch isn't tied to the transaction in that sense. It's not a lock, designed to protect the integrity of the transaction; it's a latch, designed to protect the integrity of the memory. Handling the lock behavior, snapshot versions, and so on — that's all separate from this, but it may increase the amount of work that needs to be done by the process that has taken out the latch.

Once the latch has been released, the 3,300 transaction can get in with its own EX latch and insert its row of data, updating the header and offset accordingly, as seen in Figure 7-15 and Figure 7-16.

```
PAGE HEADER:


Page @0x00000002F3994000

m_pageId = (1:73)                     m_headerVersion = 1              m_type = 1
m_typeFlagBits = 0x0                  m_level = 0                     m_flagBits = 0x8000
m_objId (AllocUnitId.idobj) = 84      m_indexId (AllocUnitId.idInd) = 256
Metadata: AllocUnitId = 72057594043432960
Metadata: PartitionId = 72057594039042048
Metadata: ObjectId = 245575913        m_prevPage = (0:0)              Metadata: IndexId = 0
pminlen = 12                          m_slotCnt = 3                   m_nextPage = (0:0)
m_freeData = 141                      m_reservedCnt = 0               m_freeCnt = 8045
m_xactReserved = 0                    m_xdesId = (0:0)                m_lsn = (32:78:2)
m_tornBits = 0                        DB Frag ID = 1                  m_ghostRecCnt = 0


Allocation Status

GAM (1:2) = ALLOCATED                 SGAM (1:3) = ALLOCATED
PFS (1:1) = 0X61 MIXED_EXT ALLOCATED   50_PCT_FULL                    DIFF (1:6) = CHANGED
ML (1:7) = NOT MIN_LOGGED

DATA:

Slot 0, Offset 0x60, Length 15, DumpStyle BYTE

Record Type = PRIMARY_RECORD          Record Attributes = NULL_BITMAP    Record Size = 15

Memory Dump @0x000000001380A060

0000000000000000:   10000c00 01000000 64000000 020000          ........d......

Slot 1, Offset 0x6f, Length 15, DumpStyle BYTE

Record Type = PRIMARY_RECORD          Record Attributes = NULL_BITMAP    Record Size = 15

Memory Dump @0x000000001380A06F

0000000000000000:   10000c00 02000000 c8000000 020000          ........È......

Slot 2, Offset 0x7e, Length 15, DumpStyle BYTE

Record Type = PRIMARY_RECORD          Record Attributes = NULL_BITMAP    Record Size = 15

Memory Dump @0x000000001380A07E

0000000000000000:   10000c00 03000000 2c010000 020000          ..........,......

OFFSET TABLE:

Row - Offset
2 (0x2) - 126 (0x7e)
1 (0x1) - 111 (0x6f)
0 (0x0) - 96 (0x60)
```

FIGURE 7-15

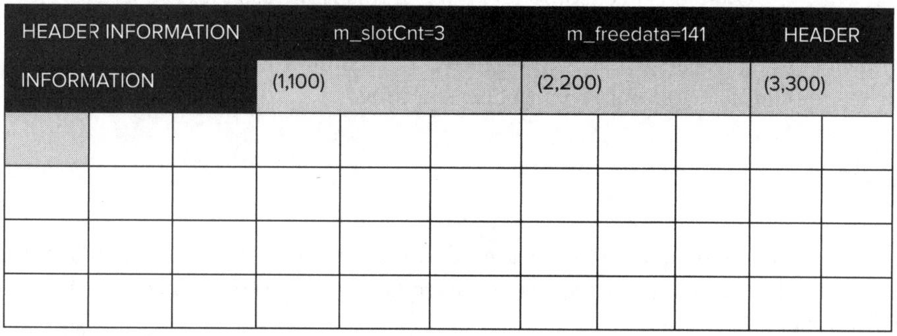

HEADER INFORMATION		m_slotCnt=3			m_freedata=141			HEADER	
INFORMATION		(1,100)			(2,200)			(3,300)	

FIGURE 7-16

In short, without latching, data is lost. With latching, it's not. It's that simple. Regardless of what kind of isolation level is being used by the transaction, SQL Server protects data with latches.

LATCH TYPES

As you learned in the preceding section, latches exist to protect in-memory data. There are hundreds of different types of latch, most of which you are unlikely to encounter in any meaningful way when you are working with SQL Server. While latch waits will occasionally show up in sys.dm_os_wait_ stats, you normally have to actively search for them. As a rule, they don't come to you.

Typically, latches are divided into two distinct categories in SQL Server. They either serve the buffer pool, in which case they are known as *BUF latches* (showing up as PAGELATCH or PAGEIOLATCH in sys.dm_os_wait_stats and aggregated into the BUFFER latch class in sys.dm_os_latch_stats), or they don't, in which case they are grouped under the non-buffer (*Non-BUF*) heading. This is a slight generalization, but it's adequate for our purposes here.

If you run the following query, you will get a list of more than 150 latch types (code file Ch7LatchTypes.sql):

```
SELECT  *
FROM    sys.dm_os_latch_stats;
```

If you order this data by any of the three numeric columns, you'll see that by far the most common latch type is BUFFER. If you look at the contents of sys.dm_os_wait_stats, you'll see latches that are prefixed with LATCH_, PAGELATCH_ and PAGEIOLATCH_.

The LATCH_ waits are all for the Non-BUF types. There are many of these, ensuring that the database engine can handle many of the operations it needs to perform. If you look through those latch types in sys.dm_os_latch_stats, you will see things such as BACKUP_FILE_HANDLE latches, SERVICE_BROKER latches, and even VERSIONING latches, which may be involved in your transactions depending on the isolation level.

The PAGELATCH_ latches are like those you saw in the example earlier. Data from a user object is needed, and to ensure that it can be written or read consistently, a latch is acquired. These buffer latches can be applied to all kinds of pages, including Page Free Space (PFS), Global Allocation Map (GAM), Shared Global Allocation Map (SGAM), and Index Allocation Map (IAM) pages.

The PAGEIOLATCH_ latch types are used when data is being moved from disk into RAM. An I/O operation is in play when a I/O latch is needed. In some ways, this is the easiest type latch wait to troubleshoot, as high PAGEIOLATCH wait times imply that the I/O subsystem cannot keep up. If this is the case, and you can't mitigate the problem through I/O reduction or increased RAM, you have a nice argument for buying that faster storage you've been wanting.

LATCH MODES

Latch modes are far easier to contemplate than lock modes. I'm sure you remember from Chapter 6 that nasty big matrix of lock compatibilities. Latches have far fewer modes, and compatibility is much more straightforward.

If you query sys.dm_os_wait_stats as follows (code file Ch7LatchModes.sql), you'll see the different modes listed there. This query is looking at the PAGELATCH_ latches, but you could use it for PAGEIOLATCH_ or LATCH_ instead and see the same latch modes. They are the two character combinations following the underscore.

```
SELECT   *
FROM     sys.dm_os_wait_stats
where wait_type like 'PAGELATCH%';
```

Six latch modes are listed, usually in the following order: NL, KP, SH, UP, EX, DT. While there's no guarantee they'll appear in this order if you don't specify an ORDER BY clause, this is the order you'll likely see.

NL

NL is an internal Null latch. You don't need to consider it. It essentially means no latch is being used, so it isn't even recorded under normal conditions.

KP

KP is a Keep latch, used to indicate that a particular page is needed for something and shouldn't be destroyed.

SH

This refers to a Shared latch, which is needed to read the data from a page.

UP

This is an Update latch, which indicates that a page is being updated, but not the table data within it. This is not related to the T-SQL UPDATE statement, which requires an Exclusive latch (the next mode discussed). Update latches are more common for internal operations, such as maintaining PFS pages or updating the checksum bits on a page. Because the type of data being updated is not needed to service queries, it is compatible with a shared latch, but not another Update latch.

EX

When data is being explicitly changed or added, an Exclusive latch is required. This is the most common type of latch for troubleshooting purposes, as two EX latches cannot be held on the same page at the same time. While this is also true of UP latches, EX latches are the more common of the two.

DT

The presence of this latch, the Destroy latch, means that the page is in the process of being removed from memory. A page that is deleted picks up a DT latch from the lazywriter process while the record of the page is removed. Bear in mind that this does not necessarily mean that the data is being deleted — it may simply be removed from the buffer cache, with a copy of the data still residing on the disk. However, multiple steps are involved in removing a page from the buffer cache, as the SQL Server engine maintains a hash table that lists which pages are currently in memory (otherwise, it wouldn't know the memory address of the page). The DT latch cannot be taken out if any other kind of latch is on the page, which makes the KP latch much more significant. A page that is needed but isn't yet being read or written would use a KP latch to prevent the DT latch from being acquired.

Latch Compatibility

The five latch types (ignoring the internal NL latch) are compatible as shown in Table 7-1. Note how much simpler it is than the lock compatibility equivalent.

TABLE 7-1: Latch Types

	KP	SH	UP	EX	DT
KP	Y	Y	Y	Y	N
SH	Y	Y	Y	N	N
UP	Y	Y	N	N	N
EX	Y	N	N	N	N
DT	N	N	N	N	N

A page that has an EX latch on it can have a KP latch applied, but not any other type. Similarly, the only type of latch that can exist on a page that needs an EX latch applied is a KP latch. Unlike the lock compatibility table, there are no surprises in the latch compatibility table.

Despite the simplicity of this table, be sure you feel comfortable with the various scenarios that are possible. Consider the page with the shared latch that allows an update latch to be acquired on it (for an internal process to make a change to non-user data), but not an exclusive latch (which would mean that actual data was changing). Consider the page that is being destroyed and doesn't allow anything else to come near it; and the update latch, which prevents other update latches.

Grant Order

In any system, particularly as the number of processor threads grows, a number of requests will be queued for a particular page. For example, a number of pages might be inserting data into a table while others are reading that data, and the data may need to be moved from disk, and so on.

For a page that has no latches on it, the first process that wants a latch will be granted one. That's straightforward; but when more processes start coming along, the behavior is slightly different. A KP latch will skip the queue completely — unless there is a DT latch on the page, a KP latch will jump ahead and keep it alive.

Other latches will wait, joining the queue (even if there is compatibility between the two — another slight difference between lock behavior and latch behavior). When the current latch is released, the first latch in the queue can be granted, but here something special happens. Any other latch in the queue that is compatible with that first latch (which is being granted) will be allowed, even if there are incompatible locks in front of it. It's like the nightclub bouncer who takes the first person in the queue but also looks through it for anyone else who can be let in. This way, the next latch type in line is always granted, but there's an opportunity for other latches to jump in through the closing door at the same time. Typically, latches are taken out for short periods, so the incompatible latches shouldn't have to wait for too long, depending on what's going on. The algorithm might not seem fair, but it does make sure that concurrency can apply when possible.

Latch Waits

You've already looked at wait types such as `PAGELATCH_EX` and `PAGEIOLATCH_SH`, but there's more to discuss about this in order to provide a complete picture of the information in `sys.dm_os_wait_stats`. As described earlier, some latches can come into contention with one another. This is intended and necessary as part of the need to serialize access. However, as with locking, this does raise the prospect of blocking, and consequently latch waiting.

A *latch wait* can be defined as a latch request that cannot be granted immediately. This could result from one of two reasons. First, the latch is already being accessed. As stated earlier, new latches are evaluated at the closure of the existing request. The second reason follows from the first. When the wait list is accessed following the closure of the previous latch, the next wait in that list may be a conflicting lock with other waits. If you refer back to the grant order example, when an EX request is processed, no other latch may be granted at the same time.

Unfortunately, there are side effects to keeping latches lightweight. They do not provide full blocking task information when forced to wait. Blocking task information is only known when the latch is held in one of the write latch modes — namely, UP, EX, and DT. Given that only one task can hold a latch in one of these modes at any one time, identifying it as the blocker is relatively straightforward. Suppose the blocker is a read latch (either KP or SH) — this latch could be held by many tasks simultaneously, so identifying the task that is the blocker is not always possible. When the blocker is known, all waiting tasks will report that the one task is the cause of the block. Logically, then, the wait type is that of the requester, not the blocker.

It is possible for this blocking information to change during a single task's wait. Consider this example: A UP latch has been granted. Another task has requested a DT latch and therefore has been forced to wait. At this point the blocker is reported, as the latch held is a UP latch. By definition this can only be a single task. Before the UP latch has been released, a KP latch sneaks in and is granted (remember that KPs don't respect the FIFO rules). The UP latch is then released, leaving the KP in place to do its thing. It can no longer be guaranteed that this KP is the only latch in play. The DT latch is still forced to wait because the KP is already there. However, now there is no serialized write latch mode in effect and the blocking information is lost. What can be said though at this point is that the blocker is either a KP latch or a SH latch.

It is also possible for a task to be shown to block itself in certain scenarios (although it is somewhat of an illusion, as the blocking is probably being done by internal threads that belong to the database engine rather than the actual task). This is due to the asynchronous nature of data access. Again, this is probably best illustrated with an example. Consider this scenario: A read request is made to the Buffer Manager, but when the hash table is checked, it is found that the page doesn't exist in memory. An I/O request is scheduled and a `PAGIOLATCH_EX latch` is taken (assume granted) on a BUF structure to allow the page to be read into the data page for the buffer. The task that initiated the request will then submit an SH latch to read the data. However, this can appear as being blocked by the EX latch if there is a lag retrieving the page from disk.

SUPERLATCHES/SUBLATCHES

If you think about what kinds of pages would have latches applied to them frequently, it's easy to consider the exclusive latches on insert pages; but a far more commonly latched page would be the root page of a frequently used index. Every time a seek is performed on an index, the root page must be read to help point the way to the page containing the rest of the data. Even tables that are frequently written to have a lot of shared access (for reading) on the root page of the indexes on those tables. The root pages probably don't need to change very often at all, but they need to be read repeatedly.

The queuing method of accepting all compatible latches each time the latching check is done only helps so far. It's still a lot of work to manage all this. Enter the SuperLatch (or sublatch). SuperLatches improve the performance of systems with 32 or more logical processors by promoting a single latch into an array of sublatches, one for each CPU core. This way, each core can easily acquire a sublatch without having to apply the shared latch to the page, because it's already taken out.

The PSS SQL blog site has some useful diagrams showing how this looks, which they have generously let us use here (see Figure 7-17 and Figure 7-18) from `http://blogs.msdn.com/b/psssql/archive/2009/01/28/hot-it-works-sql-server-superlatch-ing-sub-latches.aspx`.

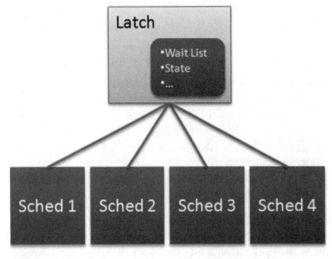

FIGURE 7-17

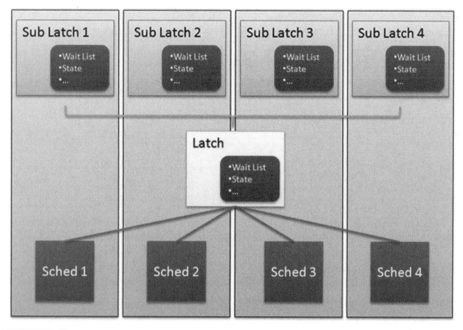

FIGURE 7-18

In the original scenario, there would be a single latch with a wait list of items trying to reach it. When the latch is released, the single wait list can be examined for compatible latches again, and the shared latch re-acquired. As a SuperLatch, the SuperLatch remains acquired, and each sublatch is handled by a processor. The sublatch then resides inside a single-processor microcosm, in a cache local to the CPU, sort of like the chair in your house when you're the only person home — so that processor has much freer access to the page as long as the sublatch is shared.

The problem appears when a processor needs an exclusive latch. To do this, the SuperLatch must coordinate with all the sublatches to ensure that they're all converted to exclusive latches when the time is right. It's a lot more expensive than acquiring a regular exclusive latch; so if this happens often enough, the SuperLatch is demoted to an ordinary latch. SuperLatches are useful, but only on pages that are almost always read-only.

MONITORING LATCHES AND SPINLOCKS

In terms of monitoring latches, you've already been introduced to some of the DMVs. There's more to monitoring latches than just DMVs, though. Performance Monitor also offers useful informa-tion about latches, as do extended events, which also provide information about spinlocks. Another option is to use memory dumps, but those are not covered here.

DMVs

The DMVs covered earlier are a useful point of reference. You should familiarize yourself with the contents of sys.dm_os_wait_stats, sys.dm_os_latch_stats, and sys.dm_os_spinlock_stats, and be comfortable with the output they provide. In addition, `sys.dm_os_waiting_tasks` will display a list of any tasks that are currently waiting on a resource, providing a useful `session_id` column that can be used to hook into other useful DMVs for information about sessions and the like.

sys.dm_os_wait_stats

This DMV has five columns.

- ➤ `wait_type`
- ➤ `waiting_tasks_count`
- ➤ `wait_time_ms`
- ➤ `max_wait_time_ms`
- ➤ `signal_wait_time_ms`

The first three were described earlier. `max_wait_time_ms` shows the largest wait time for a single wait since the DMV was cleared. `signal_wait_time_ms` is less relevant for latches, although it does get used if threads hit spinlock barriers.

sys.dm_os_latch_stats

This DMV has four columns.

- ➤ `latch_class`
- ➤ `waiting_requests_count`
- ➤ `wait_time_ms`
- ➤ `max_wait_time_ms`

These columns have all been described earlier.

sys.dm_os_spinlock_stats

This DMV has six columns.

- ➤ `name`
- ➤ `collisions`
- ➤ `spins`
- ➤ `spins_per_collision`
- ➤ `sleep_time`
- ➤ `backoffs`

A collision is recorded when a spinlock tries to acquire a resource but finds it unavailable. As a result, the spinlock starts spinning. This increases the spins but the collision has already been recorded. Usefully, this DMV also provides a `spins_per_collision` column, saving the user from doing the calculation.

I'm sure you can imagine that the number of spins is potentially quite large. Let's just say that it's a good thing that this column is a bigint type, which handles numbers up to 19 digits long. I don't think the correct technical term is actually "gazillions," but it feels right when you take a look at this DMV on busy systems that have been up for a while.

The `sleep_time` and `backoffs` columns simply report the amount of time that has been spent sleeping on spinlocks, and the number of backoffs.

Performance Monitor

Performance Monitor provides several useful counters to keep an eye on. Figure 7-19 shows a typical screenshot containing the list of counters in the SQLServer:Latches category for a machine.

FIGURE 7-19

Table 7-2 describes these counters.

TABLE 7-2: Useful Performance Monitor Counters

COUNTER	DESCRIPTION
Average Latch Wait Time (ms)	Average latch wait time (in milliseconds) for latch requests that had to wait
Latch Waits/sec	Number of latch requests that could not be granted immediately and had to wait before being granted
Number of SuperLatches	Number of latches that are currently SuperLatches
SuperLatch Demotions/sec	Number of SuperLatches that have been demoted to regular latches
SuperLatch Promotions/sec	Number of latches that have been promoted to SuperLatches
Total Latch Wait Time (ms)	Total latch wait time (in milliseconds) for latch requests that had to wait in the last second

These performance counter values are also available using the DMV `sys.dm_os_performance_counters` (see Figure 7-20) (code file `Ch7Monitoring.sql`):

```
SELECT *
FROM sys.dm_os_performance_counters
WHERE object_name LIKE '%Latches%';
```

```
select *
from sys.dm_os_performance_counters
where object_name like '%Latches%'
```

	object_name	counter_name	instance_name	cntr_value	cntr_type
1	SQLServer:Latches	Latch Waits/sec		1281939	272696576
2	SQLServer:Latches	Average Latch Wait Time (ms)		187379	1073874176
3	SQLServer:Latches	Average Latch Wait Time Base		1281939	1073939712
4	SQLServer:Latches	Total Latch Wait Time (ms)		187379	272696576
5	SQLServer:Latches	Number of SuperLatches		0	65792
6	SQLServer:Latches	SuperLatch Promotions/sec		0	272696576
7	SQLServer:Latches	SuperLatch Demotions/sec		0	272696576

FIGURE 7-20

Note that although the `object_name` field appears to end in the string `'Latches'`, this field is actually stored as nchar(256), rather than nvarchar(256), so there is a large amount of whitespace at the end, and that last `%` is needed.

Extended Events

Chapter 13 is dedicated to the topic of extended events, so this section simply explains which extended events are available for latches and spinlocks. If you open the New Session Wizard for Extended Events from SQL Server 2012 Management Studio, you will reach a screen from which you select the events you wish to capture. After reaching this, first scroll the Event library section to reveal the Channel drop-down box. Then, as shown in Figure 7-21, check Debug, which is unchecked by default.

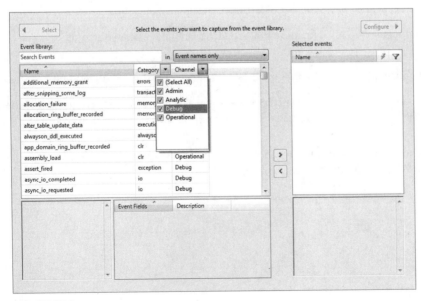

FIGURE 7-21

Now you can search for spinlock and latch to find a list of extended events related to these areas, as described in Table 7-3.

TABLE 7-3: Spinlock and Latch Extended Events

EXTENDED EVENT	DESCRIPTION
spinlock_backoff	Spinlock backoff
spinlock_backoff_warning	Occurs when a spinlock backoff warning is sent to the Error Log
latch_acquire_time	Time taken to acquire a latch
latch_demoted	Occurs when a SuperLatch is demoted to an ordinary latch
latch_promoted	Occurs when a latch is promoted to a SuperLatch
latch_suspend_begin	Occurs when the executing task must suspend while waiting for a latch to become available in the requested mode
latch_suspend_end	Occurs when the executing task is resumed after waiting for a latch
latch_suspend_warning	Occurs when there is a timeout waiting for a latch possibly causing performance problems

You should now be able to create an XE session collecting these events. Bear in mind that you would typically expect to see many more latch_acquire_time events occurring than the other event types, and you might not want to bother collecting them.

LATCH CONTENTION EXAMPLES

All of the code in this section uses the Ch7Examples.sql code file.

Earlier in the chapter, you saw a contrived example demonstrating why a latch is necessary. This section looks at a couple of examples demonstrating contention issues involving latches and spinlocks. Some of these examples are borrowed from various presentations involving the SQLCAT team at SQLBits events in the U.K., and we are indebted to Thomas Kejser in particular for his work on these.

Inserts When the Clustered Index Key Is an Identity Field

A lot of advice suggests using an identity field for the clustered index on a table. Certainly there are benefits to doing this. An identity field is typically an int or bigint type, making it relatively small compared to some other candidates for primary keys, in particular uniqueidentifier fields, which can cause frequent page splits, as well as being overly large, especially because clustered index keys appear in nonclustered indexes as well.

However, for tables that use identity fields for clustered index keys, when the number of inserts scales up, the final page will become "hot," and contention could occur.

Consider the scenario in which a lot of processor cores are trying to insert data into the same page. The first session to reach the page in question will obtain a PAGELATCH_EX latch; but in the same moment, a large number of other threads might also be trying to acquire a PAGELATCH_EX latch. There would also be PAGELATCH_SH latches acquired at the higher index levels, to allow these pages to be traversed. If the insert needs to tip onto a new page, then a PAGELATCH_EX would be required at the next index level higher.

If sys.dm_os_waiting_tasks were queried during heavy inserts, it would likely show PAGELATCH_EX waits, with the resource_description column showing the page of note. The page could be examined, with DBCC PAGE, and identified as the table under stress.

The point here is not to make a case against ever using an identity field for a clustered index. In many systems, it's still an excellent idea. However, if you're seeing a large amount of latch contention during busy periods of insertion into such a table, then this design choice may certainly be a contributor to the predicament.

The solution has to move the activity away from the hotspot of insertion. While this could be done by simply replacing the identity field with a new uniqueidentifier field, populated with newid() values, the same goal can be achieved in other ways. One way of spreading the load sufficiently without losing the benefits of having a small clustered index, with the data nicely arranged in a b-tree, is to introduce partitioning. This way, the table is spread across a number of b-tree structures, instead of just one. With a bit of planning, the activity can be spread across the partitions. There may still be a hotspot for each partition, but this could well be enough to relieve the stress on the problem page.

The following example assumes that eight partitions are wanted, but you could choose whatever number suited your needs. All the partitions can be put on the same filegroup; this exercise is not designed to use partitions to spread the table across multiple filegroups, but merely to make additional b-tree structures to store the table.

```
CREATE PARTITION FUNCTION pf_spread (TINYNT) AS RANGE LEFT FOR VALUES
(0,1,2,3,4,5,6);
CREATE PARTITION SCHEME ps_spread AS PARTITION pf_spread ALL TO (PRIMARY);
```

To spread the data across your various partitions, you simply need to introduce into the table a column that causes the data to be distributed. In this case, ID % 8 will do nicely:

```
ALTER TABLE MyStressedTable
ADD PartID AS CAST(ID % 8 AS TINYINT) PERSISTED NOT NULL;
```

Once this is done, the clustered index simply needs to be created on the partitions:

```
CREATE UNIQUE CLUSTERED INDEX cixMyStressedTable (ID, PartID) ON ps_spread(PartID);
```

Now, inserts will be cycled around the eight partitions, which should enable many more inserts to be done before latch contention occurs. Going back to the analogy using the chairs at a party, this partitioning provides seven more chairs. If the number of threads being used to perform the inserts is such that there is now a very small number of threads per b-tree, then the likelihood of contention is very much reduced.

Of course, additional partitions might translate into more work finding data using the ID field. A query that simply filters on the ID field would need to search all eight partitions, despite the fact that you can see a correlation between the ID and the partition. To avoid having to search across all the partitions, code such as

```
SELECT *
FROM dbo.MyStressedTable
WHERE ID = @id;
```

should be changed to

```
SELECT *
FROM dbo.MyStressedTable
WHERE ID = @id
AND PartID = CAST(@id % 8 AS TINYINT);
```

Queuing

Another typical scenario that can exhibit large amounts of latch contention is a system designed to allow queuing, for similar reasons to the last example, although exhibited in a slightly different way, and certainly resolved with a different method.

Most queues are handled using a table, with numerous inserts used to push items onto the queue, and deletes using TOP to enable quickly locating the earliest row in the table. Techniques such as using the OUTPUT clause can help with concurrency, but as the load increases this kind of design can still end up showing latch contention issues.

Certainly there would be PAGELATCH_EX waits in the leaf levels, as in the last example; but from time to time, activity in the leaf levels would cause similar activity through the higher levels of the b-tree, even up to the root. This means there is potential for contention between the inserts and deletes, even if they are at opposite sides of the b-tree. A representation of this can be seen in Figure 7-22.

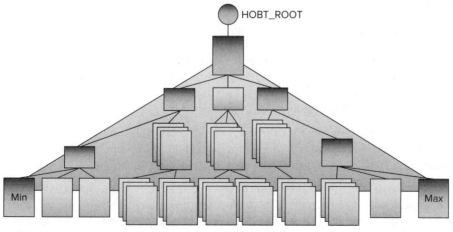

FIGURE 7-22

It's interesting to note at this point that some of the changes required at the higher levels of a b-tree when performing inserts and deletes are simply not required when performing updates. Unless the update causes a page split by being larger than the earlier page, and provided the clustered index key values for the row being updated don't change, an update command should not need to affect the higher levels of the clustered index at all. This is similar to changing information in the page of a book. The table of contents need not change if only the information in a particular paragraph is being updated, and no extra pages are being introduced.

To that end, one method to avoid this kind of latch contention is to pre-populate a table with a number of fixed-length columns, and then cycle through them with updates, using two sequences to help the queuing stored procedures to know which value is at the top of the queue, and which one is at the end. It is important to gauge the maximum length of the queue. The impact on the b-tree of needing to perform inserts is significant, and should be avoided with a little planning.

An approach such as this can work nicely:

```
CREATE SEQUENCE dbo.seqQueuePush START WITH 1 CACHE 1000;
CREATE SEQUENCE dbo.seqQueuePop START WITH 1 CACHE 1000;
```

Unless specified otherwise, sequences are created using the bigint type, starting at the lowest possible. Because the maximum bigint is extremely large, it might be a little nicer to start with 1 and work up. Either way, it's important to have your queue start empty, with both sequences at the same number. A cache is used to avoid a bottleneck on generating the next number. You should experiment to see what size cache suits your particular queuing system.

As well as markers to indicate the locations of the beginning and end of your queue, you need a table structure to hold it. For example, if you anticipate needing to be able to handle 10,000 messages in the queue, you should create 10,000 positions using placeholder messages. This enables the b-tree to grow to the appropriate size before the system is under load.

The following code will create the queue, and populate it with the 10,000 placeholder items.

```
CREATE TABLE dbo.MyQueue (ID INT, Available BIT, Message CHAR(7000));
INSERT dbo.MyQueue
SELECT TOP (10000) ROW_NUMBER() OVER (ORDER BY (SELECT 1))-1, 1, ''
FROM sys.all_columns t1, sys.all_columns t2;
```

The message has been chosen at 7,000 characters, as it fits nicely within a single page. Note that it is CHAR(7000), not VARCHAR(7000), as the row should be fixed length. You do not want to implement compression at this point either. A bit column is used to indicate whether or not the position in the queue is taken, in case the queue fills up completely.

These 10,000 slots are numbered from 0 to 9,999. Your ever-increasing sequences will far exceed this range, but the modulo function will provide a mapping, enabling the sequence numbers to roll around to the start every 10 thousand entries.

When message 3,549,232 arrives, it would be pushed into slot 9232. If message 3,549,019 is being popped out at the time, it would be found in slot 9,019. After these two operations, the sequences would be ready to tell the system that the next slot for a push would be position 3,549,233, and for a pop it would be 3,549,020. Any delay in processing the messages that are being popped off the queue would be fine as long as the size of the queue doesn't stretch beyond 10,000.

Pushing a message onto the queue is therefore as simple as incrementing the sequence, performing a modulo 10,000 on the sequence number to discover into which slot the message should be pushed, and running an UPDATE command to put the message into that appropriate slot:

```
DECLARE @pushpos INT = NEXT VALUE FOR dbo.seqQueuePush % 10000;
UPDATE dbo.MyQueue SET Message = @msg, Available = 0
WHERE ID = @pushpos;
```

To pop a message from the queue, code such as this could be used:

```
DECLARE @poppos INT = NEXT VALUE FOR dbo.seqQueuePop % 10000;
UPDATE dbo.Queue SET Message = '', Available = 1
OUTPUT deleted.Message
WHERE ID = @poppos;
```

Some testing could be performed to ensure that the queue is not empty, but this technique can certainly enable up to 10,000 messages in the queue at any one time, and spread a heavy load across a large number of pages. Most important, negative impact on the higher levels of the b-tree, caused by performing inserts and deletes, can be avoided.

An environment that leverages the efficiency of updates in this way has already been seen in this chapter. There was data that needs to be updated very quickly, and updates are used rather than inserts — as shown in Figure 7-23, the DMV sys.dm_os_latch_stats:

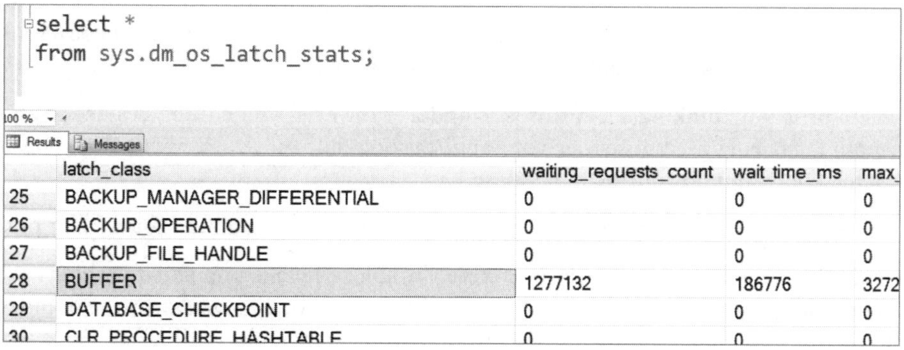

```
select *
from sys.dm_os_latch_stats;
```

	latch_class	waiting_requests_count	wait_time_ms	max_
25	BACKUP_MANAGER_DIFFERENTIAL	0	0	0
26	BACKUP_OPERATION	0	0	0
27	BACKUP_FILE_HANDLE	0	0	0
28	BUFFER	1277132	186776	3272
29	DATABASE_CHECKPOINT	0	0	0
30	CLR_PROCEDURE_HASHTABLE	0	0	0

FIGURE 7-23

It does not contain any kind of ID field. The only fields are latch_class, waiting_requests_count, wait_time_ms, and max_wait_time_ms; and yet the data is always returned in order, and the order is meaningful. The BUFFER class is always row 28. ACCESS_METHODS_HOBT_VIRTUAL_ROOT is always row 5 (this is a non-buffer latch that exhibits waits when root splits are needed, which would occur if a traditional delete/insert queue had been implemented).

You may have noticed when querying this DMV that many of the entries are zero, but the entries are still there. This is different to, say, sys.dm_db_index_usage_stats, which only includes a row once an index is used for a scan, seek, lookup, or update operation.

The sys.dm_os_latch_stats DMV is like your queue structure. It needs to be able to respond extremely quickly, as do many of the internal mechanisms within SQL Server. To that end, it is much quicker to set bits than to squeeze them in. Incrementing a counter that is already in place is a significantly better option than trying to preserve space until it is needed, if the speed of recording the data is to be maintained.

UP Latches in tempdb

It is possible that the resource your request is waiting on might be in tempdb, rather than the database you have designed. You can see this by looking at the `wait_resource` field in `sys.dm_exec_requests` and, in particular, the first number, which indicates the database. The number 2 means that tempdb has the problem.

If `PAGELATCH_UP` waits are seen on the first page in any of the files in tempdb — that is, page 2:1:1 or 2:4:1 (essentially, 2:N:1 for any N) — then this indicates that the PFS (Page Free Space) page is exhibiting latch contention. This can be confirmed by looking at `sys.dm_os_buffer_descriptors`:

```
SELECT page_type
FROM sys.dm_os_buffer_descriptors
WHERE database_id = 2 AND page_id = 1;
```

A common reaction to any kind of contention in tempdb is to increase the number of data files it uses. It is good practice to have more than one tempdb data file in a multi-threaded environment, but continually adding new files isn't necessarily the best approach to resolve this problem.

The `PFS_PAGE` resource must be updated whenever data is inserted into a table without a clustered index — that is, a heap. This doesn't imply that a heap is necessarily bad; there are many positive things about storing data outside b-trees. However, the `PFS_PAGE` must be consulted whenever an insert is done, to locate a page with enough free space for the insert.

At this point you're probably thinking, "But this is tempdb." However, you haven't designed your database for tempdb; it's being used to service your application, and you've already made sure that you don't have latch contention in your own database.

One common cause of this type of contention is the use of multi-statement table-valued functions.

A multi-statement table-valued function declares a table variable, which is populated within the code of the function definition. Finally, the `RETURN` command is issued, which returns the populated table variable to the user. Examples of this can be seen in SQL Server Books Online.

This is in contrast to an inline table-valued function, which is handled very differently.

Like a scalar function, a multi-statement table-valued function is executed in a separate context. It is no coincidence that both methods use `BEGIN` and `END` and in many ways are more similar to a stored procedure. An inline function does not use `BEGIN` and `END`, and is more similar to a view in that the subquery within is extracted into the outer query, not simply the results. The tempdb database is used to store the results of multi-statement table-valued functions, and it is here that contention could occur.

Imagine a scenario in which a multi-statement table-valued function is used in a correlated subquery, such as an `EXISTS` clause, or in the `SELECT` clause. Without the ability to perform simplification on the function, the Query Optimizer may well need to call the function many times. This is commonly seen in scalar functions used in the `WHERE` clause, but it can also be seen when a multi-statement table-valued function is used outside the `FROM` clause.

The storage used by tempdb for the results of a multi-statement table-valued function must be managed, which involves the PFS_PAGE resource (using UP latches, because the information being updated is not table data, which would require an EX latch), as it determines where new records can be placed, and it marks them as free once the results have been consumed by the outer query. Even a single statement can end up having such a function called many times, causing contention even within a single query.

I'm sure you can imagine some of the ways to avoid this contention. Inline equivalents can be useful; and restructuring the query to avoid using the function in an EXISTS or SELECT clause can also be effective. That's because latch contention is not just about the database design, but also about the way in which queries are written.

Spinlock Contention in Name Resolution

Unfortunately, developers do not always qualify their object names in their queries. This is particularly common in older applications, originally written in SQL Server 2000 or earlier, before schemas were introduced, but it also occurs in many other systems. It's very easy to assume that dbo is the only schema used, and to omit the dbo. prefix in table names — using, for example

```
SELECT * FROM Customers;
```

instead of

```
SELECT * FROM dbo.Customers;
```

This is a simple error to make, and you may not notice any discernible effect on your system until it needs to scale. However, if you don't specify the schema, the system needs to do a couple of quick checks. It has to determine your default schema, and it has to check whether there is a table with that name in your default schema. If not, it has to check the dbo schema to see if that's what you meant.

All this can happen very quickly — so quickly that a spinlock is used. It would be rare to find that a spinlock could not be acquired immediately on such an operation, but you may well see this occurring on a system under significant load. The contention appears on the SOS_CACHESTORE spinlock type. Fortunately, it's simple to resolve: Just ensure that you always fully qualify your table names.

SUMMARY

Latch contention is not something that can be controlled by hints in the same way that locks can. Latches are designed to protect the very internal structures within SQL Server that hold data, and they are absolutely necessary.

As the demands on your data increase, with more and more processor threads needing access, even latches can start to contend for resources. Good design decisions, both schema design and query design, can typically prevent these problems, however, and you should be able to avoid most latch contention issues through appropriate planning and awareness.

Knowing Tempdb

WHAT'S IN THIS CHAPTER?

➤ How SQL Server uses tempdb for internal and user-created temporary objects

➤ Avoiding and troubleshooting common tempdb issues

➤ How to monitor and tune tempdb performance

➤ Using configuration best practices to increase the performance and availability of tempdb

WROX.COM CODE DOWNLOADS FOR THIS CHAPTER

The wrox.com code downloads for this chapter are found at `http://www.wrox.com/remtitle.cgi?isbn=1118177657` on the Download Code tab. The code is in the Chapter 8 download and individually named according to the names throughout the chapter.

INTRODUCTION

This chapter is about the system database called tempdb, which is used for storing temporary objects and has been a key component of SQL Server since its inception. Beginning with SQL Server 2005, however, the role of tempdb has been brought to the forefront with a plethora of new features and optimizations that depend on temporary objects.

All these features have increased the visibility and requirement for good tempdb performance, which is why we have dedicated a full chapter to a thorough grounding in what it is used for, how to troubleshoot issues, and how it should be configured.

The first section looks at what makes tempdb special, which SQL Server components use it, and specifically how it is used. The next section covers common issues and how to troubleshoot them, which sets the scene for the configuration recommendations that follow. Finally, you'll find an especially useful best practices section at the end of the chapter.

NEW FOR SQL SERVER 2012

The only major change for tempdb in SQL Server 2012 is support for file placement on local storage within a Failover Cluster Instance. You can read about why and how you might do that in the "Configuration Best Practices" section of this chapter.

OVERVIEW AND USAGE

You can think of tempdb as the "scratch" database for SQL Server; it's a temporary data store used by both applications and internal operations. It is very similar to other databases in that it has a data file and a log file and can be found in SQL Server Management Studio, but it does have some unique characteristics that affect how you use and manage it.

The first fact to note is that everyone using an instance shares the same tempdb; you cannot have any more than one within an instance of SQL Server but you can get detailed information about who is doing what in tempdb using DMVs, which are discussed in the section on troubleshooting space issues later in the chapter.

The following features and attributes should be considered when learning about, using, tuning, and troubleshooting tempdb:

> ➤ Nothing stored in tempdb persists after a restart because tempdb is recreated every time SQL Server starts. This also has implications for the *recovery* of tempdb — namely, it doesn't need to be done. See the following sidebar.

TEMPDB HAS FEWER LOGGING OPERATIONS

When you change a value in a normal database, both the old value and the new value are stored in the transaction log. The old value is used in case you need to roll-back the transaction that made the change (undo), and the new value is used to roll-forward the change during recovery (redo) if it hadn't made it to the data file before the restart (see dirty pages and checkpoints in Chapter 1).

You still need to be able to undo a change in tempdb but you'll never need to redo the change as everything is thrown away on restart. Therefore, tempdb doesn't store the redo information, which can result in significant performance gains when making many changes to big columns compared to a user database.

➤ Tempdb is always set to "Simple" recovery mode, which, if you remember from Chapter 1, means that transaction log records for committed transactions are marked for reuse after every checkpoint. This means you don't need to back up the transaction log for tempdb, and in fact, you can't back up tempdb at all.

➤ Tempdb can only have one filegroup (the PRIMARY filegroup); you can't add more.

➤ Tempdb is used to store three types of objects: user objects, internal objects, and the version store.

User Temporary Objects

All the code in this section uses the Ch8_1TempDBTempObjects.sql code file.

To store data temporarily you can use local temporary tables, global temporary tables, or table variables, all of which are stored in tempdb (you can't change where they're stored). A local temporary table is defined by giving it a prefix of # and it is scoped to the session in which you created it. This means no one can see it; and when you disconnect, or your session is reset with connection pooling, the table is dropped. The following example creates a local temporary table, populates it with one row, and then selects from it:

```
CREATE TABLE #TempTable ( ID INT, NAME CHAR(3) ) ;
INSERT  INTO #TempTable ( ID, NAME )
VALUES  ( 1, 'abc' ) ;
GO
SELECT  *
FROM    #TempTable ;
GO
DROP TABLE #TempTable ;
```

Global temporary tables can be seen by all sessions connected to the server and are defined by a prefix of ##. They are used in exactly the same way as local temporary tables, the only difference being that everyone can see them. They are not used very often because if you had a requirement for multiple users to use the same table, you're more likely to implement a normal table in a user database, rather than a global temporary table. Here is exactly the same code just shown but implemented as a global temporary table:

```
CREATE TABLE ##TempTable ( ID INT, NAME CHAR(3) ) ;
INSERT  INTO ##TempTable ( ID, NAME )
VALUES  ( 1, 'abc' ) ;
GO
SELECT  *
FROM    ##TempTable ;
GO
DROP TABLE ##TempTable ;
```

As you can see, the only difference is the prefix; both local temporary tables and global temporary tables are dropped when the session that created them is closed. This means it is not possible to create a global temporary table in one session, close the session, and then use it in another.

A table variable is used similarly to a local temporary table. The differences are explored in the next section. Here is the same sample again, this time implemented as a table variable:

```
DECLARE @TempTable TABLE ( ID INT, NAME CHAR(3) ) ;
INSERT  INTO @TempTable ( ID, NAME )
VALUES  ( 1, 'abc' ) ;
SELECT  *
FROM    @TempTable ;
```

The syntax for declaring a table variable is slightly different from a temporary table; but a more important difference is that table variables are scoped to the batch, rather than the session. If you kept the GO batch delimiter as in the previous examples, then an "object does not exist" error would be raised for the last SELECT statement because the table variable would not exist in the scope of the statement.

Temp Tables vs. Table Variables

All the code in this section uses the `Ch8_2TempTableAndTVStats.sql` code file.

Having touched on the concept and scope of temporary tables and table variables in the previous section, the mechanism used to store temporary results usually boils down to the differences in features between a temporary table (#table) and a table variable.

Statistics

The major difference between temp tables and table variables is that statistics are not created on table variables. This has two major consequences, the first of which is that the Query Optimizer uses a fixed estimation for the number of rows in a table variable irrespective of the data it contains. Moreover, adding or removing data doesn't change the estimation.

To illustrate this, executing the code below and looking at the properties of the table scan in the actual execution plan will give you the properties shown in Figure 8-1. To understand the example you need to first understand the Query Optimizer, statistics, and execution plans, which are covered in Chapter 1 and Chapter 5.

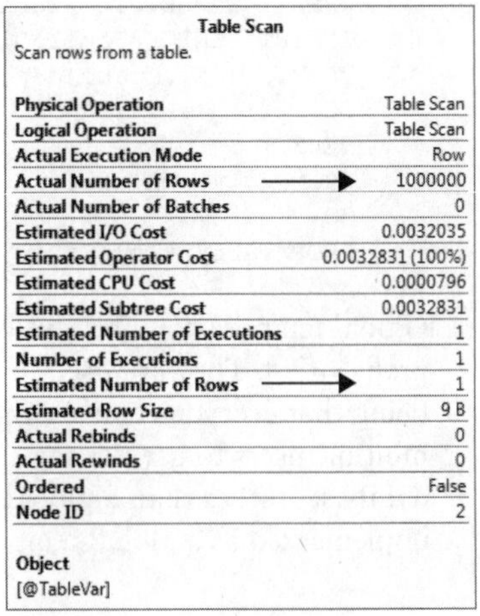

Table Scan	
Scan rows from a table.	
Physical Operation	Table Scan
Logical Operation	Table Scan
Actual Execution Mode	Row
Actual Number of Rows	1000000
Actual Number of Batches	0
Estimated I/O Cost	0.0032035
Estimated Operator Cost	0.0032831 (100%)
Estimated CPU Cost	0.0000796
Estimated Subtree Cost	0.0032831
Estimated Number of Executions	1
Number of Executions	1
Estimated Number of Rows	1
Estimated Row Size	9 B
Actual Rebinds	0
Actual Rewinds	0
Ordered	False
Node ID	2
Object	
[@TableVar]	

FIGURE 8-1

```
DECLARE @TableVar TABLE ( c1 INT ) ;
INSERT INTO @TableVar
SELECT TOP 1000000 row_number( ) OVER ( ORDER BY t1.number ) AS N
FROM   master..spt_values t1
CROSS JOIN master..spt_values t2 ;

SELECT  COUNT(*)
FROM    @TableVar ;
```

Note that the Query Optimizer based the plan on an estimation of one row being returned, whereas 1 million rows were actually returned when it was executed. Regardless of the number of rows in the table variable, the Query Optimizer will always estimate one row because it has no reliable statistics with which to generate a better estimation, and this could cause a bad execution plan to be used.

You can do the same test but with a temporary table instead by executing this code:

```
CREATE TABLE #TempTable ( c1 INT ) ;
INSERT INTO #TempTable
SELECT TOP 1000000 row_number( ) OVER ( ORDER BY t1.number ) AS N
FROM    master..spt_values t1
CROSS JOIN master..spt_values t2 ;

SELECT  COUNT(*)
FROM    #TempTable ;
```

The properties for the table scan in this scenario are shown in Figure 8-2, which indicates an accurate row estimate of 1000000.

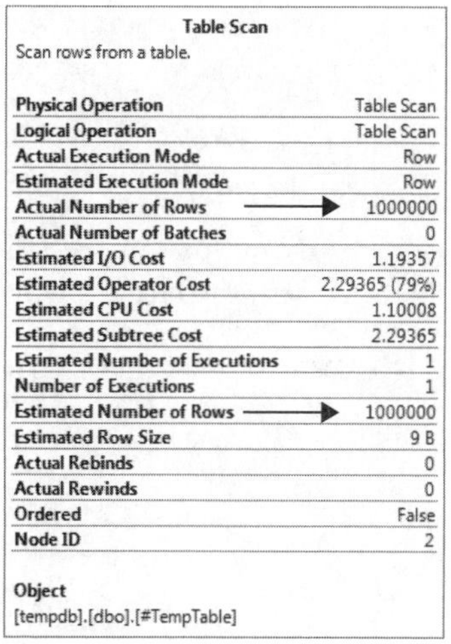

Indexes

You can't create indexes on table variables although you can create constraints. This means that by creating primary keys or unique constraints, you can have indexes (as these are created to support constraints) on table variables.

Even if you have constraints, and therefore indexes that will have statistics, the indexes will not be used when the query is compiled because they won't exist at compile time, nor will they cause recompilations.

Schema Modifications

Schema modifications are possible on temporary tables but not on table variables. Although schema modifications are possible on temporary tables, avoid using them because they cause recompilations of statements that use the tables.

Table Scan	
Scan rows from a table.	
Physical Operation	Table Scan
Logical Operation	Table Scan
Actual Execution Mode	Row
Estimated Execution Mode	Row
Actual Number of Rows	1000000
Actual Number of Batches	0
Estimated I/O Cost	1.19357
Estimated Operator Cost	2.29365 (79%)
Estimated CPU Cost	1.10008
Estimated Subtree Cost	2.29365
Estimated Number of Executions	1
Number of Executions	1
Estimated Number of Rows	1000000
Estimated Row Size	9 B
Actual Rebinds	0
Actual Rewinds	0
Ordered	False
Node ID	2
Object	
[tempdb].[dbo].[#TempTable]	

FIGURE 8-2

Table 8-1 provides a brief summary of the differences between temporary tables and table variables.

TABLE 8-1: Temporary Tables versus Table Variables

	TEMPORARY TABLES	TABLE VARIABLES
Statistics	Yes	No
Indexes	Yes	Only with constraints
Schema modifications	Yes	No
Available in child routines including sp_executesql	Yes	No
Use with INSERT INTO ... EXEC	Yes	No
In memory structures	No	No

TABLE VARIABLES ARE NOT CREATED IN MEMORY

There is a common misconception that table variables are in-memory structures and as such will perform quicker than temporary tables. Thanks to a DMV called `sys.dm_db_session_space_usage`, which shows tempdb usage by session, you can prove that's not the case. After restarting SQL Server to clear the DMV, run the following script to confirm that your `session_id` returns 0 for `user_objects_alloc_page_count`:

```
SELECT  session_id,
        database_id,
        user_objects_alloc_page_count
FROM    sys.dm_db_session_space_usage
WHERE   session_id > 50 ;
```

Now you can check how much space a temporary table uses by running the following script to create a temporary table with one column and populate it with one row:

```
CREATE TABLE #TempTable ( ID INT ) ;
INSERT  INTO #TempTable ( ID )
VALUES  ( 1 ) ;
GO
SELECT  session_id,
        database_id,
        user_objects_alloc_page_count
FROM    sys.dm_db_session_space_usage
WHERE   session_id > 50 ;
```

The results on my server (shown in Figure 8-3) indicate that the table was allocated one page in tempdb.

session_id	database_id	user_objects_alloc_page_count
51	2	1

FIGURE 8-3

Now run the same script but use a table variable this time:

```
DECLARE @TempTable TABLE ( ID INT ) ;
INSERT  INTO @TempTable ( ID )
VALUES  ( 1 ) ;
GO
SELECT  session_id,
        database_id,
        user_objects_alloc_page_count
FROM    sys.dm_db_session_space_usage
WHERE   session_id > 50 ;
```

session_id	database_id	user_objects_alloc_page_count
51	2	2

FIGURE 8-4

As shown in Figure 8-4, using the table variable caused another page to be allocated in tempdb, so table variables are not created in memory.

Table variables and temporary tables are both likely to be cached, however, so in reality, unless your server is memory constrained and you're using particularly large tables, you'll be working with them in memory anyway.

Whether or not you use temporary tables or table variables should be decided by thorough testing, but it's best to lean towards temporary tables as the default because there are far fewer things that can go wrong.

I've seen customers develop code using table variables because they were dealing with a small amount of rows, and it was quicker than a temporary table, but a few years later there were hundreds of thousands of rows in the table variable and performance was terrible, so try and allow for some capacity planning when you make your decision!

Internal Temporary Objects

Internal temporary objects are objects used by SQL Server to store data temporarily during query processing. Operations such as sorts, spools, hash joins, and cursors all require space in tempdb to run. You can read more about query processing in Chapter 5.

To see how many pages have been allocated to internal objects for each session, look at the `internal_object_alloc_page_count` column in the `sys.dm_db_session_space_usage` DMV. You'll find more details on looking at tempdb usage in the "Troubleshooting Common Issues" section later in the chapter.

The Version Store

Many features in SQL Server 2012 require multiple versions of rows to be maintained, and the *version store* is used to store these different versions of index and data rows. The following features make use of the version store:

➤ **Triggers** — These have used row versions since SQL Server 2005, rather than scan the transaction log as they did in SQL Server 2000.

➤ **Snapshot Isolation and Read-Committed Snapshot Isolation** — Two new isolation levels based on versioning of rows, rather than locking. You can read more about them in Chapter 6.

➤ **Online Index Operations** — Row versioning to support index updates during an index rebuild.

➤ **MARS (Multiple Active Result Sets)** — Row versioning to support interleaving multiple batch requests across a single connection. You can search SQL Server Books Online for more information on this.

Version Store Overhead

The overhead of row versioning is 14 bytes per row, which consists of a transaction sequence number referred to as an *XSN* and a row identifier referred to as a *RID*. You can see this illustrated in Figure 8-5.

FIGURE 8-5

The XSN is used to chain together multiple versions of the same row; the RID is used to locate the row version in tempdb.

The 14-byte overhead doesn't reduce the maximum possible row size of 8,060 bytes, and it is added the first time a row is modified or inserted in the following circumstances:

➤ You're using snapshot isolation.

➤ The underlying table has a trigger.

➤ You're using MARS.

➤ An online index rebuild is running on the table.

It is removed in these circumstances:

➤ Snapshot isolation is switched off.

➤ The trigger is removed.

➤ You stop using MARS.

➤ An online index rebuild is completed.

You should also be aware that creating the additional 14 bytes could cause page splits if the data pages are full and will affect your disk space requirement.

Append-Only Stores

The row versions are written to an append-only store of which there are two; index rebuilds have their own version store and everything else uses the common version store. To increase scalability, each CPU scheduler has its own page in the version store to store rows, as illustrated in Figure 8-6 with a computer that has four CPU cores. See Chapter 5 for more information about CPU cores and schedulers.

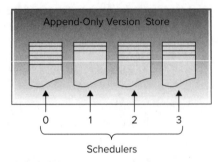

FIGURE 8-6

You can view the entire contents of the version store using the sys.dm_tran_version_store DMV, but use it with care as it can be resource intensive to run.

For an example demonstrating how row versioning is used, Figure 8-7 illustrates an example of multiple read and write transactions operating under snapshot isolation.

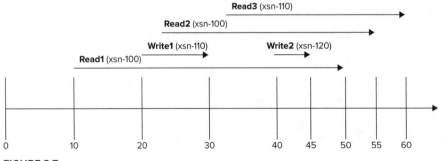

FIGURE 8-7

Along the bottom of the diagram a timeline is represented from 0 to 60; the horizontal arrows represent the duration of a specific transaction. The sequence of events occurs like this:

1. At timeline 10 a transaction called Read1 starts and reads the row associated with XSN-100.

2. At 20 another transaction called Write1 starts, which wants to modify the row. Snapshot isolation guarantees a repeatable read for Read1 and ensures that any new readers can read committed data at the point a write starts. Therefore, it copies the rows associated with XSN-100 to the version store and allows Write1 to modify the row under XSN-110.

3. Read2 starts before Write1 has committed, so the version chain is traversed from XSN-110 to XSN-100 in the version store to get the last committed value.

4. Read3 starts *after* Write1 has committed and reads the value from XSN-110.

5. Write2 now starts and wants to modify the row. Read1 and Read2 still need the version under XSN-100 and Read3 needs the version under XSN-110, so a new version is created for XSN-120, and XSN-110 is moved to the version store in tempdb.

6. Write2 commits XSN-120.

7. Read1 completes, but XSN-100 is still being used by Read2.

8. Read2 completes and XSN-100 is now stale.

9. Read3 completes and XSN-110 is now stale.

A background thread removes stale versions of rows from tempdb every minute, so at that point only the result of the write operation carried out by transaction Write2 will be stored and no previous versions will be available or stored in tempdb.

Figure 8-8 represents the state of the row on the data page and the versions stored in tempdb at timeline 0. You can see that the only available result is the currently committed value as of XSN-100.

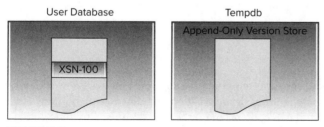

FIGURE 8-8

Figure 8-9 shows the state at timeline 45. Two versions are being maintained in tempdb to provide a repeatable read for the Read1, Read2, and Read3 transactions.

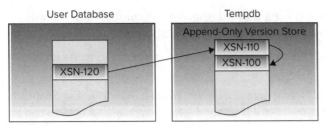

FIGURE 8-9

Figure 8-10 shows timeline 60. All transactions that required previous versions to maintain the snapshot isolation level have now completed, so the stale versions stored in tempdb have been cleaned up by a background thread.

> **NOTE** *You'll find more in-depth information on snapshot isolation, including its uses and its drawbacks, in Chapter 6.*

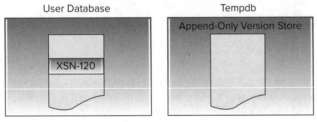

FIGURE 8-10

TROUBLESHOOTING COMMON ISSUES

The unique nature of tempdb as a shared resource for temporary objects makes it more prone to specific performance problems than other databases. This section describes the most common issues that tempdb is vulnerable to and how to troubleshoot or even avoid them.

Latch Contention

Compared to a normal database, tempdb's use as a temporary storage area makes the workload pattern likely to contain a disproportionate amount of the creation and destruction of many small objects. This type of workload can lead to latch contention on the pages required to allocate objects in a database.

If you've read Chapter 7 on latches, then you know that a latch is a short-term synchronization lock used by SQL Server to protect *physical* pages — it's covered only briefly here for the sake of context.

You can't influence latching behavior by changing the isolation level or by using "hints," as you can with normal locks; latches are used automatically behind the scenes to protect pages in memory from being modified by another task while the content or structure is being changed or read from disk.

Allocation Pages

When you create an object such as a temporary table in tempdb, it needs to be allocated space in exactly the same way as creating a table in a normal database. You need to be aware of three pages in the allocation process: Page Free Space, Global Allocation Map, and Shared Global Allocation Map, all of which are covered in the following sections.

PFS (Page Free Space)

The PFS page stores 1 byte of information for each page, indicating how much free space is on it and what it's used for, which means that a single PFS page can store information about roughly 64MB of pages. Therefore, you'll find a new PFS page at close to 64MB intervals throughout a database data file.

The first page on any database data file is always a PFS page, so it's easy to spot the page in an error message. If you see "2:1:1" anywhere, it's referring to the first page on the first data file in database_id 2, which is tempdb; "5:3:1" would be the first PFS page in file_id 3 in database_id 5.

GAM (Global Allocation Map)

The GAM page tracks 1 bit per *extent* (an extent is eight pages), indicating which extents are in use and which are empty. SQL Server reads the page to find free space to allocate a full extent to an object.

Storing only 1 bit for each extent (instead of 1 byte per page like the PFS page) means that a single GAM page can track a lot more space, and you'll find a new GAM page at roughly 4GB intervals in a data file. However, the first GAM page in a data file is always page number 2, so "2:1:2" would refer to the first GAM page in tempdb.

SGAM (Shared Global Allocation Map)

The SGAM page (pronounced *ess*-gam) also stores 1 bit per extent but the values represent whether the extent is a mixed extent with free space or a full extent. SQL Server reads this page to find a mixed extent with free space to allocate space to a small object.

A single SGAM can track 4GB of pages, so you'll find them at 4GB intervals just like GAM pages. The first SGAM page in a data file is page 3, so "2:1:3" is tempdb's first SGAM page.

Allocation Page Contention

Imagine that you take an action within an application that needs to create a temporary table. To determine where in tempdb to create your table, SQL Server will read the SGAM page (2:1:3) to find a mixed extent with free space to allocate to the table.

SQL Server takes out an exclusive latch (latches are covered in Chapter 7) on the SGAM page while it's updating the page and then moves on to read the PFS page to find a free page within the extent to allocate to the object.

An exclusive latch will also be taken out on the PFS page to ensure that no one else can allocate the same data page, which is then released when the update is complete.

This is quite a simple process (but maybe not to explain) and it works very well until tempdb becomes overloaded with allocation requests. The threshold can be hard to predict and the next section describes several things you can do to proactively avoid it.

The issue itself manifests as a PAGELATCH wait, with 2:1:1 or 2:1:3 as the resource description. Figure 8-11 shows contention on the allocation pages because multiple users are trying to allocate many objects at the same time.

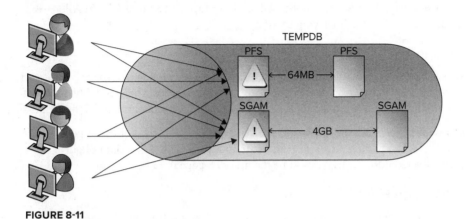

FIGURE 8-11

Allocation Page Contention: An Example

All the code in this section uses the Ch8_3TempdbContention.sql code file.

In order to demonstrate page contention I've created a couple of stored procedures and a table in an empty database called tempdbdemo. If you want to step through the example yourself, we have provided all the necessary steps and scripts in the associated code file.

```
-- Create stored procedure that creates a temp table, a clustered index and
populates with 10 rows
-- The script expects a database called tempdbdemo to exist
USE [tempdbdemo] ;
GO
CREATE PROCEDURE [dbo].[usp_temp_table]
AS
    CREATE TABLE #tmpTable
        (
          c1 INT,
          c2 INT,
          c3 CHAR(5000)
        ) ;
    CREATE UNIQUE CLUSTERED INDEX cix_c1 ON #tmptable ( c1 ) ;
    DECLARE @i INT = 0 ;
    WHILE ( @i < 10 )
        BEGIN
            INSERT  INTO #tmpTable ( c1, c2, c3 )
            VALUES  ( @i, @i + 100, 'coeo' ) ;
            SET  @i += 1 ;
        END ;
GO
-- Create stored procedure that runs usp_temp_table 50 times
CREATE PROCEDURE [dbo].[usp_loop_temp_table]
AS
```

```
SET nocount ON ;
DECLARE @i INT = 0 ;
WHILE ( @i < 100 )
    BEGIN
        EXEC tempdbdemo.dbo.usp_temp_table ;
        SET @i += 1 ;
    END ;
```

The `usp_temp_table` stored procedure creates a table in tempdb with three columns and a unique clustered index on Column 1. The table is then populated with 10 rows. The `usp_loop_temp_table` stored procedure runs the `usp_temp_table` procedure 100 times.

To simulate multiple users trying to run the same procedure at the same time, I'm going to use a tool called *OStress,* which is part of a download called RML Utilities.

> **NOTE** *At the time of writing, RMLUtilities has a dependency on SQL Native 10 which comes with the SQL Server 2008 client tools. Fortunately, you can just download it for free from here and install it alongside SQL Server 2012:* `http://www.microsoft.com/en-us/download/details.aspx?id=16978` *(Look for* Microsoft SQL Server 2008 R2 Native Client).
>
> *RMLUtilities can be found here:* `http://www.microsoft.com/en-us/download/details.aspx?id=4511`

For the purpose of the demo I'm just going to use OStress very simply to run the `usp_loop_temp_table` procedure using 300 connections. The aim is to simulate 300 people running a stored procedure that recursively calls another stored procedure 100 times.

OStress needs to be run from the command prompt:

```
C:\"Program Files\Microsoft Corporation"\RMLUtils\ostress -Schristianvaio\NTK12 -E
-Q"EXEC demo.dbo.usp_loop_temp_table;" -ooutput.txt -n300
```

Of course, *christianvaio\NTK12* is my SQL Server instance name, so change it to your own if you're following along.

While OStress is running, take a look at the `sys.dm_os_waiting_tasks` DMV using the following script, reproduced here with the kind permission of Robert Davis (`http://www.sqlsoldier.com/wp/sqlserver/breakingdowntempdbcontentionpart2`):

```
WITH TASKS
AS (SELECT session_id,
           wait_type,
           wait_duration_ms,
           blocking_session_id,
           resource_description,
    PageID = Cast(Right(resource_description, Len(resource_description)-
    Charindex(':', resource_description, 3)) As Int)
    From sys.dm_os_waiting_tasks
           Where wait_type Like 'PAGE%LATCH_%'
           And resource_description Like '2:%')
```

```
SELECT session_id,
       wait_type,
       wait_duration_ms,
       blocking_session_id,
       resource_description,
       ResourceType = Case
            When PageID = 1 Or PageID % 8088 = 0 Then 'Is PFS Page'
            When PageID = 2 Or PageID % 511232 = 0 Then 'Is GAM Page'
            When PageID = 3 Or (PageID - 1) % 511232 = 0 Then 'Is SGAM Page'
            Else 'Is Not PFS, GAM, or SGAM page'
       End
       From Tasks ;
```

The script is filtered on all PAGELATCH waits and shows you for each page whether or not it's PFS, GAM, or SGAM. Most of the time when you have contention, it will be on the first allocation pages but this script is more thorough as it will detect any of these pages throughout the file.

You should see results similar to those shown in Figure 8-12.

	session_id	wait_type	wait_duration_ms	blocking_session_id	resource_description	ResourceType
1	51	PAGELATCH_UP	73	NULL	2:1:1	Is PFS Page
2	75	PAGELATCH_UP	72	NULL	2:1:1	Is PFS Page
3	76	PAGELATCH_EX	79	NULL	2:1:329	Is Not PFS, GAM, o
4	91	PAGELATCH_UP	69	NULL	2:1:1	Is PFS Page
5	98	PAGELATCH_UP	69	NULL	2:1:1	Is PFS Page
6	115	PAGELATCH_UP	69	NULL	2:1:1	Is PFS Page
7	121	PAGELATCH_UP	62	NULL	2:1:1	Is PFS Page
8	122	PAGELATCH_EX	52	NULL	2:1:122	Is Not PFS, GAM, o
9	123	PAGELATCH_EX	53	NULL	2:1:122	Is Not PFS, GAM, o

Query executed successfully. CHRISTIANVAIO\NTK12 (11.0 RTM) christianVAIO\christia... master 00:00:00 291 rows

FIGURE 8-12

At the time this snapshot of sys.dm_os_waiting_tasks was taken, 291 tasks (from 300 connections) were waiting for a PAGELATCH, and you can see several examples of 2:1:1 (which is the PFS page), so there is evidence of allocation page contention.

Resolving and/or Avoiding Allocation Page Contention Problems

All the code in this section uses the Ch8_4TempDBContentionResolution.sql code file.

Once you've determined that you're suffering from allocation page contention in tempdb (or even if you're not sure), you have a few different ways to reduce the likelihood of it happening.

Multiple Tempdb Data Files

If you're a DBA rather than a developer, you might be tempted to opt for this solution first. Recall that there is a set of allocation pages at the start of each data file, so if you have more than one file and can balance the load between them you'll be less likely to get a hotspot on the allocation pages compared to a single file.

It's a good best practice to have multiple tempdb files for your instance anyway because doing so is a simple, risk-free way of reducing the likelihood of contention occurring.

Tempdb works with multiple data files by using a *proportional fill* algorithm to try to balance the amount of free space across all the files. The effect of this is to favor the file with the most free space until it equals all the other files. This is a bad scenario if you're trying to balance the allocation requests evenly across the files, so you need to ensure that all the tempdb data files are the same size. This is illustrated in Figure 8-13.

> **NOTE** *You can learn more about how to configure multiple tempdb data files in the last major section of this chapter, "Configuration Best Practices."*

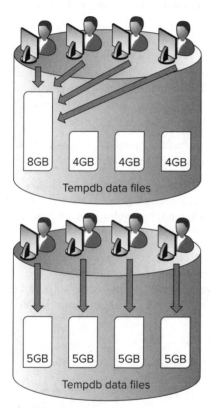

FIGURE 8-13

To determine whether simply adding more files can make a measurable difference to the contention example from the previous section, you can configure the server to have four equally sized tempdb data files. It's not important for them to be on separate drives because you're not doing it to improve I/O performance but simply to have more allocation pages.

You can modify the following the script for your own environment to configure the data files, which are all on the same disk.

```
ALTER DATABASE tempdb
MODIFY FILE (name=tempdev,size=512MB) ;
GO
ALTER DATABASE tempdb
ADD FILE (name=tempdev2,size=512MB,filename='D:\data\tempdev2.ndf') ;
```

```
GO
ALTER DATABASE tempdb
ADD FILE (name=tempdev3,size=512MB,filename='D:\data\tempdev3.ndf') ;
GO
ALTER DATABASE tempdb
ADD FILE (name=tempdev4,size=512MB,filename='D:\data\tempdev4.ndf') ;
```

Run through the demo again and see if it makes a difference. Try adding more and more files to see the effect.

Adding more files in this example will help reduce contention and will even remove it if you add enough files, but you can get easier gains by checking the code.

Temporary Object Reuse

This optimization is a little-known feature called *temporary object reuse*. If you're a developer and you manage the code rather than the server, the first thing you'll likely look at is optimizing the code, rather than reviewing server best practices. In most scenarios changing the code yields the best performance improvements anyway, so it's not a bad starting approach.

Beginning with SQL Server 2005, it's possible for SQL Server to cache temporary object definitions so that they can be reused if the same object needs to be created again. To be more specific, one IAM page (Index Allocation Map) and one extent are cached.

Objects that are reused don't have to be allocated new space and therefore won't contribute to any allocation problems. Optimizing your code to ensure that your temporary tables are being cached will help to reduce any potential problems.

SQL Server tries to cache temporary tables by default, so the first thing you need to check is whether or not SQL Server is caching yours. To do so, you can run your code in a loop and monitor the difference between the "temp table creation rate" Performance Monitor counter at the start and end of the loop. Fortunately, Sunil Agarwal from Microsoft has written a nice wrapper script that does it for us:

```
SET NOCOUNT ON ;
GO
DECLARE @table_counter_before_test BIGINT ;
SELECT  @table_counter_before_test = cntr_value
FROM    sys.dm_os_performance_counters
WHERE   counter_name = 'Temp Tables Creation Rate' ;
DECLARE @i INT = 0 ;
WHILE ( @i < 10 )
    BEGIN
        EXEC tempdbdemo.dbo.usp_loop_temp_table ;
        SELECT  @i += 1 ;
    END ;
DECLARE @table_counter_after_test BIGINT ;
SELECT  @table_counter_after_test = cntr_value
FROM    sys.dm_os_performance_counters
WHERE   counter_name = 'Temp Tables Creation Rate' ;
PRINT 'Temp tables created during the test: '
    + CONVERT(VARCHAR(100), @table_counter_after_test
    - @table_counter_before_test) ;
```

To use the script yourself simply change the stored procedure name you want to test from `usp_loop_test_table` to whatever code you want.

If the code you want to test is complicated, you might want to set the loop iterations to 1 the first time you run this script just to be sure how many *different* temporary tables are created. Once you know that, you can set it back to 10 loop iterations as in the example.

The example code indicates that only one temporary table creation statement is called many times, so if the value returned from the above script is more than 1, then you can be confident that you're not getting temporary object reuse.

Running the script provides the following result:

```
Temp tables created during the test: 1000
```

During 10 executions, 1,000 temporary tables were created, so you can conclude that the table isn't being cached (remember that the looping procedure executes the procedure creating the temp table 100 times, 10 * 100 = 1,000).

There's obviously a problem in the example code somewhere, so what you need to determine now is under what circumstances SQL Server *will* cache temporary tables, so you know whether any changes can be made to the code.

Temporary objects will be cached as long as the following obtains:

➤ Named constraints are not created.

➤ DDL (Data Definition Language) statements that affect the table, such as CREATE INDEX or CREATE STATISTICS, are not run after the table has been created.

➤ The object is not created using dynamic SQL; using sp_executesql, for example.

➤ The object is created inside another object such as the following:

    ➤ Stored procedure

    ➤ Trigger

    ➤ User-defined function

    ➤ The return table of a user-defined table-valued function

If you look back at the code for `usp_temp_table` you'll notice that a unique clustered index is created after the table definition, which breaks the rules for cached temporary objects:

```
CREATE UNIQUE CLUSTERED INDEX cix_c1 ON #tmptable ( c1 ) ;
```

All is not lost, however, because you can utilize a constraint within the temporary table definition to achieve the same results without breaking the rules for temporary object caching. The next code listing shows the new definition with the old CREATE INDEX statement commented out.

```
USE [tempdbdemo] ;
GO
CREATE PROCEDURE [dbo].[usp_temp_table]
AS
```

```
CREATE TABLE #tmpTable
    (
        c1 INT UNIQUE CLUSTERED,
        c2 INT,
        c3 CHAR(5000)
    ) ;
--CREATE UNIQUE CLUSTERED INDEX cix_c1 ON #tmptable ( c1 ) ;
DECLARE @i INT = 0 ;
WHILE ( @i < 10 )
    BEGIN
        INSERT  INTO #tmpTable ( c1, c2, c3 )
        VALUES  ( @i, @i + 100, 'coeo' ) ;
        SET @i += 1 ;
    END ;
GO
```

Here, a unique clustered constraint has been added to the c1 column, which SQL Server will enforce internally by using a clustered index, so you can keep exactly the same functionality.

Testing the new stored procedure using the temporary table creation test now returns the following result:

```
Temp tables created during the test: 1
```

The stored procedure has been successfully optimized for temporary object reuse, but what effect will it have on the allocation page contention example earlier in this chapter? Run through the workload again and see for yourself.

This example has shown you two ways to tackle a tempdb page contention issue: adding more data files and temporary object reuse. Taking advantage of temporary object reuse doesn't remove the issue because of the large number of concurrent connections trying to use the object name, so adding additional tempdb data files is still required to balance the allocation requests.

Trace Flag 1118

This trace flag was introduced in SQL Server 2000 to help alleviate contention on the SGAM page (2:1:3) by disabling mixed extent allocations in *all* databases.

You might remember from earlier in the chapter that SGAM pages track mixed extents that have free space available. Every time you create a new table that's not big enough to fill an extent (which happens a lot in tempdb), the SGAM page is read to find a mixed extent with enough free space to allocate to your table.

The effect of enabling this trace flag is that every object you create will be allocated its own extent (a *uniform* extent). The only downside to this is the extra disk space that's needed because every table needs at least 64KB; although that's unlikely to be an issue on most systems.

SQL Server 2008 introduced an improved algorithm for allocating space in mixed extents, so you'll be unlikely to encounter this issue often if at all with SQL Server 2012.

Even though you're unlikely to find SGAM contention in SQL Server 2012, trace flag 1118 still works exactly the same: It disables mixed extent allocations.

> **NOTE** *While you probably won't ever need to use 1118 to reduce SGAM contention, the fact that it forces only uniform extents to be allocated can be used to increase performance under very heavy workloads, so it might be worth testing if you're tuning that kind of environment.*

Monitoring Tempdb I/O Performance

Troubleshooting SQL Server implies a *reactive* activity; an issue has occurred that now needs to be fixed. That may be true but one of the differences that separates an average SQL Server professional from a good one is knowing about a problem *before* it has an impact on a live system.

You should be aware by now of tempdb's importance to the overall health of an entire instance, so it shouldn't be a hard sell to realize the benefits of being proactive and monitoring tempdb to get early warning of potential problems before they affect a production system. This section covers the specifics of monitoring tempdb I/O: What you should be looking at and what thresholds should prompt you to do something.

The speed at which requests to store and retrieve data are processed against tempdb is important to the overall performance of any SQL Server instance and can even be critical where tempdb is either heavily used or part of an important business process.

Whether you have tempdb on local storage or a SAN (storage area network), on a RAID10 volume or RAID1, the simplest way to check I/O system performance is to look at the latency of I/O requests. You'll find a lot more detailed information about storage, including SANs, RAID levels, and benchmarking performance, in Chapter 4.

There are two methods for measuring disk latency: using Performance Monitor (see Chapter 10) and using SQL Server DMVs. Which one you should choose depends on how you want to monitor performance and how accurate you need it to be.

Performance Monitor

The PerfMon counters that you should be interested in are as follows:

➤ Avg. Disk sec/Transfer

➤ Avg. Disk sec/Read

➤ Avg. Disk sec/Write

You'll find these grouped under Logical Disk, which shows the logical drives and drive letters presented in Windows as you would see them in Explorer; and Physical Disk, which shows the drives as Windows sees them internally. Which group you get the counters from won't matter in most cases — I tend to use the Logical Disk counters because it's easier to work with drive letters.

The counters themselves all provide the average latency in milliseconds for I/O requests. "Avg. Disk sec/Transfer" is the combined average for both reads and writes to a drive. This counter provides the simplest measurement for regular long-term monitoring.

"Avg. Disk sec/Read" and "Avg. Disk sec/Write" separate the requests into read and write measurements, respectively, that can be useful for determining how to configure disk controller cache (see Chapter 4). For example, if you're seeing poor read performance and excellent write performance, you might want to optimize the cache for reads.

SQL Server DMVs

Monitoring the performance of a disk volume using Performance Monitor is a useful indicator of a potential storage performance issue, but you can get a further level of granularity from SQL Server itself. The following script (code file: Ch8_5ReadAndWriteLatency.sql) uses the sys.dm_io_virtual_file_stats DMV to calculate the read and write latency for all database files that have been used since the SQL Server service was last started.

```
SELECT  DB_NAME(database_id) AS 'Database Name',
        file_id,
        io_stall_read_ms / num_of_reads AS 'Avg Read Transfer/ms',
        io_stall_write_ms / num_of_writes AS 'Avg Write Transfer/ms'
FROM    sys.dm_io_virtual_file_stats(-1, -1)
WHERE   num_of_reads > 0
        AND num_of_writes > 0 ;
```

You can see part of the output from running the script on a busy production SQL Server in Figure 8-14. Tempdb has four data files with file_id's 1, 3, 4, and 5, and a transaction log with file_id 2. All the data files have the same read and write latency, which is a positive indicator that the I/O is balanced across all the files, and all the results indicate good performance from tempdb.

Database Name	file_id	Avg Read Transfer/ms	Avg Write Transfer/ms
master	1	11	3
master	2	6	2
tempdb	1	7	5
tempdb	2	4	3
tempdb	3	7	5
tempdb	4	7	5
tempdb	5	7	5

FIGURE 8-14

Thresholds

Microsoft suggests the following performance thresholds for disk latency on drives containing SQL Server database files:

Database data files:

➤ **Target:** <10ms

➤ **Acceptable:** 10–20ms

➤ **Unacceptable:** >20ms

Database log files:

➤ **Target:** <5ms

➤ **Acceptable:** 5–15ms

➤ **Unacceptable:** >15ms

You should use these thresholds for guidance only because some systems will never be able to achieve the target latency. If you don't have any performance issues with your application and you're seeing latency of 20ms, then it's not so important; but you can still look at Chapter 4 to see if there's anything you can do to optimize your existing storage investment.

Using 20ms is a good rule of thumb target on most systems unless SQL Server is spending a lot of time waiting for I/O requests.

Troubleshooting Space Issues

All the code in this section uses the `Ch8_6TempDBSpaceIssues.sql` code file.

It was mentioned at the beginning of this chapter that all the databases on an instance have to share only one tempdb; this makes it even more important to understand who is doing what in tempdb, so Microsoft provides three DMVs to enable you to do just that.

sys.dm_db_file_space_usage

This DMV provides a view of the number and types of pages that are allocated in tempdb by file, allowing you to see the distribution of pages across your data files.

You can also use this DMV to total the values across all the files to get a single view of the breakdown of tempdb usage, which can help you narrow down the scope of the problem in the event of unexpected usage. Here is an example script for this:

```
SELECT  SUM(total_page_count)*8/1024 AS 'tempdb size (MB)',
        SUM(total_page_count) AS 'tempdb pages',
        SUM(allocated_extent_page_count) AS 'in use pages',
        SUM(user_object_reserved_page_count) AS 'user object pages',
        SUM(internal_object_reserved_page_count) AS 'internal object pages',
        SUM(mixed_extent_page_count) AS 'Total Mixed Extent Pages'
FROM    sys.dm_db_file_space_usage ;
```

Example results from the preceding script are shown in Figure 8-15. Note that user, internal and version pages are from uniform extents only.

	tempdb Size (MB)	tempdb pages	in use pages	user object pages	internal object pages	version store pages	mixed extent pages
1	256	32768	320	128	8	0	184

FIGURE 8-15

sys.dm_db_task_space_usage

This DMV provides details of tempdb usage for currently running tasks. The values are set to 0 at the start of the task and deleted when the task completes, so it's useful for troubleshooting live issues with currently executing tasks. For example, the following script will give you the top five sessions currently using space in tempdb, ordered by the total amount of space in use:

```
SELECT TOP 5 *
FROM    sys.dm_db_task_space_usage
WHERE   session_id > 50
ORDER BY user_objects_alloc_page_count + internal_objects_alloc_page_count
```

sys.dm_db_session_space_usage

When a task completes, the values from sys.dm_db_task_usage are aggregated by session, and these aggregated values are viewable using sys.dm_db_session_space_usage.

The following example code demonstrates how to use this DMV, showing you all the sessions in order of total tempdb usage:

```
SELECT  *
FROM    sys.dm_db_session_space_usage
WHERE   session_id > 50
ORDER BY user_objects_alloc_page_count + internal_objects_alloc_page_count DESC ;
```

The output won't include any currently executing tasks, so it's not very useful for a live issue; but you can look up the session_id in sys.dm_exec_requests to gather information about who's using that session_id, such as their login details; the server they're connecting from; and the application they are using.

CONFIGURATION BEST PRACTICES

Because several of the issues addressed in this chapter have required configuration changes, this section consolidates all the best practices for configuring tempdb. You won't just find prescriptive rules here, but also the background to the recommendations and guidance on how to choose the best configuration for any particular environment. In particular this section covers the following:

➤   Where to place tempdb

➤   Initial sizing and autogrowth

➤   Configuring multiple files

Tempdb File Placement

It's quite a well-known best practice to separate data, transaction logs, and tempdb, and if you knew that already, are you sure you know why? The origin of this recommendation lies with the separation of types of workload between different physical storage, i.e. separate physical disks.

This is still a valid recommendation for environments where you can guarantee that separation, but more commonly we see customers deploying SQL Server in a shared storage environment, where physical separation is much harder to achieve and usually isn't even necessary for performance reasons.

It is still a good idea however to maintain separation to help with manageability so that potential problems are easier to isolate. For example, separating tempdb onto its own logical disk means that you can pre-size it to fill the disk (see tempdb sizing later in the chapter) without worrying about space requirements for other files, and the more separation you implement the easier it is to correlate logical disk performance to specific database files.

At the very minimum you should aim to have one logical disk for data files, one for transaction log files, and one for tempdb data files. I prefer to keep the tempdb data files on their own drive so they can be sized to fill the drive and place the tempdb log files with the user database log files where there should be enough free disk space for unexpected autogrow events for any log file.

Local Tempdb for Failover Cluster Instances

Until SQL Server 2012, a failover cluster instance of SQL Server required *all* its database files to be on shared disk resources within the cluster. This was to ensure that when the instance failed over to another node in the cluster, all its dependent disks could be moved with it.

As you've already read at the beginning of the chapter, nothing in tempdb persists after a restart and it's effectively recreated every time. The failover process for a clustered instance involves a restart of SQL Server so nothing in tempdb needs to be moved across to the other node and there's no technical reason why tempdb should be on a shared disk.

In SQL Server 2008 R2 you could force tempdb onto a local disk but it wasn't supported; in SQL Server 2012 it's fully supported and very straightforward to implement. All you need to do is use ALTER DATABASE like this:

```
USE master ;
GO
ALTER DATABASE tempdb
MODIFY FILE (NAME = tempdev, FILENAME = 'D:\tempdbdata\tempdb.mdf') ;
GO
ALTER DATABASE tempdb
MODIFY FILE (NAME = templog, FILENAME = 'E:\tempdblogs\templog.ldf') ;
GO
```

You will see messages after execution that look like this:

```
Local directory 'D:\tempdbdata\tempdb.mdf'is used for tempdb in a clustered
server. This directory must exist on each cluster node and SQL Server
service has read/write permission on it.
The file "tempdev" has been modified in the system catalog. The new path
will be used the next time the database is started.
Local directory 'E:\tempdblogs\templog.ldf' is used for tempdb in a
clustered server. This directory must exist on each cluster node and SQL
Server service has read/write permission on it.
The file "templog" has been modified in the system catalog. The new path
will be used the next time the database is started.
```

That's all there is to it. All you need to remember is that you need to have the same path available on all cluster nodes, and the service account needs to have read/write permission so that tempdb can start after failover.

Why Might a Local tempdb Be Useful?

There are two reasons why you might want to move tempdb from a shared disk to a local disk, and both are related to performance.

The first reason is that the relatively recent increase in cost effective, ultra-fast solid-state storage (see Chapter 4) presents an opportunity to achieve significant performance gains on servers experiencing heavy tempdb usage. The challenge prior to SQL Server 2012 was that solid-state storage cards, like those provided by FusionIO and Texas Instruments, plug straight into a server's motherboard to avoid all the overhead of traditional storage buses. This made it very difficult to use them at all in failover cluster instances and now they can be used for the discrete task of running tempdb.

The second reason you might want to use a local tempdb is to take I/O requests off your shared storage to improve the performance of the shared storage. We used this to great effect for one customer who was really at the peak of their SANs performance capacity; a FusionIO card was placed in each node of several failover clusters and all tempdb activity was re-directed locally. Even though tempdb performance was never bad before, the result was a significant reduction in load against the SAN which extended its life by an additional six months.

Tempdb Initial Sizing and Autogrowth

A default installation of any SQL Server edition will create a tempdb database with an 8MB data file and a 1MB transaction log file. For a lot of SQL Server installations these file sizes won't be enough, but they are configured to autogrow by 10% as needed. You can see the properties window for tempdb on a default installation of SQL Server 2012 Developer Edition in Figure 8-16.

FIGURE 8-16

Although the autogrow feature enables a more hands-off approach to maintaining many SQL Server installations, it's not necessarily desirable because the files cannot be used while they are autogrowing, and it can lead to fragmentation of the files on the hard disk, leading to poor performance.

This is a recommendation that would apply to any SQL Server database, but for tempdb it's even more relevant. When you restart your SQL Server instance, tempdb is re-created (files will be reused if they already exist) and sized to the value specified in the database properties, which as you've just seen is only 8MB for the data file and 1MB for the log file by default.

We've reviewed many SQL Server installations with tempdb files of tens of GBs that have autogrown to that size and have the default properties set. The next time SQL Server is restarted, tempdb will be just 8MB and will have to start autogrowing all over again.

Figure 8-17 illustrates an example scenario of tempdb sizing.

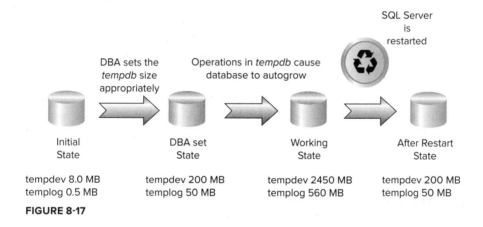

FIGURE 8-17

In this case, you can see the size of the initial files, which the DBA has set to 200MB and 50MB. The workload running against SQL Server has then caused the tempdb files to autogrow to 2450MB and 560MB.

SQL Server is then restarted and tempdb returns to 200MB and 50MB, as set by the DBA, and would have to autogrow again to fulfill the workload.

To What Size Should Tempdb Be Set?

This is obviously a difficult question to answer without more details about the workload, but there is still some guidance that you can use. First of all, unless you're running SQL Server Express, set tempdb to be bigger than the default; that's an easy one.

Next, if you can give tempdb its own disk, then configure it to almost fill the drive. If nothing else will ever be on the drive, then you're better off setting it to be larger than you'll ever need. There's no performance penalty, and you'll never have to worry about autogrow again.

If you can't put tempdb on its own disk, then you'll need to manage size and autogrow a bit more closely. You could just let it autogrow for a while and then manually set it to be a bit larger than what it grows to, or you could just make it a reasonable size in relation to your other databases and set large autogrow amounts.

To What Size Should Autogrow Be Set?

If you've moved tempdb to its own drive and configured it to almost fill the disk, then arguably you don't need to enable autogrow. That would be a reasonable choice in this scenario, but it may be worth leaving it on if you still have a small amount of disk space left over.

The best way to think of autogrow for any database, not just tempdb, is as a last resort. Your databases should be sized appropriately so they don't need to autogrow, but you still configure it just in case you need it.

Using fixed-growth amounts is generally a better approach for autogrow because it makes autogrow events more predictable. Autogrowing a 10GB transaction log by 10%, for example, will take a long time and will affect the availability of the database.

The Instant File Initialization (IFI) feature in Windows Server 2003 and later can make things a bit easier for autogrowing the data files, but it doesn't work for log files because of the way they are used.

IFI is used automatically by SQL Server if the service account is a local administrator (which it shouldn't be as a security best practice) or if the account has the Manage Volume Maintenance Tasks advanced user rights. To give the service account the necessary rights, you can use the Local Group Policy Editor, shown in Figure 8-18, by running gpedit.msc.

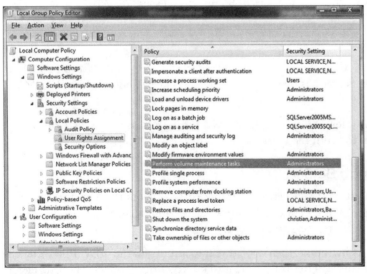

FIGURE 8-18

Once IFI is working, you can set autogrow to be large fixed amounts for data files. 50MB or 500MB are good values depending on the size of the database, but any size is created virtually instantly so you avoid any downtime.

> **NOTE** *If you've configured multiple data files and you want to allow autogrow, consider enabling trace flag 1117, which will force all data files to grow uniformly so you don't break the load balancing between files.*

For transaction log files, however, you need to be a lot more conservative and use a figure that balances the time it takes to autogrow and the usefulness of the extra space. Autogrowing by 1MB, for example, is quick, but you might need to do it so often that it becomes a bottleneck. Autogrowing by at least 10MB for the transaction log is a good place to start, but you may need it to be higher to provide enough space to avoid autogrowing again quickly. The best option is to avoid autogrowing in the first place by correctly sizing the files.

Configuring Multiple Tempdb Data Files

The use of multiple data files as an aid to reducing allocation contention problems for tempdb was covered earlier in the chapter. Another reason you might want to use multiple data files is to increase the I/O throughput to tempdb — especially if it's running on very fast storage.

When you create multiple data files they will all be in the primary filegroup and SQL Server uses a proportional fill algorithm to determine which file to use for each request to create an object. If all the files are exactly the same size, then SQL Server uses the files in a "round robin" fashion, spreading the load equally across the files. This is, of course, exactly what you want.

Microsoft recommends *up to* a 1:1 mapping between the number of files and logical CPUs because during testing of massive workloads they've seen performance benefits, even with hundreds of data files.

A more pragmatic approach however, is to have a 1:1 mapping between files and logical CPUs *up to eight*, and then add files if you continue to see allocation contention or if you're looking to push the I/O subsystem harder. The performance benefit from adding files diminishes each time, and in our experience, eight is the sweet spot, especially if you're implementing this as a pro-active measure.

Whether or not you configure multiple data files as a best practice on all your SQL Servers or just on those for which you've detected issues is a choice only you can make. However, you might want to configure them on all the servers you work with as a proactive measure, as it's hard to see a downside.

SUMMARY

This chapter introduced the concept of, and many uses for, the tempdb database in SQL Server 2012, as well as some of the most common problems you might encounter and how to avoid them.

The key points from this chapter are as follows:

➤ Three types of objects can be found in tempdb: user-created, internally created, and the version store.

➤ Latch contention is a common problem even in SQL Server 2012, but it is easy to resolve and even avoid.

➤ You should familiarize yourself with the following DMVs for help in troubleshooting urgent tempdb space issues:

    ➤ `sys.dm_db_file_space_usage`

    ➤ `sys.dm_db_task_space_usage`

    ➤ `sys.dm_db_session_space_usage`

➤ Appropriately sizing and configuring tempdb should be paramount for any SQL Server installation to avoid performance issues later.

PART II
Troubleshooting Tools and Lessons from the Field

▶ **CHAPTER 9:** Troubleshooting Methodology and Practices

▶ **CHAPTER 10:** Viewing Server Performance with PerfMon and the PAL Tool

▶ **CHAPTER 11:** Consolidating Data Capture with SQLdiag

▶ **CHAPTER 12:** Bringing It All Together with SQL Nexus

▶ **CHAPTER 13:** Diagnosing SQL Server 2012 Using Extended Events

▶ **CHAPTER 14:** Enhancing Your Troubleshooting Toolset with PowerShell

▶ **CHAPTER 15:** Delivering a SQL Server Health Check

▶ **CHAPTER 16:** Delivering Manageability and Performance

▶ **CHAPTER 17:** Running SQL Server in a Virtual Environment

Troubleshooting Methodology and Practices

INTRODUCTION

SQL Server is a complex product, often tightly integrated with mid-tier and end-user applications. Problems can be many and varied, and the scope of a database administrator (DBA) is broad, covering storage, servers, networking, applications, and meeting business requirements. DBAs often find themselves supporting third-party and in-house-developed applications with varying levels of maturity and robustness. There are no fixed requirements for Transact-SQL development, and application developers often overlook the performance and scalability of code they write. This chapter provides DBAs with guidance based on mature patterns for troubleshooting complex issues and complements the technical aspects of this book.

This chapter focuses on a data-driven methodology for troubleshooting SQL Server problems, consisting of the following three steps (the data collection and analysis may require multiple iterations until the problem's cause is identified):

1. Define the problem.

2. Iterate through:

   ➤ Data collection

   ➤ Data analysis

3. Validate and implement resolution.

Investing time and effort to develop and refine a troubleshooting methodology helps improve the efficiency and speed with which you troubleshoot problems. Much like planning a trip, the route and endpoint may vary, but identifying the destination and developing an approach to planning an efficient route is a distinct and different skill from driving itself. As you plan subsequent journeys, you can refine your approach, becoming more adept at determining the quickest route and better at estimating the length of time it takes between breaks and optimal departure time.

Troubleshooting SQL Server problems is similar to planning a long car trip. Whereas the rest of this book focuses on how the engine works and the troubleshooting skills themselves, this chapter will help you develop a methodology for troubleshooting, which is as important as the tangible troubleshooting skills themselves.

The book provides one approach for troubleshooting, which you can use to develop or refine your own approach. As you do so, consider roles and responsibilities, communication, reporting, and seeking external help. Reaching a successful resolution can often be achieved by more than one route. Identifying the path of least resistance while achieving the goal is the hallmark of a database professional experienced in troubleshooting complex issues.

APPROACHING PROBLEMS

Developing a professional methodology to managing problems will lead to a less stressful time at work, help make work more rewarding, and differentiate you from others. Although SQL Server is a discrete technology, it is often the case that when problems occur, uncertainty arises regarding the root cause, and problem scope is rarely well-defined. As such, issues can be passed around support teams with little progress or ownership.

This section of the chapter describes a set of ten principles you can use in order to clearly and efficiently identify and resolve problems with SQL Server. Although many of the details here are not specific to SQL Server problems, they are good practices for troubleshooting many types of complex IT issues.

Ten Steps to Successful Troubleshooting

The following steps provide a detailed methodology for successful and efficient incident resolution. They intentionally separate identification of the root cause and issue resolution. These are different tasks, and many situations require equal (or greater) effort to identify the root cause of an issue versus actually fixing it. Indeed, the fix itself may be trivial, but knowing exactly which fix to make is completely dependent on accurately understanding the problem and its cause; therefore, accurate root cause diagnosis is vital.

To get in front of a complex issue — that is, understand it and resolve it — use the following ten steps:

1. **Define the problem** — Establish a clear problem statement. The objective is to capture in one or two sentences a summary of the technical problem and success criteria. A detailed explanation will likely be required later, but aim initially to create a concise summary for circulation to interested parties.

2. **Ascertain the problem's impact** — The business stakeholders and sponsors often don't want to know technical details. They want to know the operational and financial impact of the incident. This must be categorized and monetized to the furthest extent possible. For example, if you had a website outage, you should estimate the cost to the organization — e.g., $10,000/ hour. If degraded service is likely, how much will it cost in lost revenue or reputation? If the incident prevents employees from completing their work (e.g., call center workers are unproductive), this can be estimated by the cost of wages plus operational impact (e.g., $10/ hour for 50 call center employees plus any overtime to make callbacks).

3. **Engage the correct resources** — These could be internal or external. In many enterprise scenarios, it is necessary to formally engage internal resources from other disciplines, such as storage operations, application support, and incident management. There may be external suppliers or third parties who should be engaged, such as hardware manufacturers, software vendors, or implementation consultants. Ensure that all participants are briefed with the same problem description and have a good understanding of the success criteria.

4. **Identify potential causes** — Meet all necessary parties (physically or virtually) to share the problem description, its impact, and any troubleshooting steps already performed. Consider proposed options to mitigate the impact or work around the problem. Identify any possibility to minimize the immediate impact to the business while a long-term solution is sought.

5. **Plan and coordinate tasks across teams** — Develop a plan, consisting of a number of hypotheses and a number of scenarios that may cause or influence the problem. Seek to prove or disprove each hypothesis by assigning it to a team with the skills and experience necessary to prove the hypothesis and reach a conclusion. — The intention is to narrow the focus by eliminating components that are not causing the problem, until eventually the problem component is found. Iterate around this method until the hypotheses are proven or disproven.

6. **Select a communication plan and review** — Document the plan and agree who will keep management, end users, and the technical team updated. Mutually agree on a time to reconvene, (e.g., every 2 hours or 4 hours may be appropriate). In scenarios with geographically dispersed teams, maintaining an open conference call to assist troubleshooting can be useful, but it's still important to plan and execute regular reviews.

7. **Identify root cause** — After a number of iterations (each iteration should be isolated, repeatable, and have narrow scope),you will have disproved a number of hypotheses, and hopefully proved one. Once the cause of the problem is understood, progress to the next step to find a fix.

8. **Determine solution** — This step involves identifying a resolution to the defined and understood cause of the problem.

9. **Test and implement** — Even if the problem does not exist in the test or pre-production environment, implement the fix there first. This involves making the identified change and confirming no undesired impact, then deploying to the production environment. If possible, ensure a rollback position and be prepared to invoke this plan if necessary.

10. **Review** — Post-mortem analysis will help prevent further recurrence of this issue or new issues in the future and can be used to identify other vulnerable systems within the organization which should be fixed, and will improve the troubleshooting approach to ensure it is as optimized and efficient as possible.

The ten steps outlined above and described in more detail in the following sections describe a troubleshooting approach you can adapt and simplify as desired. Not all problems require full formal engagement, but adopting an approximation of these disciplines can help you prioritize other activities, such as monetizing the impact of problems and defining a clear problem statement.

Behavior and Attitude

In addition to employing a good troubleshooting approach, adopting a positive attitude with moderate determination and persistence to identify the root cause and resolve issues definitely helps. A positive attitude leads to better quality results, faster resolution, and it will reduce the stress level for you and co-workers during the troubleshooting process. Using a consistent approach to resolving problems by decomposing them scientifically is a proven and effective method, and many of these aspects are within your control.

The following behaviors and attitudes are characteristic of the most effective database professionals when troubleshooting complex problems:

➤ **Remain calm** — Stay objective, no matter how urgent the problem. Project confidence and calmness to your peers, end users, and management, even if they show signs of stress or panic. This reassures them that you are in control and able to resolve the problem. These people are more likely to give you the time and space necessary to investigate and resolve the issue if they trust your capability.

➤ **Remember that problems are never random** — Problems with computers happen for a reason. When you don't understand the reason, the cause may seem random, but there is always an explanation. Intermittent or infrequent problems in particular appear random; seek to identify patterns or correlating events that could lead to the circumstances that cause the problem.

➤ **Avoid prejudice** — Never assume that you know how to solve a problem until you have a problem description and have done some basic testing. It is not necessary to provide an instant answer; the correct answer with a short delay trumps a quick, inaccurate answer. This habit also builds your credibility with management as a reliable and capable engineer.

➤ **Avoid looking for fixes** — Ensure that finding the cause is your first priority! The people around you will be pressing hard for a fix or an estimated time to fix. The fix is the goal, but you must first lay the foundation by understanding the cause.

➤ **Think ahead** — Proactively consider potential blockers. If you may need to restore the database, start the tape retrieval process in parallel with troubleshooting. This reduces overall downtime and impact if you do need to revert to the backup.

Success Criteria

Having defined the problem, recognizing its resolution is usually relatively straightforward. Nonetheless, explicitly agreeing on a set of success criteria helps to structure troubleshooting steps and provide a positive test case scenario. Otherwise, what constitutes problem resolution can be subjective.

With performance problems, for example, it can be difficult to reach a consensus about what constitutes good-enough performance, which can mean different things to different people. From a DBA's perspective, it's often the case that the first few optimizations realize the most performance gains, with each subsequent performance improvement harder to achieve — meaning more effort, more fundamental schema changes, and smaller incremental performance improvement. For this reason, it's important to agree on the performance objective and when to stop tuning.

Unfortunately, it's common to see an enterprise spend a lot of time troubleshooting numerous issues that have nothing to do with the main source of the problem. Avoid this by defining both the problem and the success criteria, and seeking agreement with the sponsor; that way, expectations are clear and understood by all parties.

Working with Stakeholders

Stakeholders are a group of people usually consisting of business management, IT management, owners, shareholders, and anyone with an interest in the success or failure of the organization. Most business stakeholders want problems resolved as fast as possible using the fewest possible resources, and managers often feel under pressure to provide answers to users, their superiors, and external stakeholders such as customers, investors, auditors, or the media.

When managers are not well informed or they don't have confidence in the incident team, this can lead to the undesirable behavior of micro-management. These are the managers who hover, requesting constant updates and generally inhibiting the troubleshooting process. You can avoid this, however, by proactively handling an incident to ensure both that stakeholders have the information they need and that they receive regular updates.

Broadly speaking, managers look first for a solution, then the cause. Database professionals should first attempt to understand the cause, then identify a solution. These opposing approaches can lead to friction, so it's important to recognize them and respect each other's priorities.

To minimize friction with management, try enlisting their help by nominating a single spokesperson for the incident. Request that they communicate with stakeholders and anyone who isn't directly involved in troubleshooting the problem. Agree on a schedule for providing updates and stick to that schedule to reduce distractions, such as requests for information. Identify one person to whom you will provide updates, letting that person communicate with anyone else who needs the information. If more than one person is directly involved in the technical aspects of troubleshooting, nominate just one technical person to talk to the management contact.

Managers can also help by gathering information to determine the problem's real impact on the business. As a guideline, try to establish the following:

➤ How severely is the system affected?

➤ How many users cannot work?

> ➤ Is money being lost? If so, quantify the amount.

> ➤ What is the visibility of the issue?

> ➤ Are external customers affected?

> ➤ Could any regulatory or compliance obligations be breeched?

> ➤ How serious are the consequences if the problem persists?

Management can also be enlisted to identify mitigating factors. Are any options available to run a degraded service such as manual systems that enable some operations to continue? Encourage managers to generate ideas for a short-term tactical solution while the root cause is investigated and a resolution implemented.

Managers might also be helpful in engaging third parties, initially to make contact and open a dialog, and, in situations in which escalation is required, to engage the right resources to advance a solution. Each of these factors can be used to help shape the solution.

Service-Level Agreements

A service-level agreement (SLA) forms an agreement between IT and the business or between an outsourcer and an organization. The SLA should define availability and performance metrics for key business applications. SLAs often include metrics for response and resolution times in the event of an incident. These agreements are non-functional requirements and useful for managing business expectations in terms of application performance, availability, and response time in the event of an incident.

Two terms commonly used in storage solution design can be borrowed and adapted to most other areas of IT and business agreements: *recovery point objective (RPO)* and *recovery time objective (RTO)*. Both can be included within an SLA to govern the data loss and recovery period following an incident.

RTO refers to the amount of time a solution can be down before the system is recovered. This varies according to the type of failure — for example, in the event of a single server failure in a failover cluster, the RTO could reasonably be 1–2 minutes; in the event of a total site loss, it might reasonably be four hours. This RTO metric essentially governs how long IT has to restore service in the event of various types of failures.

RPO refers to how much data loss can be tolerated without impact to the business. In the SQL Server world this commonly determines the frequency of transaction log backups. If, for example, the RPO were five minutes, you would need to take log backups every five minutes to ensure a maximum data loss of the same duration. Combining these facets of an agreement, it would be fairly common for a DBA to agree to configure five-minute log backups, and log shipping to a second location with an RPO of 15 minutes and an RTO of four hours. This would mean bringing the disaster recovery location online within four hours and ensuring a maximum data loss duration of 15 minutes. Agreeing to these objectives ahead of time with the business is an important part of setting and managing expectations.

Engaging External Help

It is not always necessary or possible to solve a problem with external assistance if there is a lack of knowledge, experience or time. Knowing who and when to call are important aspects of successful troubleshooting. Often, the objection to hiring a consultant, specialist, or support provider, or to open a support request with Microsoft Customer Service and Support (CSS), is financial. In reality, many problem scenarios can be much more expensive to resolve without external help. The time, resources, and opportunity costs of taking a long time to solve a problem, solving it in an inappropriate or inefficient way, or not solving it at all can be high. Ensure that all factors are taken into consideration when deciding if and when to engage outside help.

In some situations, it may be cheaper to engage help immediately — e.g., when the day rate for a consultant is half the cost of revenue loss per day; in this scenario it may make sense to bring in a consultant immediately. For example, it may be most beneficial to engage a specialist for problems related to rarely used features, as an organization might not have deep expertise with such features.

Besides cost, another barrier to enlisting external help is a desire to be perceived by the organization as the expert in a particular feature or technology. This can be quite short-sighted, particularly if an incident is causing revenue or reputation damage to the organization. Knowing when to ask for help is a valuable trait, and engaging an external resource also provides the opportunity to learn and increase the value you deliver to the business. Using external resources also provides a firsthand opportunity to see different approaches to troubleshooting, which can be more valuable than the technical skills themselves.

Certain types of problems are well suited for outside help. One such example is database corruption. This can be a serious problem, and many urban legends and "common wisdom" surround the best approach to resolving corruption problems, and mistakes could easily make a problem worse, without solving the underlying cause of the problem.

If you do engage support, whether it's from CSS, a consultant, or another outside assistance, you will need to provide them with some basic information. Consider the following as a starting point:

➤ Environment overview (network diagram, application architecture)

➤ Problem statement and steps to reproduce

➤ success criteria

➤ Key stakeholders

➤ Steps already taken to resolve issue and outcome

➤ Windows System and Application Event Logs and SQL Server Error Logs

➤ Profiler trace containing the problem (if possible)

➤ SQLDiag output if it will add value

DEFINING THE PROBLEM

Investing time to understand the problem and application environment often leads to a higher-quality and faster problem resolution. While it is tempting to focus on immediately resolving the problem, complex problems are rarely resolved until causes are fully understood. A thorough understanding of the configuration, patterns, and characteristics of the problem will position you well for resolving the problem.

To learn about the problem, you need to identify the major software and hardware components, review the impact of recent changes, and understand the specific circumstances that cause the problem condition to occur. The following section provides a framework for these aspects. Decomposing the problem into constituent components will help isolate the cause of the problem and identify bottlenecks.

Guidelines for Identifying the Problem

Use the following guidelines to fully comprehend the exact problem you are facing:

➤ Construct a diagram of the end-to-end application environment.

➤ Obtain visibility of major hardware components, paying special attention to components that may complicate troubleshooting, such as geographically dispersed configurations, local caching, and network load balancing (NLB). Network load balancers can mask a problem with an individual server because the problem server may only serve traffic for 25% of requests (assuming four active servers); therefore, occurrences of the problem can appear random or inconsistent.

➤ Gather all relevant logs to a single location:

➤ Windows and System Event logs

➤ SQL Server Error Logs

➤ Dump files

➤ Application logs

➤ Construct a timeline of activities and events leading up to the failure.

➤ Retrieve change logs, including any information relating to changes before the problem occurred and any changes or steps carried out in an attempt to resolve the problem.

➤ Understand the steps necessary to reproduce the problem. If possible, ensure that you have a repeatable process to reproduce the problem and validate on a test environment if possible.

➤ Agree on success criteria. Where the problem is repeatable, this is easy. With intermittent problems this can be more difficult, although agreeing to a period of non-occurrence may be valid (e.g., before troubleshooting the problem occurred daily, so if one week passes without the problem you can consider the issue resolved).

➤ Understand log context, (e.g., client, middle tier, or SQL Server). Pay attention to the time zone on each machine. It may be necessary to synchronize the time zones for data from multiple sources.

➤ Understand the rhythm of the business. This enables you to determine whether the current workload is typical, a seasonal spike, or an unusual pattern.

➤ Capture any situations when the problem does not occur. Understanding these scenarios can be useful in refining the scope of the problem too.

Part of understanding the problem is understanding why the issue is occurring now. If this is a new system, perhaps you haven't seen this level of load on the system before. If it is an existing system, review your change control documents to see what has changed recently on the system. Any change, even if seemingly unrelated, should be reviewed. This can mean any alteration, no matter how small, such as a Windows or SQL Server patch, a new policy or removed permission, a configuration option, or an application or database schema change.

Isolating the Problem

Are you certain the problem is related to the database tier? How do you know it's a database problem? Many problems begin life as an application behavior or performance issue, and there may be other software components or interactions that could affect the database platform.

Once you have a good understanding of the problem, decompose it into manageable elements; isolating each component enables you to focus on the problem area fast. The intention of this approach is to eliminate or incriminate each area of the environment. Approach troubleshooting as a series of mini-experiments, each looking to prove or disprove that a specific feature or component is functioning correctly.

The following list describes what to look for when troubleshooting each major problem category:

➤ **Connectivity issues** — Does the problem only occur with one protocol, such as named pipes or TCP/IP? Are some applications, users, client workstations, or subnets able to connect while others cannot? Does the problem occur only with double hops, whereas direct connections work? Will local connections work but remote connections fail? Is the problem related to name resolution (does `ping` by name work)? Could network routing be the issue (check `ping` or `tracert`)? Can you connect using the dedicated administrator connection (DAC)? Try to connect with SQL Authentication as well as using a domain account.

➤ **Performance issues** — For a performance problem you need to determine if the problem is on the client, the middle tier, the server on which SQL Server runs, or the network. If it is an application performance problem, it is essential to establish how much time is consumed in the database tier; for example, if application response time is 10 seconds, is 1 second or 9 seconds consumed by the database response time? Capture slow-running stored procedures, execute these directly on the server, and confirm execution times.

➤ **Hardware bottlenecks** — Identify resource contention around disk, CPU, network, or memory. Using wait stats analysis and the tools discussed in this book, identify the top N worst queries by contended resource (disk, memory, or CPU) and investigate further.

➤ **SQL Server issues** — As well as hardware contention, SQL Server has finite internal resources, such as locks, latches, worker threads, and shared resources such as tempdb. Isolate these problems with wait stats analysis and DMVs, then investigate queries that are causing the resource consumption.

➤ **Compilation issues** — If possible, identify one user query that is slow, the most common causes are insufficient resources. This could be caused by a sub-optimal query plan as a result of missing or outdated statistics, or inefficient indexes. Analyze the plan cache to help identify this problem.

Performance Bottlenecks

Performance troubleshooting involves identifying the bottleneck. This may be done live on the system, or via a post-mortem review by analyzing data collected during problem occurrence. This is often an iterative process, each cycle identifying and resolving the largest bottleneck until the problem is resolved. Often, fixing one bottleneck uncovers another and you need to start the troubleshooting cycle again with the new bottleneck.

Memory

If you identify a SQL Server memory bottleneck, you have several options to improve performance. The first is to increase physical memory or change the memory configuration. Another approach is to review queries and optimize performance to consume less memory.

If you decide to increase the memory available to SQL Server, you could consider adding more physical memory, or increasing the memory assignment for virtual machines (VMs). Improving the use of existing memory without adding more is often more scalable and yields better results. While x86 (32-bit) systems are becoming less common, if you are running SQL Server 2005 or 2008 on 32-bit systems or VMs, consider using the Address Window Extension (AWE) or /3GB to increase the buffer pool available to SQL Server (the AWE feature was discontinued in SQL Server 2012). However, if you do see memory contention on a x86 server, consider a plan to migrate to an × 64 system to resolve this issue. The × 64 platform provides increased virtual memory and better memory management.

Aside from physical memory and server configuration, significant performance gains can be made through query tuning to reduce memory requirements. Identify queries that require significant memory grants, such as sorts or hashes, and review the query plans for these scenarios. Try to identify better indexes, and avoid table scans and other operations that force a large number of rows to be read from disk and manipulated in memory.

CPU

CPU problems could be sustained or occasional spikes. Occasional CPU spikes, especially for a small number of CPUs, can often be safely ignored. Wait statistics record the resource SQL Server or a query is waiting on. Capturing wait statistics information can prove a useful tool in understanding resource bottlenecks and to identify whether CPU contention is the cause of performance problems. Consider server build and configuration options to improve CPU performance, such as increasing the number and speed of CPU cores. In terms of configuration options, review the maximum degree of parallelism to ensure it is optimal for the intended workload.

In many situations, overall performance may be acceptable while the server demonstrates high CPU. As with memory, once you have established CPU is the dominant wait type, identify the top 10 worst-performing queries by CPU and then work through each of these in turn. Look at the query execution plan and identify expensive CPU operations, such as hash joins, sorts, and computed columns. Look for opportunities to reduce CPU workload with new indexes, consolidated indexes, XML indexes, or to improve query design.

Storage I/O

Storage input/output (I/O) is typically the slowest resource within a server (memory and CPU are orders of magnitude quicker). Therefore, optimizing the storage solution design and configuration (ensuring the solution performs optimally) as well as being considerate with I/O requests (making fewer I/O requests) is essential to achieve scalable systems with good performance. Review the PerfMon disk counters for Average Disk Sec/Read and Average Disk Sec/Write to verify that the time to make a read or write is ideally below 20 milliseconds for OLTP systems, higher for decision support systems. Generally speaking, if storage is performing slower than this, database performance will be affected. When reviewing storage performance, consider the end-to-end solution. Following are some elements that may affect performance:

➤ RAID levels

➤ Disk types (enterprise flash Disk, SCSI)

➤ Dedicated or shared disk arrays

➤ Connectivity (InfiniBand, Fibre Channel, iSCSI)

➤ HBA cache and queue settings

➤ HBA load balancing policy (active; active vs. active; or passive)

➤ NTFS cluster size

➤ Layout and isolation of data, index, log, and tempdb files

➤ Storage cache and controllers policy

In addition to ensuring optimal storage performance, be smart with I/O and ensure that the database is not making unnecessary requests. Reviewing and optimizing a query plan to eliminate index scans and replace them with seeks can often deliver an order of magnitude benefit in I/O reduction. It is common to overwhelm the storage solution with inefficient queries, saturating controllers and cache on the storage array.

Reduce I/O workload by improving indexes for more efficient access, make sure statistics are current, tune or increase memory to improve cache performance, or alter queries to avoid unnecessary I/O. Rationalize and consolidate indexes to minimize the overhead of index maintenance. Use Profiler or DMVs to identify the worst-performing queries by reads and writes. In addition, use STATISTICS IO to identify batches within a query that contain high logical I/Os. Usually, identifying the table or view that has the highest number of logical I/Os is sufficient to identify the table or view requiring optimization.

Network

Network bottlenecks can look like SQL Server performance problems. When query results are not sent or received by the client as fast as SQL Server can send them, SQL Server can appear slow. Often a particular function within an application is described as slow. In this case, you should try to determine the database interaction used by this functionality.

SQL Server Profiler can find which stored procedures, functions, and queries are executed when the application feature is accessed. Sometimes this indicates that each query executes quickly, but either very many queries are executed or there is a large delay between the calls to each query. The latter case usually indicates that the performance problem is somewhere outside of SQL Server.

> **CONSIDER DISABLING TCP CHIMNEY**
>
> TCP Chimney is a network interface card (NIC) technology that by default allows servers to offload some TCP workload to the network card itself. This works well on desktop PCs and application servers, but database servers often transfer large amounts of data to clients.
>
> In this scenario, the offload activity may overwhelm the NIC, and the processing capability on the network card can become a bottleneck. Disable TCP offloading using the NETSH command utility and NIC drivers.

If you are able to narrow the problem down to a single stored procedure as the main contributor to the problem, break that stored procedure down into individual queries. Often there will be a single query within that procedure — this is the area to focus on for tuning and optimization.

DATA COLLECTION

When the problem is defined and well understood, and the success criteria have been agreed upon, the next step is to gather data. What data you should gather depends on the problem and what (if any) work has already been completed.

It is critical that decisions about remedial action are based on data. Decisions or recommendations without the foundation of empirical data are simply guesses or assumptions. Gathering data is an iterative process that may require several iterations before the complete problem is captured and a conclusive decision can be reached. As mentioned earlier, ensure that stakeholders understand that sufficient data will be required ahead of any recommendations and problem resolution. These stakeholders must also understand the value and long-term benefits of quantitative analysis and evidence-based decisions. Clearly explaining your methodology helps to win their confidence in the process and its outcome.

Since data collection is so important in identifying the root cause, the following section provides an approach around data collection and specific guidance to ensure the data collection objectives are met.

Focused Data Collection

Only rarely is complete fault information provided when an incident is escalated. The nature of databases means serverwide problems are more immediately obvious, and support teams are notified rapidly. High-impact database problems reach support teams by phone or walk-up much faster than automated alerts or formal support-ticket escalation. Typically, escalated support cases contain insufficient data to make any kind of decision, and further analysis is required before any kind of remediation can begin. In the early minutes (sometimes hours) of these incidents, information can be vague while the cause of the problem is unknown. At this point, the scope of the issue is often the complete solution, consisting of all components of the solution.

During this time, it can be useful to adopt a top-down approach to troubleshooting by starting with Performance Monitor (PerfMon). PerfMon has the advantage of being a serverwide diagnostics tool, and it can be useful in identifying or indemnifying the database tier as the root cause of the problem.

The divide-and-conquer method is especially useful when troubleshooting performance problems. This approach takes the complete end-to-end application environment and selects a midpoint between the client and the database server to determine whether the performance problem exists at that point. Based on the outcome, you can then focus on the problem half and iterate through it until the problem component is identified. This approach can work particularly well with the database tier, as calling a number of stored procedures to validate database functionality and responsiveness can be a useful junction in identifying or absolving SQL Server as the cause of the performance problem.

Understanding Data Gathering

Data gathering is a balance between collecting sufficient information to capture the problem and not collecting so much data that the collection process itself affects system performance or there is simply too much data to analyze efficiently.

> **BLACK BOX TRACING**
>
> Consider a scenario with an intermittent problem for which there is no clear pattern to occurrences. *Black box tracing* creates a server-side trace, writing trace data to a circular log file that contains data for a specified time period (e.g., 1 hour or 4 hours). If the problem event occurs again and the trace is stopped before the occurrence of the problem is overwritten in the log (this could be automated), the trace will contain the problem. You can also look a setting up in Extended Events to help with this (Chapter 13).

If the problem can be reproduced it will be much easier to collect data and refine the scope rapidly. If it occurs in a predictable pattern, it is usually possible to restrict data collection to a short period of time and gather all necessary data.

Conversely, if the problem happens infrequently or without pattern, a different strategy is required. Often it isn't possible to start data capture when the problem occurs because events occurring just before the problem starts may be important. Therefore, consider using a black box circular trace to enable a continuous lightweight trace that can be stopped when the problem occurs.

Tools and Utilities

The following list summarizes some of the most commonly used data collection tools and analysis utilities. Subsequent chapters contain additional details covering when and how to use each of these tools:

➤ **PerfMon** — Performance Monitor (PerfMon) ships with Windows and can be used to gather information on server resources and services. It can track serverwide information such as CPU and memory usage, I/O statistics, and network activity. Several SQL Server-specific counters can be useful for various troubleshooting and monitoring scenarios.

➤ **Profiler** — SQL Server Profiler can be used to capture statement-level information from within the database engine.

➤ **XEvents** — Extended Events are a lightweight event-driven data-capture feature that can assist troubleshooting while minimizing the monitoring footprint.

➤ **PSSDiag** — This is a wrapper around SQLDiag, PerfMon, and other add-ins. SQLDiag can do anything that PSSDiag can do, but it is not pre-packaged with all the add-ins that PSSDiag may be configured with. PSSDiag is usually configured by a Microsoft support engineer and sent to help troubleshoot a specific problem. It is specific to a certain version of SQL Server, and the add-ins are usually architecture specific (x86 or x64).

➤ **SQLDiag** — SQLDiag ships with SQL Server. It can be used to gather basic environmental information such as the SQL Server Error Logs, Event Logs, and SQL Server configuration settings. It can also be used to capture time-synchronized Profiler and PerfMon information (see Chapter 11).

➤ **Event Logs (Application, System, and Security)** — These logs are often useful, displaying which errors, warnings, and informational messages have occurred in the recent past.

➤ **Application logs** — If the application instrumentation includes writing Error Log output or diagnostic information, these logs can be useful for identifying the cause of a problem.

➤ **User dumps** — If you see an exception in the SQL Server Error Logs, you should also see a mini-dump file with the extension .mdmp. This can be used by Microsoft CSS to help determine why the exception occurred.

➤ **NetMon** — This is a network sniffer that is used to look at data as it is sent over the network. It is often used to diagnose connectivity or Kerberos problems.

➤ **CMS** — Central Management Server is a feature with SQL Server Management Studio and provides a method of storing your SQL Server registrations in a central database. It can be useful in a troubleshooting scenario because you don't have to remember specific SQL Server instance names and passwords — they are already stored in CMS. In addition, you can execute commands against groups of CMS servers at once.

➤ **Management Data Warehouse** — This SQL Server Management Studio tool is used for performance trending. You can use it to collect and consolidate various data over time, which you can then analyze to see how performance has changed.

➤ **Policy-Based Management (PBM)** — PBM can be used to validate whether predetermined standards have been followed. Some policies can prevent certain actions from ever occurring.

DATA ANALYSIS

After data collection, data analysis is the second iterative activity required to identify the problem's root cause. It may be necessary to perform data analysis multiple times for a single problem, including data from multiple sources and formats. The typical starting point is to review PerfMon output to identify bottlenecks or contention with I/O, CPU, memory, or the network resources. Often, once the main bottleneck is resolved, another will appear. At this point it is important to understand the success criteria and SLAs to have a clear goal and know when to stop troubleshooting.

The following list describes several tools and utilities you can use to analyze the data collected:

➤ **SQL Nexus** — This tool, available from `www.codeplex.com`, imports data into a SQL Server database and generates reports showing the most common performance issues based on that data. It takes Profiler, PerfMon, and PerfStats as input. For example, it can show all statements captured in the trace that were blocked for more than 30 seconds. SQL Nexus is commonly used to show the stored procedures or queries that had the highest duration, were executed most frequently, or used the highest cumulative CPU. With stored procedures, it is possible to drill down to get more specific information on duration and other statistics about individual queries within the stored procedure. SQL Nexus is a great tool for taking a large amount of data and quickly locating pain points that require more thorough examination. You can read all about it in Chapter 12.

➤ **Profiler** — Profiler can be used to replay statements if the right events were captured. A Replay template built into Profiler can be used to capture those events. This is useful to test the same queries repeatedly against a database to which changes have been made, such as modifying indexes and altering file layout. The impact/benefits of these changes can be measured relative to the overall workload using this consistent set of replay workload. Profiler can also be useful for troubleshooting security and connectivity problems.

➤ **PerfMon** — Performance Monitor can be used to isolate CPU, memory, I/O, or network bottlenecks. Another use is to help determine whether SQL Server is the victim of another process (such as anti-virus apps or device drivers), consuming resources such that SQL Server performance is affected.

➤ **Database Tuning Advisor (DTA)** — The DTA can take as input either an individual query or an entire trace workload. It makes recommendations for possible index or partitioning changes that can be tested. Never implement suggestions from DTA without thorough review in the context of the total workload. Analysis with DTA is most effective when a complete workload can be captured in a trace and processed.

➤ **SQL Server Data Tools** — Provides an integrated environment for developers to create, edit and deploy database schemas. A full discussion of the product is well beyond the scope of this section.

➤ **Debugger** — It is possible to debug stored procedures from SQL Server Management Studio beginning with SQL Server 2008.

COUNTING THE COST OF PERFORMANCE PROBLEMS

Performance problems are rarely caused by a single large query executing on a server. More often, the query with the highest cumulative cost is a relatively short and fast query, but one that might be executed thousands of times per minute. A stored procedure that takes 200 ms to execute and is called thousands of times per minute will have a greater impact on server performance than a single query that takes 1.5 seconds to complete. As such, focus your attention on queries with the highest cumulative cost.

When analyzing data, use aggregates to consider the total cumulative time (duration, CPU, read/writes, etc.), rather than identifying the single longest-running query. You can use the Performance Dashboard reports or SQL Nexus to identify these queries.

VALIDATING AND IMPLEMENTING RESOLUTION

Once the solution has been identified, it should be validated through testing and implemented in production. This process should be as controlled and disciplined as the iterations of collecting and analyzing data. A production problem does not justify a cavalier attitude toward production changes, and professionalism must be maintained even under pressure.

Validating Changes

Changes should always be made in a test environment prior to production. In an ideal scenario, the problem can be reproduced in the test environment, which provides an opportunity to confirm, or validate, that the fix has the desired impact. It is also important to carry out confidence tests to ensure that the change has no undesired impact.

Testing Changes in Isolation

If possible, test each change in isolation. Changing several settings at once can make it harder to identify which change resolved the problem or caused other issues. In addition, it can be harder to roll back multiple changes than single, individual changes. Ensure that you have a thorough understanding of the consequences of any change, including rollback options.

Implementing Resolution

The final step is to implement the resolution in production. Ensure that the change is documented and any impact (such as service restarts) communicated. Note the behavior of the database or application before and after the change, as well as exactly what change was made. Ensure that the success criteria are met once the resolution is implemented, and share your results with the stakeholders.

Once the resolution is implemented and the solution is stabilized, carry out post-mortem analysis and ensure that the root causes are communicated to relevant parties. Identify any other vulnerable systems within the organization and communicate any lessons learned that may help you avoid a recurrence of similar problems in the future.

SUMMARY

Confidence and control are critical to successful troubleshooting. Developing a methodology that can be consistently applied and refined is a valuable skill that enhances your value to an organization.

Your attitude, knowledge of when and whom to ask for help, and ability to communicate with management and stakeholders are essential skills. In many job roles these skills are as important as technical skills to a successful career.

It doesn't matter if you are investigating a performance problem, resolving a security issue, or fixing a connectivity problem. Use each scenario as an opportunity to implement and refine your troubleshooting approach.

Define the problem, understand the exact circumstances under which the problem manifests itself, and identify the problem's potential impact on the organization. Consider the end-to-end application, hardware, and software scenario. Use the divide-and-conquer technique to isolate the problem, eliminating or incriminating each component of the problem until you find the root cause. After the cause is understood, develop a fix to resolve the issue, and then test it to validate that it doesn't cause any undesirable consequences before implementing it in production.

10

Viewing Server Performance with PerfMon and the PAL Tool

WHAT'S IN THIS CHAPTER?

➤ When and how to use Windows Performance Monitor

➤ Prescriptive guidance on problem counters

➤ Using PAL for log analysis

➤ Using other log analysis tools

WROX.COM CODE DOWNLOADS FOR THIS CHAPTER

There are no code downloads for this chapter.

INTRODUCTION

Performance Monitor, often referred to as PerfMon, is a tool that provides performance data useful for narrowing the scope of a problem. This data is frequently used as a first point of call for troubleshooting — providing server-wide diagnostics information, PerfMon can be used to eliminate components as the cause of a problem.

PerfMon is often used interactively to provide a real-time view of server performance and resource utilization (such as CPU, memory, and disk activity). PerfMon may also be useful for post-mortem analysis, whereby logs can be configured to record data continuously, rollover, or start/stop at specific intervals. DBAs often find the tool useful when troubleshooting intermittent problems or identifying a problem outside SQL Server (either a hardware problem or a Windows issue).

Engineers familiar with PerfMon typically know a handful of PerfMon counters that can provide an overview of server performance and health. Experienced engineers, well practiced with PerfMon, often take an iterative approach — adding and removing counters as the scope of a problem becomes more refined and troubleshooting is more focused.

It's important to know when and how PerfMon can be useful, as it provides different data from SQL Profiler, extended events, or dynamic management views (DMVs).

Users unfamiliar with PerfMon often look at the data generated in the performance log and ask numerous questions about it, such as the following: Is x value acceptable? Why is my system running so slow? What does "normal" look like? How can I tell if there's a problem? This chapter will help you answer such questions in three ways:

➤   By providing and explaining the key counters and thresholds for issues

➤   By helping you gather a baseline from a healthy server

➤   By demonstrating the tools available to assist in analyzing performance logs

After reading this chapter you should have a good understanding of how to use PerfMon, including which counters to monitor and what values are acceptable. Additionally, you'll be aware of a selection of tools and utilities to help with log analysis.

PERFORMANCE MONITOR OVERVIEW

PerfMon provides server-wide real-time and logged performance monitoring. First introduced with Windows NT 4.0, the core features and user interface have barely changed from the first Microsoft Management Console (MMC) snap-in. In Windows Server 2003 the tool was renamed to System Monitor, although the data logging functionality of System Monitor retained the name Performance Monitor. In Windows Server 2008, PerfMon was incorporated into Reliability and Performance Monitor.

You can use Performance Monitor for many common tasks:

➤   View real-time performance data on your server.

➤   See performance data represented visually.

➤   Record performance data over an extended time frame.

➤   Quantify the performance impact of hardware or software changes.

➤   Save and export performance data.

➤   Fire alerts based on performance thresholds.

➤   Compare performance data from different servers.

➤   Capture a baseline set of performance counters for trending and troubleshooting over time.

Reliability and Performance Monitor

PerfMon in Windows Server 2008 brings a new look and a new name for the parent snap-in, Reliability and Performance Monitor, although real-time performance monitoring retains the PerfMon name.

Reliability and Performance Monitor comprises three components: Monitoring Tools, Data Collector Sets, and Reports. This chapter focuses on Performance Monitor and Data Collector Sets. Monitoring Tools comprises Performance Monitor (PerfMon), which is the tool of choice when investigating server-wide or resource problems; and Reliability Monitor, which reports on system stability.

Resource Overview

Once Reliability and Performance Monitor is launched, the Resource Overview screen is displayed showing real-time performance data. The Resource Overview provides a visual representation of each of the four key hardware elements: CPU, Disk, Network, and Memory. Each element can be expanded to reveal a list of processes, listed in descending order by resource type; for example, when CPU is expanded, all processes are listed ordered by Average CPU descending, as shown in Figure 10-1.

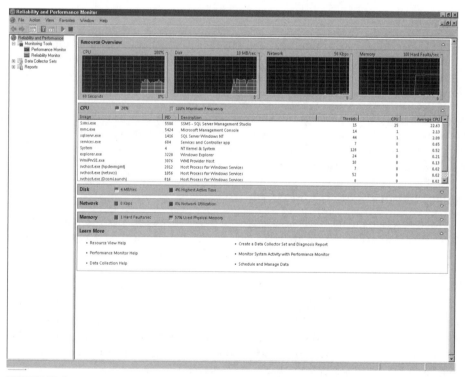

FIGURE 10-1

In addition to the four individual performance graphs displayed across the top of the Resource Overview, each resource element displays two mini-performance bars. It's worth noting that for CPU, when looking at this on your own PC, the green bar displays the current CPU utilization and the blue bar displays the maximum CPU frequency. Some computers may have maximum CPU frequency less than 100% when operating in energy-saving modes. If you're interested in reading further — there's more detail on CPU performance and powersaving mode in Chapter 2. The Memory resource element displays hard (page) faults per second in the green bar (more on hard page fault later in this chapter), and the percentage of physical memory in use is shown in blue.

Data Collector Sets

Data Collector Sets combine all the information necessary for common problem diagnostics, including event tracing, performance counters, and configuration (Registry and WMI classes). Administrators can create Data Collector Sets with providers enabled for trace and counter data. Once a collector set has been defined, it is stored in Reliability and Performance Monitor. This enables starting and stopping the collector at any point in the future without recreating it, or it can be controlled on a schedule.

Three pre-defined system Data Collector Sets are included: LAN Diagnostics, System Diagnostics, and System Performance. Each collects performance counters, trace data, and system configuration for common troubleshooting scenarios.

Reliability Monitor

Reliability Monitor provides a system stability chart. Here, events such as hardware failures, or application or Windows failures, are tracked against a timeline. The data presented by Reliability Monitor provides access to failure activity information, plotted against a time chart to facilitate correlation between failure events and system activity (software installation or uninstallation, etc.).

The chart displayed by Reliability Monitor plots the *System Stability Index*, a rating system reflecting reliability where 10 is a stable server and 1 is considered an unstable server. The purpose of the System Stability Index is to assist in correlating a decrease in system stability with a specific change (such as a new device driver or a hotfix installation).

PerfMon Usability in Windows Server 2008

There are some user interface enhancements for PerfMon in Windows Server 2008 (compared with Windows Server 2003 and earlier). There are relatively minor changes between Windows Server 2008 and the R2 release; this section contains a summary of the highlights.

Auto-Scaling Counters

In early versions of Windows Server, counter values were often either off the top of the PerfMon graph or dwarfed by other counters — neither situation enabled users to easily see changes in these values. This made scaling counters a painful process of trial and error, as each counter had to be selected in turn in an attempt to choose a reasonable value to scale the counter by. The process was made much simpler in Windows Server 2008 because users could select a group of counters, right-click, and choose "Scale selected counters." Windows then adjusted the scale of each counter to a reasonable value so that all lines are plotted in or around the middle of the graph.

> **NOTE** *Always be aware of auto-scaling in PerfMon. Check the scaling of counters before comparing multiple counters, particularly when comparing between servers. Auto-scaling can adjust instances of the same counter to use different scales.*

Show/Hide Counters

Another minor but useful enhancement to PerfMon in Windows Server 2008 enabled the showing or hiding of counters on the graph. This is useful when monitoring in real time because many counters can be captured and fewer can be displayed. Showing and hiding counters means the data (including min, max, and average values) is still recorded but it can be displayed as needed, which is also faster than adding counters.

New PerfMon Counters for SQL Server 2012

As shown in Table 10-1, a number of new PerfMon counters are available in SQL Server 2012. Some of these provide logging for new features such as AlwaysOn and FileTable, and some are more detailed counters related to memory utilization.

First introduced in SQL Server 2008, the Deprecated Features PerfMon counter provides a chance to capture deprecated features, reducing the risk of issues with future projects when upgrading from SQL Server 2012. Deprecated features are features that still operate although they will be removed in a future version.

TABLE 10-1: New PerfMon Counters for SQL Server 2012

COUNTER		DESCRIPTION
Availability Replica	Bytes Received from Replica/sec	Total bytes received from the availability replica
	Bytes Sent to Replica/sec	Total bytes sent to the availabilty replica
	Bytes Sent to Transport/sec	Total bytes sent to transport for the availabilty replica
	Flow Control Time (ms/sec)	Time, in milliseconds, messages waited on flow control in the last second
	Flow Control/sec	Number of flow control initiated in the last second
	Receives from Replica/sec	Total receives from the availability replica
	Resent Messages/sec	Number of messages being resent in the last second
	Sends to Replica/sec	Total sends to the availability replica
	Sends to Transport/sec	Total sends to transport for the availability replica

continues

TABLE 10-1 *(continued)*

COUNTER		DESCRIPTION
Batch Resp Statistics	Batches >=000000ms & <000001ms	Number of SQL Batches with a response time greater than or equal to 0ms but less than 1ms
	Batches >=000001ms & <000002ms	Number of SQL Batches with a response time greater than or equal to 1ms but less than 2ms
	Batches >=000002ms & <000005ms	Number of SQL Batches with a response time greater than or equal to 2ms but less than 5ms
	Batches >=000005ms & <000010ms	Number of SQL Batches with a response time greater than or equal to 5ms but less than 10ms
	Batches >=000010ms & <000020ms	Number of SQL Batches with a response time greater than or equal to 10ms but less than 20ms
	Batches >=000020ms & <000050ms	Number of SQL Batches with a response time greater than or equal to 20ms but less than 50ms
	Batches >=000050ms & <000100ms	Number of SQL Batches with a response time greater than or equal to 50ms but less than 100ms
	Batches >=000100ms & <000200ms	Number of SQL Batches with a response time greater than or equal to 100ms but less than 200ms
	Batches >=000200ms & <000500ms	Number of SQL Batches with a response time greater than or equal to 200ms but less than 500ms
	Batches >=000500ms & <001000ms	Number of SQL Batches with a response time greater than or equal to 500ms but less than 1,000ms
	Batches >=001000ms & <002000ms	Number of SQL Batches with a response time greater than or equal to 1,000ms but less than 2,000ms
	Batches >=002000ms & <005000ms	Number of SQL Batches with a response time greater than or equal to 2,000ms but less than 5,000ms
	Batches >=005000ms & <010000ms	Number of SQL Batches with a response time greater than or equal to 5,000ms but less than 10,000ms

COUNTER		DESCRIPTION
	Batches >=010000ms & <020000ms	Number of SQL Batches with a response time greater than or equal to 10,000ms but less than 20,000ms
	Batches >=020000ms & <050000ms	Number of SQL Batches with a response time greater than or equal to 20,000ms but less than 50,000ms
	Batches >=050000ms & <100000ms	Number of SQL Batches with a response time greater than or equal to 50,000ms but less than 100,000ms
	Batches >=100000ms	Number of SQL Batches with a response time greater than or equal to 100,000ms
Database Replica	File Bytes Received/sec	Amount of filestream data received by the availability replica for the database
	Log Bytes Received/sec	Amount of logs received by the availability replica for the database
	Log remaining for undo	The amount of log in kilobytes remaining to finish the undo phase
	Log Send Queue	Amount of logs in kilobytes waiting to be sent to the database replica
	Mirrored Write Transactions/sec	Number of transactions that wrote to the mirrored database in the last second, that waited for log to be sent to the mirror
	Recovery Queue	Total number of hardened log in kilobytes that is waiting to be redone on the secondary
	Redo blocked/sec	Number of times redo gets blocked in the last second
	Redo Bytes Remaining	The amount of log in kilobytes remaining to be redone to finish the reverting phase
	Redone Bytes/sec	Amount of log records redone in the last second to catch up the database replica
	Total Log requiring undo	The amount of log in kilobytes that need to be undone
	Transaction Delay	Number of milliseconds transaction termination waited for acknowledgement per second

continues

TABLE 10-1 *(continued)*

COUNTER		DESCRIPTION
FileTable	Avg time delete FileTable item	Average time, in milliseconds, taken to delete a FileTable item
	Avg time FileTable enumeration	Average time, in milliseconds, taken for a FileTable enumeration request
	Avg time FileTable handle kill	Average time, in milliseconds, taken to kill a FileTable handle
	Avg time move FileTable item	Average time, in milliseconds, taken to move a FileTable item
	Avg time per file I/O request	Average time, in milliseconds, spent handling an incoming file I/O request
	Avg time per file I/O response	Average time, in milliseconds, spent handling an outgoing file I/O response
	Avg time rename FileTable item	Average time, in milliseconds, taken to rename a FileTable item
	Avg time to get FileTable item	Average time, in milliseconds, taken to retrieve a FileTable item
	Avg time update FileTable item	Average time, in milliseconds, taken to update a FileTable item
	FileTable db operations/sec	Total number of database operational events processed by the FileTable store component per second
	FileTable enumeration reqs/sec	Total number of FileTable enumeration requests per second
	FileTable file I/O requests/sec	Total number of incoming FileTable file I/O requests per second
	FileTable file I/O response/sec	Total number of outgoing file I/O responses per second
	FileTable item delete reqs/sec	Total number of FileTable delete item requests per second
	FileTable item get requests/sec	Total number of FileTable retrieve item requests per second
	FileTable item move reqs/sec	Total number of FileTable move item requests per second

COUNTER		DESCRIPTION
	FileTable item rename reqs/sec	Total number of FileTable rename item requests per second
	FileTable item update reqs/sec	Total number of FileTable update item requests per second
	FileTable kill handle ops/sec	Total number of FileTable handle kill operations per second
	FileTable table operations/sec	Total number of table operational events processed by the FileTable store component per second
Memory Broker Clerks	Internal benefit	The internal value of memory for entry count pressure, in ms per page per ms, multiplied by 10 billion and truncated to an integer
	Memory broker clerk size	The size of the the clerk, in pages
	Periodic evictions (pages)	The number of pages evicted from the broker clerk by last periodic eviction
	Pressure evictions (pages/sec)	The number of pages per second evicted from the broker clerk by memory pressure
	Simulation benefit	The value of memory to the clerk, in ms per page per ms, multiplied by 10 billion and truncated to an integer
	Simulation size	The current size of the clerk simulation, in pages
Memory Node	Database Node Memory (KB)	Amount of memory the server is using on this node for database pages
	Foreign Node Memory (KB)	Non NUMA-local amount of memory on this node
	Free Node Memory (KB)	Amount of memory the server is not using on this node
	Stolen Node Memory (KB)	Amount of memory the server is using on this node for purposes other than database pages
	Target Node Memory (KB)	Ideal amount of memory for this node
	Total Node Memory (KB)	Total amount of memory the server has committed on this node

Getting Started with PerfMon

PerfMon is a component of Reliability and Performance Monitor which can be launched from Start ⇨ All Programs ⇨ Administrative Tools. Alternatively, just type **perfmon** into the Run box and press Enter.

As mentioned earlier, PerfMon is a Windows monitoring tool, and as such it can be used to monitor any application — from Microsoft Exchange to Windows itself. When an application is installed, performance counters are registered and you can monitor the counters in real time or trace them to a log file. PerfMon isn't designed specifically for SQL Server, so you need to add the relevant Windows and SQL Server counters to a log file in order to view resource utilization and SQL Server activity.

Monitoring Real-Time Server Activity

One of the most common uses for PerfMon is viewing real-time server activity. PerfMon provides data instantly on system workload, performance, and resource consumption. By reading the data presented by PerfMon, you can rapidly narrow the scope of a problem.

Within Reliability and Performance Monitor, select Performance Monitor from the Monitoring Tools folder. You'll be presented with a line chart plotting percentage of processor time from your own computer, as shown in Figure 10-2. In this section, you'll add a few counters to get a feel for CPU, disk, and memory activity on your PC.

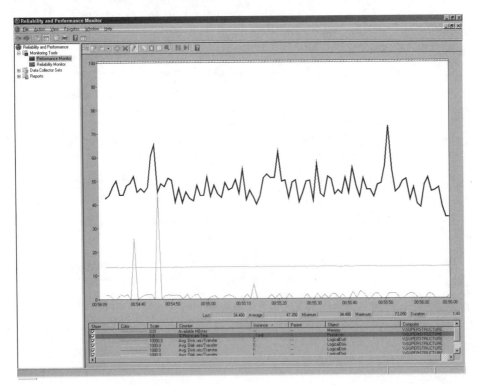

FIGURE 10-2

Right-click anywhere in the chart area and choose Add Counters. From here you can choose from hundreds of counters to monitor! Scroll through the list of counters until you see Memory and expand the Memory counter. Select Available Mbytes and click Add. Next, scroll to locate the LogicalDisk counter and select Avg. Disk sec/Transfer. If you have multiple disks, select each disk individually from the instance list and click OK as shown in Figure 10-3.

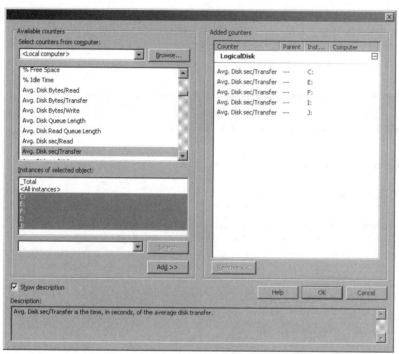

FIGURE 10-3

The counters will be added to the performance graph immediately and as the red timeline moves across the screen, each counter will be populated with data.

Note a couple of pointers: Organize the columns so you can read each row more easily; press Ctrl+H to enable highlighting for a selected counter — this means the line graph is highlighted. Select all counters, right-click, and choose Scale Selected Counters to ensure they are all displayed within the screen.

Mostly you'll want to monitor a server (rather than your own workstation), and it's possible to use PerfMon to monitor a remote server by typing the server name from the Add Counters dialog. If you're adding a lot of counters, the graph can become a little unwieldy because individual counters become difficult to read. If so, you have three options: Remove nonrequired counters, hide nonrequired counters (uncheck Show button), or use a report view instead of the line graph (select Report from the mini drop-down on the top menu bar).

Starting Out with Data Collector Sets

Data Collector Sets are groups of data-gathering tools. They can include kernel tracing, performance logs, and configuration data. Three Data Collector Sets are provided out-of-the-box, including a system performance collector that consists of a kernel trace and a PerfMon log. To utilize a pre-defined data collector, select Data Collector Sets ⇨ System, right-click System Performance, and select Start.

The system performance collector runs for 60 seconds. When collection has finished, navigate to Reports ⇨ System ⇨ System Performance, and choose the latest report. As shown in Figure 10-4, the report presents data in a very readable layout.

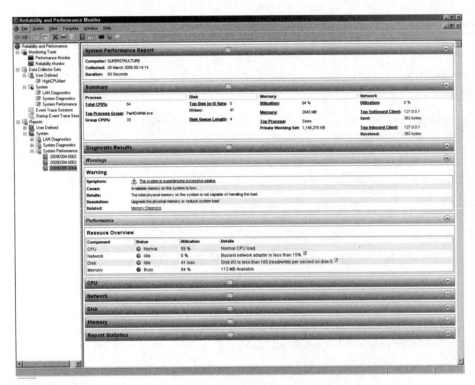

FIGURE 10-4

The System Performance report begins with a summary of the four key resources: CPU, Disk, Memory, and Network. Figure 10-4 shows memory utilization at 94% and the diagnostic results indicate excessive paging and low memory, recommending either adding more memory or reducing system load. The Resource Overview section shows memory status with a red traffic signal, highlighting a memory issue.

The small effort required to start the system performance collector, wait 60 seconds, and launch the report results in a conclusive initial investigation. In this case, the top process shown in the memory summary is SSMS (SQL Server Management Studio), and the next step would be to identify the problem session and resolve the issue.

Working with Data Collector Sets

In addition to the provided Data Collector Sets, you can also create user-defined Data Collector Sets consisting of your own counters and settings. Real-time monitoring is great when a quick snapshot is required, but it can be difficult to identify patterns and trends when observing a server "live." It's usually more convenient to capture performance data to a file and then analyze that log file — either manually or using one of the tools you'll look at later in this chapter. This section walks through configuring a user-defined Data Collector Set to monitor system performance.

User-defined Data Collector Sets in Windows Server 2008 replace the Performance Logs and Alerts from Windows 2000/2003 but the principle is the same. To access them, from Reliability and Performance Monitor select Data Collector Sets. Right-click User Defined and choose New ➪ Data Collector Set. A short wizard launches to create the new collector set. The first choice is to create from a template or create manually. Creating a collector set from a template provides three template collectors: Basic, System Diagnostics, and System Performance. You can use these templates as a starting point, adding and removing counters as required. Because these templates are Windows-generic, there's nothing especially interesting about them from a SQL Server perspective. Therefore, choose the second option, Create manually (Advanced), and give the new collector a useful name, as shown in Figure 10-5.

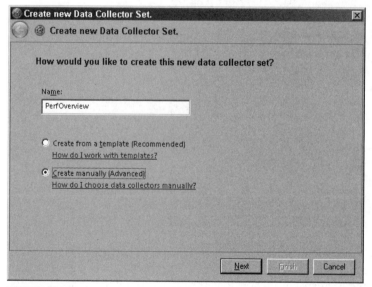

FIGURE 10-5

The next step is to select Create Data Logs or Performance Counter Alerts. In most situations you'll use the Performance Counter data log because you will likely be interested in gathering some system-wide performance data, rather than use PerfMon to fire an alert when a threshold is exceeded. Three types of data can be captured in the data log, as summarized in Table 10-2.

TABLE 10-2: Data Collector Set Logging Options

LOG TYPE	DESCRIPTION
Performance counter	Provides performance data for most aspects of Windows and SQL Server
Event trace data	Uses event tracing for Windows to provide low-level operating system tracing
System configuration information	Captures Registry keys

After selecting Create Data Logs, select the Performance counter log type and click Next to continue. Now you'll add a small selection of interesting counters to get an overview of system performance. Click Add, and select all counters as shown in Figure 10-6. Leave the sample interval at 15 seconds; the impact of the sampling interval is covered in the next section.

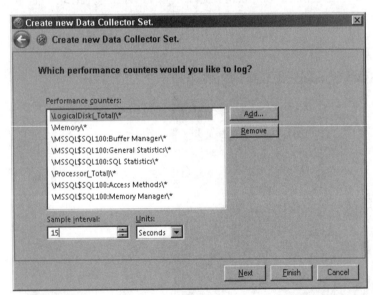

FIGURE 10-6

After adding the counters, select a folder to store the trace data. Ensure there is sufficient space on the disk to hold the trace file (the size depends on how long the trace is running but normally 2GB of free space should be fine for a few hours of tracing). Click Next when you have entered a location for the logs. At the final confirmation dialog, click Finish to create the collector.

Starting, Stopping, and Scheduling Collectors

At this point, the data collector has been defined, but no data has actually been captured because the collector has not been started. To start a collector, right-click on the collector name and choose

Start. Collectors with no stop condition configured will run until they are stopped manually. To stop the collector, right-click on the collector name and choose Stop. Collectors can be started and stopped as a whole, but performance logs or traces within a collector cannot be started independently of the collector. Define a new collector if this is required.

You can schedule collectors using the Schedule tab on the collector properties. When combined with a stop condition, both starting and stopping a collector can be fully scheduled.

Configuring Collector Properties

There are two points of interest in the properties dialog. One is the Directory tab, where you can change the folder used to store the log files. The other is the Stop Condition tab, which enables administrators to configure the duration of the collector — in seconds, minutes, hours, days, or weeks. Once the time configured in the stop condition has elapsed, the collector is automatically stopped.

Other points of interest on the collector properties dialog include the Schedule tab, which as it suggests enables administrators to schedule the start of the collector. There's also a Task tab, where you can configure a task to run when the data collector stops, such as sending a MSG (new version of NET SEND) on completion.

Configuring Properties for Performance Counters

You may have noticed that there is no place in the collector properties to add or remove PerfMon counters — that's because they are found in the Performance Counter properties. Because collectors can contain multiple data sources (listed in the right-hand pane), these properties are specific to each log type. Locate the Performance Counter log (usually named DataCollector01) and double-click it to show the properties.

Use the Performance Counter properties to modify log parameters, such as adding and removing counters, and changing log format and sample interval. The File tab contains further settings, including a checkbox to prefix log files with the computer name; this is particularly useful when comparing logs from multiple servers because it saves time opening files to identify the source server.

PerfMon Log Formats

There are four options for PerfMon log format: Comma Separated, Tab Separated, SQL, and Binary. The Binary log (BLG) type is the default and is suitable for most situations. Choosing SQL will require a data source name (DSN) to connect to SQL Server. There are some performance considerations when using this method because you want to limit the impact of monitoring to genuine users or server activity, and outputting trace data to the same instance being monitored is unlikely to help. Performance log files can be imported into a database post-capture for easier/better analysis, so avoid logging directly to SQL Server, unless there's a good reason to do so and you're confident you understand any impact on the monitored instance.

Using the Relog.exe tool it's possible to manipulate log files, converting files between types; and if you're working with large log files, you can narrow the time frame or extract some interesting counters.

Remotely Running PerfMon

Like many server management tools, an instance of PerfMon can be connected to a remote server for remote monitoring. This avoids the need to connect via Remote Desktop and may reduce the overhead of monitoring on the target server.

To run PerfMon against a remote server, when adding counters, specify the target server name, replacing <Local computer> in the "Select counters from computer" drop-down box (see Figure 10-7). In order to use PerfMon remotely, you'll need to be a Local Administrator on the target server, and the remote registry service should be running.

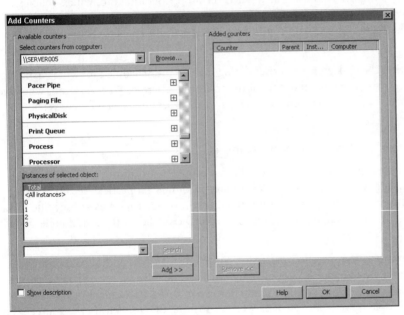

FIGURE 10-7

Factors to Consider When Running PerfMon

Monitoring servers adds overhead but it can be necessary. All data capture tools impose some cost to the target server. Our challenge is to resolve an incident (often performance related) while minimizing the overhead. When monitoring, you should consider performance implications with a view to reducing overhead and minimizing two main risks:

➤ Making problems worse

➤ Affecting data capture

PerfMon counters are themselves updated by the application, even when not consumed by PerfMon. Therefore, any performance overhead with PerfMon is only usually encountered when polling (or sampling) these counters and when writing these to disk if a collector has been set up.

The overhead of using PerfMon to monitor normal servers with regular workload is typically minimal. Performance becomes a discussion point when monitoring servers operating in time-sensitive environments (e.g., trading or reservation platforms) or with servers suffering acute performance problems — those in which the monitoring overhead could tip the server over the edge.

Because reading PerfMon counters is the only real overhead of concern, you should consider network time and disk activity during monitoring. If you can perceive performance degradation when running PerfMon, you can quickly and easily stop logging and measure any performance improvement.

> **NOTE** *One of the challenges with many performance problems is that you must obtain a PerfMon log to identify the cause of the problem. Without a log, engineers and managers can observe poor application performance and hypothesize about potential causes and remedies, but performance data is needed in order to diagnose the problem and take remedial action.*
>
> *Frequently, you just have to accept the risk and overhead of running PerfMon because there simply is no better way to obtain performance data that will help solve a problem.*

The Impact of Running PerfMon

PerfMon is a lightweight tool and its impact on any given server is partly related to how PerfMon is configured, but it is also dependent on the workload of that server while PerfMon is running. To illustrate this scenario, consider two servers: Server A is suffering under heavy workload with 99% CPU utilization and poor disk performance, while server B currently runs with 20% CPU and good disk response times. In this case, it's likely that the impact to server A is greater because PerfMon could consume 1% or 2% available CPU capacity, whereas that same amount added by PerfMon to server B will have negligible detectable impact.

Many organizations attempt to reduce the risk and impact to systems by monitoring during periods of low activity — e.g., during lunch or late afternoon — when user volumes and activity are typically lower, but this is usually the worst idea! It is essential to capture data while the problem is happening, not on either side of the problem (typically when concurrency is at its peak). Additionally, the worse the problem, the easier it is to spot. Often problems are accentuated with user activity, so if they're more likely to occur and be worse when they do happen, you've got the best chance possible to capture a log containing them.

There are three key factors to consider when determining the impact of PerfMon: sample interval, number of counters, and disk performance. The following sections take a brief look at each.

Sample Interval

The sample interval controls the frequency with which PerfMon polls counters to read their values. The more often PerfMon samples, the greater the impact to the server and the more log data generated. The default is 15 seconds, which is usually fine when tracing for a few hours only; when tracing over longer periods, reducing the sample interval reduces both the overhead of PerfMon and the size of the file generated.

Consider a situation in which you have a busy system with a high workload but very short transactions — sampling every 60 seconds could miss many of these very short transactions. The sample interval can affect the shape of the data, so always be aware of it and the overall monitoring window when reviewing performance logs, especially when looking at min, max, and average values. Take into account system activity and usage patterns to ensure that the log is representative of typical workload.

Number of Counters

A consideration with similar impact to sample interval, more counters results in a higher cost to sample and store those counter values. Most instance counters have a _TOTAL counter, which is a total of the individual counter instances combined. In some cases, such as for disk counters, this total is of limited use, as usually the details about each disk (instance) counter are required to identify disk performance problems. The total can hide problems, because an average might look healthy; but a very busy disk could be masked by several other disks with little activity.

Disk Performance

When capturing performance data using Data Collector Sets, consider where the log files will be stored. The objective is to minimize the impact to SQL Server; log performance data to a file on disk (not a database); and, where available, use a disk that will not contend with any databases — i.e., avoid any disks where data or log files are stored.

PerfMon logs grow in a linear and predictable pattern (unlike SQL Profiler trace files, which are workload dependent); for example, sampling 100 counters every 15 seconds for 5 minutes might create a 2MB PerfMon log file, so it would be reasonable to estimate that logging 100 counters for six hours would generate a 144MB log file. Generally, I try to avoid capturing data to a system drive, as the implications of filling that drive are much greater than when logging to a nonsystem drive.

Servers Suffering Very Poor Performance

When capturing PerfMon logs on servers with acute performance problems, run PerfMon as cautiously as possible to reduce the impact while still harvesting performance data. Here are some guidelines:

➤ Run PerfMon remotely.

➤ Reduce the sampling interval.

➤ Include as few counters as possible.

➤ Log to disk.

Common PerfMon Problems

You may sometimes encounter problems with PerfMon itself — specifically, counters could be missing, they might not be displayed correctly, or there could be problems connecting to servers remotely. This section contains a brief summary of some common issues and how to resolve them.

Using PerfMon on 64-bit Systems Using WOW

When running x64 Windows with x86 SQL Server, you're using Windows on Windows (WOW), which means x64 Windows is emulating an x86 environment to host x86 SQL Server. If you're using x64 Windows and x64 SQL Server, this section isn't relevant to you.

When PerfMon runs on an x64 host, none of the counters pertaining to x86 applications are available because the x64 PerfMon cannot load x86 counters. You can overcome this by launching the x86 version of the Microsoft Management Console (MMC) with the PerfMon snap-in. Run the following to launch the PerfMon x86 from an x64 Windows computer:

```
mmc /32 perfmon.msc
```

> **NOTE** *If you're running SQL Server in a Windows on Windows (WOW) mode — i.e., x86 SQL Server on x64 Windows — you'll be unable to run PerfMon remotely from other x64 machines because the remote Registry service is an x64 process; therefore, counters are visible only to x86 processes.*

Remote Monitoring Fails

If you're trying to monitor remote servers without any success, the most likely cause is permissions problems. Try the following troubleshooting tips:

➤ Ensure that the account is local administrator on the target server.

➤ Confirm NetBIOS access to the target server.

➤ Ensure that the remote Registry service is running on the target server.

➤ Ensure that no local security policy or Active Directory group policy is restricting access.

SQL Server Counters Are Missing

When you open PerfMon, you might find that there are no SQL Server counters available in the counter list. This problem occurs more often on clustered instances. If counters are missing, check the SQL Server Error Log and the Windows Event Application log to determine whether any errors are logged regarding the failed counters. If there are no errors in either log, you can unload the counters as follows:

```
unlodctr mssqlserver
```

Once the counters have been unloaded, verify the path to `sqlctr.ini` and use the following command to reload the counters:

```
lodctr C:\Program Files\Microsoft SQL Server\MSSQL10.1\MSSQL\Binn\sqlctr.ini
```

As with any change, test the process on a nonproduction server to gain confidence in the process (even if there is no problem on the test server, you can still test the commands). After reloading the counters, if they still aren't listed, use the following process to rebuild them.

Counters Are Missing or Numbers Appear Instead of Names

If when you attempt to add performance counters the list contains numbers instead of counter names, the counters could have been corrupted by a process incorrectly modifying the Registry. This problem can be overcome by rebuilding the counters, a process explained in detail in Microsoft KB article 300956 at `http://support.microsoft.com/kb/300956`.

GETTING MORE FROM PERFORMANCE MONITOR

This section builds on the introduction to PerfMon, providing specific counters and prescriptive guidance on acceptable counter thresholds. With so many counters available, it can be difficult to know which to use when; and no single counter is sufficient for making any decisions or recommendations. Typically, a variety of PerfMon counters are used to construct a picture of workload and resource consumption.

> **NOTE** *Your aim when troubleshooting is to narrow your focus as quickly as possible to zoom in on the problem. To do this effectively, you should use an iterative approach, whereby each iteration has a specific objective or component, such as disk or memory, to eliminate or incriminate. At the end of each data-gathering cycle and log analysis (an iteration), you should be able to say with some certainty that a particular component of the solution has been ruled in or ruled out as the problem source.*

This section looks at hardware, operating system, and SQL Server bottlenecks, considering each major component in order of problem likelihood: memory, disk, and CPU. You'll also learn about SQL Server performance counters in order to provide a plan for using PerfMon to identify specific SQL Server problem conditions.

Bottlenecks and SQL Server

A bottleneck is any resource that significantly restricts database performance. There will always be bottlenecks of one kind or another — the goal is to ensure that no single component significantly delays the entire transaction processing system. Identifying bottlenecks enables you to prioritize your troubleshooting; there may be numerous problems, but a clear and specific bottleneck provides an area of focus. This section examines some different types of bottlenecks and provides some prescriptive guidance that can help you identify resource contention. It's normal for an active database server to read and write from disk lots where locking and blocking is part of normal usage patterns; however, when any one resource or component consumes a significant portion of query completion time, this could cause a problem.

SQL Server performance is closely related to server performance because query processing duration is dependent on sufficient memory, disk, and CPU performance. SQL Server depends on each of these resources, so they are listed in order of likelihood of causing a problem; but each should be configured correctly and performing well to service SQL Server and provide optimal transaction throughput for the hardware.

Types of Bottlenecks

Most bottlenecks can be categorized as one of two types: configuration-based or schema-based. Each of these categories can cause bottlenecks within each resource type (CPU, memory, and disk). Although there are many potential problem scenarios, most server-wide or instance-wide bottlenecks tend to be configuration-based, whereas database schema bottlenecks are database design issues, specific to an individual database (common issues may include schema normalization, index selection, and statistics).

Configuration-Based Bottlenecks

SQL Server doesn't require any specialized knowledge to install, and most of the default values are sufficient for most deployments. When performance and scalability are critical issues, many optimizations can be made — both to the operating system and to SQL Server. Knowing which to change and when is key to getting the most from the hardware and SQL Server itself — see Chapter 15 for lots more detail in this area.

Configuration-based bottlenecks include any operating system configuration, such as memory settings, including /3GB and /PAE; I/O performance tuning, such as disk sector alignment; and HBA queue depth optimization. Additionally, there are many SQL Server configuration-based optimizations, such as disk and log file placement, database auto-growth settings, and any `sp_configure` options.

Schema-Based Bottlenecks

Schema bottlenecks are application-specific, as they relate to the schema of a specific database (whereas configuration bottlenecks are server-wide or instance-wide). In most cases, the best time to optimize the schema is during application design because schema changes have the least impact on the application when it is still under development. Schema-based bottlenecks illustrate why performance testing must be included as an integral part of software build projects, as it can be incredibly difficult to retrofit performance to an application that's already live.

Schema-based bottlenecks include normalization problems, whereby the schema is either overnormalized, requiring denormalization, or not fully normalized — i.e., the tables contain duplicate data. Additional schema-based bottlenecks include missing or surplus indexes, missing statistics and poor choice of clustering key (such as using a GUID instead or an incrementing identity column).

Prescriptive Guidance

This section includes details about valuable PerfMon counters to include when troubleshooting each resource type, and prescriptive guidance for "healthy" counter values. The prescriptive guidance can serve as a baseline indicator of problems and highlight any significant resource problems early in the troubleshooting cycle, but you should also use other evidence you gather before making a decision or recommendation to form an action plan. As mentioned earlier, no single item of evidence is usually enough to form a complete picture of a problem.

Each section contains a table with details about the main PerfMon counters for each resource group, a description of what to look for, and a value for a problem condition. Finding a counter value that falls within the problem condition threshold warrants further investigation.

Investigating CPU Problems

The availability of CPU cycles to service SQL Server in a timely manner is critical to database server performance. Configuration-based CPU bottlenecks may include max degree of parallelism, the cost threshold of parallelism, and mis-configured CPU hyperthreading. Changing from default configuration and the optimum setting for each of these configuration options is scenario dependent, it can be challenging to be presceptive and cover all potential scenarios — there are often edge cases and exceptions.

Kernel Mode and Application Mode

It's important to recognize the difference between kernel mode consumption and application mode consumption because this concept will provide an important and useful indicator when troubleshooting. It applies to both CPU and memory consumption.

Kernel mode refers to internal Windows operating system operations whereby the kernel has unrestricted access to system hardware, such as the full memory address range, external devices, and so on.

Application mode (also known as user mode) is responsible for everything else, including running applications such as SQL Server. All user-mode applications access hardware resources through the executive, which runs in kernel mode. An application requiring disk I/O submits the request through the kernel-mode executive, which carries out the request and returns the results to the requesting user-mode process.

CPU Performance Counters

SQL Servers suffering from performance problems caused by high CPU usage is a common performance issue. It can be easy to identify the high-consumption Windows process as sqlservr.exe using Task Manager, but the counters shown in Table 10-3 will provide additional information to assist in troubleshooting further.

The performance data should be captured for at least a few minutes to ensure the sample is representative. If there is an intermittent problem or when gathering a baseline, a longer data capture period will result in more meaningful results.

TABLE 10-3: Key CPU PerfMon Counters

COUNTER		WHAT TO LOOK FOR	PROBLEM CONDITION
Processor	% Processor Time	Percent of total time the CPUs are busy servicing productive requests	>80%
Processor	% Privileged Time	Percent of total CPU time spent servicing kernel-mode requests	>30%
Process	% Processor Time (sqlservr)	Percent of total time SQL Server spent running on CPU (user mode + privilege mode)	>80%
Process	% Privilege Time (sqlservr)	Percent of total time SQL Server was executing in privilege mode	>30% of % Processor Time (sqlservr)

Common Causes of CPU Problems

This section describes three common causes of high CPU usage conditions:

➤ **Missing Statistics or Outdated Statistics** — The Query Optimizer is dependent on relevant statistics to determine a good execution plan. Therefore, missing or outdated statistics could cause the Query Optimizer to select a sub-optimal plan, causing excessive CPU consumption.

➤ **Missing Indexes** — A lack of useful indexes can result in a high-CPU condition. SQL Server is dependent on meaningful indexes to retrieve data efficiently, and missing indexes often cause excessive CPU utilization. A lack of useful indexes can result in expensive operations, such as hash joins and sorts that could be avoided with improved indexes.

➤ **Excessive Recompilation** — Poor plan reuse can cause a high-CPU condition whereby SQL Server consumes excessive CPU cycles while generating query plans. Recompilations can be caused by ad hoc or dynamic queries or by a lack of memory (procedure cache), causing plans to be dropped from cache.

Investigating Memory-Related Problems

SQL Server performance is closely related to the availability and performance of sufficient memory. SQL Server configuration-related memory settings include the following:

➤ sp_configure

    ➤ Min/max server memory

    ➤ AWE Enabled

    ➤ Min memory per query

➤ Windows

    ➤ /3GB, /USERVA, /PAE (in 32-bit environments)

➤ Lock Pages in Memory privilege

Typically, using the Windows Task Manager doesn't provide the best measure of the memory consumed by SQL Server. Using PerfMon is a more reliable method of measuring memory consumption, since this includes all types of memory allocation that can be made by SQL Server. You can also refer back to Chapter 3 for more details on memory.

Types of Memory Pressure

SQL Server can suffer from internal or external memory pressure, and understanding how to identify and troubleshoot each will enable more targeted troubleshooting. External memory pressure occurs most often when SQL Server is running on a shared computer and several processes are competing for memory. In this situation, Resource Monitor within SQL Server Operating System (SQLOS) receives a signal from Windows to request that SQL Server reduce its committed memory. This causes SQL Server to recalculate its target commit level, and reduce it if necessary.

Internal memory pressure occurs when multiple SQL Server resources compete with each other for memory. This typically causes SQL Server to shrink the data cache, which can impact server performance. Use the DBCC MEMORYSTATUS command to gain visibility of SQL Server memory consumption.

Virtual Address Space

Every Windows process has its own virtual address space (VAS), the size of which varies according to processor architecture (32-bit or 64-bit) and the operating system edition. The VAS is a fixed-size resource that can be exhausted (even on 64-bit computers) while physical memory is still available.

Memory Performance Counters

Table 10-4 outlines the PerfMon counters that are key to gathering information about memory availability and consumption.

TABLE 10-4: Key Memory PerfMon Counters

COUNTER		WHAT TO LOOK FOR	PROBLEM CONDITION
Memory	Available Mbytes	Amount of free physical memory in MB; values below 100MB could indicate external memory pressure or a max server memory setting that's too high.	<100MB
Memory	Pages/sec	A high value doesn't necessarily mean a problem; review this counter if you suspect external memory pressure and always consider in the context of other memory counters.	<500
Memory	Free System Page Table Entries	Page Table Entries are most likely to become depleted (and therefore a bottleneck) on x86 servers, particularly where /3GB or /USERVA switches are used.	<5000
Paging File	% Usage, % Usage Peak	Generally, workload increases the demand for virtual address pace (VAS), which increases the demand for Page File. Heavy reliance on page file use is usually an indication of memory problems. The threshold will depend on the size of your pagefile. See Chapter 3 for sizing details.	>70%
MSSQL Buffer Manager	Page Life Expectancy	Duration, in seconds, that a data page resides in the buffer pool. A server with sufficient memory has high page life expectancy. Watch the trend of this counter over time. Overall it should stay stable or trend higher. Frequent dips of the value can indicate memory pressure.	<300 seconds
MSSQL Buffer Manager	Buffer Cache Hit Ratio	Percent of page requests satisfied by data pages from the buffer pool. Page Life Expectancy is a better overall indicator of buffer pool health.	<98%
MSSQL Buffer Manager	Lazy Writes/ sec	Number of times per second SQL Server relocates dirty pages from buffer pool (memory) to disk	>20

Disk or Storage-Related Problems

SQL Server read/write performance is closely related to the ability of Windows to retrieve and write data pages to disk efficiently.Efficient and timely data access is dependent on both configuration-based and schema-based factors, such as data and log file sizing and placement, useful indexes, and index fragmentation.

Disk and storage performance can be a hugely complex and protracted exercise, and one that is often confused by unclear terminology and logical abstractions that make it hard to identify root cause. However, regardless of storage hardware, disk layout, or path configuration, the only aspect of real interest is the time required to read or write from disk because this is a great indicator of whether disk access performance is likely to cause SQL Server problems.

Typically, once disk access has been identified as a bottleneck, tools more specialized than PerfMon must be employed to provide a lower level of detail on bottlenecks. Most SAN vendors provide performance-monitoring tools that help diagnose issues with storage controllers, cache performance, and physical disk service time. These tools provide further diagnosis on the over-utilized component and performance bottleneck.

Disk performance problems have wide and varied potential resolutions, including extensive disk reconfiguration, such as changing RAID level, disk group membership, and strip size. You can also make many enhancements within SQL Server, including right-sizing data and log files; pre-allocating space; and, for very large databases, table partitioning. Table 10-5 describes the main PerfMon counters to check for disk performance.

TABLE 10-5: Key Disk PerfMon Counters

COUNTER		WHAT TO LOOK FOR	PROBLEM CONDITION
Physical Disk	Avg. disk sec/Read	Average time, in seconds, to complete a read from disk	>0.010 Sub-optimal >0.020 Poor
Physical Disk	Avg. disk sec/Write	Average time, in seconds, to complete a write to disk	>0.010 Sub-optimal >0.020 Poor

SQL Server Performance Problems

Sometimes server hardware resources do not cause bottlenecks, but application performance is still bad. In this situation, it's possible that internal SQL Server resources can become exhausted or depleted. Table 10-6 describes the principal counters for monitoring internal SQL Server resources.

TABLE 10-6: Key SQL Server PerfMon Counters

COUNTER		WHAT TO LOOK FOR	PROBLEM CONDITION
MSSQL SQL Statistics	Batch Requests/sec	Number of T-SQL batches processed by SQL server; higher is better. Useful for a baseline and should be considered when making any comparisons.	>1000 Indicates a server with high activity
MSSQL SQL Statistics	SQL Compilations/sec	Number of batches requiring plan compilations per second. High compilations indicate either poor plan reuse or many ad hoc queries.	>20% Batch Requests/sec
MSSQL SQL Statistics	SQL Recompilations/sec	Number of statement recompiles per second	>20% Batch Requests/sec
MSSQL General Statistics	Processes Blocked	Number of currently blocked processes	Investigate when >0
MSSQL Locks	Lock Waits/sec	Number of user requests waiting for locks per second. Can be indicative of blocking.	>0
MSSQL Locks	Lock Timeouts/sec	Number of lock timeouts per second; anything greater than 1 should be investigated.	>0
MSQQL Transactions	Free Space in tempdb (KB)	Reports free space in tempdb in KB	<100MB

Wait Stats Analysis

SQL Server wait stats record the amount of time SQL Server spends waiting for each resource. A number of these wait types are exposed as PerfMon counters:

➤ Lock waits

➤ Log write waits

➤ Network I/O waits

➤ Non-page latch waits

➤ Page I/O latch waits

➤ Page latch waits

➤ Waits for the worker

Although it may be easier to access these wait stats from the DMVs within SQL Server, collecting them as part of a system-wide data-gathering exercise with PerfMon minimizes the logistics effort involved in collecting the information.

Getting a Performance Baseline

A performance baseline is simply a PerfMon log from a time frame representing "normal" performance, retained for future review. The PerfMon log should contain counters that build a complete picture of hardware and SQL Server resources during a representative workload period.

The performance baseline can provide answers to questions that an individual would otherwise be unable to answer. On occasions when there are any performance problems, the baseline is available for comparison; and by mapping the SQL Server batch requests per second against other values, it will be possible to identify and compare problem server activity per workload with the workload of a known good data capture.

The baseline should be continually maintained; otherwise, configuration changes or tuning optimizations could alter the output and invalidate any comparison. It's useful to get into the habit of taking a fresh baseline on a regular basis.

PERFORMANCE ANALYSIS OF LOGS

The Performance Analysis of Logs (PAL) tool is a free utility for analyzing PerfMon counter logs and creating reports highlighting important areas by severity. The report color-codes counters to display problem areas based on thresholds defined by subject matter experts in the support teams at Microsoft.

It was written and is maintained by Clint Huffman, a Premier Field Engineer at Microsoft, and supports most major Microsoft server products. It reduces the amount of time required to review and analyze PerfMon logs by automating this analysis, saving you time by quickly highlighting potential problem areas requiring further investigation.

Getting Started with PAL

PAL is available from Microsoft's open-source community project, CodePlex. PAL has been tested on computers running Windows 7 x 64 and using the English-US locale. It can run on x86 operating systems, but x64 is recommended when processing large log files.

The tool was originally developed using VBScript, COM, the Microsoft Log Parser tool, and the Microsoft Office 2003 Web Components (OWC11). The latest version of PAL at the time of writing is 2.3.2; it has three prerequisites, each is free and publicly available:

➤ Windows PowerShell 2.0 or greater

➤ .NET Framework 3.5 Service Pack 1

➤ Microsoft Chart Controls for .NET Framework 3.5

You can download PAL from `http://pal.codeplex.com`.

After you have downloaded and opened PAL, the tabs located across the top of the utility act as steps in the wizard. Navigating through each of these steps and populating the required information is all that is necessary to process a PerfMon log. The following steps will help get you started with PAL:

1. Once installed, launch PAL from the Start menu. The Welcome page will be displayed, as shown in Figure 10-8.

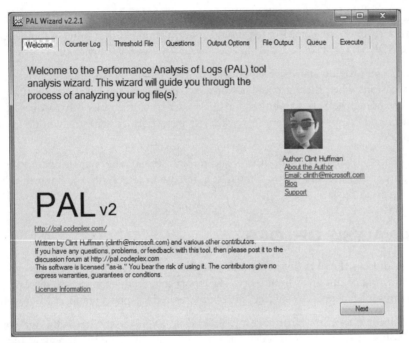

FIGURE 10-8

USING THE EXPORT FEATURE TO CREATE A LOG TEMPLATE

If you don't have an existing PerfMon log to analyze, consider exporting a threshold file to create a counter log template. To do this, choose the Threshold File tab from the PAL interface, select the SQL Server 2005/2008 template, and click the Export to PerfMon Template File button. Export the template with an .XML extension for use on Windows 7 or Windows Server 2008 target machines.

2. Select the Counter Log tab and browse to select the PerfMon log (see Figure 10-9).

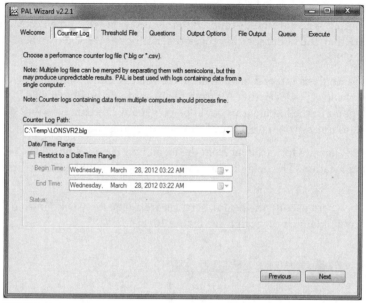

FIGURE 10-9

3. Click Next or select the Threshold File option from the top menu bar (see Figure 10-10). Select the required Threshold File from the drop-down selection box. The current release doesn't have a SQL Server 2012 template, so the SQL Server 2005/2008 template will provide the closest match (these templates can be configured/adapted as required).

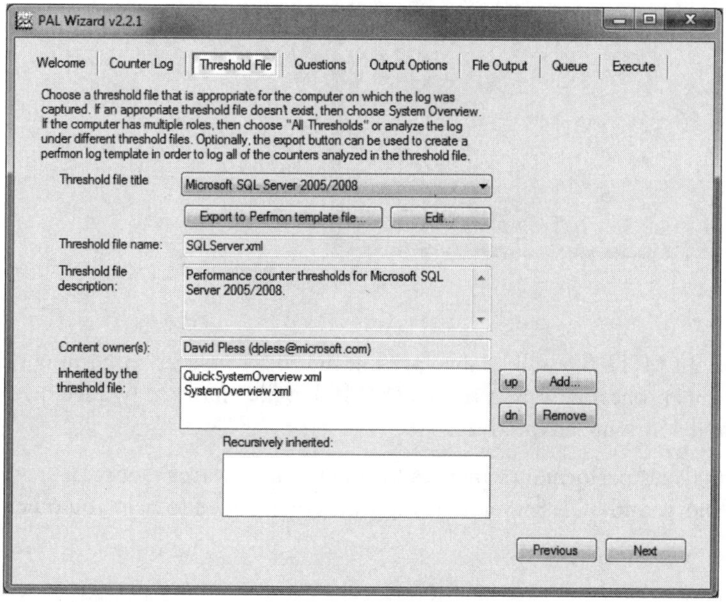

FIGURE 10-10

4. On the Questions tab there are five additional questions to answer. Responding to these questions will provide output with thresholds tailored to the server on which the PerfMon log was captured. Ensure that you count logical processors, not physical sockets, when choosing the number of CPUs.

5. Click Next or choose the Analysis Interval menu item. Here you can control the interval used by PAL to analyze the log files. Selecting All from the drop-down box means PAL will analyze every data point in the log file (this could be very many) and analysis will be lengthy. Leave this as Auto unless you have a specific reason to change it.

6. Click Next or choose the Output Options item from the menu bar. Here it's possible to control the output types and location. The default settings are usually good unless something specific is required.

7. Move to the Execute tab, where usually the default settings are adequate. Click Finish to begin log analysis, which will launch the script (see Figure 10-11).

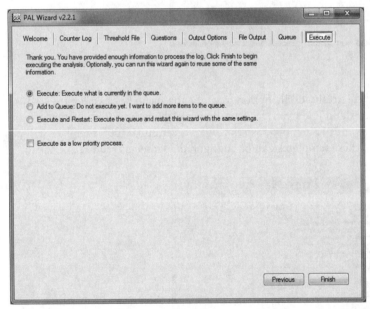

FIGURE 10-11

Once the PAL tool has finished, an MHT file will be displayed in Internet Explorer containing the results. To get an idea of what this process entails, a recent 254MB log file analyzed by PAL on a quad-core computer took around 45minutes to analyze.

The report produced by PAL analyzes performance metrics for the key hardware resources: Processor, Network, Disk, Memory, and SQL Server. The report is color-coded to help you quickly identify problem areas.

OTHER PERFMON LOG ANALYSIS TOOLS

This section evaluates common tools for managing, manipulating, and interpreting PerfMon logs. Because PerfMon logs can be saved or converted to comma-separated value (CSV) files, there are many options for data analysis, including loading the file into SQL Server, or analyzing it with Microsoft Excel or almost any other data manipulation tool.

Using SQL Server to Analyze PerfMon Logs

Analyzing large quantities of performance logs with SQL Server can be a useful solution when data analysis through other methods could be cumbersome and labor intensive. The data load process from CSV files could simply make use of the ad hoc Import/Export Wizard launched from SQL Server Management Studio, or alternately this process could be automated and scheduled.

SQL Server can't read the native binary log file (BLG) file type, so you should either write PerfMon logs to a log file as a CSV file type or use the Relog utility to convert the file post-capture (more detail to follow) from BLG to CSV. It is also possible for PerfMon to log directly to a SQL Server database through a DSN, although there is additional overhead with this process, which can be avoided by logging to file.

Analyzing PerfMon logs from within a database has the benefit of data access through the familiar language of T-SQL, which means problems should be easier to identify, and you can write queries looking for specific problem conditions. Here's an example where three counters could be used to identify a low-memory condition:

➤ Available memory less than 100MB

➤ Page life expectancy less than 60 seconds

➤ Buffer cache hit ratio less than 98%

If the PerfMon logs have already been imported into SQL Server, the following query could be used to identify any instance during the data capture window when the low memory condition existed:

```
SELECT *
FROM subset
WHERE Mem_Avail_Bytes < 1000000
AND Buff_Mgr_PLE < 60
AND Buff_Cache_Hit_Ratio < 98
```

This example should be modified to reflect the table and column names specified during the data import, but the concept could be adapted for any number of scenarios. Additionally, this method could be used to manage performance data across a number of servers, and Reporting Services could be used to present the data.

Combining PerfMon Logs and SQL Profiler Traces

A feature first available in SQL Server 2005 was the capability to combine PerfMon logs with SQL Profiler traces. Using Profiler to combine logs in this way enables the viewing of T-SQL code that's running on the server, combined with the hardware impact of running the code, such as high CPU or low memory.

The combined view presents a time axis that can be navigated, by selecting a moment when a CPU spike occurred; the Profiler trace automatically relocates to the T-SQL that was executing at the time of the spike.

Using Relog

Relog can be used to create new log files with a new sampling rate or a different file format than existing PerfMon logs. Relog was first included in Windows XP, and it can be useful when handling large logs or many surplus counters are included. Additionally, there are situations when a log contains data for many hours but the time frame of interest is much shorter; Relog can assist in extracting the interesting time window for easier analysis. Table 10-7 shows a summary of Relog parameters.

TABLE 10-7: Summary of Relog Parameters

OPTION	DESCRIPTION
-?	Displays context-sensitive help
-a	Appends output to the existing binary file
-c <path [path ...]>	Filters counters from the input log
-cf <filename>	Filters file listing performance counters from the input log. The default is all counters in the original log file.
-f <CSV|TSV|BIN|SQL>	Specifies the output file format
-t <value>	Writes only every nth record into the output file. The default is to write every record.
-o	Specifies the output file path or SQL database
-b <dd/MM/yyyy HH:mm:ss[AM|PM]>	Begin time for the first record to write into the output file
-e <dd/MM/yyyy HH:mm:ss[AM|PM]>	End time for the last record to write into the output file
-config <filename>	Settings file containing command options
-q	Lists performance counters in the input file
-y	Answers yes to all questions without prompting

The following sections demonstrate three example scenarios in which Relog would be useful, including the syntax used.

Extracting Performance Data for a Specific Time Window

This technique can be useful when using PerfMon to log over many hours or days. Were a problem to occur, for example, at 10:30 a.m. on March 15, it would be useful to extract the time frame from 10:00 to 11:00 to provide a manageable log size, without losing any data points. The command looks as follows:

```
Relog Server001_LOG.blg -b 15/03/2012 10:00:00 -e 15/03/2012 11:00:00 -o
Server001_LogExtract.blg
```

Extracting Specific Performance Counters

Sometimes monitoring tools or other engineers gather logs containing extraneous counters. In these situations, you can extract specific counters for analysis using Relog. The Relog parameter -c enables counters to be specified. In the following example only the memory-related counters would be extracted to a newly created log file:

```
Relog Server001_Log.blg -c "\Memory\*" -o Server001Memory_Log.blg
```

Furthermore, it is possible to perform more complex filtering by passing Relog a text file containing a subset of counters from the original performance log. The following command can be used to extract those counters specified in filter file from the original log:

```
Relog Server001_Log.blg -cf CounterList.txt -o Server001Overview_Log.blg
```

The preceding example requires CounterList.txt to contain a single counter per line with the counters to be extracted.

Converting Log Files to New Formats

PerfMon creates log files in a binary log format (BLG) by default. In some situations it can be desirable to convert a performance log to a new format to enable applications other than PerfMon to read the log. For example, this can be useful when importing the data to SQL Server or analyzing performance in Excel. The following example shows how to convert the BLG file to a CSV file:

```
Relog Server001_Log.blg -f CSV -o Server001_Log.csv
```

Using LogMan

LogMan can be used to schedule the starting and stopping of logs. This can be a useful alternative to using the Windows AT scheduler or the scheduler functions available within PerfMon. The great benefit of using LogMan is that you can centrally control the start and stop of Performance monitoring. Using LogMan, it's possible to define a data collector and copy that collector to multiple servers from a single, central location. Table 10-8 summarizes the LogMan command-line actions. The syntax is as follows:

```
logman [create|query|start|stop|delete|update|import|export] [options]
```

TABLE 10-8: Summary of LogMan Usage

VERB	DESCRIPTION
Create	Creates a new data collector
Query	Queries data collector properties. If no name is given, all data collectors are listed.
Start	Starts an existing data collector and sets the begin time to manual
Stop	Stops an existing data collector and sets the end time to manual
Delete	Deletes an existing data collector
Update	Updates properties of an existing data collector
Import	Imports a Data Collector Set from an XML file
Export	Exports a Data Collector Set to an XML file

The following example creates a collector named DBOverviewLog, which contains all Processor, Memory, and LogicalDisk counters with a sample interval of 30 seconds and a max log file size of 254MB:

```
Logman create counter "DBOverviewLog" -si 30 -v nnnn -max 254 -o
"D:\logs\DBOverview" -c "\Processor(*)\*" "\Memory(*)\*" "\LogicalDisk(*)\*"
```

Table 10-9 describes the four options available with LogMan, including the useful -s parameter, which enables the collector to be created, started, and stopped on remote computers.

TABLE 10-9: LogMan Options

OPTION	DESCRIPTION
-?	(a) Displays context-sensitive help
-s <computer>	(b) Performs the command on the specified remote system
-config <value>	(c) Setting file containing command options
-ets	(d) Sends commands to Event Trace Sessions directly without saving or scheduling

Using LogMan it's possible to script collection for a baseline data set from an entire application environment. This could be incredibly useful when doing performance testing, baselining application performance, or troubleshooting live problems.

Using LogParser

LogParser is a simple to use yet powerful tool for log file analysis, popularized for analyzing logs from IIS web servers. LogParser can be used to examine a range of log types and can provide output in various forms. Once installed, LogParser enables pseudo-SQL querying of log files! This can be great when searching Windows Event Logs, IIS logs, or PerfMon logs.

LogParser is part of the Windows Resource Kit and available as a standalone download from `www.microsoft.com/en-us/download/details.aspx?displaylang=en&id=24659`. PerfMon logs must be converted to CSV (using Relog) prior to analysis with LogParser.

SUMMARY

This chapter provided you with details on when and how to use PerfMon to capture server performance data. You read specific guidance on prescriptive counters to help identify common issues with poorly performing SQL servers. Additionally, the chapter provided guidance on using the PAL tool to analyze performance logs, as well as other log manipulation tools such as Relog, LogMan, and LogParser for log analysis.

11

Consolidating Data Capture with SQLdiag

WHAT'S IN THIS CHAPTER?

➤ Collecting data for analyzing SQL Server performance

➤ Getting friendly with SQLdiag

➤ Using SQLdiag Configuration Manager

➤ Employing Best Practices

WROX.COM CODE DOWNLOADS FOR THIS CHAPTER

There are no code downloads for this chapter.

THE DATA COLLECTION DILEMMA

One of the biggest issues a SQL Server professional faces when troubleshooting a complex SQL Server problem is the data collection task. The classic catch-22 situation always presents itself: installing data collection utilities on the server versus not collecting all the required data to address the root cause of the problem at hand.

The most common dilemma encountered is using a single tool to capture the required set of data simultaneously when faced with a critical production issue. Unless and until there are tools that enable quick configuration capabilities, we are left gambling with the prospect of continued service unavailability and missing service-level agreements while trying to configure the data collection tools. Seasoned SQL Server professionals have their own toolset handy, which they consider to be their equivalent of a superhero's utility belt and which serves them well at the time of a crisis situation.

Once you have successfully fought the demons inside your SQL Server environment that were wreaking havoc and causing the problems, you will be tasked with identifying the root cause of the issue. Identifying the root cause in itself is not a bad thing. However, this noble task may soon take an ill-fated turn when you realize that the data required to perform a complete post-mortem analysis is missing. When battling with a critical production service-related issue, it is possible that the data necessary for post-mortem analysis is not collected, as the need of the moment is to restore service as soon as possible. This makes it highly pertinent to have a data collection utility in place, one which not only collects all the necessary data required given a particular situation but also is easily configurable at the drop of a hat!

The *SQLdiag*, which started shipping with SQL Server 2005, is a utility used to collect diagnostic data from a SQL Server instance. It is a general-purpose diagnostics utility that can be run as a console application or a service. SQLdiag can help you collect SQL Server Profiler traces, Windows Performance Monitor logs, and outputs of various VBScript, T-SQL, and DOS scripts through an extensible interface exposed by the SQLdiag Configuration Manager. This close knit integration of data collection capabilities makes SQLdiag a "must have" tool in the SQL Server professional's repertoire.

The data that is collected by the SQLdiag utility can be imported into a SQL Server database using *SQL Nexus,* a GUI tool for providing an aggregated view of the data collected in a report format. Chapter 12 explains how you can derive maximum benefit from SQL Nexus.

AN APPROACH TO DATA COLLECTION

In this section, we will delve into specifics of how data can be collected to analyze the performance of your SQL Server instance. Basically, SQL Server data analysis can be done in the following ways:

➤ *Baseline Analysis* — A baseline of your SQL Server instance will tell you what the resource usage for the SQL Server instance in question looks like on an average at a particular time of the day. You will know if the delta difference that you see for a particular set of data has a positive or a negative connotation only if you the appropriate baselines established for your SQL Server instance. When you have an existing baseline available, then it makes sense to capture data during the problem period for a short period of time in order to establish a comparative study between the current start and an established baseline. This enables you to look for seemingly innocuous patterns in the data that might prove to be the root cause of your SQL Server troubles. This is what is referred to as a baseline analysis.

➤ *Bottleneck Analysis* — The second option, bottleneck analysis, is the approach to which most SQL Server professionals are accustomed. This is used when a baseline is not readily available or an available baseline is not pertinent to the current state of the environment. In such a situation, you need to collect data both for a period when the issue is not occur-ring and during the period when the problem manifests itself. Then the two sets of data are compared to weed out the difference and the symptoms that were exhibited when the problem occurred. The ideal scenario for a bottleneck analysis is to start data collection a little before the problem manifests itself, capturing the transition period from a serenely functional SQL Server environment to an environment that raises all sorts of red lights on service-level scorecards. Sometimes, we have to be content with a comparative analysis and compare two sets of data collection, which may not even belong to the same environment. This may sound appalling but is a harsh reality in the production world scenario where it is not always feasible to add additional workload or bring in new executables to collect diagnostic data. Bottleneck analysis helps you arrive at the top N bottlenecks that your SQL Server instance is experiencing by identifying the road-blocks which are preventing the smooth functioning of your SQL Server instance.

This requires some precise data collection capabilities, along with various other requirements like knowing which system catalogs to query, what tools to run to collect the required data, etc. The next few pages in this chapter will help you understand how developing a friendship with SQLdiag can prove beneficial when a SQL Server crisis arises. The following section will explain how SQLdiag can be used to configure and collect diagnostic data within a few minutes.

GETTING FRIENDLY WITH SQLDIAG

There are two times when you collect data for troubleshooting a SQL Server issue:

➤ You are faced with a critical problem in your production environment and the data collection is being done to identify and fix the root cause.

➤ You are trying to reproduce an issue for which sufficient data was not collected initially to ascertain a definitive root cause.

The latter scenario is always a cumbersome process because you might end up playing the waiting game for intermittent issues. The frustration of such waiting for the actual issue to occur can become more excruciating due to the overhead of managing the data that diagnostics tools collect when left running.

This is where SQLdiag becomes a SQL Server professional's best friend, living up to the adage that "a friend in need is a friend indeed." SQLdiag is a command-line utility that is available by default in `C:\Program Files\Microsoft SQL Server\110\Tools\Binn`. This assumes that the binary installation path of the SQL Server instance on the machine was done on the C: drive.

> **NOTE** *If you have SQL Server 2005 or SQL Server 2008/2008 R2 instances installed on the server, you will find the SQLdiag utility available under the* `C:\Program Files\Microsoft SQL Server\90\Tools\Binn` *or* `C:\Program Files\Microsoft SQL Server\100\Tools\Binn` *folders, respectively.*

You can run SQLdiag in three modes:

➤ Snapshot mode using the /X command line parameter

➤ As a command-line application by specifying one or more command-line parameters

➤ As a service

Each of the aforementioned modes is explained in detail in the following sections of the chapter along with the scenario which suits the data collection mode.

> **WARNING** *The user who runs SQLdiag must be a member of the Windows Administrators group and a member of the SQL Server sysadmin fixed server role. When the /G command-line switch is specified, on startup SQLdiag does not enforce SQL Server connectivity checks or verify that the user is a member of the sysadmin fixed server role. Instead, SQLdiag defers to Windows to determine whether a user has the appropriate rights to gather each requested diagnostic. If /G is not specified, SQLdiag checks whether the user is a member of the Windows Administrators group; if not, it will not collect SQL Server diagnostics. If the machine has User Account Control (UAC) enabled, an elevated command prompt should be used to run SQLdiag to prevent possible access denied errors.*

Using SQLdiag in Snapshot Mode

When SQLdiag is run in snapshot mode, it collects a snapshot of all the configured diagnostic data (mentioned in the SQLdiag configuration file discussed in the next section) and then shuts down automatically. If you execute SQLDIAG /X from a command prompt window, the SQLdiag utility creates a SQLDIAG folder in the Binn folder, containing all the data it collected. You will additionally find an "internal" folder containing log files created by the utility, along with the XML configuration file that it used to collect the data, among other files. This method of collecting data is quite useful when you want a quick snapshot of the state of the SQL Server instance. You get a plethora of information ranging from SQL Server and Windows configuration, errors encountered recently, waits experienced by the database engine and much more.

After data collection is completed, the utility shuts down automatically with the message SQLDIAG Collection complete. Collector exiting. A default snapshot data collection collects the following information:

➤ SQL Server default traces

➤ MSINFO32 output in a text file

➤ A *<MachineName>_<InstanceName>*_sp_sqldiag_Shutdown.OUT text file, which contains the following data:

  ➤ All Errorlogs

  ➤ Output of various system stored procedures, such as sp_configure, sp_who, sp_lock, sp_helpdb, to obtain the SQL Server instance and database configuration details

  ➤ Output of various DMVs and system catalogs, such as sys.sysprocesses, sys.dm_exec_sessions, and sys.dm_os_wait_stats, to obtain additional information, with the following being of key importance:

> ➤ Insight into the instance's memory usage

> ➤ A snapshot of the current values for all the SQL Server PerfMon counters

> ➤ A snapshot of the SQL Server wait statistics

> ➤ Status of the sessions and requests active on the SQL Server instance. along with the associated input buffers

> ➤ Status of the SQL Server schedulers

Using SQLdiag as a Command-line Application

Before looking at the basics of running a SQLdiag data collection, you should first understand the anatomy of the SQLdiag configuration file in order to appropriately configure the various data collectors for capturing diagnostic data. Figure 11-1 shows a screenshot of the key elements in the SQLDIAG.XML configuration file.

```xml
<?xml version="1.0" standalone="true"?>
- <dsConfig xsi:noNamespaceSchemaLocation="SQLDiag_Schema.Xsd" xmlns:xsi="http://www.w3.org/2001/XMLSchema-instance" xmlns:pssd="http://tempuri.org">
  - <Collection casenumber="SRX000000000000" setupver="3.0.1.7">
    - <Machines>
      - <Machine name=".">
        - <MachineCollectors>
          - <EventlogCollector shutdown="true" startup="false" enabled="false">
            - <Eventlogs>
                <EventlogType name="Application" enabled="true"/>
                <EventlogType name="Security" enabled="true"/>
                <EventlogType name="System" enabled="true"/>
              </Eventlogs>
            </EventlogCollector>
          - <PerfmonCollector enabled="false" maxfilesize="256" pollinginterval="5">
            + <PerfmonCounters>
            </PerfmonCollector>
          </MachineCollectors>
        - <Instances>
          - <Instance name="*" user="" ssver="11" windowsauth="true">
            - <Collectors>
                <SqldiagCollector shutdown="true" startup="false" enabled="true"/>
                <BlockingCollector enabled="false" maxfilesize="350" pollinginterval="5" filecount="1"/>
              + <ProfilerCollector enabled="false" maxfilesize="350" pollinginterval="5" filecount="1" template="_GeneralPerformance90.xml">
              + <CustomDiagnostics>
              </Collectors>
            </Instance>
          </Instances>
        </Machine>
      </Machines>
    </Collection>
  + <Analysis>
</dsConfig>
```

FIGURE 11-1

SQLdiag Configuration File Key Elements

➤ The full-stop (.) for the *Machine Name* value signifies that the data collection is to be done from the local machine (i.e., the machine from where the SQLdiag execution was initiated).

➤ The asterisk (*) for the *Instance Name* value specifies that the utility should collect data from all instances installed on the machine.

➤ The *EventlogCollector* element specifies whether the Windows Event Logs need to be collected and if so, whether they should be collected when the utility starts up or shuts down, or both.

➤ The *PerfmonCollector* element specifies whether PerfMon data will be collected, and the *pollinginterval* and *maxfilesize* parameter values define the time interval between two consecutive samples and the maximum size of the .blg PerfMon file, respectively.

➤ The *SqldiagCollector* element specifies whether the utility will collect the SQLdiag output file, discussed earlier in the "Using SQLdiag in Snapshot Mode" section.

➤ The *ProfilerCollector* element specifies the SQL Server Profiler events to be captured, along with all the Profiler trace configuration settings. Note that SQLdiag always captures a server-side Profiler trace to ensure minimal impact of a Profiler trace capture on the SQL Server instance.

➤ The *BlockingCollector* element enables trace flag 1222 to facilitate the capture of deadlock graphs in the SQL Server Error Log.

You can control the collectors used by SQLdiag using the XML templates. Every collector can be enabled or disabled using <enabled=true> or <enabled=false> within the configuration file. Use either your favorite text editor to modify the XML configuration file or even Management Studio, which supports XML document editing.

> **WARNING** *Don't delete collectors from the XML files, as SQLdiag will subsequently fail to load the XSD if the XML file doesn't match.*

If you are wondering what happened to the CustomDiagnostics variable explanation, it is covered in the section "Using SQLdiag Configuration Manager." The following code snippet shows all the parameters that the SQLdiag utility can accept.

```
Usage: sqldiag [START | STOP | STOP_ABORT] [/O outputpath] [/I cfgfile] [/M machine1
[machine2 machineN]|@machinelistfile] [/Q] [/C #] [/G] [/R] [/U] [/N #] [/A appname]
[/T {tcp[,port]|np|lpc|via}] [/X] [/L] [/B YYYYMMDD_HH:MM:SS] [/E YYYYMMDD_HH:MM:SS]
```

Now take a look at how each of these parameters is used, along with some best practices to prevent the data collection effort from becoming an accessory to a performance degradation crime.

SQLdiag Parameter List

➤ START | STOP | STOP_ABORT — START and STOP are used to start and stop the data collection, respectively. STOP_ABORT is used when data collection needs to be terminated immediately without waiting for all the collectors to complete, which proves quite useful when your data collection might start competing for resources with a production workload or your data collection has exceeded your intended data collection time window.

➤ /O outputpath — This specifies the directory in which the utility will write the collected data. It is advisable to use a local disk on which SQL Server database files do not reside.

➤ /I cfgfile — This specifies the configuration file to be used for the data collection. The default configuration file is always SQLDiag.Xml.

➤ `/M machinename` or `machinelist file` — This is a comma-separated list indicating the machines from which the utility should collect data. This parameter is rarely used, as remote data collection should be avoided. A machine name provided using this parameter overrides the machine name value in the configuration file.

➤ `/Q` — Runs in quiet mode and prevents any prompts

➤ `/C` — This specifies the compression option, which can be useful when you are collecting diagnostic data for long periods of time, especially for the large PerfMon and Profiler trace files. `/C 1` directs SQLdiag to compress the output folder files using NTFS compression.

➤ `/G` — Connectivity checks are skipped when this switch is specified, and data collection is prevented only due to lack of permission or connectivity issues. SQLdiag will not collect data by default if the user running the utility is not a member of the Windows Administrators group on the server.

➤ `/R` — Registers the utility as a service

➤ `/U` — Unregisters the utility as a service

➤ `/N` — This parameter defines how SQLdiag controls management of the output folder. `/N 2` renames the existing output folder (if present) and instead writes to the output path specified. This can be a helpful option when you perform a data collection for a specific period of time and the captured data is analyzed later. This scenario requires preservation of the output folder and not an overwrite of the existing data. The default option is to overwrite.

➤ `/A appname` — Provides an application name for the utility and enables the option of running multiple concurrent data collection executables with different application names.

➤ `/T` — Tells SQLdiag to connect to the SQL Server instance using a specified protocol such as TCP, Named Pipes, Local Procedure Call, or Virtual Interface Adapter. Various environments are secure and only allow connections using a specific port or protocol. In such scenarios, this parameter comes to the rescue and facilitates the important data connection required to collect diagnostic information.

➤ `/L` — Specifies running the data collection in continuous mode. This has to be defined in conjunction with either a start time or an end time using the `/B` or `/E` parameters. This parameter enables collecting data around the clock when you don't know when the problem will occur or it occurs intermittently. This ensures that SQLdiag collects the data even if you are not around monitoring the server during the data collection period.

➤ `/B` and `/E` — These specify the starting and ending times of the data collection, respectively. These two parameters can be used together to collect data while troubleshooting an issue that occurs during a specific time period. They enable you to schedule your data collection without being logged onto the server when the issue occurs at inconvenient hours of the day. The date and time format for these parameters is `YYYYMMDD_HH:MM:SS` and you can even specify the time using a + sign. For example, `/B +02:00:00` specifies that data collection should start two hours from the time the command is issued.

➤ `/P` — Sets the support folder path. By default, `/P` is set to the folder in which the SQLdiag executable resides. This folder contains SQLdiag support files, such as the XML configuration file, Transact-SQL scripts, and other files that the utility uses during diagnostics collection.

Now that you are familiar with the parameters, a few examples of their values and behaviors are shown when used in conjunction with other parameters:

The following command tells SQLdiag to start data collection at 12:01AM on 25th December, 2012, and terminate data collection after two hours with a specific output folder. /G parameter will skip connectivity checks.

```
SQLDIAG /O D:\SQLDIAG_Data\ /G /B 20121225_00:01:00 /E +02:00:00
```

The command prompt window will display the following line on successful execution of the above code indicating that SQLdiag is successfully initialized:

```
SQLDIAG Begin time 20121225_00:01:00 specified.  Waiting
```

The following command instructs SQLdiag to collect data using a configuration file with file compression. The application name will be shown as DemoDiag with quiet mode enabled to suppress any prompts.

```
SQLDIAG /O D:\SQLDIAG_Data\ /A DemoDiag /Q /I D:\SQLDIAG_Custom.xml
```

The following lines are what you will see in the command prompt window when SQLdiag initializes successfully:

```
DIAG$DemoDiag Collector version

IMPORTANT:  Please wait until you see 'Collection started' before attempting to
reproduce your issue
```

> **NOTE** *When attempting to collect diagnostic data, always wait for the message "SQLdiag Collection started. Press Ctrl+C to stop" to appear (in a green font) in the command prompt window before attempting to reproduce a problem scenario for which diagnostic data needs to be collected.*

The time required for SQLdiag to initialize varies according to the state of the Windows machine from which the data is being collected. Because some of the servers used to collect diagnostic data may be under severe stress in terms of physical resources, it may take a little more time than usual to complete the initialization phase. Even the shutdown of the SQLdiag utility is extended due to custom diagnostics configured. The most common sources of delays are as follows:

➤ Large SQL Server Error Logs collected during shutdown

➤ The long time taken to collect MSINFO32 output

➤ T-SQL scripts captured during shutdown, which take a long time to execute

The SQLdiag console output and the verbose log of the utility can be found in the `internal` folder of the output directory in the files `##console.log` and `##SQLDIAG.LOG`, respectively. When the utility experiences a failure or does not behave as expected, these two files can provide you with additional insight about why the failure occurred.

> **WARNING** *Do not shut down the data collection process using the exit button of the command prompt window. This can cause your Profiler traces or PerfMon files to be orphaned, compounding an already existing problem. The easiest way to detect this scenario is that your Profiler and PerfMon files will continue to grow in size and you will be unable to move or delete the files. The profiler trace can be easily stopped using the* sp_trace_setstatus *command. However, the orphaned PerfMon files are a different story. Most often, you can only correct this by restarting the SQL Server service, which is definitely not a good scenario to run into when operating on a production environment.*

Using SQLdiag as a Service

The third way you can collect data using SQLdiag is with a Windows service. You can use the /R parameter to register the utility as a service, and /U to unregister the tool as a service. You can use the /A switch to register SQLdiag as a service with a unique name. Figure 11-2 shows the properties of the SQLdiag utility registered as a service. The following command registers SQLdiag as a service with the name DIAG1:

```
SQLDIAG /R /A DIAG1
```

As you can see, the SQLdiag service registration appends DIAG$ to the service name when the /A parameter is used to provide the application name. If you choose to only use the /R switch, then the service is named SQLDIAG as shown in Figure 11-3.

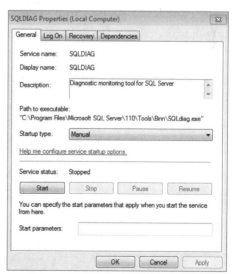

FIGURE 11-2   **FIGURE 11-3**

Note that service registration is done using the `Log On As` account as `Local System`. The majority of environments in which you will be using SQLdiag as a service will likely not have SQL Server sysadmin privileges granted to the `Local System` account. Therefore, after registering the utility as a service, you will need to change the service account to an account that has Administrator rights on the Windows machine and sysadmin privileges on the SQL Server instance(s) to which the service will connect.

> **WARNING** *If you run the service using a user account that is not part of the Windows Administrator group or the sysadmin role of SQL Server without the /G switch, you will get the following message in the Windows Application Event Log:*
>
> ```
> Warning: User SYSTEM is not a member of the sysadmin role on <SQL
> Server instance name>. Diagnostics for <SQL Server instance name>
> will not be collected
> ```

The next decision you need to make is which parameters you want to specify for the service. While registering the service, you can provide parameters as appropriate. In the following example, SQLdiag is being registered as a service:

```
'C:\Program Files\Microsoft SQL Server\110\Tools\Binn\sqldiag.exe' /R /I
C:\SQLDIAG_Data\SQLDIAG_Custom.XML /O 'C:\SQLDIAG_Data'
```

A successful service registration reports the message "SQLDIAG Service installed. Exiting." Note that in the above command, we needed to specify the path of the configuration file and the output folder, as well as to ensure that the right set of configuration options are used and the diagnostic data collected is captured in the correct folder.

> **WARNING** *The aforementioned success message is reported if you have multiple versions of SQLdiag available on the machine even if the SQL Server 2012 SQLdiag was not used for the service registration. This happens because your environment path variable points to the path of an older version of SQLdiag from another SQL Server 2005, 2008, or 2008 R2 installation, before the SQL Server 2012 path was added to the environment variable. Once you start the SQLdiag service, the following error will be reported in the SQLdiag log as well as in the Windows Application Event Log:*
>
> ```
> SQLDIAG . Function result: 87. Message: The parameter is incorrect.
> SQLDIAG Invalid SQL Server version specified.  SQL Server version
> 11 is not supported by this version of the collector
> ```

The above message signifies that an older version of SQLdiag was used to connect to a SQL Server 2012 instance. When you start the SQLdiag service, it uses the parameters specified during service registration to collect the required data based on information present in the configuration file. You can view events reported by the SQLdiag service by looking at the Windows Application Event Log, shown in Figure 11-4.

Level	Date and Time	Source	Event ID	Task Category
Information	4/20/2012 1:47:06 AM	SQLDIAG	50206	None
Information	4/20/2012 1:47:06 AM	SQLDIAG	50206	None
Information	4/20/2012 1:47:05 AM	SQLDIAG	50206	None
Information	4/20/2012 1:45:17 AM	SQLDIAG	50206	None
Information	4/20/2012 1:45:16 AM	SQLDIAG	50206	None
Information	4/20/2012 1:45:16 AM	SQLDIAG	50206	None
Information	4/20/2012 1:45:16 AM	SQLDIAG	50206	None

Event 50206, SQLDIAG

General | Details

2012/04/20 01:47:06.79 SQLDIAG Collection complete. Collector exiting

FIGURE 11-4

Configuring and Running SQLdiag on a Failover Cluster

When configuring a data collection package for a SQL Server failover cluster instance with Diag Manager, you need to remember a few salient points:

➤ Specify the SQL virtual server name as Machine Name.

➤ Specify the SQL Server instance name in the Instance Name text box. For a default failover cluster instance, enter **MSSQLSERVER**.

➤ Once you have the package configured, it is a best practice to run the SQLdiag data collection utility from the node that is the current owner of the SQL Server resource.

When running SQLdiag in the default configuration on a multi-instance failover cluster, the command window will show numerous errors in red. This is because the default configuration file, SQLDIAG.XML, has not been changed to collect data from a specific failover cluster instance. SQLdiag automatically detects the cluster and gathers logs and configuration information for every virtual server and instance. Errors are displayed in the command window because SQLdiag attempts to connect to each instance at every virtual server, resulting in several failures.

In this case, either configure the SQLDiag.XML file with the required target's virtual server name or ignore these errors. If any errors are displayed, they can be safely ignored. Likewise, the log file (##SQLDIAG .LOG) is usually easier to read and interpret to identify errors that can be safely ignored. A few of the ignorable messages actually have the text "you can usually safely ignore this" enclosed in parentheses.

USING SQLDIAG CONFIGURATION MANAGER

If you recognize the term PSSDIAG, then you have been around the SQL Server world for quite some time now and have worked on various SQL Server issues that required Microsoft engineers to collect diagnostic data using the PSSDIAG tool. You would also be familiar with saving PSSDIAG in a secure location and going through the XML configuration file to review the additional data that the PSSDIAG tool collects. In 2011, the Microsoft SQL Server Support team released a public version of the coveted Configuration Manager used for setting up data collection using SQLdiag, available on the CodePlex website, Microsoft's free open source project hosting site, under the name *Pssdiag/ Sqldiag Manager*. This means that you no longer need to painstakingly modify XML configuration files in a text editor. This tool is provided on an as-is basis by Microsoft. This tool provides you with the capability of using a graphical user interface to configure your data collection rather than having to painstakingly modify a XML configuration file.

> **NOTE** *As-is support means that you are free to download the tool and use it for your data collection needs. However, Microsoft Support does not support the tool and the only medium of support you have is to post a question or issue on the tool's codeplex homepage.*

The tool has the following prerequisites:

➤ .NET Framework 2.0

➤ Windows 2003 Server/XP or above

HOW TO INSTALL THE PSSDIAG/SQLDIAG MANAGER

1. Visit the Pssdiag/Sqldiag Manager home page by browsing to
   `http://diagmanager.codeplex.com/`.

2. Click the Downloads tab.

3. Download the setup.10.5.1.202.zip file after accepting the license agreement.

4. Extract the files and run the installation using setup.exe.

In order to understand why this tool, hereafter referred to as *Diag Manager*, is so important to data collection related to SQL Server issues, the following list describes the many ways in which it extends your data collection capabilities:

➤ It relies on the SQLdiag collector engine to provide a collection of PerfMon, Profiler trace, msinfo32, error logs, Windows event logs, T-SQL script output, and registry exports.

➤ It ships with a ready-to-use set of custom collectors.

➤ It provides an interface for cutomization of the PerfMon and Profiler trace collection along with the capability to add your own custom collectors.

➤ It will package all your files into a single cab file for the machine from which you intend to collect data.

➤ The custom collectors shipped will collect data that can be analyzed by the SQL Nexus tool.

> **NOTE** *If you encounter any issues while using the tool, you can file it using the Issue Tracker link on the home page of the Diag Manager tool on CodePlex. If you have any questions, you can start a new discussion using the Discussions link.*

Diag Manager is a 32-bit tool whose default installation location is as follows:

➤ **64-bit** — `C:\Program Files (x86)\Microsoft\Pssdiag`

➤ **32-bit** — `C:\Program Files\Microsoft\Pssdiag`

Once you have installed Diag Manager, you can find the program under All Programs ➪ PSSDIAG ➪ PSSDIAG Configuration Manager.

> **NOTE** *The Diag Manager does not have a specific SQL Server 2012 tab. You can use the SQL Server 2008 tab for configuring the data collection for SQL Server 2012. All of the configurations that are available under the SQL Server 2008 tab work for SQL Server 2012 instances.*

Configuring SQLdiag Data Collection Using Diag Manager

After launching the tool, the GUI will provide various configuration options, as shown in Figure 11-5.

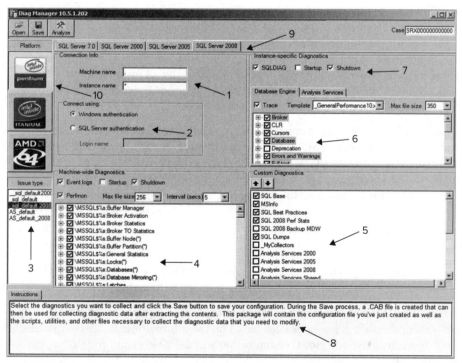

FIGURE 11-5

The arrows in Figure 11-5 show the different configuration options in the UI that enable you to easily customize your data collection. Some of the configuration options will be familiar to you from the "SQLdiag Configuration File Key Elements" list of this chapter.

Now take a look at what the Diag Manager UI allows you to customize. The first task is to select the platform: x86, x64, or IA64 (arrow 10 in Figure 11-5). Then you can choose the SQL Server version using the appropriate tabs. SQL Server 7.0 and SQL Server 2000 configurations (arrow 9 in Figure 11-5) are not supported by this tool.

> **WARNING** *If you forget to select the platform or the SQL Server version and need to make a change later or post the customizations made, you will lose any changes made and the options will default to the template selected.*

Now that you know how to select the right platform and SQL Server version, consider some key areas in the tool. The *Issue Type* section (arrow 3 in Figure 11-5) available in the leftmost pane of the UI is the list of templates you can use for configuring the data collection, with some events and collectors pre-configured. You could start with the `sql_default_2008` collector and edit them as appropriate for your data collection needs.

The *Connection Info* (arrow 1 in Figure 11-5) box is where you provide the machine name and the SQL Server instance name from which you intend to collect the diagnostic data. The full-stop (.) and asterisk (*) for the machine name and instance name, respectively, direct the configured SQLdiag package to collect data from all the SQL Server instances installed on the local machine. The best configuration practice here is to always provide a machine name and an instance name. The considerations mentioned in the section "Configuring and Running SQLdiag on a Failover Cluster" for configuring SQLdiag on a cluster apply here as well.

After providing the machine name and instance name, you can select the authentication used to permit collection of the data, Windows or SQL Server authentication. If you choose SQL Server authentication, you can only provide the username (arrow 2 in Figure 11-5). You will be prompted for the password at runtime. The `##SQLDIAG.log` file will contain the following information when you use SQL Server authentication for logging into the SQL Server instance:

```
Password:
User prompted for password at runtime
SQLDIAG Initialization starting...
```

The next section is *Machine-wide Diagnostics* (see Figure 11-6 and arrow 4 in Figure 11-5), which enables you to configure the PerfMon data collection by specifying the following:

➤ **The different PerfMon counters (arrow 4 in Figure 11-5) that you want to collect** — By default, a set of counters is pre-populated based on the information present in the selected template. You can enable additional counters that you deem necessary for analyzing your problem scenario. It is always a good practice to collect all the SQL Server Performance Monitor counters so that you do not miss any relevant information required for your data analysis. Furthermore, the overhead of collecting PerfMon data is the lowest compared to the other data collectors.

➤ The maximum file size and interval at which you want to collect the data samples

➤ Configuration of the Windows Event Log collection

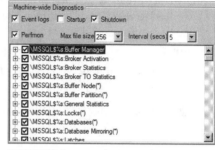

The next step is to configure the Profiler trace. This can be done using the *Instance-specific Diagnostics* (arrow 7 in Figure 11-5) section of the tool, used for configuring database engine/analysis server trace (arrow 6 in Figure 11-5) and collection of SQLdiag output. Here you can configure a trace for the database engine and SQL Server Analysis Services instance. Based on the SQL Server version selected, you will see the Profiler trace events populated in the list, which you can configure for your data collec-

FIGURE 11-6

tion along with the Profiler trace rollover size. Collection of the SQLdiag diagnostic script can be enabled or disabled from this section.

> **WARNING** *Although you can right-click on a Profiler event and add filters from this section, you shouldn't use this option, as the trace filter will not be honored when added to the XML configuration file.*

The last section in the Diag Manager is *Custom Diagnostics* (arrow 5 in Figure 11-5), which provides a list of pre-built custom collectors that are already available for data collection. In addition to this, you can extend the data collection, as described in more detail in the section "Understanding the Custom Diagnostics." The *Instructions* (arrow 8 in Figure 11-5) tab at the bottom of the Diag Manager UI provides an explanation of all the Custom Diagnostics options when you click on them.

> **NOTE** *If you need to configure a SQLdiag collection for a RunAs User (RANU) SQL Server Express instance, refer to the steps provided at* http://troubleshootingsql.com/2011/05/19/tools-tips-and-tricks-5 -sqldiag-and-ranu/.

Adding Trace Filters to a SQLdiag Configuration

Normally, Profiler trace filters are added to a SQL Server data collection to reduce the amount of diagnostic data that is collected by SQLdiag. For example, you could add a filter on SPID to collect only trace events which pertain to a particular Session ID. Note that the text filters add CPU overhead to the data collection as there is a significant CPU overhead for evaluating text-based filters as opposed to integer filters. However, if you collect a Profiler trace using a SQLdiag configuration XML file, then you need to follow these steps:

1. Start SQLdiag on the server.The options to start SQLdiag can be found in the "Using SQLdiag as a Command-line Application" section of this chapter.

2. Find out the Trace ID of the Profiler trace running using `fn_trace_getinfo` function or `sys.traces` view.

3. Stop the trace using `sp_trace_setstatus` without deleting the definition.

4. Use the Trace ID obtained from step 2, and use the `sp_trace_setfilter` stored procedure to set the filter. Refer to "SQL Profiler Data Columns" in SQL Server Books Online for the Data Column numbers.

5. To verify that the filter is active, use the `fn_trace_filterinfo` function.

6. When you are satisfied that the filter is active, start the trace data collection using `sp_trace_setstatus`.

The following T-SQL Commands can be used toSet a Filter for SPID = 52 for TraceID = 2 once the SQLdiag has been initialized:

```
select * from sys.traces — To get the trace id
EXEC sp_trace_setstatus 2,0 — Stops the trace but doesn't delete the trace definition
from the server
EXEC sp_trace_setfilter 2, 12, 0, 0, 52 — Add a filter for SPID = 52
EXEC sp_trace_setstatus 2,1 — Start the trace again
select * from fn_trace_getfilterinfo(2) — Get information about the filters set for the
trace
```

Understanding the Custom Diagnostics in SQLdiag

This section looks at the different categories of custom diagnostics available out-of-the-box in the Diag Manager. The extensibility of SQLdiag using Diag Manager is a very compelling reason for all SQL Server professionals to add this tool to their repertoire. The T-SQL, VBScript and DOS commands used by the custom diagnostics configurations are available in the `C:\Program Files\Microsoft\Pssdiag\CustomDiagnostics` folder.

> **NOTE** *If you have installed Diag Manager on a 64-bit machine, then instead of* `Programs Files` *you will be looking for the* `Program Files (x86)` *folder.*

General Custom Diagnostics

The *SQL Base* custom collector is used to add tasks that should be executed for every type of SQL Server data collection. This custom collector runs before any other custom collector task. One of the group's primary purposes is to define global parameters that may be of general use in other task groups. This collector also collects basic configuration information from the registry, system configuration information, the status of the PAE switch, and the trace flags active on the target SQL Server instance.

All the output files have the prefix "`SERVER_SQL_Base_*`."

The *MSINFO* custom collector collects the msinfo32 output from the target machine.

The *SQL Best Practices* custom collector collects outputs of various scripts to check the following:

➤ NTFS compression on SQL Server database files

➤ Hypothetical indexes on the databases (if any)

➤ Use of the /3GB and /PAE switch in the BOOT.INI file

➤ Information about all the SQL Server Profiler traces active on the target SQL Server instance

All the output files have the prefix "`SERVER_SQL_Best_Practices_*`."

SQL 2008 Perf Stats

The most common customization that SQL Server professionals and Microsoft engineers add to SQLdiag is to collect SQL Server blocking diagnostics. You might already be familiar with the configuration option to capture blocking information. This information can be collected using the *SQL 2008 Perf Stats* custom diagnostic option. This section describes why this custom diagnostic is not just about collecting blocking information on your SQL Server instance as seen below. Note that the scripts available in the download section work for SQL Server 2012 instances as well.

However, if you intend to capture the SQL Perf Stats script manually, then you need to get the latest Perf Stats script, available from CodePlex at `http://sqlnexus.codeplex.com/wikipage?title=Sql2005PerfStatsScript&ProjectName=sqlnexus`. After downloading it, follow these steps:

1. Click Page Info from the navigation bar.

2. Scroll down to locate the File Attachments section.

3. Locate `PerfStatsScript2008R2.zip` and download the file.

4. After extracting the zip file, you will find the files shown in Figure 11-7.

Name	Type	Compressed size	Password ...	Size
SQL_2008_Perf_Stats.sql	Microsoft SQL Server Que...	14 KB	No	98 KB
SQL_2008_Perf_Stats_Snapshot.sql	Microsoft SQL Server Que...	5 KB	No	20 KB
SQLDiagPerfStats_Detailed_Trace2008.XML	XML Document	15 KB	No	209 KB
SQLDiagPerfStats_Trace2008.XML	XML Document	15 KB	No	202 KB
SQLDiagReplay2008.xml	XML Document	15 KB	No	209 KB
StartSQLDiagDetailed_Trace2008R2.cmd	Windows Command Script	1 KB	No	1 KB
StartSQLDiagForReplay2008R2.cmd	Windows Command Script	1 KB	No	1 KB
StartSQLDiagTrace2008R2.cmd	Windows Command Script	1 KB	No	1 KB

FIGURE 11-7

The `SQL_2008_Perf_Stats_Snapshot.sql` script collects information about your SQL Server instance's top resource-consuming queries, missing indexes information with the `CREATE INDEX` scripts along with resource consuming query hashes. Query hash was a new feature added in SQL Server 2008 and later versions to create a hash value for the queries which use different literal parameter values. The output of this script is collected twice: once when SQLdiag starts and once when it is stopped.

The `SQL_2008_Perf_Stats.sql` script captures various DMV outputs and blocking information periodically using a delay of ten seconds with the `WAITFOR DELAY` command.

The output of both aforementioned scripts can be imported into a SQL Server database using the SQL Nexus tool for data analysis. The bonus here is the fact that this custom diagnostic also collects the output of the System Health Session Extended Event session, which is an Extended Event session that runs by default on SQL Server 2008 instances and later.

> **NOTE** *This custom diagnostic is the equivalent of the* SQL 2005 Perf Stats *custom collector used for SQL Server 2005 instances to collect similar diagnostic information.*

Backing Up Diagnostic Data Already Available

The *SQL 2008 Backup MDW* custom collector performs a backup of any Management Data Warehouse database that you might have configured on the SQL Server instance. When you Save the SQLdiag configuration, a pop-up window will prompt you for the Management Data Warehouse database name, as show in Figure 11-8.

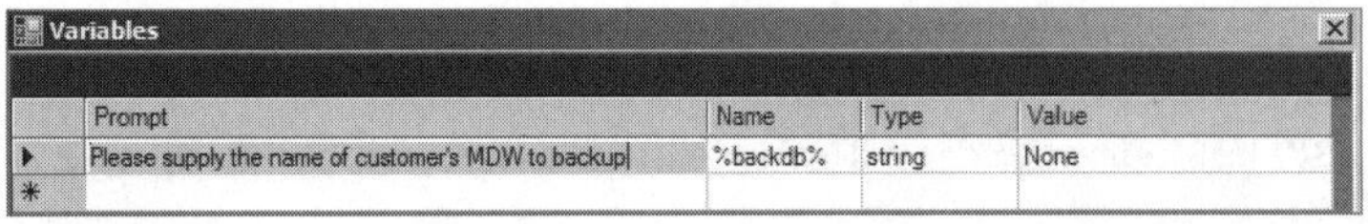

	Prompt	Name	Type	Value
▶	Please supply the name of customer's MDW to backup	%backdb%	string	None
＊				

FIGURE 11-8

The *SQL Dumps* custom collector collects all the mini-dump (`SQLDumpXXXX.mdmp`) files, symptom dump text files (`SQLDump*.txt`) and the exception log file. The collector skips any dump file larger than 10MB and limits the dumps collected to 70MB. The dump files skipped will be the older dump files.

> **WARNING** *Both the custom collectors can bloat your SQLdiag output folder, so these collectors should be enabled only when required. A Management Data Warehouse database backup can be significantly large if it stores data for a large number of instances or contains a large amount of historical data.*

Analysis Services Custom Collectors

The Diag Manager provides four different types of collectors for Analysis Services. Three collectors are specific to a given Analysis Services version, and the fourth is a shared collector that collects general diagnostics from an Analysis Services instance:

- ➤ Analysis Services 2000
- ➤ Analysis Services 2005
- ➤ Analysis Services 2008
- ➤ Analysis Services Shared

The Analysis Services 2008 and Analysis Services Shared works for SQL Server 2012 Analysis Services installed in the multi-dimensional model. If you are interested in viewing what these collectors collect, you can find details by right-clicking on the collector and selecting the Details option as shown in Figure 11-9.

FIGURE 11-9

Feature-Specific Custom Diagnostics

The Diag Manager also provides you with some feature-specific custom collectors that can be very helpful when you are troubleshooting a particular SQL Server scenario or feature.

The *Database Mirroring* custom collector collects information from various system DMVs and catalogs for the database mirroring configuration and status of the mirrored databases. In addition, the database mirroring collector connects the database mirroring partner and witness to collect the configuration data that it collected from the target instance on which SQLdiag is running. To ensure that all the data is collected, you would need to ensure that the account running the SQLdiag has permissions to collect the database mirroring configuration information from the mirror and witness. Note that there are no new custom collectors available for collecting data specific to Availability Groups for SQL Server 2012 as yet. However, you can write your own collector by defining a new custom collector under the *_MyCollectors* option discussed later in this chapter.

> **WARNING** *The collector assumes that the account running SQLdiag will be able to log into all the SQL Server instances as a sysadmin using Windows authentication.*

The *Full Text Search* custom collector collects the full-text search configuration and the full-text catalog details for each database that is full-text enabled.

The *Linked Server Configuration* custom collector collects information about the available linked server providers on the target machine, and configuration information about all the linked servers configured on the target SQL Server instance.

> **WARNING** *The T-SQL scripts used by the aforementioned collectors make use of the* xp_cmdshell *extended stored procedure, which will result in errors reported in the SQLdiag log file if* xp_cmdshell *is not enabled on the target SQL Server instance. If* xp_cmdshell *cannot be enabled on the target SQL Server instance due to compliance or security reasons, then the information that couldn't be collected can be manually collected.*

The *SQL 2005 tempdb Space and Latching* custom collector can be used to troubleshoot SQL Server issues pertaining to tempdb contention. The T-SQL script used by this collector collects tempdb usage and statistics in a loop during the entire duration of the SQLdiag data collection. The collector uses the following DMVs and system catalogs to collect the diagnostic information:

➤ sys.dm_db_file_space_used

➤ sys.dm_db_session_file_usage

➤ sys.dm_db_task_space_usage

➤ sys.sysprocesses

➤ sys.dm_os_waiting_tasks

The *SQL Blocking* custom collector enables the trace flag 1222 during the initialization phase of SQLdiag, which ensures that deadlock information is written to the SQL Server Error Log. Note that this collector does not collect blocking information from the target SQL Server instance. Information about the blocking chains observed need to be captured by using the *SQL 2008 Perf Stats* custom collector.

The *SQL Memory Error* custom collector collects diagnostic information about the target SQL Server instance's memory usage, which can be useful while troubleshooting SQL out-of-memory issues.

> **WARNING** *Some of the data captured by these custom diagnostics will not be captured when running SQLdiag from a remote machine. This is one of many reasons why it is recommended to run SQLdiag from the machine on which the SQL Server instance is installed.*

The *SQL Agent* custom collector collects all the SQL Server Agent logs and the backup of the MSDB database from the target SQL Server instance. This can result in the output folder becoming very large, and can dramatically increase the time it takes for the SQLdiag shutdown phase, which would be directly proportional to the size of the MSDB database. It is probably a good idea to collect the relevant data from the MSDB database tables if the MSDB database is quite large.

Capturing Extended Events

The *XEvents Waits* custom collector enables you to configure Extended Events (XEvents) data collection on the target SQL Server instance. By default, the collector has three XEvent sessions for capturing information for page latch waits experienced on the target instance. You can view configuration details of the collector by right-clicking on the XEvent Waits custom collector and clicking Details as shown in Figure 11-10.

	Enabled	Name	Type	Collection Point	Wait	Command	Polling Interval (secs)
⊞	☑	Start Xevent	TSQL_Script	Startup	No	XEventStart.sql	0
⊞	☑	LATCH_SH waits	Utility	Shutdown	Yes	sqlcmd.exe -S%server_instance% -iLATCH_SH_WAITS.sql -E -o"%output_na	0
⊞	☑	LATCH_EX waits	Utility	Shutdown	Yes	sqlcmd.exe -S%server_instance% -iLATCH_EX_WAITS.sql -E -o"%output_na	0
▶ ⊞	☑	LATCH_UP waits	Utility	Shutdown	Yes	sqlcmd.exe -S%server_instance% -iLATCH_UP_WAITS.sql -E -o"%	0

FIGURE 11-10

For example, assume there is a need to capture wait information for all PAGEIOLATCH waits. PAGEIOLATCH_* waits are encountered when the SQL Server database engine experiences an I/O sub-system related wait condition. Most commonly high wait-times experienced by these wait types signify storage sub-system related latencies. Figure 11-11 shows what the final configuration would look like. This would require the addition of two custom events:

➤   A startup event that will execute a T-SQL script to create and start the XEvent session that will capture the wait information for all PAGEIOLATCH waits

➤   A utility-type collector that will execute a T-SQL script when the SQLdiag utility is shut down to collect the data captured by the XEvent session into an XML file

	Enabled	Name	Type	Collection Point	Wait	Command	Polling Interval (secs)
⊞	☑	Start Xevent	TSQL_Script	Startup	No	XEventStart.sql	0
⊞	☑	LATCH_SH waits	Utility	Shutdown	Yes	sqlcmd.exe -S%server_instance% -iLATCH_SH_WAITS.sql -E -o"%output_na	0
⊞	☑	LATCH_EX waits	Utility	Shutdown	Yes	sqlcmd.exe -S%server_instance% -iLATCH_EX_WAITS.sql -E -o"%output_na	0
⊞	☑	LATCH_UP waits	Utility	Shutdown	Yes	sqlcmd.exe -S%server_instance% -iLATCH_UP_WAITS.sql -E -o"%output_na	0
⊞	☑	PAGEIOLATCH	TSQL_Script	Startup	No	XEventStart - Copy.sql	0
▶ ⊞	☑	PAGEIOLATCH Stop	Utility	Startup	Yes	sqlcmd.exe -S%server_instance% -iPAGEIOLATCH.sql -E -o"%output_name%.xml"	0

FIGURE 11-11

One of the new additions to SQL Server 2012 Management Studio is the UI for Extended Events. You can use the UI to configure your custom Extended Events session. Once the session is configured, it will be available under the Sessions folder, as shown in Figure 11-12.

This new addition to Management Studio enables you to extend your customization options by adding an Extended Event collection to

FIGURE 11-12

your SQL Server data collection arsenal. Once you have configured the required set of events, you can script out the Extended Event session and use the acquired T-SQL script to set up your own XEvent collection while configuring a SQLdiag collection using the _MyCollectors custom collector described in the following section.

Adding Your Own Custom Collectors

Now that you have looked at the myriad of pre-configured data collectors for various scenarios and features, you might be wondering what happened to the specific data collection that was required for an issue you were troubleshooting in your SQL Server environment. If the previously described custom collectors do not satisfy your data collection requirements, then you can configure your own custom collector using the _MyCollectors custom collector.

Consider an example in which you needed to collect the space usage of the folders in the default data folder of SQL Server. This information was to be collected during startup of the data collection using a PowerShell script. The following PowerShell Script will capture the disk space usage for all the folders in the folder specified below:

```
$startFolder = 'C:\Program Files\Microsoft SQL Server\MSSQL11.MSSQLSERVER\MSSQL\DATA'
$colItems = (Get-ChildItem $startFolder | Measure-Object -property length -sum)
'$startFolder -- ' + '{0:N2}' -f ($colItems.sum / 1MB) + ' MB'

$colItems = (Get-ChildItem $startFolder -recurse | Where-Object
{$_.PSIsContainer -eq $True} | Sort-Object)
foreach ($i in $colItems)
    {
        $subFolderItems = (Get-ChildItem $i.FullName |
        Measure-Object -property length -sum)
        $i.FullName + ' -- ' + '{0:N2}' -f ($subFolderItems.sum / 1MB) + ' MB'
    }
```

Assume that the preceding code was saved into a file called space.ps1. Then you would right-click on _MyCollectors and add a Utility task as shown in Figure 11-13.

Enabled	Name	Type	Collection Point	Wait	Command
☑	Get Disk Space	Utility	Shutdown ▾	OnlyOnShutdown	powershell.exe -File ".\space.ps1" -NoLogo -NonInteractive >"Pshell_DiskSpace.OUT"

FIGURE 11-13

When data collection is completed, a file named <Machine Name>__MyCollectors_Get_Disk_Space_Shutdown_DiskSpace.OUT would appear in the output folder. If you looked at the configuration file after saving the settings using Diag Manager, you would find that the XML node that has the custom collector configuration would look like the following code snippet:

```
<CustomDiagnostics>
  <CustomGroup name='_MyCollectors' enabled='true' />
  <CustomTask enabled='true' groupname='_MyCollectors' taskname='Get Disk
```

```
Space' type='Utility' point='Shutdown' wait='OnlyOnShutdown' cmd='powershell.exe -File
&quot;.\space.ps1&quot; -NoLogo -NonInteractive  &gt; &quot;PShell_DiskSpace.OUT&quot; '
pollinginterval='0' />
            </CustomDiagnostics>
```

> **NOTE** *Before saving the package configuration, you must add your custom scripts (in the preceding example,* `space.ps1`) *to the* `C:\Program Files\Microsoft\Pssdiag\CustomDiagnostics\_MyCollectors` *folder.*

Saving and Using a SQLdiag Configuration

Now that you know how to configure the SQLdiag collection based on the data you need to collect, this section describes how to save the configuration package, as this tool was released to work with SQL Server 2008 R2, 2008, and 2005 versions. When you click the Save button, the dialog shown in Figure 11-14 will appear, providing the location of the cabinet (.cab) file and the XML configuration file. You can change the path of the two files as appropriate.

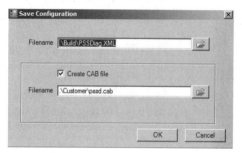

When you click OK, the dialog shown in Figure 11-15 will appear for selecting either SQL Server 2008 R2 or SQL Server 2008, in case you were configuring the data collection using the SQL Server 2008 tab in the Diag Manager.

FIGURE 11-14

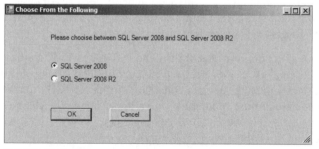

FIGURE 11-15

> **NOTE** *The preceding configuration steps work for all releases of SQL Server 2005 and later. Because we are discussing data collection configuration for SQL Server 2012 instances, you should select the SQL Server 2008 tab when you start your configuration. When the dialog is provided for choosing the SQL Server version while saving the cabinet file, choose the SQL Server 2008 R2 option.*

By default, the cabinet file generated is located at `C:\Program Files\Microsoft\Pssdiag\Customer` with the name `pssd.cab`. This cabinet file stores all the necessary supporting files required to collect the data for all the enabled data collectors configured by you. The `pssd.cab` file can now be copied to the target machine from which you want to collect the diagnostic data.

When you extract the cabinet file, you will find a `pssdiag.cmd` file, which calls the SQLdiag executable to collect data using the `PSSDIAG.XML` configuration file. Before you start the data collection, you need to modify the `PSSDIAG.XML` file, changing the `ssver` value to 11 from 10.50, as shown in the following example. This directs the SQLdiag utility to collect diagnostic data from a SQL Server 2012 instance.

```
<Instance name='MSSQLSERVER' windowsauth='true' ssver="11" user=''>
```

Now you are all ready to collect diagnostic data using SQLdiag by executing the `pssdiag.cmd`, which is a DOS batch command file, to start the data collection.

> **WARNING** *If you had a SQL Server instance from a release earlier than SQL Server 2012 already installed on the machine before the RTM version of SQL Server 2012 was installed, then you need to do one of two things. Either edit your environment PATH variable to ensure that the SQL Server 2012 SQLdiag path precedes any other directories containing older versions of the SQLdiag executable, or modify `pssdiag.cmd` and hard-code the SQL Server 2012 SQLdiag path.*

EMPLOYING BEST PRACTICES

Now that you have learned the intricacies of using SQLdiag, this section describes a set of best practices that will not only help you collect the right set of data, but also help you minimize the performance overhead of data collection on the target SQL Server instance(s).

One common best practice is to keep multiple configurations of the `pssd.cab` file already configured for various scenarios, such as high CPU usage, SQL Server timeouts, long-running queries, and so on. This enables you to avoid the hassle of configuring the data collection during a crisis situation. All you would need to do is extract the contents of the cabinet file into a folder and make changes to the `PSSDIAG.XML` configuration file for the `Machine Name`, `Instance Name`, and `ssver` values. After this quick modification is done, you are ready to collect your required diagnostic data.

> **WARNING** *Do not mix-and-match SQLdiag/PSSDIAG configuration files sent by Microsoft CSS engineers with those you have generated with the public version of the Diag Manager UI. This can lead to unwanted errors, as Microsoft engineers might add other custom diagnostics to the data collection utility based on the issue they were troubleshooting on your servers, whose supporting files are not available in the version of Diag Manager you downloaded from CodePlex.*

Gearing Up for Long-Term Data Collection

Sometimes there is a need to collect data for prolonged periods for intermittent issues whose occurrence is hard to predict. You are forced to run data collection around the clock to ensure that all relevant data is captured for the next occurrence of the issue. This raises the question of when the data collection should be started or stopped. The Diag Manager provides such an option through another custom diagnostic option called Delete Old Trace Files. This custom diagnostic deletes all but the N most recent Profiler (.trc) files and PerfMon (.blg) files. When you click Save in the Diag Manager UI, you are prompted to provide the number of trace and PerfMon files that should be retained, as shown in Figure 11-16. This gives you the flexibility to run data collection for long periods without running out of drive space.

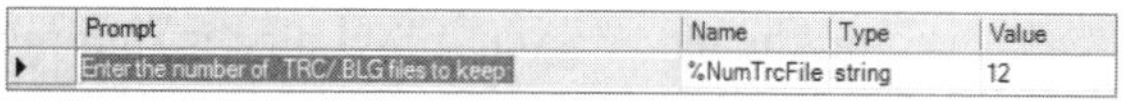

Prompt		Name	Type	Value
▶	Enter the number of TRC/ BLG files to keep	%NumTrcFile	string	12

FIGURE 11-16

> **WARNING** *The number of trace files corresponds to a fixed amount of disk space used, but not to a fixed amount of time captured. It is always a good idea to run SQLdiag for a brief period during peak hours to estimate the rate of Profiler trace events generated and the disk space consumed for about 10–15 minutes. This enables you to form a rough approximation of the time span of the activity that will be captured before the data is overwritten. The PerfMon files do not increase as rapidly in size as the Profiler trace files. The Profiler trace collection is by far the most resource intensive data collection component in SQLdiag.*

In addition to this, you can exercise other options for long-term data collection that enable you to retain more trace files without running out of disk space:

➤ Reduce the set of Profiler events being captured. The following section elaborates on this topic.

➤ Use the /c2 command-line parameter to enable background NTFS compression of the output files generated.

➤ Consider using the /N, /E, and /L command-line parameter to restart data collection at a specific time every day, with a new output folder created for each restart of the data collection. The older folder can be deleted if the issue for which the data collection was initiated did not occur.

➤ Consider using SQLdiag's built-in NT service support. This can be quite helpful when you cannot keep a remote desktop session open on your server for a long period of time. If you are using the command line option to initialize SQLdiag, then you will end up needing to keep a session active so that the console window doesn't close. By running SQLdiag as a service, you do not have to worry about any such restrictions!

➤ Add more local disk space. This is an obvious option but it's not always viable or possible.

The following are *not* recommended as methods to deal with space constraints on the target machine where you are capturing data:

➤ **Attempting to trace to a network drive or UNC path or using the client-side Profiler UI from a remote machine** — This method of tracing is highly detrimental to SQL Server performance and should be avoided at all costs! SQLdiag always captures a server-side Profiler trace. The destination output folder should always be a local drive!

➤ **Attempting to run SQLdiag remotely in an attempt to minimize space usage on the server** — This isn't useful because Profiler traces are always captured locally on the server (even if SQLdiag is running remotely).

Filtering Out the Noise

The prime reason why the size of a SQLdiag data collection balloons out of proportion or the target SQL Server performance degrades while capturing diagnostic data is the high number of redundant or irrelevant Profiler events added to the data collection configuration.

The following list provides guidelines on when to avoid certain Profiler event categories which generate a high number of events when added to the set of profiler events being captured by SQLdiag. This can lead to a high amount of chatter in the trace files captured without adding value to the analysis:

➤ `Broker` — None of the events in the Broker category are required unless you are troubleshooting an issue related to Database Mail or Service Broker in SQL Server 2005 or above. However, the Broker event category can generate a lot of noise if you have Service Broker/Database Mail configured on the server and are using it heavily.

➤ `Cursors` — If the client application or provider that connects to your SQL Server instance uses server-side cursors, then this event category can lead to an unmanageable amount of data collected that will take you ages to sift through. The `sp_cursor*` calls will be captured either way in your Stored Procedure event classes, which makes it a moot point to track `CursorOpen`, `CursorClose`, and `CursorExecute` through this event category for general-performance issues. The only useful events in this event category are `CursorImplicitConversion` (which enables you to track implicit conversion of requested nonsupported cursor types by the SQL Server database engine) and `CursorRecompile` (which helps you track down T-SQL cursor recompiles due to schema changes). You would want to use the events in this category only when troubleshooting a specific cursor-related issue.

➤ `Locks` — This event category generates the highest amount of activity. `Lock:Acquired` and `Lock:Released` event classes (if captured) can make your data analysis more difficult than scaling Mount Everest. If you need to track the number of locks for each session, then it is done best outside the Profiler using DMVs such as `sys.dm_tran_locks`. However, this event category has some useful event classes:

    ➤ `Lock: Deadlock` and `Lock: Deadlock Chain` — Helpful when troubleshooting deadlock issues on a SQL Server instance

    ➤ `Lock: Timeout` and `Lock: Timeout (timeout > 0)` — Help troubleshooting timeout-related issues due to lock blocking

➤   `Lock: Escalation` — This one is debatable. It helps track down lock escalations but on servers that have a high number of these, this can become a high frequency event.

➤ `OLEDB` — Unless you are sure, based on the symptoms shown regarding the issue, that OLEDB calls need to be traced, you shouldn't be collecting any event from this event category except for OLEDB errors. Therefore, if your OLEDB provider were returning a large number of errors, you would be able to track it down using the `HRESULT` obtained from this event class.

➤ `Query Notifications` — The same logic used earlier for the `Broker` event category applies to this event category.

➤ `Scans` — This might be useful when you are doing a repro of sorts on a test or development environment, but on a production server this is a strict no-no as you will end up collecting more noise than any useful data for analysis purposes! Capturing this event unless and until absolutely required is a very easy way to bloat your profiler trace file size very quickly! You should be able to determine, looking at the plans, whether there was a table/index scan without having to capture a separate noisy event in the Profiler traces.

➤ `Security Audit` — This is a very good event category when troubleshooting security or permissions-related issues on a SQL Server instance. For performance-related issues, this is just plain noise! The events under this category are fired nineteen-to-the-dozen on a SQL Server instance, which just bloats your Profiler trace size rather than do anything useful! The two truly useful events in this category are `Audit: Login` and `Audit: Logout`, which help track the session's connection settings and other attributes, such as host name, user name, etc.

➤ `Transactions` — This event category also has a lot of noise events that aid more in bloating Profiler trace size rather than doing anything useful. In particular, don't capture the `Transaction Manager` (`TM:*`) event classes unless you are troubleshooting an issue related to Begin/Commit/Rollback that is taking a long time to complete. The `SQLTransation` event is quite useful for troubleshooting deadlock-related issues, as it helps track transaction begin and commit/rollback and nest levels for a given session. The `DTCTransaction` event class is useful for troubleshooting DTC transaction, related issues and tracking the different states of a DTC transaction.

➤ `Performance Event` — This is one of the most widely used event categories among Microsoft SQL Server Support Engineers for troubleshooting query performance issues. That's because this event category helps you capture query plans. There are several different event classes in this category for capturing query plans, which can be divided into two types based on data you can obtain from these events:

     ➤ **Compile-time details** — `Showplan All`, `Showplan XML`, and `Showplan Text` (occurs during query execution but does not contain runtime details like rows returned) and `Showplan XML For Query Compile` and `Showplan All For Query Compile` (shows the compile-time query plan). These two events can be very useful when you want to capture a query plan for timeout-related issues, as the other events that show the execution time query plans may not be generated when you are dealing with query timeouts. Therefore, if you are not facing any timeouts and need the query plans with runtime details, you need not capture any of the afore-mentioned events. The Query Compile event classes (especially the XML events) are required when you are trying to nail down compilation-related issues and want to determine the resources (CPU/memory) consumed during query compilation.

➤ **Runtime details** — `Showplan Statistics Profile` and `Showplan XML Statistics Profile` show the query plan with runtime details in text and XML format, respectively. Based on whether you prefer sifting through text or XML, you could capture either one. XML events are not the best in terms of reducing the size of the Profiler traces captured.

Following are some other high-frequency event classes, which can be excluded as well from your profiler trace configuration unless the issue that you are troubleshooting warrants the collection of these events:

➤ `SP:CacheMiss`, `SP:CacheInsert`, `SP:CacheRemove`, and `SP:CacheHit` — These events are helpful when tracking procedure cache plan caching issues; otherwise, you are going to be dealing with a lot of noise in the Profiler traces if these events are captured, as one of these events occurs every time a plan is looked up in the procedure cache.

➤ `TSQL: Prepare SQL`, `TSQL: Exec Prepared SQL`, `TSQL: Unprepare SQL` — These are useful for troubleshooting issues with prepared SQL calls from providers but should be avoided unless and until you are confident that the problem is due to how the SQL statement is being prepared.

Alert-Driven Data Collection with SQLdiag

Another way to minimize the amount of time you need to run the data collection utility is to be aware of the symptoms associated with your problem period. Troubleshooting intermittent issues is always tricky; you must tread the fine line between the necessary evil of collecting diagnostic data and running the risk of antagonizing your customers or users with even further degraded performance. The preceding tips can help you avoid unwanted phone calls when you are trying to be the Good Samaritan by helping to get the server back up and running while it is reduced to a crawl due to a performance bottleneck.

An alert eye can spot symptoms like high CPU usage, a high number of lock timeouts, or a high number of blocking chains during a problem period, any of which can become your trigger point to start the data collection. SQL Server Agent can monitor and automatically respond to events, such as messages from SQL Server, specific performance conditions, and Windows Management Instrumentation (WMI) events. The response to such an alert can be a job that starts the SQLdiag data collection through the use of command-line parameters. Not only is this a smart way of collecting data, it will minimize the amount of time you spend praying that the issue will occur while you are staring at a dashboard, monitoring the SQL Server instance's performance metrics. Unfortunately, Murphy's Law has a unique way of rearing its head, so the chances are high that the bottleneck that brings your SQL Server instance to its knees will appear at the most inopportune moment possible. You can go one step further and send out e-mails or pager alerts when the data collection begins, to ensure that necessary attention is given to the issue at the correct time.

SUMMARY

SQLdiag, configured properly with the right set of custom collectors, can be a one-stop shop for SQL Server professionals for collecting diagnostic data for analyzing and determining the root cause of complex SQL Server problems. These are the same tools that are used by the Microsoft SQL Server CSS team to collect and analyze data from SQL Server instances that they are troubleshooting. When you add SQL Nexus to the mix, you increase the chances of performing correlated analysis, which is essential for building a sound hypothesis and arriving at the root cause of a SQL Server issue.

12

Bringing It All Together with SQL Nexus

WHAT'S IN THIS CHAPTER?

➤ Getting familiar with SQL Nexus

➤ Loading data into a Nexus database

➤ Analyzing the aggregated data

➤ Customizing SQL Nexus

➤ Common issues and how to resolve them

WROX.COM CODE DOWNLOADS FOR THIS CHAPTER

There are no code downloads for this chapter.

INTRODUCING SQL NEXUS

SQL Nexus is a tool used by SQL Server professionals and Microsoft engineers to aggregate SQL Trace data, performance monitor logs, and the output of various T-SQL scripts into a single SQL Server database. This chapter explains how the data collected by SQLdiag, covered in Chapter 11, can be imported into a SQL Server database and then analyzed with the help of existing reports in SQL Nexus. SQL Nexus is a free tool available on the Microsoft CodePlex site and is provided on an as-is basis. This means that the Microsoft Support team does not support SQL Nexus and any issues related to the tool need be posted on the discussion forum of the tool's home page on the CodePlex site.

> **NOTE** *This chapter assumes that the concepts discussed earlier in this book are already understood or have been read so that the analysis patterns discussed later in this chapter are clearly understood.*
>
> *SQL Trace refers to both trace files captured using the client side SQL Profiler and the server-side SQL Trace.*

SQL Nexus uses three components:

➤ **RML Utilities** (also known as ReadTrace) — A tool to aggregate data collected by SQL Trace files and import them into a SQL Server database. The download link to the tool is available using the following link: `http://blogs.msdn.com/b/psssql/archive/2008/11/12/cumulative-update-1-to-the-rml-utilities-for-microsoft-sql-server-released.aspx`.

➤ **Relog** — An executable that can extract data present in performance counter logs. It is also available on the Microsoft download site.

➤ **Rowset Importer** — A component available with the SQL Nexus download on CodePlex that can parse data present in the output of the T-SQL scripts of the custom diagnostics and SQL PerfStats script (see Chapter 11). The parsed data is then imported into the SQL Nexus database.

> **NOTE** *Some of the tools discussed in this chapter are due to be updated for SQL Server 2012 in the near future. When they are, we will release additional material on the website for this book explaining the enhancements and new features.*

GETTING FAMILIAR WITH SQL NEXUS

This chapter is based on SQL Nexus 3.0.0.0, which at the time of writing is the most current version available on the Microsoft CodePlex site, the open-source community website for Microsoft. The SQL Nexus home page has links to download the tool along with the source code, and a discussion forum and issue tracker where you can post your comments and questions about any issues faced while working with the tool.

Prerequisites

Note the following to-do items before you start using SQL Nexus:

➤ Install the Microsoft SQL Server 2008 SP1 Report Viewer control to view the aggregated reports using the client-side reports available in the tool.

➤ Install the RML Utilities so that SQL Nexus can import the SQL Traces.

➤ If you'll be using SQL Server 2012 for the database repository, install SQL Server 2008 Native Client, which is available as a free download as part of the Microsoft SQL Server 2008 Feature Pack on the Microsoft Downloads site.

➤ Verify that .NET Framework 2.0 is installed on your machine. If you are unsure of the .NET framework versions installed on your machine, then you can check if the `<system drive>\Windows\Microsoft.NET\Framework64` folder (for 64-bit) or the `<system drive>:\Windows\Microsoft.NET\Framework` contains the `v2.0.*` folder on your machine.

➤ Use a SQL Server 2012 or lower database engine to import the collected data.

> **WARNING** *We do not recommend loading your collected data into a production SQL Server instance as this would lead to resource intensive operations associated with the import competing with your production workload.*

Once you have fulfilled the preceding requirements, you can download the latest release from the SQL Nexus page on CodePlex (`http://sqlnexus.codeplex.com/`) and launch the tool using `sqlnexus.exe`. No steps are required to install the tool. After launching it, you will be prompted to provide the SQL Server instance name and the credentials to connect to the instance on which you want to import the data. The default database for this tool is *sqlnexus*. Figure 12-1 shows the landing page of the SQL Nexus tool.

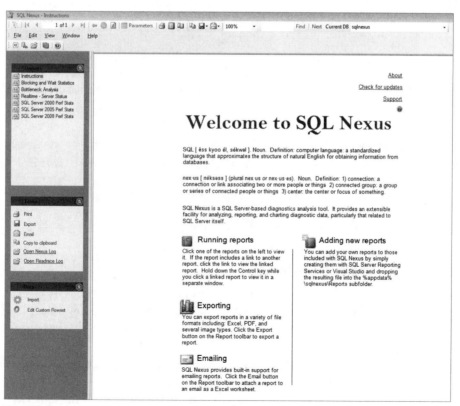

FIGURE 12-1

Figure 12-1 displays the Tasks option (on the left) which provides you with the option to import the data using the `Import` link. After clicking this option, you will be presented with the Data Import dialog shown in Figure 12-2.

There are three importers for SQL Nexus, as shown in Figure 12-3.

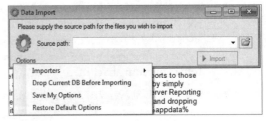

FIGURE 12-2

➤ **BLG Blaster** — This imports the PerfMon and sysmon files that you collect as part of your data collection into two tables (refer to Chapter 10 for more information about how to capture data with PerfMon):

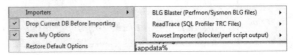

FIGURE 12-3

➤ `[dbo].[CounterData]` — Stores the performance counter data which was collected by SQLdiag or another performance monitoring tool

➤ `[dbo].[CounterDetails]` — Stores information about the counters that were configured for the data collection

➤ **ReadTrace** — This importer uses `ReadTrace.exe` to import the data from SQL Traces into the SQL Nexus database. All the imported data from the SQL Traces is available in the objects under the `ReadTrace` schema.

➤ **Rowset Importer** — This importer parses the output of the T-SQL scripts and imports them into the relevant database tables. Output from the SQL Server Perf Stats script (see Chapter 11) makes up the bulk of the data imported into the SQL Nexus database tables.

> **NOTE** *Currently, no reports are available for the Performance Monitor data that is imported into the SQL Nexus database. You can either write T-SQL queries to view and aggregate the import data or create your own custom reports for viewing the PerfMon data.*

Loading Data into a Nexus Database

Every time you launch SQL Nexus you're presented with a dialog to connect to SQL Server. The SQL Server instance to which you connect is used to store the results from processing a data collection. SQL Nexus is an "offline" analysis tool, which means it analyzes data that has already been collected.

When you connect to a SQL Server instance, SQL Nexus looks for a database called "sqlnexus." If it is found, then the Recovery Model is set to Simple to ensure that the transaction log doesn't need to be managed through transaction log backups during the data import process. If the sqlnexus database doesn't exist, then one is created with a 50MB data file.

> **NOTE** *Please refer to Chapter 11 for details about what data you need to capture for analyzing a bottleneck or troubleshooting a performance issue on your SQL Server instance.*

Once you have provided the output directory location of the data collected by SQLdiag or manually collected diagnostic data, click the Import button. This initiates the import, and the relevant importers will be called to extract, parse, and import the relevant data into the appropriate tables. A summary of each of the files processed and the importers activated is displayed in the same dialog after the import is initiated.

> **NOTE** *For security reasons, the* `*.trc` *files are created with the same Windows security permissions as the database data files. In most environments this means that you don't have read permission to the files, which will cause the import to fail. Check the permissions on all the* `*.trc` *files in the SQLDiag Output folder and assign the account running the import into the SQL Nexus database Read & Execute permissions where appropriate.*

If you run into any errors or exceptions while importing the data, you can view the SQL Nexus log file, which is located at `%temp%/sqlnexus.000.log` on the machine on which you are running SQL Nexus. This log file can be attached to the Discussion/Issue Tracker pages available on the SQL Nexus CodePlex site in case you are not able to resolve the issue. You can also browse through the existing discussions and issues listed on the site, which contains answers to the most commonly asked questions about the tool.

The BLG Blaster and the Rowset Importer are relatively straightforward in their tasks, but the ReadTrace importer warrants a special mention here. Figure 12-4 shows the different options available for the ReadTrace importer.

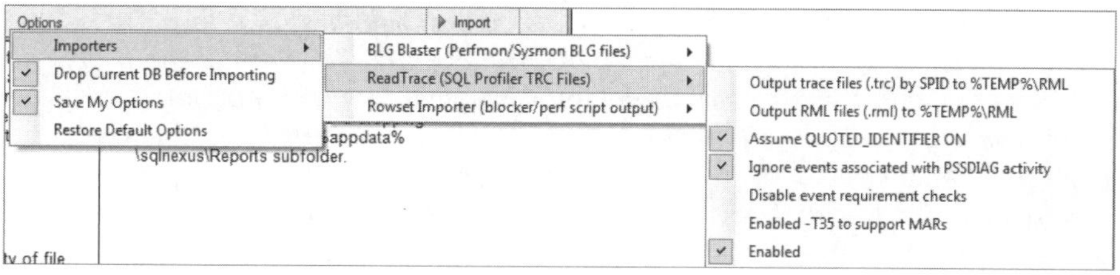

FIGURE 12-4

The following list describes each of these options:

➤ **Output trace files (.trc) by SPID to %TEMP%\RML** — This is a helpful option when you want to extract the events associated with each SPID/Session ID into individual SQL Trace files.

➤ **Output RML files (.rml) to %TEMP%\RML** — This option is useful when you want to generate Replay Markup Language (RML) files. RML is an XML-like format that is used for replay and data exchange with the OSTRESS utility (which is discussed later in the chapter). The .TRC events are broken down into sequences of RML nodes. This enables OSTRESS to replay the activity.

➤ **Assume QUOTED_IDENTIFIER ON** — RML Utilities performs normalization of the queries submitted to the database engine to generate Hash IDs for unique normalized SQL Server texts. If this option is set to OFF, then the normalization parsing is done by using QUOTED IDENTIFIER OFF semantics. The default setting is ON.

➤ **Ignore events associated with PSSDIAG activity** — This is another useful option for reducing the noise that results from capturing T-SQL queries executed by the PSSDIAG executable during the diagnostic data capture. This is accomplished using the HOSTNAME filter parameter for ReadTrace and can be further configured if ReadTrace is run separately.

➤ **Disable event requirement checks** — RML Utilities requires the capture of starting and completed events in order to create accurate aggregation data. If the necessary events are not captured, then the SQL Trace import will fail to import any data into the ReadTrace schema tables as the default behavior. This can be overridden for trace files so that they can be imported into a SQL Nexus database.

➤ **Enabled -T35 to support MARS** — Note that this trace flag is for the ReadTrace executable and is not a SQL Server instance trace flag. RML Utilities provides partial support for MARS (Multiple Active Result Sets) connections wherein a MARS session is made to appear as separate sessions. The formula used is [(Session Id * 10) + BatchId]. This enables basic performance analysis capabilities. Enabling this option also disables RML output processing. When this option is enabled, SQL Nexus calls ReadTrace with the parameters -T35 and -f.

> **WARNING** *There is a caveat when generating RML files or TRC files for individual Sesison IDs/SPIDs with SQL Nexus, as the default output location is the TEMP folder on your machine, which invariably points to your system drive. Unless you have edited the* TEMP *environment variable to point to a different location, you could quickly run out of disk space when analyzing large amounts of diagnostic data. You can overcome this, however, by using* ReadTrace.exe *separately to load the SQL Trace files into the SQL Nexus database.*

The destination for the imported data is by default a database called sqlnexus, which is created when SQL Nexus connects to a SQL Server instance. This database can store diagnostic data collected from only one instance at a time, so it is re-created each time you run an import. If you want to keep the results of previous imports, then you need to take a database backup before the next import, or you can create a new database for each import. This can be done using the drop-down box for the database, available in the top right-hand corner of the SQL Nexus UI window. If you select the New Database option, the dialog shown in Figure 12-5 appears, into which the diagnostic data can be loaded. If you try to import diagnostic data into a database that has prior SQL Nexus data,

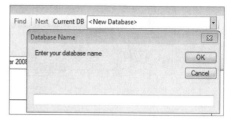

FIGURE 12-5

then you will be prompted each time to overwrite the database. You then have two options: Either overwrite the database and lose the existing imported data in the database, or choose not to overwrite and create a new database to import the data.

> **NOTE** *Creating a new database to import diagnostic data is a good practice, as it helps with comparative analysis through T-SQL queries or* `Reporter.exe`, *which is shipped with RML Utilities. You will find that the later sections of this chapter discuss the usage of this tool in detail.*

If you face an issue with SQL Nexus while importing the data, there are two places to look depending on the type of error that you encountered. If you face an issue with the Rowset Importer, which is responsible for importing the text files; or with relog.exe, which is responsible for the PerfMon data import, then you can click the Open Nexus Log option under Tasks (see Figure 12-6) to view the SQL Nexus log file. The SQL Nexus log file is located in your temp folder, which can be accessed using the `%temp%` environment variable from the Run prompt.

If you run into an issue while importing the SQL Trace files, then click the Open ReadTrace Log option (as shown in Figure 12-6), which is located in the `%temp%/RML` folder of your machine. This file is not only useful for troubleshooting import issues, but also helps you determine the parameters passed to the ReadTrace executable in case you want to run the import manually for different sets of trace files.

FIGURE 12-6

Analyzing the Aggregated Data

Now that you have loaded the diagnostic data successfully into a SQL Nexus database, this section describes how you can leverage the existing set of reports available in SQL Nexus. The welcome screen of SQL Nexus has a Reports pane on the left from which you can pick the reports you want to view. If the report doesn't contain the set of data necessary to render it, then the pop-up shown in Figure 12-7 will appear.

FIGURE 12-7

> **NOTE** *A conscious decision was made to remove the Realtime Server Status report for SQL Server 2008 instances and later. It is meant for use only with SQL Server 2005 instances.*

Three sets of reports are available:

➤ SQL Server 2000 Perf Stats

➤ SQL Server 2005 Perf Stats

➤ SQL Server 2008 Perf Stats

The SQL Server 2008 Perf Stats report works for diagnostic data collected from all SQL Server 2008 instances and later. You will see a set of reports available as shown in (see Figure 12-8) once this report has rendered successfully.

SQL Server 2008 Perf Stats Reports	
Report	**Description**
Blocking and Wait Statistics	Blocking and wait statistics
Bottleneck Analysis	Bottlneck Analysis
Query Hash	This report is for Query hash. It is only available in 2008
Spin Lock Stats	This report reports spinlock stats

FIGURE 12-8

> **NOTE** *If you captured blocking information using the* `sp_blocker_pss08` *stored procedure (see Microsoft KB 271509), then you need the SQL Server 2000 Perf Stats report to view the blocking reports, as these reports are designed to use the set of data collected by the "old" blocker script. The SQL Server 2005/2008 Perf Stats report was designed for data collection done using the SQL Perf Stats family of scripts. The Bottleneck Analysis and the Blocking and Wait Statistics reports only work if the SQL Server 2005/2008/2008 R2 Perf Stats scripts have been used to capture diagnostic data. The existing SQL Server Perf Stats script available on the CodePlex website can collect blocking and wait statistics information from SQL Server 2012 instances as well.*

Let's first consider the non-Profiler trace aggregation reports available under SQL Server 2008 Perf Stats Reports. The *Bottleneck Analysis* report provides three sets of input:

➤ SQL process vs. system CPU utilization, including other processes retrieved from the `sys.dm_os_ring_buffers` DMV

➤ Bottleneck analysis graph based on the different waits captured using the SQL 2005/2008 Perf Stats script

➤ A table summarizing the different waits by category, with an aggregated weightage of each wait category observed during the period of data collection

As shown in Figure 12-9, the first two sections of the Bottleneck Analysis report indicate no high CPU usage on the server from which the diagnostic data was collected. However, a lock-blocking issue was uncovered during the data collection period. With a single glance at the report, you can deduce a plethora of information about a system not previously inspected. This is why SQL Nexus is so widely used by SQL Server professionals: It provides quick insight into the diagnostic data collected from a SQL Server environment. Of course, you still need to draw your own correlations from the reports; the tool only acts as a medium for providing the relevant inputs needed for analysis.

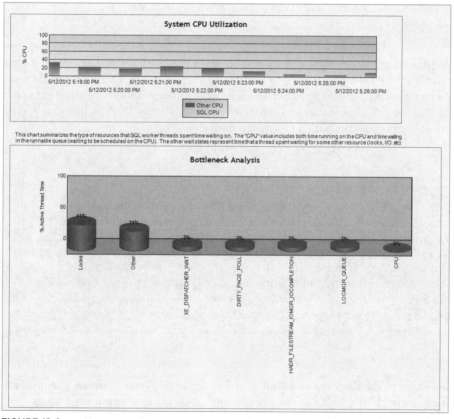

FIGURE 12-9

The second nugget of information that you will find in this report is the graphical query, which gives you an aggregated view of the different waits observed, grouped into categories. In Figure 12-10, note that 41% of the total waits observed on the SQL Server instance are attributed to locks. Therefore, based on a single report, you can determine that the SQL Server instance had a blocking bottleneck. The next step is to drill down into the data to ascertain the finer details about the blocking bottleneck.

Wait Category	Total Wait Time (ms)	% Total Wait Time (ms)	Wait Time (ms) per Sec
Locks	3286093	41%	5878
Other	2471675	31%	4416
XE_DISPATCHER_WAIT	599942	7%	1073
DIRTY_PAGE_POLL	557901	7%	998
HADR_FILESTREAM_IOMGR_IOCOMPLETION	557552	7%	997
LOGMGR_QUEUE	557812	7%	997
CPU	124	0%	0
Total	8031099	100%	14359

FIGURE 12-10

The table shown in Figure 12-10 has a drill-through option for each wait category other than CPU. Clicking any of these wait categories will take you to another report containing details about the wait category recorded from the `sys.dm_exec_requests` output captured by the SQL 2005/2008 Perf Stats script.

The Bottleneck Analysis report provides a quick way to gauge the bottlenecks that were experienced on the SQL Server instance from which the diagnostic data was collected. This report enables you to ascertain whether the bottleneck is a red herring. The drill-through option helps you get granular information about the wait category that you are interested in analyzing further. In short, you can easily identify your top bottlenecks with a few mouse clicks!

> **NOTE** *The CPU wait category is uniquely different from the other wait categories. It classifies the amount of time taken by requests utilizing the CPU and requests waiting for CPU quantum, which is the smallest unit of execution time, within the same group. Therefore, if you have a system that has a CPU bound SQL Server workload, then you might find CPU to be the top wait category even though you don't see a 100% CPU usage. This is not necessarily a problem, and you will have to perform a certain amount of due diligence before identifying queries with high CPU usage as the culprit(s).*

Shifting our focus now to the Blocking and Wait Statistics report, this report shows a snapshot of the top wait categories, along with a list of any blocking chains that were reported when when the SQL Server 2005/2008 Perf Stats were collecting data. Figure 12-11 shows an example of the report.

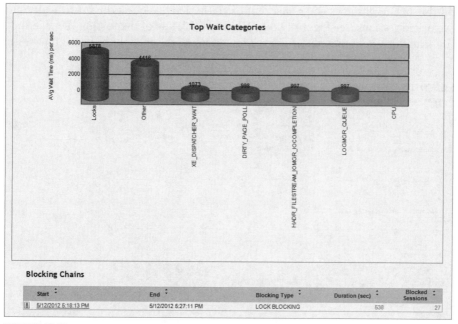

FIGURE 12-11

The list of blocking chains reported contains two additional levels of detail that provide more information about the head blocker and the blocking chain associated with the head blocker at a particular point in time (see Figure 12-12). The head blocker session information, along with the different snapshots available, is displayed in the first drill-through level. Clicking any of the runtime hyperlinks will take you to the second drill-through level, which displays the status of the different sessions active for the data collected at that time.

Blocking Chain Statistics

Head Blocker Session ID	52	Blocking Duration (sec)	538	
Blocking Start	5/12/2012 5:18:13 PM	Max Blocking Chain Size	27	
Blocking End	5/12/2012 5:27:11 PM			

Head Blocker Statistics

Program Name	Microsoft SQL Server Management Studio - Query	Transaction Type	1-Read/write
Host Name		Transaction Isolation	2-Read Committed
NT User		Transaction Name	user_transaction
Login Name		Trans Start (Duration)	5/12/2012 5:16:33 PM (627 sec)
		# Open Transactions	1

Head Blocker Runtime Summary (Session ID 52)

Runtime	Blocker Task State	Blocker Wait Category	Wait Time (ms)	Blocker Query Duration (ms)	Blocked Tasks	Blocker Command	Most Recent Head Blocker Query
2012-05-12 17:18:13.160	not running		0		1	AWAITING CMD	update dbo.tblAwesom...
2012-05-12 17:18:24.173	not running		0		1	AWAITING CMD	update dbo.tblAwesom...

FIGURE 12-12

The second drill-through level shows you a snapshot of all the active requests and their wait times, along with any blocked sessions (see Figure 12-13). You can click any of the Session ID hyperlinks to get additional information about that particular session, along with the input buffer of that session.

Detail for Session ID 52 at 5/12/2012 5:18:44 PM

Program Name	Microsoft SQL Server Management Studio - Query	Transaction Type	1-Read/write
Host Name		Transaction Isolation	2-Read Committed
NT User		Transaction Name	user_transaction
Login Name		Trans Start (Duration)	5/12/2012 5:16:33 PM (131 sec)
Last Query Start/End	5/12/2012 5:16:36 PM / 5/12/2012 5:16:36 PM	# Open Transactions	1
Wait Type			
Wait Time (ms)	0		
Resource Description			
Procedure	NULL		
Query	update dbo.tblAwesomeSauce set b = dateadd(mi,1,b)		

update dbo.tblAwesomeSauce set b = dateadd(mi,1,b)

Runtime Snapshot

Snapshot Time: 2012-05-12T17:18:44.810

Session ID	Task State	Command	Blocking Session ID	Wait Type	Wait Duration (ms)	Wait Resource	Query	Request CPU (ms)
52	NULL	NULL			0		update dbo.tblAwesomeSauc...	
53	SUSPENDED	SELECT	52	LCK_M_S	90986	KEY: 7:7205759403904 2048 (8194443284a0)	select a,b,c from dbo.tbl...	0

FIGURE 12-13

The Blocking and Wait Statistics report helps you drill down into the blocking chains observed during the data collection period. Even if you did not collect SQL Trace files, the SQL Server 2005/2008 Perf Stats script captures a sufficient amount of detail to give you an idea of who was blocking what and why. Armed with the 3Ws, you can make good progress pinpointing the head blocker in your environment.

The two reports just discussed provide information to track down most common blocking and bottleneck scenarios without having to write a single T-SQL query on the aggregated data imported into the SQL Nexus database. There are other reports available to enable additional insight into data analysis. The second report is the Query Hash report (available on clicking the SQL Server 2008 Perf Stats report), which uses the `query_hash` value introduced in SQL Server 2008 and later versions for tracking down similar queries. The data is collected by the SQL Server 2008 Perf Stats Snapshot script, which runs when the SQLDIAG collection starts and ends. This report provides insight into TOP CPU, Duration, and Logical Reads queries found on your SQL Server instance during the data collection. The information is retrieved from the `sys.dm_exec_query_stats` DMV, which stores aggregate performance statistics for cached query plans. This is an important point to keep in mind, as the problem query would not appear in this report if the query plan was not cached or had been removed from the cache. You can refer Chapter 5 to understand when plans are removed from the procedure cache.

The Spinlock Stats report aggregates all the top spins/collision counts experienced during the data collection by the SQL Perf Stats script and provides a graphical view of the top categories. This report is available on clicking the SQL Server 2005/2008 Perf Stats report (Figure 12-8). This report is not very widely used but it has proven to be very helpful when diagnosing niche performance issues which are not obvious by viewing the aggregated data in the reports discussed above.

> **NOTE** *A spinlock is a lightweight locking mechanism where access to a resource is expected to be held for a very short time. Rather than yielding the processor when the lock request is unsuccessful, a spinlock will loop and periodically check to see if access is available. You can read more about spinlocks in Chapter 7.*

Familiarizing Yourself with the RML Utilities Reports

Having looked at the available reports for the non-Profiler-related data, this section examines the reports available for the SQL Trace data that was imported into the SQL Nexus database. The SQL Trace data, as mentioned earlier in this chapter, is imported by the ReadTrace executable. There are a set of reports which are available within SQL Nexus when RML Utilities is installed under the report heading ReadTrace_Main report.

> **NOTE** *If you are unable see the ReadTrace_Main report after installing RML Utilities, then follow the second step mentioned in Issue #1 in the section "Resolving Common Issues," later in this chapter.*

The ReadTrace_Main report gives you an aggregated view of the different batches that were executed during the SQL Trace collection along with a line graph which shows the changes in duration, CPU usage, reads, and writes for all the batches that were captured in the SQL Trace files as shown in Figure 12-14.

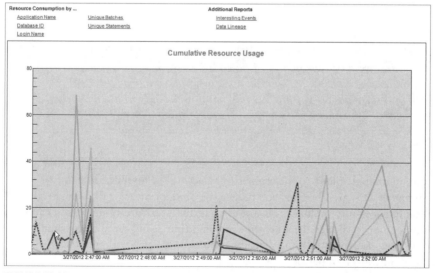

FIGURE 12-14

The second half of the report, shown in Figure 12-15, provides a table and an aggregated summary of all the data imported from the SQL Trace files. The Interval Start column has a drill-through option that displays the TOP N queries aggregated by CPU usage, duration, writes, and reads for that time interval. If you use the Unique Batches or Unique Statements hyperlinks available at the top of the ReadTrace_Main report, you can view a list of the top resource-consuming queries from the entire duration of the data collection. If you do drill through into the details of each query, you will find two options — namely, drilling down by batch and statement.

> **WARNING** *One common pitfall with RML Utilities is assuming that a batch always has statements associated with it. It is true that a batch will have one or more T-SQL statements; but if the statements do not have* SP:StmtStarting *and* SP:StmtCompleted, *then the batch will not have an entry in the* ReadTrace .tblStatements *table, which is where the Unique Statements report goes to fetch data for rendering the report.*

Show/Hide	Scale	Counter	Average	Minimum	Maximum	Total
▶	1	Batches Started	5.56	0	31	200
▶	1	Batches Completed	5.42	1	30	195
▶	1	Attentions	0.00	0	0	0
▶	0.000001	Duration (µs)	5,805,516.36	0	68,544,638	208,998,589
▶	0.01	CPU (ms)	618.00	0	4,567	22,248
▶	0.0001	Reads	10,884.81	0	155,646	391,853
▶	0.01	Writes	30.00	0	1,005	1,080

⊟ View Details

Interval Start ⇕	Interval End ⇕	Batches Started ⇕	Batches Completed ⇕	Attentions ⇕	Duration (µs) ⇕	CPU (ms) ⇕	Reads ⇕	Writes ⇕
2:45:56 AM	2:46:00 AM	5	4	0	976,113	280	165	2
2:46:00 AM	2:46:04 AM	14	15	0	549,751	170	1,234	1
2:46:08 AM	2:46:12 AM	2	2	0	175,559	40	46	2
2:46:12 AM	2:46:16 AM	2	2	0	561,792	200	310	5
2:46:20 AM	2:46:24 AM	9	6	0	130,415	20	43	0

FIGURE 12-15

> **NOTE** *The duration time reported for data collected from SQL Server 2005 instances and later is always measured in microseconds, whereas the CPU time is reported in milliseconds. Forgetting this information is likely to invoke the wrath of the developer whose query you erroneously pinpointed as the culprit!*

You also have the option to apply filters to the reports by selecting the application name or database ID or login name. This greatly helps you reduce the amount of noise that you need to sift through, enabling you to zoom into the data relevant to your analysis. Additionally, you can use the Parameters tab in the toolbar to change the start time and end time using the sliders available. This also helps in zooming into and analyzing a problem time period rather than looking at the entire duration of the data collection period.

The Interesting Events report, shown in Figure 12-16, identifies different events that occurred during the data collection that might provide some insight into your troubleshooting efforts. The report groups the events by type and then by runtime intervals, displaying a grouping of all the interesting events that were captured during the specified time interval that you are analyzing. Examples include query cancellations (Attentions), sort warnings, hash warnings and exceptions. The Parameters tab provides you with the functionality of narrowing down the time window that you are interested in.

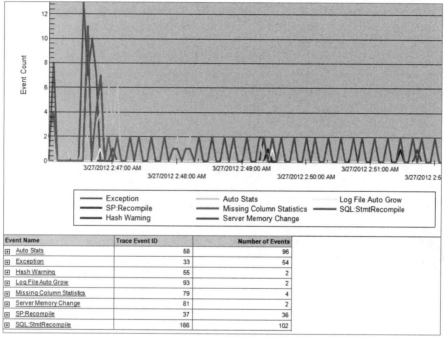

FIGURE 12-16

When you look into the reports showing information about the unique batches or unique statements, you can drill through by clicking on the batch or the query. This gives you a view of the CPU usage, duration, reads, and writes recorded for each execution within the time interval. You can also view the query plan and the query text for the batch or statement using the drill-through options.

FIGURE 12-17

All the reports discussed so far include the functionality to be exported in the formats shown in Figure 12-17 using the Export option available in the SQL Nexus UI.

If you do use the Export option, Access Control Lists (ACLs) are applied to the reports to prevent unauthorized access. The user exporting the report will be the only one who has full-access on the exported report. The user of Reporter has ultimate responsibility for propagation of the data.

Comparative Analysis Report Generated by Reporter.exe

To view the preceding reports, you can also use the Reporter executable, which is available under the `C:\Program Files\Microsoft Corporation\RMLUtils` folder, which can be launched by double-clicking the `Reporter.exe` available in the aforementioned folder. One of the really useful things that the Reporter can do for you is comparative analysis. If you have collected two sets of diagnostic data from the same SQL Server instance at different times, then you can import the SQL Trace data into two separate databases and perform an automated comparative analysis using Reporter. Once the analysis is done, it displays
a comparison chart like the one shown in Figure 12-18. The detail table at the bottom of the Comparison Overview report shows a comparison of the aggregated summary of
the queries found in both databases. The RML Utilities Help file, available after installation, has copious documentation on the reports and their usage.

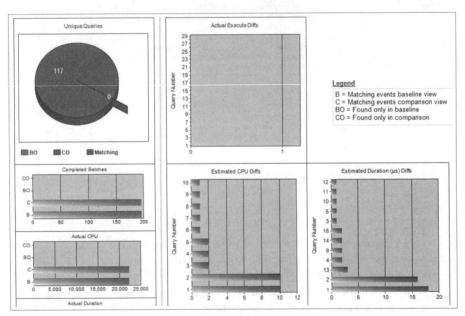

FIGURE 12-18

CUSTOMIZING SQL NEXUS

This section explains how you can add customizations to SQL Nexus and RML Utilities to help you with your analysis or *redo* tasks that you repeatedly perform during your data analysis. The following sections will help you understand the following:

➤ Importing SQL Trace files using `ReadTrace.exe`

➤ Building custom reports for SQL Nexus

➤ Running SQL Nexus using command-line options

➤ Writing your own T-SQL query to facilitate quicker data analysis

➤ Running stress tests on your SQL Server instance using `OSTRESS.EXE`

Using ReadTrace.exe

SQL Nexus provides you with the option to break down the activity of each SPID into individual `.trc` files, but they can only be directed to the `%TEMP%\RML` folder on your machine. You have two options: Change the `%TEMP%` environment path on your machine to a different drive or use the `ReadTrace.exe` to generate the `.trc` files in the required path. The first option is a bit drastic as a change in the temp environment variable will affect all applications running under the user's context. Sometimes, the free disk space of your system drive may not be sufficient to accommodate all the session specific Trace files generated by `ReadTrace.exe`. This warrants for the use of the command-line options that the executable provides. A third option, available with RML Utilities, is the capability to add SPID, Hostname, and Application filters while importing the data to reduce the size of the session specific Trace files generated by `ReadTrace.exe`. The `ReadTrace.exe` can be accessed from the RML Utilities command prompt. Some of the default values for the common parameters required for ReadTrace to import a SQL Trace file are mentioned below:

➤ `-o` — Output files to be generated in the current directory unless otherwise specified

➤ `-s` — If the `-s` parameter is not specified, the default option is to connect to the default SQL Server instance installed on the machine.

➤ `-d` — Loads SQL Trace data into a database called `PerfAnalysis` unless a database name is explicitly mentioned for this parameter value

➤ `-E` — Uses Windows authentication while connecting unless otherwise specified

One of the situations in which you might need to use ReadTrace.exe separately to import SQL Trace data into a SQL Nexus database is when you are analyzing a deadlock. When analyzing deadlocks, the deadlock graph is not sufficient to determine why a lock is still held by that session and why that session acquired the lock on the object in the first place. At that point, you need to track down the sequence of statements executed by the session. To do so, you can use the following command to import the data for the sessions involved in the deadlock. This command imports the SQL Trace data into a database called `dbRMLUtilDemo` by filtering only on activities for SPID 53 and 55:

```
readtrace -S. -E -ddbRMLUtilDemo
-I"D:\RML\RMLUtil_demo.trc" -A"!SQLCMD" -s53 -s55 -MF -o"D:\RML\output" -f
```

The preceding command also excludes events generated by queries executed through the SQLCMD utility, which is what PSSDIAG or SQLDIAG uses to execute the T-SQL queries to collect the diagnostic data. Additionally, individual trace files for each SPID/Session ID will be generated in the `D:\RML\output` folder. You can also add hostname filters using the `-H` parameter.

> **NOTE** *You can use* `Readtrace.exe /?` *from the RML Utilities command prompt to look at the parameters available or use the RML Utilities Help file to get the list of parameters.*

Building Custom Reports for SQL Nexus

Another option you have is to build custom reports for the tables available in the SQL Nexus database. The report structure itself is quite simple. It uses the Shared Data Source, `sqlnexus.rds`, so that the database context can switch when you change the database name using the drop-down menu in the SQL Nexus tool. Once you have the custom reports built, you can drop them in the following folder: `%appdata%\SQLNexus\Reports`. SQL Nexus automatically picks up these reports when it is launched. If you are familiar with designing reports for SQL Server Reporting Services, then this will be a piece of cake for you. You can build your reports using a Visual Studio Reporting Services project. When you build the report project, you need to ensure that the target server version for the project is set to "SQL Server 2008" or "SQL Server 2008 R2 or later."

Running SQL Nexus Using the Command Prompt

This option is only rarely used but it can be very powerful when automating your diagnostic data analysis. Using `sqlnexus.exe /?` from a command prompt window will return the list of command-line parameters that the tool can accept. The following command will import the diagnostic data into a `sqlnexus_cmd` database by picking up the files to be imported from the `C:\temp\sqldiag\output` folder. `/X` will cause SQL Nexus to exit after importing the diagnostic data into the database:

```
Sqlnexus.exe /S. /D"sqlnexus_cmd" /E /I"C:\temp\sqldiag\output" /X
```

Remember that the settings you saved while running SQL Nexus the last time you ran it in the GUI are used when the command-line options are specified.

Creating Your Own Tables in the SQL Nexus Database

Let's assume that you decided to collect the output of a T-SQL script that is not part of the default collectors provided by the Pssdiag and Sqldiag Manager. After the diagnostic data has been collected you need to pore through pages and pages of textual data manually, using your favorite text editor, to create a useful hypothesis about the issue that you are troubleshooting. This is another scenario in which SQL Nexus turns out to be your best friend, as it can import the data into a table, enabling you to run queries on the imported data and saving you valuable time.

The Rowset Importer is responsible for importing data from text files into a SQL Nexus database. SQL Nexus provides a way to extend this functionality to other text files containing diagnostic data through the Edit Custom Rowset option, which is available in the left hand pane of the tool's main page. Figure 12-19 shows the Manage Custom Rowset dialog that is launched when you click the Edit Custom Rowset link.

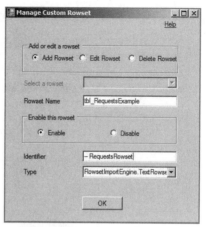

FIGURE 12-19

Here you can specify the table name (`Rowset Name`) into which the data needs to be imported (`tbl_RequestsExample` in this case) and the `identifier` for the data that needs to be imported (– `RequestsRowset` in this case). The Identifier is the most important key here, as this tells the Rowset Importer how to recognize the data that you want to import. This means that before your `SELECT` query spews out the diagnostic data into the output file, it should be preceded by a `PRINT` statement with the Identifier name that you specified while creating your custom rowset. For the example shown in Figure 12-19, the output of the diagnostic query would be preceded by the following:

```
print '—RequestsRowset'
```

If you attempt to import query outputs that have columns with a data type length greater than 8000, the import will fail with the following error in the SQL Nexus log file:

```
SQLNexus Information: 0: RowsetImportEngine Error: An unexpected error has
occurred: System.Data.SqlClient.SqlException: The size (8192) given to the
column 'query_text' exceeds the maximum allowed for any data type (8000).
```

SQL Nexus 3.0.0 doesn't give you the option to add your own column data types using the UI. The custom rowset that you define in the Manage Custom Rowset dialog treats all columns as `varchar`. To change this behavior, modify `C:\Users\<user name>\AppData\Roaming\sqlnexus\TextRowsetsCustom.xml` directly to add or modify the data types that you want.

Keep in mind the following points while using a custom rowset:

➤ If you have data that is larger than `varchar(8000)` in the result sets collected, then be sure to modify the `TextRowsetsCustom.xml` file before you import the data.

➤ Give each rowset that you collect a unique identifier. You don't want the importer to mix-and-match the data you are importing.

➤ Add a runtime column using `GETDATE()` or a variable for scripts capturing data in a loop to ensure that you can track the trend easily without having to second-guess it.

➤ All columns that are collected in the result set(s) have to be named.

➤ Avoid CR/LFs (Carriage Returns/Line Feeds) in the result set (i.e., don't use `CHAR(13)` in your T-SQL script while capturing the data, as this seriously confuses the importer because it treats CR/LFs as end-of-row indicator).

➤ Either capture the data directly into a file by running the data collection script from Management Studio or use the `sqlcmd –W` parameter if you are capturing the data using `sqlcmd`. The `–W` ensures that trailing spaces from the result sets are removed.

Writing Your Own Queries

If you still want to go that extra mile with SQL Nexus, you can write your own T-SQL queries to fetch and aggregate the data available in the SQL Nexus tables. The following query returns an aggregation of the SUM of all the CPU/Duration/Reads/Writes that completed execution during the time the SQL Trace files were captured:

```
select a.hashid,b.OrigText,
SUM(a.duration) as SumDuration,
SUM(a.Reads) as SumReads,
SUM(a.Writes) as SumWrites,
SUM(a.CPU) as SumCPU,
MAX(a.duration) as MAXDuration,
MAX(a.Reads) as MAXReads,
MAX(a.Writes) as MAXWrites,
MAX(a.CPU) as MAXCPU,
MIN(a.duration) as MINDuration,
MIN(a.Reads) as MINReads,
MIN(a.Writes) as SumWrites,
MIN(a.CPU) as MINCPU,
AVG(a.duration) as AVGDuration,
SUM(a.Reads) as AVGReads,
Sum(a.Writes) as AVGWrites,
SUM(a.CPU) as AVGCPU,
GROUPING(a.hashid) as [GroupNo]
from readtrace.tblBatches a
inner join readtrace.tblUniqueBatches b
on a.HashID = b.HashID
where EndTime is not null
group by  a.hashid,b.OrigText WITH ROLLUP
```

If you are feeling adventurous, then feel free to write queries to slice and dice the data present in the SQL Nexus tables. This not only helps you to reduce the amount of time needed to perform a repetitive task during data analysis, but also helps you become familiar with the schema of the tables. Once you are as familiar with the table schema in the SQL Nexus database as your own backyard, you will find that troubleshooting common SQL Server performance issues is not such a daunting task after all if the required data has been captured already. As they often say, knowing is half the battle!

The OSTRESS Executable

OSTRESS is a scalable, ODBC-based application that can stress or replay database commands. You can specify a query via a command-line parameter, .SQL script, or .RML file. Replay mode uses .RML files generated by ReadTrace as it processes SQL Server trace files. Tools such as SQLCMD or OSQL are not practical for a stress-testing scenario because it requires a separate process for each thread and it is difficult to control. If you don't want to write your own stress-testing code, then the OSTRESS executable shipped with RML Utilities is a great alternative! The Distributed Replay Client, which is a new SQL Server 2012 feature, can also be helpful, but if you don't have a SQL Server 2012 instance handy with Distributed Replay configured, then OSTRESS can be a very useful utility. It is a command-line-based tool that you can run as part of an automated process or a test script.

> **NOTE** *You need SQL Server Native Client 10.0 installed on your machine to use OSTRESS. This can be downloaded from the latest SQL Server 2008 Feature Pack available on the Microsoft Downloads site.*

The following code snippet applies filters for Sesison IDs 51, 52, and 53, and excludes events generated by an application named SQLDIAG or hostname MyLaptop. The output folder will contain the .RML files for SPID 51, 52, and 53, which can be used by OSTRESS for generating load.

```
readtrace -S. -E -ddbRMLUtilDemo
-I"D:\RML\RMLUtil_demo.trc" -A"!SQLCMD" -s51 -s52 -s53 -o"D:\RML\output"
-H"!MyLaptop" -A"!SQLDIAG
```

In addition to stress testing, you may want to interject random events. An example of such an event would be to introduce a timeout after a specified amount of time. OSTRESS is designed especially for this type of stress scenario. It is also useful for reproducing and stressing query cancellations (attention signals) whereby either a query time-out or cancellation has been issued by the client, as well as many other actions. The RML Utilities Help file has detailed documentation about the utility.

Things to Remember About OSTRESS

➤ OSTRESS parameters are case sensitive.

➤ Parameters must be separated with the hyphen (-) or forward slash (/) character.

➤ Parameters that contain spaces or special characters should be enclosed in quotation marks.

➤ White space is not permitted between the parameter indicator and its value.

OSTRESS gives you the unique capability to specify the number of connections and iterations for a particular query or queries present in an RML file. The following example executes SELECT @@VERSION against the default instance using 50 threads with 100 iterations each:

```
Ostress.exe -Q"Select @@VERSION" -oc:\temp\output -n50 -r100
```

> **NOTE** *Using* ostress.exe -? *from the RML Utilities command prompt will return a list of the parameters available for the OSTRESS executable. You might also want to add the location of the SQL Nexus and RML Utilities directories to your* %PATH% *environment variable so that you can use these utilities from any command prompt window, obviating the need to fully qualify their path or browse to the directory containing these EXEs.*

RESOLVING COMMON ISSUES

This section describes the most common issues that users of RML Utilities and SQL Nexus face, including the best way to resolve them.

Issue #1

While trying to import a SQL Trace file using SQL Nexus, you might get the following error in the SQL Nexus log file:

```
"The system cannot find the file specified (System)"
Program Location:
    at System.Diagnostics.Process.StartWithCreateProcess(ProcessStartInfo startInfo)
    at System.Diagnostics.Process.Start()
    at System.Diagnostics.Process.Start(ProcessStartInfo startInfo)
    at ReadTrace.ReadTraceNexusImporter.DoImport() in
C:\jacklidocs3\cprsrc\main\src\sqlnexus_pass\ReadTraceNexusImporter\
ReadTraceNexusImporter.cs:line 364
    at sqlnexus.fmImport.DoImport() in
C:\jacklidocs3\cprsrc\main\src\sqlnexus_pass\sqlnexus\fmImport.cs:line 557
```

This message could appear for either of the following reasons:

➤   Your RML Utilities version is older than the current version. If so, install the latest version of RML Utilities.

➤   Your RML Utilities location is not registered with SQL Nexus. To correct this, navigate to `C:\Program Files\Microsoft Corporation\RMLUtils` and from the command prompt execute `orca.exe /R`.

Issue #2

When you run Reporter with the default settings, you get the following error:

```
Server: (local) Error: 4060 Severity: 11 State: 1 Line: 65536 Source: .Net
SqlClient Data Provider
Cannot open database "PerfAnalysis" requested by the login. The login failed.
```

When you launch Reporter, which is part of the RML Utilities installation, the `PerfAnalysis` database is the default database to which it will attempt to connect. You need to change the name of the baseline database to the database into which you imported the SQL Trace files using SQL Nexus in order to generate reports and avoid the preceding error message.

Issue #3

If you are unable to view the Blocking and Wait Statistics report or the Bottleneck Analysis report, or you receive the error "Database doesn't have the necessary data to run this report," then the required data is not present in the SQL Nexus database tables required to render the report. This seems obvious enough from the error message, but you need to determine whether sufficient data is present to render these reports. This pop-up message was added to the utility after a large number of SQL Nexus users reported exceptions or blank reports because the required data was not present in the tables on which these reports depend.

The data for these reports is based on the data collected by the SQL Perf Stats script depending on the version of the SQL Server instance from which you are collecting data. The file that normally contains the data needed to generate the preceding reports has the following naming convention: `<ServerName>__SQL_2005_Perf_Stats_Startup.OUT` or `<ServerName>__SQL_2008_Perf_Stats_Startup.OUT`. Ensure that this file has collected at least two snapshots of the outputs of the T-SQL queries present in the SQL Server 2005/2008 PerfStats script. The check that is done to report this error confirms whether data is present in the following tables in the Nexus database:

➤ `tbl_Requests`

➤ `tbl_blocking_chains`

➤ `tbl_notableActiveQueries`

These tables are not populated if the SQL Server Perf Stats script output is not found by the SQL Nexus engine while importing the data. The lack of data in these tables results in the above error.

Another common pitfall is use of the `sp_blocker_pss08` stored procedure to collect blocking-related data from SQL Server 2005 and later instances. If you have collected blocking data using this stored procedure, then you need to use the SQL 2000 Perf Stats report to view the aggregated data, as it is imported into a different table called `tbl_sysprocesses` as the import process associated with the output of this script doesn't create the aforementioned tables.

Issue #4

When you click the UniqueStatements link in the ReadTrace_Main report in SQL Nexus, you get an exception that has the following error excerpt:

```
Must declare the scalar variable "@StartTimeInterval".
```

This error is reported in the exception message that is raised in SQL Nexus as well. The issue is not with SQL Nexus but with the RML Utilities report. You can get this issue under the following conditions:

➤ There are no entries in the `readtrace.tblStatements` and `readtrace.tblTimeIntervals` tables.

➤ You are using an older version of ReadTrace (RML Utilities).

This issue occurs when you click the UniqueStatements report link and without specifying any parameters for the Start Time and the End Time.

> **NOTE** *You can send an e-mail to* `sstlbugs@microsoft.com` *and request the latest build for RML Utilities with the ReadTrace and SQL Nexus log file as attachments.*

SUMMARY

The SQL Nexus tool can enable you to reduce the time it takes to analyze collected diagnostic data by aggregating and importing the data into a SQL Server database. The graphical reports shipped with SQL Nexus help you in drawing pertinent hypotheses for the most common SQL Server performance problems within a few minutes. The tool is widely used by SQL Server professionals to diagnose SQL Server performance issues for their customer environments.

Identifying the right set of data to be collected is always the first step of the process, a task discussed in Chapter 11. Once you have that data, analyzing it to draw the right set of conclusions to form a spot-on hypothesis is critical. SQL Nexus is just the tool to aid you in creating your hypothesis! SQL Nexus' value will become obvious when you have to sift through gigabytes of diagnostic data within a short period of time. That is when you realize that having the diagnostic data in a database table(s) with indexes built on them can be a time and life (or job) saver.

13

Diagnosing SQL Server 2012 Using Extended Events

WHAT'S IN THIS CHAPTER?

➤ Introduction to Extended Events

➤ Why you should start using Extended Events

➤ Creating Extended Events sessions in SQL Server 2012

➤ Viewing data captured by Extended Events

WROX.COM CODE DOWNLOADS FOR THIS CHAPTER

There are no code downloads for this chapter.

INTRODUCTION TO EXTENDED EVENTS

If you're familiar with recent versions of SQL Server, then it's likely you'll have heard of Extended Events, also known as XE or XEvents, and you know that it's a diagnostics feature built into the database engine. For most people, however, their knowledge of it is not much more than that. The lack of a need to use it and a challenging command set in the first release in SQL Server 2008 meant that learning to use it was often a low priority on people's "to do" list.

Fortunately, SQL Server 2012 should change that, as not only has the product's documentation made it clear that Extended Events is set to become one of SQL Server's primary diagnostic tools in future versions, but also, and perhaps more important, a graphical user interface for it is now part of SQL Server Management Studio. No longer does a complex set of T-SQL commands need to be understood before you can use the feature.

The objective of this chapter is to introduce you to the Extended Events feature in SQL Server 2012 using its new graphical user interface. After reviewing how Extended Events work and the terminology it uses, you'll see how easy it is to start capturing diagnostic information, and how to start doing things that previous generations of tools like Profiler and SQLTrace both did and didn't let you do. Finally, you'll look at how to analyze the data that Extended Events captures.

GETTING FAMILIAR WITH EXTENDED EVENTS

Before looking at Extended Events, it's worth thinking about why you might want to read this chapter. After all, if you've survived this long without using Extended Events, then you might be tempted to skip this chapter and read about something you're more familiar with. The next few paragraphs should both introduce you to the feature and demonstrate some of the reasons why reading the remainder of the chapter would be useful. Note that the purpose of this chapter is to provide a high-level overview of getting started with Extended Events, rather than an in-depth examination of its internals or advanced features, for which you can find excellent community contributions online.

Extended Events is a database engine feature that captures troubleshooting information about events you're interested in finding out more about. However, unlike previous generations of tools, it has very little overhead on the system it's monitoring, not capturing diagnostic data until an event is triggered by a very specific set of configured database engine events. This differs from tools, such as Profiler or SQLTrace for which, even with clever filters, you typically need to capture large volumes of event-related data, and then manually match your troublesome event's occurrence to other sources of data you capture around that time.

In fact, it's almost certain that if you've previously done any diagnostics work in SQL Server you'll have used the SQLTrace or Profiler tools, and it's these technologies specifically that Microsoft is aiming to replace with Extended Events (eventually).

Unlike SQLTrace or Profiler, the "sit and wait" approach of Extended Events enables you to capture only the data that's of interest to you, reducing both the volume of data that needs reviewing and the load you place on SQL Server. Of course, you can still use Extended Events to capture large amounts of data for a very broad range of events if that's what you want — in fact, its flexibility is another of its benefits.

Another benefit just briefly mentioned is that unlike previous generations of debugging tools, using Extended Events adds very little overhead to the system being monitored, both because of how it does the actual monitoring and how it then records the data it subsequently captures. Indeed, from its very inception, Extended Events was designed to be lightweight and therefore something you can use on servers with even the heaviest of workloads; that's not something you could say about previous tools like Profiler.

In addition to the more traditional use of Extended Events by DBAs and developers for trouble-shooting performance, security, and functionality issues, Windows system administrators can also hook into Extended Events as a source of debugging data about what SQL Server is doing. In fact, Extended Events are very closely related to a hardcore debugging system called Event Tracing for Windows, which will be familiar to people who debug Windows at the kernel level. Therefore, if you're in any of these categories, you'll likely find this chapter interesting and useful.

WHY YOU SHOULD BE USING EXTENDED EVENTS

While Extended Events have been around since the release of SQL Server 2008, they have not been as popular as one might expect for such a powerful troubleshooting feature. You might still be wondering then if now is a good time to begin using them. This section addresses that question by reviewing three of the primary reasons why people are now using Extended Events, along with some examples demonstrating when you might choose to use them.

SQL Server Roadmap

The first reason to consider using Extended Events now is driven by Microsoft's diagnostic tools road map for SQL Server. According to Microsoft, the tools most people currently use for troubleshooting, SQL Trace and Profiler, are slated for retirement in a future version of SQL Server. Their replacement, as you can probably guess, is Extended Events; and even SQL Server 2012 includes new functionality for Extended Events, whereas SQL Trace is starting to be left behind. Fortunately, it's very likely that whatever you do today with Profiler you can also do with Extended Events.

If after using SQL Server for many years you've built up a library of Profiler based monitoring sessions, all is not lost, as there are several migration options and aids available for you. Microsoft provides some migration mappings in some SQL Server DMVs for people who want to migrate between the Profiler and Extended Events, while boB "The Tool Man" Taylor has recently released an actual conversion tool called SQL PIE (Profiler Into Events) that will be downloadable soon from Codeplex.

Graphical Tools

The second reason to use Extended Events now is that SQL Server 2012 delivers out-of-the-box what Extended Events in SQL Server 2008 lacked, a graphical user interface (GUI). Unlike other new SQL Server features that were embedded in SQL Server Management Studio, the adoption of Extended Events was hindered by this lack of a GUI. Instead, learning a new T-SQL command set stood in the way of using them, along with the need to know how to query XML data. Although a GUI tool was written by a community member for SQL Server 2008, you had to be interested enough in Extended Events to find and then use it. Even now, you can probably begin to see why Microsoft had to deliver improvements in SQL Server 2012 if they were ever going to realistically be able to retire the SQL Trace components.

Fortunately, Microsoft did respond, and SQL Server 2012 includes a native graphical interface for Extended Events built into SQL Server Management Studio. Now it's possible to create, deploy, and monitor reasonably complex Extended Events sessions without having to use any T-SQL commands or query XML data. Of course, there are always benefits if you choose to do that, but they're no longer compulsory as they were in SQL Server 2008.

Low Impact

Finally, if the preceding two reasons aren't enough to persuade you to begin using Extended Events, then consider the nearly zero overhead that using them has on SQL Server. Extended Events is often called "lightweight" for good reasons. First, it is embedded deep within the SQL Server engine, which means it requires far less code to function compared to older tools that connect to SQL Server like a regular user does before they send event data. Second, although other tools such as Profiler may try to limit the amount of data they request, they tend to use inherently inefficient mechanisms within SQL Server that often results in capturing more data than is needed.

Instead, Extended Events take a reactive approach, only collecting and sending data to their target when a previously configured situation being monitored for occurs. If that event doesn't happen, then the SQL Server engine will not capture or store any event data. Microsoft has measured just how lightweight the events architecture that Extended Events use actually is, and determined that 20,000 events per second firing on a server with a 2 GHz Pentium CPU and 1GB of memory consumed less than 2% of the CPU's resource — and that's on a very old specification server!

Of course, it's always possible to configure anything badly and suffer undesirable consequences, including with Extended Events, so low overhead should not be an excuse to avoid planning and testing their deployment into your production environments. In fact, it's even possible to purposely configure an Extended Events session to stop SQL Server when a specific event occurs; it's that powerful! However, to do that, you would have to deliberately configure that very specific action to occur, so don't worry that you could accidentally stop SQL Server.

When You Might Use Extended Events

Having discussed some of the reasons why you might want to use Extended Events, this section considers what you might use it for. If you're already familiar with tools like Profiler and SQL Trace, then you will already be familiar with these examples based on your current monitoring:

➤ Troubleshooting blocking and deadlocking

➤ Finding long-running queries

➤ Tracking DDL operations

➤ Logging missing column statistics

After you start to explore some of the more advanced capabilities of Extended Events, you'll see it's just as easy to track events such as the following:

➤ Long-running physical I/O operations

➤ Statements that cause specific wait stats to occur

➤ SQL Server memory pressure

➤ AlwaysOn Availability Groups events

WHAT ARE EXTENDED EVENTS?

To clarify what Extended Events are, they are a feature within the SQL Server database engine that enables SQL Server to watch for and then respond to specific database engine events occurring. These events could be as simple as a user logging in or something more technical such as a long-running I/O operation. When a watched for event occurs, the Extended Event session performs an *action*, which is typically to gather additional information about what has just happened. For example, when a long I/O operation occurs, you might want to record the SQL Server statement to which the event was related. All the information collected is sent to a *target* where it's stored. This could be something as simple as a flat file, but Extended Events also provides a few advanced storage options that can process the collected data rather than just store it. Figure 13-1 provides an illustration of this basic process.

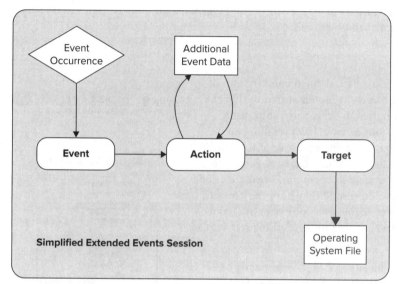

FIGURE 13-1

Where the Name Extended Events Comes From

Although the name Extended Events provides a clue as to what it's about, it is not as prescriptive as something like Resource Governor. The Extended Events feature within SQL Server takes its name partly from a high-performance troubleshooting feature in the Windows operating system called Event Tracing for Windows (ETW), a low-level debugging tool that exposes kernel-level events generated by applications or device drivers. It is normally used by developers during development and troubleshooting. Some SQL Server tuning experts use it to obtain very detailed performance data from Windows. ETW has been around since Windows Server 2000, and it introduced the Windows kernel concepts of controllers, providers, and consumers of event data, terminology that's still used today.

Rather than get very technical, it is sufficient to know that the Extended Events feature was built on the fundamental design principles of ETW, in terms of both its architectural design and its object-naming conventions. The events it refers to are simply "things that happen" within your system, such as a query being executed, a physical file being read, or a memory request being granted — similar to what you are used to seeing in Profiler, but there are more of them, covering more areas. Fortunately for us, SQL Server hides all this low-level complexity and just exposes objects and commands that we can relate to as database professionals.

Extended Events Terminology

Hopefully, by now you're beginning to understand the powerful foundations upon which Extended Events is built upon, and why and how you might use it. If not, don't worry, as you'll be looking at some examples demonstrating when and how to use this feature in the next section. Before that, however, this section reviews the terminology that Extended Events uses. Like all SQL Server features, Extended Events has its own names for objects and methods, and this section should serve as a comprehensive glossary for them.

Sessions

An Extended Events session is a user-defined combination of events, actions, filters, and targets, which is stored within the SQL Server instance, although SQL Server also ships with some of its own system sessions as well. Each session can be configured to start either manually on request or automatically when SQL Server itself starts. Once a session is started, it tells the Extended Events engine to begin monitoring for the specified events, and what to do should they happen. You can think of the Extended Events engine as a controller and coordinator within the SQL Server engine for everything related to Extended Events.

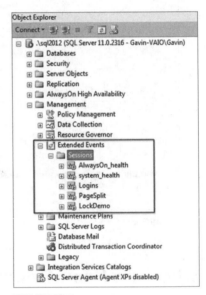

FIGURE 13-2

You can create a session using either T-SQL commands or, new in SQL Server 2012, the GUI available through SQL Server Management Studio. Using the GUI, you can create, manage, and view sessions and their captured data entirely through SQL Server Management Studio. It is this new GUI tool that we focus on using in this chapter. Figure 13-2 shows you where in SQL Server Management Studio you can find it and any sessions that may have been configured.

In this case, five sessions are currently configured, four of which are running. You can stop and start them, as well as find additional options, by right-clicking on a session, as shown in Figure 13-3.

Of the five sessions shown, note that Logins, PageSplit, and LockDemo are user-defined sessions; the other two are system-defined sessions that SQL Server uses internally to provide both itself and administrators with system information. The session AlwaysOn_health looks for expected and unexpected changes to AlwaysOn Availability Groups so they can be displayed in the AlwaysOn dashboard. The system_health session is very similar to the default trace SQL Server also has, a "black box" critical event recorder that can be used to retrospectively diagnose critical system issues.

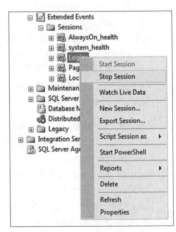

FIGURE 13-3

Sadly, the SQL Server Management Studio interface for Extended Events appears only when you connect to an instance of SQL Server 2012. Although Extended Events existed in SQL Server 2008, you need to use one of the graphical tools created by SQL Server community members in order to connect to SQL Server 2008 instances and manage the Extended Events sessions, or use the T-SQL commands.

Events

An event, like its name suggests, is something that happens within SQL Server that you're interested in finding out more about. Events are defined by specific points in the SQL Server source code; and whenever a running task reaches one, a check is performed to determine whether the Extended Events engine currently has a session watching for that event to happen. If so, then the task is suspended while the Extended Events engine performs the session's actions, something you'll learn more about in a moment.

Checking for an event and then executing the session's actions happen synchronously, meaning the user's running task is halted until the actions are completed. Fortunately, the processes that perform these steps are very fast and efficient, which is why Extended Events is often described as being lightweight. Therefore, despite being synchronous, the overhead of this feature is very small; and regular usage even on production systems is not normally associated with lower performance.

> **NOTE** *Actions are covered in more depth in a few paragraphs, but for now assume that the configured action in the example is to get the text of the SQL Server statement that caused the event to occur.*

Because the events we can monitor are written into the SQL Server source code, it's not possible for us as end users to add our own, although Microsoft contends that it can ship custom events if needed. For example, Microsoft support engineers have said they can ship Extended Events modules to an end user for monitoring very specific errors. Despite that being a well-publicized option, these extra modules are certainly not downloadable; nor are we aware of anyone actually using them.

To store the event definitions and their internal code, the Extended Events engine uses its own storage containers, called *packages*. Several of these packages ship with SQL Server 2012, far more than were included with SQL Server 2008, and Microsoft can ship others as just mentioned. If you want to know what packages are available, you can query the names from one of the many DMVs that Extended Events provides. The following query is one example:

```
select name, description from sys.dm_xe_packages
```

On the RTM release of SQL Server 2012, the preceding returns the following results:

```
name         description
package0     Default package. Contains all standard types, maps, compare
             operators, actions and targets
sqlos        Extended events for SQL Operating System
```

```
XeDkPkg      Extended events for SQLDK binary
sqlserver    Extended events for Microsoft SQL Server
SecAudit     Security Audit Events
ucs          Extended events for Unified Communications Stack
sqlclr       Extended events for SQL CLR
filestream   Extended events for SQL Server FILESTREAM and FileTable
sqlserver    Extended events for Microsoft SQL Server
```

For those of you familiar with SQL Server's other features, you'll likely have spotted a package called SecAudit and associated it with the auditing feature within SQL Server. The auditing feature uses Extended Events itself as the mechanism to capture and log SQL Server event activity requested by security administrators. However, this package has extra security protection around it, so you can't view or use any of its content yourself.

The events themselves, which you're able to monitor for using Extended Events, are also visible through a DMV. They are stored with other Extended Events data so a where clause is needed:

```
select name, description from sys.dm_xe_objects where object_type = 'event'
order by name
```

If you're familiar with Profiler or SQL Trace, then you are already familiar with some of the event names that the preceding query returns. If not, many of the event names are self-explanatory, such as sql_batch_completed, database_created and login. As you begin to browse through the long list, however, you'll begin to see some of the newer monitoring capabilities that Extended Events offers, including events such as page_compression_attempt_failed, availability_replica_state_change, and wait_info.

For those of you who want to migrate away from using Profiler, it's possible to look up the name of the Profiler events you're familiar with and find their equivalent in Extended Events through the mapping query shown here:

```
select t.trace_event_id as 'Trace Event ID', t.name as 'Trace Event Name',
       x.xe_event_name as 'XE Event Name'
from   sys.trace_events t
join   sys.trace_xe_event_map x
on     t.trace_event_id = x.trace_event_id
```

Event Fields

Once you understand what an event is, the concept of an event field is easily understood. Whereas an event is something that occurs, an event field is a piece of data about that event. For example, some of the event fields for the sql_statement_starting event are line_number, offset, offset_end, and statement, all pieces of data that could be useful in diagnosing an expensive statement. You can query the list of event fields for an event from the Extended Event DMVs, as shown in the following example query for the event fields just mentioned:

```
select  c.name, c.description
from    sys.dm_xe_object_columns c
join    sys.dm_xe_objects o on o.name= c.object_name
where   o.name = 'sql_statement_starting'
```

You probably noticed from the query results that the number of event fields for an event is relatively small, far smaller than you might expect in order to do any comprehensive troubleshooting. If the event for which you want to capture data doesn't provide the information you need in the fields associated with it, don't panic. One of the benefits of Extended Events is that when an event occurs, you can have the session capture additional data for you. This is done using actions.

Actions

As mentioned in the preceding section, when an event you've configured a session to monitor for occurs, it's unlikely that the event itself will provide all the data required to perform your trouble-shooting. The example just shown was `sql_statement_starting`, containing only the fields `line_number`, `offset`, `offset_end`, and `statement`, which by themselves probably aren't adequate to diagnose an issue. You would likely want some additional information, such as the session ID, the user name, or perhaps the query plan's handle.

Actions are the way that Extended Events provides you with the extra data you want about an event. You can think of the term action as meaning "go and get some additional data," as despite their name they rarely perform a task other than a data lookup. In fact, in SQL Server Management Studio, the Actions window is also called Global Fields, which is arguably a more accurate name for them. A few actions, however, do perform tasks other than a data lookup, such as creating a mini-dump or even halting SQL Server. These are technical tasks aimed at hardcore debugging; you won't find an action with a name like "Execute stored procedure" in Extended Events.

There are 48 actions, or global fields, that ship with SQL Server 2012; and like the events them-selves, they are defined in the SQL Server source code so it's not possible to add your own. You can query which are available through a provided DMV:

```
SELECT name, description  FROM sys.dm_xe_objects WHERE object_type =
'action' and capabilities_desc is null ORDER BY name
```

The results returned by the query provide the names and descriptions of the extra fields that a session can be configured to collect. As you'll see later, though, they are all listed in the SSMS interface along with all the other session options, so there's no need to remember the contents of any DMVs.

How this captured data is handled once it is collected is one of the main differences between Extended Events and other troubleshooting technologies — and a main benefit. Once an action has captured the extra data it needs, writing it to a logging destination — for example, a flat file — can be done asynchronously. When this is configured, the event's data is written to internal buffers; and the SQL Server task that caused the event can then continue. The overhead of actually writing the data to disk is offloaded to an asynchronous task, so it doesn't affect the performance of the user's query. This is one of the many reasons why this feature can be used on busy production systems. Of course, as always, there are caveats to that; and you'll look at those in the discussion of targets later in the chapter.

Filters

Filters are also known as predicates in the context of Extended Events, and both terms accurately describe their purpose, as they act like a `where` clause when a session is defined such that only events that meet certain criteria have their actions performed. For example, you may only want data to be collected when an event happens in the context of a specific database or when a specific user executed the query that caused the event. Although these may seem like reasonably high-level conditions on which to filter, you would be correct to assume that with Extended Events they can be a lot more technical, as you'll see in a moment.

Filters can delve deep into a database's internal objects, as well as a SQL Server instance's and query's runtime properties. For that reason, the most common filters you'll likely start using are for a query's runtime duration, the lock mode taken, or the object ID affected by the event. Defined filters must always evaluate as a Boolean expression; meaning you should focus on using the usual =, >, <, and <> operators.

Following are some examples of filters you might define for your sessions:

➤ For events in all user databases:

```
sqlserver.database_id > 4
```

➤ For events in all user databases not performed by a system task:

```
sqlserver.database_id > 4
and sqlserver.is_system = 0
```

➤ For queries taking longer than 10 seconds:

```
duration > 10000
```

The complete list of available filters, or *predicate sources*, as you'll see them referred to, is available by querying a DMV as shown here:

```
select name, description from sys.dm_xe_objects where object_type = 'pred_source'
```

If you're beginning to use Extended Events instead of Profiler, these filters are the ones you are likely to initially want to use; however, some filters contain internal logic that wasn't available in Profiler. For example, you can set a session to count how many times an event it monitors for occurs, and only perform an action every *n* occurrences of the event. This might be useful for something that happens so often that it's not practical to log every occurrence, but you still want to monitor it.

Finally, the way in which filters are evaluated is also more efficient than what you might be used to with other tools, as the objective is always to limit the overhead of using Extended Events as much as possible. Although filters are evaluated each time their associated events occur, they don't have to add significant overhead to the user's query execution time if they're written optimally. Extended Events use a method known as *short circuiting* to evaluate a session's filters. This means each part of the filter's definition is put in an ordered list, and each item in the list is evaluated only if the previous item evaluated to true. Therefore, if the most selective items in the filter are defined first, most of the filter may never need to be evaluated until necessary. This is very different from traditional SQL Server select queries, for which each part of the where clause is evaluated and included in the query plan before execution, regardless of the value it might actually bring to the query.

Targets

A *target* is the destination for all the information you can capture with Extended Events. However, whereas the terminology used so far has been fairly straightforward, now you start to see some terms that are less self-explanatory. In fact, it may be these terms you've seen in the past that made you think twice about using the feature. Fortunately, the SSMS interface hides some of the complexity from us.

Event Files

Event files, like their name suggests, are flat files that reside on an operating system drive and to which event data is written. They remain there until you delete them manually. The event files themselves have a default file extension of .xel and store data in a binary format that isn't human-readable without a tool such as SQL Server Management Studio. Fortunately, SSMS can open these files even if they were captured on another server. It can also export the data to a database table or a CSV file, making the data more portable if needed.

When an Extended Events session is configured to use an event file as a target, the event data is first written by the Extended Events engine to memory buffers before a second process writes it from memory to disk. This separation of processes is an important difference between Extended Events and other troubleshooting tools, as it prevents the physical writing of the data to disk from affecting performance for end users under normal circumstances. This behavior explains why event files are considered asynchronous targets.

Because Extended Events has been designed for use on servers with even the heaviest of workloads, there are several options you can configure regarding how the data is buffered and what should occur when the buffer is overwhelmed. The next three settings reviewed, memory buffer size, event retention, and maximum dispatch latency, apply to most of the targets Extended Events sessions can use, but it is useful to consider them now that you understand the potential problems a session with a full memory buffer and an event file target could have.

It's worth mentioning that the path and filename you specify when you create a session must exist otherwise the session won't start. It's often useful to create your own directory for Extended Events files, and then make sure SQL Server can read and write to it.

Memory Buffer Size

The size of the memory buffer is a configurable session option that can ultimately determine how much of a performance impact an Extended Events session has on your server, and potentially how much event data you might lose in busy conditions. For a small server with a small workload, the default maximum buffer size of 4MB is probably sufficient; but on a much busier server, you might be writing more event data to the memory buffer than your target can subsequently flush to its storage during peak periods.

As a hypothetical example, if your Extended Events session is capturing event data at the rate of 200MB/sec, but your server can only write 100MB/sec to disk, you're very quickly going to either need a lot of memory to store events before they're flushed to disk or begin discarding data from the buffer. The buffer is a First in, First out (FIFO) list, so if unflushed events need to be deleted to make room for newer events, then the oldest ones will be removed first.

That example should explain why you might choose to configure your session to use more memory, based upon your preference for what should happen if the buffer ever fills up, and therefore, how much event data you're willing to lose in order to maintain system performance for users. Exactly what events are dropped is determined by the Event Retention option.

Event Retention

What should happen if the memory buffer ever fills up is also a configurable session option, known as Event Retention. Three options determine how SQL Server should respond when the memory buffer is full and a session tries to write event data to it:

➤ `no event loss` — This option is the strictest of the possible settings and is not recommended for production environments. This setting means if the memory buffer ever fills up, end user queries must wait until there is free space in the memory buffer for their event data to be written to before they are allowed to continue. It's very similar to how SQL Trace works in that event data is never lost, but the consequences of guaranteeing that complete set of event data on a busy system can be disastrous.

➤ `single event loss` — This is the default when you create an Extended Events session. It instructs SQL Server that losing individual events is acceptable if it means the end user's query performance won't be affected like it would be with the `no event loss` option. Because the memory buffer is a FIFO list, the oldest event in the buffer is deleted to make room for the latest system activity. Although events are removed one at a time, if the Extended Events engine needs to write 500 new events to the buffer, it may have to delete the 500 oldest events first. While this sounds like a good compromise, it won't protect you from having an undersized memory buffer on a busy system, as ultimately the amount of data you lose will render your captured data worthless.

➤ `multiple event loss` — This tells SQL Server to favor protecting query performance at the expense of capturing event data on a massive scale. If the memory buffer is overwhelmed by incoming events, it can decide to completely empty the buffer rather than delete events one by one to maintain query performance. While this might mean you lose your event data, it's a good fail-safe option to have in place if you ever deploy a session on a busy server for the first time and not know what its event generation rate is likely to be.

Maximum Dispatch Latency

Now that you've seen how crucial it is to have adequate space in the memory buffer used by the Extended Events engine, you can understand why there are various options that determine what should happen if it fills up. Of course, the best solution is to ensure that it never fills up. There are two options for this: setting a very large memory buffer size or configuring the maximum dispatch latency.

If an asynchronous target is being used, it's possible that events aren't transferred from the memory buffer to the target until either the session stops and flushes the buffer, or there is memory buffer pressure that forces a flush. This shouldn't usually be a problem, but you might think it's good to keep as much free space in the memory buffer as possible in case of sudden system activity that generates a lot of event data.

This is where you can use the Maximum Dispatch Latency setting to specify the maximum amount of time event data can stay in the memory buffer before it is flushed to the target. The default is 30 seconds, which for a session with a properly sized memory buffer should be more than adequate; there's no need to change any of the default settings unless necessary. However, if you want to be cautious you can lower the maximum dispatch latency value; the minimum accepted value is 1 second.

Ring Buffer

Having looked at some of the options for sessions, we return now to some of the other targets that SQL Server allows a session to use. The ring buffer behaves much like the event file target in that it's an asynchronous target for events to be written to, and it stores them in a FIFO list. A big difference, however, is that SQL Server Management Studio doesn't provide a way to translate its XML contents into human-readable data like it does for the event file. Instead, a T-SQL query needs to be used to extract the fields you want out of the ring buffer; and while this is relatively straightforward (and demonstrated later in the chapter), it's a step back from the simplicity that the graphical user interface provides to newcomers of the feature.

Another difference of the ring buffer is that it doesn't use any physical storage — it's purely an in-memory structure, much like the memory buffer itself. Obviously, this means that data in it is lost not only when the ring buffer fills up and space has to be made for new events, but also whenever SQL Server itself is stopped. This doesn't make it suitable for reactive monitoring of historic system issues; but because you can have a target with a very low write latency that doesn't need housekeeping afterward, it is suitable for either high-level real-time monitoring of production systems or low-level controlled testing on development systems.

The ring buffer has two size parameters you can configure: either the total amount of memory it will use, or the amount of memory per event it will use. Until you understand more about how you can use the ring buffer, the default settings are more than adequate.

Event Counter

The event counter is one of three targets that don't store any of the event data sent to them but instead perform a task with it. The event counter target does what its name suggests; it counts the number of times the event occurs. Unlike some other targets, however, it doesn't require any event data or actions to be sent to it; the fact that the event has occurred is all it requires to increment the counter value it's maintaining. In order to provide an accurate event count, access to update it is serialized, so it has to be used as a synchronous target. This shouldn't cause you any performance issues though, as it's a very lightweight target that requires very little data to be sent to it.

Event counters, like the ring buffer, are in-memory structures. Therefore, their content is never written to an event file and is lost when SQL Server shuts down.

Histogram

The histogram could well be the most useful target in your early, and perhaps later, stages of troubleshooting — if only to begin identifying trends in your data that enable you to focus on a particular type of event's details.

For example, the `wait_stat` event reports every type of wait stat as they occur, but you'll probably want to know which types of wait stats occur the most often. If you were to use the event counter target, that would just tell you the total number of wait stats that have occurred so far, whereas the histogram will tell you how often each type of wait stat has occurred.

At this point, however, you begin to see where the user-friendly and quick-to-deploy side of Extended Events is countered by the programmatic T-SQL and XML-heavy side of the feature. When the histogram reports aggregated data about event activity, it uses internal identifiers rather than the friendly names we're used to in its results, as shown in Figure 13-4.

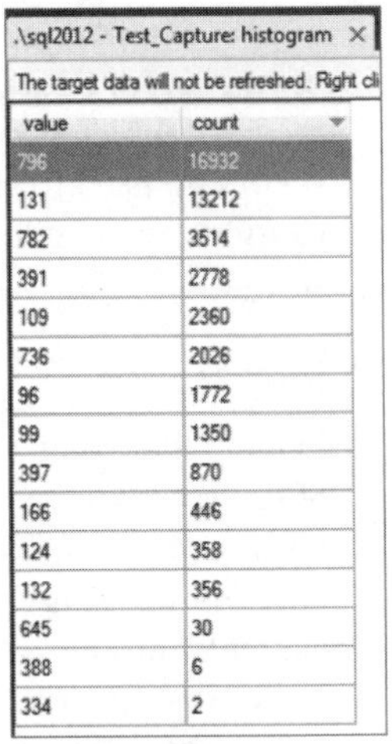
.\sql2012 - Test_Capture: histogram ×
The target data will not be refreshed. Right cli

value	count
796	16932
131	13212
782	3514
391	2778
109	2360
736	2026
96	1772
99	1350
397	870
166	446
124	358
132	356
645	30
388	6
334	2

FIGURE 13-4

This indicates that wait stats 796 and 131 are occurring the most often, but a DMV lookup is needed to know what they are:

```
select map_key, map_value from sys.dm_xe_map_values where name =
'wait_types' order by map_key
```

In this instance, you can manually look up the wait types and see they were `DIRTY_PAGE_POLL` and `LOGMGR_QUEUE`. Ultimately, you would want to query the histogram using T-SQL so you can map the values to the corresponding collected results.

Histograms are clearly useful when you're capturing data about "busy" events and need to know more about the data they're returning, but if you want to use SSMS exclusively you'll have to become familiar with some of the internal names Extended Events uses. Again, like event counters, histograms are in-memory structures, so their content is never written to an event file. Therefore, it is lost when SQL Server shuts down.

Pair Matching

The pair matching target is another event data-handling, rather than storage, target that enables you to discard two sets of related event data from your results. The example that's always used to demonstrate how this works is the data captured for the lock acquired and lock released events. If a lock is acquired but then subsequently released you're probably not interested in storing information about that having happened, and the pair matching target will discard both of those events. What you're more likely to be interested in are locks being acquired but not released by the same statement. If so, then using this target is appropriate.

Event Tracing for Windows (ETW)

This is the last target that Extended Events in SQL Server 2012 has and it is at the very hardcore end of the feature's capabilities. Using the ETW target enables SQL Server to integrate its event data with external Windows debugging software so that a complete picture of a system's performance can be captured. It's not something a SQL Server professional would typically do, but for those of you interested in the technology there are some excellent articles about it on the MSDN website.

CREATING EXTENDED EVENTS SESSIONS IN SQL SERVER 2012

By now you should have a good understanding of Extended Events terminology, how it works, and its features. Space doesn't permit covering every internal detail, capability, or feature, but you should be able to start deploying your own sessions through SQL Server Management Studio based on the examples shown here.

This section uses the new capabilities of SQL Server 2012's Management Studio to create Extended Events sessions. If you're interested in using the T-SQL commands, you'll also see how the SSMS interface can help you get started using the T-SQL commands.

Introduction to the New Session Form

SQL Server Management Studio provides two ways to create a new session: a New Session Wizard and a New Session creation form, as shown in Figure 13-5.

While the wizard option may appeal to newcomers as an easy way to get started, it's a little too lightweight in terms of functionality to be of great use, and using the more thorough New Session creation form, shown in Figure 13-6, isn't much more complicated. We recommend ignoring the wizard when you begin creating your own sessions.

FIGURE 13-5

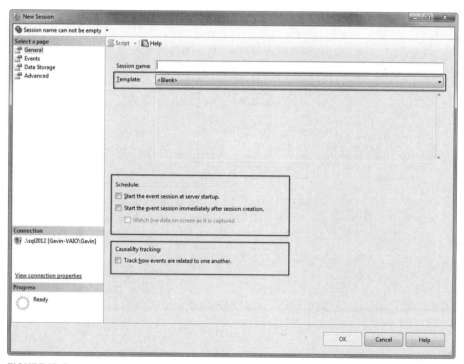

FIGURE 13-6

In addition to naming your session, such as `Deadlock_Detection`, it has the following three options (highlighted with boxes in the figure):

➤ Templates are pre-configured sessions — that is, almost ready-to-use sessions that you can deploy for common and generic situations. After selecting a template, you can configure some of the options specific to your environment, such as the event file target paths.

➤ The schedule options are self-explanatory. You can define them when you create the session or come back and configure them later.

➤ Causality Tracking is an option you might select in more complicated sessions for which you want to be able to correlate multiple events that were executed by multiple running tasks. This would rarely be required for the types of sessions you'll be creating here, so it can be ignored for now.

The Events pane, shown in Figure 13-7, is where you configure the events for which you want your session to collect data, for example, `lock_deadlock`. It is best explored using the scrollbar shown in the boxed area, although you can perform text searches as well. When you have found the events you want, you can add and remove them with the arrow buttons.

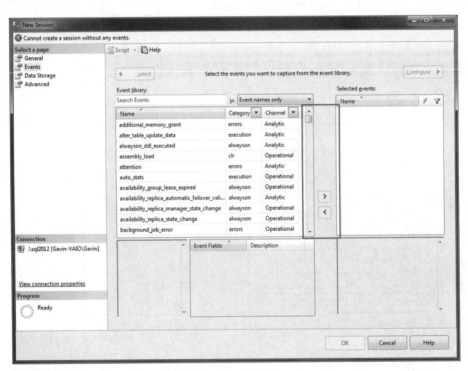

FIGURE 13-7

Once events have been added, as shown in Figure 13-8, the second half of the Events pane becomes active and you're able to click the Configure button. This reveals several tabs where additional session options can be selected, as shown in Figure 13-9. Actions, also known as global fields, can be chosen; and filters, also known as predicates, can be defined, after which you can select any optional fields that the event makes available for collection.

FIGURE 13-8

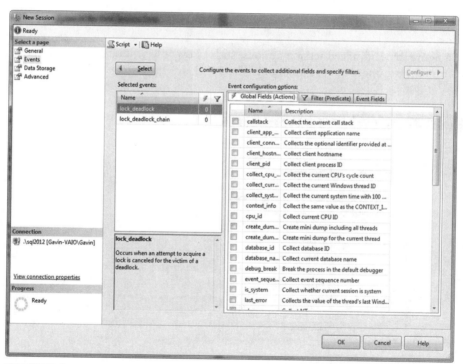

FIGURE 13-9

The form's Data Storage page, shown in Figure 13-10 with the drop-down list of available targets expanded, is where the session's targets are defined. A session can have multiple targets — for example, an event file and an event counter — and here is where you configure them. As you'll see later, the histogram targets have their own additional configuration options that become available when you add either of them.

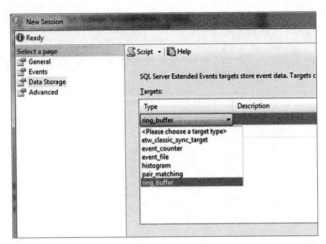

FIGURE 13-10

Finally, you can figure some advanced session options, such as Event Retention Mode and Max Memory Size, from the Advanced pane, shown in Figure 13-11.

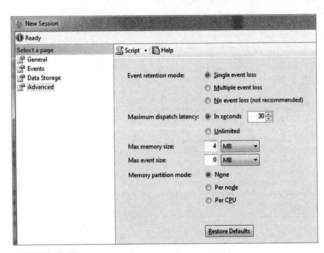

FIGURE 13-11

Monitoring Server Logins

Having looked at the session configuration interface, now you'll use it to deploy a session to capture perhaps the simplest event data SQL Server can generate, login information.

The important options for this session are highlighted with boxes in Figure 13-12. As you can see from the figure, we are configuring the `login` event to capture data from the `client_app_name` and `client_hostname` fields; not shown but selected as well is the `nt_username` global field.

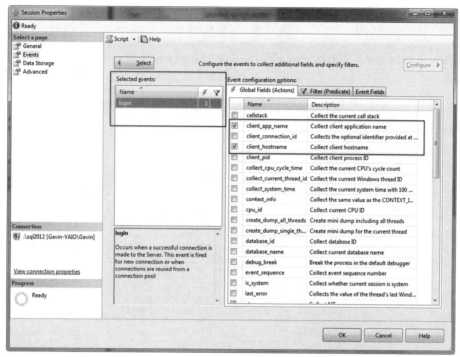

FIGURE 13-12

Once the session has been created, you may need to start it manually if you didn't set it to auto-start. To do so, right-click on the session and select Start Session.

After ensuring that the session is running, that's all you need to do to begin capturing the login information to whichever target you configured. An example of the data captured to an event file target and displayed in SSMS is shown in Figure 13-13.

Details on how to view the data captured in all these examples is described in the section "Viewing Data Captured by Extended Events," later in the chapter.

FIGURE 13-13

Monitoring for Page Splits with Extended Events

After seeing the login example in action you may be thinking that you have yet to see Extended Events do anything you couldn't do just as easily with a tool like Profiler. As you'll see in the next example, it's just as easy to capture information that has not been so easy to access previously. This example forces a clustered index to perform several page splits, demonstrating how you can use Extended Events to monitor both the page splits that are happening and which SQL Server statements caused them.

As with the previous example, Figure 13-14 shows the session configuration relevant to capturing the page split events; how you configure the rest of the session and its event file target is not so important. Also added, but not shown, is the `database_name` field; if you don't add this you'll just get the `database_id`, which may still be enough information for your troubleshooting.

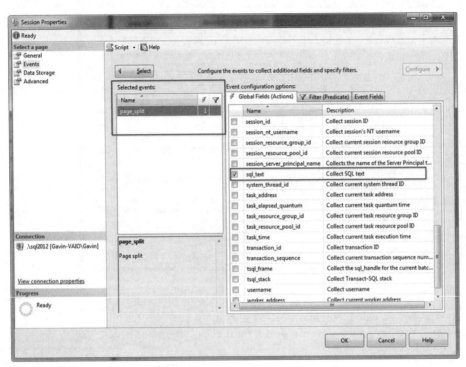

FIGURE 13-14

After creating and starting the session, it's time to force some page split activity for it to capture. The following script will set up a simple database and table before allowing you to cause page splits on demand with an `insert` statement:

```
create database PSDemo
go
use PSDemo
go

create table t1 (ID uniqueidentifier default newid(),
val1 char(8000), val2 char(37))
go
create clustered index idx_t1 on t1(ID)
go
```

```
insert t1 (val1, val2) values ('X','Y')
go

-- Repeat this insert statement as often as you want to cause splits
insert t1 (val1, val2) (select val1, val2 from t1)
go
```

After executing the script you'll be able to see just how frequently page splits occur as a database begins to be populated, especially with a table design that was chosen to exaggerate the frequency of page splits. An example of one of the page split events captured is shown in Figure 13-15.

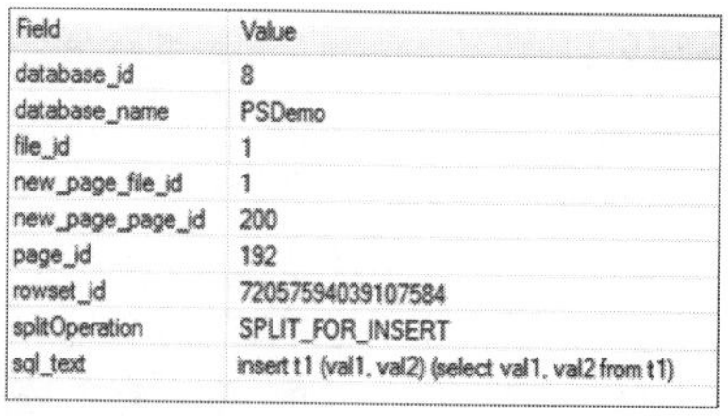

Field	Value
database_id	8
database_name	PSDemo
file_id	1
new_page_file_id	1
new_page_page_id	200
page_id	192
rowset_id	72057594039107584
splitOperation	SPLIT_FOR_INSERT
sql_text	insert t1 (val1, val2) (select val1, val2 from t1)

FIGURE 13-15

Counting the Number of Locks Acquired per Object

The final example you'll implement uses the histogram target to aggregate the number of locks acquired for objects in a user database as queries are executed. You might want to do this to help find locking hot spots in a database, but we're using it here because it's an easy way to demonstrate how the histogram target, and in this example the event filters, work.

The `lock_acquired` event provides all the information needed for this example, so you don't need to use any global actions or additional event fields. Instead, because SQL Server itself has a lot of background locking activity from system processes occurring, you'll use a filter to exclude the locking activity you're not interested in. The configuration for this is shown in Figure 13-16.

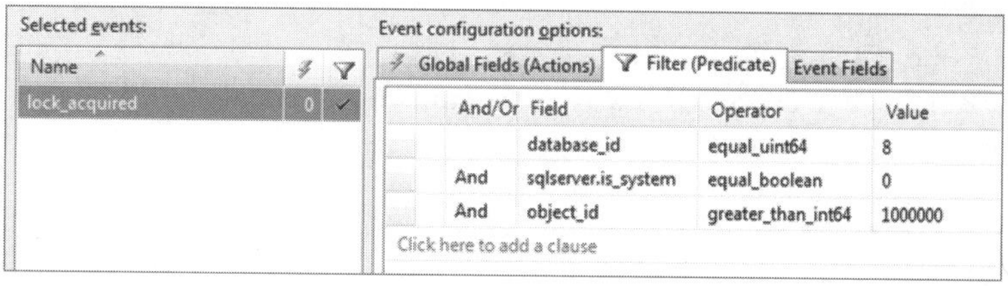

Selected events:				Event configuration options:			
Name		⚡	▽	⚡ Global Fields (Actions)	▽ Filter (Predicate)	Event Fields	
lock_acquired	0	✓		And/Or	Field	Operator	Value
					database_id	equal_uint64	8
				And	sqlserver.is_system	equal_boolean	0
				And	object_id	greater_than_int64	1000000
				Click here to add a clause			

FIGURE 13-16

If you are wondering where the filter values came from, the answer is a combination of known requirements and trial and error. One of the benefits of deploying an Extended Events session is that it's easy to stop the session, reconfigure it, and restart it if it's capturing too many or too few events (see the `object_id` filter setting shown in the screenshot). The `database_id` field was populated by executing the query `select db_id('PSDemo')`.

With the filter configured, next you add the histogram target (see Figure 13-17). This requires configuring some properties but you can use values selected from drop-down lists. You can think of the "Base buckets on" option as being like the columns in a `group by` clause of a `select` statement.

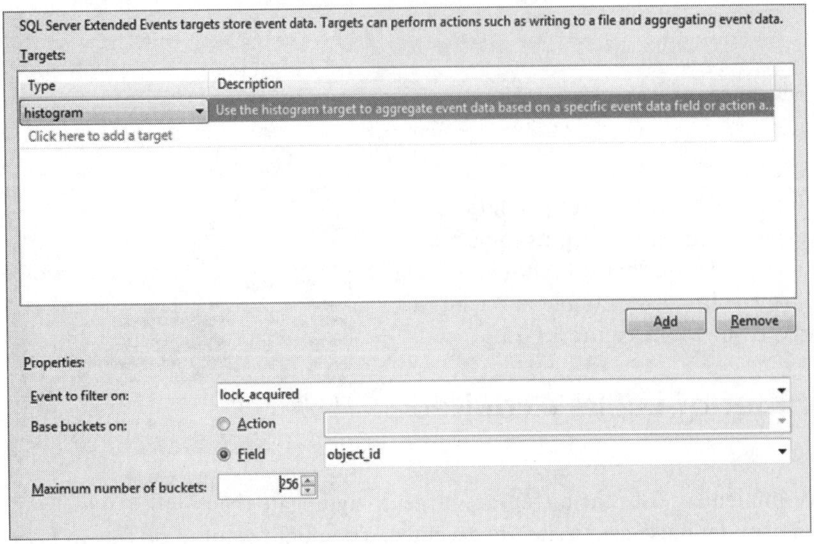

FIGURE 13-17

With the session running, you can then execute the `insert` statement from the previous example to cause locks to be acquired in your sample database:

```
insert t1 (val1, val2) (select val1, val2 from t1)
```

This produces data in the histogram that looks something like what is shown in Figure 13-18.

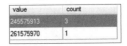

If you are wondering what the object IDs refer to in the example database, 245575913 was the actual table `t1`, while 261575970 was the default constraint that was bound to the `ID` column of table `t1`.

FIGURE 13-18

Creating Sessions Using T-SQL

It has been mentioned throughout this chapter that Extended Events has a very comprehensive set of T-SQL commands, which have deliberately not been covered in depth here. Unfortunately, their complexity has been one of the main reasons why people have not yet begun to use them, which is why this material has focused on using the SSMS interface.

However, if you want to start using the T-SQL Extended Events commands, the SSMS interface can help you get started by scripting out a session after you define it. You can do this using the Script button, which you are probably familiar with from other parts of SSMS; however, it's shown in Figure 13-19.

FIGURE 13-19

For example, a session that captures all the logout events is shown here as a T-SQL create script:

```
CREATE EVENT SESSION [LogoutEvents] ON SERVER
ADD EVENT sqlserver.logout(ACTION(sqlserver.client_app_name,
sqlserver.client_hostname,sqlserver.nt_username))
ADD TARGET package0.event_file(SET filename=N'C:\XELogs\LogoutEvents.xel')
WITH (STARTUP_STATE=ON)
GO
```

For most people reading this book, the T-SQL script will be easy to follow, and you could probably now write your own to create other sessions relatively easily. However, the strength of SSMS is that you can use it to help you learn how to write more complex scripts without getting the basics wrong. There's nothing worse than trying to get a more advanced feature to work when you've made an error with the simple parts you thought you knew well!

VIEWING DATA CAPTURED BY EXTENDED EVENTS

This section looks at how to view the data captured by Extended Events sessions. As you've seen previously in this chapter, several different types of targets can be used; and when using SQL Server Management Studio, there are different ways to view their content.

The most likely way you'll view captured data to begin with is as it happens. Viewing live data from some session targets is natively supported in SQL Server Management Studio, meaning you can watch event data being collected as it happens — just as you can in Profiler, for example.

However, once the session has stopped you might want to review the data long after it was captured, or on a totally different server or PC. SQL Server Management Studio also supports this by opening event files for viewing, in much the same way that Word opens a document file.

Finally, there are some targets, such as the ring buffer, that SQL Server Management Studio doesn't easily handle; instead, it shows the raw XML data that it holds. To extract data from this target, T-SQL queries are needed, although the same queries can also be used to query event files, so you'll be able to reuse your queries once they are written. The remainder of this chapter explains how you view the data stored in the following types of Extended Event target:

➤ Event files

➤ Memory structures, such as the event counter and histogram

➤ XML-based ring buffer

Viewing Event File Data

Using an event file as your session's target is a good choice, as it is the best choice of target given its flexibility when it comes to viewing the captured data in it. Using SQL Server Management Studio, you can view their contents both in real time as the data is being captured and as a standalone data file after the session has stopped.

Viewing Live Data

This example uses the session created earlier, which captures login events after ensuring it's started. After right-clicking on the session in SQL Server Management Studio, click the Watch Live Data option, as shown in Figure 13-20.

This opens a new tab in SQL Server Management Studio that says "Retrieving event information from server. . ." and then you will begin seeing events as they are captured. Connecting to the instance from another PC caused the events shown in Figure 13-21.

FIGURE 13-20

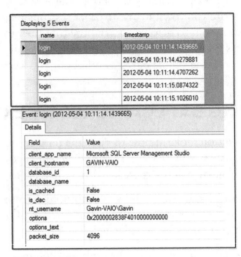

FIGURE 13-21

The output screen is divided into two parts, which are identified with boxes in the screenshot. The top box displays a list of all the events that have been captured — in this example, several login events. The bottom box shows the event and global fields captured for the event selected in the top box.

However, more information can be displayed in the top box if you'd rather see more fields when events are being captured. You can customize the view by right-clicking on the column bar at the top of the events and selecting Choose Columns (see Figure 13-22). The Choose Columns dialog will then appear (see Figure 13-23).

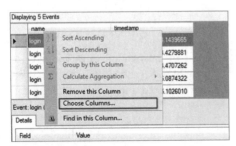

FIGURE 13-22

FIGURE 13-23

This will reconfigure the live data view to look something like what is shown in Figure 13-24.

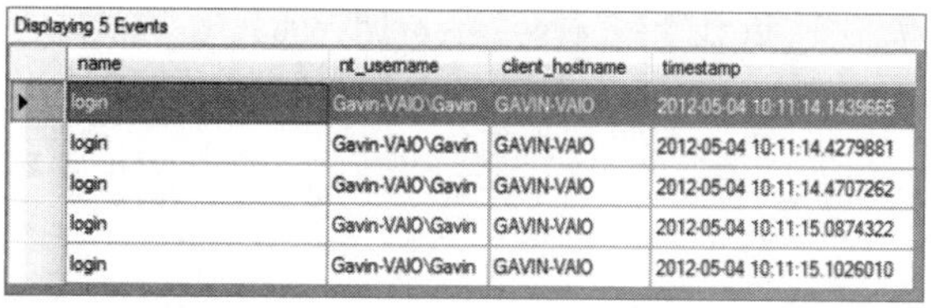

Displaying 5 Events

name	nt_username	client_hostname	timestamp
login	Gavin-VAIO\Gavin	GAVIN-VAIO	2012-05-04 10:11:14.1439665
login	Gavin-VAIO\Gavin	GAVIN-VAIO	2012-05-04 10:11:14.4279881
login	Gavin-VAIO\Gavin	GAVIN-VAIO	2012-05-04 10:11:14.4707262
login	Gavin-VAIO\Gavin	GAVIN-VAIO	2012-05-04 10:11:15.0874322
login	Gavin-VAIO\Gavin	GAVIN-VAIO	2012-05-04 10:11:15.1026010

FIGURE 13-24

Viewing Saved Data

If you've configured your session to use an event file as its target, then the captured events will also be written to disk. You can read the event file's content from disk while the session is still running, or after the session has been stopped, you might copy it from the server to your laptop.

To open the file, select File ➪ Open ➪ File within SQL Server Management Studio, from where you can then browse to wherever you keep your event files. By default, they are in the following path:

```
C:\Program Files\Microsoft SQL Server\MSSQL11.x\MSSQL\Log
```

and have a default file extension of `.xel`. Opening one of these files presents you with the same data you saw when live data was being shown.

Event files can also be queried using T-SQL. Like SQL Trace, the function `sys.fn_xe_file_target_read_file` reads an operating system file and returns it as XML-based table data. Writing queries to handle XML is something you'll become good at if you want to perform a lot of analysis on Extended Events data; but for now, the following query shows an example of how you can read the event file to see the login events you captured:

```
select event_data.value('(event/@timestamp)[1]', 'datetime2') as
[Event_Time_UTC],
            event_data.value('(event/action[@name="nt_username"]/value)[1]',
'varchar(100)') as [NT_Username],
            event_data.value('(event/action[@name="client_hostname"]/value)[1]',
'varchar(100)') as [Client_Hostname],
            event_data.value('(event/action[@name="client_app_name"]/value)[1]',
'varchar(100)') as [Client_Appname]

from (select cast(event_data as xml)
                from sys.fn_xe_file_target_read_file('C:\Program
                Files\Microsoft SQL Server\MSSQL11.SQL2012\MSSQL\Log\
                Logins_0_129805987593580000.xel', null, null, null)
                ) as results(event_data)
order by [Event_Time_UTC]
```

The preceding returns the following results:

```
Event_Time_UTC              NT_Username      Client_Hostname  Client_Appname
--------------------------- ---------------- ---------------  -------------------
2012-05-04 09:55:06.6850000 Gavin-VAIO\Gavin GAVIN-VAIO       Microsoft SQL
                                                              Server Management
                                                              Studio
2012-05-04 09:55:06.7000000 Gavin-VAIO\Gavin GAVIN-VAIO       Microsoft SQL
                                                              Server Management
                                                              Studio
```

```
2012-05-04 09:55:06.7100000 Gavin-VAIO\Gavin   GAVIN-VAIO          Microsoft SQL
                                                                   Server Management
                                                                   Studio

2012-05-04 09:55:06.7690000 Gavin-VAIO\Gavin   GAVIN-VAIO          Microsoft SQL
                                                                   Server Management
                                                                   Studio
```

The timestamp used by Extended Events is always stored in a UTC format; you may want to use the `dateadd` or similar functions to format the timestamp for your time zone. Whether or not you choose to do that depends on why you're collecting the data and whether local time information is important.

Viewing In-Memory Targets

Some of the targets are the result of calculations being performed on captured data, rather than a dump of the raw data itself — for example, the event counter. The results of these targets are still available for viewing in SQL Server Management Studio, but whereas the event file target was updated in almost real time, the in-memory targets have to be manually refreshed or scheduled to be refreshed. This is not as big a problem as it sounds, as they can still be refreshed every few seconds; you just have to configure it first.

For this example, the login session from the previous section has been reconfigured and an event counter target added. You can see this in the list of targets in SQL Server Management Studio, as shown in Figure 13-25.

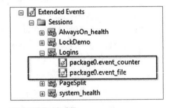

FIGURE 13-25

Once the session is running, you can right-click on the event counter target and select View Target Data. As shown in Figure 13-26, this will display the event counter's data as well as a message saying "The target data will not be refreshed. Right click the table to manually refresh or set the automatic refresh interval." Right-clicking will show that you can have it auto-refresh anywhere between every five seconds and every hour.

You can view the results from the histogram target in the same way that you viewed the event counter just shown; however, because these are in-memory data structures, their results aren't written to the event file or in

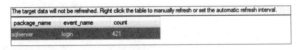

FIGURE 13-26

fact kept anywhere once the session is stopped. This is perhaps where analysis of an event file using T-SQL after testing may be more appropriate.

Querying a Ring Buffer Using T-SQL

Finally, this section consolidates what you've just seen in the previous two sections to query an in-memory target — in this case, a ring buffer — using T-SQL. The most likely reason you'd want to do this is because the ring buffer stores its results only in an XML format, so they have to be turned into relational data before you can analyze them further.

Ring buffers are stored in a DMV called `sys.dm_xe_session_targets`, and it's from here you query their content. This final example has created a session called `Logins_rb` to write its data to a ring buffer target. To create this yourself, create a new session with the options highlighted in Figure 13-27 and Figure 13-28.

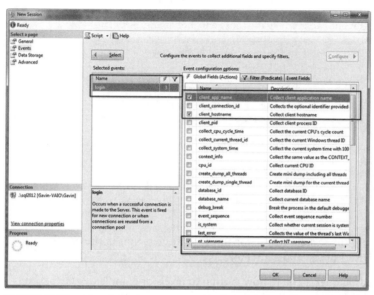

FIGURE 13-27

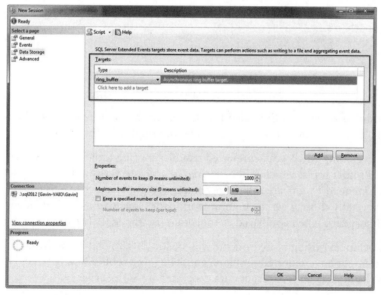

FIGURE 13-28

Once you have started the session and the ring buffer has started having event data written to it, it's possible to query its content using a DMV to extract its content in a meaningful format, as shown in the following query:

```
select  events.value('(event/@timestamp)[1]', 'datetime2') as [Event_Time_UTC],
        events.value('(event/action[@name="nt_username"]/value)[1]',
        'varchar(100)') as [NT_Username],
        events.value('(event/action[@name="client_hostname"]/value)[1]',
        'varchar(100)') as [Client_Hostname],
        events.value('(event/action[@name="client_app_name"]/value)[1]',
        'varchar(100)') as [Client_Appname]
from    (select event_data.query('.') as events
         from
         (select    cast(target_data as xml) as target_data
          from sys.dm_xe_session_targets xt
          join sys.dm_xe_sessions xs
          on xs.address = xt.event_session_address
          where xs.name = 'Logins_rb'
          and xt.target_name = 'ring_buffer' ) as data
          cross apply target_data.nodes ('RingBufferTarget/event') as
          results(event_data)) as tab (events)
order by [Event_Time_UTC]
```

The results the query returns are the same as those for the other targets you've previously queried; the difference is their source isn't a physical file anymore.

As you can see from the preceding query, you're now getting to levels of complexity far beyond what a newcomer to Extended Events would be dealing with. However, if that's something you're interested in investigating further, then I recommend reading the blog posts of the SQL Server community's Extended Events expert Jonathan Kehayias. Not only has Jonathan published some great detailed articles about Extended Events but also some invaluable scripts as well; in fact the previous query was based on one of Jonathan's.

```
http://sqlskills.com/blogs/jonathan/category/Extended-Events.aspx
```

SUMMARY

This chapter discussed a number of aspects of Extended Events, and at this point you should know enough to start using them and making them a central part of your troubleshooting toolkit.

Extended Events are rapidly becoming Microsoft's preferred troubleshooting tool for SQL Server, replacing the SQL Trace and Profiler tools, which will be retired in a future version. Even now, while all these tools are available, Extended Events are rapidly becoming the preferred choice to trouble-shoot production systems, especially those with the highest workloads. The load using Extended Events is minimal, indeed almost zero when compared to tools that use the SQL Trace feature.

Additionally, Microsoft has begun exposing more in-depth diagnostic data to end users through Extended Events. Events that might have required development debugging tools a few years ago can now be accessed as easily as the most high-level event data generated by SQL Server.

For newcomers to the feature, for whom this chapter was written, SQL Server 2012 delivers strong incentive to begin using the feature: native graphical user interface tools built into SQL Server Management Studio. These tools are more than adequate for configuring and managing your first and even subsequent Extended Events sessions.

Finally, users who want to get the most from Extended Events have begun to see how the data captured by sessions can be queried using regular T-SQL and its XML handling functions.

14

Enhancing Your Troubleshooting Toolset with PowerShell

WHAT'S IN THIS CHAPTER?

➤ Introducing PowerShell

➤ Getting started with PowerShell

➤ Using PowerShell to investigate server issues

➤ Proactively tuning SQL Server performance with PowerShell

WROX.COM CODE DOWNLOADS FOR THIS CHAPTER

The wrox.com code downloads for this chapter are found at www.wrox.com/remtitle
.cgi?isbn=1118177657 on the Download Code tab. The code is in the Chapter 14 download
and individually named according to the names throughout the chapter.

INTRODUCING POWERSHELL

System administrators are realizing the productivity gains that can be achieved from
PowerShell, the unified scripting environment provided by Microsoft. Reusing scripts of
commonly executed tasks is much faster and less error prone than repeatedly clicking
through dialogs.

PowerShell was first unveiled to the world at the Microsoft Professional Developers Conference
with a code name of Monad in 2003. Following a beta release, version 1 was officially released
in 2006, and since then PowerShell has become a deeply integrated component of Windows.
Indeed, SQL Server 2012 takes PowerShell so seriously that PowerShell 2.0 is a prerequisite,
and SQL Server will not install if PowerShell is not already installed on the system. The initial

SQL Server and PowerShell integration that started out with the SQL Server Database Engine now provides support for SSIS and SSAS in SQL Server 2012. PowerShell is also still in active development, which proceeds rapidly; the PowerShell 3.0 release is expected in late 2012.

This chapter looks at the latest version of PowerShell available at the time of writing, version 2.0, and demonstrates why it is such a useful tool for your troubleshooting toolset. You'll see how simple it is to construct scripts for use in your environment that can be run with minimal impact on system performance. Even better, you can save these scripts for later use. That way, when you find yourself in the heat of a production issue, you will have all your diagnostic scripts ready to run quickly and effectively.

GETTING STARTED WITH POWERSHELL

PowerShell is an object-oriented, command-line and scripting engine created by Microsoft and built on top of the .NET Framework. PowerShell provides full access to COM, WMI, the Windows Registry, and the .NET Framework.

The PowerShell product team created a design that enables developers to extend and enhance the environment with new cmdlets, providers, and modules. This deep Windows integration out-of-the-box and the extensibility of the framework means that you can create scripts to perform nearly any conceivable task.

You can think of PowerShell as an alternative view of your environment, as opposed to the familiar GUI experience. Every time you run a cmdlet, PowerShell responds with a result that you can evaluate and investigate further; and because everything returned is an object, you can drill down for further details. You can run cmdlets repeatedly and scroll through their history in the command window to see how you got to where you are. If you find you are repeatedly running the same pattern of cmdlets, you can package them up into a script or function and reuse complex composite scripts of cmdlets with a single new script or function name.

As mentioned earlier, PowerShell operates on objects. This is a very important aspect of its design that makes life simpler for you because you can take the results of one cmdlet and pass them straight into the next cmdlet as input. This is known as the *pipeline* and it differentiates PowerShell from other command shells, which have traditionally relied on text streams.

The productivity benefits that result from using PowerShell — automating repetitive tasks and reducing errors — are obvious, but PowerShell is also great for investigation and troubleshooting; and its command-line interface is useful when you are trying to investigate an issue. Imagine a situation in which you need to investigate a poorly performing server that you have not worked on before. With the following simple command you can quickly identify where the server resources are being consumed. This example shows how you can determine the top ten processes consuming the most CPU resources:

```
Get-Process | Sort-Object cpu -Descending | Select-Object -First 10
```

This simple statement has taken all the processes running on the computer, sorted them by CPU utilization descending, and then selected the top 10 processes. You don't have to wait for a user interface to load, which eliminates putting additional strain on the server.

Another troubleshooting question you may wish to find out is when the computer last booted up. You can also achieve this with a simple script (code file: PS_LastBootTime01.PS1):

```
$wmiBootTime = (get-wmiobject Win32_OperatingSystem).lastbootuptime;
[DateTime]$lastBootUpTime =
[Management.ManagementDateTimeConverter]::ToDateTime($wmiBootTime);
$uptime = (Get-Date) - $lastBootUpTime;
Write-Host $lastBootUpTime;
Write-Host $uptime;
```

In the preceding example I created a variable and stored the last boot-up time, which is initially a string when retrieved from WMI. I then converted it into a DateTime object. I calculated the uptime by using the Get-Date cmdlet, subtracting the date on which the machine was rebooted. I then displayed the last boot-up time and the uptime in the console.

You can build a suite of such statements and scripts that you want to run later, and you can easily package them into a script that you can run on a server. Don't worry if these scripts look a little daunting right now. This chapter explains in detail how scripts are composed, and by the end of it, you will have enough knowledge to understand numerous useful cmdlets and scripts to help with troubleshooting and diagnostics.

The PowerShell Environment

PowerShell 2 is pre-installed on Windows 7 and Windows Server 2008 R2 operating systems. Although PowerShell can be installed onto earlier versions of Windows, it is not immediately obvious from where you can obtain the download. This is because the actual product name that is indexed by all the popular Internet search engines is "Windows Management Framework," not PowerShell. You can find the PowerShell download from the following link: http://support.microsoft.com/kb/968929.

Once installed, you can either use PowerShell in interactive command-line mode (the shell), or use a script editor to create script files containing multiple statements to execute. To launch the interactive command line, run PowerShell.exe or find the "Windows PowerShell" shortcut that is installed in your Start menu. There is an alternate icon in the Start menu called "Windows PowerShell Modules"; this is similar to the standard "Windows PowerShell" item, but while loading the shell it also imports all the modules in the PowerShell Modules folder. The following PowerShell variable allows you to discover where the PowerShell modules are located on your machine:

```
$env:PSModulePath
```

The environments variable contains many configuration settings on your system. You can discover all of them by listing the contents of the variable as shown below:

```
PS > get-childitem env:
```

When you install PowerShell packs as part of Windows features, the PowerShell modules will be installed here, which provides a quick way to ensure that every Windows feature with PowerShell support installed has all its functionality available to you when you load the command line.

All the commands that you will be familiar with from cmd.exe are available, such as DIR. You will also have access to a wealth of new commands that are provided with PowerShell; these commands are commonly known as *cmdlets*.

PowerShell ships with a host application, the PowerShell Integrated Scripting Environment (ISE). This is installed by default in Windows 7 and can be enabled by installing the "Windows PowerShell Integrated Scripting Environment (ISE)" feature on Windows Server 2008 R2. The PowerShell ISE enables you to create script files, which by convention have an extension of .PS1. You can also debug and run scripts from within this environment; although this is a significant improvement from using Notepad and the command window in PowerShell 1, there is still room for improvement.

I prefer to use PowerGUI, a free PowerShell Scripting Environment that is available for download from www.powergui.org. PowerGUI also offers a wealth of additional cmdlets that have been written by the PowerGUI community, providing functionality that is not available out-of-the-box with PowerShell. If you also use Visual Studio, you're in luck, because Adam Driscoll has created a Visual Studio, extension (VSX) for PowerShell that uses PowerGUI. You can download the VSX from http:/visualstudiogallery.msdn.microsoft.com/ 01516103-d487-4a7e-bb40-c15ec709afa3; this extension enables you to create, debug, and manage scripts within the Visual Studio IDE.

A growing community of users has contributed additional cmdlets and modules. The best known and supported set of community functionality is available at http://pscx.codeplex.com. The PowerShell Community Extensions (PSCX) utility is worth downloading and keeping locally because it contains numerous cmdlets, functions, and modules to facilitate your work with respect to many aspects of Windows. A set specific to SQL Server, known as the SQL PowerShell Extensions, is available from http://sqlpsx.codeplex.com.

Security was an important consideration when the product team created PowerShell. With such an integrated and extensible scripting and command-line interface, it was critical to consider how users would be protected from unauthorized scripts executing. A key feature of this is the Execution Policy, which is a systemwide configuration that specifies the type of scripts that can be executed on the computer. Table 14-1 summarizes the four possible values for the Execution Policy.

TABLE 14-1: PowerShell Execution Policies

EXECUTION POLICY	DESCRIPTION
Restricted	No scripts can be run. Windows PowerShell can be used only in interactive mode.
AllSigned	Only scripts signed by a trusted publisher can be run.
RemoteSigned	Downloaded scripts must be signed by a trusted publisher before they can be run.
Unrestricted	No restrictions; all scripts can be run.

You can check the current status of the Execution Policy on your computer with the Get-ExecutionPolicy cmdlet. The following example shows how my computer is currently configured.

As you can see in the example below, the machine is set up so that downloaded scripts must be signed to run, but scripts created on the computer don't have to be signed to run.

```
PS > Get-ExecutionPolicy
RemoteSigned
```

The Basics — Cmdlets, Variables, Advanced Functions, and Modules

PowerShell is created upon a few core building blocks. A thorough understanding of these constituent parts will make understanding the environment a lot easier, so the following sections describe these core components.

Cmdlets

Cmdlets follow a naming convention to assist with identification. This convention is [*Name*]-[*Verb*], such as `Get-Process`, `Get-Help`, and `Remove-Item`.

Cmdlets are .NET classes that provide a single piece of functionality and are either provided with the PowerShell environment or provided by .NET developers and installed into the environment. They can take PowerShell objects as input and provide PowerShell objects as output. This ability to take and return PowerShell objects enabled the framework creators to offer what's known as a pipeline. Using pipelines, you can construct single lines of PowerShell that contain multiple cmdlets, each passing the output as input to the next, with cmdlets participating in the pipeline separated by the bar operator (|). Very powerful functionality can be composed in a single line of PowerShell using this functionality. The following example uses the `Get-Process` cmdlet to list all the running processes on the computer, and then the output of the `Get-Process` cmdlet is connected to the `Export-Csv` cmdlet, which exports the list of processes to a CSV file:

```
Get-Process | Export-Csv .\processes.csv -NoTypeInformation
```

Discovering functionality is important in the command line because unlike in a GUI where you can visually scan through the menu items, you need to instead use discoverability tools that are provided with PowerShell. The first cmdlet to be aware of is `Get-Help`. `Get-Help` takes one parameter `CmdletName` or `TopicName`. You can also provide a few properties: `-examples` to display the examples; `-detailed` to get further information; and `-full` for all the technical information. The following example uses `Get-Help` to retrieve all the information about the `Get-Process` cmdlet:

```
Get-Help Get-Process -full
```

In order to "`Get-Help`" you need to know the cmdlets that are available, and PowerShell provides the `Get-Command` cmdlet for just that purpose. If you are trying to find all the cmdlets available within a module, you can specify the module name to filter the results to only the commands that exist within the module. The module name for SQL Server 2012 is SQLPS, so you can find all the cmdlets provided with SQL Server 2012 with the following:

```
Get-Command -Module sqlps
```

If you don't have the sqlps module available the cmdlets will return nothing. You can make the module available for use by importing it as shown below:

```
Import-Module sqlps
```

Aliases enable cmdlets to have different names, behavior embraced by the PowerShell team. As mentioned earlier, for example, DIR is available in PowerShell. It isn't in fact the DIR command you'll find in the cmd.exe but rather a PowerShell Cmdlet called Get-ChildItem that has been aliased to DIR for backward compatibility. Interestingly Get-ChildItem is also aliased to LS, which is the equivalent command on UNIX platforms.

Variables

After you have written cmdlet statements in PowerShell, you need to be able to store data so that it can be retrieved and manipulated further through your scripts. PowerShell provides variables to store data within PowerShell. Variables always start with a $ symbol, followed by the name you choose. For example, to store the top 10 processes by CPU usage you can use the following:

```
$TopTenProcessesByCPU = Get-Process | Sort-Object cpu -Descending | Select-Object -
First 10
```

Now that the value is stored in a variable, it is available for retrieval and further use through your script.

You can discover all the variables that are available using the Get-Variable cmdlet. Table 14-2 shows some of the more important variables that were returned after I ran this on my machine.

TABLE 14-2: Common PowerShell Variables

VARIABLE NAME	DESCRIPTION
$_	Current item in the pipeline
$args	Array of arguments
$Error	Array of errors
$FALSE	Boolean False
$HOME	Folder containing the current user's profile
$Host	This is a reference to the host of this runspace.
$null	References to the null variable always return the null value. Assignments have no effect.
$PID	Current process ID
$PROFILE	Path to the active Profile

`$PSCulture`	Culture of the current Windows PowerShell session
`$PSEmailServer`	Variable to hold the Email Server. This can be used instead of the `HostName` parameter in the `Send-MailMessage` cmdlet.
`$PSHOME`	Parent folder of the host application of this Runspace
`$PSUICulture`	UI Culture of the current Windows PowerShell Session
`$PSVersionTable`	Version information for current PowerShell session
`$PWD`	PowerShell Working Directory
`$StackTrace`	Detailed StackTrace for the last error
`$TRUE`	Boolean True

The most important variable to familiarize yourself with is `$_`, which is the current object in the pipeline. This is very handy when you want to iterate through all the items that are being sent through the pipeline. The following example uses a `Where-Object` cmdlet to filter the output on every process that has been passed along the pipeline where the `WorkingSet` of the current process in the pipeline is greater than 100MB:

```
Get-Process | Where-Object {$_.WorkingSet -gt 100MB}
```

Note that this example uses the `-gt` comparison operator. PowerShell provides a set of comparison operators that need to be used when comparing objects. Table 14-3 lists the commonly used comparison operators.

TABLE 14-3: PowerShell Equality Operators

OPERATOR	DESCRIPTION
`-eq`	Equal to
`-ne`	Not equal to
`-gt`	Greater than
`-ge`	Greater than or equal to
`-lt`	Less than
`-le`	Less than or equal to
`-like`	Matches using the (*) wildcard character

continues

TABLE 14-3 *(continued)*

OPERATOR	DESCRIPTION
-notlike	Does not match using the (*) wildcard character
-match	Matches a string using a regular expression
-notmatch	Does not match a string using a regular expression
-contains	Includes an identical value
-notcontains	Does not include an identical value
-band	Bitwise AND
-bor	Bitwise OR
-bxor	Bitwise XOR

It is often useful to know the makeup of a variable. You can discover the structure of an object using the Get-Member cmdlet. The following code demonstrates the creation of a new string object and then passing it into the Get-Member cmdlet:

```
PS > [String]$NewString | Get-Member
```

Knowing the members available on an object is very useful because you can start using them. For instance, in the following example I have a Statement string and want to return the last word. By inspecting the members on the $Statement variable, I can see that there is a Length property, an IndexOf method, and a Substring method, which I can use together to return the part of the string I'm interested in (code file: PS_StringManipulation01.PS1):

```
$Statement = "PowerShell Rocks"
$Statement.SubString($Statement.IndexOf(" ") + 1, $Statement.Length -
$Statement.IndexOf(" ") - 1)
```

Advanced Functions

Once you have used a snippet of PowerShell code a few times you'll probably want a way of refactoring that code into something that you can reuse easily. Fortunately, PowerShell 2.0 makes this very easy to accomplish with a new feature called *advanced functions*. I'm going to use a trivial example to demonstrate this functionality. Assume that you regularly filter the Get-Process cmdlet for all processes starting with SQL, and you want to be able to return all these processes with a simple cmdlet named Get-SQLProcess. The following code listing shows how this advanced function is created:

```
function Get-SQLProcess
{
<#
.SYNOPSIS
Retrieves processes starting with the term SQL

.DESCRIPTION
The Get-SQLProcess function uses the Get-Process Cmdlet to retrieve all the
processes
that start with SQL from the local computer.
#>
    [CmdletBinding()]
    Param()
    Process
    {
    Get-Process SQL*
    }
}
```

After this code has been executed by the PowerShell environment, you'll be able to call this function; and because it uses the CmdletBinding attribute, which differentiates the advanced function from a standard function, PowerShell will treat it like a compiled cmdlet — meaning it will have autocomplete and be listed among the available cmdlets. I've also written some simple documentation for the preceding example, so this function now has help as well. The following listing shows the documentation that is displayed for this function when Get-Help is called on it:

```
PS > Get-Help Get-SQLProcess

NAME
    Get-SQLProcess

SYNOPSIS
    Retrieves processes starting with the term SQL


SYNTAX
    Get-SQLProcess [<CommonParameters>]


DESCRIPTION
    The Get-SQLProcess function uses the Get-Process Cmdlet to retrieve all the
    processes that start with SQL from the local computer.


RELATED LINKS

REMARKS
    To see the examples, type: "get-help Get-SQLProcess -examples".
    For more information, type: "get-help Get-SQLProcess -detailed".
    For technical information, type: "get-help Get-SQLProcess -full".
```

Modules

Modules are another new feature introduced in PowerShell 2.0. Before modules were available, developers who wanted to introduce new functionality into PowerShell were required to use snap-ins, which were created in the C# programming language, compiled, and then imported into the PowerShell host. This was difficult and required the assistance of an experienced C# developer to introduce new functionality. Modules are designed to make this easier, as a module is a package that can contain members such as cmdlets, providers, functions, variables, aliases, and so on. There are four types of module, described in the following sections.

Script Modules

A PowerShell script that has a .PSM1 file extension is known as a *script module*. Modules contain PowerShell script that can be shared within an organization and, if required, further afield. Adding advanced functions as shown in the last section enables the script author to create cmdlet-like functionality and share it.

Script modules are the most accessible way to create a module because any valid PowerShell script can simply be saved into a file with a .PSM1 extension and then be used as any other module type.

Binary Modules

A binary module contains compiled .NET code and is compiled into an assembly (.dll). This is essentially a replacement for the snap-in functionality provided in PowerShell 1.0. The disadvantage of using binary modules is that the assistance of an experienced C# developer was required to create the modules. However, if significant intellectual property is contained within the module, this may be the best approach because the code can be obfuscated before it is distributed.

Manifest Modules

Manifest modules are used to describe the contents of a module. They can contain the prerequisites (PowerShell version, .NET Framework version, etc.); processing directives such as scripts; formats; and type properties. Restrictions can be applied, such as members of the module to export. This is useful when creating a clean API for others to share. By convention, manifest files have a .psd1 extension, and formatting and type files have a .psxml extension.

Dynamic Modules

Dynamic modules are created on demand using the New-Module cmdlet. These modules live in memory only for the session in which the PowerShell host is active, and because of this transient nature they are not exposed through the Get-Module cmdlet.

Working with Modules

To identify the modules available on your system, you can use the Get-Module cmdlet with the -ListAvailable parameter, which returns a list of all the modules that can be imported into the session. The following example shows the SQL modules available on my system:

```
PS > get-module -listavailable sql*

ModuleType Name                    ExportedCommands
---------- ----                    ----------------
Manifest   SQLASCMDLETS            {}
Manifest   SQLPS                   {}
```

Once you have identified a module that you would like to use, you can import it using the `Import-Module` cmdlet. You need to provide the name of the module if it is listed in the available modules or by entering the full path of the module. When importing a module, there is a parameter called `-DisableNameChecking` that prevents PowerShell from checking the members' verbs against a predefined, approved list from the PowerShell product team.

SQL Server 2012 comes with two modules, SQLPS and SQLASCMDLETS; the following example script imports both modules into the active session:

```
Import-Module SQLPS,SQLASCMDLETS -DisableNameChecking
```

I like to inspect the cmdlets that are available when importing a module for the first time so that I can find out what I can do with the module. This is possible using the `Get-Command` cmdlet with the `-module` parameter to filter the cmdlets listed to only those for the given module. The following example shows the cmdlets available within the SQLASCMDLETS module:

```
PS SQLSERVER:\> Get-Command -Module SQLASCMDLETS

CommandType      Name
-----------      ----
Cmdlet           Add-RoleMember
Cmdlet           Backup-ASDatabase
Cmdlet           Invoke-ASCmd
Cmdlet           Invoke-ProcessCube
Cmdlet           Invoke-ProcessDimension
Cmdlet           Invoke-ProcessPartition
Cmdlet           Merge-Partition
Cmdlet           New-RestoreFolder
Cmdlet           New-RestoreLocation
Cmdlet           Remove-RoleMember
Cmdlet           Restore-ASDatabase
```

If you no longer want to reference a module imported into a session, you can remove it using the `Remove-Module` cmdlet, providing the name of the module you wish to remove.

Signing PowerShell Scripts

Modules are designed to be shared and should therefore be digitally signed so that users who have locked down their computer with `Set-ExecutionPolicy` will still be able to execute the script — unless the computer is locked down to Restricted, in which case no scripts can be executed. Signing a script is an involved process requiring code-signing certificates and is outside the scope of this book, but you can obtain more information from TechNet magazine at the following link: http://technet.microsoft.com/en-us/magazine/2008.04.powershell.aspx.

Working Remotely

In the first version of PowerShell users were constrained to working on a local computer. This was OK if you had a single computer to manage, but many administrators work with multiple servers in complex computing environments, and it is a major limitation to remote onto each computer in order to use PowerShell. This was recognized and addressed in version 2.0, when WinRM was launched. WinRM is a Windows service that runs on the target computer and allows a remote computer running PowerShell 2.0 to communicate with it and execute PowerShell 2.0 scripts from the local computer.

From an administrator's perspective, this opens up a wealth of possibilities — from the simplicity of now having a single management computer from which to operate, to being able to construct a full monitoring framework within PowerShell.

To set up PowerShell remoting you must have PowerShell 2.0 installed on all the participating computers. There are a couple of steps that you must perform to have everything running:

1. On the target computer, run PowerShell as Administrator (this step won't work if you are not running with elevated privileges). Run the `Enable-PSRemoting -force` cmdlet to set up the WinRM (Windows Remote Management) service and the firewall configuration to allow remoting commands to pass through:

```
PS WSMan:\localhost\Client> Enable-PSRemoting -force
WinRM already is set up to receive requests on this machine.
WinRM has been updated for remote management.
Created a WinRM listener on HTTP://* to accept WS-Man requests to any IP on
this machine.
WinRM firewall exception enabled.
```

2. On the target computer, ensure that the computer from which you'll be executing scripts is a trusted host by using the TrustedHosts command, as shown here:

```
PS C:\> cd wsman:\localhost\client
PS WSMan:\localhost\Client> Set-Item TrustedHosts SQL2012 -Force
PS WSMan:\localhost\Client> Get-Item TrustedHosts
   WSManConfig: Microsoft.WSMan.Management\WSMan::localhost\Client

Name                    Value
----                    -----
TrustedHosts            SQL2012
```

After completing these steps you can run remote scripts. You can do this interactively with the `New-PSSession` cmdlet and then enter the remote session with the `Enter-PSSession` cmdlet. Alternately, you can invoke scripts on the remote machine with the `Invoke-Command` cmdlet. I like to test the remote session using `Invoke-Command` and request the hostname to ensure that I've connected to the remote computer correctly, as shown in the following example:

```
Invoke-Command -Session $sessions -ScriptBlock {Hostname}
```

What's New in SQL Server 2012

Prior to SQL Server 2012, the SQL Server team created a PowerShell mini-shell called SQLPS. This has changed in SQL Server 2012; SQLPS is now a standard PowerShell 2.0 host and imports the SQLPS module. This makes life a lot easier if you are already using a standard PowerShell host because you too can use import-module SQLPS and SQLASCMDLETS to gain all the SQL Server provider functionality within another PowerShell host.

SQL Server 2012 ships with the following 40 cmdlets:

SQLPS CMDLETS	SQLASCMDLETS CMDLETS
Add-SqlAvailabilityDatabase	Add-RoleMember
Add-SqlAvailabilityGroupListenerStaticIp	Backup-ASDatabase
Backup-SqlDatabase	Invoke-ASCmd
Convert-UrnToPath	Invoke-ProcessCube
Decode-SqlName	Invoke-ProcessDimension
Disable-SqlHADRService	Invoke-ProcessPartition
Enable-SqlHADRService	Merge-Partition
Encode-SqlName	New-RestoreFolder
Invoke-PolicyEvaluation	New-RestoreLocation
Invoke-Sqlcmd	Remove-RoleMember
Join-SqlAvailabilityGroup	Restore-ASDatabase
New-SqlAvailabilityGroup	
New-SqlAvailabilityGroupListener	
New-SqlAvailabilityReplica	
New-SqlHADREndpoint	
Remove-SqlAvailabilityDatabase	
Remove-SqlAvailabilityGroup	
Remove-SqlAvailabilityReplica	
Restore-SqlDatabase	
Resume-SqlAvailabilityDatabase	
Set-SqlAvailabilityGroup	
Set-SqlAvailabilityGroupListener	
Set-SqlAvailabilityReplica	
Set-SqlHADREndpoint	
Suspend-SqlAvailabilityDatabase	
Switch-SqlAvailabilityGroup	
Test-SqlAvailabilityGroup	
Test-SqlAvailabilityReplica	
Test-SqlDatabaseReplicaState	

Of these cmdlets, 22 are for managing the new High Availability features and Analysis Services, which I'm not covering in this chapter. The other notable cmdlets from a troubleshooting and performance perspective are for backup and restore. SQL Server Backup and Restore cmdlets are a welcome addition to SQL Server 2012; previously, as a script author you had two options:

➤ `Invoke-SQL` and write T-SQL that you execute from a PowerShell script.

➤ Load the SMO objects and use the backup and restore functionality provided through the SMO library. This was my preferred approach but it requires a significant scripting effort, somewhere in the neighborhood of 20–50 lines of script to handle a typical backup or restore scenario.

Backup-SqlDatabase

The following script shows how simple database backups can be using the SQL Provider and the new `Backup-SqlDatabase` script to iterate through all the databases, creating a folder for each one and then generating a backup based on a timestamp (code file: `PS_SQLBackup01.PS1`):

```
foreach($database in (Get-ChildItem))
{
    $dbName = $database.Name
    $timeStamp = Get-Date -FORMAT yyyyMMddHHmmss
    $backupFolder = "c:\backups\$dbName"

    if((Test-Path $backupFolder) -eq $False)
    {
        New-Item -type directory -path $backupFolder
    }

    Backup-SqlDatabase -Database $dbName -BackupFile "$backupFolder\$dbName-
    $timeStamp.bak"
}
```

Restore-SqlDatabase

The new cmdlets also make restoring a database very straightforward. The following script demonstrates how to restore the Adventure Works database:

```
Restore-sqldatabase -Database AdventureWorks '
-BackupFile "C:\Backups\AdventureWorks\AdventureWorks-20120220005537.bak"
```

You may notice the "`'`" character after AdventureWorks. This is not a mistake or a typo. It is a continuation character; which means that you can type a line in the PowerShell command line, press return, and PowerShell will continue accepting input for the previous line. This is very useful when single statements become too long to read comfortably.

More than 40 parameters are available for `Restore-SqlDatabase`, enabling the creation of some very complex restore scripting. Anything that is possible within the SQL Server Management Studio user interface or through T-SQL is available here, with the added benefit of simple file management. This makes complex restores using multiple files, such as restoring many log files, a relative breeze.

USING POWERSHELL TO INVESTIGATE SERVER ISSUES

PowerShell provides full integration with the Windows Management Instrumentation (WMI) framework, The WMI framework is a very powerful method for querying the Windows system to find detailed information. Traditionally, it has not been easy to gain access to WMI, and this was mainly done via a programming interface. PowerShell opens up access to WMI making it a useful resource for your troubleshooting efforts.

Interrogating Disk Space Utilization

In this example, you are going to see how to make use of one of the WMI win32-logicaldisk classes to retrieve information about disk space utilization on the server. Initially, the raw information provided by the class will be returned and then the data will be used to produce a detailed analysis of disk space available:

```
Get-wmiobject win32_logicaldisk
```

Running the Get-WmiObject cmdlet and providing the win32_logicaldisk class returns the following results on my computer:

```
DeviceID     : C:
DriveType    : 3
ProviderName :
FreeSpace    : 105582891008
Size         : 128742060032
VolumeName   :

DeviceID     : D:
DriveType    : 5
ProviderName :
FreeSpace    : 0
Size         : 45471744
VolumeName   : VBOXADDITIONS_4.
```

The default list view of the results is not very readable for this output, but you can improve it by formatting the output as a table:

```
Get-wmiobject win32-logicaldisk | format-table -autosize
```

On my computer this statement produces the following output:

```
DeviceID DriveType ProviderName    FreeSpace          Size VolumeName
-------- --------- ------------    ---------          ---- ----------
C:               3                 105582891008 128742060032
D:               5                            0     45471744 VBOXADDITIONS_4.
```

You may want to filter this information so that you are only displaying fixed disks. This can be achieved by using a Filter parameter to filter the disks returned to be fixed disks only:

```
Get-WmiObject Win32_logicaldisk -Filter   "DriveType = 3" | Format-Table -autosize
```

This is getting better, but the results are being presented with the free space and the size in bytes. I can't remember the last time when bytes were a meaningful unit of measure for a hard disk, so you can modify the script to format the output in GB (code file: PS_DiskInfo01.PS1):

```
$diskinfo = Get-WmiObject Win32_logicaldisk -Filter  "DriveType = 3"
$diskinfo | foreach-object {$_.FreeSpace = $_.FreeSpace / 1GB; '
$_.Size = $_.Size / 1GB}
$diskinfo | format-table -autoSize
```

We are now presented with a table that shows the total capacity of the drive and the available space in GB, as shown when run on my system below:

```
DeviceID       : C:
DriveType      : 3
ProviderName   :
FreeSpace      : 388
Size           : 466
VolumeName     : OS

DeviceID       : H:
DriveType      : 3
ProviderName   :
FreeSpace      : 303
Size           : 466
VolumeName     : DATA
```

Interrogating Current Server Activity

When checking whether a remote computer is responsive, a good first place to investigate is the ping response. Using the win32_pingstatus WMI class, this is relatively straightforward. The data returned from this class is structured and can then be used within other parts of the investigation or recorded back to disk in a file, e-mailed to a recipient, or stored within a database. The following example checks the status code (0 if successful) of a ping test on as server called SQL2012 (replace SQL2012 with a machine name on your network):

```
Get-WmiObject win32_pingstatus -Filter "Address='SQL2012'" '
| Select-Object statuscode
```

Assuming a status code of 0 is returned from the server, you can now turn your attention to services running on the computer. To find out which services are running, execute the following:

```
Get-Service | Where-Object { $_.Status -eq 'Running' }
```

The Get-Service cmdlet is very handy for simple service queries. Unfortunately, it doesn't provide access to every property on the service. I often find it useful to see the Service State and the Start Mode. Fortunately, this information is available on the Win23_Service WMI class; and the following script shows an example of querying this class to find services that start automatically with Windows but are currently stopped. This may be useful if a server is not behaving as expected and you suspect that a service that is usually started at boot time is currently not running.

```
Get-WmiObject -Class Win32_Service -Property Name,State,StartMode -Filter
"StartMode='Auto' AND State='Stopped'" '
| Select-Object -Property Name,StartMode,State
```

Finding out which processes are active is useful during troubleshooting. Often, a process has run away with CPU or memory and is therefore putting pressure on the system, causing other vital services to be starved of resources. Once again PowerShell jumps to the rescue with Get-Process, which returns process information. A busy system will have many processes running, so I like to run two queries — the first finds the top 10 processes by CPU utilization, and the second finds the top 10 processes by memory utilization. The following example queries the top 10 processes by CPU utilization and displays the results from my SQL2012 Virtual Machine:

```
PS C:\> get-process | Sort-Object CPU -Descending | Select-Object -First 10
```

Handles	NPM(K)	PM(K)	WS(K)	VM(M)	CPU(s)	Id	ProcessName
388	50	41052	56776	222	48.50	3660	iexplore
783	53	41408	58104	287	28.92	2452	explorer
889	78	101688	144016	548	27.94	2208	Ssms
914	47	196188	216300	639	27.03	2252	powershell
57	7	1352	5072	70	12.00	3580	notepad
637	55	58648	73928	621	7.56	3028	SQLPS
564	43	16048	29524	177	5.97	3396	iexplore
39	6	2028	5036	57	2.97	3008	conhost
223	17	7816	17984	111	1.02	3968	notepad
79	9	1392	4480	71	0.19	2632	VBoxTray

This isn't a busy system, so the usual suspects such as Internet Explorer (iexplore) and Windows Explorer (explorer) are high in the list. The following example shows a similar query, this time querying by memory utilization:

```
PS C:\> get-process | Sort-Object WS -Descending | Select-Object -First 10
```

Handles	NPM(K)	PM(K)	WS(K)	VM(M)	CPU(s)	Id	ProcessName
639	88	444404	308232	-502		1268	sqlservr
816	47	200100	220736	640	28.13	2252	powershell
818	77	99328	143800	547	28.22	2208	Ssms
618	52	101812	74352	1906		1452	ReportingServicesService
637	55	58648	73928	621	7.56	3028	SQLPS
784	54	41748	58472	288	29.61	2452	explorer
388	50	40948	56748	221	48.52	3660	iexplore
1690	54	75844	54556	674		1312	msmdsrv
1061	52	28388	35400	432		848	svchost
311	26	31896	33084	534		1336	SMSvcHost

In this case, the processes consuming the largest working set of memory are different from the processes consuming the most CPU. Finding processes that are using excessive CPU or memory gives you a scope for further investigation.

Interrogating for Warnings and Errors

When a server is not behaving as expected, an error has often occurred. Inspecting the Windows Event Log is a good place to start an investigation into what may have gone wrong. PowerShell has full support for the Windows Event Log. The Get-EventLog cmdlet lists all the items within an Event Log. The following example shows the list of items within the application Event Log filtered to those whose source is "MSSQLSERVER" and are an error:

```
Get-Eventlog application '
| Where-Object {$_.Source -eq "MSSQLSERVER" -and $_.EntryType -eq "Error"}
```

SQL Server also has an Error Log that often contains more detailed information pertaining to SQL Server–specific issues. The following example shows how to query the SQL Server Error Log filtering the results to just the errors (code file: PS_ReadSQLErrorLog01.PS1):

```
[reflection.assembly]::LoadWithPartialName("Microsoft.SqlServer.Smo") | out-null
$server = New-Object "Microsoft.SqlServer.Management.Smo.Server" "(local)"
$server.ReadErrorLog() | Where-Object {$_.Text -like "Error:*"}
```

My machine has a single default SQL Server instance. If you are using a named instance, replace "(local)" with the name of your SQL Server instance.

Using the SQL Server Management Objects it is also possible to quickly filter the available jobs, identifying those that failed the last time they ran and are currently enabled. This is a useful script to run on a regular basis because SQL jobs often contain important management and administration tasks that are automated, and quickly identifying a failed job will save significant time diagnosing issues later. The following script example shows how to query the SMO objects for SQL Server jobs whose last run outcome failed and are still enabled (code file: PS_ReadFailedJobs01.PS1):

```
[reflection.assembly]::LoadWithPartialName("Microsoft.SqlServer.Smo") | out-null
$server = New-Object "Microsoft.SqlServer.Management.Smo.Server"  "(local)"
$server.jobserver.jobs | where-object {$_.lastrunoutcome -eq "Failed" -and
$_.isenabled -eq $TRUE}
```

Interrogating Server Performance

PowerShell 2.0 introduced integration with Windows performance counters. This means that you can quickly view all the performance counters on your machine:

```
Get-Counter -listSet * | Select-Object -ExpandProperty Paths
```

You could then find all of the SQL Server–specific counters:

```
Get-Counter -listSet * | Select-Object -ExpandProperty Paths | where-object {$_ -
like "*SQL*"}
```

It is also possible to get a sample of a performance counter:

```
Get-Counter '\Processor(*)\% Processor Time'
```

You can even leave PowerShell listening for the counter and collecting samples until you press Ctrl+C:

```
Get-Counter '\Processor(*)\% Processor Time' -continuous
```

The advantage of configuring your performance counters through PowerShell is that you can create a gold set of performance counters that you are interested in monitoring on every computer in your environment and then save the script to run on each computer, ensuring that all the computers capture the same statistics.

PROACTIVELY TUNING SQL SERVER PERFORMANCE WITH POWERSHELL

Now that you've seen some of the building blocks of PowerShell it's time to see how easy it is to combine all this together and build some more functional scripts. Remember, everything can be broken back down to cmdlets and variables; so if you find that your script is getting too complex and difficult to work with, break it back down and build it back up.

In this next section we will examine some scripts that can be used to help with SQL Server tuning as we look at index maintenance, managing disk space, and scripting out DDL data. To round the chapter off we'll look at how PowerShell scripts can be scheduled to run automatically.

Index Maintenance

To ensure maximum performance is obtained, index maintenance is an important job when managing a SQL Server. Traditionally, a DBA may have written some T-SQL to perform index maintenance, but this is not a simple task and one probably not best suited to T-SQL because of the procedural nature of the task. PowerShell offers an elegant solution to index maintenance in collaboration with the SQL Server SMO library. The following script shows how a fairly comprehensive index maintenance routine can be performed in just a few lines of PowerShell. The script iterates through all the indexes within all the tables of a user database, and based on the fragmentation level of the index performs one of three tasks (code file: PS_ManageFragmentation01.PS1):

➤   If the index is less than 5% fragmented, then do nothing because the performance benefit of maintaining the index on this occurrence is negligible.

➤   If the index is between 5% and 30% fragmented, then perform an index reorganization.

➤   If the index is greater than 30% fragmented, then perform an index rebuild.

```
[string] $ServerName = $args[0]
[string] $TargetDatabaseName = $args[1]

[Reflection.Assembly]::LoadWithPartialName("Microsoft.SqlServer.Smo") | out-null
$server = New-Object Microsoft.SqlServer.Management.Smo.Server $ServerName
$targetDB = $server.Databases[$targetDatabaseName]

foreach ($table in $targetDB.Tables)
{
```

```
foreach($index in $table.Indexes)
{
        $fragmentation = $index.EnumFragmentation()
        $averageFragmentation = $fragmentation.Rows[0].AverageFragmentation

        if($averageFragmentation -lt .05)
        {
                continue
        }

        if($averageFragmentation -ge .05 -and $averageFragmentation -lt .3)
        {
                $index.Reorganize()
                continue
        }

        $index.Rebuild()
    }
}
```

Managing Disk Space Utilization of Backups

Working with the file system is very straightforward with PowerShell. In the following example, I have created a small script that removes transaction log backups that are older than two days, differential backups that are older than eight days, and full backups that are older than 91 days. By splitting the Get-ChildItem query into three queries based on file extension and last write time, it was simply a matter of setting the number of days to subtract from the current date to define the retention period for each backup type (code file: PS_DeleteOldBackups01.PS1):

```
Get-ChildItem .\Backups -include *.trn -recurse '
        | Where-Object { $_.lastwritetime -lt (Get-Date).AddDays(-2) } '
        | Remove-Item

Get-ChildItem .\Backups -include *.dif -recurse '
        | Where-Object { $_.lastwritetime -lt (Get-Date).AddDays(-8) } '
        | Remove-Item

Get-ChildItem .\Backups -include *.bak -recurse '
        | Where-Object { $_.lastwritetime -lt (Get-Date).AddDays(-91) } '
        | Remove-Item
```

Extracting DDL Using SMO

A misplaced index or a poorly defined table definition are two examples of how changing the DDL of a database can have heavy performance implications. With this in mind, I created the following script, which can be scheduled to run once a day and will extract all the DDL objects from the database and store them on disk against the day that they were extracted. If poor performance is identified, it's easy to compare the files between days to identify whether any DDL changes caused the performance of the database to degrade.

This is a long script but it combines all the concepts and techniques discussed so far in this chapter to dump all the database objects to file (code file: PS_ExtractDDL01.PS1):

```
#Helper function to script the DDL Object to disk
function Write-DDLOutput ($filename, $object)
{
        New-Item $filename -type file -force | Out-Null
        #Specify the filename
        $ScriptingOptions.FileName = $filename

        #Assign the scripting options to the Scripter
        $Scripter.Options = $ScriptingOptions

        #Script the index
        $Scripter.Script($object)
}

#Load the SMO assembly
[reflection.assembly]::LoadWithPartialName("Microsoft.SqlServer.Smo") | out-null

#Create all the global vars we need
$Server = New-Object ("Microsoft.SqlServer.Management.Smo.Server")
$Scripter = New-Object ("Microsoft.SqlServer.Management.Smo.Scripter")
$ScriptingOptions = New-Object
("Microsoft.SqlServer.Management.SMO.ScriptingOptions")
$Scripter.Server = $Server

#Specifies the root folder that we'll store the Scripts into This will probably
become a param in future
$RootBackupFolder = "C:\SqlBackups\DDL"

#Get the day of the week so that we can create a folder for each day
$Today = [System.DateTime]::Today.DayOfWeek

#Store today's backup folder
$DDLBackupFolder = Join-Path -Path $RootBackupFolder -ChildPath $Today

#Check if today's folder exists
if ([System.IO.Directory]::Exists($DDLBackupFolder))
{
        #If it does delete it's contents
        Remove-Item (Join-Path -Path $DDLBackupFolder -ChildPath *) -Recurse
}
else
{
        #Otherwise create it
        [System.IO.Directory]::CreateDirectory($DDLBackupFolder) | Out-Null
}

#Setup the scripting options
$ScriptingOptions.AppendToFile = $true
$ScriptingOptions.FileName = $filename
$ScriptingOptions.ToFileOnly = $true
```

```
$ScriptingOptions.ScriptData = $false

#Loop through all the databases to script them out
foreach ($database in ($Server.databases | where {$_.IsSystemObject -eq $false -and
$_.IsDatabaseSnapshot -eq $false}))
{

        $databaseBackupFolder = Join-Path -Path $DDLBackupFolder -ChildPath
        $Database.Name

        #This will be the database create script
        Write-DDLOutput (Join-Path -Path ($databaseBackupFolder) -ChildPath
        ($Database.Name +  ".sql")) $database

                $ProgrammabilityBackupFolder = Join-Path -Path
                $databaseBackupFolder -ChildPath "Programmability"

                $DefaultsBackupFolder = Join-Path -Path
                $ProgrammabilityBackupFolder -ChildPath "Defaults"
                 foreach ($default in $database.Defaults)
                 {
                        #Generate a filename for the default
                        Write-DDLOutput (Join-Path -Path
                        ($DefaultsBackupFolder) -ChildPath
                        ($default.Schema + "." + $default.Name +  ".sql"))
                        $default

                 }

                #Create a folders to store the functions in
                $FunctionsBackupFolder = Join-Path -Path
                $ProgrammabilityBackupFolder -ChildPath "Functions"
                $ScalarFunctionsBackupFolder = Join-Path -Path
                $FunctionsBackupFolder -ChildPath "Scalar-valued Functions"
                $TableValuedFunctionsBackupFolder = Join-Path -Path
                $FunctionsBackupFolder -ChildPath "Table-valued Functions"

                foreach ($function in $database.UserDefinedFunctions | where
                {$_.IsSystemObject -eq $false})
                {
                        #script the functions into folders depending upon type. We're
                        only interested in scalar and table
                        switch ($function.FunctionType)
                        {
                        scalar
                        {
                                #Generate a filename for the scalar function
                                $filename = Join-Path -Path
                                ($ScalarFunctionsBackupFolder) -ChildPath
                                ($function.Schema + "." + $function.Name +  ".sql")
                        }
                        table
                        {
                                #Generate a filename for the table value function
                                $filename = Join-Path -Path
                                ($TableValuedFunctionsBackupFolder) -ChildPath
                                ($function.Schema + "." + $function.Name +  ".sql")
```

```
        }
        default { continue }
        }

        #Script the function
        Write-DDLOutput $filename $function
}

$RulesBackupFolder = Join-Path -Path
$ProgrammabilityBackupFolder -ChildPath "Rules"
foreach ($rule in $database.Rules)
{
        #Script the rule
        Write-DDLOutput (Join-Path -Path
        ($RulesBackupFolder) -ChildPath
        ($rule.Schema + "." + $rule.Name +  ".sql")) $rule
}

#Create a folder to store the Sprocs in
$StoredProceduresBackupFolder = Join-Path -Path
$ProgrammabilityBackupFolder -ChildPath "Stored Procedures"

#Loop through the sprocs to script them out
foreach ($storedProcedure in $database.StoredProcedures | where
{$_.IsSystemObject -eq $false})
{
        #script the sproc
        Write-DDLOutput ($filename = Join-Path -Path
        ($StoredProceduresBackupFolder) -ChildPath
        ($storedProcedure.Schema + "." +
        $storedProcedure.Name + ".sql"))
        $storedProcedure
}

#Create a folder to store the table scripts
$TablesBackupFolder = Join-Path -Path $databaseBackupFolder -ChildPath
"Tables"
$TableIndexesBackupFolder = Join-Path -Path
$TablesBackupFolder -ChildPath "Indexes"
$TableKeysBackupFolder = Join-Path -Path
$TablesBackupFolder -ChildPath "Keys"
$TableConstraintsBackupFolder = Join-Path -Path
$TablesBackupFolder -ChildPath "Constraints"
$TableTriggersBackupFolder = Join-Path -Path
$TablesBackupFolder -ChildPath "Triggers"

#Loop through the tables to script them out
foreach ($table in $database.Tables | where
{$_.IsSystemObject -eq $false})
{
        #Script the Table
         Write-DDLOutput (Join-Path -Path
         ($TablesBackupFolder) -ChildPath
```

```
                   ($table.Schema + "." + $table.Name +  ".sql")) $table

              foreach($Constraint in $table.Checks)
              {
                     #Script the Constraint
                     Write-DDLOutput (Join-Path -Path
                     ($TableConstraintsBackupFolder) -ChildPath
                     ($table.Schema + "." + $table.Name + "." +
                     $Constraint.Name + ".sql")) $Constraint
              }

              foreach ($index in $table.Indexes)
              {
                     #Generate a filename for the table
                     switch($index.IndexKeyType)
                     {
                            DriPrimaryKey
                            {
                                   $filename = Join-Path -Path
                                   ($TableKeysBackupFolder) -ChildPath
                                   ($table.Schema + "." +
                                   $table.Name + "." +
                                   $index.Name + ".sql")
                            }
                            default
                            {
                                   $filename = Join-Path -Path
                                   ($TableIndexesBackupFolder) -ChildPath
                                   ($table.Schema + "." +
                                   $table.Name + "." +
                                   $index.Name + ".sql")
                            }
                      }

                     #Script the index
                     Write-DDLOutput $filename $index
              }

              foreach ($trigger in $table.Triggers)
              {
                     #Script the trigger
                     Write-DDLOutput (Join-Path -Path
                     ($TableTriggersBackupFolder) -ChildPath
                     ($table.Schema + "." + $table.Name + "." +
                     $trigger.Name + ".sql")) $trigger
              }
       }

#Create a folder to store the view scripts
$ViewsBackupFolder = Join-Path -Path $databaseBackupFolder -ChildPath
"Views"
$ViewKeysBackupFolder = Join-Path -Path $ViewsBackupFolder -ChildPath
"Keys"
$ViewIndexesBackupFolder = Join-Path -Path
$ViewsBackupFolder -ChildPath "Indexes"
```

```
$ViewTriggersBackupFolder = Join-Path -Path
$ViewsBackupFolder -ChildPath "Triggers"


#Loop through the views to script them out
foreach ($view in $database.Views | where
{$_.IsSystemObject -eq $false})
{
        #Script the view
        Write-DDLOutput (Join-Path -Path
        ($ViewsBackupFolder) -ChildPath
        ($view.Schema + "." + $view.Name +  ".sql")) $view

        foreach ($index in $view.Indexes)
        {
                #Generate a filename for the table
                switch($index.IndexKeyType)
                {
                        DriPrimaryKey
                         {
                              $filename = Join-Path -Path
                              ($ViewKeysBackupFolder) -ChildPath
                              ($view.Schema + "." +
                              $view.Name + "." + $index.Name + ".sql")
                         }
                        default
                         {
                              $filename = Join-Path -Path
                              ($ViewIndexesBackupFolder) -ChildPath
                              ($view.Schema + "." + $view.Name + "." +
                              $index.Name + ".sql")
                         }
                }

                Write-DDLOutput $filename $index
        }

        foreach ($trigger in $view.Triggers)
        {
                #Script the trigger
                Write-DDLOutput (Join-Path -Path
                ($ViewTriggersBackupFolder) -ChildPath
                ($view.Schema + "." + $view.Name + "." +
                $trigger.Name + ".sql")) $trigger
        }
    }
}
```

Scheduling Script Execution

There are two methods for scheduling script execution. The first is to use Windows Task Scheduler, which is useful if you don't have SQL Server installed on the server from which you wish to execute the PowerShell script. You can simply add a new task to the Scheduler and execute PowerShell.exe, passing the script you want to execute as a parameter.

For servers on which you have SQL Server 2008 R2 or later installed, you also have the option to execute PowerShell as a SQL Server Agent job. This is easily achieved by creating a new step for a job and selecting PowerShell from the Type drop-down box. You can then enter the PowerShell script into the Command text box.

Unfortunately using PowerShell jobs in SQL Server 2008 R2 was not very useful because it would call into PowerShell version 1.0 so many scripts and modules would not work properly. If you want to execute scripts written for PowerShell 2.0 from SQL Server 2008 R2 you are best off using the execute PowerShell.exe method described earlier. Fortunately this is resolved in SQL Server 2012 because it will load PowerShell 2.0

The advantage of using the SQL Server job agent is that you may already have jobs running, and this approach enables you to manage all your jobs in one place. You can also use the logging functionality already built into the SQL Job engine to monitor the execution of the PowerShell script.

SUMMARY

This chapter introduced you to PowerShell's core concepts and provided examples of how PowerShell can be used in a troubleshooting and performance analysis scenario. The scope of possibilities for using PowerShell in a SQL Server environment are almost endless; and where the product team hasn't provided full functionality, the user community has filled the gap in the form of the SQLPSX and PSX libraries on CodePlex.

You are now aware of how you can build your own library of useful functionality within a module, and you have the tools and knowledge to share these with other members of your team or the wider population.

PowerShell is an area of administration that is still in its early stages, and it is being actively developed by the SQL Server team and the Windows team, as well as by other product groups. However, now is the perfect time to begin using this rich shell and scripting environment, and the trusted toolkit it provides, which enable you to be more efficient as a DBA and to maintain a calm and confident attitude when facing production issues.

15

Delivering a SQL Server Health Check

WHAT'S IN THIS CHAPTER?

➤ Understanding the importance of collecting diagnostic and baseline information

➤ Using instance level diagnostic queries

➤ Understanding how Microsoft releases updates for SQL Server

➤ Using database level diagnostic queries

WROX.COM CODE DOWNLOADS FOR THIS CHAPTER

The wrox.com code downloads for this chapter are found at www.wrox.com/ remtitle.cgi?isbn=1118177657 on the Download Code tab. The code is in the Ch15HealthCheck.sql download.

THE IMPORTANCE OF A SQL SERVER HEALTH CHECK

One of the first things you should do with a new or unfamiliar database server is collect as much information as possible about that server — from the details of the hardware and storage subsystem, to the operating system, up to the SQL Server instance itself. You need to know what you are dealing with — whether it is a poorly configured, "ancient" server with a completely inadequate storage subsystem, or, hopefully something much better. This information is a critical starting point for focusing your efforts to properly manage and optimize your database servers. As a database professional, there is really no excuse for not knowing the hardware and configuration details about each of your database servers.

This chapter walks you through a set of queries that you can use for your SQL Server health check, explaining what they mean and how to interpret the results. These queries start at the hardware and instance level, and then enable you to drill down to a particular database to gather more specific information about it.

One roadblock that many database administrators face in collecting this type of information is the bureaucracy within their company or organization. Quite often, someone else in a different department is in charge of provisioning and managing the actual database server hardware and operating system on the database servers. This person is usually a system administrator or system engineer. In larger organizations, a SAN administrator is often in charge of the storage subsystems. These other people, who often have different priorities than you, and usually have relatively little knowledge of SQL Server, can be big obstacles in your quest to gather important information about your database servers. They may view your information-gathering efforts as an unwelcome invasion of their territory and area of expertise, and thus may be reluctant to cooperate with you.

I have often asked other DBAs to tell me about how a particular database server is configured and what type of hardware and storage it is using, only to get vague and nearly useless answers that will not enable evaluation of a server or solve a performance problem. Many DBAs are not allowed to actually log on to the desktop of their database servers, and are completely at the mercy of their system administrator and SAN administrator for all server and storage configuration and management. Because of this, many DBAs are completely in the dark about anything they cannot easily see from SQL Server Management Studio (SSMS), and they have very little information about the details of their server hardware and storage subsystems. I think this type of organizational policy is a huge mistake, as it greatly hinders the overall effectiveness of database administrators. If you are faced with this type of situation as a DBA, you should make every effort to properly improve the matter by reaching out to your counterparts in other departments to explain what needs to be done and why it is important. Policies can often be changed, so don't just accept the situation!

However, regardless of any bureaucratic or organizational obstacles in your way, you can still use techniques from within SQL Server Management Studio (SSMS) to gather most of what you need to do a relatively comprehensive SQL Server health check. One of the most useful and easy to use techniques is to run a standard set of dynamic management view (DMV) and dynamic management function (DMF) queries to gather health-check information about your servers, instances, and databases.

RUNNING DMV AND DMF QUERIES

Since they were first introduced in SQL Server 2005, DMVs and DMFs have been useful tools for easily gathering a wealth of valuable information about your hardware, a SQL Server instance, or individual databases in an instance. With each new version of SQL Server, enhancements have been made to these DMVs and DMFs that increase their utility. SQL Server 2012 is no exception, and offers a number of completely new DMVs and DMFs that you can take advantage of during a SQL Server health check.

This set of queries is designed to be run on SQL Server 2012. Most of the queries will also work on SQL Server 2008 R2 Service Pack 1 or later, but some will not because Microsoft made a few late-breaking changes to some DMVs in SQL Server 2012. Some of the queries will also run on SQL

Server 2005, SQL Server 2008, and pre-SP1 builds of SQL Server 2008 R2; but the older your version of SQL Server, the fewer of these queries are going to work for you.

In order to run most DMV and DMF queries, you need the VIEW SERVER STATE permission on your SQL Server instance. You will already have this permission if you have system administrator rights within a SQL Server instance, but you should probably create a dedicated login and matching user that has VIEW SERVER STATE permission for use by non-administrators or monitoring applications. Once you have the rights to run DMV and DMF queries, you are ready to get started.

I strongly recommend that you run each of the queries in the following sections one at a time, after reading the background and instructions first. After you get the results of each query, take a few moments to peruse them to ensure that they make sense. Check the notes about how to interpret the results, and consider what you are seeing and whether the results seem to reinforce or contradict other results and metrics that you may have gathered. It's a good idea to save the results of these queries in individual, labeled tabs in a spreadsheet so that you have a baseline and a record of the changing results over time.

For these server- and instance-level queries, it does not really matter to which database on the instance you are connected. Once you reach the database-specific queries starting at Listing 15-32, don't forget to change your database context to the particular database you are interested in. This may seem obvious, but I have seen many people run an entire set of database-specific queries while they are still pointed at the master database. This will give you a wealth of useless information about the master database!

First, you want to find out exactly what version, edition, and build of SQL Server you have running on your instance of SQL Server. You also want to know whether it is x64 or x86 and what operating system you are running on. One very simple, non-DMV query, shown in Listing 15-1, gives you all that information, including the compile date and time of your SQL Server build.

LISTING 15-1: SQL Server and operating system information

```
-- SQL and OS Version information for current instance
SELECT @@VERSION AS [SQL Server and OS Version Info];

-- SQL Server 2012 Builds
-- Build              Description
-- 11.00.1055         CTP0
-- 11.00.1103         CTP1
-- 11.00.1540         CTP3
-- 11.00.1515         CTP3 plus Test Update
-- 11.00.1750         RC0
-- 11.00.1913         RC1
-- 11.00.2300         RTM
-- 11.00.2316         RTM CU1
-- 11.00.2325         RTM CU2
-- 11.00.2809         SP1 CTP3 (un-supported in production)
```

A sample of the results you will get from the preceding query is shown in Listing 15-2.

LISTING 15-2: SQL Server and operating system results

```
Microsoft SQL Server 2012 RC0 - 11.0.1750.32 (X64) Nov  4 2011 17:54:22 Copyright
(c) Microsoft Corporation Enterprise Evaluation Edition (64-bit) on Windows NT 6.1
<X64> (Build 7601: Service Pack 1)
```

This set of results tells you that you are using the x64 Enterprise Evaluation Edition of SQL Server 2012 Release Candidate 0 (RC0), build 1750 running on x64 Windows NT 6.1 Service Pack 1 (which could be either Windows Server 2008 R2 SP1 or Windows 7 SP1). For a production SQL Server instance, you would want to be running Windows Server 2008 R2 or Windows Server 2012, which are x64 only, rather than on Windows 7. Knowing the version, edition, and build of your SQL Server instance helps you determine what features are available within SQL Server. For example, data compression is available only in Enterprise Edition, so if you have Standard Edition or Business Intelligence Edition of SQL Server 2012, you cannot use data compression.

SQL SERVER BUILDS

Microsoft periodically (currently, every eight weeks) releases a cumulative update (CU) for SQL Server. Each update is a collection of typically 10–40 hotfixes for SQL Server that is released as an integrated setup package. About every 12–18 months, Microsoft releases a service pack for a particular major version of SQL Server, such as SQL Server 2012. When a SQL Server service pack is released, it means that you have a new release branch of that major version of SQL Server, which has its own separate cumulative updates. You need to know what release branch your SQL Server instance is on, so that you know which cumulative update to download and install.

Knowing the build number and compile date and time for your instance tells you how old your SQL Server instance is, which is very important. Microsoft originally releases a new major version of SQL Server as the *release to manufacturing (RTM)* build, which is what you get from a DVD or .iso image of the product. Many organizations install the RTM build of a major version SQL Server, but never update their SQL Server instances to a newer build, which I think is a huge mistake. I firmly believe that you should make a concerted effort to keep your SQL Server instances up to date with the most current service packs and cumulative updates.

For example, if you installed a new instance of SQL Server 2008 R2 from an .iso image that you downloaded from Microsoft, you would have Build 1600, in the RTM branch. If you then installed SQL Server 2008 R2 SP1, you would have Build 2500, in the Service Pack 1 branch. Any further cumulative updates on this instance would have to be from the Service Pack 1 branch until you moved to a later service pack for SQL Server 2008 R2.

This discussion is important for several reasons. First, if you are running on a very old build of a major version of SQL Server, you are much more likely to encounter defects that have been fixed in newer builds of that version, which makes your life as a DBA more difficult. Second, Microsoft eventually retires older release branches (usually one year after the next service pack is released). If you are on a retired release branch, there will be no more cumulative updates for that release branch; and if you ever have to call Microsoft CSS to open a support case, you will receive only limited troubleshooting support until you get on a release branch that is still fully supported. Don't let this happen to you!

Making the effort to watch for SQL Server service packs and cumulative updates, checking the fix list, downloading them, testing them, and deploying them in your production environment is a beneficial exercise for you and your organization. Deploying these updates using a planned, rolling upgrade strategy enables you to complete the deployments with minimal service interruptions, and it forces you to exercise some of your high-availability (HA), disaster-recovery (DR) infrastructure while keeping your servers up to date. I think this is much better than being a DBA who is overly hesitant to apply any SQL Server updates because you are afraid you might break something.

The next query you want to run, shown in Listing 15-3, will give you a little more information about your operating system on the database server, including the language.

LISTING 15-3: Windows information

```
-- Windows information (SQL Server 2012)
SELECT windows_release, windows_service_pack_level,
       windows_sku, os_language_version
FROM sys.dm_os_windows_info WITH (NOLOCK) OPTION (RECOMPILE);

-- Gives you major OS version, Service Pack, Edition,
-- and language info for the operating system
```

The preceding query simply gives you a little more specific information about the operating system, in a form that is easier to filter and parse than what you get from SELECT @@VERSION. Now that you know more about your operating system, you can start to gather some hardware information.

The query shown in Listing 15-4 indicates how many logical processors you have, the hyperthread ratio of the processors, how many physical CPUs you have, and how much physical memory you have in your database server. It also indicates whether you are running in a virtual machine and when SQL Server was last started. Unfortunately, the hyperthread ratio does not distinguish between logical and physical cores in each physical processor. For example, the laptop used to write this chapter on is a dual-core processor with hyperthreading, and the hyperthread ratio is 4. If my laptop were a quad-core without hyperthreading, my hyperthread ratio would also be 4. Especially with the new, core-based licensing in SQL Server 2012 Enterprise Edition, it is important to distinguish between true physical cores and logical cores. Fortunately, the next two queries will help clear up this confusion.

LISTING 15-4: Hardware information

```
-- Hardware information from SQL Server 2012 (new virtual_machine_type_desc)
-- (Cannot distinguish between HT and multi-core)
SELECT cpu_count AS [Logical CPU Count], hyperthread_ratio AS [Hyperthread
Ratio],cpu_count/hyperthread_ratio AS [Physical CPU Count],
physical_memory_kb/1024 AS [Physical Memory (MB)],
affinity_type_desc, virtual_machine_type_desc, sqlserver_start_time
FROM sys.dm_os_sys_info WITH (NOLOCK) OPTION (RECOMPILE);

-- Gives you some good basic hardware information about your database server
```

The query shown next in Listing 15-5 simply reads the SQL Server Error Log to get the manufacturer and model number of your database server. If you are a true hardware geek like me, simply knowing that you have a Dell PowerEdge R710 server tells you quite a bit by itself, without having to look anything else up. Otherwise, you can do some research with your favorite search engine to find out more details about your server after you know the manufacturer and model number.

LISTING 15-5: Server manufacturer and model

```
-- Get System Manufacturer and model number from
-- SQL Server Error log. This query might take a few seconds
-- if you have not recycled your error log recently
EXEC xp_readerrorlog 0,1,"Manufacturer";

-- This can help you determine the capabilities
-- and capacities of your database server
```

Knowing the manufacturer and model of your database server enables you to find out important things about it, such as how many processor sockets it has, how many memory slots it has, and how many and what type of PCI-E expansion slots it has. It also tells you what type of processors (Intel or AMD), and what generation(s) of processors, that server model supports.

Now that you know how many physical processors and how many logical cores are visible to your database server, you need to find out the exact model number of the processor(s) in your database server. Once you know this, you can use your favorite search engine to determine each processor's exact specifications, including how many physical cores it has, whether it supports hyperthreading, TurboBoost, or TurboCore, how large the L2 and L3 cache is, and the rated clock speed of the processor. The query in Listing 15-6 returns the processor description and the rated clock speed from the Windows Registry.

LISTING 15-6: Processor description

```
-- Get processor description from Windows Registry
EXEC xp_instance_regread
'HKEY_LOCAL_MACHINE',
'HARDWARE\DESCRIPTION\System\CentralProcessor\0',
'ProcessorNameString';

-- Gives you the model number and rated clock speed of your processor(s)
```

It is very important to know the rated clock speed of the processors in your database server, as it is possible that your processors are not running at their full speed at all times due to some form of power management. By default, Windows Server 2008 and Windows Server 2008 R2 use the Balanced Windows Power Plan. This means that when the processors are not under a high workload, they reduce their clock speed to reduce their electrical power usage. This is great for extending the battery life on laptops, and it is good for reducing electrical power usage in desktop systems and even web servers. Unfortunately, power management is not such a great option for database servers. That's because when the processor sees a sudden increase in workload, it responds by increasing the clock speed back to full speed. That sounds good so far, but this response to the spike in the workload does not happen quickly enough to avoid a negative effect on query performance. Some short duration, relatively inexpensive queries may not even trigger the throttle-up mechanism, so they are executed while the processor is still running at reduced speed.

In my experience, I have typically seen a 20–25% hit to performance for OLTP workloads when using the Windows default Balanced power plan instead of the High Performance power plan. It depends on which processor you are using, with Intel Nehalem and Westmere processors (see Chapter 2, "Demystifying Hardware") being particularly vulnerable. Even with the High Performance power plan, it is still possible that your database server is being affected by hardware power management, controlled from the main system BIOS.

To avoid this problem, first make sure your database servers are using the High Performance power plan, not the Balanced power plan. This setting can be changed dynamically, with no reboot of Windows required. Second, use CPU-Z, a free tool available from cpuid.com to determine the actual clock speed at which your processors are running. If you are using the High Performance power plan and your processor is still not running at full speed, you need to go into the main system BIOS and change its power management settings to either OS control, or to be disabled completely. Depending on your organization, you may have to get your system administrator to make this change for you, as it requires a reboot of the server to get into the main BIOS configuration.

Now that you know a little more about your hardware and whether you are getting the full benefit of the money you spent on it, it is time to collect some information about the SQL Server Services that are installed on the instance. In SQL Server 2008 R2 Service Pack 1 and later, and in SQL Server 2012, you can learn quite a bit about which SQL Server Services are installed and how they are configured and running from the query shown in Listing 15-7.

LISTING 15-7: SQL Server Services information

```
-- SQL Server Services information from SQL Server 2012
SELECT servicename, startup_type_desc, status_desc,
last_startup_time, service_account, is_clustered, cluster_nodename
FROM sys.dm_server_services WITH (NOLOCK) OPTION (RECOMPILE);

-- Gives you information about your installed SQL Server Services,
-- whether they are clustered, and which node owns the cluster resources
```

The preceding query tells you exactly which SQL Server Services are installed, their startup type, whether they are running, which account credentials they are using, when they last started, whether they are clustered, and what node they are running on in the cluster. This is all good information to know, and it is very easy to find out with this new DMV. Next, you can get some information about the SQL Server Error Log with the query shown in Listing 15-8.

LISTING 15-8: SQL Server Error Log information

```
-- Shows you where the SQL Server error log is located and how it is configured
SELECT is_enabled, [path], max_size, max_files
FROM sys.dm_os_server_diagnostics_log_configurations WITH (NOLOCK)
OPTION (RECOMPILE);

-- Knowing this information is important for troubleshooting purposes
```

This query gives you the file path to the SQL Server Error Log (which is simply a text file that you can open in Notepad in an emergency). If your SQL Server Service ever fails to start, the first place you should look is in the SQL Server Error Log. Of course, if your SQL Server Service is not running, you won't be able to run this query, so you should run it ahead of time and store the results in your server run book. Next, you will find out whether your database server is using Windows Clustering, with the query shown in Listing 15-9.

LISTING 15-9: Operating system cluster information

```
-- Get information about your OS cluster
--(if your database server is in a cluster)
SELECT VerboseLogging, SqlDumperDumpFlags, SqlDumperDumpPath,
       SqlDumperDumpTimeOut, FailureConditionLevel, HealthCheckTimeout
FROM sys.dm_os_cluster_properties WITH (NOLOCK) OPTION (RECOMPILE);

-- You will see no results if your instance is not clustered
```

This query returns some configuration information about your Windows cluster. If it returns no information, then your operating system on the database server is not clustered (you have a standalone instance), in which case you can skip the query shown in Listing 15-10.

Otherwise, if you are using a cluster, you can use the query shown in Listing 15-10 to get some useful information about your cluster nodes.

LISTING 15-10: Cluster node information

```
-- Get information about your cluster nodes and their status
-- (if your database server is in a cluster)
SELECT NodeName, status_description, is_current_owner
FROM sys.dm_os_cluster_nodes WITH (NOLOCK) OPTION (RECOMPILE);

-- Knowing which node owns the cluster resources is critical
-- Especially when you are installing Windows or SQL Server updates
```

This query returns all your cluster nodes, including their status and whether they own the cluster resources. For example, if you have a three-node cluster, this query would return three rows and indicate which node currently owned the SQL Server instance. This is actually important information to know if you are getting ready to do some maintenance on the cluster, such as installing a

SQL Server cumulative update, as you would want to first install it on a node that does not own the cluster resources as part of a rolling update.

Next, you want to start gathering some additional information about how your SQL Server instance is configured, which you can do with the query shown in Listing 15-11.

LISTING 15-11: Instance configuration values

```
-- Get configuration values for instance
SELECT name, value, value_in_use, [description]
FROM sys.configurations WITH (NOLOCK)
ORDER BY name OPTION (RECOMPILE);

-- Focus on
-- backup compression default
-- clr enabled (only enable if it is needed)
-- lightweight pooling (should be zero)
-- max degree of parallelism
-- max server memory (MB) (set to an appropriate value)
-- optimize for ad hoc workloads (should be 1)
-- priority boost (should be zero)
```

This query returns current configuration values for a fairly large number of instance-level properties. Some of these properties can be changed using the SSMS graphical user interface, but they can all be changed using the sp_configure system stored procedure.

You should focus on a few key configuration values, which include backup compression default, clr enabled, lightweight pooling, max degree of parallelism, max server memory (MB), optimize for ad hoc workloads, and priority boost. Of these, the first two values that you typically want to change from their default values are backup compression default and optimize for ad hoc workloads (see Chapter 3), both of which should be enabled by setting them to 1. Next, I suggest setting max server memory (MB) to an appropriate, non-default value, taking into account which SQL Server components are installed and running on your SQL Server instance. The idea behind this is to ensure that memory is reserved for the operating system and other SQL SERVER components, like SQL Server Integration Services (SSIS), so there is sufficient memory for them to operate properly.

In SQL Server 2008 R2 and earlier, the max server memory (MB) setting controlled only the memory used by the SQL Server buffer pool, but in SQL Server 2012 it controls overall memory usage by most other Database Engine components, which means you can probably set the max server memory (MB) setting a little bit higher on SQL Server 2012 than in previous versions (See Chapter 3).

If any databases running on your instance use CLR assemblies, you will have to enable CLR integration by setting clr enabled to 1. Otherwise, it should not be enabled, as it uses some resources on your database server and will increase your attack surface. Most other instance configuration options should usually be left at their default values, unless you have a good reason to change them and you know what you are doing.

> **NOTE** *Whenever I see every instance-level property set at its default value, I know that the DBA or other administrator who installed and/or manages this instance is inexperienced or perhaps just an "accidental DBA" who does not understand which instance settings should be changed. It is also possible that this person was just too busy to change anything from the default settings or does not pay sufficient attention to detail (a critical trait for a great DBA).*

Next, you are going to find out a little bit about the network configuration settings on the database server with the query shown in Listing 15-12.

LISTING 15-12: TCP Listener information

```
-- Get information about TCP Listener for SQL Server
SELECT listener_id, ip_address, is_ipv4, port, type_desc, state_desc, start_time
FROM sys.dm_tcp_listener_states WITH (NOLOCK) OPTION (RECOMPILE);

-- Helpful for network and connectivity troubleshooting
```

This DMV, which was added in SQL Server 2008 R2 SP1, tells you which TCP ports are being used by the TCP Listener — for T-SQL, the Service Broker, and database mirroring. This is useful information for troubleshooting general network connectivity and firewall issues. It is also useful for investigating connectivity issues with SQL Server AlwaysOn availability replicas.

The next query, shown in Listing 15-13, provides SQL Server–related information collected from the Windows Registry, using the sys.dm_server_registry DMV that was added in SQL Server 2008 R2 SP1.

LISTING 15-13: SQL Server Registry information

```
-- SQL Server Registry information
SELECT registry_key, value_name, value_data
FROM sys.dm_server_registry WITH (NOLOCK) OPTION (RECOMPILE);

-- This lets you safely read some SQL Server related
-- information from the Windows Registry
```

This query, which was added in SQL Server 2008 R2 SP1, gives you quite a bit of useful information about your SQL Server instance, such as which network protocols are enabled, where the SQL Server main executable is located, and where the SQL Server Agent executable is installed. This is safer and easier to use than the old xp_instance_regread extended stored procedure, although it admittedly does not allow you to query as many different values.

Next, to investigate whether this instance of SQL Server has been generating any memory dumps, you can use the query shown in Listing 15-14.

LISTING 15-14: SQL Server memory dump information

```
-- Get information on location, time and size of any memory dumps from SQL Server
SELECT [filename], creation_time, size_in_bytes
FROM sys.dm_server_memory_dumps WITH (NOLOCK) OPTION (RECOMPILE);

-- This will not return any rows if you have
-- not had any memory dumps (which is a good thing)
```

This query, which was also added in SQL Server 2008 R2 SP1, tells you if and when your SQL Server instance has generated any memory dumps. Hopefully, you will not see any results for this query. If you do, start looking in the SQL Server Error Log(s) that correspond to the times for the SQL Server memory dumps to see if you can find any relevant information about what happened to generate the memory dump. You should also look at the Windows Event logs, and maybe even get ready to open a support case with Microsoft.

Next, to find out how many databases are running on your SQL Server instance, and where they are located, use the query shown in Listing 15-15.

LISTING 15-15: Database filenames and paths

```
-- File Names and Paths for Tempdb and all user databases in instance
SELECT DB_NAME([database_id])AS [Database Name],
       [file_id], name, physical_name, type_desc, state_desc,
       CONVERT( bigint, size/128.0) AS [Total Size in MB]
FROM sys.master_files WITH (NOLOCK)
WHERE [database_id] > 4
AND [database_id] <> 32767
OR [database_id] = 2
ORDER BY DB_NAME([database_id]) OPTION (RECOMPILE);

-- Things to look at:
-- Are data files and log files on different drives?
-- Is everything on the C: drive?
-- Is TempDB on dedicated drives?
       -- Are there multiple data files?
```

This query returns the file paths and sizes for the data and log files for all the user databases and tempdb. If the type_desc column is ROWS, that means you have a data file, whereas LOG means a transaction log file. This query tells you how many user databases are running on the instance and how large they are, which gives you some idea of the complexity of the server's workload.

You should be looking to see whether the data and log files are on different drive letters. Some SAN administrators like to provision just one large LUN, which makes it harder to track what is going on from SQL Server and Windows. You also want to ensure that tempdb is not running on the C: drive of the database server (which is what happens with a default standalone installation of SQL Server). You can also see whether there are multiple tempdb data files instead of just one (See Chapter 8), and whether the larger user databases have multiple data files instead of just one large data file.

Next, you are going to discover some key database properties for all the databases on the instance, using the query shown in Listing 15-16.

LISTING 15-16: Database property information

```
-- Recovery model, log reuse wait description, log file size, log usage size
-- and compatibility level for all databases on instance
SELECT db.[name] AS [Database Name], db.recovery_model_desc AS [Recovery Model],
db.log_reuse_wait_desc AS [Log Reuse Wait Description],
ls.cntr_value AS [Log Size (KB)], lu.cntr_value AS [Log Used (KB)],
CAST(CAST(lu.cntr_value AS FLOAT) / CAST(ls.cntr_value AS FLOAT)AS DECIMAL(18,2)) *
100 AS
[Log Used %], db.[compatibility_level] AS [DB Compatibility Level],
db.page_verify_option_desc AS [Page Verify Option], db.is_auto_create_stats_on,
db.is_auto_update_stats_on, db.is_auto_update_stats_async_on,
db.is_parameterization_forced,
db.snapshot_isolation_state_desc, db.is_read_committed_snapshot_on,
is_auto_shrink_on, is_auto_close_on
FROM sys.databases AS db WITH (NOLOCK)
INNER JOIN sys.dm_os_performance_counters AS lu WITH (NOLOCK)
ON db.name = lu.instance_name
INNER JOIN sys.dm_os_performance_counters AS ls WITH (NOLOCK)
ON db.name = ls.instance_name
WHERE lu.counter_name LIKE N'Log File(s) Used Size (KB)%'
AND ls.counter_name LIKE N'Log File(s) Size (KB)%'
AND ls.cntr_value > 0 OPTION (RECOMPILE);

-- Things to look at:
-- How many databases are on the instance?
-- What recovery models are they using?
-- What is the log reuse wait description?
-- How full are the transaction logs ?
-- What compatibility level are they on?
```

This query returns all the databases on the instance, including the system databases. For each database, a number of important database properties are listed. First is the recovery model for the database, which can be SIMPLE, FULL, or BULK-LOGGED. Knowing the recovery model for each of your user databases is critically important! Next, you get the log reuse wait description for each database, which tells you what is preventing the active portion of the transaction log from being reused.

One of the most common mistakes made by novice DBAs is to have a database running in the default recovery model of FULL without taking regular transaction log backups. When this happens, the transaction log eventually fills up completely and attempts to autogrow the transaction log file (if autogrow is enabled). If the transaction log is able to autogrow, it continues to do so each time it fills up, until at some point it completely fills up the disk where it is located. When this happens, you will have a read-only database until you do something to correct the issue. While this is happening, your log reuse wait description for that database will show up as LOG BACKUP.

Regularly monitoring your log reuse wait description for each database also alerts you about other problems you need to investigate. For example, if you are using database mirroring and there are any problems with mirroring (such as not being able to send the log activity to the mirror or not being able to apply the log activity fast enough on the mirror), you will see a log reuse wait description of DATABASE MIRRORING. Other common log reuse wait descriptions that bear further investigation include REPLICATION and ACTIVE TRANSACTION.

This query also tells you how large your transaction log file is for each database, and how full it is, which is good information to know! I don't like to see a transaction log become more than 50% full. If that is happening, you can either make the transaction log file bigger or take more frequent transaction log backups.

Finally, you are retrieving a number of other important database-level properties for each database on the instance, including the compatibility level, the page verify option, auto create statistics, auto update statistics, auto update statistics asynchronously (See Chapter 5), forced parameterization, and the snapshot isolation level.

Next, the results of the query shown in Listing 15-17 indicate which database files are seeing the most I/O stalls.

LISTING 15-17: I/O stall information by database file

```
-- Calculates average stalls per read, per write,
-- and per total input/output for each database file.
SELECT DB_NAME(fs.database_id) AS [Database Name], mf.physical_name,
io_stall_read_ms, num_of_reads,
CAST(io_stall_read_ms/(1.0 + num_of_reads) AS NUMERIC(10,1)) AS
[avg_read_stall_ms],io_stall_write_ms,
num_of_writes,CAST(io_stall_write_ms/(1.0+num_of_writes) AS NUMERIC(10,1)) AS
[avg_write_stall_ms],
io_stall_read_ms + io_stall_write_ms AS [io_stalls], num_of_reads + num_of_writes
AS [total_io],
CAST((io_stall_read_ms + io_stall_write_ms)/(1.0 + num_of_reads + num_of_writes) AS
NUMERIC(10,1))
AS [avg_io_stall_ms]
FROM sys.dm_io_virtual_file_stats(null,null) AS fs
INNER JOIN sys.master_files AS mf WITH (NOLOCK)
ON fs.database_id = mf.database_id
AND fs.[file_id] = mf.[file_id]
ORDER BY avg_io_stall_ms DESC OPTION (RECOMPILE);

-- Helps determine which database files on
-- the entire instance have the most I/O bottlenecks
```

This query lists each database file (data and log) on the instance, ordered by the average I/O stall time in milliseconds. This is one way of determining which database files are spending the most time waiting on I/O. It also gives you a better idea of the read/write activity for each database file, which helps you characterize your workload by database file. If you see a lot of database files on the same drive that are at the top of the list for this query, that could be an indication that you are seeing disk I/O bottlenecks on that drive. You would want to investigate this issue further, using Windows Performance Monitor metrics such as Avg Disk Sec/Write and Avg Disk Sec/Read for that logical disk. After you have gathered more metrics and evidence, talk to your system administrator or storage administrator about this issue. Depending on what type of storage you are using (See Chapter 4), it might be possible to improve the I/O performance situation by adding more spindles, changing the RAID controller cache policy, or changing the RAID level. You also might consider moving some of your database files to other drives if possible.

Now, using the query shown in Listing 15-18, you are going to see which user databases on the instance are using the most memory.

LISTING 15-18: Total buffer usage by database

```
-- Get total buffer usage by database for current instance
SELECT DB_NAME(database_id) AS [Database Name],
COUNT(*) * 8/1024.0 AS [Cached Size (MB)]
FROM sys.dm_os_buffer_descriptors WITH (NOLOCK)
WHERE database_id > 4 -- system databases
AND database_id <> 32767 -- ResourceDB
GROUP BY DB_NAME(database_id)
ORDER BY [Cached Size (MB)] DESC OPTION (RECOMPILE);

-- Tells you how much memory (in the buffer pool)
-- is being used by each database on the instance
```

This query will list the total buffer usage for each user database running on the current instance. Especially if you are seeing signs of internal memory pressure, you are going to be interested in knowing which database(s) are using the most space in the buffer pool. One way to reduce memory usage in a particular database is to ensure that you don't have a lot of missing indexes on large tables that are causing a large number of index or table scans. Another way, if you have SQL Server Enterprise Edition, is to start using SQL Server data compression on some of your larger indexes (if they are good candidates for data compression). The ideal candidate for data compression is a large static table that is highly compressible because of the data types and actual data in the table. A bad candidate for data compression is a small, highly volatile table that does not compress well. A compressed index will stay compressed in the buffer pool, unless any data is updated. This means that you may be able to save many gigabytes of space in your buffer pool under ideal circumstances.

Next, you will take a look at which user databases on the instance are using the most processor time by using the query shown in Listing 15-19.

LISTING 15-19: CPU usage by database

```
-- Get CPU utilization by database
WITH DB_CPU_Stats
AS
(SELECT DatabaseID, DB_Name(DatabaseID) AS [DatabaseName],
 SUM(total_worker_time) AS [CPU_Time_Ms]
 FROM sys.dm_exec_query_stats AS qs
 CROSS APPLY (SELECT CONVERT(int, value) AS [DatabaseID]
            FROM sys.dm_exec_plan_attributes(qs.plan_handle)
            WHERE attribute = N'dbid') AS F_DB
 GROUP BY DatabaseID)
SELECT ROW_NUMBER() OVER(ORDER BY [CPU_Time_Ms] DESC) AS [row_num],
```

```
          DatabaseName, [CPU_Time_Ms],
          CAST([CPU_Time_Ms] * 1.0 / SUM([CPU_Time_Ms])
          OVER() * 100.0 AS DECIMAL(5, 2)) AS [CPUPercent]
FROM DB_CPU_Stats
WHERE DatabaseID > 4 -- system databases
AND DatabaseID <> 32767 -- ResourceDB
ORDER BY row_num OPTION (RECOMPILE);


-- Helps determine which database is
-- using the most CPU resources on the instance
```

This query shows you the CPU utilization time by database for the entire instance. It can help you characterize your workload, but you need to take the results with a bit of caution. If you have recently cleared the plan cache for a particular database, using the DBCC FLUSHPROCINDB (database_id) command, it will throw off the overall CPU utilization by database numbers for the query. Still, this query can be useful for getting a rough idea of which database(s) are using the most CPU on your instance.

The next query, shown in Listing 15-20, is extremely useful. It rolls up the top cumulative wait statistics since SQL Server was last restarted or since the wait statistics were cleared by using the DBCC SQLPERF ('sys.dm_os_wait_stats', CLEAR) command.

LISTING 15-20: Top cumulative wait types for the instance

```
-- Isolate top waits for server instance since last restart or statistics clear
WITH Waits AS
(SELECT wait_type, wait_time_ms / 1000. AS wait_time_s,
100. * wait_time_ms / SUM(wait_time_ms) OVER() AS pct,
ROW_NUMBER() OVER(ORDER BY wait_time_ms DESC) AS rn
FROM sys.dm_os_wait_stats WITH (NOLOCK)
WHERE wait_type NOT IN (N'CLR_SEMAPHORE',N'LAZYWRITER_SLEEP',N'RESOURCE_QUEUE',
N'SLEEP_TASK',N'SLEEP_SYSTEMTASK',N'SQLTRACE_BUFFER_FLUSH',N'WAITFOR',
N'LOGMGR_QUEUE',N'CHECKPOINT_QUEUE', N'REQUEST_FOR_DEADLOCK_SEARCH',
N'XE_TIMER_EVENT',N'BROKER_TO_FLUSH',N'BROKER_TASK_STOP',N'CLR_MANUAL_EVENT',
N'CLR_AUTO_EVENT',N'DISPATCHER_QUEUE_SEMAPHORE', N'FT_IFTS_SCHEDULER_IDLE_WAIT',
N'XE_DISPATCHER_WAIT', N'XE_DISPATCHER_JOIN', N'SQLTRACE_INCREMENTAL_FLUSH_SLEEP',
N'ONDEMAND_TASK_QUEUE', N'BROKER_EVENTHANDLER', N'SLEEP_BPOOL_FLUSH',
N'DIRTY_PAGE_POLL', N'HADR_FILESTREAM_IOMGR_IOCOMPLETION',
N'SP_SERVER_DIAGNOSTICS_SLEEP'))

SELECT W1.wait_type,
CAST(W1.wait_time_s AS DECIMAL(12, 2)) AS wait_time_s,
CAST(W1.pct AS DECIMAL(12, 2)) AS pct,
CAST(SUM(W2.pct) AS DECIMAL(12, 2)) AS running_pct
FROM Waits AS W1
INNER JOIN Waits AS W2
ON W2.rn <= W1.rn
GROUP BY W1.rn, W1.wait_type, W1.wait_time_s, W1.pct
HAVING SUM(W2.pct) - W1.pct < 99 OPTION (RECOMPILE); -- percentage threshold

-- Clear Wait Stats
-- DBCC SQLPERF('sys.dm_os_wait_stats', CLEAR);
```

This query will help you zero in on what your SQL Server instance is spending the most time waiting for. Especially if your SQL Server instance is under stress or having performance problems, this can be very valuable information. Knowing that your top cumulative wait types are all I/O related can point you in the right direction for doing further evidence gathering and investigation of your I/O subsystem. However, be aware of several important caveats when using and interpreting the results of this query.

First, this is only a rollup of wait types since the last time your SQL Server instance was restarted, or the last time your wait statistics were cleared. If your SQL Server instance has been running for several months and something important was recently changed, the cumulative wait stats will not show the current actual top wait types, but will instead be weighted toward the overall top wait types over the entire time the instance has been running. This will give you a false picture of the current situation.

Second, there are literally hundreds of different wait types (with more being added in each new version of SQL Server), and only a small number of them are documented in SQL Server Books Online. There is a lot of bad information on the Internet about what many wait types mean, and how you should consider addressing them. Bob Ward, who works for Microsoft Support, is a very reliable source for SQL Server wait type information. He has a SQL Server Wait Type Repository available online at `http://blogs.msdn.com/b/psssql/archive/2009/11/03/` `the-sql-server-wait-type-repository.aspx` that documents many SQL Server wait types, including what action you might want to take to alleviate that wait type.

Finally, many common wait types are called *benign* wait types, meaning you can safely ignore them in most situations. The most common benign wait types are filtered out in the NOT IN clause of the health check query to make the results more relevant. Even so, I constantly get questions from DBAs who are obsessing over a particular wait type that shows up in this query. My answer is basically that if your database instance is running well, with no other signs of stress, you probably don't need to worry too much about your top wait type, particularly if it is an uncommon wait type. SQL Server is always waiting on something; but if the server is running well, with no other warning signs, you should relax a little.

Next, using the query shown in Listing 15-21, you are going to look at the cumulative signal (CPU) waits for the instance.

LISTING 15-21: Signal waits for the instance

```
-- Signal Waits for instance
SELECT CAST(100.0 * SUM(signal_wait_time_ms) / SUM (wait_time_ms) AS NUMERIC(20,2))
 AS [%signal (cpu) waits],
CAST(100.0 * SUM(wait_time_ms - signal_wait_time_ms) / SUM (wait_time_ms) AS
NUMERIC(20,2)) AS [%resource waits]
FROM sys.dm_os_wait_stats WITH (NOLOCK) OPTION (RECOMPILE);

-- Signal Waits above 15-20% is usually a sign of CPU pressure
```

Signal waits are CPU-related waits. If you are seeing other signs of CPU pressure on your SQL Server instance, this query can help confirm or deny the fact that you are seeing sustained cumulative CPU pressure. Usually, seeing signal waits above 15–20% is a sign of CPU pressure.

Now you will take a look at which logins have the most open database connections, using the query shown in Listing 15-22.

LISTING 15-22: Login count information

```
--  Get logins that are connected and how many sessions they have
SELECT login_name, COUNT(session_id) AS [session_count]
FROM sys.dm_exec_sessions WITH (NOLOCK)
GROUP BY login_name
ORDER BY COUNT(session_id) DESC OPTION (RECOMPILE);

-- This can help characterize your workload and
-- determine whether you are seeing a normal level of activity
```

This query is one way to gauge whether you are seeing a normal level of activity on your database server. You can look at the number of connections for each login (especially if you use application-level logins) to determine whether you are seeing a normal workload. For example, if one of your logins typically sees about 150 active connections but you are seeing 350 connections for that login, then you probably have good reason to suspect that your workload has changed and your database server may be working harder than usual.

This query is also good for troubleshooting and confirming database connectivity. If you are seeing active connections for particular logins, then you know that at least some web or application servers are able to connect using that login. You can also use the old DBA trick of using a Microsoft Data Link (.udl file) to verify connectivity from a remote server.

You can easily create a Microsoft Data Link file on any machine running Windows 2000 or newer by creating a new, empty text file and then changing the file extension from .txt to .udl. Then you can double-click on the .udl file and you will open a Data Link Properties dialog. After you enter valid login credentials for the database server and database that you want to connect to, you can click on the Test Connection button to verify that you can make a database connection to that database on that server. This is a good troubleshooting tool that you can use on a web server or application server that does not require any development tools to be installed to verify connectivity from that server to the database server.

Next, using the query shown in Listing 15-23, you will take a look at some current task and pending I/O count information.

LISTING 15-23: Average Task Count information

```
-- Get Average Task Counts (run multiple times)
SELECT AVG(current_tasks_count) AS [Avg Task Count],
AVG(runnable_tasks_count) AS [Avg Runnable Task Count],
AVG(pending_disk_io_count) AS [Avg Pending DiskIO Count]
FROM sys.dm_os_schedulers WITH (NOLOCK)
WHERE scheduler_id < 255 OPTION (RECOMPILE);

-- Sustained values above 10 suggest further investigation in that area
-- High Avg Task Counts are often caused by blocking or other resource contention
-- High Avg Runnable Task Counts are a good sign of CPU pressure
-- High Avg Pending DiskIO Counts are a sign of disk pressure
```

This is one query that you will want to run multiple times in quick succession, as the values returned change very frequently, depending on your workload and how your SQL Server instance is running. Any value for these three columns that stays above 10 for a sustained period is cause for some concern. The Average Task Count (per CPU scheduler) is a good indicator of your overall workload level. Sustained high Average Task Counts are often caused by blocking or other resource contention. The Average Runnable Task Count indicates how many tasks are waiting for CPU time on each CPU scheduler. It is a very reliable indicator of CPU pressure. The Average Pending DiskIO Count measures how many pending I/O operations are on each CPU scheduler, so it is a good indicator of overall I/O pressure. This value in particular will jump around a lot as your I/O subsystem is under stress. For all three of these columns, lower values are better than higher values.

The next query, shown in Listing 15-24, will return your CPU utilization history over the last 256 minutes, in one-minute intervals.

LISTING 15-24: CPU utilization history

```
-- Get CPU Utilization History for last 256 minutes (in one minute intervals)
-- This version works with SQL Server 2008 and above
DECLARE @ts_now bigint = (SELECT cpu_ticks/(cpu_ticks/ms_ticks)
                          FROM sys.dm_os_sys_info WITH (NOLOCK));

SELECT TOP(256) SQLProcessUtilization AS [SQL Server Process CPU Utilization],
               SystemIdle AS [System Idle Process],
               100 - SystemIdle - SQLProcessUtilization
               AS [Other Process CPU Utilization],
               DATEADD(ms, -1 * (@ts_now - [timestamp]),
               GETDATE()) AS [Event Time]
FROM (SELECT record.value('(./Record/@id)[1]', 'int') AS record_id,
    record.value('(./Record/SchedulerMonitorEvent/SystemHealth/SystemIdle)[1]', 'int')
    AS[SystemIdle],record.value('(./Record/SchedulerMonitorEvent/SystemHealth/
    ProcessUtilization)[1]','int')
            AS [SQLProcessUtilization], [timestamp]
        FROM (SELECT [timestamp], CONVERT(xml, record) AS [record]
          FROM sys.dm_os_ring_buffers WITH (NOLOCK)
          WHERE ring_buffer_type = N'RING_BUFFER_SCHEDULER_MONITOR'
          AND record LIKE N'%<SystemHealth>%') AS x
      ) AS y
ORDER BY record_id DESC OPTION (RECOMPILE);

-- Look at the trend over the entire period.
-- Also look at high sustained Other Process CPU Utilization values
```

This query shows the recent CPU utilization history for your database server, recorded in one-minute increments. That means it can miss a short spike of CPU activity, but I don't think that's really a big problem. You should be more interested in the trend over the last four hours than worry about sub minute spikes. The query gives you CPU utilization by the SQL Server Database Engine, and the sum of all other processes that are running on the database server (the "Other Process CPU Utilization" column). This gives you an idea of CPU pressure caused by SQL Server versus other sources such as management or monitoring software. Ideally, your mission-critical database servers are dedicated SQL Server instances with virtually nothing else running on the machine besides SQL

Server. If you see Other Process CPU Utilization above 5% for a sustained period, you should investigate what else is using CPU on your database server.

After looking at your CPU utilization history, it is a good idea to see what is happening with the physical memory at the operating-system level on your database server. You can do that using the query shown in Listing 15-25.

LISTING 15-25: Operating system memory information

```
-- Good basic information about OS memory amounts and state
SELECT total_physical_memory_kb, available_physical_memory_kb,
       total_page_file_kb, available_page_file_kb,
       system_memory_state_desc
FROM sys.dm_os_sys_memory WITH (NOLOCK) OPTION (RECOMPILE);

-- You want to see "Available physical memory is high"
-- This indicates that you are not under external memory pressure
```

This query tells you how much physical memory is in the server, how much physical memory is available, how large the operating system page file is, and how much space is available in the page file. It also signals whether the operating system is low on physical memory, which would mean that SQL Server was under external memory pressure. It is rare to see the operating system signaling that is under severe memory pressure, especially if you have set the max server memory (MB) instance-level setting in SQL Server to an appropriate value that leaves enough memory available for the operating system.

After looking at memory usage at the operating-system level, you are going to want to take a look at what is happening with SQL Server's internal memory usage, which you can do using the query shown in Listing 15-26.

LISTING 15-26: SQL server memory information

```
-- SQL Server Process Address space info
--(shows whether locked pages is enabled, among other things)
SELECT physical_memory_in_use_kb,locked_page_allocations_kb,
       page_fault_count, memory_utilization_percentage,
       available_commit_limit_kb, process_physical_memory_low,
       process_virtual_memory_low
FROM sys.dm_os_process_memory WITH (NOLOCK) OPTION (RECOMPILE);

-- You want to see 0 for process_physical_memory_low
-- You want to see 0 for process_virtual_memory_low
-- This indicates that you are not under internal memory pressure
```

This query tells you how much memory is actually being used by the SQL Server Database Engine. This information is more reliable than what is displayed in Windows Task Manager. It also tells you whether this SQL Server instance is using locked pages in memory. Finally, it indicates whether the SQL Server process is signaling that it is low on physical or virtual memory.

One classic way of measuring whether SQL Server is under internal memory pressure is to look at its Page Life Expectancy (PLE) (See Chapter 3, "Understanding Memory"), which you can do using the query shown in Listing 15-27.

LISTING 15-27: Page Life Expectancy information

```
-- Page Life Expectancy (PLE) value for default instance
SELECT cntr_value AS [Page Life Expectancy]
FROM sys.dm_os_performance_counters WITH (NOLOCK)
WHERE [object_name] LIKE N'%Buffer Manager%' -- Handles named instances
AND counter_name = N'Page life expectancy' OPTION (RECOMPILE);

-- PLE is one way to measure memory pressure.
-- Higher PLE is better. Watch the trend, not the absolute value.
```

This query returns the current Page Life Expectancy (PLE) value, in seconds, for the default instance of SQL Server. PLE is a measurement of how long SQL Server expects to keep in the SQL Server buffer pool before it is flushed or evicted. Higher PLE values are better than lower PLE values. You should develop an awareness of the normal range of PLE values for your more important SQL Server instances. That will help you identify a current PLE that is abnormally high or low.

Microsoft has a long-standing recommendation of 300 as a threshold for acceptable PLE, which is often debated in the SQL Server community. One thing that everyone does agree on though is that a PLE value of less than 300 is quite bad. Modern database servers with high amounts of physical memory typically have much higher PLE values than 300. Instead of focusing on the current PLE value, watch the trend over time.

After looking at Page Life Expectancy, you are going to want to look at Memory Grants Outstanding, using the query shown in Listing 15-28.

LISTING 15-28: Memory Grants Outstanding information

```
-- Memory Grants Outstanding value for default instance
SELECT cntr_value AS [Memory Grants Outstanding]
FROM sys.dm_os_performance_counters WITH (NOLOCK)
WHERE [object_name] LIKE N'%Memory Manager%' -- Handles named instances
AND counter_name = N'Memory Grants Outstanding' OPTION (RECOMPILE);

-- Memory Grants Outstanding above zero
-- for a sustained period is a secondary indicator of memory pressure
```

This query returns the current value for Memory Grants Outstanding for the default instance of SQL Server. Memory Grants Outstanding is the total number of processes within SQL Server that have successfully acquired a workspace memory grant (refer to Chapter 3). You want this value to be zero if at all possible. Any sustained value above zero is a secondary indicator of memory pressure due to queries that are using memory for sorting and hashing. After looking at Memory Grants Outstanding, you should also look at Memory Grants Pending (which is a much more important indicator of memory pressure), by using the query shown in Listing 15-29.

LISTING 15-29: Memory Grants Pending information

```
-- Memory Grants Pending value for default instance
SELECT cntr_value AS [Memory Grants Pending]
FROM sys.dm_os_performance_counters WITH (NOLOCK)
WHERE [object_name] LIKE N'%Memory Manager%' -- Handles named instances
AND counter_name = N'Memory Grants Pending' OPTION (RECOMPILE);

-- Memory Grants Pending above zero
-- for a sustained period is an extremely strong indicator of memory pressure
```

This query returns the current value for Memory Grants Pending for the default instance of SQL Server. Memory Grants Pending is the total number of processes within SQL Server that are waiting for a workspace memory grant. You want this value to be zero if at all possible. Any sustained value above zero is an extremely strong indicator of memory pressure. Especially if you see any signs of internal memory pressure from the previous three queries, take a closer look at the overall memory usage in SQL Server by running the query shown in Listing 15-30.

LISTING 15-30: Memory clerk information

```
-- Memory Clerk Usage for instance
-- Look for high value for CACHESTORE_SQLCP (Ad-hoc query plans)
SELECT TOP(10) [type] AS [Memory Clerk Type],
       SUM(pages_kb) AS [SPA Mem, Kb]
FROM sys.dm_os_memory_clerks WITH (NOLOCK)
GROUP BY [type]
ORDER BY SUM(pages_kb) DESC OPTION (RECOMPILE);

-- CACHESTORE_SQLCP   SQL Plans
-- These are cached SQL statements or batches that
-- aren't in stored procedures, functions and triggers
--
-- CACHESTORE_OBJCP   Object Plans
-- These are compiled plans for
-- stored procedures, functions and triggers
--
-- CACHESTORE_PHDR    Algebrizer Trees
-- An algebrizer tree is the parsed SQL text
-- that resolves the table and column names
```

This query gives you a good idea of what (besides the buffer cache) is using large amounts of memory in SQL Server. One key item to look out for is high values for CACHESTORE_SQLCP, which is the memory clerk for ad hoc query plans. It is quite common to see this memory clerk using several gigabytes of memory to cache ad hoc query plans.

If you see a lot of memory being used by the CACHESTORE_SQLCP memory clerk, you can determine whether you have many single-use, ad hoc query plans using a lot of memory in your procedure cache by running the query shown in Listing 15-31.

LISTING 15-31: Single-use ad-hoc queries

```
-- Find single-use, ad-hoc queries that are bloating the plan cache
SELECT TOP(20) [text] AS [QueryText], cp.size_in_bytes
FROM sys.dm_exec_cached_plans AS cp WITH (NOLOCK)
CROSS APPLY sys.dm_exec_sql_text(plan_handle)
WHERE cp.cacheobjtype = N'Compiled Plan'
AND cp.objtype = N'Adhoc'
AND cp.usecounts = 1
ORDER BY cp.size_in_bytes DESC OPTION (RECOMPILE);

-- Gives you the text and size of single-use ad-hoc queries that
-- waste space in the plan cache
-- Enabling 'optimize for ad hoc workloads' for the instance
-- can help (SQL Server 2008 and above only)
-- Enabling forced parameterization for the database can help, but test first!
```

This query returns the query text and size of your largest (in terms of memory usage) single-use, ad hoc query plans wasting space in your plan cache. If you see a lot of single-use, ad hoc query plans in your plan cache, you should consider enabling the instance-level optimize for ad hoc workloads setting (also see Chapter 3). This setting enables SQL Server 2008 and later to store a much smaller version of the ad hoc execution plan in the plan cache the first time that plan is executed. This can reduce the amount of memory that is wasted on single-use, ad hoc query plans that are highly likely to never be reused. Conversely, sometimes the result of enabling this setting is that more of these smaller, ad hoc plans are stored in the plan cache (because more smaller plans can fit in the same amount of memory as fewer, larger plans), so you may not see as much memory savings as you anticipated.

Even so, we don't see any good reason not to enable this setting on all SQL Server 2008 and later instances. When I talked to one of the developers at Microsoft who worked on this feature a couple of years ago, the only downside to this setting that she could see was a scenario in which you had several identical ad hoc query plans that would be executed between two and ten times, in which case you would take a small hit the second time the plan was executed. That seems like an edge case to me.

DATABASE-LEVEL QUERIES

After running all the server- and instance-level queries, you should have a fairly good idea of which database or databases are the most resource intensive on a particular instance of SQL Server. In order to get more details about a particular database, you need to switch your database context to that database and run a set of database-specific queries. The code in Listing 15-32 shows how to switch your database context using T-SQL. Be sure to change the name of the database to the name of the database that you are interested in investigating further.

LISTING 15-32: Switching to a user database

```
-- Database specific queries  ******************************************************

-- **** Switch to a user database *****
USE YourDatabaseName;
GO
```

This code merely switches your database context to the named database. Be sure to change the name to the database that you want to look at. Many people make the mistake of running these queries while connected to the master system database. If you do that, you will get a lot of mostly useless information about your master database.

After you are sure you are pointing at the correct database, you can find out how large it is with the query shown in Listing 15-33.

LISTING 15-33: Database file sizes and space available

```
-- Individual File Sizes and space available for current database
SELECT name AS [File Name], physical_name AS [Physical Name], size/128.0 AS [Total
Size in MB],
size/128.0 - CAST(FILEPROPERTY(name, 'SpaceUsed') AS int)/128.0 AS [Available Space
In MB], [file_id]
FROM sys.database_files WITH (NOLOCK) OPTION (RECOMPILE);

-- Look at how large and how full the files are and where they are located
-- Make sure the transaction log is not full!!
```

This query shows you where the data and log files for your database are located. It also returns how large and how full they are. It is a good way to help monitor and manage your data and log file sizing and file growth. I don't like to see my data files getting too close to being 100% full, and I don't like to see my log files getting more than 50% full. You should manually manage the growth of your data and log files, leaving autogrow enabled only for an emergency.

The next query, shown in Listing 15-34, shows a DMV that enables you to focus solely on your log file size and space used.

LISTING 15-34: Transaction log size and space used

```
-- Get transaction log size and space information for the current database
SELECT DB_NAME(database_id) AS [Database Name], database_id,
CAST((total_log_size_in_bytes/1048576.0) AS DECIMAL(10,1))
AS [Total_log_size(MB)],
CAST((used_log_space_in_bytes/1048576.0) AS DECIMAL(10,1))
AS [Used_log_space(MB)],
CAST(used_log_space_in_percent AS DECIMAL(10,1)) AS [Used_log_space(%)]
FROM sys.dm_db_log_space_usage WITH (NOLOCK) OPTION (RECOMPILE);

-- Another way to look at transaction log file size and space
```

This query, using a DMV introduced in SQL Server 2008 R2 Service Pack 1, enables you to directly query your log file size and the space used, as a percentage. It would be relatively easy to use this DMV to write a query that could be used to trigger an alert when a percentage of log file usage that you specify is exceeded. Of course, if you are properly managing the size of your transaction log, along with how often you take transaction log backups when you are in the FULL recovery model, you should not run into problems that often. The obvious exceptions are if something happens with database mirroring, replication, or a long-running transaction that cause your transaction log to fill up despite frequent transaction log backups.

The next query, shown in Listing 15-35, will enable you to gather some I/O statistics by file for the current database.

LISTING 15-35: I/O statistics by file for the current database

```
-- I/O Statistics by file for the current database
SELECT DB_NAME(DB_ID()) AS [Database Name],[file_id], num_of_reads, num_of_writes,
io_stall_read_ms, io_stall_write_ms,
CAST(100. * io_stall_read_ms/(io_stall_read_ms + io_stall_write_ms)
AS DECIMAL(10,1)) AS [IO Stall Reads Pct],
CAST(100. * io_stall_write_ms/(io_stall_write_ms + io_stall_read_ms)
AS DECIMAL(10,1)) AS [IO Stall Writes Pct],
(num_of_reads + num_of_writes) AS [Writes + Reads], num_of_bytes_read,
num_of_bytes_written,
CAST(100. * num_of_reads/(num_of_reads + num_of_writes) AS DECIMAL(10,1))
AS [# Reads Pct],
CAST(100. * num_of_writes/(num_of_reads + num_of_writes) AS DECIMAL(10,1))
AS [# Write Pct],
CAST(100. * num_of_bytes_read/(num_of_bytes_read + num_of_bytes_written)
AS DECIMAL(10,1)) AS [Read Bytes Pct],
CAST(100. * num_of_bytes_written/(num_of_bytes_read + num_of_bytes_written)
AS DECIMAL(10,1)) AS [Written Bytes Pct]
FROM sys.dm_io_virtual_file_stats(DB_ID(), NULL) OPTION (RECOMPILE);

-- This helps you characterize your workload better from an I/O perspective
```

This query returns the number of reads and writes for each file in your database. It also returns the number of bytes read and written for each file in the database, and the number of read I/O and write I/O stalls for each file in the database. Finally, it breaks down the read/write ratio and read/write I/O stall ratio into percentage terms. The point of all this information is to help you better characterize your I/O workload at the database-file level. For example, you might discover that you are doing a lot more writes to a particular data file than you expected, which might be a good reason to consider using RAID 10 instead of RAID 5 for the logical drive where that data file is located. Seeing a lot of I/O stalls for a particular database file might mean that the logical drive where that file is located is not performing very well or simply that the database file in question is particularly active. It is definitely something to investigate further.

Next, with the query shown in Listing 15-36, you are going to take a look at the transaction log Virtual Log File (VLF) count.

LISTING 15-36: Virtual Log File count

```
-- Get VLF count for transaction log for the current database,
-- number of rows equals the VLF count. Lower is better!
DBCC LOGINFO;

-- High VLF counts can affect write performance
-- and they can make database restore and recovery take much longer
```

This query simply tells you how many VLFs you have in your transaction log file. Having a large number of VLFs in your transaction log can affect write performance to your transaction log. More important, it can have a huge effect on how long it takes to restore a database, and how long it takes a database to become available in a clustering failover. It can also affect how long it takes to recover a database when your instance of SQL Server is started or restarted. What is considered a large number of VLFs?

I don't like to see more than a couple of hundred VLF files in a transaction log. For the most part, having fewer VLFs is better than having a large number, but I don't worry too much until I start getting more than 200-300. The most common way to get a high VLF count is when you create a database in FULL recovery model with the default settings for the size and autogrowth increment for the transaction log file, and then you don't take frequent transaction log backups. By default, you start out with a 1MB transaction log file that is set to grow by 10% when autogrow kicks in after the 1MB file fills up completely. The now 1.1MB file will quickly fill up again, and autogrow will make it 10% larger. This happens repeatedly; and each time the transaction log file is grown, more VLFs are added to the transaction log. If the growth amount is less than 64MB, then 4 VLFs will be added to the transaction log. If the growth amount is between 64MB and 1GB, then 8 VLFs will be added to the transaction log. Finally, if the growth amount is over 1GB, then 16 VLFs will be added to the transaction log.

Knowing this, you can see how a 1MB transaction log file can grow and end up with tens of thousands of VLFs. The way to avoid this is to manually manage your transaction file size, and to change the autogrow increment to a more reasonable value. That way you will have fewer growth events (whether manual or autogrows), and therefore a lower VLF count. With a relatively large and active database, I recommend setting the autogowth increment to 8000MB. This way, you only need a few growth events to grow the transaction file to a sufficiently large size, which keeps the VLF count much lower.

Picking a good size for your transaction log file depends on a number of factors. First, how much write activity do you think your database will see with its normal workload? You want to figure out how much transaction log activity is generated in an hour, in terms of MB or GB. One easy way to determine this is to take an uncompressed transaction log backup every hour for a full day. This gives you a good idea of your average and peak log generation rates. Make sure that your transaction log file is large enough to hold at least eight hours of normal activity, and consider when and how often you do maintenance activity such as reorganizing or rebuilding indexes, which generate a lot of transaction log activity. Creating new indexes on large tables and loading or deleting a lot of data also creates a lot of transaction log activity.

You should also consider how often you are going to run transaction log backups (in order to help meet your Recovery Point Objective [RPO] and Recovery Time Objective [RTO]). If you need to run very frequent transaction log backups, you may be able to have a somewhat smaller transaction log file. This also depends on how large your database is and how long it takes to do a full database backup. While a full database backup is running, transaction log backups will not clear the log file. If you have a very slow I/O subsystem and a very large database, your full database backups may take a long time to complete. You want to size your transaction log file to be large enough that it never has to autogrow. One disadvantage to having an extremely large transaction log file (besides wasting some disk space) is that it will take quite a bit longer to restore a copy of your database, as Windows cannot use Windows Instant File Initialization on log files.

If you discover that you have a very high number of VLFs in your transaction log file, you should take a transaction log backup and then immediately shrink the transaction log file — not the entire database, just the transaction log file. After you do this, check your VLF count. It may have not gone down by much, depending on the prior activity and state of your transaction log. If this is the case, simply repeat the transaction log backup and transaction log file shrink sequence several times until you get the VLF count down. By this time, your transaction log file will probably be very small, so you are going to want to immediately grow it back in reasonable increments to a reasonable size, based on the factors previously discussed. Keep in mind that if you decide to grow your transaction file in 8000MB increments and you have a slow I/O subsystem, you may see a performance impact during the file growth operation, as Windows Instant File Initialization does not work on transaction log files.

At this point, it is time to start looking at the query activity on this particular database, using the query shown in Listing 15-37.

LISTING 15-37: Top cached queries by execution count

```
-- Top cached queries by Execution Count (SQL Server 2012)
SELECT qs.execution_count, qs.total_rows, qs.last_rows, qs.min_rows, qs.max_rows,
qs.last_elapsed_time, qs.min_elapsed_time, qs.max_elapsed_time,
SUBSTRING(qt.TEXT,qs.statement_start_offset/2 +1,
(CASE WHEN qs.statement_end_offset = -1
     THEN LEN(CONVERT(NVARCHAR(MAX), qt.TEXT)) * 2
 ELSE qs.statement_end_offset END - qs.statement_start_offset)/2)
AS query_text
FROM sys.dm_exec_query_stats AS qs WITH (NOLOCK)
CROSS APPLY sys.dm_exec_sql_text(qs.sql_handle) AS qt
ORDER BY qs.execution_count DESC OPTION (RECOMPILE);

-- Uses several new rows returned columns
-- to help troubleshoot performance problems
```

This query simply returns cached queries ordered by execution count. This is useful for getting an idea about your typical workload. Knowing which queries are executed the most often, along with their range of execution times and range of rows returned can be very useful information. Having the query text available enables you to run a query in SSMS, where you can look at the execution plan and the I/O statistics to determine whether there are any tuning opportunities.

Next, you will take a look at a similar query that focuses on cached stored procedures. This query is shown in Listing 15-38.

LISTING 15-38: Top cached stored procedures by execution count

```
-- Top Cached SPs By Execution Count (SQL Server 2012)
SELECT TOP(250) p.name AS [SP Name], qs.execution_count,
ISNULL(qs.execution_count/DATEDIFF(Second, qs.cached_time, GETDATE()), 0)
AS [Calls/Second],
qs.total_worker_time/qs.execution_count AS [AvgWorkerTime],
```

```
qs.total_worker_time AS [TotalWorkerTime],qs.total_elapsed_time,
qs.total_elapsed_time/qs.execution_count AS [avg_elapsed_time],
qs.cached_time
FROM sys.procedures AS p WITH (NOLOCK)
INNER JOIN sys.dm_exec_procedure_stats AS qs WITH (NOLOCK)
ON p.[object_id] = qs.[object_id]
WHERE qs.database_id = DB_ID()
ORDER BY qs.execution_count DESC OPTION (RECOMPILE);

-- Tells you which cached stored procedures are called the most often
-- This helps you characterize and baseline your workload
```

This query returns the top cached stored procedures ordered by execution count. It can help you determine which stored procedures are called most often, and how often they are called. Knowing this is very helpful for baseline purposes. For example, if you know that your most frequently executed stored procedure is normally called 50 times/second, but you later see it being called 300 times/second, you would want to start investigating. Perhaps there was a change to your application(s) that is causing them to call that stored procedure much more often. It might be by design, or it might be a defect in the application, introduced in a recent update. It is also possible that your applications are suddenly seeing more load, either from legitimate users or from a denial-of-service attack.

One thing to keep in mind when examining all these queries that are looking at cached stored procedures is that the stored procedures may have gone into the cache at different times, which skews the numbers for these queries. You should always look at the cached_time in the query results (see Listing 15-39) to see how long the stored procedure has been in the cache.

LISTING 15-39: Top cached stored procedures by average elapsed time

```
-- Top Cached SPs By Avg Elapsed Time (SQL Server 2012)
SELECT TOP(25) p.name AS [SP Name], qs.total_elapsed_time/qs.execution_count
AS [avg_elapsed_time], qs.total_elapsed_time, qs.execution_count,
ISNULL(qs.execution_count/DATEDIFF(Second, qs.cached_time,
GETDATE()), 0) AS [Calls/Second],
qs.total_worker_time/qs.execution_count AS [AvgWorkerTime],
qs.total_worker_time AS [TotalWorkerTime], qs.cached_time
FROM sys.procedures AS p WITH (NOLOCK)
INNER JOIN sys.dm_exec_procedure_stats AS qs WITH (NOLOCK)
ON p.[object_id] = qs.[object_id]
WHERE qs.database_id = DB_ID()
ORDER BY avg_elapsed_time DESC OPTION (RECOMPILE);

-- This helps you find long-running cached stored procedures that
-- may be easy to optimize with standard query tuning techniques
```

This query captures the top cached stored procedures by average elapsed time. This is useful because it can highlight long-running (on average) stored procedures that might be very good tuning candidates. If you can make some changes to a stored procedure that previously took 90 seconds that result in it returning in 5 seconds, you will look like a magician to your boss. Conversely, if a long-running query is executed only once a day, optimizing it will not really help your overall workload as much as you might expect. This query is somewhat less sensitive to the cached_time issue, as you are sorting by average elapsed time.

Next, you are going to look at the most expensive stored procedures from an overall CPU perspective, with the query shown in Listing 15-40.

LISTING 15-40: Top cached stored procedures by total worker time

```
-- Top Cached SPs By Total Worker time (SQL Server 2012).
-- Worker time relates to CPU cost
SELECT TOP(25) p.name AS [SP Name], qs.total_worker_time AS [TotalWorkerTime],
qs.total_worker_time/qs.execution_count AS [AvgWorkerTime], qs.execution_count,
ISNULL(qs.execution_count/DATEDIFF(Second, qs.cached_time, GETDATE()), 0)
AS [Calls/Second],qs.total_elapsed_time, qs.total_elapsed_time/qs.execution_count
AS [avg_elapsed_time], qs.cached_time
FROM sys.procedures AS p WITH (NOLOCK)
INNER JOIN sys.dm_exec_procedure_stats AS qs WITH (NOLOCK)
ON p.[object_id] = qs.[object_id]
WHERE qs.database_id = DB_ID()
ORDER BY qs.total_worker_time DESC OPTION (RECOMPILE);

-- This helps you find the most expensive cached
-- stored procedures from a CPU perspective
-- You should look at this if you see signs of CPU pressure
```

This query returns the top cached stored procedures ordered by total worker time. Worker time relates to the CPU cost of a query or stored procedure. Especially if you see signs of CPU pressure from looking at your top cumulative wait types or your CPU utilization history, you should look very closely at the results of this query to figure out which stored procedures were the most expensive from a CPU perspective. The reason you sort by total worker time is because this takes into account the total CPU cost of the stored procedure since it has been cached. You might have a stored procedure that is not particularly expensive for a single execution that is called very frequently, resulting in a very high overall CPU cost.

With this query, you do need to pay particular attention to the cached_time column for each stored procedure. The length of time that a stored procedure has been in the cache can have a huge effect on its cumulative cost figures. That's why I like to periodically clear out the procedure cache so that the stored procedures that are part of my regular workload will be recompiled and go back into the cache at nearly the same time. This makes it much easier to accurately interpret the results of all these stored procedure cost queries. It also has the benefit of clearing out single-use, ad hoc query plans that may be wasting a lot of space in your cache.

Next, the query shown in Listing 15-41 will provide some information about your cached stored procedures from a logical reads perspective.

LISTING 15-41: Top cached stored procedures by total logical reads

```
-- Top Cached SPs By Total Logical Reads (SQL Server 2012).
-- Logical reads relate to memory pressure
SELECT TOP(25) p.name AS [SP Name], qs.total_logical_reads
AS [TotalLogicalReads], qs.total_logical_reads/qs.execution_count
AS [AvgLogicalReads],qs.execution_count,
ISNULL(qs.execution_count/DATEDIFF(Second, qs.cached_time, GETDATE()), 0)
AS [Calls/Second], qs.total_elapsed_time,qs.total_elapsed_time/qs.execution_count
AS [avg_elapsed_time], qs.cached_time
FROM sys.procedures AS p WITH (NOLOCK)
INNER JOIN sys.dm_exec_procedure_stats AS qs WITH (NOLOCK)
ON p.[object_id] = qs.[object_id]
WHERE qs.database_id = DB_ID()
ORDER BY qs.total_logical_reads DESC OPTION (RECOMPILE);


-- This helps you find the most expensive cached
-- stored procedures from a memory perspective
-- You should look at this if you see signs of memory pressure
```

This query returns the top cached procedures ordered by total logical reads. Logical reads equate to memory pressure, and indirectly to I/O pressure. A logical read occurs when a query finds the data that it needs in the buffer pool (in memory). Once data is initially read off of the I/O subsystem, it goes into the SQL Server buffer pool. If you have a large amount of physical RAM and your instance-level max server memory setting is at an appropriately high level, you will have a relatively large amount of space for the SQL Server buffer pool, which means that SQL Server is much more likely to subsequently find what it needs there, rather than access the I/O subsystem with a physical read.

If you are seeing signs of memory pressure, such as persistently low page life expectancy values, high memory grants outstanding, and high memory grants pending, look very closely at the results of this query. Again, you need to pay close attention to the cached_time column to ensure that you are really looking at the most expensive stored procedures from a memory perspective.

After I have identified the top several stored procedure offenders, I like to run them individually (with appropriate input parameters captured from SQL Server Profiler) in SSMS with the SET STATISTICS IO ON command enabled and the graphical execution plan enabled. This enables me to start troubleshooting why the queries in the stored procedure are generating so many logical reads. Perhaps the queries are doing implicit conversions that cause them to ignore a perfectly valid index, or maybe they are using T-SQL functions on the left side of a WHERE clause. Another common issue is a clustered index or table scan due to a missing index. There are many possible reasons why a query has a very large number of logical reads.

If you are using SQL Server 2008 or later and you have Enterprise Edition, you should take a look at SQL Server data compression. Data compression is usually touted as a way to reduce your I/O utilization requirements in exchange for some added CPU utilization. While it does work very well for that purpose (with indexes that are good candidates for compression), it can also reduce your memory pressure in many cases. An index that has been compressed will stay compressed in the buffer pool, until the data is updated. This can dramatically reduce the space required in the buffer pool for that index.

The next query, shown in Listing 15-42, looks at the most expensive stored procedures from a physical reads perspective.

LISTING 15-42: Top cached stored procedures by total physical reads

```
-- Top Cached SPs By Total Physical Reads (SQL Server 2012).
-- Physical reads relate to disk I/O pressure
SELECT TOP(25) p.name AS [SP Name],qs.total_physical_reads
AS [TotalPhysicalReads],qs.total_physical_reads/qs.execution_count
AS [AvgPhysicalReads], qs.execution_count, qs.total_logical_reads,
qs.total_elapsed_time, qs.total_elapsed_time/qs.execution_count
AS [avg_elapsed_time], qs.cached_time
FROM sys.procedures AS p WITH (NOLOCK)
INNER JOIN sys.dm_exec_procedure_stats AS qs WITH (NOLOCK)
ON p.[object_id] = qs.[object_id]
WHERE qs.database_id = DB_ID()
AND qs.total_physical_reads > 0
ORDER BY qs.total_physical_reads DESC,
qs.total_logical_reads DESC OPTION (RECOMPILE);

-- This helps you find the most expensive cached
-- stored procedures from a read I/O perspective
-- You should look at this if you see signs of I/O pressure or of memory pressure
```

This query returns the top cached stored procedures ordered by total physical reads. Physical reads equate to disk I/O cost. A physical read happens when SQL Server cannot find what it needs in the SQL Server buffer pool, so it must go out to the storage subsystem to retrieve the data. No matter what kind of storage you are using, it is much slower than physical memory.

If you are seeing signs of I/O pressure, such as I/O-related wait types in your top cumulative wait types query, or high times for disk seconds/read in Windows Performance Monitor, examine the results of this query very closely. Don't forget to consider how long a stored procedure has been in the cache by looking at the cached_time column. A very expensive stored procedure that was just recently cached will probably not show up at the top of the list compared to other stored procedures that have been cached for a long period of time.

After identifying the top several stored procedure offenders, run them individually (with appropriate input parameters captured from SQL Server Profiler) in SSMS with the SET STATISTICS IO ON command enabled and the graphical execution plan enabled. This will help you determine why the queries in the stored procedure are generating so many physical reads. Again, after you have exhausted standard query-tuning techniques to improve the situation, you should consider using SQL Server data compression (if you have Enterprise Edition) to further reduce the amount of data being read off of the I/O subsystem. Other options (besides standard query tuning) include adding more physical RAM to your server and improving your I/O subsystem. Perhaps you can add additional spindles to a RAID array, change the RAID level, change the hardware cache policy, and so on.

Next, take a look at the most expensive cache stored procedures for logical writes. To do that, use the query shown in Listing 15-43.

LISTING 15-43: Top cached stored procedures by total logical writes

```
-- Top Cached SPs By Total Logical Writes (SQL Server 2012).
-- Logical writes relate to both memory and disk I/O pressure
SELECT TOP(25) p.name AS [SP Name], qs.total_logical_writes
AS [TotalLogicalWrites], qs.total_logical_writes/qs.execution_count
AS [AvgLogicalWrites], qs.execution_count,
ISNULL(qs.execution_count/DATEDIFF(Second, qs.cached_time, GETDATE()), 0)
AS [Calls/Second],qs.total_elapsed_time, qs.total_elapsed_time/qs.execution_count
AS [avg_elapsed_time], qs.cached_time
FROM sys.procedures AS p WITH (NOLOCK)
INNER JOIN sys.dm_exec_procedure_stats AS qs WITH (NOLOCK)
ON p.[object_id] = qs.[object_id]
WHERE qs.database_id = DB_ID()
ORDER BY qs.total_logical_writes DESC OPTION (RECOMPILE);

-- This helps you find the most expensive cached
-- stored procedures from a write I/O perspective
-- You should look at this if you see signs of I/O pressure or of memory pressure
```

This query returns the most expensive cached stored procedures ordered by total logical writes, meaning simply the stored procedures that are generating the most write activity in your database. You might be surprised to see SELECT type stored procedures show up in this list, but that often happens when the SELECT procedures INSERT intermediate results into a temp table or table variable before doing a later SELECT operation.

Especially with OLTP workloads that see a lot of intensive write activity, you should pay attention to the results of this query. As always, consider the cached_time column before making any judgments. After you have identified the actual top offenders in this query, talk to your developers to see if perhaps they are updating too much information, or updating information too frequently. I would also be looking at the index usage on your most frequently updated tables. You might discover that you have a number of nonclustered indexes that have a high number of writes, but no reads. Having fewer indexes on a volatile, write-intensive table will definitely help write performance. After some further investigation and analysis, you might want to drop some of those unused indexes.

From a hardware perspective, adding more physical RAM to your server might help even out your write I/O workload a little bit. If SQL Server has more RAM in the buffer pool, it will not have to issue automatic checkpoints to write to the data file(s) quite as often. Going longer between automatic checkpoints can help reduce total write I/O somewhat because more data in the same data pages might have been modified over that longer period of time. A system that is under memory pressure will also be forced to have the lazy writer write dirty pages in memory to the disk subsystem more often.

Finally, improving your I/O subsystem, especially the LUN where your transaction log is located, would be an obvious step. Again, adding more spindles to the RAID array, changing from RAID

5 to RAID 10, and making sure your RAID controller hardware cache is used for writes instead of reads will all help write performance.

Next, you will take a look at the most expensive statements within your cached stored procedures for average I/O, using the query shown in Listing 15-44.

LISTING 15-44: Top statements by average I/O

```
-- Lists the top statements by average input/output
-- usage for the current database
SELECT TOP(50) OBJECT_NAME(qt.objectid) AS [SP Name],
(qs.total_logical_reads + qs.total_logical_writes) /qs.execution_count
AS [Avg IO],SUBSTRING(qt.[text],qs.statement_start_offset/2,
(CASE
 WHEN qs.statement_end_offset = -1
 THEN LEN(CONVERT(nvarchar(max), qt.[text])) * 2
 ELSE qs.statement_end_offset
 END - qs.statement_start_offset)/2) AS [Query Text]
FROM sys.dm_exec_query_stats AS qs WITH (NOLOCK)
CROSS APPLY sys.dm_exec_sql_text(qs.sql_handle) AS qt
WHERE qt.[dbid] = DB_ID()
ORDER BY [Avg IO] DESC OPTION (RECOMPILE);

-- Helps you find the most expensive statements for I/O by SP
```

This query identifies the most expensive cached statements for I/O, ordered by average I/O. If your system is showing any signs of I/O pressure, you should definitely take a look at the results of this query. Even if you are not seeing I/O pressure, it never hurts to be aware of which statements within your stored procedures are causing the most I/O pain.

Next, using the query shown in Listing 15-45, you will look for nonclustered indexes that have more writes than reads.

LISTING 15-45: Possible bad nonclustered indexes

```
-- Possible Bad NC Indexes (writes > reads)
SELECT OBJECT_NAME(s.[object_id]) AS [Table Name], i.name AS [Index Name],
i.index_id,user_updates AS [Total Writes],
user_seeks + user_scans + user_lookups AS [Total Reads],
user_updates - (user_seeks + user_scans + user_lookups) AS [Difference]
FROM sys.dm_db_index_usage_stats AS s WITH (NOLOCK)
INNER JOIN sys.indexes AS i WITH (NOLOCK)
ON s.[object_id] = i.[object_id]
AND i.index_id = s.index_id
WHERE OBJECTPROPERTY(s.[object_id],'IsUserTable') = 1
AND s.database_id = DB_ID()
AND user_updates > (user_seeks + user_scans + user_lookups)
AND i.index_id > 1
ORDER BY [Difference] DESC, [Total Writes] DESC, [Total Reads] ASC OPTION
(RECOMPILE);

-- Look for indexes with high numbers of writes
```

```
-- and zero or very low numbers of reads
-- Consider your complete workload
-- Investigate further before dropping an index!
```

This query returns all nonclustered indexes in the current database, along with their total writes and total reads ordered by the difference between the number of writes and the number of reads. The idea here is to find indexes that have a lot of writes and very few (or zero) reads. An index that is only written to, but never used for reads, is not useful at all. You are paying the cost to maintain the index, but you are receiving no benefit. Having many "unused" indexes on a table hurts your insert/update/delete performance, and it makes your table and database need more space in the data file(s). It also makes backups and restores take longer to complete.

Keep in mind that these read and write statistics reflect only the period since this instance of SQL Server has been running. Depending on how long your instance has been running, you may not have seen your complete workload yet. For example, some indexes may be used only for monthly reporting queries, meaning they might have a lot more writes than reads during the rest of the month. If you dropped an index like that based on the results of this query, you could cause some serious performance issues when it comes time to run those reporting queries.

In other words, use some caution and common sense before you start dropping indexes solely based on the results of this query. You should always do some further investigation and analysis before you drop an index on an important database.

Next, using the query shown in Listing 15-46, you will look for indexes that SQL Server thinks you would benefit from adding to this database.

LISTING 15-46: Missing indexes by index advantage

```
-- Missing Indexes current database by Index Advantage
SELECT user_seeks * avg_total_user_cost * (avg_user_impact * 0.01)
AS [index_advantage],
migs.last_user_seek, mid.[statement] AS [Database.Schema.Table],
mid.equality_columns, mid.inequality_columns, mid.included_columns,
migs.unique_compiles, migs.user_seeks, migs.avg_total_user_cost,
migs.avg_user_impact
FROM sys.dm_db_missing_index_group_stats AS migs WITH (NOLOCK)
INNER JOIN sys.dm_db_missing_index_groups AS mig WITH (NOLOCK)
ON migs.group_handle = mig.index_group_handle
INNER JOIN sys.dm_db_missing_index_details AS mid WITH (NOLOCK)
ON mig.index_handle = mid.index_handle
WHERE mid.database_id = DB_ID() -- Remove this to see for entire instance
ORDER BY index_advantage DESC OPTION (RECOMPILE);

-- Look at last user seek time, number of user seeks
-- to help determine source and importance
-- SQL Server is overly eager to add included columns, so beware
-- Do not just blindly add indexes that show up from this query!!!
```

This query shows you what SQL Server considers to be "missing indexes" ordered by a calculated column called index_advantage. The idea here is that anytime the SQL Server query optimizer determines that a particular index not present in the database would help reduce the cost of a query, it will note that fact. Over time, as your workload runs on your database server, you will likely see a growing number of proposed new indexes returned when you run this query. I strongly caution you to not get overly enthusiastic about creating new indexes based solely on the results of this query. Many people have proudly told me that they wrote a script that automatically creates every single index that SQL Server identifies in this query, which is a huge mistake!

Instead, you should consider a number of factors before you start adding new indexes to your tables. First, consider what type of workload you have and how volatile your table is. If you have an OLTP type of workload, with a lot of writes to your table, you should be much more hesitant about adding new indexes, as more indexes will slow down your insert/update/delete performance on that table. Second, you should look at the `last_user_seek` column to get an idea of whether this "missing" index would really affect your normal workload. If your `last_user_seek` is from a few seconds or a few minutes ago, it is more likely to be part of your normal workload. If it is from a few days or a few weeks ago, it is more likely to be from an ad hoc query or a reporting query, and I would be much less inclined to add that index. You should also look at the `user_seeks` column to get an idea of how many times SQL Server has determined it would need this index, along with the `avg_user_impact` and `avg_total_user_cost` columns to help assess how important the index really might be.

You should also consider your existing indexes on the table in question. In many cases this query will recommend a new index that is almost an exact duplicate of an existing index. You need to apply some judgment and common sense and consider your complete workload before you start adding new indexes based solely on the results of this query. Finally, you should be aware that if you make any kind of index change on a particular table, the missing index statistics for that table will be cleared out, and it will take some time (as your workload is running) for the missing index statistics to show any information for that table. To understand how this could bite you, suppose you had a table that needed three new indexes to help an important part of your normal work-load. After a thorough analysis, you decide to add the first index. After that index is added, you run this query again, and no results are returned for the table in question. This might lead you to conclude that SQL Server does not need the other two indexes, which would probably be incorrect. You just need to wait for a period of time, depending on your workload, to see whether SQL Server really needs any more indexes on the table. You can use the query shown in Listing 15-45 along with this query to help zero in on which indexes are really needed on each table.

Next, you will look for missing index warnings in the cached execution plans for stored procedures in this database, using the query shown in Listing 15-47.

LISTING 15-47: Missing index warnings for cached plans

```
-- Find missing index warnings for cached plans in the current database
-- Note: This query could take some time on a busy instance
SELECT TOP(25) OBJECT_NAME(objectid) AS [ObjectName],query_plan,
cp.objtype, cp.usecounts
FROM sys.dm_exec_cached_plans AS cp WITH (NOLOCK)
CROSS APPLY sys.dm_exec_query_plan(cp.plan_handle) AS qp
WHERE CAST(query_plan AS NVARCHAR(MAX)) LIKE N'%MissingIndex%'
AND dbid = DB_ID()
```

```
ORDER BY cp.usecounts DESC OPTION (RECOMPILE);

-- Helps you connect missing indexes to specific stored procedures or queries
-- This can help you decide whether to add them or not
```

This query returns information about cached execution plans that have "missing index" warnings. It will give you the stored procedure name, the query plan, and the use count for that cache execution plan. This can help you decide whether a particular "missing index" is really important or not. You should use this query along with the query shown in Listing 15-46 to help determine whether you should add any new indexes to a particular table.

Next, using the query shown in Listing 15-48, you can find out which tables and indexes are using the most space in the SQL Server buffer pool.

LISTING 15-48: Buffer usage by table and index

```
-- Breaks down buffers used by current database
-- by object (table, index) in the buffer cache
SELECT OBJECT_NAME(p.[object_id]) AS [ObjectName],
p.index_id, COUNT(*)/128 AS [Buffer size(MB)],  COUNT(*) AS [BufferCount],
p.data_compression_desc AS [CompressionType]
FROM sys.allocation_units AS a WITH (NOLOCK)
INNER JOIN sys.dm_os_buffer_descriptors AS b WITH (NOLOCK)
ON a.allocation_unit_id = b.allocation_unit_id
INNER JOIN sys.partitions AS p WITH (NOLOCK)
ON a.container_id = p.hobt_id
WHERE b.database_id = CONVERT(int,DB_ID())
AND p.[object_id] > 100
GROUP BY p.[object_id], p.index_id, p.data_compression_desc
ORDER BY [BufferCount] DESC OPTION (RECOMPILE);

-- Tells you what tables and indexes are
-- using the most memory in the buffer cache
```

This query indicates which indexes and tables in the current database are using the most memory in the SQL Server buffer pool. It also shows you whether the index is using any form of data compression. If you see an index that is using a large amount of space in the buffer pool, you should investigate whether that index might be a good candidate for SQL Server data compression, assuming that you have SQL Server 2008 or later Enterprise Edition.

An ideal data compression candidate would be a large, static table that has highly compressible data. In such a case, you might see as much as a 10:1 compression ratio, meaning the compressed index would take up far less space in the buffer pool, and in the data file on disk. In my experience, I have typically seen anywhere from 2:1 up to 4:1 for average compression ratios. A poor data compression candidate would be a smaller, highly volatile table containing data that does not compress very well. In that case, you would most likely be better off without using data compression.

Next, you will find out the size (in terms of row counts) and the data compression status of all the tables in this database, using the query shown in Listing 15-49.

LISTING 15-49: Table names, row counts, and compression status

```
-- Get Table names, row counts, and compression status
-- for the clustered index or heap
SELECT OBJECT_NAME(object_id) AS [ObjectName],
SUM(Rows) AS [RowCount], data_compression_desc AS [CompressionType]
FROM sys.partitions WITH (NOLOCK)
WHERE index_id < 2 --ignore the partitions from the non-clustered index if any
AND OBJECT_NAME(object_id) NOT LIKE N'sys%'
AND OBJECT_NAME(object_id) NOT LIKE N'queue_%'
AND OBJECT_NAME(object_id) NOT LIKE N'filestream_tombstone%'
AND OBJECT_NAME(object_id) NOT LIKE N'fulltext%'
AND OBJECT_NAME(object_id) NOT LIKE N'ifts_comp_fragment%'
AND OBJECT_NAME(object_id) NOT LIKE N'filetable_updates%'
GROUP BY object_id, data_compression_desc
ORDER BY SUM(Rows) DESC OPTION (RECOMPILE);

-- Gives you an idea of table sizes, and possible data compression opportunities
```

This query returns all your table sizes, including row count and data compression status (for the clustered index), ordered by row counts. It is a good idea to have a notion of how many millions or billions of rows are contained in the larger tables in your database. This is one indirect way of keeping tabs on the growth and activity of your database. Knowing the compression status of the clustered index of your largest tables is also very useful, as it might uncover some good candidates for data compression. As previously discussed, SQL Server data compression can be a huge win in many scenarios if you are able to take advantage of it with Enterprise Edition.

Next, using the query shown in Listing 15-50, you can find out the last time that statistics were updated for all indexes in the database.

LISTING 15-50: Last statistics update for all indexes

```
-- When were Statistics last updated on all indexes?
SELECT o.name, i.name AS [Index Name],STATS_DATE(i.[object_id],
i.index_id) AS [Statistics Date], s.auto_created,
s.no_recompute, s.user_created, st.row_count
FROM sys.objects AS o WITH (NOLOCK)
INNER JOIN sys.indexes AS i WITH (NOLOCK)
ON o.[object_id] = i.[object_id]
INNER JOIN sys.stats AS s WITH (NOLOCK)
ON i.[object_id] = s.[object_id]
AND i.index_id = s.stats_id
INNER JOIN sys.dm_db_partition_stats AS st WITH (NOLOCK)
ON o.[object_id] = st.[object_id]
AND i.[index_id] = st.[index_id]
WHERE o.[type] = 'U'
ORDER BY STATS_DATE(i.[object_id], i.index_id) ASC OPTION (RECOMPILE);

-- Helps discover possible problems with out-of-date statistics
-- Also gives you an idea which indexes are most active
```

This query returns the name and several other properties for every clustered and nonclustered index in your database, sorted by the date on which statistics on that index were last updated. This can help you track down performance problems caused by out of date statistics that could be causing the SQL Server Query Optimizer to choose a poorly performing execution plan. I like to use this query to discover whether I have old statistics on my more volatile and important tables in the database.

Unless you have a compelling reason not to, it is usually a very good idea to have SQL Server automatically create statistics and automatically update them as the data changes in your tables. Especially for OLTP workloads, I usually like to enable the Auto Update Statistics Asynchronously database setting, which allows the Query Optimizer to use existing statistics while new ones are being generated (instead of waiting for the new ones to be created). This can give you more predictable query performance instead of taking a big performance hit during a statistics update operation.

> **NOTE** *It is also a good practice to manually update statistics on a periodic basis as part of your regular database maintenance. Even under Auto Update Statistics, statistics are not updated the moment data changes. To keep the update frequency from conflicting with normal query workloads, the auto update is only triggered when a certain threshold of data change has occurred. Performing periodic manual statistics updates ensures you always have up to date statistics.*

Next, using the query shown in Listing 15-51, you will find out which indexes in the current database have the most fragmentation.

LISTING 15-51: Fragmentation information for all indexes

```
-- Get fragmentation info for all indexes
-- above a certain size in the current database
-- Note: This could take some time on a very large database
SELECT DB_NAME(database_id) AS [Database Name],
OBJECT_NAME(ps.OBJECT_ID) AS [Object Name],
i.name AS [Index Name], ps.index_id, index_type_desc,
avg_fragmentation_in_percent, fragment_count, page_count
FROM sys.dm_db_index_physical_stats(DB_ID(),NULL, NULL, NULL ,'LIMITED') AS ps
INNER JOIN sys.indexes AS i WITH (NOLOCK)
ON ps.[object_id] = i.[object_id]
AND ps.index_id = i.index_id
WHERE database_id = DB_ID()
AND page_count > 500
ORDER BY avg_fragmentation_in_percent DESC OPTION (RECOMPILE);

-- Helps determine whether you have fragmentation in your relational indexes
-- and how effective your index maintenance strategy is
```

This query returns every table and index in the current database, ordered by average fragmentation level. It filters out indexes that have fewer than 500 pages, as fragmentation in very small tables is not something you typically have to worry about. Depending on the size of your tables and indexes, and your hardware, this query could take some time to run. This query uses the LIMITED mode option (which is the default if no mode option is specified) when it runs, so it will return less information, but take less time to run than the DETAILED mode.

This query is useful because it can show you the overall condition of your indexes as far as fragmentation goes relatively quickly. Heavily fragmented indexes can reduce your I/O performance and your query performance for some types of queries. It can also increase the space required by your data files.

If you see indexes that have more than 10% fragmentation, you need to decide whether to reorganize them or simply rebuild them. Reorganizing an index is always an online operation, and it can be stopped at any time. It can take longer than simply rebuilding an index and it may not reduce the fragmentation as much as rebuilding the index will. Rebuilding an index can be either an online operation or an offline operation, depending on several factors. The first factor is whether you have SQL Server Standard Edition or SQL Server Enterprise Edition.

If you have Standard Edition, rebuilding an index is always an offline operation. If you have Enterprise Edition, your index rebuild operations can be online or offline depending on a few more factors. With SQL Server 2012, you can rebuild clustered indexes in online mode, regardless of what data types your table contains. With earlier versions of SQL Server, you cannot rebuild a clustered index in online mode if your table has any lob data types, such as nvarchar (max).

After you reorganize or rebuild indexes that are heavily fragmented, you may free up a considerable amount of space within your data file(s). The data file will still be the same size, but more free space will be available. This is a good thing! Strongly resist any urge you may have to shrink your data files to reclaim that disk space. Shrinking data files is a very resource-intensive operation that has the unfortunate side-effect of heavily fragmenting your indexes. Do not let your system administrator or SAN administrator talk you into shrinking data files or entire databases on a regular basis.

Finally, don't make the common mistake of simply rebuilding all your indexes on a regular basis, whether they need it or not. This is a huge waste of resources on your database server. You can find many good index maintenance scripts on the Internet. One very well regarded one was developed and is maintained by Ola Hallengren which you can get from here: http://ola.hallengren.com.

SUMMARY

In this chapter, you walked through a set of 51 queries that enable you to gather a wealth of useful information about your database server — starting at the hardware level, then at the instance level, and finally at the individual database level. For each query, you have read the underlying rationale for why you would want to run the query and what you can expect to discover. You should now be able to interpret the results of each query, and in many cases also be able to respond to them. For some queries, I provided a more extended discussion of my thoughts and experiences regarding best practices for the area covered by the query.

The purpose behind this detailed examination of queries is that as a database professional, you should be keenly aware of what is going on with your database servers — from the hardware and storage subsystem, to the instance configuration and health, and finally to the properties and performance of your most important individual databases. I believe that you should run this set of queries on every single database server and instance for which you are responsible, saving the results as a baseline. I have never failed to find problems or opportunities for improvement on a database server after running these queries. You should also be able to find and correct many issues in your environment based on what you discover from them.

After you get a baseline, and work on correcting the initial problems that you discover, get in the habit of periodically running these queries again to discover anything new that crops. A busy database server is a very complex system. You will often find that after you make a change to alleviate a performance bottleneck, the bottleneck simply moves to another part of the system. Even if you have modern, high-performance hardware on a properly configured database instance, with a well-tuned database, you will see changes over time as your data volumes grow and your workload increases or simply changes. After reading this chapter, you have a very good set of tools that you can use to discover and address this inevitable change process.

16

Delivering Manageability and Performance

WHAT'S IN THIS CHAPTER?

➤ SQL Server manageability

➤ Policy-based management

➤ Automating policy management

➤ Microsoft tools for managing SQL Server

WROX.COM CODE DOWNLOADS FOR THIS CHAPTER

The wrox.com code downloads for this chapter are found at `www.wrox.com/remtitle .cgi?isbn=1118177657` on the Download Code tab. The code is in the Chapter 16 download and individually named according to the names throughout the chapter.

IMPROVE EFFICIENCY WITH SQL SERVER MANAGEABILITY FEATURES

This chapter provides information for database administrators who are responsible for database environments consisting of a large number SQL Servers. It provides guidance on tools and techniques to improve efficiency and effectiveness as a DBA by utilizing some of the manageability features of SQL Server.

In many organizations, the number and variety of SQL Server instances, combined with a lack of proper management, means the operational DBA team can be very busy with reactive tasks. In these situations it can be difficult to invest the time required to address the root cause, standardize the environment, and reduce the flow of break/fix support incidents.

The topic of manageability is broad and means different things to different groups of people. Manageability can mean developing build and deployment standards, rationalizing high-availability technologies, and implementing standardized database maintenance procedures. The benefits of effective manageability are fewer problems and quicker resolution when they do occur, and fast response time to new business requests.

MANAGEABILITY ENHANCEMENTS IN SQL SERVER 2012

This section provides a brief overview of manageability enhancements in SQL Server 2012. The first important change to mention is several enhancements to the *database restore* usability— including the addition of a visual timeline for point-in-time restore. This means it's possible to point the restore database wizard at a folder that can contain full, differential, and log backups; and, using a sliding timescale bar, select the point required for restore. The wizard will construct the correct restore command based on the sequence and precedence required to complete the point-in-time restore. Furthermore, the Page Restore dialog provides the capability to easily restore corrupt pages from a database backup, and to roll forward transaction logs.

Another important manageability enhancement can be found in the *Database Engine Tuning Advisor (DTA)*. In previous releases, the DTA has required a query or Profiler trace in order to provide recommendations to improve performance. In SQL Server 2012, the DTA can use the plan cache as a source for tuning. This saves effort and may improve the usefulness of the recommendations.

A common manageability problem with database migrations and database mirroring has been resolved through a new concept introduced in this version: *contained databases*. The contained database solution addresses the issue whereby SQL Server logins can become orphaned when migrating a database between servers or SQL Server instances. The contained database addresses this by enabling users to connect to the database without authenticating a login at the database engine level. This provides a layer of abstraction from the SQL Server instance and therefore mobility. Similarly, the concept of *partially contained databases* separates application functionality from instance-level functionality. This provides mobility but it lacks some features; for example, replication, change tracking, or change data capture cannot be utilized, as these require interaction with instance- or management-level objects, which are outside the database and cannot currently be contained within the database.

The *data-tier application (DAC or DACPAC)*, first introduced in SQL Server 2008, did not enjoy widespread adoption. One of the reasons why the uptake was limited was because the deployment method for schema upgrades was cumbersome and not practical for anything beyond a small database. The DACPAC schema upgrade process was impractical because a side-by-side approach was used, whereby a new database was created (with a unique name) alongside the existing database; database migration took place; and then the original database was dropped; and the new, temporary database was renamed to the proper database name. This process has been improved, and the new DAC upgrade process uses an in-place upgrade that simplifies the old method.

Finally, there are a number of enhancements in SQL Server Management Studio that improve functionality and usability, including improvements to IntelliSense and new breakpoint functionality.

POLICY-BASED MANAGEMENT

The Policy-Based Management (PBM) feature, introduced in SQL Server 2008, enables DBAs to enforce standards and automate health-check-type activities across an entire SQL Server environment. The PBM feature provides a framework for DBAs to enforce organizational standards for naming conventions, security, and configuration settings, and to provide regular reports and alerts on these conditions.

The PBM feature requires an initial investment in terms of understanding the mechanics and implementation, but the benefits of the solution can be quickly realized through rapid deployment and automation across an entire organization. Therefore, the return on investment (ROI) of the initial investment required to configure and implement the platform can be rapid. In addition, many DBAs carry out morning checks, and automating a lightweight 15-minute morning check could save more than 65 hours per year! Clearly, the benefits of automation — including scalability and consistency — present a strong business case for investing effort in a solution such as PBM.

Overview

Policy-Based Management provides a mechanism for DBAs to manage configuration and deployment standards and compliance within the SQL Server environment. Managing compliance reduces variation within an organization, which in turn reduces the complexity and effort required to support and maintain the provisioning of benefits, such as reduced resolution time for issues and efficiencies in terms of the effort expended for such issues.

The types of policy that can be implemented by PBM include database-levels checks, such as ensuring that Auto Close and Auto Shrink are disabled, enforcing object-naming conventions, and ensuring that instance-level configuration options, such as Max Degree of Parallelism and Max Server Memory, are correctly configured.

Three key aspects of PBM are required to get started:

➤ **Facet** — Object properties for checks (e.g., database, login, or server). Facets are fixed and cannot be added or changed.

➤ **Condition** — Evaluates to `true` or `false`, and contains logic to validate a setting or option; e.g., to confirm AutoClose is `false`

➤ **Policy** — Applies a condition on a target, determines policy mode, such as evaluate or prevent

In addition, using conditions can be a powerful way to refine the targets for policies. This can be useful in situations where different policies or best practices apply to different servers within an environment. A good example is the database data and log file autogrow settings. It's a common best practice to specify the growth increment based on a fixed size, rather than a percentage, to avoid disk fragmentation and minimize the synchronous file grow operation. However, it can be difficult to build a one-size-fits-all policy for the optimal file growth increment, as many organizations host databases with files ranging between a couple of megabytes to several terabytes.

To account for these variations, you can use conditions to create policies that ensure best practice compliance for data and log file growth, as shown in Table 16-1.

TABLE 16-1: PBM Conditions

DATA AND LOG FILE SIZE	GROWTH INCREMENT
<100MB	100MB
>100MB and <10GB	500MB
>10GB	1GB

When defining each policy, it's possible to choose an evaluation mode that determines the effect of the policy; Table 16-2 summarizes the options.

TABLE 16-2: Policy Evaluation Modes

EVALUATION MODE	DESCRIPTION
On Demand	Policies are evaluated manually by a DBA, as required.
On Schedule	A pre-defined schedule controls when policies are evaluated.
On Change Prevent	The policy will actively prevent an action that could cause a condition to evaluate false (only where rollback is possible).
On Change Log Only	Allows a change that will cause a false evaluation, but logs the change

Getting Started with PBM

This section describes the steps required to get a PBM deployment up and running. Three phases are required: defining a condition, creating a policy, and evaluating this policy against a local machine. The following steps establish a condition and policy:

1. Launch SQL Server Management Studio and select Management ⇨ Policy Management.

2. Right-click on Conditions and choose New Condition.

3. Type the condition name **Auto Close Disabled**.

4. Using the Facet drop-down list, Select Database Performance.

5. In the Expression pane, select the field name @AutoClose, verify that the operator shows the equals sign (=), and choose the value False (as shown in Figure 16-1). Click OK.

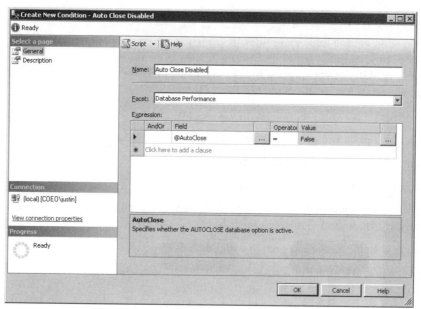

FIGURE 16-1

6. Right-click on Policy and choose Create New Policy.

7. Specify the policy name **Database – Auto Close**.

8. Using the Check condition drop-down list, select the Auto Close Disabled condition.

9. Verify that the Against Targets options shows a check alongside Every Database.

10. Ensure that the Evaluation Mode shows On demand, and Server restriction is None.

11. Click OK.

Now expand the policies folder, right-click on the policy named Database – Auto Close, and choose Evaluate. The report will display a list containing one row for each database on the instance, and hopefully each will display a green check indicating compliance. Enable the Auto Close option for one database and then reevaluate the policy to confirm it is functioning correctly.

Now you should see a single database listed with a red cross mark, indicating noncompliance. Alongside the noncompliant database is a checkbox; mark this checkbox as enabled. Then click the Apply button in the lower-right corner of the dialog. Clicking the Apply button does two things: It changes the database property to Disable Auto Close, and it reevaluates the policy to show a compliant database (green) now.

This example demonstrates how effective PBM can be in identifying and resolving configuration issues within an environment. If this policy were scheduled, it could find and fix any sub-optimal configuration within an environment. A clear benefit of this level of automation is that if any new configuration issue is introduced — either through a change to an existing database or through a new database in the environment — compliance could be ensured on the next policy evaluation.

Using Conditions as Server Restrictions

This section focuses on adding more logic to a policy by using the server restrictions options. To enhance the intelligence of the Auto Close policy described in the previous example, it may be useful to target this policy only at SQL Servers running the Standard or Enterprise Edition. This will avoid the possibility of spurious alerts for instances of SQL Server Express.

The following steps will create a condition and assign it as a restriction to the policy created earlier:

1. Right-click on Conditions and choose New Condition.

2. Enter the name **SQL Server Standard or Enterprise Edition**.

3. Using the Facet drop-down box, choose Server.

4. In the Expression pane, choose the field named @EngineEdition, choose the equals operator, and select Standard from the Value drop-down box.

5. Click to add a new clause to the Expression using the OR operator.

6. Choose again the field @EngineEdition, use the equals operator, and select EnterpriseOrDeveloper from the Value drop-down box.

7. Click OK.

8. Locate the policy for Database – Auto Close and choose Properties.

9. Using the Server Restriction drop-down box, select the Condition named SQL Server Standard or Enterprise Edition.

The next time this policy is evaluated it will detect the SQL Server edition, and this policy will be evaluated only against servers running Standard or Enterprise Editions. In order to leverage the value of these policies, it's necessary to define a Central Management Server, import the policies, and evaluate against the environment. The next section describes the process and steps required to successfully configure the environment and evaluate the policies.

Enterprise Policy Evaluation

The architecture for the Policy-Based Management framework consists of a Central Management Server where policies are stored; server groups, which are logical containers for servers; and server registrations, which are connections to the target database servers. Once the Central Management Server is defined and each instance registered, policies can be evaluated against entire groups of servers with ease, and reports can be generated showing compliance status.

The first step is to configure a Central Management Server. This server is typically used as a repository for policies and to host the schedules for policy evaluation.

To configure a Central Management Server:

1. Launch SQL Server Management Studio and choose View ➪ Registered Servers.

2. Expand Database Engine and in the expanded view that appears, right-click on Central Management Servers and select Register Central Management Server. The New Server Registration dialog, shown in Figure 16-2, will appear.

3. Type the name of the instance that will host your Central Management Server in the "Server name:" field of the New Server Registration dialog. You can optionally give this Registered server a friendly name in the registered server name and registered server description text fields in this dialog. Click Save after you have select the hosting instance.

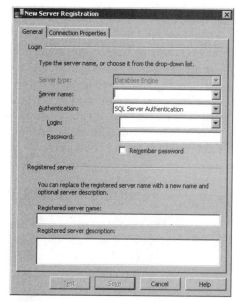

FIGURE 16-2

Now that your Central Management Server is created, you'll want to add servers to it. It is a best practice to create various server groups for the different groupings of servers in your environment (e.g. Production, Test, Development). To create a Server Group right-click on the Central Management Server you just created and choose New Server Group, enter the name **Production**, and click OK.

Register each production instance within the group named Production by right clicking on the server group and choosing New Server Registration. The instances must be able to communicate directly with the Central Management Server, so you will want to point specify connection details to connect to the instance in the New Server Registration dialog.

If policies were created on an instance other than the Central Management Server, you need to transfer them, which you can do using a simple export/import process. To export the policies from the source instance, right-click and choose Export, and specify a name and location on disk. One XML file is created for each policy exported.

To import policies to the Central Management Server, right-click on the server name and choose Central Management Server Actions, and then select Import Policies from the submenu. Navigate to the folder location and select the policy files to import.

To evaluate the policies, right-click on the Central Management Server to evaluate for all registered servers, or right-click on the group name to evaluate for servers within the group, and choose Evaluate Policies from the menu. Choose the source (specify the Central Management Server) and check the policies to evaluate using the left-hand checkboxes. Click Evaluate in the bottom-right corner and verify the output.

NAMING CONVENTIONS FOR POLICIES

Consider defining a naming convention standard for conditions and policies. It helps to organize policies by using the target in the name; for example, any policies for databases can include the prefix "Database" in the policy name, and server-wide policies can be prefixed with "Server."

Automating Best Practice Checks with PBM

Microsoft and the SQL Server community have established many best practices concerning SQL Server and database design, configuration, and deployment. Typically, a best practice is a deviation from a standard or default configuration to improve some aspect of the solution — performance, reliability, maintainability, and so on. Because SQL Server is an application platform and can be deployed and used in many different ways, use of these best practices is often hotly debated. As such, there are may be exceptions to these best practices, whereby a given recommendation may apply only in some situations, or some additional qualifications or conditions are required to determine whether the best practice is applicable.

> ### ORGANIZING POLICIES USING CATEGORIES
>
> The PBM feature has an option to populate metadata for each policy. This includes a category, a description, and a hyperlink to further information. One particularly useful field is Category, which can be used to separate policies based on their purpose, e.g., best practices, organization standards, or bad configurations. The categories can be used to sort policies during evaluation and improve manageability.

This section provides guidance on implementing policies to automate checks for best practices. It is not intended to define a best practice, or to provide a full set of health-check policies.

There are several benefits to defining and automating health-check policies — in particular scalability and reuse of the solution. You can execute the checks on a schedule, and any deviation or omission will be highlighted immediately. Additionally, these checks can be scaled across an entire estate to which new servers or additional environments are added with relatively little effort.

Database — Check Last Backup

This check ensures that a successful full backup occurred in the past 24 hours. The approach used in this condition could easily be adapted for use with transaction log backups.

First, create a new condition using the name **Last Good Backup**. In the Facet field, select Database maintenance. Choose the field @LastBackupDate and use the operator >=. Next, in the Value field, click the ellipses (. . .) to launch the Advanced Edit dialog. This dialog permits entry of a T-SQL statement. Enter the following, click OK, and save the condition:

```
DateAdd('day', -1, GetDate())
```

Next, create a new policy named **Database — Recent Backup**, and select the check condition Last Good Backup that you created earlier. Initially, set the Evaluation Mode to On demand. All other settings should remain at their default. Click OK to complete creation of the policy.

Database — Data and Log File Auto-Grow Increments

This policy checks the auto-growth increments for data and log files to ensure they are optimized given the database size. This particular policy is a good example of how the optimal value for the auto-growth increment varies according to the size of the database. It would be unreasonable to grow a 10MB log file by anything more than a few MB. Similarly, it would be unreasonable to grow a 100GB data file by anything less than 1GB.

To get started with this policy example, create the four conditions shown in Table 16-3. Figure 16-3 shows values for a medium data check condition.

TABLE 16-3: Example Autogrow Conditions

CONDITION NAME	FACET	FIELD	OPERATOR	VALUE (KB)
Optimized Autogrow — Small Data	Data File	@Growth	>	5120
Optimized Autogrow — Small Log	Log File	@Growth	>	5120
Optimized Autogrow — Medium Data	Data File	@Growth	>	102400
Optimized Autogrow — Medium Log	Log File	@Growth	>	102400

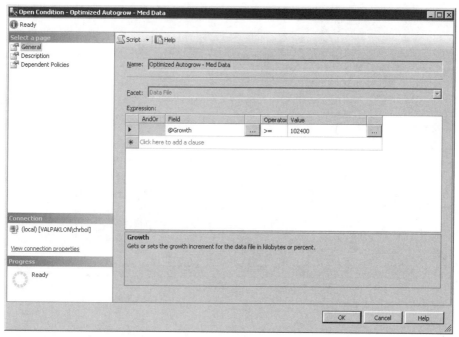

FIGURE 16-3

Before creating the policies, four further conditions are required that will be used in the target to ensure that each policy is applied against the correct database (see Figure 16-4). Table 16-4 summarizes the additional conditions required.

TABLE 16-4: Additional Conditions for Filtering Targets

CONDITION NAME	FACET	AND/OR	FIELD	OPERATOR	VALUE
Log file 1GB or greater with KB growth	Log File		@Size	>=	102400
		And	@GrowthType	=	KB
Log file with KB growth	Log File		@GrowthType	=	KB
Data File 1GB or greater with KB growth	Data File		@Size	>=	102400
		And	@GrowthType	=	KB
Data File with KB growth	Data File		@GrowthType	=	KB

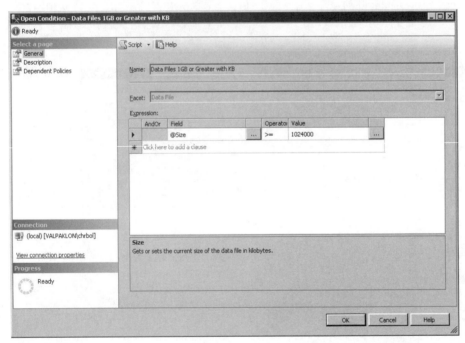

FIGURE 16-4

Once these conditions are created, the next and final step is to create the policies. Four policies are required, and these policies will connect the check condition to the target conditions and specify the evaluation mode for the policy. Table 16-5 summarizes the four policies required. Figure 16-5 shows an example dialog using the Small Data condition.

TABLE 16-5: Example File Autogrow Policies

POLICY NAME	CHECK CONDITION	AGAINST TARGETS
Database — Log File Autogrow Amount	Optimized Autogrow — Small Log	Log Files with KB Growth Type Log file in Every Database
Database — Data File Autogrow Amount	Optimized Autogrow — Small Data	Data Files with KB Growth Type File in Every FileGroup in Every Database
Database — Medium Data Autogrow	Optimized Autogrow — Medium Data	Data Files 1GB or greater with KB file in Every FileGroup in Every Database
Database — Medium Log Autogrow	Optimized Autogrow — Medium Log	Log Files 1GB or greater with KB LogFile in Every database

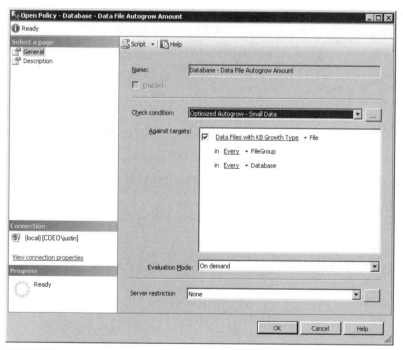

FIGURE 16-5

Creating these eight conditions and four policies enables the automated policy evaluation to ensure that small databases have KB growth increments, and databases with data or log files larger than 1GB have autogrow set to 1GB or larger.

SQL Server — Max Degree of Parallelism

The intention of this policy is to ensure that the sp_configure option for Max Degree of Parallelism (MaxDoP) has been optimized (i.e., the current running value is nondefault) on any server with more than four CPUs.

Implementing this policy as described requires two conditions and one policy. The first condition will be used as a check condition to verify that the MaxDoP setting is correct. The second condition will be used as a server restriction to ensure that the policy applies only to servers with more than four CPUs. Finally, the policy will bring together the check condition and the restriction condition and determine the evaluation mode.

Start by creating the check condition shown in Figure 16-6.

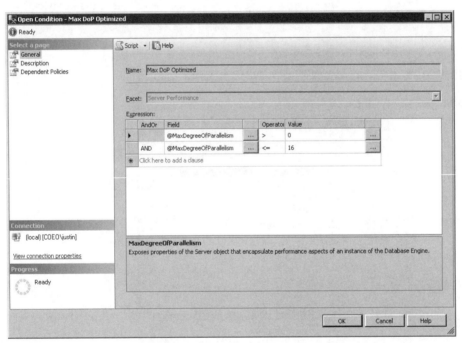

FIGURE 16-6

Next, create a new condition that will be used for the server restriction. Create a new condition named **Greater than 4 CPUs**, using the facet Server. In the Expression pane, use **@Processors**, and set the Operator and Value to **>4**.

The final step is to create the policy. Use the name **SQL Server — MaxDoP** and choose the check condition and server restriction conditions created earlier. The policy should look like what is shown in Figure 16-7.

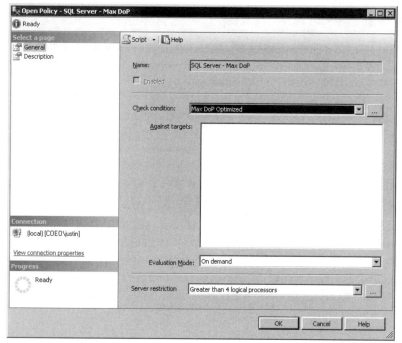

FIGURE 16-7

In summary, these three policy examples — check last full backup, autogrow settings, and MaxDoP — provide a framework of conditions and policies that can be used in a number of scenarios. You can also adapt and apply this foundation to most types of health-check policies, and scale it out to meet a variety of objectives for PBM.

Enforcing IT Standards with PBM

This section considers scope when using Policy-Based Management (PBM) to report and potentially enforce organization IT standards within the database. Many organizations suffer from staff turnover, lack of adherence, and missing or conflicting standards for object naming conventions.

There is potentially an overlap between the policies in this section and those in the preceding best practices section. Arguably some of these policies are best practices, but when adopting these conventions as organizational standards, PBM can be used to enforce these policies. That is to say, PBM could prevent a developer or administrator from making a change that is noncompliant with the organization's standards.

In order to configure a policy to utilize the On Change: prevent evaluation mode, the facet must support Data Definition Language (DDL) changes.

OUT-OF-THE-BOX BEST PRACTICE POLICIES

SQL Server provides a number of best practice policies. You can import these policies, which are located in the Program Files folder. These policies provide a useful starting point, although they often require modification to achieve the desired outcome.

Object Naming Conventions

Naming conventions are a good area in environments with a lot of best practice guidance. However, an organization needs to determine which approach will best suit its needs.

One commonly used convention is to prefix all stored procedures with the characters **'usp_'**. This clearly identifies these as user-created stored procedures, thereby differentiating them from system stored procedures.

To do so, create a condition, choose a meaningful name, and select the Stored Procedure facet. In the Expression pane, choose the field @Name, use the LIKE operator, and type **'usp_%'** in the Value field, as shown in Figure 16-8.

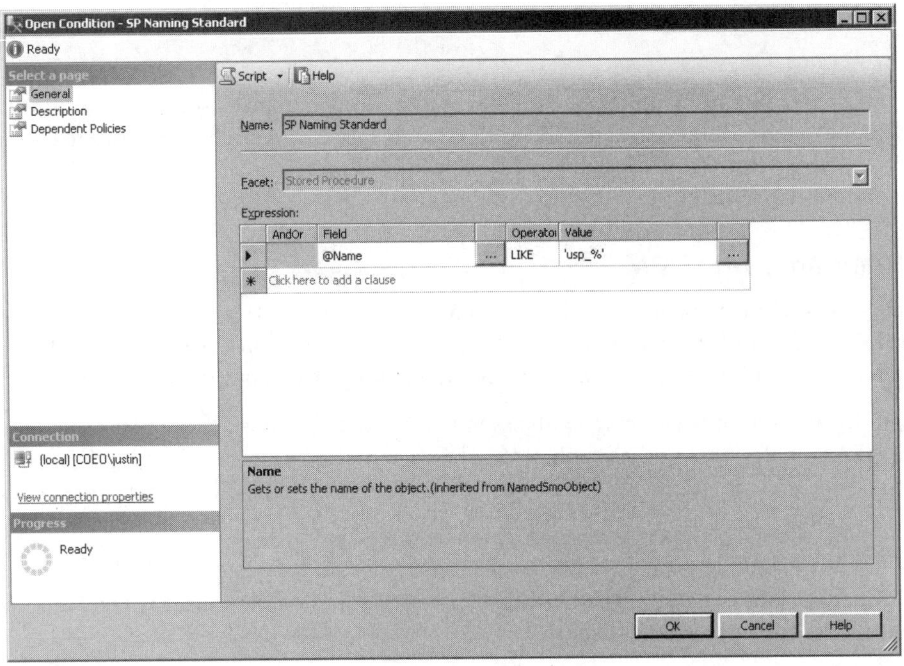

FIGURE 16-8

Once the condition has been created, create a new policy and select the check condition created earlier. In the Against targets pane, choose Every Stored Procedure in Every database. If desirable, change the Evaluation Mode to On change: prevent. This will cause an error and rollback for any CREATE PROCEDURE statement that does not comply with the naming convention. Figure 16-9 shows the policy configuration.

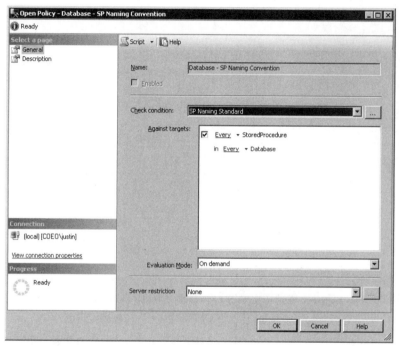

FIGURE 16-9

Clustered Indexes

This is a potentially contentious topic, although many DBAs and some organizations mandate that every table must have a clustered index. The following steps describe how to create the condition and policy for reporting through PBM.

First, create a new condition, specify a meaningful name, and choose the facet named Table. Select the field @HasClusteredIndex, use the equals operator, and choose the value True.

Next, create a policy and select every table in every database for the targets. The facet used in this condition does not support enforcing the condition, so the Evaluation mode options are On Demand or On Schedule. Figure 16-10 shows the policy configuration.

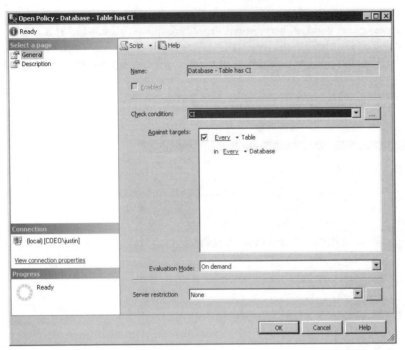

FIGURE 16-10

Enterprise Policy Management Framework

The Enterprise Policy Management Framework (EPMF) provides centralized compliance reporting for Policy-Based Management solutions. It is currently available only for SQL Server 2008.

The EPMF provides a set of reports that enable easy identification of policy failures, organized by policy category and over time. The solution is easy to deploy and configure, and further leverages investment in the Policy-Based Management infrastructure and knowledge.

You can download the EPMF and keep an eye out for SQL Server 2012 updates here: http://epmframework.codeplex.com/.

OTHER MICROSOFT TOOLS FOR MANAGING SQL SERVER

This section describes manageability tools for SQL Server other than those included with the product. There is a significant industry in creating tools that help in the development and management of databases and servers, and Microsoft has invested heavily in enterprise deployment, configuration, and monitoring tools for the entire application platform, including SQL Server. Several years ago, Microsoft defined a set of acceptance criteria for all server-based products, stating they must ship with a monitoring management pack (originally called Microsoft Operations Manager, or MOM, and now renamed System Center Operations Manager, or SCOM), which means customers can add application-specific monitoring to their monitoring platform.

Since the SQL Server database platform has become more mature, many customers focus on reducing total cost of ownership (TCO) and delivering better value to the business by improving service levels and reducing deployment times for new services. The benefit driving more widespread adoption of these technologies is breadth of coverage. For example, an increasing number of customers are deploying Hyper-V in some capacity within the data center, and it is very easy to add monitoring and alerting via the System Center Operations Manager.

The next step in the evolution of the data center is the private cloud concept. Typically these deployments are created and standardized using a virtualization platform. Compared to the traditional server purchase and provisioning cycle, this can drastically reduce both the cost per server (or virtual machine) and the provisioning time required.

System Center Advisor

The System Center Advisor (SCA) is a cloud-based subscription service that provides configuration reviews and feedback. Part of the System Center manageability product family, it offers detailed customer-specific guidance based on server configuration, and leverages best practices and field knowledge from the Microsoft Customer Service and Support (CSS) organization.

The tool is intended to consolidate the features of other products such as Windows Server Update Service (WSUS) and the Best Practice Analyzer (BPA), and to close the gap between best practice guidance and advice provided by CSS. As a result, SCA provides customers with specific, actionable recommendations.

SCA supports SQL Server 2008, SQL Server 2008 R2 and SQL Server 2012, running on Windows Server 2008 and Windows Server 2008 R2. You can find out more and try it out here:
`http://www.microsoft.com/en-in/server-cloud/system-center/advisor-overview.aspx`.

There is also a Microsoft KB article to be aware of for SQL Server 2012 which can found here:

How to configure SQL Server 2012 to allow for System Center Advisor monitoring:
`http://support.microsoft.com/kb/2667175`.

LICENSING SYSTEM CENTER ADVISOR

System Center Advisor is available to customers with Software Assurance (SA) as a value-added service — without any additional charge. Other than purchasing Software Assurance, there's currently no licensing model for using System Center Advisor.

Microsoft does not offer System Center Advisor through a typical cloud pay-as-you-go subscription, or through the Service Provider License Agreement (SPLA) models.

It's important to understand under which circumstances you would use SCA, as approaching the tool with accurate expectations is more likely to result in a satisfactory experience. Although SCA does provide a lot of useful information, it isn't a performance analysis tool or a live monitoring tool, and it has no real-time data capture or alerting features. Here's a summary of the environments that can be monitored at the time of writing:

➤ Windows Server 2008 and later

    ➤ Active Directory

    ➤ Hyper-V Host

➤ General operating system

➤ SQL Server 2008 and later

    ➤ SQL Engine

➤ Exchange Server 2010

➤ SharePoint Server 2010

SCA functionality is based on periodic configuration snapshots, taken over time. It reports configuration changes and missing or new updates. Note that SCA will not monitor CPU utilization, disk space, memory, or any other operational monitoring counters or thresholds. For these purposes, SCA can be used to supplement any operational monitoring, rather than replace such tools.

It supports an evolving knowledge base, acquired from the field experience of Microsoft CSS, supporting SQL Server deployments. The SCA knowledge base will expand to include rules (recommendations) for service packs, cumulative updates, Quick Fix Engineering (QFE) releases, and configuration changes that resolve new issues — identified and resolved after a product is in the in-life product life cycle phase. The recommendations provided are far more specialized than anything that can be provided through traditional software update models such as Windows Server Update Service (WSUS), which does not contain the configuration view or logic to determine applicability of updates with the same level of sophistication provided by SCA.

Topology

Although the SCA is a cloud-based service, two components require on-premise installation. However, this process is streamlined and relatively non-intrusive. Two roles must be deployed on-premise: Gateway and Agent.

Each environment requires a Gateway that uses certificate-based authentication to upload data to the web service. The Gateway collects and uploads monitoring data captured from each Agent. The Gateway must be in the same security zone (Active Directory domain or trusted domain) as the servers to be monitored. Additionally, the Gateway must have Internet connectivity to complete the data upload to the web service.

Each server that will be monitored with SCA requires an Agent installation. If the server is not in the same domain as the Gateway, the Gateway and certificate must also be installed on the server. Additionally, the Agents must have network communication with the Gateway. The data collection process runs approximately every 24 hours; once the deployment is complete, you can check the following day to ensure that the server is displayed correctly in the web console.

Reporting

The alerting and administration for SCA is accessed via the web portal found at
`http://www.systemcenteradvisor.com`. The web console provides an easy-to-use overview of

the environment's current status, using colors to indicate alert severity (critical, warning, without alert) and specifying the area affected (SQL Server and Windows), as shown in Figure 16-11. The Overview page also shows server status, which displays any nonreporting Agents.

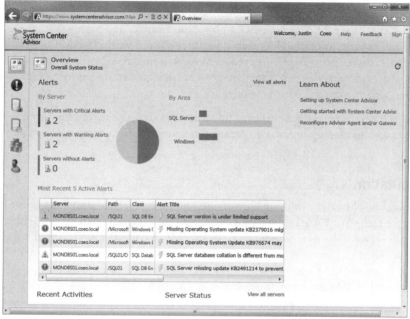

FIGURE 16-11

Displayed in the left-hand navigation area are five additional tabs, which are summarized in Table 16-6.

TABLE 16-6: SCA Home Page Icons

WEB CONSOLE TAB	DESCRIPTION
Alerts	Displays all open alerts, grouped by server and severity. Alerts can be sorted and managed (closed or ignored) using this interface.
Configuration: Current Snapshot	Shows each parameter captured in the snapshot of each server. Servers can be selected from a drop-down.
Configuration: Change History	Changes ordered by dates, where server name and properties are displayed.
Servers	Lists servers under monitoring, shows role (Gateway or Agent) and the gateway used for reporting.
Account	Used to manage the SCA configuration, users, etc.

In addition to using the web console for monitoring, SCA can also be configured to send e-mail notifications of new SCA alerts.

System Center Operations Manager

The System Center Operations Manager (SCOM) product is Microsoft's enterprise monitoring tool and part of the Systems Center suite. SCOM provides a powerful, flexible, and highly configurable platform for building a monitoring solution. However, it requires a lot of work. In addition, the management packs for SQL Server provided by Microsoft have been updated (rather than rewritten) across several versions of SQL Server. As such, the management packs often use legacy technologies and don't provide optimal feature coverage for new releases.

The bottom line is that you need to make a significant investment in terms of designing, deploying, configuring, tuning, and developing in order to create a meaningful monitoring solution with SCOM.

Design and Implementation

The System Center Operations Manager solution consists of a number of key components (some of which are shared with the technology used in System Center Advisor), including an Agent, which must be installed on each server to be monitored; the Gateway, which collects monitoring data; the Root Management Server (RMS), where the data is stored and aggregated and alerts are generated; and the Console, which is where DBAs and systems engineers can manage an environment. Figure 16-12 shows a typical SCOM deployment scenario.

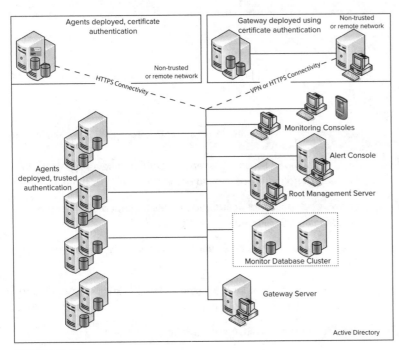

FIGURE 16-12

The Agent must be installed onto each target server that will be monitored, and communication must be enabled with its gateway. If the target server and gateway are not in the same security zone (i.e., not in the same domain or in a workgroup), then certificates must be used to provide authentication between the target server and gateway. Each server can report to up to six management groups.

The Gateway role is both a security boundary and an architectural scalability point. Given that the SCOM platform is designed to scale to monitor many thousands of devices, the RMS may become a point of contention if all devices were set up to report directly to this host. Instead, the Gateway servers provide a point of scale-out for the monitoring infrastructure. Additionally, in scenarios in which organizations operate from multiple locations or use different security zones, gateway servers can be used as a security boundary and as a point of aggregation for data flowing to the RMS. Agents are "homed" to a given Gateway, and a PowerShell script can be used to provide a failover Gateway, providing a fault-tolerant solution.

The top tier in the hierarchy is the Root Management Server (RMS), which is the central point for configuration and changes (new agents and rules or monitors). The RMS server must be able to communicate with all Gateway servers; and if no Active Directory trust exists, certificate authentication must be configured.

Rules and Monitors

Two types of checks are carried out by SCOM: rules and monitors. Both collect data, and understanding the difference between them is crucial for determining which should be used.

A monitor is a near real-time operation, and the only way to alter the health state of a managed object. Additionally, the health state changes automatically once the condition is resolved. An example is low disk space; once space is released, the monitor will resolve automatically. Collected data is not stored.

A rule is typically used to collect data about a specific object (e.g., Avg Disk Transfer/sec for a storage performance baseline). Rules may also be useful to create an alert without affecting health state. These alerts must be resolved manually. Collected data is stored in the data warehouse.

Alerts

The final fundamental SCOM concept to understand is alerts. An alert is not an e-mail or page notification, but an event that can be triggered by a monitor or rule. Alerts are displayed in the SCOM Console, under the Alerts tab where they are sorted in order of priority by default. A notification is a method of communication — such as e-mail, SMS, or pager — fired on an alert.

Calibration is the process of tuning alerts to ensure the correct level of sensitivity. An environment can contain vastly different database workloads, Windows and SQL Server configuration settings, and optimization, so the concept of a healthy server can also vary. Alert calibration refines thresholds on a per-server basis to ensure that alerts are meaningful.

Alert tuning takes the form of overrides, which modify thresholds from the standard to customize the values of a given rule or monitor for a specific server or group (e.g., All Windows 2008 Logical Disks or All SQL Server 2008 databases).

When creating overrides, it is useful to store these outside the "sealed" management packs that are provided by Microsoft. This provides isolation between the pre-packaged, downloaded management packs and anything that is organization or server specific. Define an organization standard for naming the management packs where overrides are saved — for example, you could create a new MP for the Windows Server 2008 R2 customizations and name it Windows Server 2008 R2 — Overrides. This clearly delimits the in-box and custom functionality.

Importing Management Packs

The Windows and SQL Server management packs (MPs) are published by Microsoft, version controlled, and released for public consumption free of charge. Download the latest version and import it into SCOM. Any dependencies between management packs are indicated at the time of import. The MP download includes a Word document that is a guide to describe the setup process, rules, and monitors, and contains any last-minute breaking changes.

The import/export functionality can also be used as a backup and recovery method for custom management packs in case a management pack rollback is required.

> **SCOM AND SQL AGENT**
>
> By default, the SCOM alerts will alert only on job failure. If there is a step failure but the "On failure" job step is set to continue, then no alert is raised. This is the out-of-the-box behavior and may be changed if required.

Management Pack Authoring

The greatest value derived from any monitoring process is the creation of health checks that identify key aspects of the application platform and provide detailed data collection. As such, SCOM is a great platform to develop this custom monitoring in the form of *management pack authoring.*

One such example for SQL Server is checking for the most recent full backup, a feature that isn't included out-of-the-box. This is a good example in which SCOM can alert based on SQL Agent job failures; however, in some situations SQL Agent is disabled, the database maintenance job schedule becomes disabled, or for some reason the backup job does not run. Without proactive monitoring to check for the last good backup, situations like these could continue unnoticed for some time. This is a good scenario in which authoring a custom monitor to check for the backup event would be useful.

SUMMARY

This chapter provided an overview of manageability in SQL Server 2012. You learned about several enhancements, including improvements to the database restore wizard, contained databases, SQL Server Management Studio functionality, and the Database Tuning Advisor.

You also worked through detailed examples demonstrating how to implement Policy-Based Management in order to provide an organization-wide configuration and reporting solution.

Next, you looked at some Microsoft tools for managing SQL Server, including the cloud-based service System Center Advisor, for configuration and patching guidance; and the on-premise enterprise monitoring solution, System Center Operations Manager, for operational monitoring and alerting.

Finally, you saw that there are numerous ways to achieve the same result in your monitoring efforts. For example, this chapter demonstrated the methods required to define a check for the last recent good backup using Policy-Based Management or System Center Operations Manager. Understanding the strengths of these tools and comparisons such as this should help you select the right tool for the job for SQL Server manageability.

The most important concept of manageability in SQL Server 2012 is that it is made easier by these tools, and developing good manageability habits is the best way to ensure the health of your environment.

17

Running SQL Server in a Virtual Environment

WHAT'S IN THIS CHAPTER?

➤ Why virtualize a server?

➤ Common virtualization products

➤ Virtualization concepts

➤ Extended features of virtualization

➤ Managing contention

➤ Identifying candidates for virtualization

➤ Architecting successful virtual database servers

➤ Monitoring virtualized database servers

WROX.COM CODE DOWNLOADS FOR THIS CHAPTER

The wrox.com code downloads for this chapter are found at `www.wrox.com/remtitle .cgi?isbn=1118177657` on the Download Code tab. The code is in the Chapter 17 download and individually named according to the names throughout the chapter.

THE SHIFT TO SERVER VIRTUALIZATION

Of all the innovations in server technology over the last 10 years, in my view virtualization has had the biggest impact, and made the biggest improvements, to server computing. Although 64-bit architectures, multi-core processors, and solid-state drives have revolutionized their niches of the industry, only virtualization has fundamentally changed the way we can choose to deploy, manage, and protect server workloads.

Today, it's likely then that the IT environments you use have virtualized servers in them. While a few years ago these servers might have run the smaller workloads such as domain controllers and print servers, today the capability of virtualization technology means you are more likely to also find mission critical servers with high workloads, such as database servers, being virtualized.

This chapter's aim is to review the concepts of virtualization technology, some of the products that run virtualized servers, their features, benefits and some of their limitations.

Finally, we'll consider how you can deploy SQL Server 2012 successfully in a virtual environment and monitor it post go-live.

Where later parts of the chapter show examples of server virtualization being used, Microsoft's Hyper-V feature has been used; this is because its terminology and interface will be more familiar to SQL Server professionals who are new to server virtualization, and an evaluation of Windows Server, which provides access to it, is available as a download from Microsoft.

AN OVERVIEW OF VIRTUALIZATION

A typical textbook definition of virtualization defines the concept of sharing a single physical resource between multiple isolated processes, by presenting each with their own virtual version of the physical resource. For example, several virtualized instances of Windows can run concurrently on a single physical server, each believing they have exclusive access to the server's hardware. One of the many benefits of doing this is to increase the physical server's overall utilization, therefore increasing the value the physical server delivers.

A simple real-world example of deploying virtualization is to have a single physical server hosting four virtual servers.

Let's assume that the physical server has four CPU cores, 16GB of memory, and the necessary virtualization software to run virtual servers installed on it.

In our example, four virtual servers can then be created by the virtualization software and each configured to have four virtual CPUs and 3GB of memory.

By default, none of the virtual servers are aware of each other, let alone that they are sharing the physical server's hardware between them — nor would they know in our example that each physical CPU core has potentially been allocated twice (8 physical cores but 16 virtual CPUs allocated).

When the four virtual servers are running concurrently, the virtualization software manages access to the physical server's resources on an "as and when needed" basis.

In a well-configured environment, we could expect the person who configured the virtual servers to know that no more than two of them would ever need to use all of their CPU resources at any one time. Therefore, the physical host should always be able to satisfy requests by the virtual servers to use all of their allocated CPU resources without having to introduce any significant scheduling overhead.

In a badly configured environment, there might be a need for three virtual servers to use all of their allocated CPU resources at the same time. It's when this happens that performance could begin to degrade for each of the virtual servers, as the virtualization software has to start scheduling access to the physical server's resources; a quart has to be made out of a pint pot!

However, as you can probably already see, if the virtual server workloads in this example were correctly sized and their workloads managed, then a significant amount of data center space, power, cooling, server hardware, CPUs, and memory can be saved by deploying one rather than four physical servers.

This "deploy only what you actually need" approach provided by virtualization explains why the technology moved so quickly from being deployed in the development lab to enterprise data centers. In fact, other than smartphone technology, it's hard to find another technological innovation in recent years that has been adopted so widely and rapidly as virtualization has.

This rapid adoption is highly justifiable; virtualization brought IT departments an efficient data center with levels of flexibility, manageability, and cost reduction that they desperately needed, especially during the server boom of the mid-2000s and then the recession of the late 2000s. Moreover, once virtualization is deployed and the benefits of replacing old servers with fewer new servers are realized, the technology then goes on to deliver more infrastructure functionality — and interestingly, functionality that wasn't available with traditional physical servers.

Indeed, it's rare to find a SQL Server environment now which *doesn't* use virtualization technologies in some way. In larger environments, companies might only be deploying it on developer workstations or in the pre-production environment; but increasingly I am finding small, mid-size, and even large infrastructures that are hosting their entire production environment in a virtualized manner.

History of Virtualization

The concepts of the virtualization technology that people are deploying today are nothing new, and you can actually trace them back to IBM's mainframe hardware from the 1960s! At the time, mainframe hardware was very expensive, and customers wanted every piece of hardware they bought to be working at its highest capacity all of the time in order to justify its huge cost. The architecture IBM used partitioned a physical mainframe into several smaller logical mainframes that could each run an application seemingly concurrently. The cost saving came from each logical mainframe only ever needing to use a portion of the mainframe's total capacity. While hardware costs would not have decreased, utilization did, and therefore value increased, pleasing the finance director.

During the 1980s and 1990s, PC-based systems gained in popularity; and as they were considerably cheaper than mainframes and minicomputers, the use of virtualization disappeared from the technology stack for a while. However, in the late 1990s, VMware, a virtualization software vendor, developed an x86-based virtualization solution that enabled a single PC to run several operating system environments installed on it concurrently. I remember the first time I saw this running and was completely baffled! A backup engineer had a laptop running both Windows and Linux on it; from within Windows you could watch the virtual server boot with its own BIOS and then start up another operating system. At the time, very few people knew much about the Linux operating system, especially me, so the idea of running it on a Windows laptop looked even more surreal!

This example was a typical use of VMware's original software in the late 1990s and early 2000s, and for a few years, this was how their small but growing customer base used their technology. It was only a few years later that a version of their virtualization software hosted on its own Linux-based operating system was released and data center hosted server-based virtualization solutions began appearing.

Fundamentally, this server-based virtualization software is the basis of the platform virtualization solutions we use today in the biggest and smallest server environments.

The Breadth of Virtualization

When we talk about virtualization today, it is mostly in terms of physical servers, virtual servers, and the virtualization software known as a hypervisor, all terms this chapter defines later. However, your data center has probably had virtualization in it in some form for a long time, for the reasons we mentioned earlier — to help increase the utilization of expensive and typically underused physical hardware assets.

Today, most Storage Area Network hardware, SANs, use virtualization internally to abstract the storage partitions they present a server with from their physical components, such as the different speed hard drives it might use internally for storing data on.

While a system administrator will see an amount of usable storage on a storage partition the SAN creates for them, the exact configuration of the physical disks that store the data are hidden, or abstracted, from them by a virtualization layer within the SAN.

This can be a benefit for system administrators, allowing them to quickly deploy new storage while the SAN takes care of the underlying technical settings. For example, modern SANs will choose to store the most regularly used data on fast disks and the less frequently used data on slower disks. Yet, the data accessed most frequently might change over time, but by using virtualization, the SAN can re-distribute the data based on historic usage patterns to optimize its performance without the system administrator knowing.

Of course, this may not always be appropriate, a DBA might ask to use storage with consistent performance metrics; but like all virtualization technologies, once the product's options and limitations are known, an optimized configuration can be used.

Cisco and other network vendors also use virtualization in their network hardware. You may wonder how a collection of network cables and switches could benefit from virtualization, but the concept of virtual LANS (VLANs) enables multiple logical networks to be transmitted over a common set of cables, NICs and switches, removing the potential for duplicated network hardware.

Finally, believe it or not, SQL Server still uses memory virtualization concepts that date back to the Windows 3.1 era! Windows 3.1 introduced the concept of virtual memory and the virtual address spaces, and as discussed in Chapter 3 of this book, it is still core to the Windows memory management architecture that SQL Server uses today. By presenting each Windows application with its own virtual memory address space, Windows (rather than the application) manages the actual assignment of physical memory to applications. This is still a type of virtualization where multiple isolated processes concurrently access a shared physical resource to increase its overall utilization.

Platform Virtualization

Having looked at the background of virtualization and some of the reasons to use it, this section clarifies what the term platform virtualization means, as it's the focus for the rest of this chapter.

Platform virtualization is a type of hardware virtualization whereby a single physical server can concurrently run multiple virtual servers, each with its own independent operating system, application environment and IP address, applications, and so on.

Each virtual server believes and appears to be running on a traditional physical server, with full access to all of the CPU, memory, and storage resources allocated to it by the system administrator. More importantly, in order for virtualization technology to work, the virtual server's operating system software can use the same hardware registers and calls, and memory address space, which it would use if it were running on a dedicated physical server. This allows software to run on a virtual, rather than physical, server without being recompiled for a different type of hardware architecture.

Cloud Computing

It's almost impossible to read technology news these days without seeing references to cloud computing, and more commonly private clouds and public clouds. One of the advantages of cloud computing is that new servers can be deployed very quickly, literally in just minutes, and to do this they use platform virtualization. While this chapter won't go into how cloud computing works, it's worth remembering that at the technology layer, virtualization is a key enabler of this technology revolution.

Private Clouds

In summary, private clouds are usually a large and centrally managed virtualization environment deployed on-premise, typically in your data center. The virtualization management software they use often has management features added that allow end users to provision their own new servers through web portals, and for the dynamic allocation of resources between virtual servers. A key benefit for businesses too is the ability to deploy usage-based charging models that allow individual business departments or users to be charged for their actual usage of a virtual server, as well as allowing more self-service administration of server infrastructures.

Public Clouds

Public clouds, more often referred to as just cloud computing, are very similar to private clouds but are hosted in an Internet connected data center that is owned and managed by a service provider rather than an internal IT department. They allow users from anywhere in the world to deploy servers or services, through non-technical interfaces such as a web portal, with no regard for the underlying physical hardware needed to provide them. Microsoft's Windows Azure service is an example of a cloud computing service.

WHY VIRTUALIZE A SERVER?

"Why would you want to virtualize a server?" is a question I surprisingly still hear, particularly from people with no experience of having used virtualization technology. A typical follow-on comment is often "I've heard you can't virtualize database servers."

A few years ago, that question and comment were probably worth asking when IT teams were discussing virtualization of servers running SQL Server. SQL Server is a resource hungry application that needs particularly large amounts of memory and fast storage to process big workloads, and a few years ago, virtualization technology sometimes struggled to deliver those resources. As an example, some of the ways virtualization software presented storage to a virtual server meant it was inherently slow, and some virtualization software architecture meant it could only assign relatively low amounts of memory to a virtual server. Because of these issues, it was quite a few years before organizations I worked in considered mixing SQL Server with virtualization.

However, these technical limitations quickly disappeared, so the pace of adoption increased, justified by benefits that business and technical teams couldn't ignore any longer. The following sections describe the main benefits of using virtual servers:

Business Benefits

Selling the idea of virtualization to a business is easy; in fact, it's too easy. Even worse, I've had finance directors tell me that I can design *only* virtualized infrastructures for them regardless of what the IT teams want — or, more worryingly, need! From a business perspective, the major driver for using virtualization is obviously cost reduction. While the cost of physical servers has dropped over time, the number we need has increased, and increased quite quickly too. Today, even a relatively small business requires several servers to deploy products such as Microsoft's SharePoint Server or Exchange Server, with each server performing perhaps a compartmentalized role or high-availability function. Therefore, even though server hardware became more powerful, their "average utilization" dropped — and often to very low values. For example, I'm willing to bet that if you checked one of your domain controllers, its average CPU utilization would constantly be under 30%. That means there's 70% of its CPU utilization that could be used for something else.

Therefore, it was no surprise when even systems administrators, IT managers, and CIOs started to question why they had 10 servers running at 10% utilization and not 1 running at 100%. The potential cost savings, often described by businesses as *the savings from consolidation,* can be realized with virtualization by migrating from multiple underutilized servers to a single well-utilized server. In addition to cost savings, other benefits of consolidation can have a big impact on a business too. For example, at one company where I worked, we virtualized a lot of older servers because the facilities department couldn't get any more power or cooling into a data center.

In reality, the savings aren't as straightforward as the 10 times 10% utilization example, but it does demonstrate why both business teams and technical teams began taking a big interest in virtualization.

Technical Benefits

For IT teams, adopting virtualization has also meant needing to learn new skills and technologies while changing the way they've always worked to some degree. However, despite these costs, IT teams across the world have embraced and deployed virtualization solutions even though it likely represented the biggest change in their way of working for a generation. This section looks at the benefits that drove this adoption.

One of the main benefits comes from consolidation. Before virtualization was available, data centers had stacks of servers hosting lightweight roles, such as domain controllers, file servers, and small database servers. Each of these functions had to either share a physical server and operating system with another function or have its own dedicated physical server deployed in a rack. Now, using virtualization we can potentially deploy dozens of these low-utilization functions on a single physical server, but still give each its own operating system environment to use. Consequently, server hardware expenditure decreases, but also equally and perhaps more importantly, so do power, cooling, and space costs.

Another technical benefit comes from how virtual servers are allocated resources, such as memory and CPU. In the virtual world, providing sufficient physical server resources are available, creating a new virtual server is purely a software operation. When someone wants a new server deployed, no one would need to install any physical memory, storage, or CPU hardware, let alone a completely new physical server.

Likewise, an existing virtual server can have additional resources such as extra CPUs or memory allocated to it at the click of a mouse — providing the physical host server has the capacity—then the next time the virtual server reboots it will see and be able to use the additional resources.

Both deploying a new virtual server and allocating addition resources can be done in seconds, drastically increasing the flexibility of the server environment to react to planned and un-planned workloads.

Encapsulation

The final technical advantage we'll discuss is a benefit of something virtualization does called *encapsulation*. Despite how they appear to the operating system and applications running within the virtual server, when virtual servers are created, their data is stored as a set of flat files held on a file system; therefore, it can be said that the virtual server is "encapsulated" into a small set of files. By storing these flat files on shared storage, such as a SAN, the virtual servers can be "run" by any physical server that has access to the storage. This increases the level of availability in a virtual environment, as the virtual servers in it do not depend on the availability of a specific physical server in order to be used.

This is one of the biggest post-consolidation benefits of virtualization for IT teams because it enables proactive features to protect against server hardware failure, regardless of what level of high availability support the virtual server's operating system or application has; more about these are discussed in the Virtualization Concepts section. This type of feature won't usually protect against an operating system or database server crashing, but it can react to the physical server the virtual server was running on un-expectedly going offline.

This level of protection does incur some downtime however, as the virtual server needs to be restarted to be brought back online. For those looking for higher levels of protection, VMware's Fault Tolerance feature lock-steps the CPU activity between a virtual server and a replica of it; every CPU instruction that happens on one virtual server happens on the other.

The features don't stop there. Some server virtualization software allows virtual servers to be migrated from one physical server to another without even taking them offline, which is known as online migration and is covered in the "Virtualization Concepts" section of this chapter. This feature can be critical to reducing the impact of planned downtime for a physical server as well, whether it is for relocation, upgrading, etc.

There are, as you'd expect, limitations to how this can be used, but generally it's a very popular feature with system administrators. The "Extended Features of Virtualization" section of this chapter discusses more about these features.

SQL Server 2012 and Virtualization

Many people ask me how SQL Server behaves when it's virtualized. The answer is that it should behave no differently to when it runs on a physical server, especially when it's deployed in a properly resourced virtual environment, just like you would do with a physical server. However, virtualized instances of SQL Server still need adequate, and sometimes large, amounts of CPU, memory, and storage resources in order to perform well. The challenge with virtualization is making sure the resources SQL Server needs to perform adequately are always available to it.

Additionally, virtual servers running SQL Server can benefit from some of the features that encapsulation brings, which we've just discussed; however, it's at this point that some virtualization features, such as snapshotting a virtual server, which we'll discuss later in this chapter, Microsoft does not support using with SQL Server.

However, regardless of all the resource allocation activity that happens between the physical server and virtualization software, it's true to say that SQL Server itself does not change its behavior internally when run in a virtualized environment. That should be reassuring news, as it means that SQL Server will behave the same way whether you run it on a laptop, a physical server, or a virtual server. Nor are any new error messages or options enabled within SQL Server because of it running on a virtual server, with the exception of Dynamic Memory support that's described in a moment. That's not to say that you don't need to change how you configure and use SQL Server once it is virtualized; in fact, some of the server resource configurations are more important in the virtual world, but they are still all configured with the standard SQL Server tools.

The one feature in SQL Server 2012 that does automatically get enabled on start-up as a consequence of being in a virtual environment is hot-add memory support. This feature was released in SQL Server 2005 and originally designed to support physical servers that could have hundreds of gigabytes of memory and large numbers of processors, yet could still have more added without them being powered down or rebooted. Once additional memory had been plugged in and the server hardware had brought it online, Windows and SQL Server would then auto-detect it and begin making use of it by expanding the buffer pool. While this sounds like a clever feature, I suspect very few users ever had both the right hardware and a need to use it, so the feature never gained widespread use.

Fast-forward a few years and Microsoft's Hyper-V virtualization technology shipped a new feature called Dynamic Memory. By monitoring a virtual server's Windows operating system, the Dynamic Memory feature detects when a virtual server is running low on memory; and if spare physical memory is available on the host server, it allocates more to the virtual server. When this happens, the hot-add memory technology in Windows and SQL Server recognize this new "physical memory" being added and dynamically reconfigure themselves to use it — without needing to reboot Windows or restart SQL Server.

This behavior was available in the Enterprise and Data Center Editions of SQL Server 2008, but support for it has expanded in SQL Server 2012 to include the Standard Edition. This expanded support demonstrates how closely Microsoft wants its virtualization software, operating system, and database server software to work together. The expectation by Microsoft is that use of this feature will become routine once it's made available to the Standard Edition of SQL Server.

Limitations of Virtualization

Like all technologies, virtualization has limits, restrictions, and reasons not to use it in certain situations. Some virtualization vendors would like you to virtualize every server you have, and in fact, some now even claim that today that's possible. However, this all-virtual utopia is likely to be challenged by your applications, IT team, and budget.

Why might you not virtualize a new or existing server? The original reason people didn't virtualize has rapidly disappeared in recent years: a perceived lack of support from application vendors. In hindsight, I attribute lack of adoption more to a fear of not knowing what effect virtualization might have on their systems, rather than repeatable technical issues caused by it. The only actual problems I've heard of are related to Java-based applications, but fortunately they seem rare and SQL Server doesn't use Java.

Another rapidly disappearing reason for restricting the reach of virtualization is the resource allocation limitations that hypervisors put on a virtual server. Despite VMware's technology supporting a virtual server with as many as 8 virtual CPUs and as much as 255GB of memory as far back as 2009, most people weren't aware of this and assumed virtual servers were still restricted to using far less than their production servers needed. As a result, it was domain controllers, file servers, and other low-memory footprint workloads that were usually virtualized in the early phases of adoption.

Today, the capabilities of virtualization software has increased considerably; VMware's software and Windows Server 2012 now support 32 virtual CPUs and 1TB of memory, per virtual server! This means even the most demanding workloads can be considered for virtualization. The only current exceptions are what are considered to be "real time" workloads — that is, applications that process or control data from an external source that expects reactions or outputs within a specific number of milliseconds rather than a certain number of CPU clock cycles. To do this normally, the application requires constant access to CPU resources, which is something that virtualization software by default removes. You can enable support for real-time workloads in some virtualization software but doing so removes some of the management flexibility and resource utilization benefits virtualization has.

COMMON VIRTUALIZATION PRODUCTS

If you search for virtualization products using your favorite search engine, you'll get dozens of results for different products, and many opinions about which is best. While it's true that the virtualization marketplace is crowded, there are still only a handful of vendors that offer production-ready server virtualization products. Developers, testers, and DBAs may already be familiar with a wider range of virtualization products, such as Oracle's Virtual Box and VMware Workstation, but VMware and increasingly Microsoft have the lion's share of the virtualized data center marketplace. This section looks at the primary server virtualization products available, and some of the virtualization support that hardware vendors have built into their products in recent years.

VMware

Regardless of what any other virtualization vendor's marketing department may tell you, in my experience more businesses currently use VMware for their server virtualization platforms than any other. In my view, the main reason for this is because for a long time, VMware was almost the only vendor selling production grade virtualization software, and they also created the features that today, we expect every virtualization vendor to provide by default.

VMware's current server virtualization product set, vSphere, consists of two components: the VMware vSphere Hypervisor, also known as ESXi, and the enterprise virtual environment management platform, vSphere.

VMware's basic hypervisor software is available free of charge, even for production environments, and it supports running and managing a reasonable number of virtual servers on it — not bad for a free product. However, its feature set and manageability are quite limited when compared to capabilities of the VMware tools designed for the enterprise; for example, it supports only 32GB of memory in the physical host server. Nonetheless, for smaller environments or those new to virtualization, this product is often sufficient and can significantly reduce the deployment costs associated with VMware's larger vSphere product.

To provide an enterprise-scale and feature-rich virtualization solution, VMware couples its hypervisor with the vSphere management platform. This not only provides significantly more management and reporting functionality, but also increases scalability and availability. The other major difference is that groups of physical host servers running the VMware hypervisor are managed collectively, blurring the boundaries between individual server resources and a cluster of host servers as VMware refers to it.

While production environments can be deployed using just VMware's hypervisor, most of the businesses I work with have invested in the vSphere infrastructure to get the fuller feature set not available in the standalone hypervisor. The software is often expensive and it requires a strong commitment to virtualization, but it has been successful enough to make VMware the size of company it is today. That said, however, Microsoft is offering ever-increasing levels of virtualization functionality in the Windows operating system, and VMware will be forced at some point to reconsider the cost models and feature sets of its products.

> **NOTE** *VMware was the first vendor to adopt a licensing model based on memory size for its products, having decided that the traditional "per-CPU" model traditionally used by the industry was becoming outdated in 2011. Such a bold move wasn't entirely successful, however, and subsequent tweaking was needed to appease a surprised marketplace.*

Microsoft Hyper-V

Until very recently most of us probably didn't think of Microsoft as a virtualization software vendor although they have in fact produced desktop virtualization software, such as VirtualPC and Virtual Server, for a number of years now. Sadly for Microsoft, my experience showed they were the kind of products that were loved by those who used them but unknown to everyone else.

First released as a role within Windows Server 2008, Hyper-V was intended to bring Microsoft's new server virtualization capabilities to the massive Windows Server marketplace. This was an excellent product marketing decision, as anyone new to and curious about server virtualization now had the technology bought and paid for in their server operating system. No longer would they have to research, select, and download a product before installing it — more often than not on a dedicated physical server.

Hyper-V is more than just a software feature which gets installed within Windows though, it's a component which sits deep within the operating system itself, and in some areas is closer to the physical hardware than Windows itself is once Hyper-V is enabled. It's this low-level code that allows Hyper-V to schedule all of the different CPU requests its virtual servers make and allocate them CPU time so they can run.

Not all of the reaction to Hyper-V's initial release was good for Microsoft though. The first version suffered from the usual inadequacies of v1.0 software we've become used to. In fact, it wouldn't be unfair to say that the version that shipped with Windows Server 2008 was unsuitable for most production workloads. However, progress was made in making people aware that Microsoft was entering the server virtualization market.

Significant improvements were made to Hyper-V in Windows Server 2008 R2 and again with Service Pack 1. Live migration, dynamic storage, Dynamic Memory, and enhanced processor feature support made deploying Hyper-V in a busy production environment a reality. It is likely that many of the people who have chosen to adopt Hyper-V have done so because of Microsoft's dominance and reputation with other applications, along with the pricing model.

In the same way that VMware offers a hypervisor product and an enterprise management platform, vSphere, so does Microsoft. System Center Virtual Machine Manager is a suite of management tools designed to manage large Hyper-V environments, as well as deploy, orchestrate, and monitor private clouds. Known sometimes as just VMM, it's not as widely adopted as vSphere, but I suspect that will change as Hyper-V is adopted by more and more enterprise-scale customers. System Centre Virtual Machine Manager 2012 has been released with many private cloud management capabilities built into it and will be core to Microsoft's server products strategy over the next few years.

Windows Server 2012 enhances Hyper-V's capabilities with a compelling update of the feature. Its virtual servers will support up to 32 virtual CPUs and 1TB of memory each, while support for replication of virtual servers will offer new high availability capabilities.

Xen

Of the three server virtualization products covered in this section, XEN is undoubtedly the rarest and least widely adopted. Xen was the output of a research project by the University of Cambridge in the early 2000s, and its legacy was an open-source hypervisor. Although the open-source version still exists, a number of commercial versions are also available. Citrix Systems now owns and sells a commercial version of it known as XenServer, while the technology has also been adopted by vendors such as Sun and Oracle. Of more interest, however, is its adoption by a number of cloud service providers such as Amazon and Rackspace, demonstrating that cloud technology does not differ fundamentally from on-premise technology.

Hardware Support for Virtualization

While we can very easily see and interact with the virtualization software we install on our servers, what we can't see is that the CPUs inside our servers now have components built into them to assist with virtualization. In the same way that CPUs had specific logic and components added to them to support floating-point and multimedia operations, they now have similar features built into them to help make virtualization software run faster. For example, Intel's Extended Page Tables feature provides support for second-level address translation (SLAT). SLAT helps optimize the translation of a virtual server's memory addresses to physical server memory addresses through the use of cached lookup tables.

Both AMD and Intel provide these features but with different names. AMD's CPUs have feature sets called AMD-V and Rapid Virtualization Indexing (RVI) now built-in, while Intel's CPUs have built-in features called VT-x and EPT. Although it isn't necessary to know the specific roles of these components, a SQL Server professional should understand that the latest generations of virtualization software work only on server's with these CPU features available. However, that shouldn't be a problem, as I haven't seen a server for a few years now that doesn't have them built-in.

VIRTUALIZATION CONCEPTS

Like any technology, virtualization covers a minefield of new terminology, features, and capabilities. To make things even more complicated, different vendors often use different terms for the same item. To help remove that ambiguity, this section covers the main terms and features commonly used by virtualization software currently being deployed.

Host Server

The host server, shown in Figure 17-1, is called the physical server deployed within the virtual environment. Today people use standard x64-based servers, such as an HP DL360, which are usually configured with a large number of CPU cores, large amounts of memory, some local disks for the hypervisor, and host bus adapters for access to storage area network (SAN) storage. The only difference between a host server and other servers is that its installed operating system's only function is to manage the physical server's resources to allow multiple virtual servers to run concurrently on the same physical hardware, rather than directly run application software such as SQL Server.

FIGURE 17-1

Hypervisor

By this point in the chapter, you will be familiar with the term virtualization software which we've used, and you will have seen how important that is to providing virtual servers. One of the components of that software is the hypervisor.

The hypervisor's role is to coordinate the hosting and running of a number of virtual servers and manage the allocation of the host server's physical resources between them. For example, on a host server with 4 physical CPU cores, the hypervisor enables a number of currently running virtual servers to behave as though each one has access to four physical CPU cores, known as virtual CPUs (see Figure 17-2).

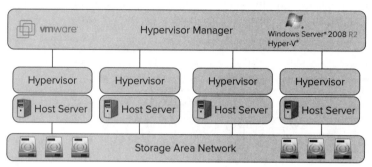

FIGURE 17-2

What happens during periods of high workloads when there isn't enough physical CPU resource to satisfy all of the virtual server requests for CPU time is perhaps one of the most performance sensitive qualities of a hypervisor. The last thing you want is for virtual servers to become slow just because one specific virtual server is busy, although this problem has yet to be eliminated and can still happen with some hypervisors.

How the hypervisor manages these situations varies between vendors. At a high level, they track how much CPU time a virtual server has used recently, and use that data, along with system administrator configured priority information known as shares or weighting, to determine in what order a queue of requests for CPU time should be processed during periods of high demand.

VMware has an extra feature built into their hypervisor's CPU scheduling algorithms called relaxed co-scheduling. The purpose of this is to identify which particular virtual CPUs in a multi-CPU virtual server are the ones needing to do the work so it can avoid supplying un-required physical CPU time to the virtual server; the principle being that lots of smaller workloads are easier to find CPU resources for than a single large workload.

When installing VMware's server virtualization software, the hypervisor is installed directly on the host server as its operating system; you don't, for example, install Windows first. Those who deploy VMware's hypervisor will actually see a custom Linux installation boot to then run a set of VMware services, but it's a self-contained environment that doesn't allow application software to be installed. Meanwhile, users of Hyper-V will install a regular installation of the Windows Server software and then add the Hyper-V role to the server. Installing this role is more than just adding some components to the operating system; though, when the Hyper-V hypervisor gets installed it actually becomes the server's operating system. The Windows installation that was installed on the server now gets converted to become a virtual server that is run by the newly installed Hyper-V hypervisor. This all happens transparently, but it is why Microsoft recommends not using the host server's operating system for anything other than Hyper-V services.

Virtual Server (or Guest Server or Virtual Machine)

The running of *virtual servers*, also called *guest servers* or *virtual machines*, is the sole purpose of a virtual environment. Each virtual server has very similar properties to a traditional physical server in that it will have a number of virtual CPUs, an amount of memory, and a quantity of virtual hard drives assigned to it. "Inside" the guest server, a regular operating system such as Windows Server 2008 will be installed on drive C: — just like a physical server would. Figure 17-3 shows a diagram representing the relationship between the hypervisor and the guest servers.

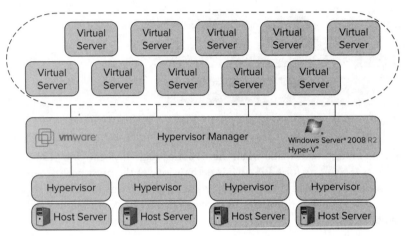

FIGURE 17-3

Inside virtual servers the hypervisor normally has a set of tools installed, often called client, or integration, services. These provide a level of integration between the virtual server and its hypervisor that wouldn't otherwise be possible, such as sharing files between hypervisor and client or perhaps synchronizing the system time with the host server.

However, also installed is a driver that, on command from the hypervisor, can begin consuming specific quantities of memory within the virtual server. We discuss more about these in the "Demand-Based Memory Allocation" section of this chapter but for now it's sufficient to say its purpose is to be allocated memory within the virtual server so some of the physical memory the virtual server was previously using can be re-allocated by stealth to another virtual server.

It's called a balloon driver because it inflates as needed to consume memory within the virtual server's operating system. Its purpose is not to actually use the memory but to set it aside to ensure that nothing else within the virtual server is using it.

In comparison with the virtualization software and technology, there's very little to say about virtual servers, and that's a good thing, as the idea of virtualization is to make the fact they're not running on a physical server invisible to them.

While virtual servers can be configured to "run" on different physical host servers using technologies like online migration that we'll cover in the next section, at any point in time, a running virtual server is assigned to a specific physical host server. Virtual servers cannot be allocated and use physical server resources, such as memory, from multiple physical host servers.

EXTENDED FEATURES OF VIRTUALIZATION

Now that you are familiar with some of the fundamental concepts of virtualization, this section looks at some of the more advanced features and capabilities the technology offers. This is where the unique magic of the technology begins to appear, as some of these concepts simply weren't available to traditional physical servers for all the time we were using them. While a hypervisor's primary function is to "run" a virtual server and grant it the resources it requires as it needs them, the current versions of VMware and many of Microsoft's server virtualization products also provide many of the features discussed in the following sections.

Snapshotting

Snapshotting a virtual server is very similar to how SQL Server's own snapshot function works. In principle, the hypervisor suspends the virtual machine, or perhaps requires it to be shut down, and places a point-in-time marker within the virtual machine's data files. From that point on, as changes are made within the virtual machine's virtual hard drive files, the original data is written to a separate physical snapshot file by the hypervisor. This can have a slight performance overhead on the I/O performance of the virtual server and, more important, require potentially large amounts of disk space because multiple snapshots can be taken of a virtual server, each having its own snapshot file capturing the "before" version of the data blocks. However, a copy of all of the pre-change data gets saved to disk.

Having these snapshot files available to the hypervisor enables it, upon request, to roll back all the changes in the virtual server's actual data files to the state they were in at the point the snapshot was taken. Once completed, the virtual server will be exactly in the state it was at the point in time the snapshot was taken.

While this sounds like a great feature which can offer a level of rollback functionality, it is un-supported by Microsoft for use with virtual servers running SQL Server. Microsoft gives more information about this in the Knowledge Base article 956893; however, until Microsoft supports its use, snapshotting should not be used with virtual servers running SQL Server.

High-Availability Features

You read earlier that encapsulation means that a virtual server is ultimately just a collection of files stored on a file system somewhere. These files can normally be broken down into the virtual hard drive data files, as well as a number of small metadata files that give the hypervisor information it needs to "run" the virtual server, such as the CPU, memory, and virtual hard drive configuration. Keeping these files in a centralized storage location — a SAN, for example — enables several different host servers to access the virtual server files. The trick that the file system and hypervisor have to perform is controlling concurrent read/write access to those files in a way that prevents corruption and two host servers running the same virtual server at once.

Support for this largely comes from the file systems they use; VMware, for instance, has a proprietary VMFS file system that is designed to allow multiple host servers to both read and write files to and from the same logical storage volumes at the same time. Windows Server 2008 has a similar feature called Clustered Shared Volumes that is required in larger Hyper-V environments where multiple physical host servers concurrently run virtual servers from the same file system volume. This is a departure from the traditional NTFS limitation of granting only one read/write connection access to an NTFS volume

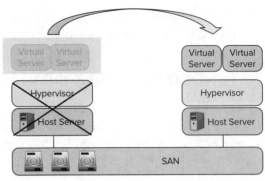

FIGURE 17-4

at a time. Ensuring that a virtual machine is only started in one place at a time is controlled by the hypervisors themselves. A system using traditional file system file locks and metadata database updates is typically used to allow or prevent a virtual server from starting (see Figure 17-4).

By the way, while the cluster shared volumes feature of Windows sounds like a great solution to numerous other requirements you might have, the technology is only supported for use with Hyper-V. Microsoft warns of unintended and unexpected results if you try to use it for anything else and you can find more information in the Microsoft TechNet article at `http://technet`
`.microsoft.com/en-us/library/dd630633%28v=ws.10%29.aspx`.

Online Migration

After you have all the files needed to run your virtual servers stored on some centralized storage, accessible by multiple physical host servers concurrently, numerous features unique to virtualization become available. The key differentiator here between the physical and virtual worlds is that you are no longer dependent on a specific physical server's availability in order for your virtual server to be available. As long as a correctly configured physical host server with sufficient CPU and memory resources is available and it can access your virtual server's files on the shared storage, the virtual server can run.

The first of these features unique to virtualization is generically described in this chapter as online migration, although Microsoft calls it Live Migration and VMware calls it vMotion for their implementations. Online migrations enable a virtual server to be moved from one physical host server to another without taking the virtual server offline.

For those unfamiliar with this technology and who can't believe what they've just read, an example should clarify the idea. In Figure 17-5, the virtual server SrvZ is currently running on the physical host server SrvA, while all of its files are stored on the SAN. By performing an online migration, you can move SrvZ to run on SrvB without having to shut it down, as shown in the second half of the diagram.

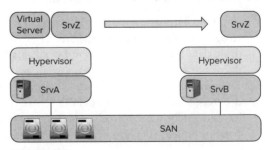

FIGURE 17-5

Why you might want to do this is a legitimate question for someone new to virtualization, especially as in the physical world this kind of server administration was impossible. In fact, server administrators receive many benefits from being able to move running virtual servers off of a specific physical host server. If a specific host requires patching, upgrading, or repairing, or perhaps has too much load, then these issues can be resolved without affecting the availability of the applications and services that the virtual servers support. Some or all of the virtual servers running on a host server can transparently be migrated to another host, freeing up the host server for maintenance.

The basic concept behind online migration is readily understandable, but some complex operations are needed to actually perform it. After the virtualization administrator identifies where the virtual server should move from and to, the hypervisor logically "joins" the two host servers and they start working together — to support not only the running of the virtual server but also its migration. Each host server begins sharing the virtual server's data files stored on the shared storage; the new host server loads the virtual server's metadata, allocates it the physical hardware and network resources it needs, such as vCPUs and memory, and, the final clever part, the hypervisor also sends a snapshot of the virtual machine's memory from the original host server to the new host server over the local area network.

Because changes are constantly being made to the memory, the process can't finish here, so at this point every memory change made on the original server needs to be copied to the new server. This can't happen as quickly as the changes are being made, so a combination of virtual server activity and network bandwidth determine how long this "synchronization" takes. As a consequence, you may need to perform online migrations during quiet periods, although server hardware, hypervisor technology, and 10GB Ethernet mean that these migrations are very quick these days. Before the last few remaining memory changes are copied from the original host server to the new host server, the hypervisor "pauses" the virtual server for literally a couple of milliseconds. In these few milliseconds, the last remaining memory pages are copied along with the ARP network addresses the virtual server uses and full read/write access to the data files. Next, the virtual server is "un-paused" and it carries on exactly what it was doing before it was migrated with the same CPU instructions and memory addresses, and so on.

If you are thinking that this pause sounds dangerous or even potentially fatal to the virtual server, in reality this technology has been tried and tested successfully — not only by the vendors themselves but also by the industry. Online migrations have been performed routinely in large service provider virtualization environments, and with such confidence that the end customer never needed to be told they were happening. Nor is this technology limited to virtual servers with low resource allocations; Microsoft has written white papers and support articles demonstrating how its LiveMigration feature can be used with servers running SQL Server. In fact, the SQLCat team has even released a white paper downloadable on their website with advice about how to tune SQL Server to make online migrations slicker and more efficient.

However, while the technology is designed to make the migration as invisible to the virtual server being migrated as possible, it is still possible for it to notice. The dropping of a few network packets is typically the most visible effect, so client connections to SQL Server can be lost during the process; or perhaps more critical, if you deploy Windows Failover Clustering on to virtual servers, the cluster can detect a failover situation. Because of this, Windows Failover Clustering is not supported for use with online migration features.

While online migrations may seem like a good solution to virtual and host server availability, keep in mind that they are on-demand services — that is, they have be manually initiated; and, most important, both the original and the new servers involved have to be available and online in order for the process to work. They also have to have the same type of CPU as well; otherwise, the difference in low level hardware calls would cause issues. You could script and then schedule an online migration, but for the purpose of this chapter we'll still consider that a manual migration. In short, while this feature is good for proactive and planned maintenance, it cannot be used to protect against unplanned downtime and host server failures.

Highly Available Virtual Servers

Understanding how online migrations work will help you understand how some of the high-availability features in hypervisors work. When comparing the high-availability features of the two most prevalent server platform hypervisors, you can see a difference in their approach to providing high availability. VMware's vSphere product has a specific high-availability feature, vSphere HA, built-in; whereas Microsoft's Hyper-V service utilizes the well-known services of Windows Failover Clustering.

Both of these HA services use the same principle as online migration in that all the files needed to start and run a virtual server have to be kept on shared storage that is always accessible by several physical host servers. This means a virtual server is not dependent on any specific physical server being available in order for it to run — other than the server on which it's currently running, of course. However, whereas online migrations require user intervention following an administrator's decision to begin the process, HA services themselves detect the failure conditions that require action.

VMware and Microsoft's approach is ultimately the same, just implemented differently. Both platforms constantly monitor the availability of a virtual server to ensure that it is currently being hosted by a host server and the host server is running it correctly. However, running according to the hypervisor's checks doesn't necessarily mean that anything "inside" the virtual server is working; monitoring that is an option available in VMware's feature where it can respond to a failure of the virtual server's operating system by re-starting it.

As an example, the hypervisor would detect a physical host server going offline through unexpected failure, causing all the virtual servers running on it to also go offline — the virtual equivalent of pulling the power cord out of the server while it's running, and then if configured to, re-start all of the virtual servers on another host server.

In this situation, whatever processes were running on the virtual server are gone and whatever was in its memory is lost; there is no preemptive memory snapshotting for this particular feature as there is for online migrations. Instead, the best the hypervisor can do is automatically start the virtual server on another physical host server when it notices the virtual server go offline — this is the virtual equivalent of powering up and cold booting the server. If the virtual server is running SQL Server, then, when the virtual server is restarted, there may well be an initial performance degradation while the plan and data catches build up, just like in the physical world.

What makes this feature exciting is the opportunity to bring some form of high availability to virtual servers regardless of what operating system or application software is running inside the virtual server. For example, you could have standalone installations of Windows and SQL Server running on a virtual server, neither of which are configured with any high-availability services, and yet now protect SQL Server against unplanned physical server failure.

This technology isn't a replacement for the application-level resilience that traditional failover clustering brings; we already saw that while the hypervisor might be successfully running the virtual machine, Windows or SQL Server may have stopped. However, this feature can provide an increased level of availability for servers that may not justify the cost of failover clustering or availability groups.

Host and Guest Clustering

To conclude this discussion of virtualization's high-availability benefits, this section explains how the traditional Windows failover clustering instances we're used to using fit in with it. Host clustering is Microsoft's term for implementing the virtual server high availability covered in the previous section; that is, should a physical host server fail, it will re-start the virtual servers that were running on it on another physical host server. It does this by using the Windows Failover Clustering services running on the physical host servers to detect failure situations and control the re-starting of the virtual servers.

Guest clustering is where Windows Failover Clustering is deployed within a virtual server to protect a resource such as an instance of SQL Server and any resource dependencies it might have like an IP address and host name.

This is deployed in the same way a Windows Failover Clustering would be in a physical server environment, but with virtual rather than physical servers.

Support from Microsoft for clustering SQL Server in this manner has been available for some time now, but adoption had been slow as the range of storage options that could be used was small. Today however, there are many more types of storage that are supported, including the SMB file share support in SQL Server 2012 and raw device mappings by VMware, which is making the use of guest clustering much more common.

Deploying SQL Server with Virtualization's High-Availability Features

When SQL Server is deployed in virtual environments, trying to increase its availability by using some of the features described becomes very tempting. In my experience, every virtualization administrator wants to use online migration features, and quite rightly so. Having the flexibility to move virtual servers between host servers is often an operational necessity, so any concerns you may have about SQL Server's reaction to being transparently relocated should be tested in order to gain confidence in the process. You might find that you agree to perform the task only at quiet periods, or you might feel safe with the process irrespective of the workload.

Likewise, the virtualization administrator is also likely to want to use the vendor's high-availability feature so that in the event of a physical host server failure, the virtual servers are automatically restarted elsewhere. This is where you need to carefully consider your approach, if any, to making a specific instance of SQL Server highly available. My advice is not to mix the different high-availability technologies available at each layer of the technology stack. This is because when a failure occurs, you only want a single end-to-end process to react to it; the last thing you want is for two different technologies, such as VMware's HA feature and Windows Failover Clustering to respond to the same issue at the same time.

MANAGING CONTENTION

In looking at some of reasons for virtualization's popularity, the preceding sections identified the concept of contention, the capability to better use previously underutilized physical resources in a server in order to reduce the total number of physical servers deployed. For the purposes of this discussion, we can split the idea of contention into two parts: good contention and bad contention.

Good Contention

Good contention is straightforward: It enables you to see positive benefits from virtualizing your servers, ultimately resulting in less time and money spent on deploying and maintaining your physical server estate.

For example, if the average CPU utilization of 6 single CPU physical servers was 10% and none of them had concurrent peak CPU usage periods, then I would feel comfortable virtualizing those 6 servers and running them as a single server with a single CPU — the logic being $6 \times 10\% = 60\%$, and therefore less than the capacity of a single server with a single CPU. I'd want to make sure there was sufficient physical memory and storage system performance available for all 6 virtual servers, but ultimately the benefit would be the ability to retire 5 physical servers.

That's a very simple example but one that most businesses can readily understand. CPU utilization is an absolute number that is usually a good reflection of how busy the server is. Conversely, sizing the server's memory is something to which you can't apply such an easy consolidation methodology to. Instead, you usually need to determine the total memory requirement of all the virtual servers you want to run on a host server and then ensure you have more than that amount of physical memory in the host. However, VMware's hypervisor complicates that by offering a memory de-duplication feature that allows duplicate memory pages to be replaced with a link to a single memory page shared by several virtual servers, but over-estimating the benefit this technology could deliver wrong can result in the performance issues you tried to avoid. For SQL Server environments that are dependent on access to large amounts of physical memory, trusting these hypervisor memory consolidation technologies still requires testing, so their use in sizing exercises should be minimized.

Bad Contention

Not all contention is good. In fact, unless you plan well you're more likely to have bad contention than good contention. To understand bad contention, consider the CPU utilization example from the preceding section: 6 servers with average CPU utilization values of 10% being consolidated onto a single CPU host server. This resulted in an average CPU utilization for the host server of around 60%. Now imagine if the average CPU utilization for two of the virtual servers jumps from 10% to 40%. As a consequence, the total CPU *requirement* has increased from 60% to 120%. Obviously, the total CPU utilization cannot be 120%, so you have a problem. Fortunately, resolving this scenario is one of the core functions of hypervisor software: How can it look like CPU utilization is 120%, for example, when actually only 100% is available?

Where does the missing resource come from? Behaviors such as resource sharing, scheduling, and time-slicing are used by hypervisors to make each virtual server appear to have full access to the physical resources that it's allocated all of the time. Under the hood, however, the hypervisor is busy managing resource request queues — for example, "pausing" virtual servers until they get the CPU time they need, or pre-empting a number of requests on physical cores while the hypervisor waits for another resource they need to become available.

How much this contention affects the performance of virtual servers depends on how the hypervisor you're using works. In a worst-case scenario using VMware, a virtual server with a large number of virtual CPUs can be significantly affected if running alongside a number of virtual servers with small numbers of virtual CPUs; this is due to VMware's use of their co-scheduling algorithm to handle CPU scheduling. Seeing multi-second pauses of the larger virtual server while it waits for sufficient physical CPU resources is possible in the worst-case scenarios, indicating not only the level of attention that should be paid to deploying virtual servers, but also the type of knowledge you should have if you're going to be using heavily utilized virtual environments.

Although that example of how VMware can affect performance is an extreme example, it does show how bad contention introduces unpredictable latency. Previously, on a host server with uncontended resources, you could effectively assume that any virtual server's request for a resource could be fulfilled immediately as the required amounts of resource were always available. However, when the hypervisor has to manage contention, a time penalty for getting access to the resource gets introduced. In effect, "direct" access to the physical resource by the virtual server can no longer be assumed.

"Direct" is in quotes because although virtual servers never directly allocate to themselves the physical resources they use in an uncontended situation, the hypervisor does not have difficulty finding the requested CPU time and memory resources they require; the DBA can know that any performance penalty caused by virtualization is likely to be small but, most important, consistent. In a contended environment, however, the resource requirements of other virtual servers now have the ability to affect the performance of other virtual servers, and that becomes un-predictable.

Demand-Based Memory Allocation

I mentioned earlier that some hypervisors offer features that aim to reduce the amount of physical memory needed in a virtual environment's host servers. Memory is still one of the most expensive components of a physical server, not so much because of the cost per GB but because of the number of GBs that modern software requires in servers. It's not surprising therefore that virtualization technologies have tried to ease the cost of servers by making what memory is installed in the server go farther. However, there is no such thing as free memory; and any method used to make memory go farther will affect performance somewhere. The goal is to know where that performance impact can occur with the least noticeable effects.

Demand-based memory allocation works on the assumption that not all the virtual servers running on a host server will need all their assigned memory all the time. For example, my laptop has 4GB of memory but 2.9GB of it is currently free. Therefore, if it were a virtual server, the hypervisor could get away with granting me only 1.1GB, with the potential for up to 4GB when I need it. Scale that out across a host server running 20 virtual servers and the potential to find allocated but un-required memory could be huge.

The preceding scenario is the basis of demand-based memory allocation features in modern hypervisors. While VMware and Hyper-V have different approaches, their ultimate aim is the same: to provide virtual servers with as much memory as they need but no more than they need. That way, unused memory can be allocated to extra virtual servers that wouldn't otherwise be able to run at all because of memory constraints.

In an ideal situation, if several virtual servers all request additional memory at the same time, the host server would have enough free physical memory to give them each all they need. If there's not enough, however, then the hypervisor can step in to reclaim and re-distribute memory between virtual servers. It may be, for example, that some have been configured to have a higher priority than others over memory in times of shortages; this is called *weighting* and is described in the next section. The rules about how much memory you can over-provision vary by hypervisor, but the need to reclaim and re-distribute memory is certainly something VMware's software and Microsoft's Hyper-V could have to do.

Re-claiming and re-distributing memory ultimately means taking it away from one virtual server to give to another, and from a virtual server that was operating as though the memory allocated to it was all theirs, and it may well have been being used by applications. When this reclamation has to happen, a SQL Server DBA's worst nightmare occurs, and the balloon driver we mentioned earlier has to inflate.

We briefly mentioned the purpose of a balloon driver in the "Virtualiztion Concepts" section of this chapter; however, to summarize its purpose, when more memory is required than is available in the host server, the hypervisor will have to re-allocate physical memory between virtual servers. It could do this to ensure that any virtual servers that are about to be started have the configured minimum amount of memory allocated to them, or if any resource allocation weightings between virtual servers need to be maintained, for example, if a virtual server with a high weighting needs more memory. Resource weightings are described in the next section.

Different hypervisors employ slightly different methods of using a balloon driver, but the key point for DBAs here is that SQL Server always responds to a low Available Megabytes value, which the inflating of a balloon driver can cause. SQL Server's response to this low-memory condition is to begin reducing the size of the buffer pool and release memory back to Windows, which after a while will have a noticeable effect on database server performance.

The advice from the virtualization vendors about how to configure their demand-based memory allocation technology for SQL Server varies. Hyper-V is designed to be cautious with memory allocations and will not allow the minimum amount of memory a virtual server needs to become unavailable, while VMware allows the memory in a host server to be over-committed. Because of the potential performance issues this can cause, VMware does not recommend running SQL Server on a host that's had its memory over-committed.

Weighting

Finally, when there is resource contention within a host server, the virtualization administrator can influence the order in which physical resources are protected, reserved, or allocated. This is determined by a weighting value, and it is used in various places throughout a virtualization environment — especially one designed to operate with contention. For example, an environment might host virtual servers for production, development, and occasionally testing. The priority may be for production to always have the resources it needs at the expense of the development servers if need be. However, the test servers, while only occasionally used, might have a higher priority than the development servers, and therefore have a weighting lower than the production servers but higher than the development servers.

IDENTIFYING CANDIDATES FOR VIRTUALIZATION

As virtualization's popularity has grown, so has the debate about which server roles can be virtualized. Some of the very broad generalizations have contained a grain of truth. Certainly for a long time there was the view that production database servers could never be virtualized but virtualization technology has developed significantly to not normally make that a problem. In fact, VMware now suggests that virtualizing 100% of an enterprise server estate is now a possibility with the latest versions of their software.

Ultimately, the only way to determine how much of your server estate can be virtualized is to adopt some high-level guiding principles before performing a detailed review of relevant performance data to ensure your virtual environment can handle your anticipated workload.

Guiding Principles

When people ask me which servers they can and can't virtualize, their question is often "what's the biggest server you'd virtualize?" My answer is always that far more factors should influence the decision than the server's size alone. This section outlines some general guiding principles that you can follow when considering virtualization. More detailed information is provided in the next section.

Server Workload

The first area is related to the server's workload. Although you might assume that this is the same as the server's size, a small server working consistently at its highest capacity may be harder to virtualize than a larger server that is often relatively idle.

Today, with a well-designed virtualization environment it's safe to work to the following design assumptions:

➤ *Quiet* server workloads can be and are routinely virtualized today. These might well be domain controllers; file servers; or the database servers for your anti-virus software, your expense tracking, or your HR system in a small to medium-size business. If the server is one whose performance doesn't require monitoring or there is no question about it always meeting its business requirements, then you can consider this a small workload.

➤ *Active* server workloads also can be and are often routinely virtualized; and as long as capacity checks for the required CPU, memory, and storage throughput are made first, these workloads usually virtualize well. This kind of server might well host your finance system's database server, where for the majority of the time a constant number of data entry users execute low-cost queries, some utilization spikes occur with ad-hoc reports, while month-end processing creates an infrequent but demanding workload. You may well already be using some performance-monitoring tools to proactively look for slowdowns in the end user experience, as well as perhaps deploying a physical server to which you know you can add more CPU or memory as needed.

> ➤ *Busy* server workloads need planning. The latest hypervisors claim to be able to accommodate them, but you need to design and tune your environment well first, in order to ensure the success promised by your virtualization vendor's marketing. These workloads reflect those servers that you already have to proactively manage, even on relatively new server hardware. In the database world, these are likely to be transactional systems that have a high throughput of order or quotes being processed, or perhaps reporting servers that routinely perform CPU-intensive server-side aggregations. These are demanding workloads that require thorough planning and testing before deploying in a virtual environment.

Gathering Sizing Data

So far we've approached the identification of "good" virtualization candidates fairly unscientifically, whereas some virtualization specialists I've worked with would have immediately started collecting performance data and analyzing it. That step is still crucial for your virtualization planning, but working through the guiding principles just described should only take a couple of moments, and it will help you to quickly identify your potential risks and concerns, or even nonstarters, and save you some time.

More detail is provided in the next section on how to use collected configuration, utilization, or performance data to help design a virtual server running SQL Server successfully, but the following list describes some data you should collect and explains why it will be useful to your planning:

> ➤ **Memory utilization** — This is one of the most important, if not the most important, piece of performance data to capture. How much memory does your database server currently have installed, how much does SQL Server currently actually use, and does SQL Server even have sufficient memory right now?
>
> Some of the counters available in Performance Monitor you can use here are probably what you already use today for monitoring SQL Server. An instance with a very high (25,000+ seconds) Page Life Expectancy is likely to be able to be virtualized with the same or perhaps less memory than it has currently without significantly affecting performance. However, if there is a very low Page Life Expectancy value consistently being seen (<1,000 seconds) then it's likely the server already has insufficient memory and I would expect the server when virtualized to have more memory than it has now. Finally, the Total and Target Server Memory counter values should also be used to determine what amount of memory is too much or too little based on the current Page Life Expectancy; it may be that not all of the server's memory is being made available for SQL Server to use.

> ➤ **CPU utilization** — This data will help you understand the server's workload patterns and identify how easy it will be for your server to coexist with other virtual servers on the same host server once virtualized. As well as collecting the Average Total CPU utilization, you should also monitor how often periods of high activity occur and how long they last. For example, you might run a recalculation job every hour that takes 10 minutes to run. In addition to collecting CPU utilization data from within Performance Monitor, you should also understand how your instance of SQL Server uses parallelism. While your current physical server might have 16 cores, running a smaller number of parallelized queries on it requires different planning than if you run a much larger number of serial queries.

➤ **Storage utilization** — This is an area often overlooked when designing virtual environments, yet it's an easy area to capture data about. The regular logical disk counters from within Performance Monitor will help you size your host server requirements when you know the average and peak period IOPS and MB/s demands of your current server in order to deliver satisfactory query times. If available, also ensure that you capture the same data from your storage subsystem. Both sets of data should show the same trends even if they show slightly different values, and will be useful in your planning.

➤ **Network utilization** — In the same way storage utilization is often overlooked, so is network utilization. The most useful Performance Monitor counter you capture here is the Mb/s throughput of the server's Network Interface Cards during peak periods, perhaps during a ETL process, backup window, or busy business period.

Consideration must also be given if the physical server currently has, or if the virtual server will have, iSCSI storage presented to it. In these situations, the iSCSI traffic is likely to be far higher than any which SQL Server itself requires, and it needs to be accommodated.

Sizing Tools

Several tools are available for gathering the data you will need to understand the resourcing requirements of your future virtual servers. The Microsoft Assessment and Planning (MAPS) toolkit can scan a specific server or an entire network to report on the software and hardware resources currently being both deployed and utilized. It even has a built-in feature to specifically advise on physical-to-virtual (P2V) migrations. VMware has a similar tool called the Capacity Planner that also analyzes a workload over a period of time and advises on the best P2V approach.

Other than these tools designed to aid P2V migrations, you may be currently using others that are already storing the kind of information you need. SQL Server's Management Data Warehouse and Utility Control Point features might be performing such roles in your environment.

Non-Performance Related Requirements

Having collected data about how hard your server may or may not need to work once it is virtualized, you should also collect information about when your server needs to work hard and, more important, be available.

For these requirements I suggest collecting the following information:

➤ **Peak workload periods** — If your database server operates according to a structured and planned routine, then knowing when you need your server to be able to work especially hard is important. Being able to plan this in a calendar format will help you visualize all your different server workloads and prevent potentially negative conflicting workloads on the same host server.

➤ **Availability requirements** — Currently, your existing server is likely deployed in a way that ensures it meets the business availability standards required of it. For example, it might be standalone or it might be clustered. Knowing what level of availability is expected of the server once it's virtualized plays a large role in determining the virtualization technologies you adopt.

ARCHITECTING SUCCESSFUL VIRTUAL DATABASE SERVERS

To ensure SQL Server works at least as well as you expect, if not better, when you deploy it on a virtual server, design considerations must be made, which often involve settings and decisions that you wouldn't have to make with a physical server deployment. These considerations, as you will see, cover a range of environment components that you may not have had to consider before, yet will sometimes have considerable influence on the performance of your database server instance.

Architecting Virtual Database Servers vs. Physical Database Servers

In the physical server world, assigning and reserving hardware resources such as CPU and memory is relatively straightforward. Ultimately, a server chassis only ever runs one instance of an operating system that has every piece of hardware resource in the server available to it. For example, if a server has 16 physical CPU cores and 32GB of memory installed in it, then Windows would also have that amount of resources available to it. This "dedicated resource" approach not only makes server design easier, it also makes troubleshooting performance issues easier, as whatever data Performance Monitor shows is the truth.

For most users of SQL Server, the introduction of storage area networks (SANs) was the first time they had to continuously depend on a shared resource. Remote network shares had previously been used for backups, but as long as their performance was "good enough" no one really questioned it. SANs, however, were different because not only were they often highly influential on SQL Server's performance, they were also usually shared among several servers at a time. This meant that the activities of one server could potentially affect the performance of all the other servers also using it. In small environments this wasn't so bad, as the DBA could probably see all the other servers connected to the SAN and quickly identify the cause of any problems; but in much larger environments the DBA had to rely on the SAN administrator to provide assurances and performance data that ruled out SAN contention as a potential cause of performance issues for SQL Server.

Most virtualization environments use SANs as their shared storage, so the scenario just described is something many administrators will be familiar with, especially those responsible for making instances of SQL Server perform as fast as possible. However, as shown in Figure 17-6, with virtualization not only is the SAN a shared resource, so is the host server's hardware resources such as the CPU and memory. Now, the DBA has to consider not only other users of the SAN affecting SQL Server's performance, but also other virtual servers running on the same physical host server.

The diagram below, shows how a visualization administrator could inadvertently allocate the same physical storage to several virtual servers, attracting performance issues if the configuration of that shared storage resource can't meet the future performance requirements of it.

Sharing resources doesn't always have to be a problem; in fact, if it is a problem then something is wrong. A correctly sized virtualization environment consisting of adequately resourced host servers and sensibly configured virtual servers should be the foundation for a very successful and

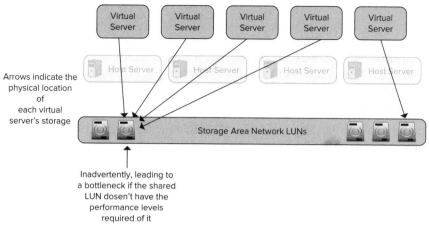

Arrows indicate the physical location of each virtual server's storage

Inadvertently, leading to a bottleneck if the shared LUN dosen't have the performance levels required of it

FIGURE 17-6

well-performing virtualization environment. However, success can be assured only by consistently adhering to and monitoring these considerations.

Virtual Database Server Design

This section covers the most important areas of a virtual server's design. Understanding these elements will ultimately help you deploy SQL Server in a virtual server successfully.

Memory

Of course, the requirement for SQL Server to have sufficient memory to deliver the performance levels expected of it isn't eliminated when it's virtualized. If anything, this requirement can become harder to fulfill because as you just saw, virtualization creates more opportunities — through contention — for memory to be taken away from SQL Server. Because the performance of SQL Server is so dependent on adequately sized and provisioned memory, it ranks first in my list of design considerations. It should be yours too.

For database servers, you should usually ensure that for every GB of memory allocated to the virtual server there is one GB of uncontended physical memory in the host server, and any future host servers the virtual server might run on for whatever reason. If your hypervisor allows it, as VMware's does, a memory reservation should be set to ensure that the virtual server always has reserved for it the memory it's allocated. This is particularly important in VMware environments where it's possible to over-allocate a host server's memory in the hope that all the virtual servers won't need it at the same time, yet performance problems might occur if they do.

Microsoft's Hyper-V technology in Windows Server 2008 R2 Service Pack 1 and later, however, offers Dynamic Memory, which enables you to allocate any unused physical memory in the host server to virtual servers should they ever be detected to have low-memory conditions. Reviewing it in the context of this chapter is interesting given its tight integration with SQL Server 2012 and the best practice white papers Microsoft is now releasing.

With Hyper-V, a virtual server could be configured to boot with 16GB assigned to it but have an upper limit memory of 32GB. If while running, the virtual server gets close to using all its initial 16GB of memory, the Hyper-V hypervisor will respond by increasing the memory allocated to the virtual server if sufficient free physical memory is available. It won't immediately assign the full 32GB, but it will slowly increase the amount the virtual server needs to eliminate the low-memory condition. As we mentioned earlier, SQL Server will then respond to the extra memory becoming available by expanding the buffer pool.

While it's good that extra memory might be available when it's most needed, care should be taken not to assume that it will always be available; or that if extra memory has been allocated, it won't be taken back by the balloon driver if a virtual server with a higher weighting needs the memory instead.

Dynamic Memory is a good way to size a new database server's memory requirement as if after a few weeks or a complete cycle of business activity the memory allocated to a database server hasn't increased above 17GB, you could be confident that 18GB, rather than 16GB, is an acceptable memory allocation for that virtual server.

VMware's memory overcommitting feature works slightly differently as the virtual server is told it has an amount of memory assigned to it but only has the memory it's currently using allocated to it. You can still size a database server's potential memory requirement, but the memory utilization data will have to come from VMware's performance counters rather than straight from those provided in Windows.

Storage

Storage is usually the second most important part of a virtual server's design in order to ensure SQL Server has the performance it needs to deliver the results expected of it.

Assigning storage to a virtual server is accomplished by attaching a virtual hard drive to it. A virtual drive is just a flat file stored and managed by the hypervisor but presented to the virtual server's operating system as though it were a physical disk. From that point, Windows can create a partition on it that is then mounted as drive D, formatted as NTFS, and so on.

When you deploy SQL Server in a physical environment you know it can benefit hugely by having multiple sets of unshared and uncontended hard drives available for its data storage. You typically see these used to distribute the system files, data files, log files, and in tempdb across different sets of spindles. The same consideration should be given to your virtualization environment's storage design, if at all possible multiple uncontended groups of physical disks should be used to place each virtual hard drive for SQL Server on. Of course, that's not always possible as some SAN's now like to pool all of their disks into one large group, in which case you should work with your storage team or vendor to understand how to get the best possible concurrent performance out of it.

Even though hypervisors have different ways of presenting storage to virtual servers, whether they use fixed or dynamic virtual disks, or raw device mappings, you ultimately need to ensure that SQL Server's I/O activity isn't negatively affected by competing workloads at the spindle level. Another possible performance impact, which is unique to virtual environments, can occur when the same set of spindles holds not only the database server's virtual hard drives but also the virtual hard drives and entirely separate virtual servers. This is a typical deployment practice for virtual environments, and for most virtual servers it is usually acceptable. However, SQL Server sometimes doesn't fit in the "usual" category — and being as sensitive as it is to storage latency, it will suffer from busy virtual hard drive storage.

Therefore, as a best practice, for *active* and *busy* servers I recommend the following storage design principles:

➤ Ensure that every logical drive within the Windows operating system is a separate virtual hard disk if you're able to place each of them on a separate physical SAN partition, known as LUNs.

➤ Test any use of thin provisioning, both at the hypervisor and storage layers, before you deploy it. Thin provisioning enables the virtual server to operate as though it has potentially much more disk space allocated to it than what has actually been provisioned for it yet. For example, in Windows we might see a 100GB logical drive but if it only has 28GB of data stored on it, then the hypervisor or the SAN may only have actually provisioned 28GB. This enables system administrators to over-allocate storage but only deploy the amount of storage required, rather than the amount provisioned, which may never be used. While this makes commercial sense, there's always an element of uncertainty regarding how much of a performance impact thin provisioning might have on SQL Server when it performs a write. I'm sure the vendors promote their thin-provisioning technologies in a way that reassures you this won't be an issue; but when you consider that the most performance-sensitive action in SQL Server can be a transaction log write, you never want to let anything unnecessarily impact the performance of that write.

➤ Consider contention on your storage infrastructure's networking. If you deploy SQL Server on a dedicated physical server and use SAN storage, then SQL Server is likely to have almost the entire capacity of the server's host bus adapter and fabric switch port dedicated to it. This helps support large numbers of concurrent reads and writes to the physical disks SQL Server needs to use. When running on a virtual server it's likely that several virtual servers will be using the host server's HBA for all their I/O activity, so it's possible that a virus scan of a mail server's file system could use the same HBA that your instance of SQL Server uses. This sharing of HBAs gets potentially even worse when blade servers are used as there might only be two HBAs for an entire chassis of 16 blade servers, and is particularly relevant as blade servers are a popular choice in medium and large virtualization environments. The easy solution to this is to ensure that your physical host server has adequate HBAs installed to support its total peak I/O workload.

As you can see, you need to consider a few additional factors when deploying storage for a virtual database server compared to a physical server, but none of them should be a challenge for an adequately resourced virtualization environment.

CPU

Configuring a virtual server's virtual CPUs, also known as vCPUs, is one of the easier tasks to perform, and until recently it was the first capacity ceiling users hit when they sized their virtual servers.

A vCPU is what is presented by the hypervisor to the virtual server as a "physical" CPU core; for example, Task Manager in a virtual server with 4 vCPUs would show 4 CPUs. However, although a vCPU acts and behaves like a physical CPU core, it doesn't perform like one. That's because there is no one-to-one mapping between a vCPU and a physical CPU core. Instead, a vCPU is a logical thread that is put on a physical CPU core's queue when it has something to execute. The more requests in the queue, the longer it takes for a thread to have its workload executed.

Additionally, another phenomenon unique to virtualization appears when a virtual server is configured with multiple vCPUs. The hypervisor knows that if a physical server has four physical CPU cores, then the operating system expects to be able to execute an instruction on all four simultaneously; a very abstract example would be SQL Server executing a parallel query across four logical CPUs, in which case SQL Server would expect all four CPUs to be available concurrently, rather than have to wait for CPUs to become available.

VMware's relaxed co-scheduling algorithm is clever enough to know that if only two of a virtual server's four vCPUs need to perform work, then only two physical CPU cores need to be found to execute the virtual server's work. This can make managing concurrent virtual server workloads more efficient to manage, as the number of physical CPU cores needed is often much lower than you would imagine. There can be issues with this approach though, when a virtual server that really does need to use a large number of virtual CPUs has to compete with a large number of smaller virtual severs with a low number of virtual CPUs. VMware's scheduling behaviors mean these smaller virtual machines can jump on and off the CPUs faster, delaying the ability to schedule the single much larger request for CPU time.

However, other hypervisors will only "run" the virtual server when enough physical CPU cores in the host server are free to run each of the vCPUs concurrently. For example, if the virtual server has four vCPUs assigned and the host server has 16 physical CPU cores, then the hypervisor would have to wait until four of the 16 physical CPU cores were available before it could process any CPU instructions from the virtual server. In this example if the host server was only running that virtual server there shouldn't be any unnecessary latency, as with 16 physical cores available there will most likely always be four available. It's only when virtual servers start competing between them for a limited number of physical CPU cores that performance problems can occur.

As a consequence of this potential for CPU access latency, a general recommendation is for virtual servers to be configured to have as few vCPUs as they actually need. That's not to say they can't have a large number if they need them, but the assumption that the more you have the faster the server will be may not always be correct.

Be aware that the virtual server itself is totally unaware of this latency, so it can only be monitored from outside of the virtual server. High CPU latency will not, for example, incur high SOS_SCHEDULER_YIELD wait stats within SQL Server.

The latest generation of hypervisors now support large numbers of vCPUs per virtual sever. VMware's vSphere 5 and Microsoft's Hyper-V in Windows Server 2012 both support assigning 32 vCPUs to a virtual server, an incredible amount of computing power but a capability that is critical to their goal of being able to virtualize any workload. My only advice is to ensure that you have adequate physical CPU cores in the host servers to support such a large number of vCPUs. The physical CPU cores in the host server should not be overcommitted — that is, try to ensure that no more than two vCPUs are assigned to running virtual servers per physical CPU core, although this limit may need to be lower in demanding workload environments.

When considering how many vCPUs to assign to your virtual database server, I recommend using previously captured performance data along with an understanding of your SQL Server workload.

If you are running a lot of queries serially, then a large number of vCPUs may not be required if the underlying clock speed of the physical CPU cores is high. However, a workload with a higher proportion of parallel queries needs additional vCPUs. Performance testing using Performance Monitor and monitoring the SOS_SCHEDULER_YIELD wait stat within SQL Server are good sources of monitoring data to determine whether you have assigned sufficient vCPUs.

Some hypervisors, such as VMware's vSphere, allow MHz limits to be placed on vCPUs, as well as a specific number of vCPUs to be allocated. For example, the virtual server may be allowed to execute four concurrent CPU threads across four vCPUs, yet each of those vCPUs may be limited to operating at 1GHz despite the fact that the clock speed of the physical CPU core it's using is much higher. This adds another level of resource control to the virtual environment but it has the potential to make performance monitoring slightly more confusing, as you'll see later in the chapter. Hyper-V has a similar CPU limiting system in place that restricts a virtual server to using a specific percentage of a physical CPU core's capability.

At the other end of the CPU sizing topic, however, is the issue of assigning too few vCPUs to a virtual server. The only recommendation I make here is to always assign at least two to any virtual server running Windows and SQL Server. Much of the code shipped by Microsoft is multi-threaded today and designed for servers with more than one logical CPU. Even the difference in the time it takes to install Windows on a virtual server with two vCPUs rather than one can be noticeable.

Networking

Networking, or rather adequate network bandwidth, is often overlooked when considering a virtual server's design, probably because it's only the source of any performance issues if the server performs lots of data transfer. My only recommendation here is that if you know that your database server transfers a lot of data over the network or is sensitive to any network latency, then ensure that you have sufficient network interface cards in the host server. In the same way that the host bus adapters needed for SAN storage can become contended, so can the NICs. Examples of SQL Server workloads that would warrant reviewing your host server's NIC sizing include large ETL imports or exports, or the use of synchronous database mirroring or AlwaysOn availability groups.

High Availability

Moving away from resource allocation but still an equally important design consideration is how, if at all, you will provide high availability for the SQL Server instance. I mentioned earlier in the chapter how virtualization provides some HA options that aren't available in the physical world. These on their own might be sufficient for delivering the level of availability your business needs, or you might need to deploy failover clustering or availability groups within SQL Server.

Before I review the HA services available to SQL Server 2012 in a virtual environment, I want to reiterate some advice provided earlier: If possible, ensure that you only ever have a single HA service monitoring, controlling, and reacting to a failure. Having just one place to look when the system goes down saves time!

The next pair of high-availability services are the same as what you would deploy with regular physical servers: AlwaysOn Failover Clustering Instances and AlwaysOn Availability Groups. For those considering deploying these on virtual servers running SQL Server, my recommendations are as follows:

➤ Configure the "server affinity" settings for your virtual servers such that the hypervisor ensures that the virtual servers that are part of your cluster or AlwaysOn availability groups are never run on the same physical host server at the same time. The idea is to protect against host server failure, so you want to remove any single points of failure.

➤ If you deploy any synchronous database mirroring, then ensure that you have adequate network bandwidth available on all the host servers on which you will run virtualized SQL Server instances.

➤ Likewise, for any servers involved in synchronous mirroring, ensure that you have adequate free physical CPU resources available on the host servers so that any latency to which vCPUs are exposed as they wait for physical CPU time is kept to a minimum.

➤ Finally, although a discussion of this is beyond the scope of this book, will your virtualization environment have any SAN-level replication deployed in order to replicate your storage system to another SAN infrastructure, typically off-site, for disaster recovery purposes? If so, you should consider whether it is using synchronous or asynchronous mirroring and what performance and data consistency impact that may have on SQL Server. It is critical to maintain storage-level transactional consistency between all the drives a SQL Server database uses; there is no point to having an updated data file drive at a storage level at the remote site if the transaction log drive is a few write transactions behind.

Operating System Enhancements

When an instance of Windows is deployed on a virtual server, other than ensuring that you have the correct hardware device drivers, there's nothing specific to virtualization that needs to be configured within the operating system other than to make sure the hypervisor's tools we discussed earlier are installed.

SQL Server Memory Configuration

Like Windows, SQL Server can also be installed on a virtual server and will operate quite successfully without any specific tuning or configuration. This is further proof of just how well a virtual server can emulate a physical server, assuming you have the resources, such as CPU and memory, available to SQL Server that it needs to run optimally for your workload.

However, you may want to consider configuring the Max Server Memory setting within SQL Server, although you'd probably do this on a well-tuned physical server as well. In SQL Server 2012 this setting now places a working limit on the total memory SQL Server uses, whereas in previous editions this only influenced the size of the buffer pool.

If you are using VMware, their recommendation is to set SQL Server's max server memory value to be based on the size of the memory reserved for the virtual server. For example, allow 2GB of memory for the operating system and assign the rest to SQL Server on a dedicated database server.

If you are deploying your virtual servers in a Microsoft Hyper-V environment, then the advice is slightly different. If you are not using Microsoft's Dynamic Memory feature, then you can be assured that whatever memory your virtual server appears to have, it actually does have, so you should configure you max server memory setting based on that value.

If you are using Dynamic Memory, then you should set the Startup RAM value in Hyper-V to represent as much memory as SQL Server will normally need, and set the Maximum RAM value to allow for any extra memory you think the virtual server might be allocated in a peak workload situation. In my experience, setting Max Server Memory to be 2GB lower than the Maximum RAM value set in the Hyper-V configuration allows SQL Server to increase its memory utilization as more memory is allocated. Note that this situation requires the Standard or Enterprise Editions of SQL Server 2012, or the Enterprise Edition of previous versions.

Common Virtualization Design Mistakes

In my role as a consultant, I regularly work with many different instances of SQL Server, an increasing number of which now run on virtual servers. Each virtual environment I see them run in has its strengths and weaknesses. The following list describes some common design decisions that have a negative impact on SQL Server:

➤ **Too many vCPUs** — As mentioned earlier, the more vCPUs a virtual server has, the longer the virtual server potentially has to wait for sufficient underlying physical CPU cores to become available in order for it to execute a CPU instruction. I've seen virtual servers running fairly light SQL Server workloads that have 4, 8, or even 16 vCPUs assigned to them "because they could" while in fact they could have performed comfortably with just two.

➤ **Unmanaged memory configurations** — Sometimes the configuration options in the hypervisor make it seem like you can assign as much memory as you like, and it will take care of finding and allocating all the memory required. There's some truth in that but you still need to account for all the memory assigned to virtual servers, even if some of the burst capability you give them is contended/shared with other virtual servers. In one environment I saw, when a virtual server running the backup software got busy at night, the performance of all the other virtual servers dropped severely! It was difficult explaining how such a simple misconfiguration completely unrelated to SQL Server was causing this. The solution is to know where all your critically needed memory will come from during the busiest of workload periods.

➤ **One big LUN with one big partition** — SQL Server, even when running in a virtual server, benefits from having multiple uncontended drives for the different types of files it uses. A default deployment option for some virtualization software is to use a single large pool of physical drives and create a single large partition on it; onto that are put all the files for the entire virtualization environment. This can quickly lead to storage hotspots, workload contention, and having to adopt the same storage configuration settings for every virtual server, such as the storage cache policy. Ideally, a SAN should be configurable so that different controller settings can be applied to different storage partitions, allowing the storage that SQL Server will ultimately use to be optimized wherever possible. It also makes performance monitoring difficult because you can't always easily identify a specific virtual server's workload. As you saw earlier, the solution here is to distribute a busy database server's storage across multiple virtual hard drives, providing they can use different groups of physical drives.

➤ **Saturated host bus adapters** — It is common to see a host server with only a single HBA running several I/O-intensive virtual servers. Not only is this a single point of failure, but the HBA can easily get saturated, causing I/O requests to be queued and introducing storage latency.

MONITORING VIRTUALIZED DATABASE SERVERS

Hopefully the previous section has given you sufficient guidance to architecting and deploying your first virtualized database servers, even if only in non-production environments. This section focuses on real-world monitoring of your virtualized database servers, identifying specific changes you may need to make to your monitoring processes and confirming which aspects of your current monitoring can remain unchanged.

Traditionally we have monitored Windows servers and servers running SQL Server with tools such as Performance Monitor. These tools have counters that are designed to expose the true utilization of a server's hardware and the operating system's demands on it. For example, we can look at the workload of a server's CPUs by monitoring the % utilization values shown in Performance Monitor. Likewise, we can see how much memory the server has both used and available by looking at similar counters. These counters were perfect in the physical server world because we knew if Windows booted up and saw 4 logical CPUs and 16GB of memory then all of that resource would be available to the operating system and usually SQL Server as well.

This can cause issues; what does 100% of CPU utilization or 8GB of available memory actually represent in the virtual world? In environments where no restriction, contention, or over-allocation of resources has been configured, some certainty can be found from performance data. In larger, more complex environments, contention ratios or memory allocation might be changing on a minute-by-minute basis.

The example shown in Figure 17-7 demonstrates how in a Hyper-V environment, the same performance metric monitored in two places can be so different because of an underlying resource limitation in place. VMware provides its own Performance Monitor counters through the VM Memory and VM Processor objects.

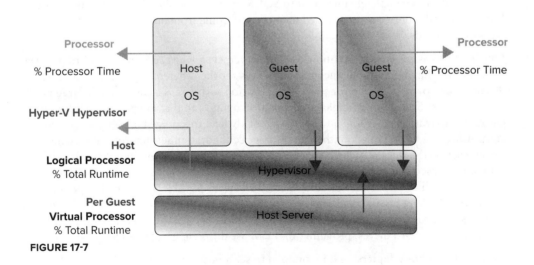

FIGURE 17-7

Information and Misinformation from Performance Monitor

Clearly, the same tools that used to reliably provide us with monitoring information can now be sources of misinformation as you'll now see.

Performance Monitor is still the most efficient way to monitor a virtual server's performance. The only caveat is to ensure that you monitor the right counters from the right source. You'll look at which specific counters to use later in this chapter.

Some Performance Monitor counters collected from within the virtual server are as valid and useful as they are on a physical server. Logical storage performance data, for example, will help you monitor the virtual server's I/O workload and enables you to measure what percentage of the host server's HBA capacity SQL Server is using, as well as ensure that SQL Server's read and write latencies are acceptable.

While the role of the hypervisor is to make the virtual server believe it is running on dedicated hardware and totally abstract it from the underlying physical hardware, some calls to specific hardware-related APIs are passed by the hypervisor straight through to the physical hardware. An example of this is retrieving technical information about the CPU that an instance of Windows is using. Figure 17-8 shows an example of information retrieved by Windows running on a Hyper-V virtual server.

wait_type	waiting_tasks_count	wait_time_ms	max_wait_time_ms	signal_wait_time_ms
PAGEIOLATCH_SH	643	13138	339	15
SOS_SCHEDULER_YIELD	13526	249	36	206

FIGURE 17-8

These hardware query requests are passed straight through to the hardware because it would be difficult for virtualization vendors to know what "artificial" value to pass back today and in the future in order to guarantee compatibility with any applications that check the version of the CPU on which they're running. This behavior enables you to put the information that Windows or a tool like CPU-Z returns into perspective, particularly as it's able to find the clock speed of the physical CPU even though the hypervisor might be limiting your access to only a portion of the available clock speed.

SQL Server wait stats are another area to consider when you are determining your sources of information or misinformation. However, even in the physical world, wait stats identify only the symptom of a system issue, not its cause. Therefore, in the virtual world they are still excellent indicators of potential issues hindering SQL Server's performance, and wait stats are a good source of information, rather than potentially misleading misinformation.

Agent job runtimes are another source of excellent information within SQL Server you can use for performance monitoring. By creating jobs that perform the same tasks with the same volumes of data repeatedly, you can compare the time they took to run today with the time they took to run yesterday.

If, for example, you have a job to back up a database approximately 20GB in size, and for six weeks it took 20 minutes to run but in the last few days it started taking longer, you may have identified a reduction in the host server's I/O capabilities. This information on its own may not be of significant operational value, but if your SQL Server instance has also started reporting a much greater occurrence of pageiolatch_xx wait stats, you may well want to start looking outside of your virtual server first.

Likewise, if you have a very CPU-intensive SQL Server agent job, then looking for changes in that job's runtime might also help you detect signs of CPU contention at the host server level.

Detecting Hypervisor Memory Reclamation

Knowing how much memory your virtual server has access to at any point in time is something you should be able find the moment you suspect a previously healthy SQL Server instance has issues. While different hypervisors have different ways to assign memory to virtual servers — based on either demand, static allocations, or host server load — they usually all use a balloon driver to reclaim memory if they ever have to start taking memory back from a virtual server.

Although Windows and SQL Server have hot-add memory features that enable you to add memory to a running instance of SQL Server, they don't have an opposite feature whereby memory can be taken away from Windows and SQL Server, yet this is sometimes a requirement in the virtual world when memory is to be reclaimed by a balloon driver.

Monitoring this reclamation happening can be tricky because the amount of "physical" memory the virtual server's operating system thinks it has never decreases. However, when the balloon driver "inflates," the amount of available memory within Windows begins to drop, and when it falls below an internal threshold SQL Server begins releasing memory to prevent the operating system from running out. Figure 17-9 shows a before and after representation of the balloon drive inflating.

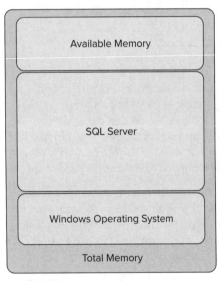
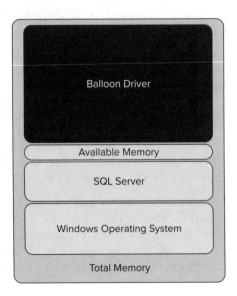

FIGURE 17-9

One way to detect changes in the allocation of the memory SQL Server is using is to look for falls in the Page Life Expectancy counter value or increases in the Pages/sec value.

If you're using Hyper-V, then another way is to query how SQL Server's memory utilization has potentially changed in response to activity by the Dynamic Memory feature. The following query returns not how much memory SQL Server is currently using but what percentage of your virtual server's memory it's using. The reason for monitoring a percentage rather than an absolute value is that the percentage is proportional to the total amount of the virtual server's memory. If the hypervisor grants the virtual server more memory at any time, you would expect the percentage of memory being used to remain constant even though SQL Server is using more memory. Likewise, if the balloon driver begins to inflate, you would expect the percentage of total memory SQL Server is using to begin to drop. You could use absolute values, but monitoring a percentage takes into account the physical memory size. The way this query works is dependant on Hyper-V's Dynamic Memory model so it won't work in VMware based environments.

```
select (m.total_physical_memory_kb /1024)
as 'Physical Memory (MB)',
convert(decimal(3,1),(convert(decimal(10,1),m.available_physical_memory_kb / 1024)
/ convert(decimal(10,1),m.total_physical_memory_kb / 1024)) * 100)
as 'Available Memory as % of Physical Memory'
from sys.dm_os_sys_memory m,sys.dm_os_sys_info i

select convert(decimal(10,1),(convert(decimal(10,1),i.committed_target_kb / 1024)
        /convert(decimal(10,1),m.total_physical_memory_kb / 1024))
        * 100) as 'Committed Target as % of Physical Memory',
        convert(decimal(3,1),(convert(decimal(10,1),i.committed_kb  / 1024)
        /convert(decimal(10,1),m.total_physical_memory_kb / 1024))
        * 100) as 'Total Committed as % of Physical Memory'
From    sys.dm_os_sys_memory m, sys.dm_os_sys_info i
```

Examples of output from this script run on a Hyper-V virtual server are shown in Figure 17-10 and Figure 17-11. The first instance was run just after SQL Server started, the second after a heavy workload when the hypervisor allocated additional memory to the virtual server using Dynamic Memory.

```
system_high_memory_signal_state system_low_memory_signal_state
-------------------------------- ------------------------------
1                                0

Physical Memory (MB) Available Memory as % of Physical Memory
-------------------- ----------------------------------------
1147                 27.6

Committed Target as % of Physical Memory Total Committed as % of Physical Memory
---------------------------------------- ---------------------------------------
35.5                                     12.9
```
FIGURE 17-10

```
system_high_memory_signal_state system_low_memory_signal_state
-------------------------------- ------------------------------
1                                0

Physical Memory (MB) Available Memory as % of Physical Memory
-------------------- ----------------------------------------
5969                 6.4

Committed Target as % of Physical Memory Total Committed as % of Physical Memory
---------------------------------------- ---------------------------------------
84.5                                     81.8
```
FIGURE 17-11

Recommended Performance Monitor Counters

I recommend monitoring the following three general groups of Performance Monitor counters to track the health of your virtual database server.

On the Host Server

Collecting performance information from the host server your SQL Server instance is running on will help you understand whether SQL Server itself should be performing as you expect it to be. For example, how busy are the host server's physical CPU cores and how much of the HBA's capacity is currently being used? It may also be necessary to collect performance data from the host server about a virtual server's resource utilization. This depends on your hypervisor but with Hyper-V, for example, a virtual server's true CPU utilization data is exposed at Virtual Processor counters on the host server. Interestingly, VMware does the opposite, exposing performance data about the host server to Performance Monitor in the virtual server.

Monitor the following performance counters on the host server:

- ➤ Percentage of physical CPU utilization
- ➤ Percentage of physical memory utilization
- ➤ Any CPU latency experienced by the hypervisor (VMware calls this CPU Ready Time)
- ➤ Total amount of memory currently allocated to the host's virtual servers
- ➤ Physical storage MB/s and IOPS that the hypervisor is using
- ➤ Physical storage read and write latency times
- ➤ Percentage of HBA bandwidth utilization
- ➤ Percentage of NIC bandwidth utilization

On the Virtual Server

Performance data gathered from within a virtual server is likely to be more meaningful if it refers to logical objects or is measuring the proportion of the virtual server's resource currently being used. For example, the % CPU utilization values that Task Manager and Performance Monitor display inside a virtual server indicate how much of the processor resource available to the virtual server is currently being used. Unfortunately, those values cannot be related to a specific physical and quantifiable hardware sizing metric — i.e., they don't indicate whether 100% is a throttled 1GHz of CPU resource or the entire native 3GHz of the physical CPU. These metrics still have value, however. If you look at Task Manager on a virtual server and see that your anti-virus software is using 60% of your CPU resource, that's an issue whether the server is virtual or physical.

The counters you should monitor here are as follows:

- ➤ % logical CPU utilization
- ➤ Total physical memory (MB)
- ➤ Available memory (MB)
- ➤ Logical storage MB/s and IOPS that the operating system is using
- ➤ Logical storage read and write latency times

On the SQL Server Instance

The monitoring you perform within SQL Server when it's running on a virtual server shouldn't be very different from your regular SQL Server monitoring. The only difference now is the potential for new or more causes of performance issues to investigate.

The DMV `sys.dm_os_sys_info` has been changed in SQL Server 2012 and offers some new columns that provide information for virtual environments. First, it confirms that SQL Server recognized that it started on a virtual server. This is shown in the `virtual_machine_type` and `virtual_machine_type_desc` columns; and although it may not seem to offer much benefit, it can be useful if you ever forget which of your servers are virtual and which are physical! The other interesting column in this DMV is `committed_kb`, which now describes the total amount of memory SQL Server is using at the time you query the DMV. This is important to know if you operate in a demand-based memory allocation environment.

The traditional performance counters you probably monitor already are included in the list of SQL Server–related performance metrics that can be used to monitor a virtual server:

➤ SQL Server file I/O latencies from `sys.dm_io_virtual_file_stats`

➤ Committed and Target Committed Memory values from `sys.dm_os_sys_info`

➤ Batch requests/sec as a benchmark of server activity levels

SUMMARY

This chapter covered a range of topics about virtualization. Although some are generic and not specifically related to SQL Server, any SQL Server professional who operates and troubleshoots in a virtual environment should understand the basics of this technology, the reasons for adoption, and the principles of designing and monitoring virtual database servers, as all of these will be crucial to your success.

The relationship between SQL Server and virtualization will grow stronger as Microsoft reacts to greater demand from customers to integrate the two more closely. The tight integration of Hyper-V's Dynamic Memory and SQL Server 2012, along with the licensing changes SQL Server has undergone in the latest release, enhance its value in virtual environments.

INDEX

Numbers

32-bit operating systems
  Address Windowing Extensions in, 54
  Diag Manager in, 307
  max worker threads in, 23
  virtual address spaces for, 57
64-bit operating systems
  Address Windowing Extensions in, 54
  Diag Manager in, 307
  max worker threads in, 23
  PerfMon in, 277
  virtual memory and, 56

A

acceptable thresholds, 230
Access Control Lists (ACLs), 340
Access Methods, 12, 16
ACID properties, 4–5, 150–153
ACLs (Access Control Lists), 340
actions in XEvents, 352, 357
active server workloads, 491
Address Window Extension (AWE), 250
ad-hoc workloads, 74–76
Advanced Micro Devices (AMD)
  CPU features by, 480
  Opteron processors by, 32–33, 35–37,
    43–46
AdventureWorks2012 database
  bulk update lock mode in, 172
  dirty reads in, 155–156
  iQuery Optimizer and, 121–122
  phantom reads in, 160

query hints in, 125
query plans in, 131
range locks in, 176
restoring, 392
affinity masks, 143–144
Agarwal, Sunil, 226
Agent, 314, 462–466
aggregate binding, 112
aggregated data analysis, 331–337
aggressive working set trimming, 73
alert-driven data collection, 322
alerts in SCOM, 465–466
algebrizer trees, 115
algebrizing, 112
allocation pages
  contention of, generally, 221–224, 229
  multiple data files in, 224–226
  temporary object reuse in, 226–228
  trace flag 1118 in, 228
AlwaysOn Availability Groups, 94
AMD (Advanced Micro Devices). *See* Advanced
    Micro Devices (AMD)
Analysis Custom Collectors, 313
append-only version stores, 218–220
application logs, 254
application mode, 280
architecture
  Access Methods in, 12
  Buffer Manager in, 12–13, 17–18
  buffer pools in, 6
  bulk-logged recovery model in, 21–22
  checkpoint process in, 19–21
  Command Parser in, 8–9
  consistency in, 4

architecture *(continued)*
  data caches in, 12–14
  database transactions and, 4–5
  dirty pages in, 18–19
  durability in, 5
  execution model in, 22–26
  explicit transactions in, 5
  full recovery model in, 21
  implicit transactions in, 5
  introduction to, 3–4
  isolation in, 5
  lazy writers in, 19
  protocol layers in, 8
  Query Executor in, 11–12
  query life cycles in, 5–7
  Query Optimizer in, 10–11
  recovery and, 18–22
  Recovery Interval in, 21
  Relational Engines in, 6
  schedulers in, 24–25
  SELECT queries in, 7–15
  Server Network Interface in, 7
  simple recovery model in, 22
  SQL Server Operating System and, 22–26
  Storage Engines in, 6
  summary of, 26–27
  TDS endpoints in, 8
  Transaction Manager in, 16–17
  UPDATE queries in, 15–18
  of virtual database servers, 494
as-is support, 305–306, 325
asterisk (*), 299
asynchronous data replication, 92–93
atomicity, 4, 150–152
attitudes, 245
authoring management packs, 466
auto_create_statistics, 117
auto_update_statistics, 117
auto_update_statistics_asynchronously,
  117
auto-growth
  in PBM, 452–455
  in tempdb, 234–237
automating best practice checks, 452–457

auto-scaling counters, 262
availability requirements, 493
Available MBytes, 72
Average Task Count, 421–422
average times, 99
AWE (Address Window Extension), 250

B

backup disk space utilization, 398
Backup MDW custom collector, 312
Backup-SqlDatabase, 392
bad contention, 489–490
bad nonclustered indexes, 436–437
Balanced Windows Power Plan, 410–411
balloon drivers, 482, 490
Base custom collector, 311
baseline analysis, 296
Batch Resp Statistics counter, 264–265
BCDR (business continuance and disaster
  recovery), 91–92, 94
BEGIN TRANSACTION, 5
behaviors, 245
benchmarks
  for AMD Opteron processors, 45–46
  Geekbench, 33–35, 50
  for hardware, 50
  for OLTP databases, 48–50
  for server models, 38, 43
  TCP. *See* TPC Benchmark E (TPC-E)
  for two-/four-socket servers, 49–50
benign wait types, 420
best plans vs. efficient plans, 10
Best Practice Analyzer (BPA), 461
Best Practices custom collector, 311
binary log (BLG) files
  analysis of, 289
  conversion of, 291
  in PerfMon, generally, 273, 319
binary modules, 388
BIOS setup, 47
black box tracing, 253
BLG (binary log) files. *See* binary log (BLG) files
BLG Blaster, 328–329

bloat, 67, 74

block-based storage systems, 85–86

Blocking and Wait Statistics reports, 334–336, 346–347

Blocking custom collector, 314

blocking reports, generally, 332

BlockingCollector, 300

bookmark lookup operators, 135

bottleneck analysis, generally, 278–279, 296–297

Bottleneck Analysis reports, 332–333, 346–347

BPA (Best Practice Analyzer), 461

breadth in virtualization, 472

Broker events, 320

BU (bulk update lock mode), 171–172

buckets, 119–120

BUF latches, 194

Buffer Manager, 12–13, 15, 17–18

buffer pools, 6, 15, 66

buffer usage, 439

build phase, 133

builds
  Average Task Count information in, 421–422
  buffer usage by database in, 418
  cluster node information in, 412–413
  CPU usage in, 418–419, 422–423
  cumulative wait types for instances in, 419–420
  database filenames/paths in, 415
  database property information in, 416–417
  Error Log information in, 412
  hardware information in, 409–410
  instance configuration values in, 413–414
  I/O stall information in, 417–418
  login count information in, 421
  memory clerk information in, 425
  memory dump information in, 415
  Memory Grants Outstanding in, 424
  Memory Grants Pending in, 425
  memory information in, generally, 423–424
  operating system cluster information in, 412
  operating system memory information in, 423
  Page Life Expectancy information in, 424
  processor description in, 410–411
  Registry information in, 414
  server manufacturer/model in, 410
  Services information in, 411
  signal waits for instances in, 420
  single-use ad-hoc queries in, 426
  TCP Listener information in, 414
  Windows information in, 409

bulk update lock mode (BU), 171–172

bulk-logged recovery model, 21–22

business benefits of virtualization, 474

business continuance and disaster recovery (BCDR), 91–92, 94

busy server workloads, 491

C

C# programming language, 388

cabinet (.cab) files, 316–317

cache stores, 119

cache thrashing, 43

cache-coherent NUMA (ccNUMA), 59

cached queries, 430

cached stored procedures
  by average elapsed time, 431–432
  by execution count, 430–431
  by total logical reads, 433–434
  by total logical writes, 435–436
  by total physical reads, 434
  by total worker time, 432

caches, memory, 65

caches of plans. See plan caches

CAL (Client Access License), 36

calm, 244

capacity optimization, 86–88

Capacity Planner, 493

Carriage Returns/Line Feeds (CR/LFs), 343

Causality Tracking, 364

causes of issues, 243

ccNUMA (cache-coherent NUMA), 59

Central Management Server (CMS), 254, 450–451

check last backup, 452

checkpoints, 19–21

classic numbering, 39

clean pages, 18

clerks, memory, 64, 267, 425

Client Access License (CAL), 36
clock speeds, 410–411
cloud computing, 473
cluster nodes, 412–413
clustered indexes, 459–460
Clustered Shared Volumes, 484
cmdlets, 382–384, 391–392
CMS (Central Management Server), 254, 450–451
CodePlex, 285, 325–327
columnstore index, 30
Command Parser, 8–9, 14
command prompts in Nexus, 342
command-line applications, 299–303
comma-separated value (CSV) files, 289
committed transactions, 5, 19
communication plans, 243
comparative analysis reports, 340
comparison operators, 385
compatibility of types, 196
compilation, 123, 250
compile-time details, 321–322
compression status, 440
concurrency. See also locks
    dangers of, generally, 153
    dirty reads and, 155–156
    double reads and, 161–162
    Halloween effect and, 162
    introduction to, 149–150
    lost updates and, 153–155
    non-repeatable reads and, 156–158
    phantom reads and, 158–160
    summary of, 179
conditions
    in Autogrow, 453–455
    for filtering targets, 454
    in MaxDoP, 456
    in Policy-Based Management, generally,
        447–448
    as server restrictions, 450
configuration
    bottlenecks due to, 279
    managing. See Configuration Manager
    in SQLdiag, 299–300
    of tempdb, 232–237

Configuration Manager
    MyCollectors custom collector in, 316–317
    Analysis Custom Collectors in, 313
    custom diagnostics in, 310–312
    Diag Manager in, 307–309
    feature-specific diagnostics in, 313–314
    introduction to, 305–307
    Profiler trace filters in, generally, 310
    saving/using in, 317–318
    SQL 2008 Backup MDW in, 312
    SQL 2008 Perf Stats in, 311–312
    XEvents data collection in, 315–316
Connection Info, 308
connectivity issues, 249
consistency, 151–152
contained databases, 446
contention
    of allocation pages, 221–229
    of latches. See latch contention
    managing, 488–491
    of spinlocks, 184–185, 209
conversion lock modes, 170–171
Cooper, Tommy, 149
co-operative scheduling, 25
Core Factor Table, 45–46
core-based licensing, 35–37
Coreinfo, 60
costs
    architecture and, 11
    of performance problems, 256
    principle of, 113
counter log templates, 286
counters
    auto-scaling, 262
    Batch Resp Statistics, 264–265
    Buffer Manager, 282
    in Data Collector Sets, 273
    Database Replica, 265
    Disk PerfMon, 283
    extracting specific performance, 291
    File Table, 266–267
    General Statistics, 284
    on host servers, 506
    Locks, 284

Memory Broker Clerks, 267
Memory Node, 267
MSSQL, 282, 284
in PerfMon, generally, 276–277, 279–284
Physical Disk, 283
show/hide, 262–263
for SQL Server 2012, 263–268
on SQL Server instances, 507
SQL Server PerfMon, 284
SQL Statistics, 284
for storage systems, 96–97
Transactions, 284
on virtual servers, 506
Windows performance, 396–397
in XEvents, 361
counting locks per object, 369–370
CPU nodes, 143–144
CPU utilization
    bad contention and, 488–489
    in Bottleneck Analysis reports, 333
    by database, 418–419
    good contention and, 488
    history of, 422–423
    virtualization and, 492
CPU wait category, 334
CPUs
    cost of queries/procedures in, 432
    logical, 23–24
    troubleshooting, 250–251, 280–281
    usage of. See CPU utilization
    virtual, 497–501
CPU-Z, 411
CR/LFs (Carriage Returns/Line Feeds), 343
CSS (Customer Service and Support), 247, 461
CSV (comma-separated value) files, 289
CU (cumulative signal) waits, 420
cumulative signal (CU) waits, 420
cumulative updates (CUs), 408–409
current numbering, 40
current server activity, 394–395
Cursors event category, 320
CUs (cumulative updates), 408–409
Custom Diagnostics, 309–312
Customer Service and Support (CSS), 247, 461

D

DAC/DACPAC (data-tier application), 446
DACs (dedicated administrator connections), 8, 24, 61
DAS (Direct Attached Storage), 79
data
    analysis of, 255–256
    caches of, 12–14
    collection of. See data collection
    in databases. See databases
    gathering of, 253–254
    loading in Nexus, 328
    replication of, 89–94
data collection
    alert-driven, 322
    approaches to, 296–297
    best practices for, 318
    data gathering in, 253–254
    Diag Manager and, 308
    dilemma of, 295–296
    filtering out noise in, 320–322
    focused, 253
    introduction to, 252
    long-term, 319–320
    Sets for. See Data Collector Sets
    SQLdiag for. See SQLdiag
    summary of, 323
    tools for, 254–255
    troubleshooting, 252–255
    utilities for, 254–255
Data Collector Sets
    introduction to, 270
    log formats in, 273
    in PerfMon, 262, 270–274
    property configuration in, 273
    in Reliability Monitor, 262
    remotely running, 274
    starting/stopping/scheduling, 272–273
    working with, 271–272
Data Definition Language (DDL). See DDL (Data Definition Language)
Data Link (.udl) files, 421
Data Loading Performance Guide, 171

data source names (DSNs), 273
data warehouses (DWs), 31, 100
database administrators (DBAs)
 counters on instances for, 507
 health checks by, 406
 on hyperthreading, 43
 index maintenance by, 397
 instance-level default settings by, 414
 liabilities of, 30
 low memory conditions and, 490
 performance improvements by, 445
 plan guides for, 129
 as storage administrators, 77
 thin provisioning and, 87
 Tick-Tock release strategy for, 41
 transaction log backups by, 416
 troubleshooting by, generally, 241
 using PerfMon, 259
 using Policy-Based Management, 447
 virtualization and, 494
 on wait types, 420
 XEvents and, 350
Database Engine Tuning Advisor (DTA), 446
Database Mirroring custom collector, 313
Database Replica counter, 265
Database Tuning Advisor (DTA), 255
database-level queries
 for buffer usage by table/index, 439
 for cached plans, 438–439
 for compression status, 440
 for file sizes/space available, 427
 in health checks, generally, 426
 for index fragmentation info, 441–442
 for I/O statistics, 428
 for missing index warnings, 438–439
 for missing indexes by index advantage, 437–438
 for possible bad nonclustered indexes, 436–437
 for procedures by average elapsed time, 431–432
 for procedures by execution count, 430–431
 for procedures by total logical reads, 433–434

for procedures by total logical writes, 435–436
for procedures by total physical reads, 434
for procedures by total worker time, 432
for row counts, 440
for statistics update for indexes, 440–441
for switching to user databases, 426–427
for table names, 440
for top cached queries, 430
for top cached stored procedures, 430–436
for top statements by average I/O, 436
for transaction log size/space used, 427–428
for Virtual Log File count, 428–430
databases
 ACID properties of, 151–153
 administrators of. See database administrators (DBAs)
 architecture in, 4–5
 file sizes in, 427
 filenames in, 415
 paths in, 415
 property information of, 416–417
 queries and. See database-level queries
 restoring usability of, 446
 space available in, 427
 in SQL Nexus, 328–331
 transactions of, 151–153
data-tier application (DAC or DACPAC), 446
Davis, Robert, 223
DBAs (database administrators). See database administrators (DBAs)
dbcc dropcleanbuffers, 18
DDL (Data Definition Language)
 Policy-Based Management and, 457
 in PowerShell, 398–403
 in tempdb, 227
deadlocks, 175
Debugger, 256
dedicated administrator connections (DACs), 8, 24, 61
defining problems. See troubleshooting
Dell PowerEdge servers, 33–35
design
 of architecture. See architecture

of SCOM, 464–465
of virtual database servers, 495–501
Destroy (DT) latches, 195–197
Diag Manager
    MyCollectors custom collector in, 316–317
    Analysis Custom Collectors in, 313
    in Configuration Manager, 307–309
    custom diagnostics in, 310–312
    feature-specific diagnostics in, 313–314
    introduction to, 306–307
    Profiler trace filters in, generally, 310
    saving/using configurations in, 317–318
    SQL 2008 Backup MDW in, 312
    SQL 2008 Perf Stats in, 311–312
    XEvents data collection in, 315–316
diagnostics
    managing. _See_ Diag Manager
    for query memory, 69–70
    SQLdiag for. _See_ SQLdiag
    XEvents for. _See_ Extended Events (XEvents)
Direct Attached Storage (DAS), 79
dirty pages, 17–19
dirty reads, 155–156
Discussion/Issue Tracker pages, 329, 337
Disk Class driver (disk.sys), 83
disk drive performance, 97–100
disk mirroring, 79–80
Disk PerfMon counters, 283
disk performance, 276
disk space utilization, 393–394
disk striping, 79–80
disk-related problems, 283
Distributed Replay Client, 344
DLLs (dynamic link libraries), 93
DMFs (dynamic management functions), 121–123, 132, 406–408
DMVs (dynamic management views)
    for Extended Event, 356–358
    hash buckets in, 119–120
    latch contention and, 183–184
    latches and, 199–201
    monitoring locks with, 163
    NUMA configurations in, 61
    optimization process in, 114

plan caches in, 66–67
queries in, 406–408
ring buffers in, 375–376
for space issues, 231–232
for spinlocks, 184–185
spinlocks and, 199–201
in SQL Server architecture, 25–26
SQL Server Registry, 414
tasks in, 145
TCP Listener, 414
for tempdb by session, 216
threads in, 145–146
for virtual environments, 507
workers in, 145
double reads, 161–162
Driscoll, Adam, 382
DSNs (data source names), 273
DT (Destroy) latches, 195–197
DTA (Database Tuning Advisor), 255, 446
Dumps custom collector, 312
durability
    Buffer Manager and, 17–18
    in locks, 151, 152–153
    in SQL Server architecture, 5
DWs (data warehouses), 31, 100
dynamic link libraries (DLLs), 93
dynamic management functions (DMFs), 121–123, 132, 406–408
dynamic management views (DMVs). _See_ DMVs (dynamic management views)
Dynamic Memory
    in Hyper-V, 476
    in virtual database servers, 496, 501
    in Xen, 479
dynamic modules, 388

E

EBs (exabytes), 56
efficient vs. best plans, 10
eMLC (enterprise MLC) flash memory, 105
encapsulation, 475
enterprise MLC (eMLC) flash memory, 105
enterprise policy evaluation, 450–451

Enterprise Policy Management Framework (EPMF), 460
equality operators, 385–386
escalation of locks, 174–175
ETW (Event Tracing for Windows), 353, 362
evaluation modes, 448
Event Retention, 360
Event Tracing for Windows (ETW), 353, 362
EventlogCollector, 299
events
    categories of, 320–322
    counters for, 361
    extended, 202–203
    fields of, 356–357
    files of, 359, 371–374
    interesting, 339
    lightweight, 351–352
    lock_acquired, 369
    logs of, 254, 304–305, 396
    T-SQL language, 8–9
    in XEvents. *See* Extended Events (XEvents)
EX (Exclusive) latches, 195–198
exabytes (EBs), 56
Exclusive (EX) latches, 195–198
exclusive lock mode (X), 168
exclusive or (XOR) calculations, 81
execution model in SQLOS, 22–26
execution plans in Command Parser, 8–9
Execution Policy in PowerShell, 382–383
explicit transactions, 5
Explorer (Windows Explorer), 395
Extended Events (XEvents)
    actions in, 357
    benefits of, generally, 351
    creating in SQL Server 2012, 363–371
    creating sessions with T-SQL, 370–371
    data collection in, 315–316
    definition of, 352–353
    dispatch latency in, 360–361
    event counters in, 361
    event fields in, 356–357
    event file data in, 371–374
    event files in, 359
    Event Retention in, 360

    events in, 355–356
    filters in, 357–358
    graphical tools in, 351
    histograms in, 361–362
    introduction to, 254, 349–350
    for latches, 202–203
    live data in, 372–373
    locks per object count in, 369–370
    low impact of, 351–352
    memory buffer size in, 359–360
    in-memory targets in, 374
    name of, 353
    New Session creation in, 363–366
    page splits monitoring in, 367–369
    pair matching in, 362
    querying ring buffers with T-SQL, 374–376
    ring buffers in, 361
    roadmap for, 351
    saved data in, 373–374
    server logins in, 366–367
    sessions in, 354–355
    for spinlocks, 202–203
    summary of, 376–377
    targets in, 359–362
    terminology in, 354–358
    viewing data captured by, 371–376
    Waits custom collector in, 315
    when to use, 352
    Windows Event Tracing in, 362
extents, defined, 221
external troubleshooting help, 247

F

facets, 447
Failover Cluster Instance, 212
failover clusters in SQLdiag, 305
FAST <number_rows>, 124
Fast Track Data Warehouse, 100
FC (Fibre Channel), 97–98
FCIP (Fibre Channel Internet Protocol), 84
FCOE (Fibre Channel Over Ethernet), 84
feature-specific custom diagnostics, 313–314
Fibre Channel (FC), 97–98

Fibre Channel Internet Protocol (FCIP), 84

Fibre Channel Over Ethernet (FCOE), 84

FIFO (First in, First out), 359, 361

file formats, 291

file placement, 232–234

File Table counter, 266–267

file-based storage systems, 85–86

FILESTREAM, 104

filtering out noise, 320–322

filters in XEvents, 357–358

First in, First out (FIFO), 359, 361

focused data collection, 253

forced parameterization, 4–5, 118

four-socket servers

    evolution of, 33–35

    selecting of, 36–38

    TPC-E benchmarks for, 49–50

fragmentation, 441–442

free buffer lists, 19

Freedman, Craig, 123, 162

ftdisk.sys (Volume Manager driver), 83

full recovery model, 21

Full Text Search custom collector, 313

full-stop (.), 299

G

/G command, 298, 301, 304

GAM (Global Allocation Map), 221

Gateway, 462–465

Geekbench, 33–35, 50

geo-clustering, 93

Global Allocation Map (GAM), 221

global temporary tables, 213

good contention, 488–489

grant order, 196–197

graphical tools, 351

graphical user interfaces (GUIs), 351, 354, 382

group binding, 112

guest clustering, 487

guest servers, 482–483

GUIs (graphical user interfaces), 351, 354, 382

H

HA (high-availability) features. *See* high-availability (HA) features

HA/DR (high-availability and disaster-recovery), 48

Hallengren, Olla, 442

Halloween effect, 162

hard page faults, 57–58

hardware

    AMD Operton processors, 43–46

    bottlenecks, 249

    comparison tools for, 48

    data warehousing and, 31

    Geekbench benchmarks for, 50

    importance of, 29–30

    information on, 409–410

    Intel processors, 35–43

    introduction to, 29

    OLAP workloads and, 31–32

    OLTP databases and, 31–32

    process vendor selection, generally, 35

    redundancy and, 46–48

    relational reporting workloads and, 31–32

    server model evolution and, 33–35

    server model selection and, 32–33

    SQL Server builds and, 409–410

    storage and, 30–35

    summary of, 51–52

    TPC Benchmark E for, 48–50

    for virtualization, 479–480

    workload types and, 30–35

hash buckets, 119–120

hash joins, 133

hash operators, 133

hash warnings, 70, 133–134

HBAs (Host Bus Adapters), 78–79, 83

health checks for SQL Server

    Average Task Count in, 421–422

    buffer usage by database in, 418

    buffer usage by table/index in, 439

    builds in, generally, 408–409

    cached plans in, 438–439

    cluster nodes in, 412–413

health checks for SQL Server *(continued)*
  compression status in, 440
  CPU usage by database in, 418–419
  CPU utilization history in, 422–423
  database file sizes/space available in, 427
  database filenames/paths in, 415
  database property info in, 416–417
  database-level queries in, 426
  DMV/DMF queries in, 406–408
  fragmentation info in, 441–442
  hardware info in, 409–410
  importance of, 405–406
  instance configuration values in, 413–414
  introduction to, 405
  I/O stall info in, 417–418
  I/O statistics by file in, 428
  login count info in, 421
  memory clerk info in, 425
  Memory Grants Outstanding in, 424
  Memory Grants Pending in, 425
  missing index warnings in, 438–439
  missing indexes by index advantage in,
    437–438
  nonclustered indexes in, 436–437
  operating system clusters in, 412
  operating system memory in, 423
  Page Life Expectancy in, 424
  procedures by average elapsed time in,
    431–432
  procedures by execution count in, 430–431
  procedures by total logical reads in, 433–434
  procedures by total logical writes in,
    435–436
  procedures by total physical reads in, 434
  procedures by total worker time in, 432
  processor description in, 410–411
  row counts in, 440
  server manufacturer/model in, 410
  signal waits for instances in, 420
  single-use ad-hoc queries in, 426
  SQL Server Error Log in, 412
  SQL Server memory in, 415, 423–424
  SQL Server Registry in, 414
  SQL Server Services info in, 411

  statistics updates for indexes in, 440–441
  switching to user databases in, 426–427
  table names in, 440
  TCP Listener in, 414
  top cached queries in, 430
  top cached stored procedures in, 430–436
  top statements by average I/O in, 436
  transaction log size/space used in, 427–428
  Virtual Log File count in, 428–430
  wait types for instances in, 419–420
  Windows info in, 409
Heap or Balanced Tree (HoBT) locks,
  166–167, 174
High Performance power plan, 411
high-availability (HA) features
  deploying SQL Server with, 487–488
  disaster recovery and, 48
  in virtual database servers, 486–487,
    499–500
  in virtualization, generally, 483–488
high-availability and disaster-recovery
  (HA/DR), 48
hints, 124
histograms, 361–362, 369–370
HoBT (Heap or Balanced Tree) locks,
  166–167, 174
Host Bus Adapters (HBAs), 78–79, 83
host clustering, 487
host servers, 480
hot-add memory support, 476
Huffman, Clint, 285
hyperthreading, 42–43
Hyper-V
  CPU utilization in, 502
  installation of, 481
  introduction to, 478–479
  memory in, 490, 495–496, 500
  PerfMon counters in, 506
  vCPUs in, 498–499
  Windows Failover Clustering in, 486
hypervisor
  memory reclamation, 504–505
  in virtualization software, 480–481
  by VMware, 478

I

IA-64, 57
IAM (Index Allocation Map), 226
IBM, 471
iexplore (Internet Explorer), 395
IFI (Instant File Initialization), 236–237
impact analysis, 243
implicit transactions, 5
Include Actual Execution Plan, 136
Index Allocation Map (IAM), 226
indexes
    maintenance of, 397–398
    missing, 281, 437–438
    spool operators for, 134
    in tempdb, 215
Indirect Checkpoint, 103
information technology (IT), 245–246, 457–460
init status, 146
initial sizing, 234–237
in-memory targets, 374
input/output (I/O). See I/O (input/output)
Instance Name, 299
instances
    configuration values for, 413–414
    counters on, 507
    cumulative wait types for, 419–420
    diagnostics specific to, 309
    Failover Cluster, 212
    name of, 299
    signal waits for, 420
Instance-specific Diagnostics, 309
Instant File Initialization (IFI), 236–237
Integrated Scripting Environment (ISE), 382
Intel processors
    classic numbering in, 39
    CPU features in, 480
    current numbering in, 40
    evolution of, 33–35
    hyperthreading in, 42–43
    overview of, 35–38
    selecting, generally, 32–33
    Tick-Tock release strategy in, 40–42
intent exclusive (UIX) locks, 170
intent lock modes (IS), (IU), (IX), 168–169

Interesting Events reports, 339
internal Null (NL) latches, 195–197
internal temporary objects, 217
Internet Explorer (iexplore), 395
Internet Small Computer Systems Interface
    (iSCSI), 84, 86
interrogation
    of current server activity, 394–395
    of disk space utilization, 393–394
    of server performance, 393–397
    of warnings/errors, 396
intervals, 275–276
I/O (input/output)
    database-level queries for, 428, 436
    Multipath, 83
    operations per second, 99
    SQLIO for, 106–109
    stall information on, 417–418
    statistics by file for current database on, 428
    storage systems, 78, 82–83, 251
    streaming, 101
    in tempdb, 229–231
    troubleshooting, 251
IOPS (I/O operations per second), 99
IS (intent lock mode), 168–169
iSCSI (Internet Small Computer Systems Interface),
    84, 86
ISE (Integrated Scripting Environment), 382
isolation
    in architecture, 5
    in locks, 151–152, 175
    testing changes in, 256
    Transaction Manager for, 16
    of troubleshooting problems, 249–250
Issue Type, 308
IT (information technology), 245–246,
    457–460
IU (intent lock mode), 168–169
IX (intent lock mode), 168–169

J

JBOD (just a bunch of disks or drives), 79, 98
join operators, 124–127, 132–134
just a bunch of disks or drives (JBOD), 79

K

Keep (KP) latches, 195–197
kernel mode, 56–57, 280
key lookup operators, 134, 135
"knee of the curve," 95
Knowledge Base article 956893, 483
KP (Keep) latches, 195–197

L

large block random access, 102
last statistics update for indexes, 440–441
latch contention
    allocation pages in, 221–229
    example of, 203–209
    indicators of, 185
    introduction to, 220–221
    measuring, 183–184
    multiple data files in, 224–226
    symptoms of, 182–183
    in tempdb, 220–228
    temporary object reuse in, 226–228
    trace flag 1118 in, 228
latches
    clustered key indexes and, 203–205
    compatibility of, 196
    contention of. See latch contention
    definitions of, 186–187
    Destroy, 195–196
    DMVs and, 199–201
    example of, 187–194
    Exclusive, 195–198
    grant order for, 196–197
    internal Null, 195–197
    introduction to, 181–182
    Keep, 195–197
    modes of, 194–198
    monitoring, 199–203
    PerfMon and, 201–202
    queueing, 205–208
    Shared, 195–197
    summary of, 210
    super/sub, 198–199
    susceptible systems and, 185–186
    symptoms of contention in, 182–183
    in tempdb, 208–209
    types of, 194–196
    UP, 208–209
    waits, 197–198
    XEvents and, 202–203
latency, 95–97
Layered Data Format (LDF) files, 152–153
lazy writers, 19
LBNs (logical block numbers), 85
LDF (Layered Data Format) files,
    152–153
least recently used (LRU) policies, 13
licensing, 35–37, 461
lightweight events, 351–352
Linked Server Configuration, 313
Little, John D.C., 95
Little's Law, 95
live data, 372–373
Live Migration, 484–485
local memory, 59
local tempdb, 233–234
local temporary tables, 213–214
Lock Manager, 16
Lock Pages in Memory (LPIM), 72–74
lock resources, 165–167
`lock_acquired` events, 369
locking hints, 124
locks
    atomicity in, 150–152
    bulk update lock mode, 171–172
    concurrency and. See concurrency
    consistency in, 151, 152
    conversion lock modes, 170–171
    database transactions and, 151–153
    deadlocks, 175
    durability in, 151, 152–153
    escalation of, 174–175
    exclusive lock mode, 168
    intent lock modes, 168–169
    introduction to, 149–150, 163
    isolation in, 151, 152
    isolation levels, 175–179
    mode compatibility for, 173–174
    modes of, 167–174

monitoring, 163–165
NOLOCK hint for, 178
read committed isolation level, 177–178
read committed snapshot isolation level, 178–179
read uncommitted isolation level, 178
repeatable read isolation level, 177
resource types, 165–167
schema modification, 168
schema stability, 168
serializable isolation level, 176–177
shared lock mode, 167
snapshot isolation level, 178
summary of, 179
transaction properties and, 150–151
update lock mode, 167
Locks event category, 320–321
Log Manager, 16
Log Parser, 293
log sequence numbers (LSNs), 20
logical block numbers (LBNs), 85
logical CPUs, 23–24
logical operators, 134
logical unit numbers (LUNs), 96, 495–497, 501
login count information
in builds in SQL Server, 421
in health checks for SQL Server, 421
LogMan, 291–292
logs
application, 254
backing up transaction, 416
binary. See binary log (BLG) files
in bulk-logged recovery model, 21–22
in Data Collector Sets, 272
Error, 412
of events, 254, 304–305, 396
formatting in PerfMon, 273
size/space used by, 427–428
in tempdb, 212
template for counter, 286
transactions, 21–22
virtual, 428–430
long-term data collection, 319–320
lookup operators, 134–135
lost updates, 153–155

low impact, 351–352
LPIM (Lock Pages in Memory), 72–74
LRU (least recently used) policies, 13
LSNs (log sequence numbers), 20
LUNs (logical unit numbers), 96, 495–497, 501

M

Machine Name, 299
Machine-wide Diagnostics, 308
manageability
enhancements for, 446
improving efficiency with, 445–446
introduction to, 445
other Microsoft tools for, 460–461
Policy-Based Management for. See Policy-Based Management (PBM)
SCOM for, 464–466
summary of, 466–467
System Center Advisor for, 461–464
management, 245–246
Management Data Warehouse, 255
management packs (MPs), 466
manifest modules, 388
manual statistics updates, 441
MAPS (Microsoft Assessment and Planning), 493
MARS (Multiple Active Result Sets), 217–218, 330
matrix of mode compatibility, 173–174
Max Degree of Parallelism (MaxDoP), 127, 456–457
Max Server Memory (MB)
in builds, 423
RAM and, 70–72
in SQL Server health checks, 413
in virtualization, 501
max worker threads, 23–24
MaxDoP (Max Degree of Parallelism), 127, 456–457
MAXDOP (n), 127
maximum dispatch latency, 360–361
maximum seek times, 99
maximum size, plan caches, 67
maximum supported physical memory, 55
MB (Max Server Memory). See Max Server Memory (MB)

MB (Min Server Memory), 70–72
MDAC (Microsoft Data Access Components), 7
MDF (Media Disk Image) files, 152–153
memory
    for ad-hoc workloads, 74–76
    bottlenecks, 250
    buffer pools, 66
    buffer size, 359–360
    caches, 65
    clerks, 64, 267, 425
    diagnostics for query, 69–70
    introduction to, 53–54
    Lock Pages in, 72–74
    Max Server, 70–72
    maximum supported physical, 55
    Min Server, 70–72
    nodes, 64, 140–143
    NUMA for, 59–62
    physical, 54–55
    plan caches for, 66–67
    pressures, 281
    problems with, 281
    query, 68–70
    Query Wait option and, 69
    sizing page files, 59
    SQL Server configurations for, 70–76
    SQL Server for, generally, 63–70
    summary of, 76
    tempdb and, 216
    utilization of, 492
    virtual, 54, 56–59, 495–501
    workspace, 68–69
Memory Broker Clerks counter, 267
Memory Error custom collector, 314
Memory Grants Outstanding, 424
Memory Grants Pending, 425
Memory Node counter, 267
Memory PerfMon counters, 282
merge joins/operators, 133
metadata, 452
Microsoft
    CodePlex by, 325
    cumulative updates by, 408–409
    Customer Service and Support by, 247, 461

    Data Link (.udl) files by, 421
    Hyper-V by. *See* Hyper-V
    manageability tools by, 460–461
    MSSSQL by. *See* MSSSQL (Microsoft SQL)
    PowerShell by. *See* PowerShell (PS)
    Windows Azure by, 473
    XEvents by, 351
Microsoft Assessment and Planning (MAPS), 493
Microsoft Data Access Components (MDAC), 7
Microsoft Management Console (MMC), 260, 277
Min Server Memory (MB), 70–72
missing
    counters, 277, 278
    indexes, 437–439
MLC (multi-layer) flash memory, 104–105
MMC (Microsoft Management Console), 260, 277
modes
    application, 280
    evaluation, 448
    kernel, 56–57, 280
    of latches, 194–198
    of locks, 167–174
    snapshot, 298–299
    user, 56–57, 280
modules, 388–389
monitoring
    for page splits, 367–369
    performance. *See* Performance Monitor
    server logins, 366–367
    virtual database servers, 502–507
monitors in SCOM, 465
MPAs (Multi-Page Allocations), 63
mpio.sys (Multipath System driver), 83
MPs (management packs), 466
MSINFO custom collector, 311
MSSSQL (Microsoft SQL)
    Buffer Manager counter, 282
    General Statistics counter, 284
    Locks counter, 284
    SERVER, 305
    SQL Statistics counter, 284
    Transactions counter, 284

multi-layer (MLC) flash memory, 104–105
Multi-Page Allocations (MPAs), 63
Multipath I/O (Input/Output), 83
Multipath System driver (mpio.sys), 83
Multiple Active Result Sets (MARS), 217–218, 330
multiple data files, 224–226, 237
multiple event loss, 360
_MyCollectors custom collector, 316–317

N

Named Pipes, 7
names
    of policies, 451
    resolution of, 112, 209
    of XEvents, 353
NAND-based flash storage, 104–105
nest loop joins, 132–134
.NET Framework, 380, 383, 388
NetMon, 254
network interface cards (NICs), 252
network load balancing (NLB), 248
networks
    balancing loads in, 248
    bottlenecks in, 252
    of servers, 7, 14
    SMB, 85–86
    of storage areas. See SANs (storage area networks)
    stretch VLAN, 94
    utilization of, 493
    of virtual database servers, 499
New Session creation forms, 363–366
Nexus
    aggregated data analysis in, 331–337
    Blocking/Wait Statistics reports in, 346–347
    Bottleneck Analysis reports in, 346–347
    command prompts for, 342
    comparative analysis reports in, 340
    custom reports for, 342
    customization of, 340–345
    data analysis in, 255

    databases in, 328–331
    defined, 296
    introduction to, 325–326
    loading data into, 328
    OSTRESS in, 344–345
    prerequisites for, 326–328
    queries in, 344
    ReadTrace.exe in, 341–342, 347–348
    Reporter.exe in, 340, 346
    RML Utilities reports in, 337–340
    SQL Trace file errors in, 346
    summary of, 348
    tables in, 342–343
    troubleshooting, 346–348
NICs (network interface cards), 252
NL (internal Null) latches, 195–197
NLB (network load balancing), 248
no event loss, 360
nodes
    cluster, 412–413
    CPU, 143–144
    memory, 64, 140–143, 267
    in NUMA, 59–60
    scheduler, 144
NOLOCK hints, 178
Non-BUF latches, 194
nonclustered indexes, 436–437
nonpre-emptive scheduling, 146
non-repeatable reads, 156–158
Non-Uniform Memory Architecture (NUMA). See NUMA (Non-Uniform Memory Architecture)
normalization, 112
NTFS Master File Table, 88
NUMA (Non-Uniform Memory Architecture)
    CPU configuration for, 61–62
    introduction to, 59–60
    soft, 142–143
    SQLOS and, 140–143
    use of, 60–61
numbers
    in AMD Operton processors, 43–45
    in Intel processors, 39–40
    in PerfMon names, 278

O

object naming conventions, 458–459
object plan guides, 129
OLAP (online analytical processing),
    30–32
OLE DB (Object Linking and Embedding
    Database), 11–12, 321
OLTP (online transaction processing)
    databases in, 48–50
    file layout in, 101
    hardware and, 31–32
    Intel processors for, 37
    introduction to, 30
    TPC-E benchmarks for, 48–50
    workloads in, 31–32
online analytical processing (OLAP), 30–32
online index operations, 217–218
online migration, 484–486
online transaction processing (OLTP). See OLTP
    (online transaction processing)
operating systems
    32-bit. See 32-bit operating systems
    64-bit. See 64-bit operating systems
    builds in, 412, 423
    health checks for, 412, 423
    information on, 407, 409
    SQLOS. See SQLOS (SQL Server Operating
        System)
    in virtual database servers, 500
operators
    bookmark lookup, 135
    comparison, 385
    equality, 385–386
    hash, 133
    for indexes, 134
    join, 124–127, 132–134
    key lookup, 134, 135
    logical, 134
    lookup, 134–135
    merge, 133
    for query plans, 132–135
    RID lookup, 134–135
    row count spool, 134
    scan, 134–135
    seek, 134–135
    spool, 134
    table spool, 134
    window spool, 134
Opteron processors
    Core Factor Table for, 45–46
    hardware in, 43–46
    numbering in, 43–45
    selection of, 32–33, 35–37
OPTIMIZE FOR, 127–128
Optimize for Ad-hoc Workloads, 74–76
Optimizer. See Query Optimizer
optimizing PerfMon, 278
orphaned PerfMon files, 303
OSTRESS, 223, 344–345
output. See I/O (input/output)

P

P2V (physical-to-virtual) migrations, 493
packages, 355
Page Free Space (PFS), 208–209, 221
Page Life Expectancy (PLE), 72, 424, 492
page table entries (PTEs), 58
PAGEIOLATCH wait types, 13
PAGELATCH_ latches, 194–195
paging, 58
Paging File counter, 282
pair matching, 362
PAL (Performance Analysis of Logs),
    285–288
parallel plans, 114–115
parameter lists, 300–303
parameterization, 117–118
parsing, 112
partially contained databases, 446
Partition Manager driver (partmgr.sys), 83
PBM (Policy-Based Management). See
    Policy-Based Management (PBM)
PCIe (Peripheral Component Interconnect
    Express), 32–33, 105
peak workload periods, 493
Perf Stats, 311–312, 332–334
PerfMon. See Performance Monitor
PerfmonCollector, 299

performance
    baselines for, 285
    bottlenecks in, 250–252
    monitoring. *See* Performance Monitor
    of storage systems, 95–96, 106–109
    troubleshooting issues with, 249
    tuning with PowerShell, 397–404
Performance Analysis of Logs (PAL), 285–288
Performance Event, 321–322
Performance Monitor
    on 64-bit systems, 277
    application mode in, 280
    auto-scaling counters in, 262
    baselines in, 285
    BLG files in. *See* binary log (BLG) files
    bottlenecks and, 278–279
    buffer pools and, 66
    configuration-based bottlenecks in, 279
    counters in, 263–268, 279–284,
      506–507
    CPU problems in, 280–281
    data analysis in, 255
    Data Collector Sets in, 262, 270–274
    Diag Manager and, 308
    disk performance in, 276, 283
    extracting counters in, 291
    file formats in, 291
    hard page faults in, 58
    Hypervisor memory in, 504–505
    introduction to, 254, 259–260
    kernel mode in, 280
    latches and, 201–202
    log analysis in, other tools for, 289–293
    log analysis in, PAL for, 285–288
    Log Parser and, 293
    LogMan and, 291–292
    memory-related problems in, 281
    missing counters in, 277–278
    numbers for names in, 278
    optimization of, 278
    prescriptive guidance for, 279–284
    problems in, 276–278
    Profiler traces and, 289–290
    real-time server activity in, 268–269
    Reliability Monitor in, 260–263
    Relog and, 290–291
    remote monitoring fails in, 277
    Resource Overview screen in, 261–262
    running, 274–276
    sample intervals in, 275–276
    schema-based bottlenecks in, 279
    server performance in, 276
    show/hide counters in, 262–263
    spinlocks and, 201–202
    SQL Server in, 283–284, 289
    starting with, 268
    storage-related problems in, 283
    summary of, 293
    time windows in, 291
    virtual address space in, 282
    virtual database servers and, 503–507
    wait stats analysis in, 284–285
    in Windows, 96, 262
    in Windows on Windows, 277
Peripheral Component Interconnect Express
    (PCIe), 32–33, 105
PFS (Page Free Space), 208–209, 221
phantom reads, 158–160
physical functions
    database servers, 494–495
    disk counters, 283
    memory, 54–55
physical-to-virtual (P2V) migrations, 493
pipelines, 380, 383
plan caches
    database-level queries for, 438–439
    introduction to, 9
    for memory, 66–67
    memory and, 74
    parameterization of, 118–119
    in Query Optimizer, 117–123
plan_handle, 115
plans
    Balanced Windows Power, 410–411
    caches of. *See* plan caches
    for capacity, 493
    communication, 243
    efficient vs. best, 10
    execution, 8–9
    guides for, 123

plans *(continued)*
    High Performance Power, 411
    introduction to, 9–11
    object, 129
    parallel, 114–115
    for queries. *See* query plans
    quick, 10
    recompilation of, 123
    for risk mitigation, 94–95
    for SQL, 129
    for templates, 129
    trivial, 10
    USE, 128
    XML, 128
platforms for virtualization, 472–473
PLE (Page Life Expectancy), 72, 424, 492
Policy-Based Management (PBM)
    auto-grow increments in, 452–455
    automating best practice checks with, 452–457
    Central Management Server in, 450–451
    check last backup with, 452
    clustered indexes in, 459–460
    conditions as server restrictions in, 450
    data analysis in, 255
    enterprise policy evaluation in, 450–451, 460
    introduction to, 447–448
    IT standards in, 457–460
    MaxDoP in, 456–457
    object naming conventions in, 458–459
    starting with, 448–449
Port driver (storport.sys), 83
possible bad nonclustered indexes, 436–437
PowerEdge servers, 33–35
PowerGUI, 382
PowerShell (PS)
    advanced functions in, 386–387
    backup disk space in, 398
    Backup-SqlDatabase in, 392
    binary modules in, 388
    Cmdlets in, 383–384
    current server activity in, 394–395
    DDL extraction in, 398–403
    disk space utilization in, 393–394
    dynamic modules in, 388
    environment of, 381–383
    index maintenance in, 397–398
    Integrated Scripting Environment in, 382
    interrogating server issues in, 393–397
    introduction to, 379–380
    manifest modules in, 388
    modules in, 388–389
    performance tuning with, generally, 397
    remote work in, 390
    Restore-sqldatabase in, 392
    scheduling script execution in, 403–404
    script modules in, 388
    server issue investigation with, 393–397
    server performance in, 396–397
    signing scripts in, 389
    SQL Server 2012 and, 389–392
    starting with, generally, 380–381
    summary of, 404
    variables in, 384–386
    warnings/errors in, 396
PowerShell Community Extensions (PSCX), 382
predicate sources, 358
pre-emptive schedulers, 25, 146
prejudice, 244
pre-optimization stage, 10
Primate Labs, 50
private clouds, 473
probe phase, 133
procedure caches, 66
processors
    afffinity with, 143–144
    AMD Operton, 43–46
    descriptions of, 410–411
    health checks for, 410–411
    by Intel, 35–43
    selecting, generally, 35
products for virtualization, 477–480
Professional SQL Server 2008 Internals and Troubleshooting, 54, 57
Profiler
    _MyCollectors custom collector in, 316–317
    Analysis Custom Collectors in, 313
    custom diagnostics in, 310–312

data analysis in, 255
feature-specific diagnostics in, 313–314
introduction to, 254, 310
in PerfMon, 289–290
saving/using configurations in, 317–318
SQL 2008 Backup MDW in, 312
SQL 2008 Perf Stats in, 311–312
trace files in, 319
trace filters in, 310–318
XEvents data collection in, 315–316
Profiler Into Events (SQL PIE), 351
ProfilerCollector, 300
proportional fill algorithms, 224
protocol layers, 8, 15
PS (PowerShell). *See* PowerShell (PS)
PSCX (PowerShell Community Extensions), 382
PSSDiag, 254
Pssdiag/Sqldiag Manager, 305–306
PTEs (page table entries), 58
public clouds, 473

Q

QFE (Quick Fix Engineering), 462
quantums, 25
queries
hints in. *See* query hints
life cycles of, 5–7
memory in, 68–70
optimization of. *See* Query Optimizer
plans for. *See* query plans
processing. *See* query processing
for ring buffers with T-SQL, 374–376
in SQL Nexus, 344
Query Executor, 11–12, 15
Query Hash reports, 336
query hints
FAST <number_rows>, 124
introduction to, 123–124
JOIN, 124–127
MAXDOP (*n*), 127
OPTIMIZE FOR, 127–128
in Query Optimizer, 123–128
RECOMPILE, 128

USE PLAN, 128
for XML plans, 128
Query Notifications, 321
Query Optimizer
algebrizer trees in, 115
auto_create_statistics in, 117
auto_update_statistics in, 117
compilation of plans in, 123
influencing, 123–129
introduction to, 113–114
parallel plans in, 114–115
parameterization in, 117–118
plan caches in, generally, 117–123
plan caches, looking into, 119–123
plan caches, parameterization in, 118–119
plan_handle in, 115
plans in. *See* query plans
query hints in, 123–128
recompilation of plans in, 118–119, 123
in SQL Server architecture, 9–11, 14
sql_handle in, 115
statistics in, 116–117
query plans
execution of, 140–147
hash operators for, 133
hash warnings and, 133–134
introduction to, 129–132
join operators for, 132–134
lookup operators for, 134–135
merge operators for, 133
nested loop join operators for, 132–134
reading, 135–140
scan operators for, 134–135
seek operators for, 134–135
spool operators for, 134
query processing
affinity masks in, 143–144
algebrizing, 112
CPU nodes in, 143–144
executing plans for, 140–147
introduction to, 111–112
memory nodes in, 140–143
optimization of. *See* Query Optimizer
parsing, 112

query processing *(continued)*
    plans in. *See* query plans
    processor affinity in, 143–144
    query hints in, 123–128
    scheduler nodes in, 144
    scheduling, 146–147
    soft NUMA in, 142–143
    SQLOS in, 140–147
    summary of, 147
    tasks in, 145
    threads in, 145–146
    workers in, 145
Query Wait option, 69
queueing, 205–208
Quick Fix Engineering (QFE), 462
quick plans, 10
quiet server workloads, 491

R

RAID (redundant array of independent disks)
    configuration of, 46–47
    disk drive latency in, 99–100
    disk mirroring and, 81–82
    disk striping and, 79–80, 82
    overhead, 100
RAM (random access memory)
    Max Server Memory for, 70–72
    NUMA configurations and, 62
    physical memory as, 54–55
    in server selection, 32–35, 38
    sizing page files and, 59
    virtual memory and, 56–58
randomness of problems, 244
range locks, 176
RANU (RunAs User), 309
Rapid Virtualization Indexing (RVI), 480
RDBMSs (relational database management
    servers), 30
read committed isolation level, 177–178
read committed snapshot isolation, 178–179, 217
read uncommitted isolation level, 178
reading query plans, 135–140
ReadTrace.exe

introduction to, 326
Nexus and, 328–331
OSTRESS and, 344
RML utilities and, 341–342
SQL Trace and, 337, 341
troubleshooting, 347–348
Unique Statements link in, 347
real-time server activity, 268–269, 332
recompilation
    excessive, 281
    query hints for, 128
    in Query Optimizer, 118–119, 123
recovery
    bulk-logged, 21–22
    checkpoint process in, 19–21
    dirty pages in, 17–19
    full, 21
    intervals in, 21
    introduction to, 18
    lazy writers in, 19
    point objectives for. *See* recovery point
        objectives (RPOs)
    simple model for, 22
    in SQL Server architecture, 18–22
    time objectives for. *See* recovery time
        objectives (RTOs)
recovery point objectives (RPOs)
    introduction to, 47–48
    for risk mitigation, 95
    in SLAs, 246
    transaction log backups for, 429
recovery time objectives (RTOs)
    introduction to, 46–48
    for risk mitigation, 95
    in SLAs, 246
    transaction log backups for, 429
redundant array of independent disks. *See* RAID
    (redundant array of independent disks)
relational database management servers
    (RDBMSs), 30
Relational Engine. *See also* query processing, 6, 15
relational reporting workloads, 31–32
relaxed co-scheduling, 481, 498
release to manufacturing (RTM) builds, 408

Reliability and Performance Monitor. *See also*
Performance Monitor
auto-scaling counters in, 262
Data Collector Sets in, 262
introduction to, 260
Reliability Monitor in, 262
Resource Overview screen in, 261–262
show/hide counters in, 262–263
in Windows Server 2008, 262
Reliability Monitor, 262
Relog
as executable, 273
log analysis in, 290–291
in Nexus, 326
remote functions
data replication, 92–93
memory, 60
monitoring fails, 277
in PowerShell, 390
running PerfMon, 274
repeatable read isolation level, 177
Reporter.exe, 340, 346
reports
blocking, 332
Blocking and Wait Statistics, 334–336,
346–347
Bottleneck Analysis, 332–333, 346–347
comparative analysis, 340
Interesting Events reports, 339
Nexus custom, 342
Query Hash, 336
relational, 31–32
RML Utilities, 337–340
Spinlock Stats, 336–337
SQL Server Reporting Services for, 30
in System Center Advisor, 462–464
System Performance, 270
resource allocation, 243
Resource Monitor, 281
Resource Overview screen, 261–262
Restore-sqldatabase, 392
results to text, 130
return on investment (ROI), 447
RIDs (row identifiers), 134–135, 217

ring buffers, 361
risk mitigation planning, 94–95
RML Utilities
comparative analysis reports in, 340
customization of, generally, 340–341
default locations in, 330–331
introduction to, 223, 326
OSTRESS and, 344–345
ReadTrace.exe in, 340–342
reports in, 337–340
.RML files in, 344
troubleshooting, 346–348
RMS (Root Management Server), 464–465
roadmap, 351
ROI (return on investment), 447
roll forward/roll back transactions, 20
ROLLBACK TRANSACTION, 5
Root Management Server (RMS), 464–465
rotational latency, 99
row count spool operators, 134
row counts, 440
row identifiers (RIDs), 134–135, 217
row versioning, 217
Rowset Importer
introduction to, 326
Nexus and, 328–329
tables in, 342–343
RPOs (recovery point objectives). *See* recovery
point objectives (RPOs)
RTM (release to manufacturing) builds, 408
RTOs (recovery time objectives). *See* recovery time
objectives (RTOs)
rules in SCOM, 465
RunAs User (RANU), 309
runnable status, 147
runnable threads, 23
running status, 147
running threads, 23
runtime details, 322
RVI (Rapid Virtualization Indexing), 480

S

S (shared lock mode), 167

SA (Software Assurance), 461
SANs (storage area networks)
    benefits of, 83–84
    data replication in, 89–92
    defined, 79
    host servers and, 480
    LUNs in, 501
    online migration and, 484
    shared array controllers in, 86–87
    storage tiering in, 88–89
    in tempdb, 229
    virtualization and, 472, 494–497
SAS (Serial Attached SCSI), 97–98
SATA (Serial Advanced Technology Attachment), 97–98, 102
saturated host bus adapters, 501
saved data, 373–374
SCA (System Center Advisor). *See* System Center Advisor (SCA)
scan operators, 134–135
Scans event category, 321
scheduling
    architecture and, 24–25
    nodes for, 144
    script execution, 403–404
    in SQLOS, 146–147
schema modification (Sch-M), 168, 215–217
schema stability (Sch-S), 168
schema-based bottlenecks, 279
Sch-M (schema modification), 168, 215–217
Sch-S (schema stability), 168
SCOM (System Center Operations Manager). *See* System Center Operations Manager (SCOM)
script execution, 403–404
script modules, 388
second-level address translation (SLAT), 480
Security Audit event category, 321
seek operators, 134–135
SELECT queries
    Access Methods for, 12
    Buffer Manager for, 12–13
    Command Parser for, 8–9
    data caches of, 12–14

introduction to, 5–7
life cycle of, 14–15
protocol layer and, 8
Query Executor for, 11–12
Query Optimizer for, 10–11
Server Network Interface for, 7
in SQL Server architecture, 7–15
TDS endpoints in, 8
sequential disk access, 100–101
Serial Advanced Technology Attachment (SATA), 97–98, 102
Serial Attached SCSI (SAS), 97–98
serializable isolation level, 176–177
Server Message Block (SMB), 85–86
Server Network Interface (SNI), 7, 14
servers
    Dell PowerEdge, 33–35
    evolution of, 33–35
    four-socket, 33–38, 49–50
    guest servers, 482–483
    host servers, 480
    investigating issues with, 393–397
    manufacturers of, 410
    models of, 32–33, 410
    performance of, 276, 396–397
    queues of, 101
    real-time activity of, 332
    relational database management, 30
    SQL Server. *See* SQL Server 2012
    two-socket, 33–38, 42, 49–50
    virtual database. *See* virtual database servers
    virtualization of, 469–470
    workloads of, 491–492
service, SQLdiag as, 303–305
Service Processor ID (SPID), 330, 341
Service Provider License Agreements (SPLAs), 461
service-level agreements (SLAs), 84, 246
sessions
    creating with T-SQL, 370–371
    in execution models, 22–23
    session_id, 22
    space usage and, 232
    in tempdb, 216
    in XEvents, 354–355, 363–366, 370–371

SGAM (Shared Global Allocation Map), 221, 228–229

Shared (SH) latches, 195–197

shared array controllers, 86

Shared Global Allocation Map (SGAM), 221, 228–229

shared lock mode (S), 167

shared memory, 7

shared with intent exclusive (SIX) locks, 170–171

shared with intent update (SIU) locks, 170

short circuiting, 358

show/hide counters, 262–263

signal waits for instances, 420

signing scripts, 389

simple parameterization, 118

simple recovery model, 22

single (SLC) flash memory, 104–105

single event loss, 360

single-use ad-hoc queries, 426

"sit and wait" approach, 350

SIU (shared with intent update) locks, 170

SIX (conversion lock mode), 170–171

sizing, 59, 492–493

SLAs (service-level agreements), 84, 246

SLAT (second-level address translation), 480

SLC (single) flash memory, 104–105

SLEEP_BPOOL_FLUSH, 21

SMB (Server Message Block), 85–86

SMP (symmetric multiprocessing), 59

SNAC (SQL Server Native Client), 7

snapshots
    introduction to, 91
    isolation in version stores, 217–220
    isolation level in locks, 178–179
    mode in SQLdiag, 298–299
    in virtualization, 483

SNI (Server Network Interface), 7, 14

soft NUMA. See also NUMA (Non-Uniform Memory Architecture), 142–143

soft page faults, 57

Software Assurance (SA), 461

solutions, testing/implementing, 244

sort warnings, 70

Space and Latching custom collector, 314

space issues, 231–232

SPID (Service Processor ID), 330, 341

Spinlock Stats reports, 336–337

spinlocks
    contention in, 184–185, 209
    definitions of, 186–187
    DMVs and, 199–201
    introduction to, 181–182
    monitoring, 199–203
    in name resolution, 209
    PerfMon and, 201–202
    summary of, 210
    susceptible systems and, 185–186
    symptoms of, 182–183
    XEvents and, 202–203

SPLAs (Service Provider License Agreements), 461

spool operators, 134

SQL Agent, 314, 462–466

SQL Base custom collector, 311

SQL Batches, 264–265

SQL Best Practices custom collector, 311

SQL Blocking custom collector, 314

SQL diagnostics. See SQLdiag

SQL Dumps custom collector, 312

SQL for PowerShell (SQLPS), 389, 391

SQL Input/Output (SQLIO), 106–109

SQL Memory Error custom collector, 314

SQL Nexus. See Nexus

SQL PIE (Profiler Into Events), 351

SQL plan guides, 129

SQL Profiler. See Profiler

SQL Server 2005, 312, 314

SQL Server 2008, 311–312

SQL Server 2012
    analyzing PerfMon logs with, 289
    bottlenecks in, 278–279
    configuring NUMA in, 61–62
    Core Factor Table in, 45–46
    Data Tools in, 256
    Enterprise Edition of, 35–37
    Error Log information in, 412
    Fast Track Data Warehouse in, 100
    health checks for. See health checks for SQL Server

SQL Server 2012 *(continued)*
    issues in, 249
    memory dump information in, 415
    memory information in, 423–424
    memory management in, 63–70
    Native Client in, 7
    new features in, 391–392
    operating system for. *See* SQLOS (SQL Server Operating System)
    PerfMon counters in, 284
    performance in, 283–284, 397–404
    Query Optimizer in. *See* Query Optimizer
    Registry information in, 414
    Services information in, 411
    using NUMA, 60–61
    virtual memory and, 500–501
    virtualization and, 476
    wait stats in, 284–285
    Wait Type Repository in, 420
SQL Server Analysis Services (SSAS), 30
SQL Server Integration Services (SSIS), 30
SQL Server Management Studio (SSMS)
    health checks in, 406
    introduction to, 129–130, 135
    query plans in, 139
    in System Performance reports, 270
    in XEvents, 359, 370–374
SQL Server Native Client (SNAC), 7
SQL Server Operating System (SQLOS). *See* SQLOS (SQL Server Operating System)
SQL Server Reporting Services (SSRS), 30
SQL Trace. *See* Trace
sql_handle, 115
SQLASCMDLETS, 389
SQLdiag
    alert-driven data collection with, 322
    Analysis Custom Collectors in, 313
    Backup MDW in, 312
    as command-line application, 299–303
    configuration file key elements in, 299–300
    Configuration Manager in, 305–307
    custom diagnostics in, 310–312
    Diag Manager in, 307–309
    on failover clusters, 305

    feature-specific diagnostics in, 313–314
    introduction to, 254, 297–298
    _MyCollectors custom collector in, 316–317
    parameter list in, 300–303
    Perf Stats in, 311–312
    Profiler trace filters in, 310–318
    saving/using configurations in, 317–318
    as service, 303–305
    snapshot mode in, 298–299
    SqldiagCollector, 300
    summary of, 323
    XEvents data collection in, 315–316
SQLIO (SQL Input/Output), 106–109
SQLOS (SQL Server Operating System)
    affinity masks in, 143–144
    architecture in, 22–26
    CPU nodes in, 143–144
    execution model in, 22–26
    introduction to, 140
    memory nodes in, 140–143
    memory pressures in, 281
    processor affinity in, 143–144
    scheduler nodes in, 144
    scheduling in, 146–147
    soft NUMA in, 142–143
    tasks in, 145
    threads in, 145–146
    workers in, 145
SQLPS (SQL for PowerShell), 389, 391
SSAS (SQL Server Analysis Services), 30
SSIS (SQL Server Integration Services), 30
SSMS (SQL Server Management Studio). *See* SQL Server Management Studio (SSMS)
SSRS (SQL Server Reporting Services), 30
stakeholders, 245–246
statistics
    Blocking and Wait, 334–336, 346–347
    last updates for indexes, 440–441
    manual updates, 441
    missing/outdated, 281
    Perf Stats, 311–312, 332–334
    in Query Optimizer, 116–117
    Spinlock, 336–337
    STATISTICS PROFILE, 131

in tempdb, 214–215
wait, 284–285
storage area networks (SANs). *See* SANs (storage area networks)
Storage Engines, 6, 15
storage systems
    AlwaysOn Availability Groups in, 94
    asynchronous data replication, 92–93
    block-based, 85–86
    capacity optimization for, 86–88
    counters for, 96–97
    data replication in, 89–91, 92–93
    disk drive latency in, 98–100
    disk drive performance in, 97–100
    file-based, 85–86
    hardware and, 30–35
    introduction to, 77–78
    I/O in, 78, 82–83, 251
    network selection for, 84–86
    PerfMon troubleshooting, 283
    performance of, 95–96, 106–109
    risk mitigation planning for, 94–95
    sequential disk access for, 100–101
    server queues in, 101
    shared array controllers in, 86
    summary of, 110
    synchronous data replication, 92
    technology for, generally, 78–82
    tiering in, 88–89
    utilization of, 493
    in virtual database servers, 496–497
    Windows Failover Clustering in, 93–94
    Windows I/O subsystems, 82–83
storport.sys (Port driver), 83
stretch virtual local area network (VLAN), 94
striped RAID, 79–80
sublatches, 198–199
success criteria, 245
superlatches, 198–199
susceptible systems, 185–186
suspended status, 147
suspended threads, 23
switching to user databases, 426–427
symmetric multiprocessing (SMP), 59

synchronous data replication, 92–94
`sys.dm_db_fi le_space_usage`, 231
`sys.dm_db_session_space_usage`, 232
`sys.dm_db_task_space_usage`, 231
`sys.dm_exec_` DMVs, 26
`sys.dm_os_` DMVs, 25–26
`sys.dm_tran_locks`, 163–165
System Center Advisor (SCA)
    for manageability, generally, 461–462
    reporting in, 462–464
    topology in, 462
System Center Operations Manager (SCOM)
    alerts in, 465–466
    design/implementation of, 464–465
    management packs in, 466
    monitors in, 465
    overview of, 464
    rules in, 465
System Center Virtual Machine Manager (VMM), 479
System Performance reports, 270
System Stability Index, 262

T

table variables. *See also* tables
    creation of, 216
    indexes in, 215
    schema modifications in, 215–217
    statistics in, 214–215
    temp tables vs., generally, 214
tables
    Core Factor Table, 45–46
    global temporary tables, 213
    hints in, 124
    local temporary tables, 213–214
    names of, 440
    NTFS Master File Table, 88
    PTEs in, 58
    spool operators for, 134
    in SQL Nexus, 342–343
    temporary, 214–217
    variables of. *See* table variables
Tabular Data Stream (TDS) endpoints, 8

targets, 230, 353, 359–362
Taylor, Bob "The Tool Man," 351
TCO (total cost of ownership), 461
TCP Chimney, 252
TCP Listener, 414
TCP/IP, 7–8, 14
TDS (Tabular Data Stream) endpoints, 8
teams for troubleshooting, 243
TechNet magazine, 389
tempdb
    allocation pages in, 221–229
    append-only version stores in, 218–220
    auto-growth in, 234–237
    configuration of, 232–237
    contention in, 221–229
    file placement in, 232–234
    GAM page stores in, 221
    indexes in, 215
    initial sizing in, 234–237
    internal temporary objects in, 217
    introduction to, 211–212
    I/O performance in, 229–231
    latches in, 208–209, 220–228
    logging operations in, 212
    memory and, 216
    multiple data files in, 224–226, 237
    overhead of version stores in, 217–218
    PFS stores in, 221
    recovery of, 212
    schema modifications in, 215–217
    SGAM page stores in, 221
    space issues in, 231–232
    statistics in, 214–215
    table variables in, 214–217
    temp tables in, 214–217
    temporary object reuse in, 226–228
    trace flag 1118 in, 228
    troubleshooting, generally, 220
    use of, generally, 212
    user temporary objects in, 213–217
    version stores in, 217–220
templates, 129, 364
temporary (temp) tables
    indexes in, 215
    memory and, 216
    schema modifications in, 215–217
    statistics in, 214–215
    table variables vs., generally, 214
temporary object reuse, 226–228
testing changes in isolation, 256
theoretical memory limits, 56
thin provisioning, 87, 497
THREADPOOL wait type, 24
threads, 145–146
Threshold File, 286–287
Tick-Tock release strategy, 40–42
tiering, 88–89
time windows, 291
top cumulative wait types, 419–420
top statements by average I/O, 436
topology in SCA, 462
total buffer usage, 418
total cost of ownership (TCO), 461
Total Server Memory, 71
TPC Benchmark E (TPC-E), 38, 43, 45–46
Trace
    defined, 326
    in Nexus, 344, 346
    ReadTrace.exe and, 337, 341
    saving files in, 319
    Spinlock Stats and, 336–337
    *.trc files in, 329
    troubleshooting, generally, 346
trace flags
    1117, 237
    1118, 228
    introduction to, 20
Transaction Manager, 16–17
transaction sequence numbers (XSNs), 217–219
transactions
    ACID properties of, 4–5
    explicit, 5
    implicit, 5
    log size/space used for, 427–428
    logging, generally, 21–22
    processing of, 10
    properties of, 150–151
Transactions event category, 321

triggers, 217–218
trivial plans, 10
troubleshooting
    approach to, 242–247
    behaviors/attitudes in, 245
    CPU problems, 250–251
    data analysis in, 255–256
    data collection in, 252–255
    data gathering in, 253–254
    defining problems in, 248–252
    external help in, 247
    focused data collection in, 253
    identifying problems in, 248–249
    implementing solutions in, 256–257
    introduction to, 241–242
    isolating problems in, 249–250
    iterative approach to, 278
    memory bottlenecks, 250
    network bottlenecks, 252
    Nexus, 346–348
    with PerfMon. *See* Performance Monitor
    performance bottlenecks, 250–252
    with PowerShell. *See* PowerShell (PS)
    service-level agreements in, 246
    space issues, 231–232
    stakeholders in, 245–246
    steps to successful, 242–244
    storage I/O bottlenecks, 251
    success criteria in, 245
    summary of, 257
    in tempdb, 220
    testing changes in isolation in, 256
    validating solutions in, 256
    virtualization issues, 501
T-SQL
    for checkpoints, 20
    in custom collectors, 314
    for explicit transactions, 5
    language events, 8–9
    in Nexus, 344
    in query processing. *See* query processing
    viewing with Profiler, 289–290
    for XEvents sessions, 354–355
tuning performance, 397–404

two-socket servers
    evolution of, 33–35
    selection of, 36–38
    Tick-Tock release history for, 42
    TPC-E benchmarks for, 49–50
type derivation, 112

U

U (update lock mode), 167
.udl (Data Link) files, 421
UIX (intent exclusive) locks, 170
UMS (User Mode Scheduler), 25
unacceptable thresholds, 230
uniform extents, 228
University of Cambridge, 479
UP latches, 208–209
update lock mode (U), 167
UPDATE queries
    Buffer Manager in, 17–18
    introduction to, 15–16
    in SQL Server architecture, 15–18
    Transaction Manager in, 16–17
USE PLAN, 128
usecounts, 74
user dumps, 254
user mode, 56–57, 280
User Mode Scheduler (UMS), 25
user temporary objects
    indexes in, 215
    internal temporary objects, 217
    introduction to, 213–214
    memory and, 216
    schema modifications in, 215–217
    statistics in, 214–215
    temp tables vs. table variables in, 214–217
    in tempdb, 213–217
user-defined Data Collector Sets, 271

V

validating solutions, 256
Van Der Valk, Henk, 101
variables, in PowerShell, 384–386

variables, table. *See* table variables
VAS (virtual address space), 56, 282
vCPUs (virtual CPUs), 497–501
VDI (Virtual Backup Device Interface), 89–90
version stores
    append-only, 218–220
    GAM page stores in, 221
    introduction to, 217
    overhead of, 217–218
    PFS page stores in, 221
    SGAM page stores in, 221
    in tempdb, 217–220
VIA (Virtual Interface Adapter), 7
VIEW SERVER STATE permissions, 407
View Target Data, 374
viewing data captured, 371–376
virtual address space (VAS), 56–58, 282
Virtual Backup Device Interface (VDI), 89–90
virtual CPUs (vCPUs), 497–501
virtual database servers. *See also* virtualization
    architecting, generally, 494
    counters for, 506–507
    CPUs in, 497–499
    design of, 495–501
    high availability in, 499–500
    Hypervisor in, 504–505
    memory in, generally, 495–496
    monitoring, 502–507
    networking in, 499
    operating system enhancements in, 500
    PerfMon and, 503–507
    physical database servers vs., 494–495
    SQL Server memory in, 500–501
    storage in, 496–497
Virtual Interface Adapter (VIA), 7
virtual local area networks (VLANs), 94, 472
Virtual Log File (VLF) count, 428–430
virtual machines (VMs), 250, 482
virtual memory, 54, 56–59
Virtual Memory Manager (VMM), 57–58
virtual servers. *See also* virtual database servers, 482–483
virtualization
    bad contention in, 489–490
    benefits of, 473–476

breadth of, 472
business benefits of, 474
cloud computing, 473
concepts in, 480–483
contention management in, 488–491
of database servers. *See* virtual database servers
encapsulation in, 475
extended features of, generally, 483
good contention in, 488–489
guest clustering in, 487
guest servers in, 482–483
hardware support for, 479–480
high-availability features, deploying SQL Server with, 487–488
high-availability features in, 483–488
highly available virtual servers, 486–487
history of, 471
host clustering in, 487
host servers in, 480
Hyper-V for, 478–479
Hypervisor in, 480–481
identifying candidates for, 491–493
introduction to, 469
limitations of, 477
non-performance requirements for, 493
online migration in, 484–486
overview of, 470–473
platform, 472–473
private clouds, 473
products for, 477–480
public clouds, 473
server workload and, 491–492
of servers, 469–470
sizing data and, 492–493
snapshotting in, 483
SQL Server 2012 and, 476
technical benefits of, 474–475
virtual servers in, 482–483
VMware for, 477–478
weighting in, 490–491
Xen for, 479
Virtualization Concepts, 475
Visual Studio extension (VSX), 382
VLANs (virtual local area networks), 94, 472

VLF (Virtual Log File) count, 428–430
VMM (System Center Virtual Machine Manager), 479
VMM (Virtual Memory Manager), 57–58
vMotion, 484
VMs (virtual machines), 250, 482
VMware
    contention and, 488–489
    CPU utilization in, 502
    high-availability features in, 486
    introduction to, 471, 477
    memory in, 490, 495–496, 500
    PerfMon counters in, 506
    relaxed co-scheduling in, 481
    vCPUs in, 498–499
    for virtualization, 477–478
    VMFS file system in, 484
Volume Manager driver (ftdisk.sys), 83
vSphere, 478, 486
VSX (Visual Studio extension), 382

W

wait types. *See also* waits
    cumulative, 419–420
    for instances, 419–420
    PAGEIOLATCH, 13
    schedulers and, 25
    SLEEP_BPOOL_FLUSH, 21
    THREADPOOL, 24
waits
    categories of, 334
    introduction to, 23
    latches, 197–198
    Query Wait option, 69
    signal, 420
    statistics on, 284–285, 334–336
    types of. *See* wait types
WAL (write-ahead logging), 16
Ward, Bob, 420
warnings, 396
Watch Live Data, 372
weighting, 490–491
window spool operators, 134
Windows Administrator group, 298, 304

Windows Event Log, 304–305, 396
Windows Explorer (Explorer), 395
Windows Failover Clustering, 93–94, 486–488
Windows information, 409
Windows I/O subsystems, 82–83
Windows Management Framework, 381
Windows Management Instrumentation (WMI), 322, 393
Windows on Windows (WOW), 277
Windows performance counters, 396–397
Windows Performance Monitor, 96, 260
Windows Remote Management (WinRM), 390
Windows Server 2003, 63
Windows Server 2008, 262
Windows Server Update Service (WSUS), 461–462
Windows Task Scheduler, 403
WinRM (Windows Remote Management), 390
WMI (Windows Management Instrumentation), 322, 393–394
worker threads, 23–24
workers, 145
workload types, 30–35
workspace memory, 68–69
WOW (Windows on Windows), 277
write-ahead logging (WAL), 16, 78
WSUS (Windows Server Update Service), 461–462

X

X (exclusive lock mode), 168
x64 platform, 56–57
Xen, 479
Xeon processors. *See* Intel processors
XEvents (Extended Events). *See* Extended Events (XEvents)
XML files
    filters and, 309
    plans in, 128
    in SQLdiag, 300, 317
XOR (exclusive or) calculations, 81
XSNs (transaction sequence numbers), 217–219

Z

zeros, 88

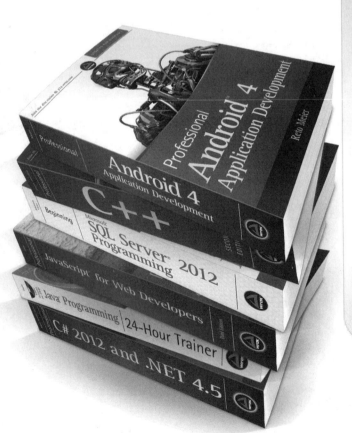